# THE
# PREACHER'S
# OUTLINE & SERMON
# BIBLE®

# REVELATION

# THE
# PREACHER'S
# OUTLINE & SERMON
# BIBLE®

### NEW TESTAMENT

### NEW INTERNATIONAL VERSION

Leadership Ministries Worldwide
Chattanooga, TN

Please address all requests for information or permission to:
Leadership Ministries Worldwide
PO Box 21310
Chattanooga, TN  37424-0310
Ph.# (423) 855-2181   FAX (423) 855-8616   E-Mail info@outlinebible.org
http://www.outlinebible.org

Library of Congress Catalog Card Number: 98-67967
ISBN Softbound Edition: 1-57407-088-6 (old) 978-1-57407-088-0 (new)

**LEADERSHIP MINISTRIES WORLDWIDE**
**CHATTANOOGA, TN**

Printed in the United States of America

2    3    4    5    6         15   16   17   18   19

## DEDICATED

To all the men and women of the world
who preach and teach the Gospel of
our Lord Jesus Christ and
to the Mercy and Grace of God

- Demonstrated to us in Christ Jesus our Lord.

   *In him we have redemption through his blood, the forgiveness of sins, in accordance with the riches of God's grace. (Ep.1:7)*

- Out of the mercy and grace of God, His Word has flowed. Let every person know that God will have mercy upon him, forgiving and using him to fulfill His glorious plan of salvation.

   *For God so loved the world that he gave his one and only Son, that whoever believes in him shall not perish but have eternal life. For God did not send his Son into the world to condemn the world, but to save the world through him. (Jn.3:16-17)*

   *This is good, and pleases God our Savior, who wants all men to be saved and to come to a knowledge of the truth. (1 Ti.2:3-4)*

6/10

## The Preacher's Outline & Sermon Bible®

is written for God's servants to use in their study, teaching, and preaching of God's Holy Word...

- to share the Word of God with the world.
- to help believers, both ministers and laypersons, in their understanding, preaching, and teaching of God's Word.
- to do everything we possibly can to lead men, women, boys, and girls to give their hearts and lives to Jesus Christ and to secure the eternal life that He offers.
- to do all we can to minister to the needy of the world.
- to give Jesus Christ His proper place, the place the Word gives Him. Therefore, no work of Leadership Ministries Worldwide—no Outline Bible Resources—will ever be personalized.

# ACKNOWLEDGMENTS AND BIBLIOGRAPHY

Every child of God is precious to the Lord and deeply loved. And every child as a servant of the Lord touches the lives of those who come in contact with him or his ministry. The writing ministries of the following servants have touched this work, and we are grateful that God brought their writings our way. We hereby acknowledge their ministry to us, being fully aware that there are many others down through the years whose writings have touched our lives and who deserve mention, but whose names have faded from our memory. May our wonderful Lord continue to bless the ministries of these dear servants—and the ministries of us all—as we diligently labor to reach the world for Christ and to meet the desperate needs of those who suffer so much.

## THE GREEK SOURCES

*Expositor's Greek Testament*, Edited by W. Robertson Nicoll. Grand Rapids, MI: Eerdmans Publishing Co., 1970.

Robertson, A.T. *Word Pictures in the New Testament*. Nashville, TN: Broadman Press, 1930.

Thayer, Joseph Henry. *Greek-English Lexicon of the New Testament*. New York: American Book Co, n.d.

Vincent, Marvin R. *Word Studies in the New Testament*. Grand Rapids, MI: Eerdmans Publishing Co., 1969.

Vine, W.E. *Expository Dictionary of New Testament Words*. Old Tappan, NJ: Fleming H. Revell Co., n.d.

Wuest, Kenneth S. *Word Studies in the Greek New Testament*. Grand Rapids, MI: Eerdmans Publishing Co., 1966.

## THE REFERENCE WORKS

*Cruden's Complete Concordance of the Old & New Testament*. Philadelphia, PA: The John C. Winston Co., 1930.

Josephus' *Complete Works*. Grand Rapids, MI: Kregel Publications, 1981.

Lockyer, Herbert. Series of books, including his books on *All the Men, Women, Miracles, and Parables of the Bible*. Grand Rapids, MI: Zondervan Publishing House, 1958–1967.

*Nave's Topical Bible*. Nashville, TN: The Southwestern Co., n.d.

*The Amplified New Testament*. (Scripture Quotations are from the Amplified New Testament, Copyright 1954, 1958, 1987 by the Lockman Foundation. Used by permission.)

*The Four Translation New Testament*. (Including King James, New American Standard, Williams - New Testament in the Language of the People, Beck - New Testament in the Language of Today.) Minneapolis, MN: World Wide Publications.

*The New Compact Bible Dictionary*, Edited by T. Alton Bryant. Grand Rapids, MI: Zondervan Publishing House, 1967.

*The New Thompson Chain Reference Bible*. Indianapolis, IN: B.B. Kirkbride Bible Co., 1964,

## THE COMMENTARIES

Barclay, William. *Daily Study Bible Series*. Philadelphia, PA: Westminster Press, Began in 1953.

Bruce, F.F. *The Epistle to the Ephesians*. Westwood, NJ: Fleming H. Revell Co., 1968.

_____. *Epistle to the Hebrews*. Grand Rapids, MI: Eerdmans Publishing Co., 1964.

_____. *The Epistles of John*. Old Tappan, NJ: Fleming H. Revell Co., 1970.

Criswell, W.A. *Expository Sermons on Revelation*. Grand Rapids, MI: Zondervan Publishing House, 1962–66.

Greene, Oliver. *The Epistles of John*. Greenville, SC: The Gospel Hour, Inc., 1966.

_____. *The Epistles of Paul the Apostle to the Hebrews*. Greenville, SC: The Gospel Hour, Inc., 1965.

_____. *The Epistles of Paul the Apostle to Timothy & Titus*. Greenville, SC: The Gospel Hour, Inc., 1964.

_____. *The Revelation Verse by Verse Study*. Greenville, SC: The Gospel Hour, Inc., 1963.

Henry, Matthew. *Commentary on the Whole Bible*. Old Tappan, NJ: Fleming H. Revell Co.

Hodge, Charles. *Exposition on Romans & on Corinthians*. Grand Rapids, MI: Eerdmans Publishing Co., 1972–1973.

Ladd, George Eldon. *A Commentary On the Revelation of John*. Grand Rapids, MI: Eerdmans Publishing Co., 1972–1973.

Leupold, H.C. *Exposition of Daniel*. Grand Rapids, MI: Baker Book House, 1969.

Morris, Leon. *The Gospel According to John*. Grand Rapids, MI: Eerdmans Publishing Co., 1971.

Newell, William R. *Hebrews, Verse by Verse*. Chicago, IL: Moody Press, 1947.

Strauss, Lehman. *Devotional Studies in Galatians & Ephesians*. Neptune, NJ: Loizeaux Brothers, 1957.

_____. *Devotional Studies in Philippians*. Neptune, NJ: Loizeaux Brothers, 1959.

_____. *James, Your Brother*. Neptune, NJ: Loizeaux Brothers, 1956.

_____. *The Book of the Revelation*. Neptune, NJ: Loizeaux Brothers, 1964.

Tasker, RVG. *The Gospel According to St. John*. "Tyndale New Testament Commentaries." Grand Rapids, MI: Eerdmans Publishing Co., 1960.

*The New Testament & Wycliffe Bible Commentary*, Edited by Charles F. Pfeiffer & Everett F. Harrison. New York: The Iverson Associates, 1971. Produced for Moody Monthly. Chicago Moody Press, 1962.

*The Pulpit Commentary*, Edited by H.D.M. Spence & Joseph S. Exell. Grand Rapids, MI: Eerdmans Publishing Co., 1950.

Thomas, W.H. Griffith. *Hebrews, A Devotional Commentary*. Grand Rapids, MI: Eerdmans Publishing Co., 1970.

_____. *Outline Studies in the Acts of the Apostles*. Grand Rapids, MI: Eerdmans Publishing Co., 1956.

_____. *St. Paul's Epistle to the Romans*. Grand Rapids, MI: Eerdmans Publishing Co., 1946.

_____. *Studies in Colossians & Philemon*. Grand Rapids, MI: Baker Book House, 1973.

*Tyndale New Testament Commentaries*. Grand Rapids, MI: Eerdmans Publishing Co., Began in 1958.

Walker, Thomas. *Acts of the Apostles*. Chicago, IL: Moody Press, 1965.

Walvoord, John. *The Thessalonian Epistles*. Grand Rapids, MI: Zondervan Publishing House, 1973.

# ABBREVIATIONS

| | | | | |
|---|---|---|---|---|
| & | = and | O.T. | = Old Testament |
| Bc. | = because | p./pp. | = page/pages |
| Concl. | = conclusion | Pt. | = point |
| Cp. | = compare | Quest. | = question |
| Ct. | = contrast | Rel. | = religion |
| e.g. | = for example | Rgt. | = righteousness |
| f. | = following | Thru | = through |
| Illust. | = illustration | v./vv. | = verse/verses |
| N.T. | = New Testament | vs. | = versus |

## THE BOOKS OF THE OLD TESTAMENT

| Book | Abbreviation | Chapters | Book | Abbreviation | Chapters |
|---|---|---|---|---|---|
| GENESIS | Gen. or Ge. | 50 | Ecclesiastes | Eccl. or Ec. | 12 |
| Exodus | Ex. | 40 | The Song of Solomon | S. of Sol. or Song | 8 |
| Leviticus | Lev. or Le. | 27 | Isaiah | Is. | 66 |
| Numbers | Num. or Nu. | 36 | Jeremiah | Jer. or Je. | 52 |
| Deuteronomy | Dt. or De. | 34 | Lamentations | Lam. | 5 |
| Joshua | Josh. or Jos. | 24 | Ezekiel | Ezk. or Eze. | 48 |
| Judges | Judg. or Jud. | 21 | Daniel | Dan. or Da. | 12 |
| Ruth | Ruth or Ru. | 4 | Hosea | Hos. or Ho. | 14 |
| 1 Samuel | 1 Sam. or 1 S. | 31 | Joel | Joel | 3 |
| 2 Samuel | 2 Sam. or 2 S. | 24 | Amos | Amos or Am. | 9 |
| 1 Kings | 1 Ki. or 1 K. | 22 | Obadiah | Obad. or Ob. | 1 |
| 2 Kings | 2 Ki. or 2 K. | 25 | Jonah | Jon. or Jona. | 4 |
| 1 Chronicles | 1 Chron. or 1 Chr. | 29 | Micah | Mic. or Mi. | 7 |
| 2 Chronicles | 2 Chron. or 2 Chr. | 36 | Nahum | Nah. or Na. | 3 |
| Ezra | Ezra or Ezr. | 10 | Habakkuk | Hab. | 3 |
| Nehemiah | Neh. or Ne. | 13 | Zephaniah | Zeph. or Zep. | 3 |
| Esther | Est. | 10 | Haggai | Hag. | 2 |
| Job | Job or Jb. | 42 | Zechariah | Zech. or Zec. | 14 |
| Psalms | Ps. | 150 | Malachi | Mal. | 4 |
| Proverbs | Pr. | 31 | | | |

## THE BOOKS OF THE NEW TESTAMENT

| Book | Abbreviation | Chapters | Book | Abbreviation | Chapters |
|---|---|---|---|---|---|
| MATTHEW | Mt. | 28 | 1 Timothy | 1 Tim. or 1 Ti. | 6 |
| Mark | Mk. | 16 | 2 Timothy | 2 Tim. or 2 Ti. | 4 |
| Luke | Lk. or Lu. | 24 | Titus | Tit. | 3 |
| John | Jn. | 21 | Philemon | Phile. or Phm. | 1 |
| The Acts | Acts or Ac. | 28 | Hebrews | Heb. or He. | 13 |
| Romans | Ro. | 16 | James | Jas. or Js. | 5 |
| 1 Corinthians | 1 Cor. or 1 Co. | 16 | 1 Peter | 1 Pt. or 1 Pe. | 5 |
| 2 Corinthians | 2 Cor. or 2 Co. | 13 | 2 Peter | 2 Pt. or 2 Pe. | 3 |
| Galatians | Gal. or Ga. | 6 | 1 John | 1 Jn. | 5 |
| Ephesians | Eph. or Ep. | 6 | 2 John | 2 Jn. | 1 |
| Philippians | Ph. | 4 | 3 John | 3 Jn. | 1 |
| Colossians | Col. | 4 | Jude | Jude | 1 |
| 1 Thessalonians | 1 Th. | 5 | Revelation | Rev. or Re. | 22 |
| 2 Thessalonians | 2 Th. | 3 | | | |

# HOW TO USE
## The Preacher's Outline & Sermon Bible®

Follow these easy steps to gain maximum benefit from The POSB.

**1** SUBJECT HEADING

**2** MAJOR POINTS

**3** SUBPOINTS
&
SCRIPTURE

**4** COMMENTARY

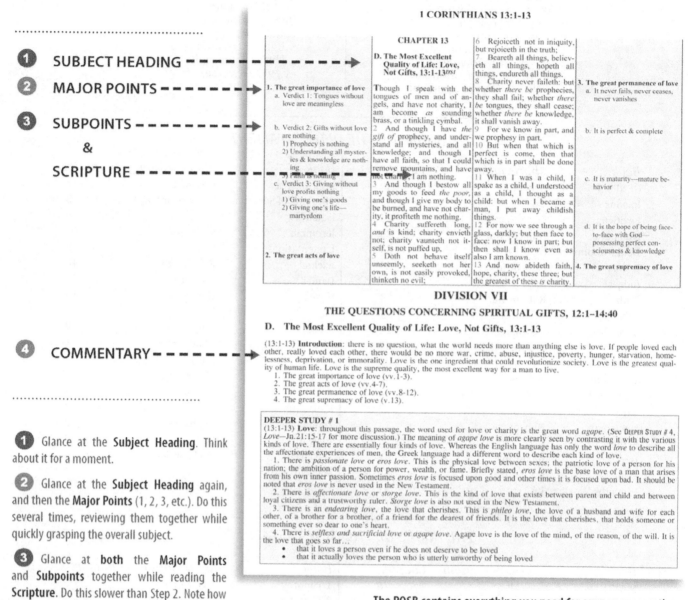

**1** Glance at the **Subject Heading**. Think about it for a moment.

**2** Glance at the **Subject Heading** again, and then the **Major Points** (1, 2, 3, etc.). Do this several times, reviewing them together while quickly grasping the overall subject.

**3** Glance at **both** the **Major Points** and **Subpoints** together while reading the **Scripture**. Do this slower than Step 2. Note how these points sit directly beside the related verse and simply restate what the Scripture is saying—in Outline form.

**4** Next read the **Commentary**. Note that the *Major Point Numbers* in the Outline match those in the Commentary. A small raised number (DS1, DS2, etc.) at the end of a Subject Heading or Outline Point, directs you to a related **Deeper Study** in the Commentary.

Finally, read the **Thoughts** and **Support Scripture** (not shown).

*As you read and re-read, pray that the Holy Spirit will bring to your attention exactly what you should preach and teach. May God bless you richly as you study and teach His Word.*

**The POSB contains everything you need for sermon preparation:**

1. **The Subject Heading** describes the overall theme of the passage, and is located directly above the Scripture (keyed *alphabetically*).

2. **Major Points** are keyed with an outline *number* guiding you to related commentary. Note that the Commentary includes "*Thoughts*" (life application) and abundant Supporting Scriptures.

3. **Subpoints** explain and clarify the Scripture as needed.

4. **Commentary** is fully researched and developed for every point.

   • **Thoughts** (in bold) help apply the Scripture to real life.

   • **Deeper Studies** provide in-depth discussions of key words.

**Woe to me if I do not preach the gospel!**
(1 Co.9:16)

# REVELATION

## INTRODUCTION

**AUTHOR**: John, the Apostle.

1. The author identifies himself as John four different times (Rev.1:1, 4, 9; 22:8).

2. The author uses several words that only John the apostle used in the Gospel of John and in the Epistles. He calls Jesus Christ the "Logos" which means *the Word* (see Rev.19:13; cp. Jn.1:1; 1 Jn.1:1). "*The Word*" is used nine times in the Gospel of John and four times in John's Epistles. He also calls Jesus Christ "*the Lamb of God*" (see Rev.5:6; 6:1; 7:9; 12:11; 13:8; 14:1; 15:3; 17:14; 19:9; 21:22. Cp. Jn.1:36.) He uses the word "*true*" (alethinos) ten times in *Revelation*. John is the only person to use the word "*tabernacle*" (skenoo). He uses it four times in *Revelation* and once in the Gospel (Rev.21:3; cp. Jn.1:14). He is also the only one to refer to the spear thrust in Christ's side (Rev.1:7; cp. Jn.19:34).

3. The early church said that John the apostle was the author. Justin Martyr said so (A.D. 150). One of the early disciples of John was a man named Polycarp. When Polycarp began his own ministry, he had a pupil or disciple named Irenaeus (died A.D. 190). Irenaeus said that Polycarp taught that John the apostle was the author. There are many others who verify the same conclusion (Canon Leon Morris. *The Revelation*. "The Tyndale New Testament Commentaries," ed. by RVG Tasker. Grand Rapids, MI: Eerdmans, 1969, p.26f). In addition to all this proof, John lived and ministered throughout Asia, the very place to which the *Revelation* was written.

**DATE**: Uncertain. Probably A.D. 95-96.

Some hold to an early date during Nero's reign (around A.D. 68); others to a later date during Domitian's reign (around A.D. 95-96). The early date is unlikely. The later date fits the circumstances much better. There are two major reasons for this.

1. John had been exiled to a rocky island in the Mediterranean, the Isle of Patmos. As far as is known, he was not exiled by the emperor Nero. Nero's persecution was more personal and local. Nero had been accused of burning Rome during a state of madness. To divert attention away from himself, he accused the Christians in Rome, and he launched an attack against them. Thousands were martyred by the most inhuman methods imaginable. The point to note is that Nero did not exile believers, he killed them. But the emperor Domitian did exile them. Domitian's persecution was a legal policy of the state and much more widespread. He made a deliberate attempt to banish Christian believers from the empire. Thus, it is much more likely that John was exiled during Domitian's reign.

2. The state of the churches pictured in *Revelation* differs from the church pictured by Paul in the 60's and 70's. *Revelation* pictures the churches as having been in existence for decades. Ephesus had lost its *first love* (Rev.2:4). Sardis was *dead* (Rev.3:1). There is a stark difference between the churches of Paul's day and the churches in the day of the *Revelation*. This definitely points toward the later date.

**TO WHOM WRITTEN**: "To the seven churches which are in Asia" (Rev.1:4; cp. 2:1-3:22). The seven churches were:

⇒ Ephesus       ⇒ Thyatira
⇒ Pergamos      ⇒ Laodicea
⇒ Smyrna       ⇒ Philadelphia
⇒ Sardis

**PURPOSE**: John had three purposes for writing *Revelation*.

1. The *immediate purpose*: to allow Jesus Christ to proclaim, "Behold, I come quickly." (Rev.2:16; 3:11; 22:7, 12, 20). The seven churches of Asia and their world needed a word of encouragement, of counsel, and of warning.

2. The *historical purpose*: to allow Jesus Christ to proclaim to His followers and to the world of every generation, "Behold, I come quickly" (Rev.2:16; 3:11; 22:7, 12, 20). God knows that every generation needs a word of encouragement, of counsel, and of warning.

3. The *godly purpose*: to give to the church and to the world "The *Revelation* of Jesus Christ" (Rev.1:1). This *Revelation* is both the unveiling of the person of Jesus Christ as the central figure of history and the unveiling of the message of His heart. He is both *the content and the unveiler* of the *Revelation*. What is the *Revelation* of Jesus Christ? The *Revelation* concerns "things which must shortly come to pass" (Rev.1:1). It concerns the Lamb, the Lord Jesus Christ Himself, who alone is worthy to open and oversee...

- the book of destiny.
- the book of the future of the world.
- the book of God's redemptive purpose.

(See outline and notes—Rev.4:1f.)

The words *the godly purpose* are chosen to describe this last point for two reasons.

   a. The picture painted by *Revelation* is that God takes an active part in the *Revelation*. God has some things to say about the future—some things to unveil, to uncover, to show to the church and to the world. It is His own *godly purpose* to unveil these events. By unveiling them, He is sending forth a word of encouragement to the world. But He is also sending forth a word of counsel and of warning. Man must heed the message of the great book of *Revelation* as well as be encouraged by it.

   b. The true title of *Revelation* is "The *Revelation* of Jesus Christ," not "The *Revelation* of John" (Rev.1:1). God's own purpose is to focus attention upon the Lamb, the Lord Jesus Christ Himself, and His ultimate triumph over the world and its ungodliness and evil. God's purpose is to show the great redemption that He is preparing for all those who truly believe and follow His Son. God's purpose is to show man that he can be saved from the terrible things that are coming upon the earth. God wants man to know that he can be saved while there is still time for him to repent. It is God's purpose to lead people to repentance and salvation; to lead them to the glorious inheritance of the great redemption that is to be given to all true followers of the Lord Jesus Christ.

**SPECIAL FEATURES**:

1. *Revelation* is "*An Apocalyptic Book*." It is the only book of Scripture that is often classified as Apocalyptic. Apocalyptic literature was literature written in the ancient world by a people under great stress. However, they were usually a people who had great hope for deliverance. The apocalyptic writings are marked by symbolism, dreams, visions, and cosmic powers that are ultimately defeated by God in a cataclysmic judgment. The authors never reveal their own names; rather they usually assign their writings to

a great character in Biblical history. Several examples are *The Book of Enoch; The Ascension of Isaiah;* and *The Assumption of Moses. The Revelation* differs from this literature in at least two respects:

    a. First, John gives his name.

    b. Second, *Revelation* is "The *Revelation* of Jesus Christ Himself." It is revealed under the inspiration of Christ Himself. Therefore, the great book of *Revelation* is Scripture; it is the very Word of God Himself.

2. *Revelation* is "*A Book of Prophecy*. It is almost completely devoted to prophecy. It has by far more prophecy than any other book of the New Testament. It is about "things which must shortly come to pass" (Rev.1:1)—about things that had not happened when they were given to John by the risen Lord.

3. *Revelation* is "*A Book of Old Testament Interpretation*." It is said that there are at least four hundred allusions to Old Testament Scriptures.

4. *Revelation* is "*A Book of Consummation*" or "*A Book of Final Things*." It deals primarily with the "Book of Destiny." The *Book of Destiny* is a book that is kept by God Himself, a book that pictures the events surrounding the climax of human history. It is a book of God's redemptive purpose (see outline and notes—Rev.4:1f).

5. *Revelation* is "*The Book Written to 'the Obedient Reader*." It gives a special promise to the obedient reader, to the person who heeds the message of *Revelation* (Rev.1:3; 22:18).

6. *Revelation* is "*The Revelation of Jesus Christ*." (See Purpose, point 3—*Introduction*.)

7. *Revelation* is "*God's Last Word to a World About to End*." (See point 4 above. See note 2—2 Pt.3:3; also see note—1 Jn.2:18.)

8. *Revelation* is "*The Book of Four Major Interpretations*."

    a. *The Preterist or Historical Interpretation*. The author is said to be writing about the events of his own day, the events of the first century. He describes only the events taking place in his own lifetime. *Revelation* is but a moral outcry against the way Rome was treating the Christian church of the first century. It has nothing to do whatsoever with prophecy. It is first century history and nothing else.

        The strength of this approach is that it forces a person to study the history and life of the early church. Most honest interpreters see the need to study the background of any writing in order to understand its message. Therefore, they make some use of this approach. Such study helps a person to learn from history. It reinforces a person's own life and enables him to better stand against the abuses of his own environment. However, the approach has several gross weaknesses.

    ⇒ It denies the prophetic message of *Revelation* when the book specifically claims to be prophecy (Rev.1:1; 4:1; 22:18).

    ⇒ It neglects the immediate message for believers of succeeding generations by limiting the message to first century believers.

    ⇒ It actually does violence to believers of succeeding generations. It limits the spiritual blessing they can receive by heeding the prophetic message of the book (Rev.1:1-3; 22:17-19).

    b. *The Idealist or Spiritualist Interpretation*. The author is said to be expressing only spiritual truths and principles. *Revelation* is said to be only a symbolic picture of the great cosmic struggle between good and evil. There is no historical background or prophetic message to the book at all.

        The strength of this view is that *Revelation* does teach great spiritual truths and principles. Of this there is little if any question. The church can learn from the message of *Revelation*. It can better understand its spiritual struggle in an antagonistic world. It can learn to love more, trust more, endure more, and hope more.

        However, the spiritual interpretation has two gross weaknesses:

    ⇒ It grossly misrepresents history and prophecy and it allows a person to neglect history and to read into the symbolic language any spiritual conclusion he wishes. There is no historical or prophetic event to guide a persons' understanding of *Revelation*. A person is left to draw his own spiritual conclusion. He can only hope he is correct.

    ⇒ Again, as in the Preterist view, there is a denial of what *Revelation* specifically claims: to be a book of prophecy.

    c. *The Continuous Historical Interpretation*. The author is said to be outlining the major events of history from the first century to the end of the world. *Revelation* is a calendar of world events as they relate to the church.

        The strength of this view is that it does show a sequence of events in the book. It forces the honest student to study the sequence and the chronological order of the events.

        The weakness of this view has shown up rather glaringly over the years.

    ⇒ There are almost as many different interpretations of the symbols in *Revelation* as there are interpreters. If the symbols of *Revelation* are picturing world history, then the writer gave no help whatsoever. There just is no clear calendar of world history in *Revelation*.

    ⇒ There is another glaring weakness. There is no calendar of world history anywhere in the Scriptures. If *Revelation* is a symbolic calendar of world history, then there is no Scripture to govern the interpretations of the prophecies in *Revelation*. A person is left to his own interpretation. There is no Scripture to interpret Scripture. But if the prophecies of *Revelation* deal primarily with the end of world history— the events surrounding the *great tribulation*, the antichrist, the millennium, and the new heavens and earth—these are taught by other Scriptures. Scripture can be tested by other Scripture.

    d. *The Futurist Interpretation*. The author is said to be predicting events that will happen as the end of the world approaches. However, the messages to the seven churches of chapters 1-3 are said to be an exception. Practically every interpreter says there is an historical background to these churches. The messages are written directly to the seven churches of Asia. But there are some who go farther and interpret each church to represent a church age—a particular period of church history leading right up to the end time.

        The strength of the Futurist view is that it takes the *Revelation* to be a book of prophecy when it claims to be a prophecy. And there is no question that the book claims to be a picture of the future.

**The *Revelation* of Jesus Christ, which God gave him to show his servants what must soon take place. He made it known by sending his angel to his servant John, (Rev 1:1)**

**After this I looked, and there before me was a door standing open in heaven. And the voice I had first heard speaking to me like a trumpet said, "Come up here, and I will show you what must take place after this." (Rev 4:1)**

**I warn everyone who hears the words of the prophecy of this book: If anyone adds anything to them, God will add to him the plagues described in this book. (Rev 22:18)**

There are several weaknesses often charged to the futurist view.

⇒ First, it is said to rob the early believers of any meaning and immediate help the author meant for them to receive. The futuristic view is said to miss any meaning and immediate help believers are to receive from its historical message. But note this: this charge misses the whole point of *hope*. It is *hope in the future*, hope in future happenings that stirs and drives man to press on and endure throughout life. Eliminate man's hope in the future and you destroy man. Therefore, this charge against the futurist interpretation of *Revelation* is wrong. The charge ignores and overlooks the very nature of man.

The future events revealed by the great book of *Revelation* give man the greatest of hopes, the very hope of eternal redemption, of being with the Lord Jesus Christ forever and ever. No greater hope and no greater message could be proclaimed than the future events proclaimed by *Revelation*. God is going to judge and eliminate all the evil and ungodly of this world and save every person who truly follows His Son, the Lord Jesus Christ.

⇒ Second, there is also the charge that great stress is often put upon arousing *fleshly curiosity*, upon *knowing about* the events of the future—that little emphasis is given to the spiritual truths for today—and that people often ignore the emphasis that *Revelation* places upon repentance and spiritual preparation for the judgment to come.

⇒ This charge is valid. There is much truth to this charge. There is within all of us a *fleshly tendency* to play God, to be recognized as knowing the future and being able to tell others what is going to happen and how to prepare for it. In addition to this, we have all seen and heard of people who focus upon future events to the neglect of the rest of Scripture. What we must do is this: *study and proclaim the whole counsel of God*. We must not neglect the *Revelation* nor any of the future events proclaimed by Scripture. But neither are we to neglect any of the other teachings of Scripture. We are to proclaim the whole counsel of God.

⇒ Third, a glaring weakness is the attempt by many to read too much into the symbolic language of *Revelation*. Some have developed a hard and fast scheme and come up with a hard and fast calendar of events that are to happen in the end time. This has brought about a tragic charge that some make their calendar of events a *test of fellowship*. And the charge is tragically true. Too many have done this. Too many display an air or attitude of superiority, of knowing more, of dogmatism—all of which rejects and alienates others—even sound Biblical believers. This of course should not be, and true believers know it. We know that fellowship is to be based only upon the essentials of the deity of Christ and of salvation, not upon the events of the end time. What we must do is love one another no matter how we may differ in our interpretation of the end time. If we do not, then we are not heeding the great message of *Revelation*. If we lose our love for Christ and for one another, then we doom ourselves even as the believers of Ephesus doomed themselves by losing their first love. We are not to base our fellowship upon how we interpret the events of *Revelation*.

This is not the reason God gave us *Revelation*. He gave us *Revelation* so that we would know what is going to happen at the end of the world and so that we can place our hope where it belongs: in the Lord Jesus Christ and in His ultimate triumph over all the evil and ungodliness of this earth.

9. *Revelation* is "*The Book That Must Be Biblically Interpreted*." What we as authors write is important and should be studied by believers, but only after the Word of God has been studied. We are the secondary sources for understanding God's Word; the Word of God itself is the primary source. There is far too much dependence upon secondary sources, and too little study of the primary source, the Bible itself. This is probably the greatest cause for the denial of the faith and of the Word of God than any other single thing. It is very difficult to deny that the Bible is the Word of God if a person truly studies and lives in the Bible. The Bible speaks for itself and it speaks powerfully. A person who denies the Bible as the Word of God has usually not lived in the study of the Bible. He has not honestly and openly studied the primary source.

The point is this: *Revelation* is a book that must be read and studied and allowed to speak for itself. It is *a book that must be Biblically interpreted*. *Revelation* is so full of symbols that a person must look elsewhere in Scripture to find out what the symbols mean in order to know what their meaning in *Revelation* is. Therefore, a person must be willing to take the time to search the Scripture if he wishes to study *Revelation*. And study it we must, for *Revelation* is part of God's Holy Word. In addition, its message is very, very special to God. It is so special that God promises a special blessing to the person who studies and heeds its great message (Rev.1:3; 22:18-19).

### PLEASE READ THIS

Remember: the purpose of **The Preacher's Outline & Sermon Bible®** is to present only what the Scripture says, not to give personal opinions. The beat of our hearts is to be true to the Word of God and to let the Word speak for itself. This we do to the best of our ability. We leave the declarations of denominational and theological positions up to the individual minister of God and to those who feel called to make such declarations. Our call with **The Preacher's Outline & Sermon Bible**® is only to *outline the Scripture and to develop the points* of the outline to the best of our ability. Our prayer is that this approach will help the minister to get into the Word of God more and more and to help him in his expounding of the Word to God's dear people.

Now, having said this, our *purpose and hope...*

- is to *outline Revelation*, letting *Revelation* speak for itself.
- is to *develop the outline points*, again letting *Revelation* speak for itself to the best of our ability.
- is to do exactly what *Revelation* says: not to add to nor take away from the message of *Revelation*. We must always remember the great danger that we who believe the Bible face: that of adding to the Word of God. Those who disbelieve the Word of God tend to deny certain parts and teachings of the Bible. But we who believe the Word of God face the danger of adding to the Word and going beyond what God has actually said. This is the reason Scripture warns us to guard against adding to as well as taking away from the message of *Revelation*. To the best of our ability, **The Preacher's Outline & Sermon Bible**® is making an attempt to do neither. Rather, our purpose, hope, and prayer is to let *Revelation* speak for itself. We are attempting to let the message do what we have attempted to do with the rest of Scripture: let it speak loudly and clearly the Word of God to us all. May God use these outlines to humble us and to lead us to commit our lives more fully to Christ Jesus our Lord and to His mission of reaching people for eternal salvation.

The *Revelation* must be allowed to speak for itself. Where it is not understood because symbolic language is used, the symbol must be searched out and explained by other Scriptures. There are at least two reasons for this.

⇒ First, God gives a special promise and warning to the reader of the *Revelation* (Rev.1:3; 22:18-19). God intended the believer to read and understand the book. It was written to be understood. It does not take a scholar to understand it. It takes a believer who seriously studies with an open and honest heart and who will let the Scripture speak for itself, not relying solely upon what other people might say. It takes a person who will depend upon the Scripture and the Holy Spirit to understand what God is saying.

Second, there are so many different interpretations that if one reads other books before reading *Revelation*, he can become confused before he ever gets around to reading *Revelation*. The book should be read and studied with an open heart. It should be allowed to speak its message without any bias—as much as is honestly possible. Serious Bible students, laymen and scholars alike—yea, all of us—must get away from reading and studying books *about* the Bible first and get back to reading and studying the *Scriptures first*.

4

THE PREACHER'S OUTLINE AND SERMON BIBLE® is unique. It differs from all other Study Bibles and Sermon Resource Materials in that every Passage and Subject is outlined right beside the Scripture. When you choose any *Subject* below and turn to the reference, you have not only the Scripture but also an outline of the Scripture and Subject *already prepared for you—verse by verse.*

For a quick example, choose one of the subjects below and turn over to the Scripture; you will find this to be a marvelous help for more *organized* and *streamlined* study.

In addition, every point of the Scripture and Subject is *fully developed in a Commentary with supporting Scripture* at the end of each point. Again, this arrangement makes sermon preparation much simpler and more efficient.

Note something else: the Subjects of *Revelation* have titles that are both Biblical and *practical.* The practical titles are often more appealing to people. This benefit is clearly seen for use on billboards, bulletins, church newsletters, etc.

A suggestion: for the *quickest* overview of *Revelation,* first read all the Division titles (I, II, III, etc.), then come back and read the individual outline titles.

---

## OUTLINE OF REVELATION

**I.  THE GREAT REVELATION TO GOD'S SERVANTS, 1:1-8**

A.  The Great Revelation, 1:1-3
B.  The Great Announcement to the Churches, 1:4-8

### VISION ONE, 1:9–3:22

**II.  THE MESSAGES OF THE GLORIFIED CHRIST TO THE SEVEN CHURCHES, 1:9–3:22**

A.  The Son of Man, the Glorified Christ, 1:9-20
B.  The Message to Ephesus: The Orthodox Church, but a Church Without Love, 2:1-7
C.  The Message to Smyrna: The Persecuted Church, 2:8-11
D.  The Message to Pergamos: The Corrupted Church That Is Married to the World, 2:12-17
E.  The Message to Thyatira: The Compromising or Permissive Church, 2:18-29
F.  The Message to Sardis: The Church with Reputation, but Dying, 3:1-6
G.  The Message to Philadelphia: The Church That Is Faithful and Alive, 3:7-13
H.  The Message to Laodicea: The Church That Is Affluent, but Lukewarm and Half-Committed, 3:14-22

### VISION TWO, 4:1–16:21

**III.  THE PICTURE OF THINGS HEREAFTER, 4:1–5:14**

In this vision two great things are seen. First, the throne of God is seen, then second, God Himself is seen holding a Book, a Book which contains the destiny of the world in the end times. However, the Book is sealed, for no one is found worthy to open and execute the events of the Book. Just when John despairs, One steps forward who is worthy, the Lamb of God, the Lord Jesus Christ, who was slain before the foundation of the earth.

A.  The Throne of God: The Focal Point of History, 4:1-11
B.  The Book of Destiny Is Sealed: The Future of the World, 5:1-4
C.  The Book of Destiny Is Opened: The Lamb Alone Is Worthy to Open the Book, 5:5-14

**IV.  THE SEVEN SEAL JUDGMENTS: EVENTS PRECEDING THE GREAT TRIBULATION, 6:1–7:17**

Christ breaks the first six seals of the Book or Scroll, not opening it yet; He just breaks the seals which bind the scroll together. As He breaks each seal, He reveals some event that is to take place immediately prior to the *great tribulation.* However, in spite of these terrible events, there is to be a remnant of believers saved, a remnant that stands fast for Christ.

A.  The Lamb Breaks the First Four Seals of the Book of Destiny: The Appearance of the Antichrist and His Power, 6:1-8
B.  The Lamb Breaks the Fifth Seal: The Slain Martyrs, 6:9-11
C.  The Lamb Breaks the Sixth Seal: The Great Day of God's Wrath Begins—The Universe Will Be Shattered, 6:12-17
D.  The Fate of Believers in the Great Tribulation (Part I): A Remnant of 144,000 From Israel Will Be Saved, 7:1-8
E.  The Fate of Believers in the Great Tribulation (Part II): A Countless Number of People Will Be Saved, 7:9-17

**V.  THE SEVEN TRUMPET JUDGMENTS: EVENTS DURING THE GREAT TRIBULATION, 8:1–11:19**

In breaking the seventh seal, an awesome revelation is made. Seven terrible judgments, called the trumpet judgments, are to be unleashed upon the earth. These are the actual events of the *great tribulation.* However, there is the prophetic message of salvation—a remnant is to be saved. The blast of the seventh trumpet brings forth an overall picture of things to come. Three of these things are of such importance they are said to be *wonders* or *signs* and they are covered in great detail.

A.  The Breaking of the Seventh Seal: Awesome Preparation for Judgment, 8:1-5
B.  The Blast of the First Four Trumpets: Natural Catastrophes, 8:6-12
C.  The Blast of the Fifth Trumpet: A Demonic-like Locust Plague, 8:13-9:11
D.  The Blast of the Sixth Trumpet: Demonic-like Military Horsemen, 9:12-21

## VI. THE SEVENTH TRUMPET IN DETAIL (PART I): TWO SPIRITUAL WONDERS STRUGGLING BEHIND THE GREAT TRIBULATION, 12:1-17

The seventh trumpet, part 1, shows that there are great spiritual and cosmic beings struggling behind the earthly scenes of history.

## VII. THE SEVENTH TRUMPET IN DETAIL (PART II): THE WAR OF THE DRAGON UPON THE EARTH, 13:1-18

The seventh trumpet, part 2, reveals just how the dragon, that old serpent the devil, carries out his attack upon God's people through human politics and religion.

## VIII. THE SEVENTH TRUMPET IN DETAIL (PART III): THE VICTORY OF THE LAMB IS ASSURED, 14:1-20

The seventh trumpet, part 3, gives much needed assurance that all things are in God's hands. The false Christ, the beast, and godless civilization will be destroyed, and the true Christ and His followers will be saved eternally.

## IX. THE SEVENTH TRUMPET IN DETAIL (PART IV): THE THIRD GREAT WONDER, THE SEVEN BOWL JUDGMENTS, 15:1–16:21

The seventh trumpet blasts forth its judgments, and the judgments come fast and furious. Why? Because they are the very last judgments. God has decided to end human history. He has decided to stop all the ungodliness and evil of this world. He can no longer take the rebellion, denial, cursing, immorality, stealing, drunkenness, sorcery, and murder of man. Therefore, Jesus Christ will destroy all the ungodly and evil of this world and do it quickly.

### VISION THREE, 17:1–20:15

## X. THE JUDGMENT OF BOTH RELIGIOUS BABYLON AND POLITICAL BABYLON, 17:1–18:24

Jesus Christ is coming back to this earth, and He is going to establish the righteousness of God forever and ever. But before He can come and establish righteousness in the earth, a few things have to be done.

⇒ All the godless and evil armies of this world have to be destroyed. This we have just seen in the former chapter (Revelation Chapter 16).

⇒ All the false religion in this world has to be destroyed. This is the discussion of the present chapter (Revelation, Chapter 17).

⇒ All the godless governments and politics and social systems of this world have to be destroyed. This will be the discussion of the next chapter (Revelation Chapter 18).

When these three things are done, then the ungodly and evil of this earth will be removed and Jesus Christ can come to earth and set up His kingdom of righteousness. As stated, the armies were destroyed in the former chapter. Now God shows us how both false religion and the godless governments and politics of this world will be destroyed.

## XI. THE GREAT MARRIAGE SUPPER OF THE LAMB, OF THE LORD JESUS CHRIST, 19:1-10

This is the great *Marriage Supper of the Lamb*, of the Lord Jesus Christ. This will be the great supper where all of heaven will be present to celebrate the union of Jesus Christ and the believers who have followed Him down through the centuries. Everyone in heaven will be there: God, Christ, believers, and the heavenly host. It will be the most celebrated and joyful event ever experienced up to that point in history. Why? Because it will be the great Marriage Supper of the Lord Jesus Christ Himself, the celebration of the very thing for which He died. It will be the first time that *all the redeemed* of all ages will come together at *one time* to honor the Lamb who was slain to redeem the universe. Because of what He has done for man, He is deserving of all the honor and praise possible. To give Him such glorious honor, God has planned the greatest celebration and banquet imaginable, the celebration of what He calls the great *Marriage Supper of the Lamb* (v.9).

## XII. THE FINAL TRIUMPH: THE MILLENNIUM USHERED IN, 19:11–20:15

This is the final triumph of Jesus Christ upon earth. Six events will take place that will bring about a new heavens and earth and that will usher in eternity. These events will bring about the very thing for which God has launched human history: the perfect fellowship and communion between God and man throughout all eternity. These six events will bring about the glorious day when believers will worship and serve God—when they will labor and work for Him throughout the whole universe and do it in perfection forever and ever.

A. The Coming of Christ as Conqueror, 19:11-16
B. The Great Battle of Armageddon, 19:17-21
C. The Great Removal and Binding of Satan, 20:1-3
D. The First Resurrection and Millennial Reign of Christ, 20:4-6
E. The Return of Satan and His Eternal Fate, 20:7-10
F. The Final Resurrection and Judgment of Unbelievers: The Great White Throne, 20:11-15

## VISION FOUR, 21:1–22:21

## XIII. THE ETERNITY OF GOD: THE NEW HEAVENS AND EARTH AND THE NEW JERUSALEM, 21:1–22:5

A. The New Heavens and the New Earth, 21:1-8
B. The New Jerusalem, The City of God (Part I): Its Description, 21:9-23
C. The New Jerusalem, The City of God (Part II): Its Citizens and Provisions, 21:24-22:5

## XIV. THE GREAT MESSAGE OF REVELATION: ELEVEN STIRRING FACTS, 22:6-21

| | CHAPTER 1 | He made it known by sending his angel to his servant John, | take place |
|---|---|---|---|
| | **I. THE GREAT REVELATION TO GOD'S SERVANTS, 1:1-8** | 2 Who testifies to everything he saw—that is, the word of God and the testimony of Jesus Christ. | **3 The revelation was given to John** <br> a. It was given by an angel <br> b. It was accurately reported by John |
| | **A. The Great Revelation, 1:1-3** | 3 Blessed is the one who reads the words of this prophecy, and blessed are those who hear it and take to heart what is written in it, because the time is near. | **4 The revelation blesses the man who reads, hears, & obeys the message** |
| **1 The revelation was given by Christ Himself** <br> **2 The revelation concerns things that must soon** | The revelation of Jesus Christ, which God gave him to show his servants what must soon take place. | | |

# DIVISION I

## THE GREAT REVELATION TO GOD'S SERVANTS, 1:1-8

### A.  The Great Revelation, 1:1-3

(1:1-3) **Introduction**: this is the great revelation of Jesus Christ. The word "revelation" (apokalupsis) means to uncover and unveil. It means to pull back a covering or a veil that is hiding something. It means to make known something; to reveal something that a person could not find out for himself. It is a revelation of truth that man could never discover for himself. This is what the book of revelation is: it is the great revelation of Jesus Christ to His servants or followers. This means a most wonderful fact: it means that there are some things that God wants us to know, some things that we could never know if we were left on our own. It means that God cares about us, that He loves us enough to reveal some things to us. And note: God cares so much for us that He has revealed a whole book of events to us. What are these events? They are events or truths that lie out in the future, that concern the end of the world. Four significant things are said about the revelation of Jesus Christ.

1. The revelation was given by Christ Himself (v.1).
2. The revelation concerns things that must soon take place (v.1).
3. The revelation was given to John (v.1-2).
4. The revelation blesses the man who reads, hears, and obeys the message (v.3).

**1** (1:1) **Revelation, The**: the revelation was given by Jesus Christ Himself. Jesus Christ is the Author of the revelation. But note: it was given to Jesus Christ by God the Father. When Jesus Christ was upon the earth, He said the following about His return and the end of the world:

> **"No one knows about that day or hour, not even the angels in heaven, nor the Son, but only the Father. (Mark 13:32)**

However, when Jesus Christ ascended into heaven, God the Father revealed these things to Christ. This is significant, for it means that the things we are about to learn did not come from man, but from *God Himself*. The revelation concerns things that *God Himself* wants us to know; therefore, He gave them to His Son and His Son has now revealed some of the things to us.

**Thought 1**. This is a stark contrast from the prophets, soothsayers, astrologers, and religionists of the world. Think of the thousands and thousands of self-proclaimed prophets and religionists upon earth. Each claims to know about God and to have some revelation from Him. But here in the Bible, in the very Word of God itself, is a whole book that has come from the Son of God, a whole book that He Himself has authored. The book concerns some very special things that God wants us to know. What are the things? This is the subject of the next point.

> **"I have much to say in judgment of you. But he who sent me is reliable, and what I have heard from him I tell the world." (John 8:26)**
>
> **For I did not speak of my own accord, but the Father who sent me commanded me what to say and how to say it. (John 12:49)**
>
> **I no longer call you servants, because a servant does not know his master's business. Instead, I have called you friends, for everything that I learned from my Father I have made known to you. (John 15:15)**
>
> **For I gave them the words you gave me and they accepted them. They knew with certainty that I came from you, and they believed that you sent me. (John 17:8)**

**2** (1:1) **End Time—Revelation, The**: the revelation concerns things that must soon take place. Note four significant facts.

1. The revelation concerns *future events*, events that are yet to happen in the end time. The events had not yet happened when Jesus Christ gave the revelation.

2. The early believers had looked for these events to take place very soon. The idea is shortly, swiftly, speedily—in their lifetime. This means that the early believers were expecting the Lord to return in their lifetime. They were doing exactly what Christ had told them to do: to look and watch for His return.

> **"Therefore keep watch, because you do not know on what day your Lord will come. (Mat 24:42)**
>
> **So you also must be ready, because the Son of Man will come at an hour when you do not expect him. (Mat 24:44)**

*"Therefore keep watch, because you do not know the day or the hour. (Mat 25:13)*

3. God's clock measures time differently than man's clock. This is clear, for it has been thousands of years since Jesus Christ gave this revelation to man. Yet He has not returned to earth and the end of the world has not yet happened. Does this mean that John was wrong in saying that the events were to shortly happen? No!

⇒ God clearly reveals that we are living in the last days, and that the events are to happen in the last days (see note, *Last Days*—2 Pt.3:3 for more discussion).

⇒ God also clearly reveals that a thousand years is as one day with Him (see note—2 Pt.3:8 for more discussion).

The point is this: the return of Christ and the end of the world are God's affairs, not man's. Therefore, the time frame of the events are bound to be based upon God's time, not man's. The events are in God's hands. In fact, based upon God's measurement of time it has been only about two days since Jesus Christ revealed the events of the revelation.

**Thought 1.** Every generation of believers must look for the return of Christ. This is exactly what He commands. He teaches that He can return any time; therefore, we are to obey Him. We are to expect His return, watch and be ready for it. But we must also realize that He may not come today. Therefore, we must plan and establish long term ministries upon the earth so that the lost can continue to be reached for Christ. The proper attitude is this: we must be expecting Christ to return today, but we must plan as though He will not come for a hundred years.

4. Jesus Christ gave the revelation to His servants. Who are His servants? Believers who *truly follow and serve Christ*. This is significant to note, for there are many who profess to believe and follow Christ and do not. The revelation is not written to them. The revelation is a *closed book* to those who do not genuinely follow Christ. It is a closed book to the world. Jesus Christ gave the revelation to His servants and His servants alone.

**Thought 1.** The revelation is not a book for the world, nor for those who profess Christ but fail to serve Him. It is a book that is written only for genuine believers. The idea is that the world cannot understand the revelation and will only mock it. Perhaps this is the reason there is often so much mockery of the things of God by the world. We who truly know Christ have too often proclaimed things to the world that were for our exhortation alone. The events revealed by Christ in this great book are for the true servants of God, not for the world. (See outlines and notes—2 Pt.3:3-7; 3:8-10; 3:11-14 for more discussion.)

*But the Counselor, the Holy Spirit, whom the Father will send in my name, will teach you all things and will remind you of everything I have said to you. (John 14:26)*
*The man without the Spirit does not accept the things that come from the Spirit of God, for they are foolishness to him, and he cannot understand them, because they are spiritually discerned. (1 Cor 2:14)*

*But solid food is for the mature, who by constant use have trained themselves to distinguish good from evil. (Heb 5:14)*
*As for you, the anointing you received from him remains in you, and you do not need anyone to teach you. But as his anointing teaches you about all things and as that anointing is real, not counterfeit—just as it has taught you, remain in him. (1 John 2:27)*
*The secret things belong to the LORD our God, but the things revealed belong to us and to our children forever, that we may follow all the words of this law. (Deu 29:29)*

**3** (1:1-2) **Revelation, The—Angel**: the revelation was given to John. John the apostle was the man chosen by Jesus Christ to receive the revelation. But note this: John had to be available. Jesus Christ always chooses a man to carry the messages of God to men. But before He can choose a man, the man has to be available. The man has to love the Lord; he has to be surrendered to Christ. John was such a man; therefore, Jesus Christ was able to choose him to receive the Word of God and to share it with the servants of God. Note two significant facts.

1. It was the angel of Christ who gave the message to John. The word *angel* means messenger. This particular angel is said to be "His angel," that is, the personal angel of Christ. The picture is that of some angel who serves Christ as His very special messenger, some angel who is appointed as the very special servant of Christ.

2. John says that he has accurately borne witness to what he saw. What did he see?

a. John saw the Word of God. The things of revelation are the Word of God. God is not far off in outer space unconcerned with man. God cares for man, cares so much that He has sent His Word to us through this book of the great revelation. We know that God cares for us because He has spoken to us: He has spoken the great message of revelation to us.

b. John saw the testimony of Jesus Christ. Jesus Christ showed John exactly what God had given Him to reveal to His followers. What John has shared in the revelation is the very testimony of Jesus Christ, the Son of God Himself.

c. John saw everything that is reported in the revelation, all the events.

**Thought 1.** It is a matter of belief. We either believe John or not. John is either telling the truth or he is lying. Which do we believe? Is Jesus Christ returning to earth? Are the events of the end time going to happen as recorded in revelation or not? Should we be watching for Christ and these events or not? If the revelation is truly the Word of God and the testimony of Jesus Christ, then we must watch and be ready, for every event will certainly take place and nothing will stop them. We shall witness every single event either from heaven or from upon the earth.

**4** (1:3) **Revelation, The—Word of God**: the revelation blesses the person who reads, hears, and obeys the message. In the early church there were, of course, no printing presses to run off copy after copy of John's letter. There was only the original copy written by him and perhaps a few other copies that had been copied by hand to be passed among the people. Therefore, the *reading* spoken of in this verse refers to the letter being read before the whole church or before special groups within the church. But note a critical point: reading is not enough. Believers must...

- *read*
- *hear* the words of this prophecy
- *take to heart* those things that are written

It is never enough to just read and hear the Word of God. We must always do what God says, obey His commandments. This is especially true when it comes to revelation. Why? Note the last statement made in verse 3: because "the time is near." The events are near, very near. Jesus Christ is returning to earth very soon. The events of the end time are about to happen. They are at hand, right over the horizon. Therefore, we must read, hear, and heed the things written in revelation. We must be looking and preparing for the coming of Christ and for the events that point toward the end of the world. The believer who does what revelation says shall be blessed ever so richly by God.

> I tell you the truth, if anyone keeps my word, he will never see death." (John 8:51)
>
> Jesus replied, "If anyone loves me, he will obey my teaching. My Father will love him, and we will come to him and make our home with him. (John 14:23)
>
> It teaches us to say "No" to ungodliness and worldly passions, and to live self-controlled, upright and godly lives in this present age, While we wait for the blessed hope—the glorious appearing of our great God and Savior, Jesus Christ, (Titus 2:12-13)
>
> But the day of the Lord will come like a thief. The heavens will disappear with a roar; the elements will be destroyed by fire, and the earth and everything in it will be laid bare. Since everything will be destroyed in this way, what kind of people ought you to be? You ought to live holy and godly lives As you look forward to the day of God and speed its coming. That day will bring about the destruction of the heavens by fire, and the elements will melt in the heat. But in keeping with his promise we are looking forward to a new heaven and a new earth, the home of righteousness. (2 Pet 3:10-13)

**Thought 1.** No genuine believer has the right to ignore or neglect revelation. Every thing said in this opening statement declares the importance of the revelation. revelation is not only to be read and heard, it is to be heeded. This means that the message can be understood by true believers.

**Thought 2.** There are seven *blesseds* or beatitudes in revelation.

⇒ The blessing or beatitude of obedience.

> **Blessed is the one who reads the words of this prophecy, and blessed are those who hear it and take to heart what is written in it, because the time is near. (Rev 1:3)**

⇒ The blessing or beatitude of eternal life.

> **Then I heard a voice from heaven say, "Write: Blessed are the dead who die in the Lord from now on." "Yes," says the Spirit, "they will rest from their labor, for their deeds will follow them." (Rev 14:13)**

⇒ The blessing or beatitude of watchfulness and purity, of watching for the Lord's return and living a pure life.

> **"Behold, I come like a thief! Blessed is he who stays awake and keeps his clothes with him, so that he may not go naked and be shamefully exposed." (Rev 16:15)**

⇒ The blessing or beatitude of heaven, of being called to the wedding supper of the Lamb.

> **Then the angel said to me, "Write: 'Blessed are those who are invited to the wedding supper of the Lamb!'" And he added, "These are the true words of God." (Rev 19:9)**

⇒ The blessing or beatitude of the resurrection, of being raised from the dead, of conquering death and living eternally with Christ.

> **Blessed and holy are those who have part in the first resurrection. The second death has no power over them, but they will be priests of God and of Christ and will reign with him for a thousand years. (Rev 20:6)**

⇒ The blessing or beatitude of obedience, of heeding the sayings of revelation.

> **"Behold, I am coming soon! Blessed is he who keeps the words of the prophecy in this book." (Rev 22:7)**

⇒ The blessing or beatitude of obedience, of keeping all of God's commandments.

> **"Blessed are those who wash their robes, that they may have the right to the tree of life and may go through the gates into the city. (Rev 22:14)**

Note the critical importance of obedience. Three of the seven blessings have to do with obeying God, with keeping His commandments—just doing what He says. Obedience cannot be overstressed. We must do what God says to do in the book of *Revelation*.

**Thought 3.** Note that the book of *Revelation* begins with a promised blessing (Rev.1:3) and closes with a promised blessing (Rev.22:7).

| | B. The Great Announcement to the Churches, 1:4-8 | by his blood, | dead |
|---|---|---|---|
| | | 6 And has made us to be a kingdom and priests to serve his God and Father—to him be glory and power for ever and ever! Amen. | c. The ruler of the kings of the earth |
| **1 Announcement 1: Grace & peace are yours** | | | d. He has redeemed us, v.5 |
| a. From God: the Eternal & unchangeable God | 4 John, To the seven churches in the province of Asia: Grace and peace to you from | | e. He has exalted us |
| | him who is, and who was, and who is to come, and from | 7 Look, he is coming with the clouds, and every eye will | **3 Announcement 3: Look, Christ comes** |
| b. From the Holy Spirit: the Servant of God | the seven spirits before his throne, | see him, even those who pierced him; and all the peoples of the earth will mourn | a. He is to be seen by all |
| c. From Jesus Christ | 5 And from Jesus Christ, who is the faithful witness, the | because of him. So shall it be! Amen. | b. He is to be seen by those who killed Him: They will mourn because of Him |
| **2 Announcement 2: Jesus Christ is the great Savior, the great Redeemer** | firstborn from the dead, and the ruler of the kings of the | 8 "I am the Alpha and the Omega," says the Lord God, | **4 Announcement 4: Christ is the Almighty God** |
| a. The faithful witness | earth. To him who loves us | "who is, and who was, and who is to come, the Al- | a. The Alpha & Omega |
| b. The first to arise from the | and has freed us from our sins | mighty." | b. Who is, was, and is to come |
| | | | c. The Almighty God |

# DIVISION I

## THE GREAT REVELATION TO GOD'S SERVANTS, 1;1-8

### B. The Great Announcement to the Churches, 1:4-8

(1:4-8) **Introduction**: this is the great announcement to the churches. Note: there were seven churches in Asia to which this great announcement was being made. The churches will be named and discussed in a later passage. When they are, it will be seen that they are representative of all churches of the Lord Jesus Christ throughout the world. For now, the great announcement is the subject to be discussed. What is the great announcement proclaimed to the churches of the world? It is fourfold.

1. Announcement 1: grace and peace are yours (v.4-5).
2. Announcement 2: Jesus Christ is the great Savior, the great Redeemer (v.5-6).
3. Announcement 3: look, Christ comes (v.7).
4. Announcement 4: Christ is the Almighty God (v.8).

**1** (1:4-5) **Grace—Peace**: announcement one—grace and peace are yours. The church must know that it can experience grace and peace.

⇒ *Grace* means the favor and blessings of God. It means that God takes an active role in our lives; that He looks after and takes care of us; that He provides all the good and beneficial things of life for us whether physical, material, or spiritual. We do not deserve the grace of God, but God loves us. Therefore, He showers us with His grace, His favor, and His blessings.

⇒ *Peace* means that we can have peace with God and with men; that we no longer have to feel that God is far way from us, nor that God is hovering over us, watching every little move that we make. God is not evil; He is not seeking every chance to condemn and punish us. God seeks only one thing with us and that is peace.

Peace also means that men no longer have to be divided, separated, and discriminated against; nor do they have to be fighting, warring, stealing, and killing each other. Man can now have peace—peace with God and peace with each other.

This is the first great declaration to the church. The great gifts of grace and peace are now available to man. But note where. It is not found among men. Neither God's grace (favor) nor the great gift of peace can be found upon earth.

Grace and peace come only from heaven, only from God and His Spirit and His Son, the Lord Jesus Christ.

1. Grace and peace come only from the eternal and unchangeable God. Note how God is described: "God *who is and who was and who is to come.*"

⇒ God is.
⇒ God was.
⇒ God is to come.

That is, God is eternal and He is unchangeable. He is the infinite God, the only living and true God. He is today as He was, and He shall be the same in the ages to come. This means the most wonderful thing: God has infinite power and knowledge. He knows that we need His grace, His care and provision, and His peace. And He has the power to give us grace and peace. All we have to do is go to Him—to Him who is the source of grace and peace.

> **But because of his great love for us, God, who is rich in mercy, made us alive with Christ even when we were dead in transgressions—it is by grace you have been saved. And God raised us up with Christ and seated us with him in the heavenly realms in Christ Jesus, in order that in the coming ages he might show the incomparable riches of his grace, expressed in his kindness to us in Christ Jesus. (Eph 2:4-7)**

> **And the peace of God, which transcends all understanding, will guard your hearts and your minds in Christ Jesus. (Phil 4:7)**

> **For the grace of God that brings salvation has appeared to all men. It teaches us to say "No" to ungodliness and worldly passions, and to live self-controlled, upright and godly lives in this present age, While we wait for the blessed hope—the glorious appearing of our great God and Savior, Jesus Christ, Who gave himself for us to redeem us from all wickedness and to purify for himself a people that are his very own, eager to do what is good. These, then, are the things you should teach. Encourage and**

rebuke with all authority. Do not let anyone despise you. (Titus 2:11-15)

He saved us, not because of righteous things we had done, but because of his mercy. He saved us through the washing of rebirth and renewal by the Holy Spirit, Whom he poured out on us generously through Jesus Christ our Savior, So that, having been justified by his grace, we might become heirs having the hope of eternal life. (Titus 3:5-7)

2. Grace and peace come from the Holy Spirit of God. Note that the Holy Spirit is called the "seven spirits." The number seven in the Bible simply means completeness, fullness, and perfection. Thus, the *seven spirits* means the Holy Spirit in all His fullness. The Holy Spirit is before the throne of God in all of His perfection and fullness. Therefore, the believer is to find grace and peace in the fullness of the Holy Spirit. It is the Spirit of God who lives within the believer in order to fill the believer with the grace and peace of God.

**Thought 1.** Our duty is to learn to walk in the Spirit; to allow Him to fill us with God's grace and peace.

And if the Spirit of him who raised Jesus from the dead is living in you, he who raised Christ from the dead will also give life to your mortal bodies through his Spirit, who lives in you. (Rom 8:11)
But the fruit of the Spirit is love, joy, peace, patience, kindness, goodness, faithfulness, Gentleness and self-control. Against such things there is no law. (Gal 5:22-23)

3. Grace and peace come from Jesus Christ. It is Christ who brought the grace and peace of God to earth. This is clearly seen in the next note.

Peace I leave with you; my peace I give you. I do not give to you as the world gives. Do not let your hearts be troubled and do not be afraid. (John 14:27)
"I have told you these things, so that in me you may have peace. In this world you will have trouble. But take heart! I have overcome the world." (John 16:33)
And are justified freely by his grace through the redemption that came by Christ Jesus. (Rom 3:24)
In him we have redemption through his blood, the forgiveness of sins, in accordance with the riches of God's grace (Eph 1:7)
For he himself is our peace, who has made the two one and has destroyed the barrier, the dividing wall of hostility, (Eph 2:14)
To the holy and faithful brothers in Christ at Colosse: Grace and peace to you from God our Father. (Col 1:2)

**2** (1:5-6) **Jesus Christ—Redemption:** announcement two—Jesus Christ is the great Savior, the great Redeemer. Five great things are declared about Jesus Christ in these two verses.

1. Jesus Christ is the faithful witness. He is the one Person we can depend upon. We can trust what Jesus Christ tells us. Jesus Christ came from God, out of heaven itself, to reveal the truth to us—the truth about God and man and man's world. What Jesus Christ has revealed can be trusted. He is the faithful witness.

I tell you the truth, we speak of what we know, and we testify to what we have seen, but still you people do not accept our testimony. (John 3:11)
Jesus answered, "Even if I testify on my own behalf, my testimony is valid, for I know where I came from and where I am going. But you have no idea where I come from or where I am going. (John 8:14)
"You are a king, then!" Said Pilate. Jesus answered, "You are right in saying I am a king. In fact, for this reason I was born, and for this I came into the world, to testify to the truth. Everyone on the side of truth listens to me." (John 18:37)

2. Jesus Christ is the first to arise from the dead. That is, He is the first to arise who never again had to die. The word "firstborn" means to be the first in rank; to be supreme and preeminent in the resurrection. Of all the people who have arisen from the dead, Jesus Christ is Supreme. It is He who is the Son of God; therefore, it is His resurrection that is the supreme and preeminent resurrection. All other people arise because He arose. All believers shall arise to live with God eternally because He arose and conquered death for us. Because He arose, we too shall arise if we *believe* that He died and arose for us.

3. Jesus Christ is the ruler of the kings of the earth. Jesus Christ has been raised from the dead and exalted to the right hand of God's throne. He and He alone has been given the seat of Sovereign rule over the earth. The world may seem chaotic and the problems too enormous to be handled. But Jesus Christ is in control, and He is able to handle it all. However, man may legitimately ask: Why does God not go ahead and come and straighten out the chaotic mess and evil of the world? God tells us as plainly as human language can say it:

The Lord is not slow in keeping his promise, as some understand slowness. He is patient with you, not wanting anyone to perish, but everyone to come to repentance. (2 Pet 3:9; cp. v.3-10)

Jesus Christ is delaying His return so that more people can be saved and live eternally with God. But some day, and from the weight of the evidence the day will be soon, Jesus Christ is returning to take over the rule of the world. He and He alone is going to rule and bring the reign of righteousness to earth. He alone is the ruler of the kings of the earth.

The earth is the Lord's, and everything in it, the world, and all who live in it; (Psa 24:1)
Lift up your heads, O you gates; be lifted up, you ancient doors, that the King of glory may come in. (Psa 24:7)
Now to the King eternal, immortal, invisible, the only God, be honor and glory for ever and ever. Amen. (1 Tim 1:17)
Which God will bring about in his own time—God, the blessed and only Ruler, the

**King of kings and Lord of lords,** (1 Tim 6:15)

**The seventh angel sounded his trumpet, and there were loud voices in heaven, which said: "The kingdom of the world has become the kingdom of our Lord and of his Christ, and he will reign for ever and ever." (Rev 11:15)**

**They will make war against the Lamb, but the Lamb will overcome them because he is Lord of lords and King of kings—and with him will be his called, chosen and faithful followers." (Rev 17:14)**

**On his robe and on his thigh he has this name written: KING OF KINGS AND LORD OF LORDS. (Rev 19:16)**

4. Jesus Christ has redeemed us. He *"loves us and has freed us from our sins by His blood"* (v.5). The word *love* is in the present tense in the Greek. This means that Jesus Christ *always loves* us. He loves us today just as He has loved us in the past. The word "freed" (lusanti) means to be loosed, set free, and released from sin. How did the blood of Jesus Christ set us free from sin?

⇒ Jesus Christ took our sins and died for them. He had lived a sinless and perfect life as a Man upon earth. Therefore, He was able to present Himself as the Ideal and Perfect Man before God. He was able to die as the ideal and perfect sacrifice. He was able to take our sins—the guilt and the judgment of our sins—upon Himself and bear the punishment for them. He was the Ideal and Perfect Man; therefore, God is able to accept His death as the ideal and perfect sacrifice for sin.

The point is this: Jesus Christ died for our sins. He actually took our sins off of us, removed them, and died for them. Therefore, we are free and loosed from sin. Sin has been removed from us. We stand before God free of sin and acceptable to Him. But remember how: by the shed blood of Jesus Christ upon the cross. It is the shed blood of Christ upon the cross—His dying for our sins—that frees us from sin.

**Who gave himself for our sins to rescue us from the present evil age, according to the will of our God and Father, (Gal 1:4)**

**In him we have redemption through his blood, the forgiveness of sins, in accordance with the riches of God's grace (Eph 1:7)**

**In whom we have redemption, the forgiveness of sins. (Col 1:14)**

**For you know that it was not with perishable things such as silver or gold that you were redeemed from the empty way of life handed down to you from your forefathers, But with the precious blood of Christ, a lamb without blemish or defect. (1 Pet 1:18-19)**

**And they sang a new song: "You are worthy to take the scroll and to open its seals, because you were slain, and with your blood you purchased men for God from every tribe and language and people and nation. (Rev 5:9)**

5. Jesus Christ has exalted us. He has actually made us to be a kingdom and priests.

⇒ By *kingdom* is meant a rule, some authority and responsibility that involves overseership, management, supervision, and governing. Believers shall rule and reign with Christ. We shall oversee and administer the affairs of the universe for Christ throughout eternity.

**Jesus said to them, "You will indeed drink from my cup, but to sit at my right or left is not for me to grant. These places belong to those for whom they have been prepared by my Father." (Mat 20:23)**

**The Spirit himself testifies with our spirit that we are God's children. Now if we are children, then we are heirs—heirs of God and co-heirs with Christ, if indeed we share in his sufferings in order that we may also share in his glory. (Rom 8:16-17)**

**Do you not know that the saints will judge the world? And if you are to judge the world, are you not competent to judge trivial cases? (1 Cor 6:2)**

**And God raised us up with Christ and seated us with him in the heavenly realms in Christ Jesus, In order that in the coming ages he might show the incomparable riches of his grace, expressed in his kindness to us in Christ Jesus. (Eph 2:6-7)**

**If we endure, we will also reign with him. If we disown him, he will also disown us; (2 Tim 2:12)**

**To him who overcomes and does my will to the end, I will give authority over the nations— 'He will rule them with an iron scepter; he will dash them to pieces like pottery' — just as I have received authority from my Father. (Rev 2:26-27)**

**I saw thrones on which were seated those who had been given authority to judge. And I saw the souls of those who had been beheaded because of their testimony for Jesus and because of the word of God. They had not worshiped the beast or his image and had not received his mark on their foreheads or their hands. They came to life and reigned with Christ a thousand years. (Rev 20:4)**

⇒ By *priests* means that we have open access into God's presence any time. Believers no longer need human priests or mediators. Believers are themselves made priests before God—all by Jesus Christ. Believers are now to offer their own prayers, praises, worship, thanksgiving, and offerings to God.

**Therefore, I urge you, brothers, in view of God's mercy, to offer your bodies as living sacrifices, holy and pleasing to God—this is your spiritual act of worship. (Rom 12:1)**

**Through Jesus, therefore, let us continually offer to God a sacrifice of**

praise—the fruit of lips that confess his name. (Heb 13:15)

You also, like living stones, are being built into a spiritual house to be a holy priesthood, offering spiritual sacrifices acceptable to God through Jesus Christ. (1 Pet 2:5)

**3** (1:7) **Jesus Christ, Return**: announcement three—look, Christ comes. This is the theme of Revelation, the coming again of Jesus Christ and the justice and judgment which He is to execute upon the earth. Jesus Christ is coming again, and when He comes, this verse says two things will happen.

1. Every eye will see Him. The glory of God is so bright and so full of light that it actually shines brighter than the sun (cp. Rev.21:23). When Jesus Christ returns, there will be a display of His glory that will surround the earth, and the reflection of the Lord's glory will be seen by every eye. Remember also there will be an innumerable host of angels and believers who are accompanying Christ back to earth. The idea is this: there will be so many that they will surround the earth. Whatever the case, Christ in all of His glory and majesty is going to return to earth, and when He returns, every eye will see Him.

2. Every person who has rejected Jesus Christ and crucified Him will mourn because of Him. This refers to all the enemies of Christ, not only to those who crucified Christ. Every person who has rebelled against Jesus Christ shall see Jesus Christ and they shall cry out in anguish because they have...

- cursed Him
- rejected Him
- ignored Him
- neglected Him
- rebelled against Him
- opposed Him

Men do not believe Jesus Christ: they reject His claim to be the Son of God, that He came from God *out of* (ek) heaven to save the world. Most persons accept that Jesus Christ was a great man and one of the greatest religious teachers of all time, but they reject His deity. They believe that man can be good enough to become acceptable to God on their own. Therefore, they reject the fact that Jesus Christ had to die for the sins of the world.

The result is going to be catastrophic: when men see Jesus Christ return to earth, they will then know that He is exactly who He claimed to be: the Messiah, the Anointed One of God, the Savior of the world. They will know that God does love the world, love it so much that He actually sent His Son to die for the sins of man. But note: when Christ returns, the idea is not that of salvation. It is that of wailing, of mourning and crying out, because of the judgment that Jesus Christ is bringing with Him. Jesus Christ, the Lord God of the universe, will be returning in glory to execute justice upon all who have rejected Him and worked evil upon the earth.

"At that time the sign of the Son of Man will appear in the sky, and all the nations of the earth will mourn. They will see the Son of Man coming on the clouds of the sky, with power and great glory. (Mat 24:30)

"When the Son of Man comes in his glory, and all the angels with him, he will sit on his throne in heavenly glory. All the nations will be gathered before him, and he will separate the people one from another as a shepherd separates the sheep from the goats. (Mat 25:31-32)

If anyone is ashamed of me and my words in this adulterous and sinful generation, the Son of Man will be ashamed of him when he comes in his Father's glory with the holy angels." (Mark 8:38)

And give relief to you who are troubled, and to us as well. This will happen when the Lord Jesus is revealed from heaven in blazing fire with his powerful angels. He will punish those who do not know God and do not obey the gospel of our Lord Jesus. (2 Th 1:7-8)

Enoch, the seventh from Adam, prophesied about these men: "See, the Lord is coming with thousands upon thousands of his holy ones To judge everyone, and to convict all the ungodly of all the ungodly acts they have done in the ungodly way, and of all the harsh words ungodly sinners have spoken against him." (Jude 1:14-15)

Look, he is coming with the clouds, and every eye will see him, even those who pierced him; and all the peoples of the earth will mourn because of him. So shall it be! Amen. (Rev 1:7)

The seventh angel sounded his trumpet, and there were loud voices in heaven, which said: "The kingdom of the world has become the kingdom of our Lord and of his Christ, and he will reign for ever and ever." And the twenty-four elders, who were seated on their thrones before God, fell on their faces and worshiped God, Saying: "We give thanks to you, Lord God Almighty, the One who is and who was, because you have taken your great power and have begun to reign. The nations were angry; and your wrath has come. The time has come for judging the dead, and for rewarding your servants the prophets and your saints and those who reverence your name, both small and great— and for destroying those who destroy the earth." (Rev 11:15-18)

I saw heaven standing open and there before me was a white horse, whose rider is called Faithful and True. With justice he judges and makes war. His eyes are like blazing fire, and on his head are many crowns. He has a name written on him that no one knows but he himself. He is dressed in a robe dipped in blood, and his name is the Word of God. The armies of heaven were following him, riding on white horses and dressed in fine linen, white and clean. Out of his mouth comes a sharp sword with which to strike down the nations. "He will rule them with an iron scepter." He treads the winepress of the fury of the wrath of God Almighty. On his robe and on his thigh he has this name written: KING OF KINGS AND LORD OF LORDS. (Rev 19:11-16, cp. v. 17-21)

He who testifies to these things says, "Yes, I am coming soon." Amen. Come, Lord Jesus. (Rev 22:20)

**4** (1:8) **Jesus Christ, Person; Deity**: announcement four—Jesus Christ is the Almighty God. Three great descriptions are given of Christ in this verse.

1. Jesus Christ is the Alpha and Omega. Alpha is the first letter of the Greek alphabet and Omega the last letter. That is, Jesus Christ is the beginning and the ending of all there is. He began all things and He shall end all things. All things find their purpose, meaning, and significance in Him. Man, the world, history—no matter how chaotic and disjointed life may seem—all things are under the control of Jesus Christ.

**Thought 1.** The exhortation is clear: we must put our trust in Jesus Christ and cast our lives upon Him. When we do, we receive the great gift of God spoken about in verse four. We receive the grace of God's care and provision and the great gift of peace, and we become safe and secure for eternity.

**I give them eternal life, and they shall never perish; no one can snatch them out of my hand. My Father, who has given them to me, is greater than all ; no one can snatch them out of my Father's hand. (John 10:28-29)**

**Peace I leave with you; my peace I give you. I do not give to you as the world gives. Do not let your hearts be troubled and do not be afraid. (John 14:27)**

**"I have told you these things, so that in me you may have peace. In this world you will have trouble. But take heart! I have overcome the world." (John 16:33)**

**But because of his great love for us, God, who is rich in mercy, Made us alive with Christ even when we were dead in transgressions—it is by grace you have been saved. And God raised us up with Christ and seated us with him in the heavenly realms in Christ Jesus, In order that in the coming ages he might show the incomparable riches of his grace, expressed in his kindness to us in Christ Jesus. (Eph 2:4-7)**

2. Jesus Christ is the Lord *who is, and who was, and who is to come.* That is, He is eternal and unchangeable. Today He is the same Person He has always been, and He shall always be the same Person.

**Thought 1.** This is a great message for man. Jesus Christ *loves us all*; He loves us as much as He loved those who lived when He first came to earth. His love is unchangeable. But remember: so are His justice and judgment. If we trust Him, we shall know His love; if we reject Him, we shall know His wrath.

**For the Son of Man is going to come in his Father's glory with his angels, and then he will reward each person according to what he has done. (Mat 16:27)**

**He also says, "In the beginning, O Lord, you laid the foundations of the earth, and the heavens are the work of your hands. They will perish, but you remain; they will all wear out like a garment. You will roll them**

**up like a robe; like a garment they will be changed. But you remain the same, and your years will never end." (Heb 1:10-12)**

**Jesus Christ is the same yesterday and today and forever. (Heb 13:8)**

**Every good and perfect gift is from above, coming down from the Father of the heavenly lights, who does not change like shifting shadows. (James 1:17)**

**Your name, O LORD, endures forever, your renown, O LORD, through all generations. (Psa 135:13)**

**Your kingdom is an everlasting kingdom, and your dominion endures through all generations. The LORD is faithful to all his promises and loving toward all he has made. (Psa 145:13)**

3. Jesus Christ is the Almighty (pantokrator). The word means the All-Controller, the All-Ruler. He is the One who controls all things and rules over all things in the whole universe. This means that Jesus Christ possesses all power: He is omnipotent, able to do anything. He controls everything: the universe and every being within the universe. He controls the atoms, protons, neutrons, and electrons of space and matter. He even controls every circumstance, event, and happening throughout the universe.

**Thought 1.** Jesus Christ is the Almighty. This means a most wonderful thing: no matter what a person goes through, if he belongs to Jesus Christ, all things will be worked out for his good. Jesus Christ will control the circumstances and twist them to the good of the believer. Nothing can snatch the believer out from under the control of Jesus Christ.

**And we know that in all things God works for the good of those who love him, who have been called according to his purpose. (Rom 8:28)**

**For I am convinced that neither death nor life, neither angels nor demons, neither the present nor the future, nor any powers, Neither height nor depth, nor anything else in all creation, will be able to separate us from the love of God that is in Christ Jesus our Lord. (Rom 8:38-39)**

**He is the image of the invisible God, the firstborn over all creation. For by him all things were created: things in heaven and on earth, visible and invisible, whether thrones or powers or rulers or authorities; all things were created by him and for him. He is before all things, and in him all things hold together. (Col 1:15-17)**

**In the past God spoke to our forefathers through the prophets at many times and in various ways, But in these last days he has spoken to us by his Son, whom he appointed heir of all things, and through whom he made the universe. The Son is the radiance of God's glory and the exact representation of his being, sustaining all things by his powerful word. After he had provided purification for sins, he sat down at the right hand of the Majesty in heaven. (Heb 1:1-3)**

**VISION ONE, 1:9-3:22**

**II. THE MESSAGES OF THE GLORIFIED CHRIST TO THE SEVEN CHURCHES, 1:9-3:22**

**A. The Son of Man, the Glorified Christ, 1:9-20**

1 **The setting—Patmos**[DS1]
  a. John was a brother & companion to the believers
    1) In trials
    2) In the kingdom
    3) In perseverance
  b. John received the Word on the island of Patmos
  c. John was in the Spirit[DS2] on the Lord's Day

2 **His loud, trumpeting voice giving instructions**

3 **His presence in the midst of the seven golden or the lampstands churches, cp. 20**

4 **His awesome & frightening appearance**
  a. With a long robe
  b. With a golden breastplate wrapped around His chest

9 I, John, your brother and companion in the suffering and kingdom and patient endurance that are ours in Jesus, was on the island of Patmos because of the word of God and the testimony of Jesus.
10 On the Lord's Day I was in the Spirit, and I heard behind me a loud voice like a trumpet,
11 Which said: "Write on a scroll what you see and send it to the seven churches: to Ephesus, Smyrna, Pergamum, Thyatira, Sardis, Philadelphia and Laodicea."
12 I turned around to see the voice that was speaking to me. And when I turned I saw seven golden lampstands,
13 And among the lampstands was someone "like a son of man," dressed in a robe reaching down to his feet and with a golden sash around his chest.
14 His head and hair were white like wool, as white as snow, and his eyes were like blazing fire.
15 His feet were like bronze glowing in a furnace, and his voice was like the sound of rushing waters.
16 In his right hand he held seven stars, and out of his mouth came a sharp double-edged sword. His face was like the sun shining in all its brilliance.
17 When I saw him, I fell at his feet as though dead. Then he placed his right hand on me and said: "Do not be afraid. I am the First and the Last.
18 I am the Living One; I was dead, and behold I am alive for ever and ever! And I hold the keys of death and Hades.
19 "Write, therefore, what you have seen, what is now and what will take place later.
20 The mystery o the seven stars that you saw in my right hand and of the seven golden lampstands is this: The seven stars are the angels of the seven churches, and the seven lampstands are the seven churches.

  c. With hair like white wool, as white as snow
  d. With eyes like a blazing fire
  e. With feet like glowing bronze
  f. With a voice like the sound of rushing waters
  g. With seven stars in His right hand
  h. With a sword in His mouth
  i. With His face shining like the sun

5 **His reassuring presence & care**
  a. John's terrified reaction
  b. Jesus' calm assurance
  c. Jesus' identification
    1) He is God—the First & the Last
    2) He is the resurrected Lord
    3) He is the Judge

6 **His clear instructions**

7 **His interpretation of the vision**

  a. The seven stars: Are seven pastors
  b. The seven lampstands: Are seven churches

---

**VISION ONE, 1:9-3:22**

# DIVISION II

## THE MESSAGES OF THE GLORIFIED CHRIST TO THE SEVEN CHURCHES, 1:9-3:22

### A. The Son of Man, the Glorified Christ, 1:9-20

(1:9-20) **Introduction**: this is the *first vision* that Christ gives John. It is a vision of Christ Himself, of Christ in His glory and exaltation. It is in this vision that the glorified Christ proclaims His message to the seven churches. But before He speaks to the churches, Christ gives John a glimpse of Himself. Christ wants believers down through the centuries to know who it is that has given these messages to the churches. Christ wants all believers to know that the message to the churches is coming from the Supreme Majesty of the universe, from One who must be heeded, from One who possesses all power and knowledge, from One who can provide and protect, assure and secure, judge and destroy. This is the vision of the Author of Revelation, of the One who has given us this awesome message of Revelation. This is the vision of the Son of Man, the glorified Christ Himself.

1. The setting—Patmos (v.9-10).
2. His loud, trumpeting voice giving instruction (v.10-11).
3. His presence in the midst of the seven golden lampstands or the churches (v.12-13).
4. His awesome and frightening appearance (v.13-16).
5. His reassuring presence and care (v.17-18).

6. His clear instructions (v.19).
7. His interpretation of the vision (v.20).

**1** (1:9-10) **John the Apostle—Patmos**: the setting for the vision was the island of Patmos (see DEEPER STUDY # 1, *Patmos*—Rev.1:9). John says three things.

1. He calls himself a brother and a companion to the believers of the churches. By *brother* he means that he is a believer even as they are believers. They are brothers in the family of God, brothers to the Lord Jesus Christ and to one another, all having been adopted into the family of God. By *companion* John means that he has lived among the believers. He has walked day by day in their midst as a companion with them. But note: John had a particular experience in mind. He had been a companion with them in their...

• day to day tribulations: trials, afflictions, persecutions, sufferings, pressure.
• day to day seeking after the kingdom: looking for the kingdom of God, longing and seeking after it.

- day to day patience: enduring and persevering against all trials and temptations; standing fast in looking for and seeking after the kingdom of God.

> **But he who stands firm to the end will be saved. (Mat 24:13)**
> **Strengthening the disciples and encouraging them to remain true to the faith. "We must go through many hardships to enter the kingdom of God," they said. (Acts 14:22)**
> **If we endure, we will also reign with him. If we disown him, he will also disown us; (2 Tim 2:12)**

2. John says that he was on the island of Patmos when Christ gave him the visions of Revelation. Note: he says that he was there for the cause of Christ; that is, he had been banished or exiled to the island for preaching the Word of God and the testimony of Christ (see DEEPER STUDY #1, *Patmos*—Rev.1:9).

3. John says that he was *in the Spirit on the Lord's day*. The *Lord's day* undoubtedly means Sunday, the first day of the week, the day that Christ was raised from the dead. *In the Spirit* means that Christ put John in a trance, that He gave John a deep spiritual experience that lifted his mind and spirit above this world and put him in the very presence of Christ Himself.

**Thought 1.** Note how God met John's need. John was alone, stranded on an island that was as barren and isolated as could be. Imagine being alone—banished from society, loved ones, and friends. But John knew Christ and Christ met his need.

> **And teaching them to obey everything I have commanded you. And surely I am with you always, to the very end of the age." (Mat 28:20)**
> **Keep your lives free from the love of money and be content with what you have, because God has said, "Never will I leave you; never will I forsake you." (Heb 13:5)**
> **Cast all your anxiety on him because he cares for you. (1 Pet 5:7)**
> **So do not fear, for I am with you; do not be dismayed, for I am your God. I will strengthen you and help you; I will uphold you with my righteous right hand. (Isa 41:10)**

---

**DEEPER STUDY # 1**

(1:9) **Patmos**: this was the island to which John the Apostle was banished.
⇒ It sat out at sea only about forty miles from the great city of Ephesus.
⇒ It sat in the midst of a group of islands called the Sporades.
⇒ It was only about ten miles long and six miles wide.
⇒ It was an isolated, barren, rocky island with hills rising to about one thousand feet.

There is little question about John being banished to the island for preaching the gospel of Christ. William Barclay gives abundant evidence for this.

---

"It was the unanimous tradition of the early Church that John was banished to the island of Patmos in the reign of Domitian.

"Tertullian says: 'The apostle John was banished to the island' (On the Prescription of Heretics, 36).
⇒ "Origen says: 'The Roman Emperor, as tradition tells us, condemned John to the island of Patmos for witnessing to the word of truth' (Homilies on Matthew).
⇒ "Clement of Alexandria tells us: 'On the death of the tyrant John returned to Ephesus from the island of Patmos' (The Rich Man's Salvation, 42).
⇒ "Jerome says that John was banished in the fourteenth year after Nero and liberated on the death of Domitian (Concerning Illustrious Men, 9).

"This would mean that John was banished to Patmos about A.D. 94 and that he was liberated about A.D. 96." (What Barclay says is outlined for clarity. *The Revelation of John*, Vol.1. "The Daily Study Bible." Philadelphia, PA: The Westminster Press, 1959, p.51.)

**Thought 1.** In the darkest hours of human need God is always there. God will meet us if we will only cast ourselves upon Him and call for Him. This was true with John when he was exiled, and it was true with others in their dark exile. The Pulpit Commentary makes the following point.
⇒ It was in exile that Jacob saw God at Bethel (Gen.35:6f).
⇒ It was in exile that Moses saw God at the burning bush (Ex.3:1f).
⇒ It was in exile that Elijah heard the still small voice (1 Kings 19:3f).
⇒ It was in exile that Ezekiel saw the glory of the Lord by the river Chedar (Ezk.1:3f).
⇒ It was in exile that Daniel saw the Ancient of days (Dan.7:9f).
(A. Plummer. *Revelation*. "The Pulpit Commentary," Vol.22, ed. by HDM Spence and Joseph S. Exell. Grand Rapids, MI: Eerdmans, 1950, p.5.)

---

**DEEPER STUDY # 2**

(1:10) **In the Spirit**: John is said to be *in the Spirit* four times (Rev.1:9-10; 4:1-2; 17:1-3; 21:9-10). These mark off the four major visions of Revelation. Note that the first vision is given by Christ coming down to John. But for the last three visions John is commanded to "come up here"; he is given the perspective of heaven upon the events which shall be hereafter.

---

**2** (1:10-11) **Jesus Christ, Exaltation—Glory**: there was the loud, trumpeting voice of the Lord giving instructions. The vision begins. John hears a *loud voice* behind him, a voice that sounded like the call of a trumpet. The idea of the trumpet is that of authority, of an overpowering and commanding voice. The Lord instructed John to write what he saw in a book and to send it to the seven churches of Asia.

**Thought 1.** Note that Christ was not giving John a message for himself, but for the church. He was to use what Christ was giving him for the edification of believers, to build them up in the faith. This is the great purpose for Revelation, the reason why it must be taught in the church: to edify and build us up in the faith.

**3** (1:12-13) **Jesus Christ—Church**: there was Christ standing in the midst of seven golden lampstands, that is, in the midst of the churches. The lampstands represent the churches (v.20). Why this symbol? Jesus Christ is the Light of the world, and it is the task of the church to hold Him forth before the world. The church is to proclaim the light of Christ to the world, and it is to do so with the brilliance and speed of light. Note that Christ stands in the midst of the candlesticks. The churches receive their light from Christ. Unless He stands in the midst of the church, the church has no light. The church must see to it that Christ is in its midst, and the church must proclaim the light of Christ to the world.

**Thought 1.** For Christ to be in the midst of the church means that the message of Christ is the very focus of the church. The message of Christ is, of course, the Word of God, the Holy Scriptures. He is the very theme of the Scriptures and it was the Scriptures that He Himself proclaimed. The church must make absolutely sure that the Holy Scriptures are read, studied, taught, and preached among its people and to the community at large.

> **The people walking in darkness have seen a great light; on those living in the land of the shadow of death a light has dawned. (Isa 9:2)**

> **In him was life, and that life was the light of men. (John 1:4)**

> **When Jesus spoke again to the people, he said, "I am the light of the world. Whoever follows me will never walk in darkness, but will have the light of life." (John 8:12)**

> **Then Jesus told them, "You are going to have the light just a little while longer. Walk while you have the light, before darkness overtakes you. The man who walks in the dark does not know where he is going. (John 12:35)**

> **For God, who said, "Let light shine out of darkness," made his light shine in our hearts to give us the light of the knowledge of the glory of God in the face of Christ. (2 Cor 4:6)**

> **For it is light that makes everything visible. This is why it is said: "Wake up, O sleeper, rise from the dead, and Christ will shine on you." (Eph 5:14)**

> **The city does not need the sun or the moon to shine on it, for the glory of God gives it light, and the Lamb is its lamp. (Rev 21:23)**

> **"You are the light of the world. A city on a hill cannot be hidden. (Mat 5:14)**

> **For this is what the Lord has commanded us: "'I have made you a light for the Gentiles, that you may bring salvation to the ends of the earth.'" (Acts 13:47)**

> **For you were once darkness, but now you are light in the Lord. Live as children of light (Eph 5:8)**

> **So that you may become blameless and pure, children of God without fault in a crooked and depraved generation, in which you shine like stars in the universe (Phil 2:15)**

**4** (1:13-16) **Jesus Christ, Exaltation—Glory**: there was the awesome and frightening appearance of Christ. Note who it is standing in the midst of the golden lampstands or churches. It is the Son of Man, Christ Himself. This means a most wonderful thing: the message of Revelation is from the Lord Himself. It is not the message of a man, not a message that we have to question and wonder about and search out to see if there is truth in it. Revelation is the message of Jesus Christ, of the exalted Lord Himself. It is a message that can be trusted, a message that is true from beginning to end. It is a message that we must heed, for it is the message of the Lord Himself.

Now, note the vision. John's vision of Christ was so awesome that it defied description. There was no human language to describe Him. All John could do was take some of the precious and awesome things of earth and say the glorified Lord is like that.

1. Jesus Christ was clothed with a robe down to His feet (v.13). This was the robe of prophets (Zech.3:4), of priests (Ex.28:4; 39:29; Lev.16:4), and of kings and princes (1 Sam.24:5, 12). The robe symbolizes the prophetic, priestly, and kingly ministry of Christ.

⇒ As prophet, Jesus Christ proclaims the Word of God to us.

⇒ As priest, Jesus Christ gives us access into the presence of God and makes us acceptable to God.

⇒ As king, Jesus Christ rules and reigns over all the affairs of the universe, and He protects and provides and works all things out for good to those who love and follow Him.

2. The chest of Jesus Christ had a gold sash strapped across it (v.13). This particular sash was something like the chestpiece or breastpiece of the high priest on which the names of his people were engraved (cp. Ex.28:4; 39:29). The sash or chestpiece covered the heart. This symbolized that Christ holds His people and His church ever so close to His heart. They are all engraved upon the chestpiece of His heart and held ever so dear by Him. (See notes—Ex.28:15-30;39:8-21 for more discussion).

> **For I am convinced that neither death nor life, neither angels nor demons, neither the present nor the future, nor any powers, Neither height nor depth, nor anything else in all creation, will be able to separate us from the love of God that is in Christ Jesus our Lord. (Rom 8:38-39)**

3. The head and hair of Jesus Christ were as white as white wool and snow (v.14). This is the picture of Christ as the Ancient of Days, as being the eternal Lord of the universe. It is possible that this is also a picture of His sinlessness and purity of mind. The spiritual warfare is fought in the mind, and Christ never sinned; He never even had one evil or negative thought that came short of God's glory. He was the sinless Son of God Himself.

> **"As I looked, "thrones were set in place, and the Ancient of Days took his seat. His clothing was as white as snow; the hair of his head was white like wool. His throne was flaming with fire, and its wheels were all ablaze. (Dan 7:9)**

> **That God was reconciling the world to himself in Christ, not counting men's sins**

against them. And he has committed to us the message of reconciliation...God made him who had no sin to be sin for us, so that in him we might become the righteousness of God. (2 Cor 5:19, 21)

Beyond all question, the mystery of godliness is great: He appeared in a body, was vindicated by the Spirit, was seen by angels, was preached among the nations, was believed on in the world, was taken up in glory. (1 Tim 3:16)

4. Jesus Christ had eyes that were like blazing fire (v.14). This symbolizes a piercing, penetrating power. He sees everywhere, even in the dark places and behind closed doors. His eyes search the innermost recesses of the heart. He knows all; He is omniscient and He is able to conquer all those who reject Him and do evil. No one will be able to hide from Him nor can anyone hide anything from Him.

His body was like chrysolite, his face like lightning, his eyes like flaming torches, his arms and legs like the gleam of burnished bronze, and his voice like the sound of a multitude. (Dan 10:6)

Nothing in all creation is hidden from God's sight. Everything is uncovered and laid bare before the eyes of him to whom we must give account. (Heb 4:13)

"I the LORD search the heart and examine the mind, to reward a man according to his conduct, according to what his deeds deserve." (Jer 17:10)

Can anyone hide in secret places so that I cannot see him?" Declares the LORD. "Do not I fill heaven and earth?" Declares the LORD. (Jer 23:24)

5. Jesus Christ had feet like glowing bronze. This symbolizes strength and perseverance. His feet are the feet that preached the gospel, the glad tidings of peace. But they are also the feet that shall tread down His enemies. His feet are also able to rush to the rescue of His people.

How beautiful on the mountains are the feet of those who bring good news, who proclaim peace, who bring good tidings, who proclaim salvation, who say to Zion, "Your God reigns!" (Isa 52:7)

His body was like chrysolite, his face like lightning, his eyes like flaming torches, his arms and legs like the gleam of burnished bronze, and his voice like the sound of a multitude. (Dan 10:6)

And how can they preach unless they are sent? As it is written, "How beautiful are the feet of those who bring good news!" (Rom 10:15)

For we do not have a high priest who is unable to sympathize with our weaknesses, but we have one who has been tempted in every way, just as we are—yet was without sin. Let us then approach the throne of grace with confidence, so that we may receive mercy and find grace to help us in our time of need. (Heb 4:15-16)

6. Jesus Christ had a voice that was like the sound of rushing waters (v.15). His voice symbolizes authority.

⇒ It sends forth the glorious message of salvation, hope, joy, confidence, and comfort.

The bride belongs to the bridegroom. The friend who attends the bridegroom waits and listens for him, and is full of joy when he hears the bridegroom's voice. That joy is mine, and it is now complete. (John 3:29)

When he has brought out all his own, he goes on ahead of them, and his sheep follow him because they know his voice. (John 10:4)

"You are a king, then!" Said Pilate. Jesus answered, "You are right in saying I am a king. In fact, for this reason I was born, and for this I came into the world, to testify to the truth. Everyone on the side of truth listens to me." (John 18:37)

For the Lord himself will come down from heaven, with a loud command, with the voice of the archangel and with the trumpet call of God, and the dead in Christ will rise first. After that, we who are still alive and are left will be caught up together with them in the clouds to meet the Lord in the air. And so we will be with the Lord forever. Therefore encourage each other with these words. (1 Th 4:16-18)

⇒ It thunders forth majestic rebuke, conviction, and judgment.

The voice of the LORD is powerful; the voice of the LORD is majestic. (Psa 29:4)

"Now prophesy all these words against them and say to them: "'The LORD will roar from on high; he will thunder from his holy dwelling and roar mightily against his land. He will shout like those who tread the grapes, shout against all who live on the earth. (Jer 25:30)

"Do not be amazed at this, for a time is coming when all who are in their graves will hear his voice And come out—those who have done good will rise to live, and those who have done evil will rise to be condemned. (John 5:28-29)

As he neared Damascus on his journey, suddenly a light from heaven flashed around him. He fell to the ground and heard a voice say to him, "Saul, Saul, why do you persecute me?" (Acts 9:3-4)

Here I am! I stand at the door and knock. If anyone hears my voice and opens the door, I will come in and eat with him, and he with me. (Rev 3:20)

7. Jesus Christ held seven stars in His right hand (v.16; cp. v.20). The seven stars symbolize the messengers, the ministers of the churches. His hand securely holds the messengers with skill and strength and comfort.

Those who are wise will shine like the brightness of the heavens, and those who lead many to righteousness, like the stars for ever and ever. (Dan 12:3)

You did not choose me, but I chose you and appointed you to go and bear fruit—fruit that will last. Then the Father will give you whatever you ask in my name. (John 15:16)

But the Lord said to Ananias, "Go! This man is my chosen instrument to carry my name before the Gentiles and their kings and before the people of Israel. (Acts 9:15)

'Now get up and stand on your feet. I have appeared to you to appoint you as a servant and as a witness of what you have seen of me and what I will show you. (Acts 26:16)

Therefore go and make disciples of all nations, baptizing them in the name of the Father and of the Son and of the Holy Spirit, And teaching them to obey everything I have commanded you. And surely I am with you always, to the very end of the age." (Mat 28:19-20)

Keep your lives free from the love of money and be content with what you have, because God has said, "Never will I leave you; never will I forsake you." (Heb 13:5)

I thank Christ Jesus our Lord, who has given me strength, that he considered me faithful, appointing me to his service. (1 Tim 1:12)

That is why I am suffering as I am. Yet I am not ashamed, because I know whom I have believed, and am convinced that he is able to guard what I have entrusted to him for that day. (2 Tim 1:12)

The Lord will rescue me from every evil attack and will bring me safely to his heavenly kingdom. To him be glory for ever and ever. Amen. (2 Tim 4:18)

8. Jesus Christ had a sharp two-edged sword coming out of His mouth (v.16). This symbolizes the Word of God and its penetrating power (cp. 2 Th.2:8).

For the word of God is living and active. Sharper than any double-edged sword, it penetrates even to dividing soul and spirit, joints and marrow; it judges the thoughts and attitudes of the heart. (Heb 4:12)

All Scripture is God-breathed and is useful for teaching, rebuking, correcting and training in righteousness, (2 Tim 3:16)

9. Jesus Christ had a face that was like the sun shining in its full strength. This symbolizes the dazzling brilliance of His presence in all of His majesty and honor and glory as God.

For the Son of Man is going to come in his Father's glory with his angels, and then he will reward each person according to what he has done. (Mat 16:27)

There he was transfigured before them. His face shone like the sun, and his clothes became as white as the light. (Mat 17:2)

And now, Father, glorify me in your presence with the glory I had with you before the world began. (John 17:5)

Meanwhile, Saul was still breathing out murderous threats against the Lord's disciples. He went to the high priest And asked him for letters to the synagogues in Damascus, so that if he found any there who belonged to the Way, whether men or women, he might take them as prisoners to Jerusalem. As he neared Damascus on his journey, suddenly a light from heaven flashed around him. He fell to the ground and heard a voice say to him, "Saul, Saul, why do you persecute me?" "Who are you, Lord?" Saul asked. "I am Jesus, whom you are persecuting," he replied. (Acts 9:1-5)

For God, who said, "Let light shine out of darkness," made his light shine in our hearts to give us the light of the knowledge of the glory of God in the face of Christ. (2 Cor 4:6)

In a loud voice they sang: "Worthy is the Lamb, who was slain, to receive power and wealth and wisdom and strength and honor and glory and praise!" (Rev 5:12)

**5** (1:17-18) **Jesus Christ—Assurance**: there was the reassuring presence and care of the Lord. John was terrified. He fell at the feet of the Lord as though he were dead. But note the calm assurance of Christ. Christ reached out with His right hand and softly and tenderly touched John, assuring Him that He was not there to consume him. Christ said four things to John.

1. "Do not be afraid" (v.17). He was declaring that He had not appeared to John in judgment but in love and care. He was appearing to commission John and to use him in the great mission of building up the churches and of reaching the lost for God.

And even the very hairs of your head are all numbered. So don't be afraid; you are worth more than many sparrows. (Mat 10:30-31)

When I saw him, I fell at his feet as though dead. Then he placed his right hand on me and said: "Do not be afraid. I am the First and the Last. (Rev 1:17)

So do not fear, for I am with you; do not be dismayed, for I am your God. I will strengthen you and help you; I will uphold you with my righteous right hand. (Isa 41:10)

But now, this is what the LORD says—he who created you, O Jacob, he who formed you, O Israel: "Fear not, for I have redeemed you; I have summoned you by name; you are mine. When you pass through the waters, I will be with you; and when you pass through the rivers, they will not sweep over you. When you walk through the fire, you will not be burned; the flames will not set you ablaze. (Isa 43:1-2)

2. "I am the First and the Last" (v.17). That is, He is the beginning and the end. He is the One who can be with a person forever—when the person is born and when he dies and during all the days in between. He can be with a person

throughout all of eternity. John need not fear the awesome, terrifying presence of Christ, for He is the eternal Lord of the universe as well as the Savior of man.

> **"I tell you the truth," Jesus answered, "before Abraham was born, I am!" (John 8:58)**
>
> **And now, Father, glorify me in your presence with the glory I had with you before the world began..."Father, I want those you have given me to be with me where I am, and to see my glory, the glory you have given me because you loved me before the creation of the world. (John 17:5, 24)**
>
> **I am the Alpha and the Omega, the First and the Last, the Beginning and the End. (Rev 22:13)**

3. "I am the Living One; I was dead; and behold, I am alive for ever and ever!" (v.18). The exalted and glorified Lord need not be feared, for He is the same Person who came to earth and died and arose for our salvation. He is exalted and dwells in the most awesome and frightening glory, but He dwells there to save us, not to condemn us. He lives for ever and ever to make us acceptable to God and to carry us through the evil and death of this world.

> **In him was life, and that life was the light of men. (John 1:4)**
>
> **The thief comes only to steal and kill and destroy; I have come that they may have life, and have it to the full. (John 10:10)**
>
> **Jesus said to her, "I am the resurrection and the life. He who believes in me will live, even though he dies; (John 11:25)**
>
> **Jesus answered, "I am the way and the truth and the life. No one comes to the Father except through me. (John 14:6)**
>
> **And who through the Spirit of holiness was declared with power to be the Son of God by his resurrection from the dead: Jesus Christ our Lord. (Rom 1:4)**
>
> **That if you confess with your mouth, "Jesus is Lord," and believe in your heart that God raised him from the dead, you will be saved. (Rom 10:9)**
>
> **Praise be to the God and Father of our Lord Jesus Christ! In his great mercy he has given us new birth into a living hope through the resurrection of Jesus Christ from the dead, And into an inheritance that can never perish, spoil or fade—kept in heaven for you, (1 Pet 1:3-4)**

4. "I hold the keys of death and Hades" (v.18). Jesus Christ is the Savior of the world. He has conquered death, and He can deliver us from judgment and Hades, of hell. He has the keys to unlock both death and hell and to deliver us from the bondage of both.

> **But it has now been revealed through the appearing of our Savior, Christ Jesus, who has destroyed death and has brought life and immortality to light through the gospel. (2 Tim 1:10)**
>
> **Since the children have flesh and blood, he too shared in their humanity so that by**

his death he might destroy him who holds the power of death—that is, the devil— And free those who all their lives were held in slavery by their fear of death. (Heb 2:14-15)

> **He will wipe every tear from their eyes. There will be no more death or mourning or crying or pain, for the old order of things has passed away." (Rev 21:4)**
>
> **"I tell you the truth, whoever hears my word and believes him who sent me has eternal life and will not be condemned; he has crossed over from death to life. (John 5:24)**
>
> **Before long, the world will not see me anymore, but you will see me. Because I live, you also will live. (John 14:19)**
>
> **He will swallow up death forever. The Sovereign LORD will wipe away the tears from all faces; he will remove the disgrace of his people from all the earth. The LORD has spoken. (Isa 25:8)**

**6** (1:19) **Revelation, The**: there were the clear instructions of Jesus Christ. Christ repeats His commission to John. He tells John to write three things. Note: these things provide an outline for the book of *Revelation*. John was to write...

- *What he had seen*: that is, the vision of the glorified Christ (chapters 1-2).
- *What is now*: that is, the state and condition of the churches (chapters 2-3).
- *What will take place later*: that is, the consummation of human history, the coming again of the Lord Jesus Christ and the end of the world (chapters 4-22).

**7** (1:20) **Church, The**: there was Christ interpreting the vision for John. The interpretation is clearly stated.

⇒ The seven stars are the angels of the seven churches. The word "angels" (angelos) means messenger as well as heavenly angels. There are several different ideas as to whom the word refers here. The weight of evidence points toward the meaning being the ministers of the churches.

⇒ The seven lampstands are symbols of the seven churches. Remember what the symbol means: the church holds forth the light of the world, the glorious light of the Lord Jesus Christ.

> **"You are the light of the world. A city on a hill cannot be hidden. (Mat 5:14)**
>
> **For this is what the Lord has commanded us: "'I have made you a light for the Gentiles, that you may bring salvation to the ends of the earth.'" (Acts 13:47)**
>
> **For you were once darkness, but now you are light in the Lord. Live as children of light (Eph 5:8)**
>
> **So that you may become blameless and pure, children of God without fault in a crooked and depraved generation, in which you shine like stars in the universe (Phil 2:15)**
>
> **You are all sons of the light and sons of the day. We do not belong to the night or to the darkness. (1 Th 5:5)**

| | CHAPTER 2 | my name, and have not grown weary. | |
|---|---|---|---|
| | **B. The Message to Ephesus: The Orthodox Church, but A Church Without Love, 2:1-7** | 4 Yet I hold this against you: You have forsaken your first love. | **4 The complaint: They had left their first love** |
| **1 The recipients** | | 5 Remember the height from which you have fallen! Re- | **5 The counsel: Remember—repent—do** |
| a. The messenger of the church | "To the angel of the church in Ephesus write: These are the words of him who holds the seven stars in his right hand and walks among the seven golden lampstands: | pent and do the things you did at first. If you do not re-pent, I will come to you and remove your lampstand from its place. | **6 The warning** |
| b. The Ephesian church^DSI | | | a. Your church, the lampstand will be re-moved |
| **2 The speaker—Jesus** | | | b. Your doctrinal purity is not enough |
| **3 The commendation** | 2 I know your deeds, your hard work and your perse-verance. I know that you cannot tolerate wicked men, that you have tested those who claim to be apostles but are not, and have found them false. | 6 But you have this in your favor: You hate the practices of the Nicolaitans, which I also hate. | |
| a. For works & labor | | 7 He who has an ear, let him hear what the Spirit says to the churches. To him who overcomes, I will give the right to eat from the tree of life, which is in the paradise of God. | **7 The promise: To the over-comers** |
| b. For steadfastness | | | |
| c. For not bearing evil | | | |
| d. For testing & rejecting false apostles | | | a. The tree of life |
| e. For persevering and not growing weary | 3 You have persevered and have endured hardships for | | b. Paradise |

# DIVISION II

## THE MESSAGES OF THE GLORIFIED CHRIST TO THE SEVEN CHURCHES, 1:9-3:22

## B. The Message to Ephesus: The Orthodox Church, but a Church Without Love, 2:1-7

(2:1-7) **Introduction**: this passage begins the great message of Christ to the seven churches of Asia. But note a signifi-cant point: verse one says that Jesus Christ is addressing the church at Ephesus, but He is in the midst of all the churches. This means a most wonderful thing: the Revelation is for all the Lord's servants and followers. He gave the Revelation so that all believers could know the things that are to take place in the end time. But note: if Jesus Christ was making the Revelation to all of His servants, why is the letter ad-dressed to only seven churches in Asia? Why was it not ad-dressed to all the churches down through the centuries? The following chart clearly shows what we are asking:

Revelation was addressed to these churches *in Asia*
- ⇒ Ephesus
- ⇒ Smyrna
- ⇒ Pergamum
- ⇒ Thyatira
- ⇒ Sardis
- ⇒ Philadelphia
- ⇒ Laodicea

Revelation was not addressed to these churches *in Asia*
- ⇒ Troas (Acts 20:5; 2 Cor.2:12)
- ⇒ Miletus (Acts 20:17)
- ⇒ Colosse (Col.1:2)
- ⇒ Hierapolis (Col.4:13)

Church history even tells us that there were other church-es in Asia beyond these eleven. John certainly knew of them all. Why then address the Revelation to only seven of the churches? There has to be a reason, for Jesus Christ was giv-ing the Revelation so that all of His servants would know about the events of the end time (v.1). What is the reason? Note that John does not say. He does not even give a hint. But two things tell us.
- ⇒ Thinking about the matter leads to one clear con-clusion. The seven churches must be *representa-*

*tive of other churches*. The characteristics that are found in these churches must be the same kind of characteristics that are found in other churches. Each of these churches must represent a certain type or kind of church. In speaking to the seven churches, Jesus Christ expects every church to identify itself and to heed the exhortation given to each. He wants all followers to heed the truths of Revelation; therefore, He has selected seven churches that are representative of all churches.
- ⇒ The *characteristics* of the churches clearly show that the churches are *representative of other churches*. The conditions that existed in each of the seven churches differed, and as we study the different types of churches in society and throughout history, we clearly see that there are seven types of churches. Therefore, in addressing the seven churches, Jesus Christ was addressing all the churches of the earth. Each church, no mat-ter its condition, can discover what kind of church it is by honestly taking inventory of its major traits and checking those traits against these seven churches. This is clearly seen as we study the messages to the churches.

The point is this: the messages to the seven churches were given for personal application. Jesus Christ expects us—all churches and all believers—to apply the messages to our own situation. Jesus Christ expects us to search our hearts and to heed the messages given to these churches. The first message is to Ephesus, an orthodox church, a church that was faithful to Christ and to the Word of God, but it was a church without love.

1. The recipients (v.1).
2. The speaker—Jesus (v.1).
3. The commendation (v.2-3).
4. The complaint: they had left their first love (v.4).

5. The counsel: remember—repent—do (v.5).
6. The warning (v.5-6).
7. The promise: to overcomers (v.7).

**1** (2:1) **Church—Minister**: there are the recipients of this letter. The letter is addressed to the minister of the church as well as to the church. This is striking, for it means that the Lord holds the minister responsible for the church and its welfare. Christ expects the minister to study and heed the message himself and to lead the believers to heed the message.

---

**DEEPER STUDY # 1**

(2:1) **Ephesus**: at its height Ephesus was the most important city along the coast of Asia Minor. Two hundred and thirty cities dotted the coast line of Asia Minor. Many had ideal harbors, but Ephesus was the queen among these coast communities. The city had been founded to command one of the main highways of Asia Minor. Its attraction was not only its natural harbor, but the rich, fertile land that covered the inland area.

Ephesus was, of course, a great commercial city. Its natural harbor and strategic location on one of the main roads of the world made it such. However, in the middle of the first century, the harbor had silted up so badly that trade had declined dramatically from the days of Ephesian glory. There had been attempts to drag the silt out, but the efforts were half-hearted and finally abandoned. The people's hearts were just not in the effort. Part of the reason for this attitude was the successful and profitable trade Ephesus enjoyed from its religious cult. The great temple of Artemis, was there. Artemis was the goddess who had a grotesque head and many breasts and focused upon the sensual pleasure of the flesh. The worshipping pilgrims found their satisfaction in prostitution with a host of priestesses who plied the cult of the goddess. A great trade of silversmiths had developed over the years, and tourist commercialism boomed year-round. This accounts for the guild of silversmiths finding the crowds an easy mark for arousing opposition against Paul (Acts 19:24). As the years went by, the great harbor silted up more and more, and the Ephesians depended more and more upon the trade that came from their religion and superstition. The natural harbor of Smyrna, which lay close by, became a more suitable port and began to take away more and more of the commercial traffic of Ephesus. As a result Ephesus became a dying city, living on its past reputation as a religious and philosophical center. The great city of Ephesus had a disease, the disease of sensual unrighteousness, and the disease did its work: it corrupted the people. The people, sensual and self-centered, lost their will and willingness to ply a commendable trade. Thus, the disease of Ephesus proved mortal. The "lampstand" of Ephesus crumbled, and the light of Ephesus died out (see Rev.2:1-7, esp. 5).

The church in Ephesus had a small beginning. When Paul visited Ephesus, he found only twelve believers in the city. They had been won to the Lord by the immature but impressive preacher Apollos. As a result they had been misinformed on the presence of the Holy Spirit; they seemed to lack a consciousness of the Spirit in the life of the believer and the awareness that He had already been sent into the world (Acts 19:1-7). After Paul's instruction to these twelve, he began to teach in the synagogue. He taught for three months. But the Jews were hardened and refused to believe. They murmured against the message. Therefore, Paul moved the church into the school of a philosopher, Tyrannus. There he preached Christ for two whole years. During this time it is said that the church was instrumental in sounding forth the Word throughout all Asia: "So that all the Jews and Greeks who live in the province of Asia heard the word of the Lord (Acts 19:10).

The Lord worked special miracles by Paul in Ephesus and the church witnessed some amazing things. From all evidence, the spectacular was necessary in order to get through to the people. As always, God did everything He could to reach a people. These experiences show the great love and movement of God toward man (see Acts 19:11-20). In viewing these accounts, we must keep the background of the city in mind. Ephesus was a hot bed of Oriental magic and superstition. The people were an emotional and sensual lot, easily moved to feelings. They were a devoted people, an expressive people, a loving people, and equally a lovable people (Rev.2:1-7, esp. 4).

As Paul preached and God worked miracles, many believed and the church grew mightily. The believers gave great evidence of changed lives by living for Christ right in the middle of an immoral and pagan society. On one occasion, the church demonstrated its new found faith by building a great bonfire and setting aflame all of its pagan and magical literature.

---

**2** (2:1) **Jesus Christ—Church**: there is the speaker, Jesus Christ Himself. Note two significant facts.

1. Jesus Christ is the One who holds the ministers of the churches in His hands. This means that the minister...

- is chosen and picked out of the world by the hand of Christ.
- is nourished and nurtured by the hand of Christ.
- is placed where he is by the hand of Christ.
- is cared for, secured, and protected by the hand of Christ.
- is given a very special closeness to Christ by being held in His hand.
- is expected to be an instrument in the hand of Christ.
- is responsible to the hand of Christ.
- is to be held accountable by the hand of Christ.

2. Jesus Christ is the One who walks in the midst of the churches or the golden lampstands. This means...

- that Christ is present in the very midst of the church.
- that Christ sees and knows all about the church.
- that Christ is present to teach and grow the church.
- that Christ is present to provide and protect the church.
- that Christ is present to guide and direct the church.
- that Christ is present as the Light of the world to give light to the church.

Note also that Christ is in the midst of *all* the churches. He has no favorites; He shows no partiality whatsoever. There are no denominations and no barriers with Christ. If a body of believers truly follows Christ, He is in their midst, right there with them.

**3** (2:2-3) **Church—Believers**: there is the commendation. The church is commended for five significant things.

1. The church *worked hard* for Christ. The Greek means to work, labor to the point of weariness, sweat, and exhaustion; to work and labor to the limit of one's ability. The church was a working church, a laboring church, a church committed to serve Christ and to serve Him to the fullest.

**Thought 1.** There is no room for laziness or lethargy in the church of Christ. Christ expects every believer to work hard for Him, to labor to the point of exhaustion. Note that Christ keeps an account of our work and labor. The idea is that He keeps a daily account: He knows every ounce of energy that we expend. He knows when we become tired and exhausted and can go no more. He also knows when we should be working and do not.

For I was hungry and you gave me something to eat, I was thirsty and you gave me something to drink, I was a stranger and you invited me in, I needed clothes and you clothed me, I was sick and you looked after me, I was in prison and you came to visit me.' (Mat 25:35-36)
In the same way, let your light shine before men, that they may see your good deeds and praise your Father in heaven. (Mat 5:16)
Command them to do good, to be rich in good deeds, and to be generous and willing to share. (1 Tim 6:18)
And do not forget to do good and to share with others, for with such sacrifices God is pleased. (Heb 13:16)

2. The church *persevered*. The word means to persevere and to be steadfast in serving Christ and in standing against all the temptations and trials of life. The church was steadfast in studying and proclaiming the gospel and in ministering to the needs of the needy.

Therefore, my dear brothers, stand firm. Let nothing move you. Always give yourselves fully to the work of the Lord, because you know that your labor in the Lord is not in vain. (1 Cor 15:58)
By standing firm you will gain life. (Luke 21:19)
You need to persevere so that when you have done the will of God, you will receive what he has promised. (Heb 10:36)
Consider it pure joy, my brothers, whenever you face trials of many kinds, Because you know that the testing of your faith develops perseverance. Perseverance must finish its work so that you may be mature and complete, not lacking anything. (James 1:2-4)
Blessed is the man who perseveres under trial, because when he has stood the test, he will receive the crown of life that God has promised to those who love him. (James 1:12)
Be patient, then, brothers, until the Lord's coming. See how the farmer waits for the land to yield its valuable crop and how patient he is for the autumn and spring rains. (James 5:7)

3. The church could not tolerate evil people. This refers to sin and evil, men who were corrupt and polluted and who lived for the world instead of living for God. The church could not tolerate the sin and shame, dirt and pollution, filth and destruction of evil.

Blessed are the pure in heart, for they will see God. (Mat 5:8)
"Therefore come out from them and be separate, says the Lord. Touch no unclean thing, and I will receive you." "I will be a Father to you, and you will be my sons and daughters, says the Lord Almighty." (2 Cor 6:17-18)
Since we have these promises, dear friends, let us purify ourselves from everything that contaminates body and spirit, perfecting holiness out of reverence for God. (2 Cor 7:1)
Have nothing to do with the fruitless deeds of darkness, but rather expose them. (Eph 5:11)
In the name of the Lord Jesus Christ, we command you, brothers, to keep away from every brother who is idle and does not live according to the teaching you received from us. (2 Th 3:6)
So that the man of God may be thoroughly equipped for every good work. (2 Tim 3:17)
Make every effort to live in peace with all men and to be holy; without holiness no one will see the Lord. (Heb 12:14)
Since everything will be destroyed in this way, what kind of people ought you to be? You ought to live holy and godly lives (2 Pet 3:11)
I will set before my eyes no vile thing. The deeds of faithless men I hate; they will not cling to me. (Psa 101:3)
I gain understanding from your precepts; therefore I hate every wrong path. (Psa 119:104)
My mouth speaks what is true, for my lips detest wickedness. (Prov 8:7)
To fear the LORD is to hate evil; I hate pride and arrogance, evil behavior and perverse speech. (Prov 8:13)

4. The church tested all the preachers and teachers of the church and rejected the false. If a teacher confessed that Jesus Christ, the Son of God, had come in the flesh, he was accepted and allowed to teach. If he denied that Jesus Christ had come in the flesh, he was not allowed to teach. The church could not tolerate false teachers and stood against all false teaching. They were loyal to Christ. They did just what Scripture exhorts: they tested the spirits of the teachers.

Dear friends, do not believe every spirit, but test the spirits to see whether they are from God, because many false prophets have gone out into the world. This is how you can recognize the Spirit of God: Every spirit that acknowledges that Jesus Christ has come in the flesh is from God, but every spirit that does not acknowledge Jesus is not from God. This is the spirit of the antichrist, which you have heard is coming and even now is already in the world. (1 John 4:1-3; cp. 1 Jn.2:22-23; Mt.7:15-20)

5. The church endured hardships, persevered for the sake of Christ's name. This is a descriptive verse, a description that touches the heart of tender believers: the church...

- persevered
- endured hardships
- did not grow weary

Why? For Christ's name sake. They did it all and endured so much for Christ's sake.

⇒ They worked and toiled to the point of exhaustion.
⇒ They endured hardships.
⇒ They did not tolerate or put up with evil.
⇒ They tested and rejected false teachers.

This is a meaningful picture of a true church, a church that has surrendered itself to the Lord Jesus Christ. It is the picture of a church that is loyal and devoted to Christ, that is orthodox through and through. It is the picture of just what a church should be. But there is one thing lacking, one devastating and destructive thing that looms ever so large in the life of the church. This is the discussion of the next note.

> **All men will hate you because of me, but he who stands firm to the end will be saved. (Mat 10:22)**
> **Whoever finds his life will lose it, and whoever loses his life for my sake will find it. (Mat 10:39)**
> **And everyone who has left houses or brothers or sisters or father or mother or children or fields for my sake will receive a hundred times as much and will inherit eternal life. (Mat 19:29)**
> **I will show him how much he must suffer for my name." (Acts 9:16)**
> **We are fools for Christ, but you are so wise in Christ! We are weak, but you are strong! You are honored, we are dishonored! (1 Cor 4:10)**
> **Therefore, since through God's mercy we have this ministry, we do not lose heart. Therefore we do not lose heart. Though outwardly we are wasting away, yet inwardly we are being renewed day by day. (2 Cor 4:1, 16)**
> **For we who are alive are always being given over to death for Jesus' sake, so that his life may be revealed in our mortal body. (2 Cor 4:11)**
> **That is why, for Christ's sake, I delight in weaknesses, in insults, in hardships, in persecutions, in difficulties. For when I am weak, then I am strong. (2 Cor 12:10)**
> **But you, man of God, flee from all this, and pursue righteousness, godliness, faith, love, endurance and gentleness. Fight the good fight of the faith. Take hold of the eternal life to which you were called when you made your good confession in the presence of many witnesses. (1 Tim 6:11-12)**
> **In everything set them an example by doing what is good. In your teaching show integrity, seriousness (Titus 2:7)**
> **You have persevered and have endured hardships for my name, and have not grown weary. (Rev 2:3)**

**4** (2:4) **Church—Love—Backsliding**: there is the complaint. The church had lost or "forsaken" its first love. This probably means two things.

1. The church and its believers had lost their feelings for Christ. The Greek says, "your love the first [love]." Believers had left their first love. Christ was no longer *first* in their lives. They were putting themselves and their own affairs first, and they were putting the church first—the programs, services, ministries, and fellowship of the church. They had become more attached to the church than they were to Christ.

⇒ They had lost their feelings of warmth and tenderness for Christ.
⇒ They had lost their sensitivity to Christ, their fervor, spark, and unction.
⇒ They were not fellowshipping and communing nor praying and sharing with Christ—not like they did when they were first converted.
⇒ They were not walking in a consciousness and awareness of Christ's presence, joying and rejoicing in Him throughout the day.

Simply stated, they were not having personal fellowship with Christ, walking and sharing with Him like they once did. They were not as attached to Christ as they had been. They were more attached to other things and other involvements of life. They loved their church and they had the right beliefs, and they were even ready to fight for the truth of Christ. But they did not love Christ, not in a personal and intimate way, not to the degree that they walked and shared with Him, fellowshipped and communed with Him all throughout the day, not in the sense that they took blocks of time and got alone with Him and prayed and shared with Him.

> **Thought 1.** Picture a young man who falls in love with a young lady. He wants to spend time with her and share with her. He wants to become attached to her and make her first in his life. This should always be our desire with Christ.

> **Because of the increase of wickedness, the love of most will grow cold, (Mat 24:12)**
> **Jesus replied, "If anyone loves me, he will obey my teaching. My Father will love him, and we will come to him and make our home with him. (John 14:23)**
> **No, the Father himself loves you because you have loved me and have believed that I came from God. (John 16:27)**
> **Grace to all who love our Lord Jesus Christ with an undying love. (Eph 6:24)**
> **Though you have not seen him, you love him; and even though you do not see him now, you believe in him and are filled with an inexpressible and glorious joy, (1 Pet 1:8)**
> **Yet I hold this against you: You have forsaken your first love. (Rev 2:4)**
> **Here I am! I stand at the door and knock. If anyone hears my voice and opens the door, I will come in and eat with him, and he with me. (Rev 3:20)**
> **"Go and proclaim in the hearing of Jerusalem: '"I remember the devotion of your youth, how as a bride you loved me and followed me through the desert, through a land not sown. (Jer 2:2)**

2. The church had lost its love for people  The church saw a rupture take place in its fellowship and in its love for one another. When the church was first founded, a deep love existed among the members (cp. Acts 20:17-38). The church had a loving heart and a helping hand—a readiness to labor together even through persecution. But something happened. What? There is no explanation. So all the negative things that rupture a fellowship or erase love are applicable: criticism, grumbling, jealousy, a selfish mind.

> **"A new command I give you: Love one another. As I have loved you, so you must love one another. By this all men will know that you are my disciples, if you love one another." (John 13:34-35)**
>
> **My command is this: Love each other as I have loved you. (John 15:12)**
>
> **Love must be sincere. Hate what is evil; cling to what is good. (Rom 12:9)**
>
> **I appeal to you, brothers, in the name of our Lord Jesus Christ, that all of you agree with one another so that there may be no divisions among you and that you may be perfectly united in mind and thought. (1 Cor 1:10)**
>
> **You are still worldly. For since there is jealousy and quarreling among you, are you not worldly? Are you not acting like mere men? (1 Cor 3:3)**
>
> **Now that you have purified yourselves by obeying the truth so that you have sincere love for your brothers, love one another deeply, from the heart. (1 Pet 1:22)**

**5** (2:5) **Repentance—Remember**: there is the counsel. The Lord counsels the church to return to him. When a church or a believer goes astray, the Lord issues the very same call that He issues here: return. Three steps are involved in returning.

1. First, remember from where you have fallen. Think back over your former love for the Lord. Remember His presence:
   ⇒ the feelings of warmth and tenderness
   ⇒ the fervor, spark, and unction
   ⇒ the fellowship and communion with Him
   ⇒ the prayer and sharing
   ⇒ the consciousness and awareness of His presence
   ⇒ the joy and rejoicing of His presence that filled your heart

Again, remember the Lord's presence, the love that existed between you and Him.

2. Second, repent: turn away from whatever has pulled you away from Christ and turn back to Christ. Something has drawn you away from Christ. You are attached to something more than you are to Christ. Something is consuming your thoughts and energies and keeping your mind from focusing upon Christ and fellowshipping and communing with Him. You are not flickering your mind to Him in prayer as you walk throughout the day. You are not sharing and communing with Him like you did. Something has replaced Him in your thoughts and attention. And you are more attached to that thing than you are to Christ. *Repent*—turn away from that attachment and turn back to Christ.

> **And saying, "Repent, for the kingdom of heaven is near." (Mat 3:2)**

> **Blessed are those who mourn, for they will be comforted. (Mat 5:4)**
>
> **I tell you, no! But unless you repent, you too will all perish. (Luke 13:3)**
>
> **Peter replied, "Repent and be baptized, every one of you, in the name of Jesus Christ for the forgiveness of your sins. And you will receive the gift of the Holy Spirit. (Acts 2:38)**
>
> **Repent, then, and turn to God, so that your sins may be wiped out, that times of refreshing may come from the Lord, (Acts 3:19)**
>
> **Repent of this wickedness and pray to the Lord. Perhaps he will forgive you for having such a thought in your heart. (Acts 8:22)**
>
> **In the past God overlooked such ignorance, but now he commands all people everywhere to repent. (Acts 17:30)**
>
> **If my people, who are called by my name, will humble themselves and pray and seek my face and turn from their wicked ways, then will I hear from heaven and will forgive their sin and will heal their land. (2 Chr 7:14)**
>
> **Let the wicked forsake his way and the evil man his thoughts. Let him turn to the LORD, and he will have mercy on him, and to our God, for he will freely pardon. (Isa 55:7)**

3. Third, do the first things that you did.
   ⇒ Begin now to flicker your mind to Christ and to take just a moment to pray. Do this all day long every so often. Acknowledge Him in all your ways, and He will make your paths straight (Pr.3:6).
   ⇒ Take set times to get alone with Christ and study His Word and pray (2 Tim.2:15; 3:16; Eph. 6:18).
   ⇒ Begin to walk just as Christ would walk if He were walking by your side—step by step and hour by hour. Do this from the moment you awaken in the morning to the moment you go to sleep at night.

**6** (2:5-6) **Warning**: there is the warning. Christ warns the church that loses its love for Him. The warning is twofold.

1. There is the warning that Christ will remove the church (the lampstand) from its place. What does this mean? It means that Christ will remove the church...
   • from being a true church.
   • from being a true representative of Christ upon earth.
   • from being a church of God's true kingdom.
   • from being in touch and in union with God.
   • from being a true light and witness to the world.
   • from being a church of the gospel of God.
   • from His presence, from the light of His presence.

This is a terrible judgment. Just how terrible can be seen by looking at the opposite of the above. If a church has been removed by Christ then it means that the church...
   • is not a true church; it is a false church.
   • is not a part of God's kingdom; it is a part of the world's kingdom.

* is not in touch and union with Christ; it is only in touch and union with the world.
* is not a true light and witness to the world; it is a false light and witness to the world.
* is not in the presence of Christ and His light; it is in the darkness of this world.
* is not a church of the gospel; it is a church with a false gospel.

**Thought 1.** How many churches have been removed by Christ? How many churches...
* are lifeless?
* are dull?
* are mechanical?
* are nothing more than form?
* lack the presence of Christ in the services?
* lack the light and witness of Christ and His power?

2. There is warning that doctrinal purity is not enough. This warning is going to be shattering to some when Christ returns. Why? Because many are doctrinally sound, but they have lost their first love for Christ. Note how doctrinally sound the Ephesian believers were.

They had stood ever so strongly against the Nicolaitans. Just who the Nicolaitans were is not known. It is thought that they stressed two things:
⇒ that Christ had done away with the law of the Old Testament and had instituted the law of Christian liberty.
⇒ that the soul and spirit of man was far more important than his body.

The results of this doctrine are clearly seen. If there is no law to govern us, then we can do what we like just so we profess to believe in Christ. And if the spirit is what really matters, then I can do what I like with my body just so I take care of my spirit.
⇒ Think how many people feel that they can live like they want just so they attend and support the church. If they attend church, they feel they can live like they want during the week.
⇒ Think how many people believe they are eternally secure because they believe in Christ, have been baptized, and belong to a church. Yet, they live like they want during the week. They continue to seek the pleasures and possessions of the world, banking and hoarding and neglecting the spread of the gospel and a world of desperate needs. There is no evidence whatsoever of repentance and of a changed and holy life—no evidence of self-denial, of the sacrifice of *all one is and has*.

The point is this: the Ephesian church had preached and taught against the error of the Nicolaitans. They had refused to allow the error to enter the church. They were doctrinally sound; they stood staunchly for the truth of Christ and the Word of God. But they lacked the main thing: love for Christ. They had lost their love for Christ.

**Thought 1.** Note two things.
1) Christ did not do away with the law; He fulfilled it. He filled it up. That is, Jesus Christ embraces the law and so much more. He is now our ideal and standard. We no longer follow the law; we follow Christ. But remember: Christ embraces the law and much more. Therefore in following Christ, we end up keeping the law and walking in far more purity

and holiness than what the law demands. (See DEEPER STUDY # 2—Mt.5:17; DEEPER STUDY # 2—Ro.8:3.)

> **"Do not think that I have come to abolish the Law or the Prophets; I have not come to abolish them but to fulfill them. (Mat 5:17)**
> **For what the law was powerless to do in that it was weakened by the sinful nature, God did by sending his own Son in the likeness of sinful man to be a sin offering. And so he condemned sin in sinful man, (Rom 8:3)**

2) The soul and spirit are important, but so is the body. We are to take care of our whole person: spirit, soul, and body. We are to keep both body and spirit pure and holy.

> **Therefore, I urge you, brothers, in view of God's mercy, to offer your bodies as living sacrifices, holy and pleasing to God—this is your spiritual act of worship. Do not conform any longer to the pattern of this world, but be transformed by the renewing of your mind. Then you will be able to test and approve what God's will is—his good, pleasing and perfect will. (Rom 12:1-2)**
> **Don't you know that you yourselves are God's temple and that God's Spirit lives in you? If anyone destroys God's temple, God will destroy him; for God's temple is sacred, and you are that temple. (1 Cor 3:16-17)**
> **Do you not know that your body is a temple of the Holy Spirit, who is in you, whom you have received from God? You are not your own; You were bought at a price. Therefore honor God with your body. (1 Cor 6:19-20)**

**7** (2:7) **Promise—Overcomers—Victory:** there is the promise to the overcomers. The word *overcomer* has the idea of conflict and struggle. The *overcomer* is a person who overcomes and conquers and gains the victory. He is the victor and conqueror. What is it that he is to overcome? Everything that pulls his heart and love away from Christ and attaches it to the world. Whatever possessions, whatever pleasures, whatever it is that has dampened the believer's first love for Christ—it is that thing that the believer must overcome.

Note that the promise is made to individual believers; therefore, all believers are to hear the messages to the churches. A church as a whole may go astray, but it is the believer who must personally overcome. How? Let him who has an ear hear what the Spirit says, and let him heed and do what the Spirit says. If he does then he will be an overcomer.

Here are the glorious promises to the overcomer.

1. The overcomer shall be allowed to eat of the tree of life. This is the tree of God, the tree that gives life, both the fullness of life and eternal life.

The tree of life is first seen in the Garden of Eden. Adam lost his right to eat of it because of his sin and disobedience to God. Thus, he was banished from the garden and cut off from eating of the tree (Gen.2:9, 16-17; 3:22-24). Now, the tree of life is given to the faithful and victorious follower of

Christ, but it is not guaranteed. Only some have a right to it (Rev.22:14), and the tree may be taken away (Rev.22:19).

And the LORD God made all kinds of trees grow out of the ground—trees that were pleasing to the eye and good for food. In the middle of the garden were the tree of life and the tree of the knowledge of good and evil. (Gen 2:9)

And the LORD God said, "The man has now become like one of us, knowing good and evil. He must not be allowed to reach out his hand and take also from the tree of life and eat, and live forever." (Gen 3:22)

She is a tree of life to those who embrace her; those who lay hold of her will be blessed. (Prov 3:18)

The fruit of the righteous is a tree of life, and he who wins souls is wise. (Prov 11:30)

When I arrived there, I saw a great number of trees on each side of the river. Fruit trees of all kinds will grow on both banks of the river. Their leaves will not wither, nor will their fruit fail. Every month they will bear, because the water from the sanctuary flows to them. Their fruit will serve for food and their leaves for healing." (Ezek 47:7, 12)

He who has an ear, let him hear what the Spirit says to the churches. To him who overcomes, I will give the right to eat from the tree of life, which is in the paradise of God. (Rev 2:7)

Down the middle of the great street of the city. On each side of the river stood the tree of life, bearing twelve crops of fruit, yielding its fruit every month. And the leaves of the tree are for the healing of the nations. (Rev 22:2)

I am the living bread that came down from heaven. If anyone eats of this bread, he will live forever. This bread is my flesh, which I will give for the life of the world." (John 6:51)

Why spend money on what is not bread, and your labor on what does not satisfy? Listen, listen to me, and eat what is good, and your soul will delight in the richest of fare. (Isa 55:2)

2. The overcomer shall become a citizen of the paradise of God. Paradise is heaven, the very dwelling place of God, the place...

- of eternal bliss and ecstasy
- of eternal perfection and life
- of eternal fulfillment and completeness
- of eternal love and joy
- of eternal peace and control
- of eternal work and pleasure
- of eternal duty and honor
- of eternal service and satisfaction

On and on the list could go. All that life is and was ever meant to be—that is what will be in the paradise of heaven. This is the glorious promise to the overcomer. (See Deeper Study # 3, *Paradise*— Lk.16:23; Deeper Study # 2— 2 Cor.12:4 for more discussion.)

Jesus answered him, "I tell you the truth, today you will be with me in paradise." (Luke 23:43)

Was caught up to paradise. He heard inexpressible things, things that man is not permitted to tell. (2 Cor 12:4)

He who has an ear, let him hear what the Spirit says to the churches. To him who overcomes, I will give the right to eat from the tree of life, which is in the paradise of God. (Rev 2:7)

**Thought 1.** The promises to the overcomer throughout this passage are meaningful. They are a dynamic challenge, a challenge to conquer whatever it is that keeps us from living for Christ.

| | | C. The Message to Smyrna: The Persecuted Church, 2:8-11 | gogue of Satan. | |
|---|---|---|---|---|
| **1** | **The recipients** | 8 "To the angel of the church in Smyrna write: These are the words of him who is the First and the Last, who died and came to life again. | 10 Do not be afraid of what you are about to suffer. I tell you, the devil will put some of you in prison to test you, and you will suffer persecution for ten days. Be faithful, even to the point of death, and I will give you the crown of life. | **4** **The counsel** |
| | a. The messenger of the church | | | a. The devil will persecute |
| | b. The Smyrna church[DS1] | | | b. Persecution will be limited |
| **2** | **The speaker—Jesus** | | | c. Do not fear, but be faithful |
| **3** | **The commendation** | 9 I know your afflictions and your poverty—yet you are rich! I know the slander of those who say they are Jews and are not, but are a syna- | 11 He who has an ear, let him hear what the Spirit says to the churches. He who overcomes will not be hurt at all by the second death. | **5** **The promise: To the overcomers** |
| | a. For afflictions | | | a. The crown of life |
| | b. For bearing poverty | | | b. The deliverance from the second death |
| | c. For spiritual wealth | | | |
| | d. For bearing slander | | | |

# DIVISION II

## THE MESSAGES OF THE GLORIFIED CHRIST TO THE SEVEN CHURCHES, 1:9-3-22

### C. The Message to Smyrna: The Persecuted Church, 2:8-11

(2:8-11) **Introduction**: the church is sometimes called upon to suffer terrible persecution. This has always been true down through history, and it was certainly true in Smyrna. The church was under heavy attack from both the community and city officials. And there was even more horrible persecution lying over the horizon (v.10). But note: the church was faithful to Christ and His mission. The church was standing fast for the truth against all attacks. It was a church in which nothing was wrong, that is, nothing of any major significance. Therefore, it was one of the few churches that Christ did not have to warn. Smyrna is the picture of just what a church should be: a dynamic witness for Jesus Christ through all circumstances no matter the trial or temptation. It is the picture of a church that loves the Lord enough to stand up for Him even when the community attacks its witness.

1. The recipients (v.8).
2. The speaker—Jesus (v.8).
3. The commendation (v.9).
4. The counsel (v.10).
5. The promise: to overcomers (v.10-11).

**1** (2:8) **Church—Minister**: there are the recipients of the letter. The letter is addressed to the minister of the church. Remember: the Greek word for angel (angelos) means both angel and messenger, that is, it can mean an earthly messenger. In the case of the church the meaning is the messenger or minister of the church. This is significant, for it means that the minister is held responsible for the church. In Smyrna's case—in the case of the persecuted church—the minister is to take the lead in standing fast against persecution.

⇒ He is to stand forth for Christ and lead his people to stand for Christ.
⇒ He is not to buckle under and deny Christ; he is to lead his people not to buckle under and deny Christ.

No matter how severe the persecution may be, the minister of the church is to lead his people to hold the banner of Christ high. Even if it means martyrdom, the minister and his people are to do what Christ says to do in this letter.

**DEEPER STUDY # 1**

(2:8) **Smyrna**: there are three historical facts that seem to have a bearing upon the message to the church.

1. Smyrna means bitter. It received its name from myrrh, one of its chief commercial products. Myrrh was a gum-like resin taken from a shrub and was very bitter. It was used in making perfume (Ps.45:8), oil (Ex.30:23), for embalming (Jn.19:39), for purification of women (Est.2:12), and for relieving and dulling pain (Mk.15:23). It should be noted that this church was experiencing what its name said: bitter sorrow, affliction, and persecution (Rev.2:9-10).

2 Smyrna was a proud city—proud of its culture, its beauty, its commercial wealth, its social life. Its citizens called it the *first city* in Asia. There was a municipal vanity among the people. Everyone tried to climb the social ladder a step further than his neighbor. Everyone wanted the first place, the highest seat, the most recognition. To these, Christ proclaims loudly and clearly, "*I am* the First and Last" (v.8); "*I am the one* who has the crown of life" (v.10).

3. Smyrna was persecuting the church severely. The city had a large number of Jews who were influential in city politics. Jews were, of course, steeped in the Old Testament and the prophecies of the Messiah. Many of the early converts to Christ were Jews. Here in Smyrna, the reaction of the Jews was severe. They reacted severely and did all they could to influence the city officials to stamp out the church. The Christian believer knew God personally and intimately; therefore, he could not worship or participate in the festivals to the god and goddesses of his day. He was marked. In some cases jobs were lost, and in all cases, social life within the city was severed. Mockery, abuse, scorn, and persecution were applied. When Jesus says He is the first and the last, it is a promise that He is with the believer through it all—from the very first to the very last (v.11). He knows what the believer is going through, for He has suffered not only the threat of death, but death itself (v.8).

**2** (2:8) **Jesus Christ—Church**: there is the speaker, Jesus Christ Himself. Christ has a very special message for the church that is suffering trouble and persecution, and His message is wrapped up in two titles.

1. Christ says that He is *the First and the Last*. He is the One supreme authority and ruler over life. Persecutors—government officials and some citizens who persecute and cause trouble for other people—may think that they hold

authority over life, but they do not. They may claim to be the first and the last, to have the final word and authority, but they are deceived. There is only one First and Last, only one supreme authority, and that is the Lord Jesus Christ, the Son of God Himself.

a. This means that all persecutors, all those who afflict and cause trouble for others, had better take heed. They shall be judged if they usurp and take the authority over human life into their own hands. There is only one authority over life, and that is the Lord Jesus Christ. Therefore, all people are to look to Him. Any person who persecutes and causes trouble for other people shall face His judgment.

**Just as man is destined to die once, and after that to face judgment, (Heb 9:27)**

b. This means that believers always have the presence of Christ with them through all the troubles and persecutions of life. Jesus Christ is the first and the last; He is always there. He is there with the believer...
- when the trouble first begins
- when the trouble is going on
- when the trouble ends

Jesus Christ is the first and the last; He spans time, all the minutes and hours of time. His presence covers all the problems, circumstances, and troubles of human life. Jesus Christ is always in charge of what happens to us. He controls the circumstances and trouble no matter what happens. Therefore, He will work all things out for our good.

**"I tell you the truth," Jesus answered, "before Abraham was born, I am!" (John 8:58)**

**"Father, I want those you have given me to be with me where I am, and to see my glory, the glory you have given me because you loved me before the creation of the world. (John 17:24)**

**And we know that in all things God works for the good of those who love him, who have been called according to his purpose. (Rom 8:28)**

**Who shall separate us from the love of Christ? Shall trouble or hardship or persecution or famine or nakedness or danger or sword? No, in all these things we are more than conquerors through him who loved us. For I am convinced that neither death nor life, neither angels nor demons, neither the present nor the future, nor any powers, Neither height nor depth, nor anything else in all creation, will be able to separate us from the love of God that is in Christ Jesus our Lord. (Rom 8:35, 37-39)**

2. Christ says that He is the One who *died and came to life again*. His death was only a passing phase, an episode He had to go through. He experienced death, but death was only a passing thing for Him. He triumphed over it. *Came to life* is aorist tense in the Greek, a once-for-all act. Once it is done, it is done—completed, finished. Jesus *came to life again*. He arose. Therefore, the message to the church at Smyrna is that no matter what they experience, it is a passing episode. Even if they experience death, it has been con-

quered. Christ has personally been there and triumphed over both pain and death. Therefore, the believer shall live forever even if he is martyred.

**"For God so loved the world that he gave his one and only Son, that whoever believes in him shall not perish but have eternal life. (John 3:16)**

**"I tell you the truth, whoever hears my word and believes him who sent me has eternal life and will not be condemned; he has crossed over from death to life. (John 5:24)**

**For my Father's will is that everyone who looks to the Son and believes in him shall have eternal life, and I will raise him up at the last day." (John 6:40)**

**No temptation has seized you except what is common to man. And God is faithful; he will not let you be tempted beyond what you can bear. But when you are tempted, he will also provide a way out so that you can stand up under it. (1 Cor 10:13)**

**The Lord will rescue me from every evil attack and will bring me safely to his heavenly kingdom. To him be glory for ever and ever. Amen. (2 Tim 4:18)**

**Since the children have flesh and blood, he too shared in their humanity so that by his death he might destroy him who holds the power of death—that is, the devil— And free those who all their lives were held in slavery by their fear of death. (Heb 2:14-15)**

**Praise be to the God and Father of our Lord Jesus Christ! In his great mercy he has given us new birth into a living hope through the resurrection of Jesus Christ from the dead, And into an inheritance that can never perish, spoil or fade—kept in heaven for you, (1 Pet 1:3-4)**

**If this is so, then the Lord knows how to rescue godly men from trials and to hold the unrighteous for the day of judgment, while continuing their punishment. (2 Pet 2:9)**

**3** (2:9) **Church—Believers**: there is the commendation. The church is commended for four things.

1. The church bore up under terrible sufferings or afflictions (thlipsin). The word means affliction, the pressure of crushing tribulation. This word indicates that the trials and persecution were most severe. But the believers were holding up under the attacks and refusing to deny Christ. They were faithful to Christ despite all the ridicule, mockery, abuse, cursing, loss of property, possible imprisonment and martyrdom.

**"Be on your guard against men; they will hand you over to the local councils and flog you in their synagogues. On my account you will be brought before governors and kings as witnesses to them and to the Gentiles. (Mat 10:17-18)**

**"Then you will be handed over to be persecuted and put to death, and you will be hated by all nations because of me. (Mat 24:9)**

"But before all this, they will lay hands on **you and persecute you. They will deliver you to synagogues and prisons, and you will be brought before kings and governors, and all on account of my name.** (Luke 21:12)

**Remember the words I spoke to you: 'No servant is greater than his master.' If they persecuted me, they will persecute you also. If they obeyed my teaching, they will obey yours also. They will treat you this way because of my name, for they do not know the One who sent me.** (John 15:20-21)

**They will put you out of the synagogue; in fact, a time is coming when anyone who kills you will think he is offering a service to God.** (John 16:2)

**For it has been granted to you on behalf of Christ not only to believe on him, but also to suffer for him,** (Phil 1:29)

**In fact, everyone who wants to live a godly life in Christ Jesus will be persecuted,** (2 Tim 3:12)

**Consider him who endured such opposition from sinful men, so that you will not grow weary and lose heart.** (Heb 12:3)

**Dear friends, do not be surprised at the painful trial you are suffering, as though something strange were happening to you. But rejoice that you participate in the sufferings of Christ, so that you may be overjoyed when his glory is revealed.** (1 Pet 4:12-13)

2. The church bore up under poverty. The idea is that of having nothing and of being destitute and beggarly. Apparently many were being forced out of their jobs and having their property confiscated as lawbreakers. What happened was this: Rome had instituted a law that said the state had to be the first loyalty of a citizen. To show that loyalty, the citizen had to proclaim his loyalty once a year. This he did by going before local government officials and making the statement, "Caesar is Lord." Of course, a true believer and follower of Christ could not do this, for there is only one Lord, the Lord Jesus Christ. This was the reason the church was being attacked so severely and suffering so much. (See DEEPER STUDY # 1, pt.3—Rev.2:12 for more discussion.)

**Jesus replied, "Foxes have holes and birds of the air have nests, but the Son of Man has no place to lay his head."** (Mat 8:20)

**Sorrowful, yet always rejoicing; poor, yet making many rich; having nothing, and yet possessing everything.** (2 Cor 6:10)

**For you know the grace of our Lord Jesus Christ, that though he was rich, yet for your sakes he became poor, so that you through his poverty might become rich.** (2 Cor 8:9)

3. The church was spiritually wealthy. They were outwardly poor, but inwardly they were rich toward the Lord and His mission. They were faithful to the Lord...
- loving Him and one another and even those who opposed them (*agape* love).
- ministering to all in need.
- studying and teaching the Scriptures.
- living righteous and holy lives.

And because of their faithfulness, they were filled with all the fullness of God's presence. God poured out upon them the riches of His grace and the fruit of His Spirit. As they walked day by day, they were filled with...
- love
- joy
- peace
- patience
- kindness
- goodness
- faithfulness
- gentleness
- self-control

God flooded them and carried them through all their trials. He strengthened and settled them, empowered and assured them with His presence, the very presence of God Himself.

**But store up for yourselves treasures in heaven, where moth and rust do not destroy, and where thieves do not break in and steal.** (Mat 6:20)

**Jesus answered, "If you want to be perfect, go, sell your possessions and give to the poor, and you will have treasure in heaven. Then come, follow me."** (Mat 19:21)

**Sell your possessions and give to the poor. Provide purses for yourselves that will not wear out, a treasure in heaven that will not be exhausted, where no thief comes near and no moth destroys.** (Luke 12:33)

**I pray also that the eyes of your heart may be enlightened in order that you may know the hope to which he has called you, the riches of his glorious inheritance in the saints, And his incomparably great power for us who believe. That power is like the working of his mighty strength,** (Eph 1:18-19)

**But because of his great love for us, God, who is rich in mercy, Made us alive with Christ even when we were dead in transgressions—it is by grace you have been saved. And God raised us up with Christ and seated us with him in the heavenly realms in Christ Jesus, In order that in the coming ages he might show the incomparable riches of his grace, expressed in his kindness to us in Christ Jesus.** (Eph 2:4-7)

**What is more, I consider everything a loss compared to the surpassing greatness of knowing Christ Jesus my Lord, for whose sake I have lost all things. I consider them rubbish, that I may gain Christ** (Phil 3:8)

**The grace of our Lord was poured out on me abundantly, along with the faith and love that are in Christ Jesus.** (1 Tim 1:14)

**In this way they will lay up treasure for themselves as a firm foundation for the coming age, so that they may take hold of the life that is truly life.** (1 Tim 6:19)

**By faith Moses, when he had grown up, refused to be known as the son of Pharaoh's daughter. He chose to be mistreated along with the people of God rather than to enjoy the pleasures of sin for a short time. He regarded disgrace for the sake of Christ as of greater value than the treasures of Egypt, because he was looking ahead to his reward.** (Heb 11:24-26)

**Listen, my dear brothers: Has not God chosen those who are poor in the eyes of the**

world to be rich in faith and to inherit the kingdom he promised those who love him? (James 2:5)

4. The church bore up under all kinds of slander. The slander came especially from the Jews of the city. There was a large community of Jews in Smyrna. We know from historians that they were very prosperous and made large gifts to the arts and to the culture development of the city. As a result they were influential with the city officials and local Roman government. As stated, it was the Jews who were stirring up so much trouble against the church. Note how they went about it: they slandered the believers. They used their tongues to...

- ridicule
- mock
- lie
- spread rumors
- accuse
- backbite

- criticize
- murmur
- talk about
- tear down
- discriminate
- divide

But note what Christ says about the slandering Jews. They may profess to be Jews, but they are not. They are the synagogue of Satan. What does this mean? The Jews were God's appointed people during the Old Testament period of history, before Christ came into the world. They were the people whom God had raised up to be His witnesses upon earth. But many of them had failed to believe and follow God. In fact, they had even killed God's Son, the Lord Jesus Christ. The Jews in Smyrna professed to be Jews, to be followers of God, but they were not. They were persecuting the real followers of God, those who believed and worshipped the Lord Jesus Christ, the Son of God Himself. Therefore they were not worshippers of God—not of the true and living God. On the contrary, they were worshippers of Satan.

**Thought 1.** This is a strong message to every church. We are either an assembly of God, of the true and living God, or of Satan. It all depends upon whether or not we worship and serve the Lord Jesus Christ. We are a true church if we proclaim and stand up for Christ in the midst of an evil and corrupt world, a world that slanders those who live righteous and godly lives.

"Whoever acknowledges me before men, I will also acknowledge him before my Father in heaven. But whoever disowns me before men, I will disown him before my Father in heaven. (Mat 10:32-33)

If anyone is ashamed of me and my words in this adulterous and sinful generation, the Son of Man will be ashamed of him when he comes in his Father's glory with the holy angels." (Mark 8:38)

If we endure, we will also reign with him. If we disown him, he will also disown us; (2 Tim 2:12)

But there were also false prophets among the people, just as there will be false teachers among you. They will secretly introduce destructive heresies, even denying the sovereign Lord who bought them—bringing swift destruction on themselves. (2 Pet 2:1)

Who is the liar? It is the man who denies that Jesus is the Christ. Such a man is the antichrist—he denies the Father and the Son. No one who denies the Son has the Fa-

ther; whoever acknowledges the Son has the Father also. (1 John 2:22-23)

Dear friends, do not believe every spirit, but test the spirits to see whether they are from God, because many false prophets have gone out into the world. This is how you can recognize the Spirit of God: Every spirit that acknowledges that Jesus Christ has come in the flesh is from God, But every spirit that does not acknowledge Jesus is not from God. This is the spirit of the antichrist, which you have heard is coming and even now is already in the world. (1 John 4:1-3)

If anyone acknowledges that Jesus is the Son of God, God lives in him and he in God. (1 John 4:15)

**4** (2:10) **Faithful—Church**: there is the counsel. Note: Christ tells the church that more persecution is coming. The devil is going to arouse the unbelievers of the world to attack them for ten days. The idea of ten is that of brevity, for just a short time. Note a significant fact: God was allowing the persecution, and the reason is given—that the believers might be tried. What does this mean? God was allowing them to be tried...

- so that they would draw closer and closer to Him and learn more from Him.
- so that their faith could be strengthened more and more and by such they could be stronger witnesses to the world. When some unbelievers saw the believers suffer for the hope of salvation, the Holy Spirit would be able to use their suffering to speak to them. (See note and DEEPER STUDY # 1—1 Pt.4:12 for more discussion.)

The counsel of Christ is a clear message to the church when it is being persecuted: do not fear but be faithful. Not to fear may seem difficult when one is in the midst of being persecuted. But we must remember who Jesus Christ is:

⇒ The First and Last: He is in charge of all events and our lives are in His hands. He is with us from the first act of persecution to the last act of persecution (see note 2, *Jesus Christ—Church—Rev.2:8* for more discussion).

⇒ The One who was died and came to life again: He is living and exalted as the Supreme Lord of the universe. He is able to take care of us and make us dynamic witnesses for Him even in the midst of terrible persecution. He will comfort and strengthen us to be faithful. He will help us to stand fast against all the trials and temptations of life.

And even the very hairs of your head are all numbered. So don't be afraid; you are worth more than many sparrows. (Mat 10:30-31)

Therefore, since through God's mercy we have this ministry, we do not lose heart. (2 Cor 4:1)

Without being frightened in any way by those who oppose you. This is a sign to them that they will be destroyed, but that you will be saved—and that by God. For it has been granted to you on behalf of Christ not only to believe on him, but also to suffer for him, (Phil 1:28-29)

**Be strong and courageous. Do not be afraid or terrified because of them, for the LORD your God goes with you; he will never leave you nor forsake you." (Deu 31:6)**

**5** (2:10-11) **Promise—Overcomer**: there is the promise to the overcomers. (See note—Rev.2:7 for more discussion.) The promise is twofold.

1. The overcomer shall receive the crown of life. This simply means the reward of eternal life, of life that goes on forever and ever. Persecutors may take our life on earth, but quicker than the eye can blink, God transfers us to heaven. Men can kill the body, but they cannot kill the soul. They cannot extinguish our lives. If we are faithful to Christ, God takes us home to heaven to live with Him eternally. He crowns us with eternal life. (See note—Jas.1:12 for more discussion.)

**Just as Moses lifted up the snake in the desert, so the Son of Man must be lifted up, That everyone who believes in him may have eternal life. (John 3:14-15)**
**Whoever believes in the Son has eternal life, but whoever rejects the Son will not see life, for God's wrath remains on him." (John 3:36)**
**Do not work for food that spoils, but for food that endures to eternal life, which the Son of Man will give you. On him God the Father has placed his seal of approval." (John 6:27)**
**I give them eternal life, and they shall never perish; no one can snatch them out of my hand. (John 10:28)**
**The man who loves his life will lose it, while the man who hates his life in this world will keep it for eternal life. (John 12:25)**
**Now this is eternal life: that they may know you, the only true God, and Jesus Christ, whom you have sent. (John 17:3)**
**And this is what he promised us—even eternal life. (1 John 2:25)**

2. The overcomer shall be delivered from the second death. What is the second death? Scripture clearly tells us.

**Then death and Hades were thrown into the lake of fire. The lake of fire is the second death. (Rev 20:14)**
**But the cowardly, the unbelieving, the vile, the murderers, the sexually immoral, those who practice magic arts, the idolaters and all liars—their place will be in the fiery lake of burning sulfur. This is the second death." (Rev 21:8)**

The second death is the lake of fire, the judgment of eternal hell and torment from the presence of God forever and ever. The believer who overcomes in persecution shall escape the second death, the lake of fire and torment. The believer may have to pass through physical death, but he will never go through the second death. He shall be transported immediately into the presence of God to live forever and ever.

Note the exhortation: he who has an ear, let him hear what the Holy Spirit says to the churches. It is the duty of every believer and every church to hear this message. We must all stand fast against the persecution of the world: ridicule, mockery, abuse, being bypassed and overlooked, neglected and ignored, being imprisoned and killed. We must be faithful. The promises are too great to lose: we shall receive the crown of life and never suffer the second death.

**Thought 1.** Note the certainty of this point: there is to be a second death. There is no question, no equivocation about the matter. It is stated simply and in a straightforward manner. There is to be a second death, a death from which all men should escape. How? By being faithful to the Lord Jesus Christ through all the trials and temptations of this life. We must be faithful to God's Son even if it means standing firm in the midst of persecution.

**The apostles left the Sanhedrin, rejoicing because they had been counted worthy of suffering disgrace for the Name. (Acts 5:41)**
**After they had been severely flogged, they were thrown into prison, and the jailer was commanded to guard them carefully. Upon receiving such orders, he put them in the inner cell and fastened their feet in the stocks. About midnight Paul and Silas were praying and singing hymns to God, and the other prisoners were listening to them. (Acts 16:23-25)**
**The Spirit himself testifies with our spirit that we are God's children. Now if we are children, then we are heirs—heirs of God and co-heirs with Christ, if indeed we share in his sufferings in order that we may also share in his glory. (Rom 8:16-17)**
**For our light and momentary troubles are achieving for us an eternal glory that far outweighs them all. (2 Cor 4:17)**
**Therefore I endure everything for the sake of the elect, that they too may obtain the salvation that is in Christ Jesus, with eternal glory. (2 Tim 2:10)**
**You sympathized with those in prison and joyfully accepted the confiscation of your property, because you knew that you yourselves had better and lasting possessions. (Heb 10:34)**
**He regarded disgrace for the sake of Christ as of greater value than the treasures of Egypt, because he was looking ahead to his reward. (Heb 11:26)**

| | | teaching of Balaam, who taught Balak to entice the Israelites to sin by eating food sacrificed to idols and by committing sexual immorality. | Balaam: It has infiltrated the church |
|---|---|---|---|
| | **D. The Message to Pergamum: The Corrupted Church That is Married to the World, 2:12-17** | | |
| **1 The recipients** | 12 "To the angel of the church in Pergamum write: These are the words of him who has the sharp, double-edged sword. | | |
| a. The messenger of the church | | | **b. The teaching of the Nicolaitans: It has infiltrated the church** |
| b. The Pergamum church*DS1* | | 15 Likewise you also have those who hold to the teaching of the Nicolaitans. | |
| **2 The speaker—Jesus** | | 16 Repent therefore! Otherwise, I will soon come to you and will fight against them with the sword of my mouth. | **5 The counsel: Repent** |
| **3 The commendation** | 13 I know where you live— where Satan has his throne. Yet you remain true to my name. You did not renounce your faith in me, even in the days of Antipas, my faithful witness, who was put to death in your city—where Satan lives. | | **6 The warning: God will come, oppose, & fight against** |
| a. For loyalty to Christ's name | | | |
| b. For doctrinal purity | | | **7 The promise: To the overcomers** |
| c. For facing martyrdom | | 17 He who has an ear, let him hear what the Spirit says to the churches. To him who overcomes, I will give some of the hidden manna. I will also give him a white stone with a new name written on it, known only to him who receives it. | a. The hidden manna |
| **4 The complaint: False doctrine & worldliness** | 14 Nevertheless, I have a few things against you: You have people there who hold to the | | b. A white stone with a new name written on it |
| a. The teaching of | | | |

# DIVISION II

## THE MESSAGES OF THE GLORIFIED CHRIST
## TO THE SEVEN CHURCHES, 1:9–3:22

### D. The Message to Pergamum: The Corrupted Church That is Married to the World, 2:12-17

(2:12-17) **Introduction**: worldliness corrupts a church. Four things cause a church to become worldly.
⇒ The church and its members begin to participate in worldly functions.
⇒ The church and its members allow worldly activities to take place in the church and in the homes of its members.
⇒ The church begins to baptize and accept people as members who have not truly repented and turned from the world to Christ.
⇒ The church and its members allow false teaching and preaching.

Nothing corrupts a church any quicker than worldliness. Pergamum was a corrupted church, a worldly church. Pergamum is the picture of the corrupted church that is married to the world.
1. The recipients (v.12).
2. The speaker—Jesus (v.12).
3. The commendation (v.13).
4. The complaint: false doctrine and worldliness (v.14-15).
5. The counsel: repent (v.16).
6. The warning: God will come, oppose, and fight against (v.16).
7. The promise: to the overcomers (v.17).

**1** (2:12) **Minister—Church**: there is the recipient of this letter. The letter is addressed to the minister of the church. If a church becomes worldly, the minister is responsible. Christ has called the minister to lead believers to a life of self-denial and holiness, to deny the possessions and pleasures of this world and live a pure and godly life. He has called the minister to lead believers to focus upon heaven and to live sacrificially. He has called the minister to teach believers to give all they are and have to reach the lost and to meet the desperate needs of the needy. Therefore, if the minister is not leading his people to live spiritual lives—if he is allowing them to follow after the pleasures and posses-

sions of the world—if he is allowing the church to become corrupted with worldliness—the minister is responsible. This is the reason this letter is sent to the minister. It is the task of the minister to proclaim the truth of sanctification and separation to a worldly church.

**DEEPER STUDY # 1**
(2:12) **Pergamum**: the city had three overriding claims to fame that seem to have had a bearing upon the message to the church.
1. Pergamum was a beautifully situated city with an air of royalty about it. It sat on top of a huge mountain, arising ever so steeply and majestically out of a beautiful valley. The city's citizens could see the Mediterranean Sea some fifteen miles away. To the approaching traveler the city struck him with a sense of stately awe and royal authority. The church had a ready picture of "Satan's throne," (v.13) of what it was to suffer persecution at the hands of a royal city under the power of the prince of this world.
2. Pergamum was one of the cultural and religious centers of the world. It had been a capital city for some 400 years. Its library was second only to Alexandria, Egypt. But the city's most prominent feature was its acropolis, rising about a thousand feet in the midst of the city. Temple after temple had been built upon it. For example, there was a temple to Asclepius, a serpent-like god of healing. It was famous for its college of medical priests. But the most famous pagan altar was built to Zeus. It was an overpowering sight, built on a huge ledge that jutted out and towered above the city. It was the largest, most ornate, and most famous altar in the world. It was forty feet high and ninety feet square. The church knew what it was to live in a pagan society, as though Satan's throne itself was there (v.13). They knew what it was to be persecuted (v.13). But they also knew what it was to place their faith in Him with the double-edged sword (v.12). They knew Him who could provide the true spiritual manna (v.17) and assure them a new name in the future (v.17).

3. Pergamum was the imperial and administrative center of Asia. As such, it was the first city in Asia to openly support imperial worship, that is, the worship of the state and its leader. What happened was this: Rome's conquest of the world had brought about peace by which food and trade and prosperity could more easily be secured. Life became much easier and more comfortable for many. As a result, a *Roman spirit* arose in many quarters. Roman government capitalized on this unifying spirit and began to center it in the Emperor Caesar himself. Gradually the government erected temples, altars, and images in Caesar's honor and he became a god. Finally, a law was issued requiring every citizen throughout the empire to go to the temple once a year and bow and say, "Caesar is Lord." To prove that a man had performed this loyal act to Rome, a written certificate was required to be in his possession. The church again knew what Christ meant when He claimed to be the One with the "double-edged sword" (v.12). They took great confidence in the fact that He knew "where they lived" (v.13). They knew what it was to live where "Satan has his throne" (v.13), and what it was to suffer martyrdom because they refused to deny Christ (v.13).

**2** (2:12) **Jesus Christ—Church**: there is the speaker, the Lord Jesus Christ Himself. A church that is corrupted by worldliness is committing a very serious crime against Christ. It is such a critical matter that Christ Himself delivers this message to the church. And note how Christ describes Himself: He is the One who has the *sharp double-edged sword* in His mouth. This means at least two things.

1. The sword of His mouth means His Word, the Word of God. The one thing needed in a worldly church is the Word of God.

⇒ The Word of God is sharp: it will cut through the most worldly and hardened heart. It will convict and convince the worldly of their sins and cut a sharp gash, separating the sinner from his sin.

⇒ The Word of God is a double-edged sword: it proclaims the law of God and the utter necessity of living a righteous life or else facing judgment and destruction. On the other side it proclaims the love and grace of God to those who separate from the world and follow the Lord Jesus Christ. As Matthew Henry says: "There is an edge to make a wound, and an edge to open a festered wound in order to its healing" (*Matthew Henry's Commentary*, Vol.6. Old Tappan, NJ: Fleming H. Revell, p.1127.)

**Take the helmet of salvation and the sword of the Spirit, which is the word of God. (Eph 6:17)**

**And then the lawless one will be revealed, whom the Lord Jesus will overthrow with the breath of his mouth and destroy by the splendor of his coming. (2 Th 2:8)**

**For the word of God is living and active. Sharper than any double-edged sword, it penetrates even to dividing soul and spirit, joints and marrow; it judges the thoughts and attitudes of the heart. (Heb 4:12)**

**In his right hand he held seven stars, and out of his mouth came a sharp double-edged sword. His face was like the sun shining in all its brilliance. (Rev 1:16)**

2. The sword of His mouth means the power and judgment of His Word. As shall be seen in the next note, the believers in Pergamum were being persecuted and some were even being martyred for their faith. Some government officials were misusing the power of the sword or execution. They were slaying innocent people, in particular believers who refused to deny Christ. Jesus Christ is proclaiming that the power of His sword—the power of His Word—is far greater. He holds the power of life and death over all men. He can speak the Word and snatch the life away from any person. Therefore, all men must heed this message. Those who do evil are hereby warned.

**Repent therefore! Otherwise, I will soon come to you and will fight against them with the sword of my mouth. (Rev 2:16)**

Note another point as well: this is a great promise to believers. If the Word of Christ is all powerful, then Christ can look after and take care of us no matter what confronts us. His power, the sword of His Word, is able to strengthen, deliver, and save us. And if it is our time to leave this world, His Word is able to transfer us right into God's presence to live perfected forever and ever.

**He has delivered us from such a deadly peril, and he will deliver us. On him we have set our hope that he will continue to deliver us, (2 Cor 1:10)**

**The Lord will rescue me from every evil attack and will bring me safely to his heavenly kingdom. To him be glory for ever and ever. Amen. (2 Tim 4:18)**

**Since the children have flesh and blood, he too shared in their humanity so that by his death he might destroy him who holds the power of death—that is, the devil— And free those who all their lives were held in slavery by their fear of death. (Heb 2:14-15)**

**Again Abner warned Asahel, "Stop chasing me! Why should I strike you down? How could I look your brother Joab in the face?" (2 Sam 2:22)**

**3** (2:13) **Church—Believers**: there is the commendation. The church is commended for three things.

1. The church was loyal to Christ's name despite the environment. The church had been established in a cesspool of worldliness, a city of people who were consumed with the pleasures, possessions, and comforts of the world. Note: Christ refers to the city as the *throne* of Satan. However, the believers were refusing to deny Christ. Once a year they could have easily made their public confession that *Caesar is Lord*, but they refused. They knew better; they knew that Christ and Christ alone was Lord. They could have gone quietly about their affairs and never mentioned Christ except when they met for worship. But this they refused to do. They wanted their loved ones, neighbors, and friends to know the salvation and hope of eternal life that was now available in Christ. Therefore, they bore testimony to Christ. They refused to deny Him. They refused to bow the knee and make a false profession to a false god, even if that god was Caesar, the state religion. They held fast to the only name that could really save them, the name of the Lord Jesus Christ.

**"Whoever acknowledges me before men, I will also acknowledge him before my**

Father in heaven. But whoever disowns me before men, I will disown him before my Father in heaven. (Mat 10:32-33)

If anyone is ashamed of me and my words in this adulterous and sinful generation, the Son of Man will be ashamed of him when he comes in his Father's glory with the holy angels." (Mark 8:38)

"I tell you, whoever acknowledges me before men, the Son of Man will also acknowledge him before the angels of God. (Luke 12:8)

That if you confess with your mouth, "Jesus is Lord," and believe in your heart that God raised him from the dead, you will be saved. For it is with your heart that you believe and are justified, and it is with your mouth that you confess and are saved. (Rom 10:9-10)

And every tongue confess that Jesus Christ is Lord, to the glory of God the Father. (Phil 2:11)

If we endure, we will also reign with him. If we disown him, he will also disown us; (2 Tim 2:12)

Who is the liar? It is the man who denies that Jesus is the Christ. Such a man is the antichrist—he denies the Father and the Son. No one who denies the Son has the Father; whoever acknowledges the Son has the Father also. (1 John 2:22-23)

If anyone acknowledges that Jesus is the Son of God, God lives in him and he in God. (1 John 4:15)

2. The church was pure in doctrine. They had not renounced their *faith in Christ*. They believed Christ and the Word of God, studied and taught it. They had neither renounced Christ nor His Word. The Word of God was being preached and taught every week from the pulpit and classes of the church.

We had previously suffered and been insulted in Philippi, as you know, but with the help of our God we dared to tell you his gospel in spite of strong opposition. For the appeal we make does not spring from error or impure motives, nor are we trying to trick you. On the contrary, we speak as men approved by God to be entrusted with the gospel. We are not trying to please men but God, who tests our hearts. You know we never used flattery, nor did we put on a mask to cover up greed—God is our witness. We were not looking for praise from men, not from you or anyone else. As apostles of Christ we could have been a burden to you, (1 Th 2:2-6)

If you point these things out to the brothers, you will be a good minister of Christ Jesus, brought up in the truths of the faith and of the good teaching that you have followed. (1 Tim 4:6)

In the presence of God and of Christ Jesus, who will judge the living and the dead, and in view of his appearing and his kingdom, I give you this charge: Preach the Word; be prepared in season and out of sea-

son; correct, rebuke and encourage—with great patience and careful instruction. (2 Tim 4:1-2)

He must hold firmly to the trustworthy message as it has been taught, so that he can encourage others by sound doctrine and refute those who oppose it. (Titus 1:9)

You must teach what is in accord with sound doctrine. (Titus 2:1)

3. The church was standing fast in persecution. At least one believer had been martyred, Antipas. Nothing is known about this dear believer other than what is recorded here. Tradition says that he was placed inside a brazen bull and slowly roasted to death (A.T. Robertson. *Word Pictures In The New Testament*, Vol.6. Nashville, TN: Broadman Press, 1933, p.305).

Note: the word "witness" (martus) is also the Greek word for martyr. A.T. Robertson says that Antipas was a witness just as Jesus said we should be (Acts 1:8). Christ gave this dear man His own title: "my faithful one" (cp. Rev.1:5; 3:14). He was faithful unto death.

**Thought 1.** This is a sharp rebuke to us today. Just think: the word witness and martyr mean the same thing. The early believers knew exactly what it meant to become a follower of Christ: it meant the commitment of all they were and had. It meant the possibility of death. As William Barclay says:

"In the early Church to be a martyr and to be a witness were one and the same thing. Witness meant so often martyrdom. An early Christian knew quite well what he was doing; as soon as he became a Christian he had made himself liable to death. Here is a rebuke to us. There are so many who are prepared to demonstrate their Christianity in Christian circles, but who are equally prepared to play down their Christianity in circles where Christianity is met with ridicule, with contempt, with indifference or with opposition. The Christian must remember that the word martus means equally martyr and witness, and that Christian witness can be, and often must be, a costly thing" (*The Revelation of John*, Vol.1, p.113f).

"Be on your guard against men; they will hand you over to the local councils and flog you in their synagogues. On my account you will be brought before governors and kings as witnesses to them and to the Gentiles. (Mat 10:17-18)

"Then you will be handed over to be persecuted and put to death, and you will be hated by all nations because of me. (Mat 24:9)

"But before all this, they will lay hands on you and persecute you. They will deliver you to synagogues and prisons, and you will be brought before kings and governors, and all on account of my name. (Luke 21:12)

Remember the words I spoke to you: 'No servant is greater than his master.' If they persecuted me, they will persecute you also. If they obeyed my teaching, they will obey yours also. They will treat you this way because of my name, for they do not know the One who sent me. (John 15:20-21)

They will put you out of the synagogue; in fact, a time is coming when anyone who kills you will think he is offering a service to God. (John 16:2)

For it has been granted to you on behalf of Christ not only to believe on him, but also to suffer for him, (Phil 1:29)

In fact, everyone who wants to live a godly life in Christ Jesus will be persecuted, (2 Tim 3:12)

Consider him who endured such opposition [hostility] from sinful men, so that you will not grow weary and lose heart. (Heb 12:3)

Dear friends, do not be surprised at the painful trial you are suffering, as though something strange were happening to you. But rejoice that you participate in the sufferings of Christ, so that you may be overjoyed when his glory is revealed. (1 Pet 4:12-13)

**4** (2:14-15) **Teaching, False—Balaam-ism—Nicolaitans:** there is the complaint. The church was guilty of false teaching and of gross worldliness. Note two charges against the worldly church.

1. The worldly church is guilty of the teaching of Balaam. What does this mean? It means that corruption and worldliness are within the church itself; it means a mixture of religion and worldliness. Balac, the Moabite king reigning adjacent to Palestine, feared Israel. To protect his kingdom, he sought the services of Balaam, a prophet, to curse Israel. When the king first approached Balaam, Balaam refused. But he accepted the second offer. Three times Balaam cursed Israel, but with no results. He then conceived an insidious plan. He would corrupt them. He suggested Moabite girls seduce Israel's men to intermarry and lead them to worship their idolatrous gods (Num.22-25; cp. 31:16). The scheme worked. And Israel, though rooted in God, became unequally yoked together with worldliness and was thereby corrupted.

Apparently what had happened in the Pergamum church was this: the church...

- had baptized some persons who had never repented and forsaken the ways of the world.
- had allowed some of the worldly to teach in the church.
- had allowed a mixed membership of believers and unbelievers: some were living separated lives of holiness and sacrificial commitment for the cause of Christ, and others were living worldly lives seeking the pleasures and possessions of this world.

The result was tragic: there were those within the church committing sexual immorality, that is, all kinds of sexual sins; and there were those participating in the drunken parties of the world, even to the point of participating in the feasts of idolatrous worshippers. (See outline and notes—1 Cor.10:14-11:1 for more discussion.)

With many other words he warned them; and he pleaded with them, "Save yourselves from this corrupt generation." (Acts 2:40)

But now I am writing you that you must not associate with anyone who calls himself a brother but is sexually immoral or greedy, an idolater or a slanderer, a drunkard or a swindler. With such a man do not even eat. (1 Cor 5:11)

Do not be yoked together with unbelievers. For what do righteousness and wickedness have in common? Or what fellowship can light have with darkness? (2 Cor 6:14)

"Therefore come out from them and be separate, says the Lord. Touch no unclean thing, and I will receive you." "I will be a Father to you, and you will be my sons and daughters, says the Lord Almighty." (2 Cor 6:17-18)

Have nothing to do with the fruitless deeds of darkness, but rather expose them. (Eph 5:11)

In the name of the Lord Jesus Christ, we command you, brothers, to keep away from every brother who is idle and does not live according to the teaching you received from us. (2 Th 3:6)

Be careful not to make a treaty with those who live in the land where you are going, or they will be a snare among you. (Exo 34:12)

Blessed is the man who does not walk in the counsel of the wicked or stand in the way of sinners or sit in the seat of mockers. (Psa 1:1)

2. The worldly church is guilty of making the false profession of the Nicolaitans (see note, pt.2—Rev.2:5-6 for discussion and verses).

**5** (2:16) **Repentance:** the counsel is to repent. The church and its believers needed to repent and to change their ways. What does this mean? The church and the true believers...

- needed to deal with those who were worldly and lead them to repentance.
- needed to change its practice of accepting people into the church just because they professed Christ. There needed to be evidence of repentance.
- needed to discipline those who refused to repent and chose to continue on in their worldly living.
- needed to stop conveying a sense of false hope and false security to unbelievers by baptizing them when they made profession without true repentance.
- needed to stop allowing the worldly to seduce, deceive, and mislead other believers in the church.

And saying, "Repent, for the kingdom of heaven is near." (Mat 3:2)

I tell you, no! But unless you repent, you too will all perish. (Luke 13:3)

Peter replied, "Repent and be baptized, every one of you, in the name of Jesus Christ for the forgiveness of your sins. And you will receive the gift of the Holy Spirit. (Acts 2:38)

Repent, then, and turn to God, so that your sins may be wiped out, that times of refreshing may come from the Lord, (Acts 3:19)

Repent of this wickedness and pray to the Lord. Perhaps he will forgive you for having such a thought in your heart. (Acts 8:22)

In the past God overlooked such ignorance, but now he commands all people everywhere to repent. (Acts 17:30)

If my people, who are called by my name, will humble themselves and pray and seek my face and turn from their wicked ways, then will I hear from heaven and will forgive their sin and will heal their land. (2 Chr 7:14)

Let the wicked forsake his way and the evil man his thoughts. Let him turn to the LORD, and he will have mercy on him, and to our God, for he will freely pardon. (Isa 55:7)

**6** (2:16) **Warning**: there is the warning. Christ warns the church that becomes worldly. He will come quickly and make war against the worldly. Note this: the Lord is not going to punish the faithful believers who are spiritual minded. He is going to punish only those who refuse to repent of their worldliness. The anger of Christ is always against the impure. Christ will never punish the spiritual members of a church; He will only punish the worldly members. Note how: with the sword of His mouth, that is, with the power of His Word. His Word is strong enough *to judge* all the worldly, no matter who they are or how many there may be.

**Thought 1.** Note this: the church as a whole is responsible for allowing worldly people to be baptized. The command of Christ is to repent and believe the gospel. True belief always involves repentance—a turning away from the world to Christ—total denial of self—the total commitment of all one is and has to Christ and His cause of world missions.

How shall we escape if we ignore such a great salvation? This salvation, which was first announced by the Lord, was confirmed to us by those who heard him. (Heb 2:3)

Let us not give up meeting together, as some are in the habit of doing, but let us encourage one another—and all the more as you see the Day approaching. (Heb 10:25)

Therefore, dear friends, since you already know this, be on your guard so that you may not be carried away by the error of lawless men and fall from your secure position. (2 Pet 3:17)

**7** (2:17) **Overcomers—Promise**: there is the great promise to the overcomers. The promise is twofold.

1. The overcomer is given the right to eat the manna or bread of heaven. This is a reference to the manna that was used to feed the children of Israel during their wilderness wanderings. God actually caused the manna or bread to be rained down from heaven upon them (Ex.16:4). The point to note is that the manna was given by God to feed them and to keep them alive during their wandering upon this earth. Now, what does the *hidden manna* mean? What is the bread of heaven? It means Christ Himself. The overcomer is given the right to feed upon Christ. This is exactly what Christ Himself said.

Jesus said to them, "I tell you the truth, it is not Moses who has given you the bread from heaven, but it is my Father who gives you the true bread from heaven. For the bread of God is he who comes down from heaven and gives life to the world." (John 6:32-33)

Then Jesus declared, "I am the bread of life. He who comes to me will never go hungry, and he who believes in me will never be thirsty. (John 6:35)

I am the living bread that came down from heaven. If anyone eats of this bread, he will live forever. This bread is my flesh, which I will give for the life of the world." (John 6:51)

This is the bread that came down from heaven. Your forefathers ate manna and died, but he who feeds on this bread will live forever." (John 6:58)

The bread or manna of God is not physical and material bread: it is spiritual. God actually promises to provide for the physical necessities of *His followers* (Mt.6:24-33). But physical and material bread is not what Christ was talking about in this passage. Physical and material bread lasts only for a short while. Once consumed, it is gone. Its satisfaction passes and man's gnawing hunger arises again. But the bread God gives is spiritual bread, that is, spiritual food for the soul (see note—Eph.1:3). It is the bread that man really needs more than anything else on earth. It is the only bread that can *permanently* feed and meet the need of man's...

- gnawing hunger
- restlessness
- emptiness
- vacuum
- loneliness
- lack of purpose, meaning, and significance

But here is the bread that comes down from heaven, which a man may eat and not die. I am the living bread that came down from heaven. If anyone eats of this bread, he will live forever. This bread is my flesh, which I will give for the life of the world." (John 6:50-51)

Jesus said to them, "I tell you the truth, unless you eat the flesh of the Son of Man and drink his blood, you have no life in you. Whoever eats my flesh and drinks my blood has eternal life, and I will raise him up at the last day. (John 6:53-54)

Just as the living Father sent me and I live because of the Father, so the one who feeds on me will live because of me. This is the bread that came down from heaven. Your forefathers ate manna and died, but he who feeds on this bread will live forever." (John 6:57-58)

The heavenly Bread, Christ Himself, gives life to man. The very purpose of bread is to give life. Bread gives life by...

- nourishing and sustaining
- satisfying
- energizing
- creating desire (the need) for more (See note— Lk.4:3-4. Cp. Neh.9:15.)
- being eaten on a regular basis

Note that Jesus Christ Himself gives life to the overcomer by doing the very same thing. Jesus Christ...

- nourishes and sustains
- satisfies
- energizes
- creates desire (the need) for more (See note—Lk.4:3-4. Cp. Neh.9:15.)
- feeds us on a regular basis

The point is clearly seen: the person who overcomes worldliness—who stops feeding upon the world—that person will be given the food of heaven itself. He will be allowed to eat the eternal bread of heaven. He will never die.

Note that manna is hidden. This simply means that Christ is hidden to the worldly people of the earth. The worldly do not see nor feed upon the bread of heaven. Christ is hidden from the worldly.

2. The overcomer is given a white stone with a new name written on it. There are an endless number of guesses about what this stone is. Only one thing is clear in this reference to it, and it is best to stick to the Scripture. The white stone is the means of being admitted into heaven, into God's presence. The overcomer is allowed into God's presence because of the white stone. Note that a new name is written upon the stone. This must mean either the name of Jesus Christ or of the believer himself.

⇒ If the name is that of Christ, then the meaning is this: the name of Jesus Christ is the only name accepted for entrance into heaven. A person must have the white stone with Christ's name written on it in order to be admitted into God's presence.

⇒ If the name is that of the believer, then the believer is given the white stone as his ticket into heaven. The stone must have his name on it in order to be admitted.

Note: the church member who has an ear must hear this message to the worldly church. He can never overcome the attacks of worldliness unless he heeds this message. Hearing and heeding is his only hope of ever conquering the seductive worldliness of this earth.

**Jesus answered, "I am the way and the truth and the life. No one comes to the Father except through me. (John 14:6)**
**For, "Everyone who calls on the name of the Lord will be saved." (Rom 10:13)**

| | E. The Message to Thyatira: The Compromising or Permissive Church, 2:18-29 | | |
|---|---|---|---|
| 1 The recipients<br>  a. The messenger of the church<br>  b. The Thyatira church<sup>DS1</sup><br>2 The speaker—Jesus<br><br>3 The commendation for deeds or works<br>  a. For love & faith<br>  b. For service & perseverance<br>  c. For expanding ministries<br>4 The complaint: Allowing a Jezebel to teach<br>  a. They tolerate a false prophetess<br>  b. They tolerate false teaching, sexual immorality, & idolatry<br><br><br><br>5 The warning to the compromising & corrupt<br>  a. To Jezebel: She shall | 18 "To the angel of the church in Thyatira write: These are the words of the Son of God, whose eyes are like blazing fire and whose feet are like burnished bronze.<br>19 I know your deeds, your love and faith, your service and perseverance, and that you are now doing more than you did at first.<br>20 Nevertheless, I have this against you: You tolerate that woman Jezebel, who calls herself a prophetess. By her teaching she misleads my servants into sexual immorality and the eating of food sacrificed to idols.<br>21 I have given her time to repent of her immorality, but she is unwilling.<br>22 So I will cast her on a bed of suffering, and I will make those who commit adultery | with her suffer intensely, unless they repent of her ways.<br>23 I will strike her children dead. Then all the churches will know that I am he who searches hearts and minds, and I will repay each of you according to your deeds.<br>24 Now I say to the rest of you in Thyatira, to you who do not hold to her teaching and have not learned Satan's so-called deep secrets (I will not impose any other burden on you):<br>25 Only hold on to what you have until I come.<br>26 To him who overcomes and does my will to the end, I will give authority over the nations—<br>27 'He will rule them with an iron scepter; he will dash them to pieces like pottery'—just as I have received authority from my Father.<br>28 I will also give him the morning star.<br>29 He who has an ear, let him hear what the Spirit says to the churches. | be cast into a bed of suffering<br>  b. To Jezebel's followers: The same fate<br>  c. The purpose for the warning<br>    1) To honor Jesus<br>    2) To execute justice<br>6 The counsel: To the faithful<br>  a. There will be no other burdens or demands made upon the faithful<br><br><br>  b. They must hold on, hold fast<br>7 The promise: To the overcomers<br>  a. They will be given authority & power over the nations<br><br><br><br>  b. They will be given the Morning Star |

# DIVISION II

## THE MESSAGES OF THE GLORIFIED CHRIST TO THE SEVEN CHURCHES, 1:9-3:22

### E. The Message to Thyatira: The Compromising or Permissive Church, 2:18-29

(2:18-29) **Introduction**: compromise will destroy a church. We live in a world of compromise where people seek their own interests at any cost. People sell their souls for the possessions, power, and pleasures of this world. People young and old alike will compromise and go along; they will do almost anything...

- to get attention
- to be popular and acceptable
- to secure their jobs
- to get promotions
- to get good grades
- to get more money
- to get bigger houses
- to live in a better neighborhood
- to get more power

On and on the list could go, but the point is clearly seen. People compromise what they know is right in order to get what they want. This was what the members of the church at Thyatira were doing. The church at Thyatira is a picture of the compromising church, a church full of believers who were compromising with the world in order to fulfill their personal desires.

1. The recipients (v.18).
2. The speaker—Jesus (v.18).
3. The commendation for deeds or works (v.19).
4. The complaint: allowing a Jezebel to teach (v.20-21).
5. The warning to the compromising and corrupt (v.22-23).
6. The counsel: to the faithful (v.24-25).
7. The promise: to overcomers (v.26-29).

**1** (2:18) **Church—Minister**: there is the recipient. The minister is responsible for the church; therefore, the Lord addresses this letter to him. The minister is to proclaim the truth to the church that is compromising with the world. If some of the members have begun to compromise with the world, it is the minister's duty to declare the Word of Christ to them, to proclaim exactly what Christ says in this message. And note how serious the problem of compromise is to Christ. Thyatira was the smallest of the seven churches, but this message is longer than any of the others. Christ has more to say to a compromising church than to any other.

**DEEPER STUDY # 1**

(2:18) **Thyatira**: there are two historical facts that seem to have a bearing upon the Lord's message to the church.

1. Thyatira was a frontier town—the least important city of the seven mentioned in Revelation. It lay on the road that stretched through a long valley between Pergamum and Sardis. It had no defensible surroundings. Its citizens could only hope to fight a delaying action for Pergamum. The church knew what it was to hope in One who could *see* all circumstances and who could trample all enemies under His foot (v. 18, 26-27). The church knew what it was to *hold on, to hold fast* (v.26-27).

2. Thyatira was renowned for its trade guilds or unions. These guilds had two prime functions: business and social. The city's two major industries were dye and wool. These products plus the major road that ran through the city

brought merchants from all over the world. The very life of the community was centered in the trade guilds or unions. Their functions often involved a meal that was usually held within the temple precincts. The social included a sacrifice to the gods and frequently ended up being a drunken immoral affair.

Note that the church knew the attraction of Jezebel's seductive teaching. This probably refers to a woman within the church who was teaching an idea that seemed to be very practical and reasonable. What was it? That believers could support the social functions of their trade guilds or unions, even if the social function was worldly. Believers had to participate in the community's social and business functions in order to secure themselves and their jobs and in order to prosper. Lowering Christian holiness and morality was necessary in order to guarantee social acceptance and the survival of one's job or business (v.20). It was felt that God would understand. But the church knew Him "whose eyes are like blazing fire" and sees all (v.18-19). It knew Him who was to trample all enemies under His feet (v.18) and who was to search the hearts of all and reward them according to their works (v.23). Note Thyatira is the city from which Lydia, the dealer of purple cloth, came (Acts 16:14, 40).

**2** (2:18) **Jesus Christ—Church**: there is the speaker, the Lord Jesus Christ Himself. Note how Christ describes Himself to the compromising church.

1. Christ declares that He is the Son of God. He is the One to whom a person owes his life. A person is not to give his life over to the world nor to anyone else. He is to give his life to the Son of God, to Jesus Christ Himself. A person is...

- to believe Christ
- to follow Christ
- to obey Christ
- to become attached to Christ
- to love Christ

No person, especially a believer, is to compromise with the world. There is to be no attachment and no love for the world. A person owes his life, all he is and has, to the Son of God.

> Then he said to them all: "If anyone would come after me, he must deny himself and take up his cross daily and follow me. (Luke 9:23)
>
> "If anyone comes to me and does not hate his father and mother, his wife and children, his brothers and sisters—yes, even his own life—he cannot be my disciple. And anyone who does not carry his cross and follow me cannot be my disciple. (Luke 14:26-27)
>
> For if you live according to the sinful nature, you will die; but if by the Spirit you put to death the misdeeds of the body, you will live, (Rom 8:13)
>
> Those who belong to Christ Jesus have crucified the sinful nature with its passions and desires. (Gal 5:24)
>
> Do not love the world or anything in the world. If anyone loves the world, the love of the Father is not in him. For everything in the world—the cravings of sinful man, the lust of his eyes and the boasting of what he has and does—comes not from the Father but from the world. (1 John 2:15-16)

2. Christ declares that His eyes are like blazing fire. Christ sees all. He sees when a person is compromising, compromising in the dark, behind closed doors, in parked cars, in the offices and houses of the world. He sees all compromise that lies, steals, cheats, commits immorality, becomes intoxicated, takes drugs. He sees all seductive teaching and misleading of people within the church. He sees and hears and rewards all according to their works (v.23). And note: He also sees and aids the faithful to stand fast when they are tempted (v.25).

> If I sinned, you would be watching me and would not let my offense go unpunished. (Job 10:14)
>
> Surely then you will count my steps but not keep track of my sin. (Job 14:16)
>
> Although you wash yourself with soda and use an abundance of soap, the stain of your guilt is still before me," declares the Sovereign LORD. (Jer 2:22)
>
> My eyes are on all their ways; they are not hidden from me, nor is their sin concealed from my eyes. (Jer 16:17)
>
> Then the Spirit of the LORD came upon me, and he told me to say: "This is what the LORD says: That is what you are saying, O house of Israel, but I know what is going through your mind. (Ezek 11:5)
>
> But they do not realize that I remember all their evil deeds. Their sins engulf them; they are always before me. (Hosea 7:2)
>
> For I know how many are your offenses and how great your sins. You oppress the righteous and take bribes and you deprive the poor of justice in the courts. (Amos 5:12)
>
> There is nothing concealed that will not be disclosed, or hidden that will not be made known. (Luke 12:2)
>
> Therefore judge nothing before the appointed time; wait till the Lord comes. He will bring to light what is hidden in darkness and will expose the motives of men's hearts. At that time each will receive his praise from God. (1 Cor 4:5)

3. Christ declares that His feet are like burnished bronze. Christ is able to step down hard upon all seductive teaching and compromise. He rules and He judges. His feet shall crush all those who compromise with the world. In addition, His feet shall crush all false teachers of compromise. The reason is clear: He is the only true spokesman and messenger of God. All others are false. Therefore, they must be judged and cursed. Note that Jezebel was claiming to be a prophetess, a spokesman, a messenger of God.

> The wise man has eyes in his head, while the fool walks in the darkness; but I came to realize that the same fate overtakes them both. (Eccl 2:14)
>
> This will take place on the day when God will judge men's secrets through Jesus Christ, as my gospel declares. (Rom 2:16)
>
> Enoch, the seventh from Adam, prophesied about these men: "See, the Lord is

coming with thousands upon thousands of his holy ones To judge everyone, and to convict all the ungodly of all the ungodly acts they have done in the ungodly way, and of all the harsh words ungodly sinners have spoken against him." (Jude 1:14-15)

Out of his mouth comes a sharp sword with which to strike down the nations. "He will rule them with an iron scepter." He treads the winepress of the fury of the wrath of God Almighty. (Rev 19:15)

They will sing before the LORD, for he comes, he comes to judge the earth. He will judge the world in righteousness and the peoples in his truth. (Psa 96:13)

**3** (2:19) **Church—Believers:** there is the commendation. Thyatira was a very active church, involved in all kinds of deeds for the Lord. And note: Christ says that He knows all about their *deeds for Him*:

> I know your deeds, your love and faith, your service and perseverance, and that you are now doing more than you did at first. (Rev 2:19)

1. There were deeds of love and faith. These would include ministries that especially showed love and strong faith. That is, ministries that concentrated upon showing care and interest, concern and provision. Such ministries would include...

- evangelism: reaching out to the lost
- the youth: growing and developing them
- the adults
- the senior adults
- the college students
- the needy
- the orphans
- the hungry
- the homeless
- the shut-ins
- the foreigners
- the prisoners
- the poor
- the single parent and child

2. There were deeds of service and perseverance. These would include ministries that demanded commitment and perseverance in order to carry them out. It would in-clude...

- lacking the money or personnel or space or some other resource, but believing God and sticking to it until the ministry was operating.
- facing opposition, but believing God and going ahead and persevering in the ministry.
- facing a difficult ministry such as visiting unbelievers or prisoners or derelicts or whatever, but trusting God and going ahead anyway.
- being required to sacrifice time or money or possessions, but doing it because one believes God.
- being tired and weary and not wanting to participate in a particular ministry, but trusting God and going ahead and persevering in it.
- feeling inadequate and incapable, but accepting the challenge, believing God, and enduring in the ministry.

3. There was even a significant growth in the ministries of the church. The church grew and expanded. It reached out more and more. It was apparently as active as it could be, ministering to the community in every way that a church should, and it continued to grow.

**Thought 1.** Think of the kind of church being described: dynamic, vibrant, alive—meeting all the social needs of the community—having all the ministries that ranged all the way from a clothes and food closet over to reaching out to the lost in a regular visitation program. The church was full of activity and energy and crowded with people. Yet, the church was a far cry from what it should have been. It was a compromising and corrupted church.

It was allowing a teacher to teach who compromised with the world, and it was allowing the worldly to be baptized and accepted into the church without repenting and separating from the pleasures, possessions, and immoralities of the world. The church appeared to be the most alive and dynamic church in the area, but it was not—not to the Lord. To the Lord the church was corrupt because of its compromise with the world. This is the discussion of the next note.

**4** (2:20-21) **Church—Backsliding—Teaching, False:** there is the complaint. The complaint immediately arouses our interest, for the name Jezebel is used. The church is charged with allowing a Jezebel to teach in the church. This means two things.

1. The church was tolerating a false prophetess to teach within the church. Note that she called herself a prophetess. She claimed that God had called and gifted her to teach and proclaim the truth. Therefore, the church appointed her as a teacher and gave her the right to teach within the church.

2. The church was tolerating *false teaching, sexual immorality, and idolatry*. This is exactly what is said in the verse.

a. First, Jezebel, the false teacher, was actually *teaching* in the church. Contrary to Christ and the Word of God, the church was allowing her to spread her false teaching.

b. Second, Jezebel, the false teacher, was being allowed to mislead and seduce the Lord's servants. She was arguing, presenting reasonable arguments, deceiving, misleading and seducing, and beguiling the servants and followers of the Lord. And the church was allowing it.

c. Third, Jezebel, the false teacher, was seducing the believers to commit sexual immorality, that is, all manner of immoral acts. How could such teaching be allowed within the church? By a very insidious teaching, and note: the teaching has continued on down through the centuries, so much so that it now infiltrates many churches. She was teaching...

- that believers could not separate themselves from the world, not entirely, not without becoming exclusive and snobbish.
- that believers needed to be sensible in dealing with the world and its functions: they needed to be participating in *some of the world's* functions in order to be friendly, keep their jobs, secure promotions, help their businesses, keep from being considered fanatical, and win the lost.

- that believers could reach the world more easily by associating and fellowshipping with the world.
- that if a person really worshipped God, he would be acceptable to God even if he did not know about Jesus Christ; that Jesus Christ is not the only way to God; that He is not the only Savior.
- that believers should attend the social functions of neighbors and fellow workers and not be exclusive and separatists.

Remember: Thyatira was renown for its trade guilds or unions. They were the center of much of the city's social and business life. Therefore, if believers did not attend these, there was a possibility that it might affect their employment and relationships with their neighbors. The argument of the false teacher, Jezebel, had a strong appeal. It would take a strong minded minister and teacher to proclaim a life of separation in such a situation.

What happened, of course, was that many of the socials became drunken and immoral parties. Believers who were present were attracted to the opposite sex and caught up in the immoral affairs just like everyone else. Believers were having immoral affairs, committing fornication.

Naturally the believers did not want to be misfits, so they would be sociable and drink and dance and participate in the activities of their neighbors. The end result was bound to happen: believers were caught up in the drunken immorality of the world. They had normal human desires just like all human beings; therefore, they were attracted to the opposite sex and some became involved in immoral affairs, committing adultery. Remember why: all because of the false teaching of Jezebel that believers must not separate themselves from the world, that they must be sensible and reasonable and not cut themselves out of the necessary business functions, socials, and pleasures of the world.

d. Fourth, Jezebel, the false teacher, was misleading seducing believers to commit idolatry. Some of the functions of the trade guilds and unions were usually held in the temple precincts of false gods. Sometimes the socials involved a simple thank-offering to the god, much like our offering of thanks at meals. The very first piece of meat was laid upon the altar to the god. Then the rest of the meat was served to the guests. Some of the believers were participating in these functions, actually participating in the functions that gave thanks to false gods. (See outline and notes—1 Cor.10:14-11:1; Ro.14:1-23 for more discussion.)

**Thought 1.** Remember what idolatry is. An idol is anything that a person puts first in his life, anything that consumes a person's mind, heart, soul, and body. An idol is that to which a person gives himself. Therefore, an idol can be...

| | |
|---|---|
| • a job | • business |
| • money | • family |
| • position | • self |
| • possessions | • sex |
| • pleasure | • knowledge |
| • sports | • power |

Some church members were apparently putting their jobs and social acceptance before God. They were attending the social functions to be socially acceptable and to secure their jobs and to prosper in the world. But the inevitable happened: they were influenced by the world and caught up in the compromise of the world. All because of some Jezebel, some false teacher in the church.

Note that Jesus Christ had given this false teacher, this Jezebel, a period to repent. This means that she knew down deep within her heart that she was teaching contrary to God's Word. But she refused to change; she refused to repent.

**If you belonged to the world, it would love you as its own. As it is, you do not belong to the world, but I have chosen you out of the world. That is why the world hates you. (John 15:19)**

**With many other words he warned them; and he pleaded with them, "Save yourselves from this corrupt generation." (Acts 2:40)**

**You, then, who teach others, do you not teach yourself? You who preach against stealing, do you steal? You who say that people should not commit adultery, do you commit adultery? You who abhor idols, do you rob temples? You who brag about the law, do you dishonor God by breaking the law? As it is written: "God's name is blasphemed among the Gentiles because of you." (Rom 2:21-24)**

**Do not conform any longer to the pattern of this world, but be transformed by the renewing of your mind. Then you will be able to test and approve what God's will is—his good, pleasing and perfect will. (Rom 12:2)**

**Since, then, we know what it is to fear the Lord, we try to persuade men. What we are is plain to God, and I hope it is also plain to your conscience. (2 Cor 5:11)**

**Do not be yoked together with unbelievers. For what do righteousness and wickedness have in common? Or what fellowship can light have with darkness? (2 Cor 6:14)**

**"Therefore come out from them and be separate, says the Lord. Touch no unclean thing, and I will receive you." "I will be a Father to you, and you will be my sons and daughters, says the Lord Almighty." (2 Cor 6:17-18)**

**Have nothing to do with the fruitless deeds of darkness, but rather expose them. (Eph 5:11)**

**In the name of the Lord Jesus Christ, we command you, brothers, to keep away from every brother who is idle and does not live according to the teaching you received from us. (2 Th 3:6)**

**No one serving as a soldier gets involved in civilian affairs—he wants to please his commanding officer. (2 Tim 2:4)**

**By faith Moses, when he had grown up, refused to be known as the son of Pharaoh's daughter. He chose to be mistreated along**

with the people of God rather than to enjoy the pleasures of sin for a short time. (Heb 11:24-25)

Do not love the world or anything in the world. If anyone loves the world, the love of the Father is not in him. For everything in the world—the cravings of sinful man, the lust of his eyes and the boasting of what he has and does—comes not from the Father but from the world. (1 John 2:15-16)

**5** (2:22-23) **Warning—Church**: there is the warning to those who compromise and are corrupted. Note five significant points.

1. There is a warning to Jezebel. She is to be cast upon a bed of suffering. This probably refers to a sexually transmitted disease or to a disease such as cirrhosis of the liver due to excess drinking. Her judgment was to match her sin, to be a direct result of her sin. She was to reap what she sowed.

For in the same way you judge others, you will be judged, and with the measure you use, it will be measured to you. (Mat 7:2)

But because of your stubbornness and your unrepentant heart, you are storing up wrath against yourself for the day of God's wrath, when his righteous judgment will be revealed. God "will give to each person according to what he has done." (Rom 2:5-6)

Do not be deceived: God cannot be mocked. A man reaps what he sows. The one who sows to please his sinful nature, from that nature will reap destruction; the one who sows to please the Spirit, from the Spirit will reap eternal life. (Gal 6:7-8)

2. There is the warning to those who gave in to Jezebel's seduction and lifestyle, to those who refused to turn to Christ and to separate themselves from the world. They were to suffer intensely. The idea is some severe affliction, deep suffering, or grave hardship.

3. The warning is to the children of Jezebel. Who are they? Real children or those who swallowed her false teaching and worldly lifestyle? In either case, they were to be killed. What does this mean?
⇒ It could mean the chastising hand of God such as fell upon some of the Corinthian believers (see outlines and notes—1 Cor.11:27-30; DEEPER STUDY # 1—1 Jn.5:16 for more discussion).

That is why many among you are weak and sick, and a number of you have fallen asleep. (1 Cor 11:30)

⇒ It could mean the second death, the judgment of eternal death when we stand face to face with Christ in the final judgment day. (See note, pt.2—Rev.2:10-11.)

4. There was still time for all of these to repent (v.22). Imagine! Christ still loved and reached out to Jezebel, this false teacher, and her followers, despite all the corruption they had caused in this great church. Christ still gave them a chance to repent. Christ said that the judgment would *only happen* if they failed to repent of their deeds.

**Thought 1.** This means a most wonderful thing: we can still repent so long as we are living on earth. No matter what we have done nor how terrible it is, Christ calls us to repentance. And if we repent, He saves us and delivers us from the judgment to come.

Repent, then, and turn to God, so that your sins may be wiped out, that times of refreshing may come from the Lord, (Acts 3:19)

Repent of this wickedness and pray to the Lord. Perhaps he will forgive you for having such a thought in your heart. (Acts 8:22)

In the past God overlooked such ignorance, but now he commands all people everywhere to repent. (Acts 17:30)

If my people, who are called by my name, will humble themselves and pray and seek my face and turn from their wicked ways, then will I hear from heaven and will forgive their sin and will heal their land. (2 Chr 7:14)

Let the wicked forsake his way and the evil man his thoughts. Let him turn to the LORD, and he will have mercy on him, and to our God, for he will freely pardon. (Isa 55:7)

"But if a wicked man turns away from all the sins he has committed and keeps all my decrees and does what is just and right, he will surely live; he will not die. (Ezek 18:21)

5. Note why Christ is going to judge those who compromise with the world and corrupt the church.

I will strike her children dead. Then all the churches will know that I am he who searches hearts and minds, and I will repay each of you according to your deeds. (Rev 2:23)

⇒ Christ is going to judge those who compromise so that all the churches may know and acknowledge that He is the Christ, the Sovereign head of the universe. He is the One who searches the minds, thoughts, and hearts of people.
⇒ Christ is going to judge those who compromise so that every person will be treated fairly and justly; so that justice will be executed within the church and the world—perfectly executed.

And that you, O Lord, are loving. Surely you will reward each person according to what he has done. (Psa 62:12)

"I the LORD search the heart and examine the mind, to reward a man according to his conduct, according to what his deeds deserve." (Jer 17:10)

For the Son of Man is going to come in his Father's glory with his angels, and then he will reward each person according to what he has done. (Mat 16:27)

For we must all appear before the judgment seat of Christ, that each one may receive what is due him for the things done while in the body, whether good or bad. (2 Cor 5:10)

Since you call on a Father who judges each man's work impartially, live your lives as strangers here in reverent fear. (1 Pet 1:17)

And I saw the dead, great and small, standing before the throne, and books were opened. Another book was opened, which is the book of life. The dead were judged according to what they had done as recorded in the books. (Rev 20:12)

"Behold, I am coming soon! My reward is with me, and I will give to everyone according to what he has done. (Rev 22:12)

**6** (2:24-25) **Faithfulness—Stedfastness**: there is the counsel to hold on, to hold fast. Note the reference to "*Satan's so-called deep secrets.*" Compromise with the world—refusing to separate from the world and to live a pure and holy life—is living in the depths of sin. It is being planted and imbedded, immersed and enmeshed in the *Satan's so-called deep secrets*, in the very depth of Satan's life-style.

But note the glorious promise to the faithful believer who has separated himself from the world and its pleasures and possessions: Christ will put no other burden upon him. What does this mean? It means two things.

1. *No other burden* can refer to the prohibition laid upon the Gentile Christians by the Jerusalem Council. They were forbidden to eat meat offered to idols (v.20; cp. Acts 15:19-29, esp, 20, 28-29).

2. *No other burden* can mean that Christ does not expect the believer to completely separate himself from the world, not in the sense that he has to live as a hermit. We are to live in the world but not of it. There are obvious pleasures and sins of the world and of the flesh that we must not touch. But there is much upon earth that we are to use and enjoy as we walk from day to day. Christ does not put the burden of extreme restrictions upon us; He only demands that we separate and have nothing to do with things that harm and destroy our bodies, minds, and souls.

Now, note the counsel: we are to hold fast until Christ comes. We are to hold on, to hold fast...

- to the commitment that we have already made to Christ.
- to the spiritual growth that we have already achieved.
- to the ministries that we have already launched.

We are not to give in to the seductions of the world no matter how appealing and attractive.

So I say, live by the Spirit, and you will not gratify the desires of the sinful nature. (Gal 5:16)

As a prisoner for the Lord, then, I urge you to live a life worthy of the calling you have received. (Eph 4:1)

Be very careful, then, how you live—not as unwise but as wise, (Eph 5:15)

Only let us live up to what we have already attained. (Phil 3:16)

Test everything. Hold on to the good. (1 Th 5:21)

But Christ is faithful as a son over God's house. And we are his house, if we

hold on to our courage and the hope of which we boast. (Heb 3:6)

Therefore, since we have a great high priest who has gone through the heavens, Jesus the Son of God, let us hold firmly to the faith we profess. (Heb 4:14)

Let us hold unswervingly to the hope we profess, for he who promised is faithful. (Heb 10:23)

Whoever claims to live in him must walk as Jesus did. (1 John 2:6)

Remember, therefore, what you have received and heard; obey it, and repent. But if you do not wake up, I will come like a thief, and you will not know at what time I will come to you. (Rev 3:3)

**7** (2:26-29) **Overcomers—Promises**: there are the promises to the overcomers. Two wonderful promises are made to the believer who overcomes and does not compromise with the world—who overcomes the seduction, sexual immorality, drunken and loose parties, idolatry, and false teaching of the world—who keeps on living and working for Christ.

1. The overcomer is given authority over the nations (cp. Ps.2:8-9). This is clearly the promise of ruling and reigning with Christ throughout eternity. The day is coming when Jesus Christ will return to earth and conquer all the forces of evil. Every knee shall bow and confess that He is the Lord God of the universe. The overcomers shall participate in that day, the glorious day of redemption with Jesus Christ. They shall be given positions of rule and service throughout the universe. They shall serve the Lord Jesus Christ in the new heavens and earth. (See note, *Rewards*—Rev.14:13; 21:24-27 for discussion).

"'Well done, my good servant!' his master replied. 'Because you have been trustworthy in a very small matter, take charge of ten cities.' (Luke 19:17)

Do you not know that the saints will judge the world? And if you are to judge the world, are you not competent to judge trivial cases? (1 Cor 6:2)

To him who overcomes, I will give the right to sit with me on my throne, just as I overcame and sat down with my Father on his throne. (Rev 3:21)

"Because he loves me," says the LORD, "I will rescue him; I will protect him, for he acknowledges my name. (Psa 91:14)

Those who are wise will shine like the brightness of the heavens, and those who lead many to righteousness, like the stars for ever and ever. (Dan 12:3)

The Sovereign LORD is my strength; he makes my feet like the feet of a deer, he enables me to go on the heights. For the director of music. On my stringed instruments. (Hab 3:19)

You are those who have stood by me in my trials. And I confer on you a kingdom, just as my Father conferred one on me, (Luke 22:28-29)

If we endure, we will also reign with him. If we disown him, he will also disown us; (2 Tim 2:12)

And from Jesus Christ, who is the faithful witness, the firstborn from the dead, and the ruler of the kings of the earth. To him who loves us and has freed us from our sins by his blood, And has made us to be a kingdom and priests to serve his God and Father—to him be glory and power for ever and ever! Amen. (Rev 1:5-6)

I saw thrones on which were seated those who had been given authority to judge. And I saw the souls of those who had been beheaded because of their testimony for Jesus and because of the word of God. They had not worshiped the beast or his image and had not received his mark on their foreheads or their hands. They came to life and reigned with Christ a thousand years. (Rev 20:4)

2. The overcomer is given the morning star. This is Jesus Christ Himself. Rev.22:16 calls Jesus, "the bright Morning Star." The hearer and overcomer is to receive Jesus Himself forever and ever, never to be away from Him again.

Note: the person who has an ear, let him hear what the Spirit says to this church. Let him separate from the world. Let him never compromise and become corrupted with the sins of the world. Let him never allow a Jezebel—a compromising or corrupt person—to teach in the church.

**CHAPTER 3**

**F. The Message to Sardis: The Church with Reputation, but Dying, 3:1-6**

| | | | |
|---|---|---|---|
| **1 The recipients**<br>a. The messenger of the church<br>b. The Sardis church[DS1]<br>**2 The speaker—Jesus**<br>**3 The complaint: Deeds**<br>a. They appear alive<br>b. But they are dead<br><br>**4 The counsel: Wake up! Strengthen what remains**<br><br><br>**5 The warning** | "To the angel of the church in Sardis write: These are the words of him who holds the seven spirits of God and the seven stars. I know your deeds; you have a reputation of being alive, but you are dead.<br>2 Wake up! Strengthen what remains and is about to die, for I have not found your deeds complete in the sight of my God.<br>3 Remember, therefore, what | you have received and heard; obey it, and repent. But if you do not wake up, I will come like a thief, and you will not know at what time I will come to you.<br>4 Yet you have a few people in Sardis who have not soiled their clothes. They will walk with me, dressed in white, for they are worthy.<br>5 He who overcomes will, like them, be dressed in white. I will never blot out his name from the book of life, but will acknowledge his name before my Father and his angels.<br>6 He who has an ear, let him hear what the Spirit says to the churches. | a. Remember & obey what you have received & heard<br>b. Repent<br>c. Know that judgment will fall unexpectedly<br>**6 The promise**<br>a. To the people not soiled: They will walk with the Lord in white<br><br>b. To the overcomers<br>1) They will be clothed in white<br>2) They will not be blotted out<br>3) They will be acknowledged by Christ before God |

# DIVISION II

## THE MESSAGES OF THE GLORIFIED CHRIST TO THE SEVEN CHURCHES, 1:9-3:22

### F. The Message to Sardis: The Church with Reputation, but Dying, 3:1-6

**(3:1-6) Introduction**: Have you ever seen a church that was dead and dying, completely lifeless? A church that was satisfied with itself, with keeping things the way they had always been? A church resting on its laurels and past history, that just reveled in what used to be? This was the church at Sardis. Sardis pictures the church that has an excellent reputation and is highly respected by the community, but it is dead and lifeless.

1. The recipients (v.1).
2. The speaker—Jesus (v.1).
3. The complaint: deeds (v.1).
4. The counsel: Wake up! Strengthen what remains (v.2).
5. The warning (v.3).
6. The promise (v.4-6).

**1** (3:1) **Minister—Church**: there are the recipients of the letter. The Lord Jesus Christ addresses the letter to the minister of the church, but He wants it proclaimed to the church as a whole. There is little hope for a dead church ever becoming alive unless the minister is set afire. There can be little awakening, little stirring, little quickening, little life within a church unless the minister is committed—totally committed—to Christ and His cause of eternal salvation. Revival is not likely unless the minister is first revived. Therefore, Christ speaks first of all to the minister.

> **Thought 1.** This is a strong point that ministers must heed. We must get into the Word and on our faces before God, evaluating our hearts to make sure we are *spiritually alive* and *revived*. As ministers of Christ, we must be living in a constant state of *awakening and revival*—a constant state that lasts on and on until the Lord comes.

**DEEPER STUDY # 1**

(3:1) **Sardis**: there are two historical facts that seem to have a bearing on the letter.

1. Sardis was a city with two sections. The first development sat on a ridge that jutted out from the side of a mountain. It was fifteen hundred feet straight up and it was impregnable, perfectly safe from any enemy. However, when the city outgrew this ridge, a second development was begun at the base of the mountain in the valley. Legend has it that gold was discovered just lying around in the river that flowed through the city. The city's history was one of wealth and security from all enemies. However, by the time John wrote Revelation, the city's flourishing wealth had passed and much of its glory had faded. The population had become flabby and soft, lethargic and complacent, living on the city's past reputation. The church knew what the Lord meant by having a name that they lived, but they were dead (v.1). They knew what it was to *have received* the best of everything, but now they needed to *repent* (v.3).

2. Sardis had been conquered only twice. Both times had been due to a false sense of security behind their impregnable fortress. They failed to post adequate watches to overlook the walls of the steep fortress. While under attack by Cyrus of Persia, a guard of Sardis was seen to drop his helmet over the steep wall and climb down the crevices to recover it. The city was taken that very night by a small band of soldiers climbing up the same crevices. Under one of the subsequent rulers to Alexander the Great, the incident was remembered, and again the city was taken in the same manner. The church knew from history what the Lord meant by "Wake up! Strengthen what remains...obey it...I will come like a thief" (v.2-3).

**2** (3:1) **Jesus Christ—Minister—Church**: there is the speaker, the Lord Jesus Christ Himself. A lifeless and dying church needs to look at Jesus Christ, at two things in particular.

1. Jesus Christ has the seven spirits of God. This is a reference to the Holy Spirit of God.

   a. The number seven means the *sevenfold ministry* of the Holy Spirit. Jesus Christ Himself spelled this out in the upper room where He revealed who the Holy Spirit was to be:

⇒ He is the Comforter, the Counselor, the other Helper (Jn.14:16).
⇒ He is the Spirit of truth (Jn.14:17).
⇒ He is the personal presence of Christ (Jn.14:18-20).
⇒ He is the very special manifestation of Christ within the believer (Jn.14:21-22).
⇒ He is the abiding presence of the Trinity (Jn.14:23-24).
⇒ He is the teacher (Jn.14:25-26).
⇒ He is the peace of Christ (Jn.14:27).

Some commentators point out that this is a reference to the sevenfold ministry of the Holy Spirit found in Isaiah.

**The Spirit of the LORD will rest on him—the Spirit of wisdom and of understanding, the Spirit of counsel and of power, the Spirit of knowledge and of the fear of the LORD— (Isa 11:2)**

⇒ The Spirit of the Lord
⇒ The Spirit of wisdom
⇒ The Spirit of understanding
⇒ The Spirit of counsel
⇒ The Spirit of power
⇒ The Spirit of knowledge
⇒ The Spirit of fear

b. The number seven also means completeness, fullness, or perfection in the Bible. Therefore, the *seven* spirits means the Holy Spirit in all His fullness.

The point is this: what a lifeless and dying church needs is the Spirit of God.

⇒ A lifeless and dying church needs to seek Christ for the Spirit of God.

**If you then, though you are evil, know how to give good gifts to your children, how much more will your Father in heaven give the Holy Spirit to those who ask him!" (Luke 11:13)**
**And I will do whatever you ask in my name, so that the Son may bring glory to the Father. You may ask me for anything in my name, and I will do it. "If you love me, you will obey what I command. And I will ask the Father, and he will give you another Counselor to be with you forever— (John 14:13-16)**

⇒ A lifeless and dying church needs to seek the life-giving, quickening power of the Spirit.

**And if the Spirit of him who raised Jesus from the dead is living in you, he who raised Christ from the dead will also give life to your mortal bodies through his Spirit, who lives in you. (Rom 8:11)**

⇒ A lifeless and dying church needs to seek the convicting power of the Spirit.

**But I tell you the truth: It is for your good that I am going away. Unless**

**I go away, the Counselor will not come to you; but if I go, I will send him to you. (John 16:7)**

⇒ A lifeless and dying church needs to seek the fruit of the Spirit.

**But the fruit of the Spirit is love, joy, peace, patience, kindness, goodness, faithfulness, Gentleness and self-control. Against such things there is no law. (Gal 5:22-23)**

⇒ A lifeless and dying church needs to seek the guidance of the Spirit.

**But when he, the Spirit of truth, comes, he will guide you into all truth. He will not speak on his own; he will speak only what he hears, and he will tell you what is yet to come. (John 16:13)**
**Because those who are led by the Spirit of God are sons of God. (Rom 8:14)**

⇒ A lifeless and dying church needs to seek revival, the Pentecostal fire of the Spirit.

**"I baptize you with water for repentance. But after me will come one who is more powerful than I, whose sandals I am not fit to carry. He will baptize you with the Holy Spirit and with fire. (Mat 3:11)**
**They saw what seemed to be tongues of fire that separated and came to rest on each of them. All of them were filled with the Holy Spirit and began to speak in other tongues as the Spirit enabled them. (Acts 2:3-4)**

⇒ A lifeless and dying church needs to seek the witnessing power of the Spirit.

**But you will receive power when the Holy Spirit comes on you; and you will be my witnesses in Jerusalem, and in all Judea and Samaria, and to the ends of the earth." (Acts 1:8)**

2. Jesus Christ has the seven stars in His hands; that is, He holds the ministers of the church in His hands. The minister is the one who is responsible for bringing about the awakening. He is held in the hand of Christ; he belongs totally to Christ. This means that he...

• has been chosen by the hand of Christ to do exactly what Christ wants.
• has been placed into the dead church by the hand of Christ.
• has been placed there for a reason: to be aroused himself and to arouse the church.

(See note 2—Rev.2:1 for more discussion.)
**You did not choose me, but I chose you and appointed you to go and bear fruit—fruit that will last. Then the Father will give you whatever you ask in my name. (John 15:16)**

The third time he said to him, "Simon son of John, do you love me?" Peter was hurt because Jesus asked him the third time, "Do you love me?" He said, "Lord, you know all things; you know that I love you." Jesus said, "Feed my sheep. (John 21:17)

But the Lord said to Ananias, "Go! This man is my chosen instrument to carry my name before the Gentiles and their kings and before the people of Israel. (Acts 9:15)

Keep watch over yourselves and all the flock of which the Holy Spirit has made you overseers. Be shepherds of the church of God, which he bought with his own blood. (Acts 20:28)

'Now get up and stand on your feet. I have appeared to you to appoint you as a servant and as a witness of what you have seen of me and what I will show you. (Acts 26:16)

Command and teach these things. (1 Tim 4:11)

Those who oppose him he must gently instruct, in the hope that God will grant them repentance leading them to a knowledge of the truth, (2 Tim 2:25)

Be shepherds of God's flock that is under your care, serving as overseers—not because you must, but because you are willing, as God wants you to be; not greedy for money, but eager to serve; (1 Pet 5:2)

"Come, let us return to the LORD. He has torn us to pieces but he will heal us; he has injured us but he will bind up our wounds. (Hosea 6:1)

So now, go. I am sending you [Moses] to Pharaoh to bring my people the Israelites out of Egypt." (Exo 3:10)

Gideon replied, "If now I [Gideon] have found favor in your eyes, give me a sign that it is really you talking to me. (Judg 6:17)

Then I heard the voice of the Lord saying, "Whom shall I send? And who will go for us?" And I [Isaiah] said, "Here am I. Send me!" (Isa 6:8)

"Son of man, I have made you a watchman for the house of Israel; so hear the word I speak and give them warning from me. (Ezek 3:17)

But if the watchman sees the sword coming and does not blow the trumpet to warn the people and the sword comes and takes the life of one of them, that man will be taken away because of his sin, but I will hold the watchman accountable for his blood.' (Ezek 33:6)

**3** (3:1) **Church—Formalism—Ritualism—Complacency:** there is the complaint. Note: there is no commendation, none whatsoever, given to this church. This means that its sin is one of the most serious problems that a church can have. What was the problem? It was a dying church, a lifeless church. But note: the church had deeds—all sorts of programs, ministries, and activities. It had so much bustling activity that it had a great reputation among other churches. Other churches looked upon the church as being progres-

sive, alive, well attended, well liked, prosperous, busy, and full of good fellowship. It had ministries for every age group and for every area of need throughout the community. It had the deeds, the right beliefs and doctrine, and it had all the ministries and activities. But note: it was dying and lifeless. However, verse two says that it was not yet totally dead; a few *living things* still remained, but they too were quickly dying. How could a church be so active and well attended and have so many ministries and yet be dying? What does this mean? It means to die spiritually; it means...

- to have a form of worship or godliness but to deny its power (2 Tim.3:5).
- to focus upon ritual, ceremony, and worship instead of Jesus Christ.
- to focus upon activities instead of Jesus Christ.
- to become formal in worship instead of alive in Christ.
- to conduct activities in order to keep the organization going instead of learning about Christ and sharing about Christ.
- to hold services and activities for social fellowship instead of for spiritual growth and edification.
- to lose one's zeal for witnessing and sharing Christ and for seeing others grow.
- to become complacent and lethargic in the study of God's Word and in prayer and spiritual growth.
- to sit in worship and Bible classes as a matter of form instead of hungering and thirsting after righteousness.
- to preach and teach as a matter of form.
- to use the ministry as a means of livelihood instead of preaching and teaching to win and grow people in Christ.

Such an active church can seldom be convinced that it is dead and lifeless because of its bustling activity. But Jesus Christ says it is dead. It is void of spiritual life and energy, void of the Spirit of God. Its works are only activities, only man-made activities and social services. The works do not have the Spirit of God and His power in them.

"Not everyone who says to me, 'Lord, Lord,' will enter the kingdom of heaven, but only he who does the will of my Father who is in heaven. (Mat 7:21)

"'These people honor me with their lips, but their hearts are far from me. (Mat 15:8)

He replied, "Isaiah was right when he prophesied about you hypocrites; as it is written: "'These people honor me with their lips, but their hearts are far from me. (Mark 7:6)

Jesus said to them, "I tell you the truth, unless you eat the flesh of the Son of Man and drink his blood, you have no life in you. (John 6:53)

And do this, understanding the present time. The hour has come for you to wake up from your slumber, because our salvation is nearer now than when we first believed. (Rom 13:11)

For the kingdom of God is not a matter of eating and drinking, but of righteousness, peace and joy in the Holy Spirit, (Rom 14:17)

You are observing special days and months and seasons and years! I fear for you, that somehow I have wasted my efforts on you. (Gal 4:10-11)

For it is light that makes everything visible. This is why it is said: "Wake up, O sleeper, rise from the dead, and Christ will shine on you." (Eph 5:14)

So then, let us not be like others, who are asleep, but let us be alert and self-controlled. (1 Th 5:6)

But the widow who lives for pleasure is dead even while she lives. (1 Tim 5:6)

Having a form of godliness but denying its power. Have nothing to do with them. (2 Tim 3:5)

They claim to know God, but by their actions they deny him. They are detestable, disobedient and unfit for doing anything good. (Titus 1:16)

"To the angel of the church in Sardis write: These are the words of him who holds the seven spirits of God and the seven stars. I know your deeds; you have a reputation of being alive, but you are dead. (Rev 3:1)

You do not delight in sacrifice, or I would bring it; you do not take pleasure in burnt offerings. The sacrifices of God are a broken spirit; a broken and contrite heart, O God, you will not despise. (Psa 51:16-17)

They remembered that God was their Rock, that God Most High was their Redeemer. But then they would flatter him with their mouths, lying to him with their tongues; (Psa 78:35-36)

The Lord says: "These people come near to me with their mouth and honor me with their lips, but their hearts are far from me. Their worship of me is made up only of rules taught by men. (Isa 29:13)

My people come to you, as they usually do, and sit before you to listen to your words, but they do not put them into practice. With their mouths they express devotion, but their hearts are greedy for unjust gain. Indeed, to them you are nothing more than one who sings love songs with a beautiful voice and plays an instrument well, for they hear your words but do not put them into practice. (Ezek 33:31-32)

alive to the Lord Jesus Christ and to the Word of God. They needed to rethink why they and the church were on earth, what their calling was, why they were meeting together as a church, why they were claiming the name of Christ and doing works and carrying on ministries in the name of Christ. Note: the words *wake up* are imperative. It is a command of Christ to the dying church. Note that the words *wake up* are also in the present tense. The believer is to awaken, become *alert*, become a follower of Jesus Christ. The believer is to always wake up and make sure he is alive spiritually.

"Therefore keep watch, because you do not know on what day your Lord will come. But understand this: If the owner of the house had known at what time of night the thief was coming, he would have kept watch and would not have let his house be broken into. (Mat 24:42-43)

"Watch and pray so that you will not fall into temptation. The spirit is willing, but the body is weak." (Mat 26:41)

What I say to you, I say to everyone: 'Watch!'" (Mark 13:37)

So be on your guard! Remember that for three years I never stopped warning each of you night and day with tears. (Acts 20:31)

And do this, understanding the present time. The hour has come for you to wake up from your slumber, because our salvation is nearer now than when we first believed. (Rom 13:11)

Be on your guard; stand firm in the faith; be men of courage; be strong. (1 Cor 16:13)

Devote yourselves to prayer, being watchful and thankful. (Col 4:2)

So then, let us not be like others, who are asleep, but let us be alert and self-controlled. (1 Th 5:6)

Be self-controlled and alert. Your enemy the devil prowls around like a roaring lion looking for someone to devour. (1 Pet 5:8)

"Behold, I come like a thief! Blessed is he who stays awake and keeps his clothes with him, so that he may not go naked and be shamefully exposed." (Rev 16:15)

**4** (3:2) **Watch**: there is the counsel. It is strong: Wake up! Strengthen what remains. Remember: the church had the services, meetings, and ministries that were needed. The church was doing the very things that it was supposed to be doing. What was wrong was the *spirit* of the people. Their spirits were not focusing upon Jesus Christ and His cause. They were...

- sitting in the services half asleep and allowing their thoughts to wander about instead of hungering for the Word of God.
- holding and attending the activities for the sake of fellowship and because it was the thing to do.

On and on the list could go. The point to see is that the people were not alive, not spiritually, not to the Lord Jesus Christ. They were attending and participating because it was the thing to do and because it gave them a sense of *religious security*. Note the twofold counsel.

1. Watch: "Rouse yourself and keep awake" (The Amplified New Testament). They need to awaken, to arouse themselves, to stir their minds and thoughts, to become alert and

2. Strengthen what remains. As stated, not all the services and activities were wrong and unneeded in the church. The church had been led by Christ to start the ministries in earlier days when the church was alive. But note: even these ministries were now dying. The believers desperately needed to arouse themselves and take hold of these ministries and put new life into them. Jesus Christ counsels: "Give immediate attention to what remains. Wake up, arouse yourselves. Strengthen these ministries now."

Shockingly, Christ says that He has not found any of their deeds perfect, that is, complete, fulfilled, or finished. Not a single ministry had been completed or carried out like it should be—not in the eyes of Christ.

But everyone who hears these words of mine and does not put them into practice is like a foolish man who built his house on sand. The rain came down, the streams rose, and the winds blew and beat against that house, and it fell with a great crash." (Mat 7:26-27)

Because of the increase of wickedness, the love of most will grow cold. (Mat 24:12)

"That servant who knows his master's will and does not get ready or does not do what his master wants will be beaten with many blows. (Luke 12:47)

How shall we escape if we ignore such a great salvation? This salvation, which was first announced by the Lord, was confirmed to us by those who heard him. (Heb 2:3)

What good is it, my brothers, if a man claims to have faith but has no deeds? Can such faith save him? (James 2:14)

Come near to God and he will come near to you. Wash your hands, you sinners, and purify your hearts, you double-minded. (James 4:8)

Anyone, then, who knows the good he ought to do and doesn't do it, sins. (James 4:17)

"A curse on him who is lax in doing the Lord's work! A curse on him who keeps his sword from bloodshed! (Jer 48:10)

**5** (3:3) **Warning**: there is the warning. The believers of a dead, lifeless church are warned to do four things.

1. They must remember *how they received and heard the gospel*; that is, they must remember how it gripped their lives with a dynamic spirit of...
- devotion
- readiness and love
- alertness and energy
- hunger and thirst
- life and vitality
- service
- witnessing
- ministry

2. They must arouse and awaken and obey the original spirit that gripped their lives.

3. They must repent. They had done wrong and sinned against Christ by losing their fervor and becoming lethargic. They desperately needed to confess their wrong and repent; they needed to turn away from their error and turn back to Christ. They needed to have prayer meetings, seeking Christ to stir their hearts and to set them aflame for Him.

4. They must know that the judgment of Christ will fall upon them if they refuse to repent, and it will fall unexpectedly. If the church and its believers refuse to watch—refuse to arouse themselves—then Christ will come upon them as a thief. And note: they will not know what hour He is coming to judge them. The idea is that Christ will come and strip them of all their valuables just like a thief. They will be left bare, without anything worthwhile. The church and its believers will be worthless, of no value or worth to Christ and His kingdom. No matter what the church and its members may think, they will be found vain, empty, and useless. They will have done no good whatsoever for the kingdom of God. Their profession will have been meaningless.

The rain came down, the streams rose, and the winds blew and beat against that house, and it fell with a great crash." (Mat 7:27)

What good is it for a man to gain the whole world, yet forfeit his soul? (Mark 8:36)

"If anyone comes to me and does not hate his father and mother, his wife and children, his brothers and sisters—yes, even his own life—he cannot be my disciple. And anyone who does not carry his cross and follow me cannot be my disciple. "Suppose one of you wants to build a tower. Will he not first sit down and estimate the cost to see if he has enough money to complete it? For if he lays the foundation and is not able to finish it, everyone who sees it will ridicule him, (Luke 14:26-29)

His work will be shown for what it is, because the Day will bring it to light. It will be revealed with fire, and the fire will test the quality of each man's work. If what he has built survives, he will receive his reward. If it is burned up, he will suffer loss; he himself will be saved, but only as one escaping through the flames. (1 Cor 3:13-15)

**6** (3:4-6) **Overcomers—Promises**: there is the promise to the overcomers. Note: there is a promise to the people who do not soil themselves as well as to the overcomers.

1. There are those who had not soiled themselves. This means there were a few faithful believers in the church. They had not defiled, dirtied, or spotted their lives with the worldliness of the day. They had kept themselves "from being polluted by the world" (Jas.1:27). They were not activity centered nor program centered, but Christ centered. They did not use the church...
- as a religious salve for their conscience
- as a social activity
- as a place for fellowship alone
- as a place for social and business contacts
- as a place to build their public image
- as a place to provide activities for the family

The faithful believers kept themselves pure. They focused upon Jesus Christ and His purpose: they were still growing spiritually and reaching out to share Christ with a needful world.

Note the promise: the faithful and pure believer "walks with Christ dressed in white." This means...
- that the faithful believer walks day by day in the presence of Christ and has the presence of Christ looking after and taking care of him—keeping him pure (white).
- that the faithful believer walks day by day and moment by moment in open confession before Christ, that he keeps himself clean by constantly confessing all sin and having Christ forgive his sins. Christ keeps him clean (white).
- that the faithful believer walks in victory and purity with Christ forever and ever.

Note that the faithful and pure believer receives this promise because he is worthy. Christ is ever so pleased that the believer focuses upon Him, his Lord; therefore, Christ loves him with a very special love and counts the believer worthy.

2. There are the overcomers. Three promises are made to the believer who keeps his spirit alive, the believer who focuses upon Jesus Christ and His spiritual purposes for the church.

a. The overcomer will be dressed in white. This is the garment of righteousness and purity, of perfection that shall be given to the believer when he enters heaven. The believer is given this garment of righteousness and purity...
- because he trusted the righteousness of Christ.
- because he followed Christ by living a righteous life.

"But when the king came in to see the guests, he noticed a man there who was not wearing wedding clothes. (Mat 22:11)

"But the father said to his servants, 'Quick! Bring the best robe and put it on him. Put a ring on his finger and sandals on his feet. (Luke 15:22)

This righteousness from God comes through faith in Jesus Christ to all who believe. There is no difference, (Rom 3:22)

God made him who had no sin to be sin for us, so that in him we might become the righteousness of God. (2 Cor 5:21)

He who overcomes will, like them, be dressed in white. I will never blot out his name from the book of life, but will acknowledge his name before my Father and his angels. (Rev 3:5)

I counsel you to buy from me gold refined in the fire, so you can become rich; and white clothes to wear, so you can cover your shameful nakedness; and salve to put on your eyes, so you can see. (Rev 3:18)

Surrounding the throne were twenty-four other thrones, and seated on them were twenty-four elders. They were dressed in white and had crowns of gold on their heads. (Rev 4:4)

After this I looked and there before me was a great multitude that no one could count, from every nation, tribe, people and language, standing before the throne and in front of the Lamb. They were wearing white robes and were holding palm branches in their hands. (Rev 7:9)

Fine linen, bright and clean, was given her to wear." (Fine linen stands for the righteous acts of the saints.) (Rev 19:8)

Abram believed the LORD, and he credited it to him as righteousness. (Gen 15:6)

I put on righteousness as my clothing; justice was my robe and my turban. (Job 29:14)

I will clothe her priests with salvation, and her saints will ever sing for joy. (Psa 132:16)

I delight greatly in the LORD; my soul rejoices in my God. For he has clothed me with garments of salvation and arrayed me in a robe of righteousness, as a bridegroom adorns his head like a priest, and as a bride adorns herself with her jewels. (Isa 61:10)

The angel said to those who were standing before him, "Take off his filthy clothes." Then he said to Joshua, "See, I have taken away your sin, and I will put rich garments on you." (Zec 3:4)

b. The overcomer will not be blotted out of the book of life. This is a book that God keeps. The picture of Scripture is this: every person's name is written in the book of life when the person is born again. But at death the names of unbelievers are erased from the book and they are judged to eternal death. The names of true believers are never touched. They receive eternal life.

However, do not rejoice that the spirits submit to you, but rejoice that your names are written in heaven." (Luke 10:20)

Yes, and I ask you, loyal yokefellow, help these women who have contended at my side in the cause of the gospel, along with Clement and the rest of my fellow workers, whose names are in the book of life. (Phil 4:3)

If anyone's name was not found written in the book of life, he was thrown into the lake of fire. (Rev 20:15)

Nothing impure will ever enter it, nor will anyone who does what is shameful or deceitful, but only those whose names are written in the Lamb's book of life. (Rev 21:27)

The LORD replied to Moses, "Whoever has sinned against me I will blot out of my book. (Exo 32:33)

May they be blotted out of the book of life and not be listed with the righteous. (Psa 69:28)

"At that time Michael, the great prince who protects your people, will arise. There will be a time of distress such as has not happened from the beginning of nations until then. But at that time your people—everyone whose name is found written in the book—will be delivered. (Dan 12:1)

c. The overcomer will be acknowledged by Christ before God. Christ will confess that He knows the believer who overcame by keeping his spirit alive and focused upon the Lord.

"Whoever acknowledges me before men, I will also acknowledge him before my Father in heaven. But whoever disowns me before men, I will disown him before my Father in heaven. (Mat 10:32-33)

"I tell you, whoever acknowledges me before men, the Son of Man will also acknowledge him before the angels of God. (Luke 12:8)

That if you confess with your mouth, "Jesus is Lord," and believe in your heart that God raised him from the dead, you will be saved. (Rom 10:9)

And every tongue confess that Jesus Christ is Lord, to the glory of God the Father. (Phil 2:11)

Who is the liar? It is the man who denies that Jesus is the Christ. Such a man is the antichrist—he denies the Father and the Son. No one who denies the Son has the Father; whoever acknowledges the Son has the Father also. (1 John 2:22-23)

If anyone acknowledges that Jesus is the Son of God, God lives in him and he in God. (1 John 4:15)

| | G. The Message to Philadelphia: The Church That Is Faithful & Alive, 3:7-13 | knowledge that I have loved you.<br>10 Since you have kept my command to endure patiently, I will also keep you from the hour of trial that is going to come upon the whole world to test those who live on the earth. | b. There will be great deliverance: From the hour of trial |
|---|---|---|---|
| 1 **The recipients**<br>a. The messenger of the church<br>b. The Philadelphian church[DS1]<br>2 **The speaker—Jesus**<br><br>3 **The commendation**<br>a. They had used the open door of evangelism & missions<br>b. They had kept Christ's Word<br>c. They had not denied the Lord's name<br><br>4 **The two great hopes**<br>a. There will be great vindication: The persecutors of the believer's will either be saved or judged | 7 "To the angel of the church in Philadelphia write: These are the words of him who is holy and true, who holds the key of David. What he opens no one can shut, and what he shuts no one can open.<br>8 I know your deeds. See, I have placed before you an open door that no one can shut. I know that you have little strength, yet you have kept my word and have not denied my name.<br>9 I will make those who are of the synagogue of Satan, who claim to be Jews though they are not, but are liars—I will make them come and fall down at your feet and ac- | 11 I am coming soon. Hold on to what you have, so that no one will take your crown.<br>12 Him who overcomes I will make a pillar in the temple of my God. Never again will he leave it. I will write on him the name of my God and the name of the city of my God, the new Jerusalem, which is coming down out of heaven from my God; and I will also write on him my new name.<br>13 He who has an ear, let him hear what the Spirit says to the churches. | 5 **The counsel: Christ is coming soon; therefore hold on, hold fast**<br>6 **The promise: To the overcomers**<br>a. Will be made a pillar in the temple of God<br>b. Will receive security<br>c. Will receive God's name<br>d. Will receive the new name of God's city<br><br>e. Will receive a new name |

# DIVISION II

## THE MESSAGES OF THE GLORIFIED CHRIST TO THE SEVEN CHURCHES, 1:9-3:22

### G. The Message to Philadelphia: The Church That Is Faithful and Alive, 3:7-13

(3:7-13) **Introduction**: Have you ever seen a church that is alive and faithful to Christ? A church that focuses upon Jesus Christ? A church that makes Jesus Christ the center of its ministries and activities? A church that focuses upon reaching and growing people for Christ? A church that focuses upon teaching people to love Christ and to love one another more and more? This was the church at Philadelphia. The very word *Philadelphia* means *brotherly love or one who loves his brother.* The believers at Philadelphia loved Christ; therefore, they gave their hearts and lives to Christ. They lived like Christ said to live and they carried out the mission of Christ upon earth. The church at Philadelphia was alive and faithful. It represents all the churches down through the ages that are alive and faithful. It shows us exactly what Christ wants a church to be. Note: there is no complaint or warning against this church. Jesus Christ has only praise and exhortation for the church that is alive and faithful.

1. The recipients (v.7).
2. The speaker—Jesus (v.7).
3. The commendation (v.8).
4. The two great hopes (v.9-10).
5. The counsel: Christ is coming soon; therefore, hold on, hold fast (v.11).
6. The promise: to the overcomers (v.12-13).

**1** (3:7) **Minister—Church**: there are the recipients of the letter. The letter is addressed to the minister of the church, but the Lord expects the minister to share it with the church. The church was alive and faithful to Christ, and it was up to the minister to keep the church focused upon the mission of Christ. The minister was the God-appointed leader to keep the church alive and faithful. The church would most likely

remain alive and faithful if the minister would...
- live in the Word of God.
- live on his face in prayer.
- preach and teach the Word of God.
- exhort the believers to live for Christ, to study the Word, pray, witness, and minister faithfully.
- lead the church to set up the ministries that would reach the lost, build up the believers, minister to the needy, and reach out to the world by supporting worldwide missions.

If the minister slacked up or failed in any of these, the church would lose some of its focus upon Jesus Christ. It would no longer be as alive or faithful as it should be. But if the minister remained diligent, alive, and faithful himself, the likelihood is that the church would stay alive and faithful to Christ. This is the reason Christ addresses the letter to the minister.

**DEEPER STUDY # 1**

(3:7) **Philadelphia**: there are five historical facts that seem to have a bearing upon the message to the church.

1. Philadelphia was founded as a border town to spread Greek culture to surrounding areas. In fact, it was situated right on the borders of Lydia, Mysia, and Phrygia. The church knew exactly what it meant to be missionary minded, to have an open door for the spread of the gospel (Rev.3:8; cp. Acts 14:27; 1 Cor.16:9; 2 Cor.2:12; Col.4:3).

2. The name Philadelphia means *brotherly love.* The very name of the church gave the believers a constant reminder: they must love one another if they were going to fulfill their missionary calling.

3. Philadelphia knew what it was to live in the midst of insecure surroundings and under constant stress and strain.

The city sat over a large earthquake fault. In A.D. 17 a terrifying earthquake hit a huge area. It completely destroyed Sardis and ten other cities. Philadelphia was spared total destruction. But for years the city was hit by unending tremors—each adding its own panic and crumbling walls to the devastation. The experience of having to constantly run in and out for safety terrorized the population. The experience was never forgotten by succeeding generations. The church knew what it was to be given the hope of becoming a "pillar in the temple of God" and the promise to the overcomer that "Never again will he leave it" (v.12).

4. Philadelphia, after its destruction by the earthquake, was given aid by the emperor Tiberius for rebuilding. In appreciation the city changed its name to Neocaesarea, the New City of Caesar. The church knew what it was to be given a new name (v.12).

5. Philadelphia had a Jewish synagogue within its city limits. The Jews claimed to be the only followers of the true God (v.9). They claimed *the keys of David*, the right to *open* and to *shut* the door to God and His kingdom (v.7). The church knew what it was to trust and know Him who alone "is true [and]...who holds the key of David [and]...opens and...shuts" (v.7).

**2** (3:7) **Jesus Christ—Church**: there is the speaker, the Lord Jesus Christ Himself. What Jesus Christ says about Himself speaks to the heart of the church that is alive and faithful.

1. Jesus Christ is *holy*. The word *holy* is a description of God Himself. Jesus Christ is claiming to have the very same nature as God the Father, to be perfectly holy even as God is perfectly holy. Remember that *holiness* means to be set apart and different from all other beings, completely and totally set apart. Christ is supremely holy. He reaches the summit of being different from all other beings. This means something significant for the church that is alive and faithful. It means they are worshipping and following God Himself by following Christ. By giving their hearts and lives to Christ, they are giving themselves to the sovereign Majesty and supreme Force of the universe, to the most holy God Himself. The church is, therefore, under His care and love. Christ Jesus, the Most Holy God, will look after and take care of the church if the church will just continue to be alive and faithful.

> Exalt the LORD our God and worship at his holy mountain, for the LORD our God is holy. (Psa 99:9)
> And they were calling to one another: "Holy, holy, holy is the LORD Almighty; the whole earth is full of his glory." (Isa 6:3)
> Can any of you prove me guilty of sin? If I am telling the truth, why don't you believe me? (John 8:46)
> Indeed Herod and Pontius Pilate met together with the Gentiles and the people of Israel in this city to conspire against your holy servant Jesus, whom you anointed. (Acts 4:27)
> Stretch out your hand to heal and perform miraculous signs and wonders through the name of your holy servant Jesus." (Acts 4:30)
> God made him who had no sin to be sin for us, so that in him we might become the righteousness of God. (2 Cor 5:21)
> For we do not have a high priest who is unable to sympathize with our weaknesses, but we have one who has been tempted in every way, just as we are—yet was without sin. (Heb 4:15)
> Such a high priest meets our need—one who is holy, blameless, pure, set apart from sinners, exalted above the heavens. (Heb 7:26)
> Who will not fear you, O Lord, and bring glory to your name? For you alone are holy. All nations will come and worship before you, for your righteous acts have been revealed." (Rev 15:4)

2. Jesus Christ is the One who is *true*. The word true (alethinos) means the true as opposed to the false, the genuine as opposed to the counterfeit, the real as opposed to the unreal. Jesus Christ is the true, genuine, and real God. He is the only living and true God. There is none other. All the other gods worshipped by men are false, counterfeit, and unreal. This, too, means a wonderful thing. God is not far off in outer space someplace, too far off to be known or reached. He is not the shadowy figure that most men imagine Him to be. God is not distant from us. He has not left us in the dark to grope and grasp and to stumble about trying to find Him. God does not hate us; He has not left us in the dark about Himself. God loves us. He has revealed Himself to us. He sent the Lord Jesus Christ to bring the truth to us. Therefore, in worshipping the Lord Jesus Christ we are worshipping the only true and living God. What the faithful church must do is continue to follow Christ, continue to make Him the focus of all that it does. When the church makes Him the center of all its ministries, activities, and meetings, then the church is following the truth—following Him who is true.

> The true light that gives light to every man was coming into the world. (John 1:9)
> The Word became flesh and made his dwelling among us. We have seen his glory, the glory of the One and Only, who came from the Father, full of grace and truth. (John 1:14)
> Jesus said to them, "I tell you the truth, it is not Moses who has given you the bread from heaven, but it is my Father who gives you the true bread from heaven. (John 6:32)
> Jesus answered, "I am the way and the truth and the life. No one comes to the Father except through me. (John 14:6)
> "I am the true vine, and my Father is the gardener. (John 15:1)
> "You are a king, then!" Said Pilate. Jesus answered, "You are right in saying I am a king. In fact, for this reason I was born, and for this I came into the world, to testify to the truth. Everyone on the side of truth listens to me." (John 18:37)
> Yet I am writing you a new command; its truth is seen in him and you, because the darkness is passing and the true light is already shining. (1 John 2:8)

3. Jesus Christ alone is the key of David, the key that "opens, [what] no one can shut, and what he shuts no one can open." What is the key of David? There is an event in the Old Testament that tells us. King Hezekiah had a faithful servant who was named Eliakim. This servant was the personal secretary to king Hezekiah; he was put in complete charge of the king's affairs. No one could gain entrance into the king's

presence without coming through Eliakim. This servant alone determined who entered the king's court. God spoke to Isaiah the prophet one day and said the following words:

> **I will place on his [Eliakim's] shoulder the key to the house of David; what he opens no one can shut, and what he shuts no one can open. (Isa 22:22)**

The key of David is the symbol of authority. Jesus Christ alone opens and shuts the door into God's court and presence. He alone determines who lives in heaven with God the Father. He alone grants entrance into the presence of God. The door into heaven is opened and closed by Him and Him alone. No other person or being has that authority. Jesus Christ alone holds the key to open and shut the door to life eternal. Therefore, the church that focuses upon Jesus Christ can be assured: it shall live forever. When the time comes, Jesus Christ shall open the door of heaven. The church that takes all its ministries, activities, and meetings and makes Jesus Christ the center of them all—that church shall live forever.

> **And he has given him authority to judge because he is the Son of Man. (John 5:27)**
> **For there is one God and one mediator between God and men, the man Christ Jesus, (1 Tim 2:5)**
> **Therefore he is able to save completely those who come to God through him, because he always lives to intercede for them. (Heb 7:25)**
> **But the ministry Jesus has received is as superior to theirs as the covenant of which he is mediator is superior to the old one, and it is founded on better promises. (Heb 8:6)**
> **For this reason Christ is the mediator of a new covenant, that those who are called may receive the promised eternal inheritance—now that he has died as a ransom to set them free from the sins committed under the first covenant. (Heb 9:15)**
> **For Christ did not enter a man-made sanctuary that was only a copy of the true one; he entered heaven itself, now to appear for us in God's presence. (Heb 9:24)**
> **To Jesus the mediator of a new covenant, and to the sprinkled blood that speaks a better word than the blood of Abel. (Heb 12:24)**
> **My dear children, I write this to you so that you will not sin. But if anybody does sin, we have one who speaks to the Father in our defense—Jesus Christ, the Righteous One. (1 John 2:1)**

**3** (3:8) **Church—Believer:** there is the commendation. This is the picture of what a church should be, the picture of a church that is alive and faithful. The Lord Jesus Christ commends this church for three things.

1. The church used the open door of evangelism and missions to reach people for Christ. The church was strategically located.
   ⇒ It was a border town that touched the borders of three other towns: Lydia, Mysia, and Phrygia. Imagine the evangelistic and mission opportunities by being surrounded with three other towns.
   ⇒ It lay on the imperial road of Rome, one of the major roads that passed from the coast and stretched right on to the east into Asia minor. Just think of the multitudes of people who passed through and visited, stayed and conducted business in the city: the businessmen, sales persons, military people, vacationers, tourists, and visiting relatives.

The point is striking: the city was so strategically located that the whole world could have been penetrated with the gospel by spreading out from the church. And note: Christ commends the church for their evangelistic and missionary work. They were reaching out. And Christ knew of their works. He had set an open door before them and they had stepped in and taken advantage of the opportunity. Because they had faithfully reached out to the lost, Christ says that He is *not going* to let anyone close the door. He is personally going to see that the door to evangelism and missions stays open.

Note one other significant fact: the church had only a little strength. This probably means that they were a small church, small in number and small in resources. This too is striking: imagine being just a small church, yet reaching out to the lost, witnessing and bearing testimony to the salvation and hope of eternal life. Imagine making such an evangelistic and mission thrust that Christ is impressed, impressed so much...

- that He commends the church for it.
- that He guarantees that the open door to evangelism and missions will always remain open. He will not allow anyone to close it.

**Thought 1.** This is the first mission of the church. The church that is alive and faithful is a church that does just what Jesus Christ did: He reached out to the lost.
⇒ This is exactly what He said about His own mission.

> **For the Son of Man came to seek and to save what was lost." (Luke 19:10)**

⇒ This is exactly what He said about the mission of His followers and church.

> **Again Jesus said, "Peace be with you! As the Father has sent me, I am sending you." (John 20:21)**

**Thought 2.** How many of our churches are strategically located? Many. In fact, most are strategically located. Some sit right in the heart of cities where teeming thousands of people live. Others sit on the main roads of cities, and others on the main roads of country and farm areas. Why then are so many of our churches not reaching out in the thrust of evangelism and missions? Why are so few of the lost being won to Christ? The church that is *alive and faithful* is a church that uses the *open door* of evangelism and missions. The believers are a people who witness and do all they can to reach the lost for Christ:

⇒ they go house to house.
⇒ they witness to fellow laborers, neighbors, friends, and family.
⇒ they are always looking for opportunities to witness and share Christ.

Therefore go and make disciples of all nations, baptizing them in the name of the Father and of the Son and of the Holy Spirit, And teaching them to obey everything I have commanded you. And surely I am with you always, to the very end of the age." (Mat 28:19-20)

He said to them, "Go into all the world and preach the good news to all creation. (Mark 16:15)

For the Son of Man came to seek and to save what was lost." (Luke 19:10)

You did not choose me, but I chose you and appointed you to go and bear fruit—fruit that will last. Then the Father will give you whatever you ask in my name. (John 15:16)

Again Jesus said, "Peace be with you! As the Father has sent me, I am sending you." (John 20:21)

But you will receive power when the Holy Spirit comes on you; and you will be my witnesses in Jerusalem, and in all Judea and Samaria, and to the ends of the earth." (Acts 1:8)

For we cannot help speaking about what we have seen and heard." (Acts 4:20)

On arriving there, they gathered the church together and reported all that God had done through them and how he had opened the door of faith to the Gentiles. (Acts 14:27)

Because a great door for effective work has opened to me, and there are many who oppose me. (1 Cor 16:9)

Now when I went to Troas to preach the gospel of Christ and found that the Lord had opened a door for me, (2 Cor 2:12)

And pray for us, too, that God may open a door for our message, so that we may proclaim the mystery of Christ, for which I am in chains. (Col 4:3)

But in your hearts set apart Christ as Lord. Always be prepared to give an answer to everyone who asks you to give the reason for the hope that you have. But do this with gentleness and respect, (1 Pet 3:15)

I know your deeds. See, I have placed before you an open door that no one can shut. I know that you have little strength, yet you have kept my word and have not denied my name. (Rev 3:8)

I will tell of the kindnesses of the LORD, the deeds for which he is to be praised, according to all the LORD has done for us— yes, the many good things he has done for the house of Israel, according to his compassion and many kindnesses. (Isa 63:7)

But if I say, "I will not mention him or speak any more in his name," his word is in my heart like a fire, a fire shut up in my bones. I am weary of holding it in; indeed, I cannot. (Jer 20:9)

Then those who feared the LORD talked with each other, and the LORD listened and heard. A scroll of remembrance was written in his presence concerning those who feared the LORD and honored his name. (Mal 3:16)

2. The church kept Christ's Word; that is, they were faithful to the Word of God. They obeyed the Lord Jesus Christ, kept His commandments. Very practically, this means...

- that they studied the Word of God.
- that they lived the Word of God.
- that they proclaimed the Word of God to believers and unbelievers alike.

I tell you the truth, if anyone keeps my word, he will never see death." (John 8:51)

"If you love me, you will obey what I command. And I will ask the Father, and he will give you another Counselor to be with you forever— (John 14:15-16)

Jesus replied, "If anyone loves me, he will obey my teaching. My Father will love him, and we will come to him and make our home with him. (John 14:23)

If you obey my commands, you will remain in my love, just as I have obeyed my Father's commands and remain in his love. You are my friends if you do what I command. (John 15:10, 14)

Now the Bereans were of more noble character than the Thessalonians, for they received the message with great eagerness and examined the Scriptures every day to see if what Paul said was true. (Acts 17:11)

"Now I commit you to God and to the word of his grace, which can build you up and give you an inheritance among all those who are sanctified. (Acts 20:32)

Do your best to present yourself to God as one approved, a workman who does not need to be ashamed and who correctly handles the word of truth. (2 Tim 2:15)

All Scripture is God-breathed and is useful for teaching, rebuking, correcting and training in righteousness, (2 Tim 3:16)

Like newborn babies, crave pure spiritual milk, so that by it you may grow up in your salvation, Now that you have tasted that the Lord is good. (1 Pet 2:2-3)

We know that we have come to know him if we obey his commands. (1 John 2:3)

3. The church confessed Christ; they did not deny the name of Christ. This means more than just witnessing for Christ. It, of course, does mean witnessing for Christ, but it means much more.

a. First, to confess Christ means that the church confesses Christ in all that it does. It means that Jesus Christ is made the focus and center...

- of all the lives of the believers.
- of all the services, meetings, ministries, programs, and activities of the church.

To confess Christ means that one lives, moves, and has his being in Christ. It means that the church does not focus upon ritual, ceremony, programs, and activities; but the church focuses upon Jesus Christ. Jesus Christ is confessed; He is made the focus, the center, the main purpose and attraction of every program and activity.

b. Second, to confess Christ also means that a person stands fast against opposition and persecution. Some in the world will always persecute true believers. They will...

- ridicule
- mock
- poke fun at
- reject
- ignore
- bypass
- curse

- imprison
- abuse
- backbite
- attack
- kill
- tempt
- take advantage of

The crowds of the world will do all they can to lead the true believer to give in and join them. But the believer is never to cave in; he is not to deny Christ. Note what Christ says: the church or the believer that is alive and faithful does not deny the name of Christ. The faithful church confesses Christ.

**"Whoever acknowledges me before men, I will also acknowledge him before my Father in heaven. But whoever disowns me before men, I will disown him before my Father in heaven. (Mat 10:32-33)**

**"I tell you, whoever acknowledges me before men, the Son of Man will also acknowledge him before the angels of God. (Luke 12:8)**

**That if you confess with your mouth, "Jesus is Lord," and believe in your heart that God raised him from the dead, you will be saved. For it is with your heart that you believe and are justified, and it is with your mouth that you confess and are saved. (Rom 10:9-10)**

**Who is the liar? It is the man who denies that Jesus is the Christ. Such a man is the antichrist—he denies the Father and the Son. No one who denies the Son has the Father; whoever acknowledges the Son has the Father also. (1 John 2:22-23)**

**If anyone acknowledges that Jesus is the Son of God, God lives in him and he in God. (1 John 4:15)**

**Thought 1.** Note how strong a church is that does these three things. The church that is alive and faithful is a church...

- that is evangelistic and mission minded.
- that keeps the Word of Christ.
- that confesses Christ in all that it does, in all of its services, meetings, programs, and activities.

**4** (3:9-10) **Church—Hope:** there is the great hope given to the church that is alive and faithful. Note how descriptive this verse is:

**I will make those who are of the synagogue of Satan, who claim to be Jews though they are not, but are liars—I will make them come and fall down at your feet and acknowledge that I have loved you. (Rev 3:9)**

The synagogue of Satan refers to the Jews who say that they follow the true God, but they do not: they reject Jesus Christ. And Jesus Christ is the Son of God, the very One who came into the world to reveal God. Therefore, to reject Jesus Christ is to reject the revelation of God, to reject God Himself. Remember who a true Jew is in the eyes of God:

⇒ a true Jew is any person who believes in Jesus Christ.

**And he received the sign of circumcision, a seal of the righteousness that he had by faith while he was still uncircumcised. So then, he is the father of all who believe but have not been circumcised, in order that righteousness might be credited to them. (Rom 4:11)**

⇒ a true Jew is not a person who claims outward racial descent. A true Jew is a person who is a Jew inwardly, who believes in the Lord Jesus Christ.

**A man is not a Jew if he is only one outwardly, nor is circumcision merely outward and physical. No, a man is a Jew if he is one inwardly; and circumcision is circumcision of the heart, by the Spirit, not by the written code. Such a man's praise is not from men, but from God. (Rom 2:28-29)**

⇒ a true Jew is a person who walks in the steps of the faith of Abraham, who walks in a faith that is placed in the Lord Jesus Christ.

**And he [Abraham] is also the father of the circumcised who not only are circumcised but who also walk in the footsteps of the faith that our father Abraham had before he was circumcised. (Rom 4:12)**

⇒ a true Jew is not a person of an earthly race, but a true Jew is a person who has the same faith that Abraham had.

**It is not as though God's word had failed. For not all who are descended from Israel are Israel. Nor because they are his descendants are they all Abraham's children. On the contrary, "It is through Isaac that your offspring will be reckoned." In other words, it is not the natural children who are God's children, but it is the children of the promise who are regarded as Abraham's offspring. For this was how the promise was stated: "At the appointed time I will return, and Sarah will have a son." (Rom 9:6-9)**

⇒ the true Israel is the church.

**Peace and mercy to all who follow this rule, even to the Israel of God [the church, believers]. (Gal 6:16)**

The point is striking: to God a Jew is not some earthly race. A Jew is a person who truly believes God, believes all the promises of God including the promise of the Messiah. A true Jew is a person who believes in the Lord Jesus Christ. Remember: God Himself gave birth to the Jewish race. He raised up the Jews to be His followers and witnesses to the human race. Therefore, to God the true Jew is a person from any earthly nation who follows and bears witness to Him.

The point is this: there were Jews in Philadelphia who were persecuting the believers. They were claiming to be Jews, the chosen people, the followers of God, but they were not. They rejected the Son of God, the very One who came to reveal God. Therefore, they were lying. They were an assembly of Satan, not of the only living and true God.

Now, with this as background, note the great hope given to the church that is alive and faithful. The hope is twofold.

1. Believers will be vindicated before all their persecutors. The persecutors of the church will either be saved or judged. Note that the Jews are going to come and fall down at the feet of the church.

   a. Believers will be vindicated because some of their persecutors will be saved (v.9). Note the verse: the Jews are going *to come and worship* with believers. This points toward the salvation of Israel in the end time. Note this closely, for it is the picture painted by Scripture.

   ⇒ In the Old Testament Israel is seen as the true follower of God and the other peoples of the world are seen coming to Israel and worshipping the God of Israel.

> This is what the LORD says: "The products of Egypt and the merchandise of Cush, and those tall Sabeans— they will come over to you and will be yours; they will trudge behind you, coming over to you in chains. They will bow down before you and plead with you, saying, 'Surely God is with you, and there is no other; there is no other god.'" (Isa 45:14)
> Kings will be your foster fathers, and their queens your nursing mothers. They will bow down before you with their faces to the ground; they will lick the dust at your feet. Then you will know that I am the LORD; those who hope in me will not be disappointed." (Isa 49:23)
> The sons of your oppressors will come bowing before you; all who despise you will bow down at your feet and will call you the City of the LORD, Zion of the Holy One of Israel. (Isa 60:14)
> I will show the holiness of my great name, which has been profaned among the nations, the name you have profaned among them. Then the nations will know that I am the LORD, declares the Sovereign LORD, when I show myself holy through you before their eyes. (Ezek 36:23)
> Then the nations will know that I the LORD make Israel holy, when my sanctuary is among them forever."' (Ezek 37:28)

   ⇒ In the New Testament the picture is reversed, and the Jews are seen coming to the church

and worshipping with the church. This means that the Jews worship the Lord Jesus Christ. (See outlines and notes—Ro.9:1-11:36, esp. 11:25-36 for more discussion and for the verses dealing with this subject.)

> As he says in Hosea: "I will call them 'my people' who are not my people; and I will call her 'my loved one' who is not my loved one," And, "It will happen that in the very place where it was said to them, 'You are not my people,' they will be called 'sons of the living God.'" (Rom 9:25-26)

**Thought 1.** The scene will be glorious: Israel (the Jews) worshipping the Messiah, the Lord Jesus Christ, right along with Gentile believers. This is the promise of the Lord to the church of Philadelphia.

Note this: the promise applies to all churches that are alive and faithful. Some of the persecutors will believe and accept the Lord Jesus Christ as their Savior. They will be won to Christ and worship right along with the believers whom they originally persecuted. This is a great promise made to the church that is faithful and alive. The task of the church is to continue to be faithful to Christ, bearing testimony and witness to Him.

> All the ends of the earth will remember and turn to the LORD, and all the families of the nations will bow down before him, For dominion belongs to the LORD and he rules over the nations. (Psa 22:27-28)

   b. Believers shall also be vindicated before all the persecutors who reject Jesus Christ. Scripture clearly states that every knee shall bow before the feet of the Lord and confess Him to be Lord.

> It is written: "'As surely as I live,' says the Lord, 'every knee will bow before me; every tongue will confess to God.'" (Rom 14:11)
> Therefore God exalted him to the highest place and gave him the name that is above every name, That at the name of Jesus every knee should bow, in heaven and on earth and under the earth, And every tongue confess that Jesus Christ is Lord, to the glory of God the Father. (Phil 2:9-11)
> Who will not fear you, O Lord, and bring glory to your name? For you alone are holy. All nations will come and worship before you, for your righteous acts have been revealed." (Rev 15:4)
> "Turn to me and be saved, all you ends of the earth; for I am God, and there is no other. By myself I have sworn, my mouth has uttered in all integrity a word that will not be revoked: Before me every knee will bow; by me every tongue will swear. (Isa 45:22-23)

2. Believers will experience a great deliverance. They will be delivered from the hour of trial that is coming upon the earth. This refers to the great distress or the great tribulation that is coming upon the earth in the end time, a period of trial that will far exceed any trial the world has ever known. Christ Himself said:

> **For then there will be great distress, unequaled from the beginning of the world until now—and never to be equaled again. (Mat 24:21)**

The great tribulation will involve two terrible forces falling upon the earth:

⇒ There will be the persecution by the antichrist.

> **He was given power to make war against the saints and to conquer them. And he was given authority over every tribe, people, language and nation. All inhabitants of the earth will worship the beast—all whose names have not been written in the book of life belonging to the Lamb that was slain from the creation of the world. (Rev 13:7-8)**

⇒ There will be the awful judgment of God against all unbelievers who reject His Son Jesus Christ.

> **Enoch, the seventh from Adam, prophesied about these men: "See, the Lord is coming with thousands upon thousands of his holy ones To judge everyone, and to convict all the ungodly of all the ungodly acts they have done in the ungodly way, and of all the harsh words ungodly sinners have spoken against him." (Jude 1:14-15)**
> **After this I heard what sounded like the roar of a great multitude in heaven shouting: "Hallelujah! Salvation and glory and power belong to our God, For true and just are his judgments. He has condemned the great prostitute who corrupted the earth by her adulteries. He has avenged on her the blood of his servants." And again they shouted: "Hallelujah! The smoke from her goes up for ever and ever." (Rev 19:1-3)**

Note that no believer need ever fear any trial, not even the trial of martyrdom. Jesus Christ says that He will deliver the believer from all trials.

⇒ Even when hated and martyred, the believer will be delivered. Physical death will have no effect upon the believer. The believer will be delivered into the very presence of God quicker than the eye can blink. The believer will never taste the torment of death. Christ was very specific about this:

> **You will be betrayed even by parents, brothers, relatives and friends, and they will put some of you to death. All men will hate you because of me. But not a hair of your head will perish. By standing firm you will gain life. (Luke 21:16-19)**

Note also that God promises to protect those believers who have to go through the tribulation. They will not suffer the judgments that God casts upon the earth. They will be protected somewhat like Israel was during the plagues that fell upon Egypt. The judgments of God will fall only upon the unbelievers. This is clearly stated:

> **They were told not to harm the grass of the earth or any plant or tree, but only those people who did not have the seal of God on their foreheads. (Rev 9:4)**

The point is striking: the hope of the believer is glorious. Jesus Christ will always deliver the believer and the church that is alive and faithful.

> **I have given you authority to trample on snakes and scorpions and to overcome all the power of the enemy; nothing will harm you. (Luke 10:19)**
> **The God of peace will soon crush Satan under your feet. The grace of our Lord Jesus be with you. (Rom 16:20)**
> **No temptation has seized you except what is common to man. And God is faithful; he will not let you be tempted beyond what you can bear. But when you are tempted, he will also provide a way out so that you can stand up under it. (1 Cor 10:13)**
> **That is why I am suffering as I am. Yet I am not ashamed, because I know whom I have believed, and am convinced that he is able to guard what I have entrusted to him for that day. (2 Tim 1:12)**
> **Now there is in store for me the crown of righteousness, which the Lord, the righteous Judge, will award to me on that day— and not only to me, but also to all who have longed for his appearing. (2 Tim 4:8)**
> **Because he himself suffered when he was tempted, he is able to help those who are being tempted. (Heb 2:18)**
> **Who through faith are shielded by God's power until the coming of the salvation that is ready to be revealed in the last time. (1 Pet 1:5)**
> **To him who is able to keep you from falling and to present you before his glorious presence without fault and with great joy— (Jude 1:24)**
> **Since you have kept my command to endure patiently, I will also keep you from the hour of trial that is going to come upon the whole world to test those who live on the earth. (Rev 3:10)**

**5** (3:11) **Hold On—Hold Fast—Jesus Christ, Return:** there is the counsel. Jesus Christ declares time and again that He is returning to earth. Note the word *soon.* Jesus Christ is coming soon. Scripture declares this time and again.

> **Let your gentleness be evident to all. The Lord is near. (Phil 4:5)**
> **For in just a very little while, "He who is coming will come and will not delay. (Heb 10:37)**
> **You too, be patient and stand firm, because the Lord's coming is near. (James 5:8)**
> **I am coming soon. Hold on to what you have, so that no one will take your crown. (Rev 3:11)**
> **"Behold, I am coming soon! Blessed is he who keeps the words of the prophecy in this book." (Rev 22:7)**

The point is this: since Christ is coming and coming soon, the faithful church must do something. It must hold on...

- to its evangelistic and missionary zeal.
- to the Word of Christ.
- to confessing and living for Christ and never rejecting Him.

Note why: because the church and its believers could lose their crown. This is the clear warning of Scripture. Believers must hold on, must hold fast. They can lose their crown if they reject Christ and commit apostasy.

> **But he who stands firm to the end will be saved. (Mat 24:13)**
> **"Therefore keep watch, because you do not know the day or the hour. (Mat 25:13)**
> **It will be good for those servants whose master finds them watching when he comes. I tell you the truth, he will dress himself to serve, will have them recline at the table and will come and wait on them. (Luke 12:37)**
> **Let us not become weary in doing good, for at the proper time we will reap a harvest if we do not give up. (Gal 6:9)**
> **You are all sons of the light and sons of the day. We do not belong to the night or to the darkness. So then, let us not be like others, who are asleep, but let us be alert and self-controlled. (1 Th 5:5-6)**
> **Therefore, prepare your minds for action; be self-controlled; set your hope fully on the grace to be given you when Jesus Christ is revealed. (1 Pet 1:13)**
> **Do not be afraid of what you are about to suffer. I tell you, the devil will put some of you in prison to test you, and you will suffer persecution for ten days. Be faithful, even to the point of death, and I will give you the crown of life. (Rev 2:10)**
> **I am coming soon. Hold on to what you have, so that no one will take your crown. (Rev 3:11)**
> **Then I heard the angel in charge of the waters say: "You are just in these judgments, you who are and who were, the Holy One, because you have so judged; (Rev 16:5)**
> **Nevertheless, the righteous will hold to their ways, and those with clean hands will grow stronger. (Job 17:9)**

**6** (3:12-13) **Overcomers—Promises**: there are the promises to the overcomer. The churches and believers who remain alive and faithful to Christ have five wonderful promises. They will receive five glorious things.

1. They will be made a pillar in the temple of God. This means that they will become a permanent part of God's house, of the eternal worship and service of heaven. And they will be a vital part, a pillar. The pillar is a symbol of...

- strength
- support
- durability
- permanence
- immortality
- a monument

> **Don't you know that you yourselves are God's temple and that God's Spirit lives in you? (1 Cor 3:16)**
> **Do you not know that your body is a temple of the Holy Spirit, who is in you, whom you have received from God? You are not your own; (1 Cor 6:19)**
> **What agreement is there between the temple of God and idols? For we are the temple of the living God. As God has said: "I will live with them and walk among them, and I will be their God, and they will be my people." (2 Cor 6:16)**
> **Built on the foundation of the apostles and prophets, with Christ Jesus himself as the chief cornerstone. In him the whole building is joined together and rises to become a holy temple in the Lord. And in him you too are being built together to become a dwelling in which God lives by his Spirit. (Eph 2:20-22)**
> **You also, like living stones, are being built into a spiritual house to be a holy priesthood, offering spiritual sacrifices acceptable to God through Jesus Christ. (1 Pet 2:5)**

2. They will receive security; they will never again have to go in or out of the city in order to be safe. They will be free from this sinful and corruptible world, free to live in heaven with God the Father and the Lord Jesus Christ. And they shall be perfected forever and ever.

> **That is why I am suffering as I am. Yet I am not ashamed, because I know whom I have believed, and am convinced that he is able to guard what I have entrusted to him for that day. (2 Tim 1:12)**
> **Now there is in store for me the crown of righteousness, which the Lord, the righteous Judge, will award to me on that day— and not only to me, but also to all who have longed for his appearing. (2 Tim 4:8)**
> **Who through faith are shielded by God's power until the coming of the salvation that is ready to be revealed in the last time. (1 Pet 1:5)**
> **Through these he has given us his very great and precious promises, so that through them you may participate in the divine nature and escape the corruption in the world caused by evil desires. (2 Pet 1:4)**
> **And this is what he promised us—even eternal life. (1 John 2:25)**
> **To him who is able to keep you from falling and to present you before his glorious presence without fault and with great joy— To the only God our Savior be glory, majesty, power and authority, through Jesus Christ our Lord, before all ages, now and forevermore! Amen. (Jude 1:24-25)**

3. They will receive God's name. This is a symbol of possession and of belonging. The believer will belong to God in an absolute and perfect sense. Others can lay claim to our lives while upon this earth. They can lay claim upon our time and energy, and some can even enslave us. But not in heaven. The name of God will be written upon us, and we will be marked forever as belonging to God. We will belong to Him totally and absolutely. Neither man nor Satan will ever again be able to touch or mark us.

To them I will give within my temple and its walls a memorial and a name better than sons and daughters; I will give them an everlasting name that will not be cut off. (Isa 56:5)

The nations will see your righteousness, and all kings your glory; you will be called by a new name that the mouth of the LORD will bestow. (Isa 62:2)

You will leave your name to my chosen ones as a curse; the Sovereign LORD will put you to death, but to his servants he will give another name. (Isa 65:15)

And when he found him, he brought him to Antioch. So for a whole year Barnabas and Saul met with the church and taught great numbers of people. The disciples were called Christians first at Antioch. (Acts 11:26)

Him who overcomes I will make a pillar in the temple of my God. Never again will he leave it. I will write on him the name of my God and the name of the city of my God, the new Jerusalem, which is coming down out of heaven from my God; and I will also write on him my new name. (Rev 3:12)

4. They will receive the name of the city of God, the new Jerusalem. They will become the citizens of the new Jerusalem, of the capital of the new heavens and earth.

But the Jerusalem that is above is free, and she is our mother. (Gal 4:26)

But our citizenship is in heaven. And we eagerly await a Savior from there, the Lord Jesus Christ, (Phil 3:20)

But you have come to Mount Zion, to the heavenly Jerusalem, the city of the living God. You have come to thousands upon thousands of angels in joyful assembly, (Heb 12:22)

But the day of the Lord will come like a thief. The heavens will disappear with a roar; the elements will be destroyed by fire, and the earth and everything in it will be laid bare. Since everything will be destroyed in this way, what kind of people ought you to be? You ought to live holy and godly lives As you look forward to the day of God and speed its coming. That day will bring about the destruction of the heavens by fire, and the elements will melt in the heat. But in keeping with his promise we are looking forward to a new heaven and a new earth, the home of righteousness. (2 Pet 3:10-13)

Then I saw a new heaven and a new earth, for the first heaven and the first earth had passed away, and there was no longer any sea. I saw the Holy City, the new Jerusalem, coming down out of heaven from God, prepared as a bride beautifully dressed for her husband. And I heard a loud voice from the throne saying, "Now the dwelling of God is with men, and he will live with them. They will be his people, and God himself will be with them and be their God. He will wipe every tear from their eyes. There will be no more death or mourning or crying or pain, for the old order of things has passed away." He who was seated on the throne said, "I am making everything new!" Then he said, "Write this down, for these words are trustworthy and true." (Rev 21:1-5)

5. They will receive the Lord's new name. What will this new name be? No one knows but God Himself, and He has not yet revealed it.

His eyes are like blazing fire, and on his head are many crowns. He has a name written on him that no one knows but he himself. (Rev 19:12)

This much we know: when Christ comes in all His majesty and glory and conquers all, we shall be marked as His servants and share in His glorious triumph. He will gain the victory for us, the victory over all enemies including the most terrible enemy of all—death and hell.

The God of peace will soon crush Satan under your feet. The grace of our Lord Jesus be with you. (Rom 16:20)

To him who overcomes, I will give the right to sit with me on my throne, just as I overcame and sat down with my Father on his throne. (Rev 3:21)

He will wipe every tear from their eyes. There will be no more death or mourning or crying or pain, for the old order of things has passed away." (Rev 21:4)

| | H. The Message to Laodicea: The Church That Is Affluent, but Lukewarm & Half-Committed, 3:14-22 | pitiful, poor, blind and naked. 18 I counsel you to buy from me gold refined in the fire, so you can become rich; and white clothes to wear, so you can cover your shameful nakedness; and salve to put on your eyes, so you can see. | dition: You are wretched, pitiful, poor, blind, naked |
|---|---|---|---|
| 1 The recipients | 14 "To the angel of the church in Laodicea write: These are the words of the Amen, the faithful and true witness, the ruler of God's creation. | | 5 The counsel |
| a. The messenger of the church | | | a. Buy spiritual gold, clothing, & eye salve |
| b. The Laodicean church*DS1* | | | |
| 2 The speaker—Jesus | | 19 Those whom I love I rebuke and discipline. So be earnest, and repent. | b. Be earnest & repent |
| 3 The complaint: Are neither cold nor hot, but lukewarm | 15 I know your deeds, that you are neither cold nor hot. I wish you were either one or the other! | | c. Hear the Lord...open your heart...fellowship with Him |
| 4 The warning: Will be spit out | 16 So, because you are lukewarm—neither hot nor cold—I am about to spit you out of my mouth. | 20 Here I am! I stand at the door and knock. If anyone hears my voice and opens the door, I will come in and eat with him, and he with me. | |
| a. Because of your false profession: Saying you are rich & in need of nothing | 17 You say, 'I am rich; I have acquired wealth and do not need a thing.' But you do not realize that you are wretched, | 21 To him who overcomes, I will give the right to sit with me on my throne, just as I overcame and sat down with my Father on his throne. | 6 The promise: To the overcomers |
| b. Because of your true con- | | 22 He who has an ear, let him hear what the Spirit says to the churches." | a. Will be enthroned |
| | | | b. Will be enthroned even as Christ is enthroned |

# DIVISION II

## THE MESSAGES OF THE GLORIFIED CHRIST
## TO THE SEVEN CHURCHES, 1:9-3:22

### H. The Message to Laodicea: The Church That Is Affluent, but Lukewarm and Half-Committed, 3:14-22

(3:14-22) **Introduction**: this is the last church addressed by Christ, and it is the worst church. Christ does not commend Laodicea at all. This is the one church about which He has nothing good to say. Imagine a church that may as well not exist—a church that has no good within its body whatsoever—a church that does no good at all. What was it that made the church so bad? So useless and worthless? Lukewarmness, which means that the church was indifferent, complacent, lethargic, self-satisfied, half-hearted, and neutral. The church and its believers were only half-way committed to Christ, only half-hearted in their worship and service for Him. Imagine! To Christ there is *no good whatsoever* in a lukewarm, half-committed believer, and most church members are lukewarm! There are few who are really *hot*, that is, really committed. Hence, this is a critical message that must be heeded by all churches and believers. We must study what Christ says to this church and heed His warning and counsel.

1. The recipients (v.14).
2. The speaker—Jesus (v.14).
3. The complaint: the church is neither cold nor hot, but lukewarm (v.15).
4. The warning: will be spit out (v.16-17).
5. The counsel (v.18-20).
6. The promise: to the overcomers (v.21-22).

**1** (3:14) **Minister—Church**: there are the recipients. Christ sends this message to the minister, for he is the one who is ultimately responsible for the state of the church. Christ expects the minister to be the first to heed the warning against lukewarmness and half-hearted commitment. Then Christ expects the minister to take the message of the Lord to the church and declare His warning to its

believers. The point to see is this: the minister is held accountable by Christ for the indifference and complacency of the believers. He expects the minister to arouse himself and repent, and to arouse the believers and lead them to repentance and whole-hearted commitment.

---

**DEEPER STUDY # 1**

(3:14) **Laodicea**: there is only one historical fact that seems to have a bearing upon this letter. Laodicea was the chief city of Phrygia—an extremely wealthy and prosperous city. It lay astride three of the most important highways of its day. It was a city of enormous wealth. The city had three particular claims to fame. It was...

* a financial and banking center
* a clothing manufacturing center
* the location of a famous medical school renown for the eye salve which it produced.

Perhaps the condition of the church in v.17—"poor, blind, and naked"—has reference to these three industries.
Paul prayed for the Laodicean church (Col.2:1-2) and wrote a letter to them (Col.2:1; 4:12-16). Archippus is said to have been the first Bishop (pastor) of the church (*The Apostolic Constitutions*, 8:46. Information from "The Pulpit Commentary," Vol.22, p.114). This seems to have some significance for what Christ says to the church, for Laodicea is a church that Christ does not commend. He has nothing good to say about the church. In writing Colossians, Paul exhorts Archippus, Laodicea's pastor: "See to it that you complete the work you have received in the Lord" (Col.4:17). The corruption and degeneration could have begun under his ministry.

**2** (3:14) **Jesus Christ**: there is the speaker, the Lord Jesus Christ Himself. Note how Christ describes Himself to the lukewarm and half-committed church and believer.

1. Jesus Christ is the "Amen." This is a title that Christ says belongs to Him. The term *Amen* is used to close prayer or to declare the truthfulness of some statement. It is a term that declares and guarantees the truth. Therefore, Jesus Christ is *the Amen*, the declaration, the guarantee of the truth. What He says is totally true and trustworthy. This means two things to a lukewarm church.

⇒ The lukewarm church can trust the promises of Christ. He will meet the needs of any church that will repent and turn from its lukewarmness and wholly commit its life to Christ.

⇒ The lukewarm church had better heed the warning of Christ. He is *the Amen*; His words of judgment will be carried out. The lukewarm church and believer will face the terrible judgment of Christ, face it just like He has pronounced it in His Word. His Word is true, completely guaranteed. What He has said will be. His pronouncement of judgment will come to pass—unquestionably. The church that ignores or neglects His Word does so at its own peril and loss.

> The Word became flesh and made his dwelling among us. We have seen his glory, the glory of the One and Only, who came from the Father, full of grace and truth. (John 1:14)
>
> Jesus answered, "I am the way and the truth and the life. No one comes to the Father except through me. (John 14:6)
>
> "You are a king, then!" Said Pilate. Jesus answered, "You are right in saying I am a king. In fact, for this reason I was born, and for this I came into the world, to testify to the truth. Everyone on the side of truth listens to me." (John 18:37)

2. Jesus Christ is the "faithful and true witness." Jesus Christ is faithful to God the Father and He bears a true witness to God the Father.

⇒ Jesus Christ is *perfectly honest*. He has not told a single lie or untruth.

⇒ Jesus Christ is also *completely honest*. He holds nothing back about the truth. He does not keep us wondering or questioning in seeking after and in knowing God. He has not kept a single thing from us that God wanted us to know about Himself.

But note: Jesus Christ is the *faithful and true witness*; He is just what the church is not. The church is lukewarm. It only tells part of the truth, only bears part of the witness. It is only half-faithful to Christ and God. What the lukewarm church needs is to get a renewed sight of Christ. They need to refocus their attention upon Jesus Christ: the only way they will ever see God is to hear the witness of Jesus Christ, the witness of Him who is faithful and true. If the church is looking at other witnesses—depending upon the rituals of baptism, church membership, ordinances, services, ceremonies, fellowship, and worship attendance to make them acceptable to God—then the church is missing the faithful and true witness of God. It is missing Christ, and to miss Christ is to doom oneself.

> I tell you the truth, we speak of what we know, and we testify to what we have seen, but still you people do not accept our testimony. (John 3:11)
>
> He testifies to what he has seen and heard, but no one accepts his testimony. (John 3:32)
>
> Jesus answered, "Even if I testify on my own behalf, my testimony is valid, for I know where I came from and where I am going. But you have no idea where I come from or where I am going. (John 8:14)
>
> In the sight of God, who gives life to everything, and of Christ Jesus, who while testifying before Pontius Pilate made the good confession, I charge you (1 Tim 6:13)
>
> And from Jesus Christ, who is the faithful witness, the firstborn from the dead, and the ruler of the kings of the earth. To him who loves us and has freed us from our sins by his blood, (Rev 1:5)

3. Jesus Christ is the "ruler of God's creation." Jesus Christ is the great Creator of the universe, the Maker and Sustainer of the universe and all that is therein. Therefore, He is the source of all—all good things, all real wealth and satisfaction, all purpose, meaning, and significance in life, all love, joy, and peace that a person experiences. Therefore, the church must not depend upon its prosperity: its rituals, ability, energy, wealth, and resources. Its only hope for life is to trust Him who is the beginning of creation, Him who alone can give the church life both abundant and eternal life. Therefore, no matter how prosperous the church, it is not the creator nor the sustainer. Christ alone creates and sustains. The church's wealth and prosperity are meaningless and useless apart from being absolutely centered in Jesus Christ.

> Through him all things were made; without him nothing was made that has been made. (John 1:3)
>
> I tell you the truth, a time is coming and has now come when the dead will hear the voice of the Son of God and those who hear will live. (John 5:25)
>
> The thief comes only to steal and kill and destroy; I have come that they may have life, and have it to the full. (John 10:10)
>
> Yet for us there is but one God, the Father, from whom all things came and for whom we live; and there is but one Lord, Jesus Christ, through whom all things came and through whom we live. (1 Cor 8:6)
>
> For by him all things were created: things in heaven and on earth, visible and invisible, whether thrones or powers or rulers or authorities; all things were created by him and for him. (Col 1:16)
>
> And you have been given fullness in Christ, who is the head over every power and authority. (Col 2:10)
>
> In the past God spoke to our forefathers through the prophets at many times and in various ways, But in these last days he has spoken to us by his Son, whom he appointed heir of all things, and through whom he made the universe. (Heb 1:1-2)

**3** (3:15) **Church—Lukewarm—Complacency—Indifference**: there is the complaint. The complaint is shocking, for it unquestionably describes most church members. What is the complaint? *Lukewarmness*. Note exactly what Christ says: the church and its members were "neither cold nor hot." This means...

- they were only lukewarm, only half-committed, only half-hearted.
- they were complacent, lethargic, self-satisfied.
- they were indifferent and neutral.

As stated, note how this so clearly describes so many church members. This is serious, even critical, for the judgment that Christ pronounces upon the lukewarm church and believer is terrible. This will be seen in the next note. For now, we need to think about how lukewarmness affects the church and its members.

⇒ A lukewarm church is only half-committed to Christ. In addition to stressing Christ, it stresses ritual, ceremony, and programs as a way to become acceptable and to please God.

> Then he said to them all: "If anyone would come after me, he must deny himself and take up his cross daily and follow me. (Luke 9:23)
> Therefore, I urge you, brothers, in view of God's mercy, to offer your bodies as living sacrifices, holy and pleasing to God—this is your spiritual act of worship. Do not conform any longer to the pattern of this world, but be transformed by the renewing of your mind. Then you will be able to test and approve what God's will is—his good, pleasing and perfect will. (Rom 12:1-2)

⇒ A lukewarm church is only half-committed to proclaiming that Jesus Christ is the Son of God.

> Who is the liar? It is the man who denies that Jesus is the Christ. Such a man is the antichrist—he denies the Father and the Son. No one who denies the Son has the Father; [but] whoever acknowledges the Son has the Father also. (1 John 2:22-23)
> Dear friends, do not believe every spirit, but test the spirits to see whether they are from God, because many false prophets have gone out into the world. This is how you can recognize the Spirit of God: Every spirit that acknowledges that Jesus Christ has come in the flesh is from God, But every spirit that does not acknowledge Jesus is not from God. This is the spirit of the antichrist, which you have heard is coming and even now is already in the world. (1 John 4:1-3)

⇒ A lukewarm church is only half-committed to teaching the Word of God.

> All Scripture is God-breathed and is useful for teaching, rebuking, correcting and training in righteousness, (2 Tim 3:16)
> Preach the Word; be prepared in season and out of season; correct, rebuke and encourage—with great patience and careful instruction. For the time will come when men will not put up with sound doctrine. Instead, to suit their own desires, they will gather around them a great number of teachers to say what their itching ears want to hear. They will turn their ears away from the truth and turn aside to myths. (2 Tim 4:2-4)

⇒ A lukewarm church is only half-committed to evangelism and missions.

> Therefore go and make disciples of all nations, baptizing them in the name of the Father and of the Son and of the Holy Spirit, And teaching them to obey everything I have commanded you. And surely I am with you always, to the very end of the age." (Mat 28:19-20)
> He said to them, "Go into all the world and preach the good news to all creation. (Mark 16:15)
> But you will receive power when the Holy Spirit comes on you; and you will be my witnesses in Jerusalem, and in all Judea and Samaria, and to the ends of the earth." (Acts 1:8)

⇒ A lukewarm church is only half-committed to stressing holy and pure living for Christ.

> "Therefore come out from them and be separate, says the Lord. Touch no unclean thing, and I will receive you." "I will be a Father to you, and you will be my sons and daughters, says the Lord Almighty." (2 Cor 6:17-18)
> Make every effort to live in peace with all men and to be holy; without holiness no one will see the Lord. (Heb 12:14)
> For it is written: "Be holy, because I am holy." (1 Pet 1:16)
> Now that you have purified yourselves by obeying the truth so that you have sincere love for your brothers, love one another deeply, from the heart. (1 Pet 1:22)

⇒ A lukewarm church is only half-committed to self-denial and sacrificial living, to stressing that its people must deny themselves and sacrificially die to self. They seldom stress that total sacrifice is demanded, that a person must give all he is and has to reach the lost and meet the desperate needs of the world.

> Jesus answered, "If you want to be perfect, go, sell your possessions and give to the poor, and you will have treasure in heaven. Then come, follow me." (Mat 19:21)
> Peter said to him, "We have left everything to follow you!" (Mark 10:28)
> After this, Jesus went out and saw a tax collector by the name of Levi sitting

at his tax booth. "Follow me," Jesus said to him, And Levi got up, left everything and followed him. (Luke 5:27-28)

Then he said to them all: "If anyone would come after me, he must deny himself and take up his cross daily and follow me. (Luke 9:23)

In the same way, any of you who does not give up everything he has cannot be my disciple. (Luke 14:33)

"I tell you the truth," Jesus said to them, "no one who has left home or wife or brothers or parents or children for the sake of the kingdom of God Will fail to receive many times as much in this age and, in the age to come, eternal life." (Luke 18:29-30)

⇒ A lukewarm church is only half-committed to the church.

Let us not give up meeting together, as some are in the habit of doing, but let us encourage one another—and all the more as you see the Day approaching. (Heb 10:25)

⇒ A lukewarm church is only half-committed to attending and staying awake and learning in the services of the church.

You diligently study the Scriptures because you think that by them you possess eternal life. These are the Scriptures that testify about me, (John 5:39)

Now the Bereans were of more noble character than the Thessalonians, for they received the message with great eagerness and examined the Scriptures every day to see if what Paul said was true. (Acts 17:11)

For everything that was written in the past was written to teach us, so that through endurance and the encouragement of the Scriptures we might have hope. (Rom 15:4)

Until I come, devote yourself to the public reading of Scripture, to preaching and to teaching. (1 Tim 4:13)

Let us not give up meeting together, as some are in the habit of doing, but let us encourage one another—and all the more as you see the Day approaching. (Heb 10:25)

⇒ A lukewarm church is only half-committed to supporting the church.

On the first day of every week, each one of you should set aside a sum of money in keeping with his income, saving it up, so that when I come no collections will have to be made. (1 Cor 16:2)

Each man should give what he has decided in his heart to give, not reluctantly or under compulsion, for God loves a cheerful giver. (2 Cor 9:7)

⇒ A lukewarm church is only half-committed to witnessing.

So do not be ashamed to testify about our Lord, or ashamed of me his prisoner. But join with me in suffering for the gospel, by the power of God, (2 Tim 1:8)

And the things you have heard me say in the presence of many witnesses entrust to reliable men who will also be qualified to teach others. (2 Tim 2:2)

But in your hearts set apart Christ as Lord. Always be prepared to give an answer to everyone who asks you to give the reason for the hope that you have. But do this with gentleness and respect, (1 Pet 3:15)

⇒ A lukewarm church is only half-committed to Bible study and prayer.

Do your best to present yourself to God as one approved, a workman who does not need to be ashamed and who correctly handles the word of truth. (2 Tim 2:15)

Like newborn babies, crave pure spiritual milk, so that by it you may grow up in your salvation, Now that you have tasted that the Lord is good. (1 Pet 2:2-3)

⇒ A lukewarm church is only half-committed to daily devotions.

For everything that was written in the past was written to teach us, so that through endurance and the encouragement of the Scriptures we might have hope. (Rom 15:4)

It is to be with him, and he is to read it all the days of his life so that he may learn to revere the LORD his God and follow carefully all the words of this law and these decrees (Deu 17:19)

The list could go on and on, but the terrible reality of lukewarmness is clearly seen. It is frightening, for lukewarmness is seen in so many churches and members.

Note what Jesus Christ says: it is better for one to be cold than lukewarm. This is utterly shocking: Christ Himself says that it is better for a person to have no commitment whatsoever to Christ than for him to be lukewarm. Why? How could this be? Because a lukewarm person does not know that he needs clothing or heat. A cold person knows he needs clothing and heat. A person must be sensitive to his need before his need can be met.

The Pharisee stood up and prayed about himself: 'God, I thank you that I am not like other men—robbers, evildoers, adulterers—or even like this tax collector. (Luke 18:11)

Jesus said, "If you were blind, you would not be guilty of sin; but now that you claim you can see, your guilt remains. (John 9:41)

Most people who profess Christ attend church only enough to salve their consciences, only enough to make them feel acceptable to God. Most people feel that God would never reject them, not in the final analysis. Most believe that God will eventually accept them into whatever kind of heaven exists in the next world. But Christ completely contradicts this. He says that all these—all the lukewarm and half-committed church members in the world—would be far better off if they made no profession at all. Being self-satisfied, feeling comfortable and respectable in one's religion, is the worst state imaginable for a person. He is the hardest person of all to arouse and set aflame for Christ. Yet, tragically this is the state of so many, the state of half-hearted commitment to Jesus Christ, the state of comfort, complacency, lethargy, indifference, and self-sufficiency.

**4** (3:16-17) **Warning—Judgment**: there is the warning. Jesus Christ warns the lukewarm and half-committed person: "I will spit you out of my mouth." This is graphic language, but it is used for a purpose. The person who claims to be a follower of Jesus Christ is claiming to be a part of His body, claiming to be nourishment for His body, a part of the growth of His body. But when the person is lukewarm, he is none of this. He is like lukewarm food, unappetizing and unwanted. Christ does not want the nourishment that such food provides. It is not fit to help in the nourishment and growth of His body. Therefore, He rejects all who are lukewarm and half-committed. There are two reasons why He rejects them.

1. The lukewarm make a false profession (v.17a). Note the verse: the church felt that it was *rich and prosperous and had need of nothing.* As stated above, the city was extremely wealthy, and practically everyone but the slaves shared in the wealth. We can tell by the very charge of Christ against the church that the believers were financially wealthy. What happened to the church is what so often happens among believers. They equated wealth and prosperity with spirituality. They felt that they had been especially blessed by God because they had been blessed with material possessions and wealth. They became...

- self-sufficient
- independent
- self-centered
- prideful
- conceited
- boastful

They carried their wealth over into their spiritual life; they confused prosperity and material blessings with spirituality and spiritual blessings. They were able to have a full staff of ministers and to have all the ministries. They were able to launch any program, to promote any activity, and to do anything the minister or church felt should be done.

⇒ They focused upon their capability instead of Christ.

⇒ They depended upon their ability instead of Christ.

⇒ They relied upon their resources instead of Christ.

Worship, Bible study, prayer, missions, witnessing, and activities—all were done as a matter of form and as a part of the normal activity of the church. There was no hunger or thirst after God, no sense of a deep-seated need, no desire for God's Word, no burden for the lost, no sense of needing to grow spiritually. Simply speaking, the church was self-sufficient and comfortable. It had the money and the members to operate and work the ministries of the church; and many of the members, being industrious business and management people, had the energy and ability. Therefore, the members operated and carried on the activities of the church, but it was all done in the energy of the flesh and of self. It was not done in the power of God's Spirit.

> **Live in harmony with one another. Do not be proud, but be willing to associate with people of low position. Do not be conceited. (Rom 12:16)**

> **So, if you think you are standing firm, be careful that you don't fall! (1 Cor 10:12)**

> **We do not dare to classify or compare ourselves with some who commend themselves. When they measure themselves by themselves and compare themselves with themselves, they are not wise. (2 Cor 10:12)**

> **If anyone thinks he is something when he is nothing, he deceives himself. (Gal 6:3)**

> **Do not be wise in your own eyes; fear the LORD and shun evil. (Prov 3:7)**

> **Many a man claims to have unfailing love, but a faithful man who can find? (Prov 20:6)**

> **Do you see a man wise in his own eyes? There is more hope for a fool than for him. (Prov 26:12)**

> **Woe to those who are wise in their own eyes and clever in their own sight. (Isa 5:21)**

> **The pride of your heart has deceived you, you who live in the clefts of the rocks and make your home on the heights, you who say to yourself, 'Who can bring me down to the ground?' Though you soar like the eagle and make your nest among the stars, from there I will bring you down," declares the LORD. (Oba 1:3-4)**

2. The lukewarm are rejected because of their true condition: they are wretched, pitiful, poor, blind, and naked. What does this mean? All of these refer to the spiritual life of the church and its believers.

a. The church was spiritually "wretched" (hotalaiporos). The word actually says *the wretched one* in the Greek. The church had its full staff and all the programs—so much so that it felt it needed nothing. But the church was really *the wretched one.* The word means to be afflicted spiritually; to be spiritually contemptible; to be spiritually inferior. In God's eyes they were spiritually lacking, very much so—so much so that they were afflicted, contemptible, and inferior.

> **For all have sinned and fall short of the glory of God, (Rom 3:23)**

> **We know that we are children of God, and that the whole world is under the control of the evil one. (1 John 5:19)**

> **Who can say, "I have kept my heart pure; I am clean and without sin"? (Prov 20:9)**

> **We all, like sheep, have gone astray, each of us has turned to his own way; and the LORD has laid on him the iniquity of us all. (Isa 53:6)**

68

b.  The church was spiritually "pitiful" (eleeinos). The word means pitied, despicable. The believers felt self-sufficient and were carrying on all the works of the church, but they were doing it in their own strength. They were *missing out* on the greatest thing in all the world: the presence of Christ and the power of Christ. They were missing out on experiencing the power of Christ working in their lives and in the church. They were to be pitied. In God's eyes they were despicable, for they were ignoring and neglecting His Son.

> If we claim to have fellowship with him yet walk in the darkness, we lie and do not live by the truth. (1 John 1:6)
> If we claim to be without sin, we deceive ourselves and the truth is not in us. (1 John 1:8)
> If we claim we have not sinned, we make him out to be a liar and his word has no place in our lives. (1 John 1:10)
> All of us have become like one who is unclean, and all our righteous acts are like filthy rags; we all shrivel up like a leaf, and like the wind our sins sweep us away. (Isa 64:6)

c.  The church was spiritually "poor" (ptochos). They felt rich and in need of nothing, but in truth they were as spiritually poor as a church and person can be.

> After he [the prodigal son] had spent everything, there was a severe famine in that whole country, and he began to be in need. (Luke 15:14)
> Remember that at that time you were separate from Christ, excluded from citizenship in Israel and foreigners to the covenants of the promise, without hope and without God in the world. (Eph 2:12)
> And constant friction between men of corrupt mind, who have been robbed of the truth and who think that godliness is a means to financial gain. (1 Tim 6:5)
> You say, 'I am rich; I have acquired wealth and do not need a thing.' But you do not realize that you are wretched, pitiful, poor, blind and naked. (Rev 3:17)
> I thought, "These are only the poor; they are foolish, for they do not know the way of the LORD, the requirements of their God. (Jer 5:4)

d.  The church was spiritually "blind" (tophlos). They could see only what was in the world: money and human ability and effort. They did not look beyond to the spiritual need of the human soul nor to the possibility of spiritual and supernatural power working within the church and the lives of people.

> But if your eyes are bad, your whole body will be full of darkness. If then the light within you is darkness, how great is that darkness! (Mat 6:23)
> The god of this age has blinded the minds of unbelievers, so that they cannot see the light of the gospel of the glory of Christ, who is the image of God. (2 Cor 4:4)
> They are darkened in their understand-

ing and separated from the life of God because of the ignorance that is in them due to the hardening of their hearts. (Eph 4:18)

e.  The church was spiritually "naked" (gumnos). They failed to see their need for the righteousness of Jesus Christ, for the clothing of Christ's righteousness. They believed they could be good enough and do enough good to become acceptable to God on their own. They felt their religious works and gifts to the church would secure God's approval. They did little thinking about their need for the righteousness of Christ and about the death of Jesus Christ for their sins.

> "But when the king came in to see the guests, he noticed a man there who was not wearing wedding clothes. 'Friend,' he asked, 'how did you get in here without wedding clothes?' The man was speechless. "Then the king told the attendants, 'Tie him hand and foot, and throw him outside, into the darkness, where there will be weeping and gnashing of teeth.' (Mat 22:11-13)
> Because when we are clothed, we will not be found naked [without the righteousness of Christ]. (2 Cor 5:3)
> "Behold, I come like a thief! Blessed is he who stays awake and keeps his clothes with him, so that he may not go naked and be shamefully exposed." (Rev 16:15)

**Thought 1.** Note that many lukewarm and half-committed persons never witness for Christ. They say that they do not witness for Christ...

*   because they want to be kind and not offend people.
*   because they are too meek and shy.
*   because there is a place for professing Christ (the church) and a place for the affairs of this world.

But note: a lukewarm commitment to Christ is nauseating to Him. He will reject all of the lukewarm and half-committed.

**5** (3:18-20) **Repentance**: there is the counsel. Christ advises the church to do three things.

1.  Christ counsels them to buy spiritual gold, spiritual clothing, and spiritual eye salve. What do each of these mean? Note what each says.
    a.  The church needed to buy spiritual gold that is purified in the fire. Remember the city of Laodicea was a banking center and a manufacturing center, extremely wealthy. Christ is teaching the church this: their wealth is not true wealth. What they need is spiritual gold, spiritual wealth. Why? So they can be truly *rich*. Gold represents spiritual riches—all the *richness and inheritance* offered by Christ—all the spiritual things that make life rich and overflowing: love, joy, peace, goodness, faith, assurance, confidence, security, hope. It is possessing all the abundance of life. Note that material possessions and wealth cannot give these things. Earthly riches cannot buy love, joy, peace, or happiness. Riches cannot keep a person healthy nor keep him alive nor erase emptiness and loneliness. This

should tell man something, but so many are so blinded by worldly wealth and possessions that they ignore it: man's great need is for spiritual gold. Above all else, we need the riches of the Spirit. Spiritual gold is the only thing that can satisfy our souls. Note where spiritual treasures are found: in Christ. If we are to be spiritually wealthy, we have to come to Christ and secure the wealth He has.

**But store up for yourselves treasures in heaven, where moth and rust do not destroy, and where thieves do not break in and steal. (Mat 6:20)**

**"Make a tree good and its fruit will be good, or make a tree bad and its fruit will be bad, for a tree is recognized by its fruit. (Mat 12:33)**

**Jesus answered, "If you want to be perfect, go, sell your possessions and give to the poor, and you will have treasure in heaven. Then come, follow me." (Mat 19:21)**

**But the fruit of the Spirit is love, joy, peace, patience, kindness, goodness, faithfulness, Gentleness and self-control. Against such things there is no law. (Gal 5:22-23)**

**What is more, I consider everything a loss compared to the surpassing greatness of knowing Christ Jesus my Lord, for whose sake I have lost all things. I consider them rubbish, that I may gain Christ (Phil 3:8)**

**In this way they will lay up treasure for themselves as a firm foundation for the coming age, so that they may take hold of the life that is truly life. (1 Tim 6:19)**

**He regarded disgrace for the sake of Christ as of greater value than the treasures of Egypt, because he was looking ahead to his reward. (Heb 11:26)**

b.  The church needed to buy white clothing. Remember the city was a clothing center, a large textile and manufacturing center. Christ is telling them this: no matter how much clothing they manufacture, they lack the real clothing. What the church needs is spiritual clothing. Why? So the shame of their spiritual nakedness will not be exposed. This refers to the righteousness of Christ, the pure righteousness of Christ that makes a person acceptable to God. A person must be clothed in the righteousness of God; he must put on the righteousness of Christ. God does not accept a person because he...
    *  is religious
    *  has been baptized
    *  belongs to the church
    *  attends worship
    *  does religious works
    *  professes Christ
    *  does good
    *  gives generously

There is only one way that a person can be acceptable to God: by being clothed in the righteousness of Jesus Christ. Christ and Christ alone is sinless. He alone is the Perfect and Ideal Man. He and He alone has made the perfect sacrifice for sins. Therefore, Jesus Christ alone is acceptable to God. If a person is to ever be acceptable to God, he has

to be clothed in the righteousness of Jesus Christ. As the Perfect and Ideal Man, the righteousness of Jesus Christ can stand for and cover all men. Therefore, when a person really believes and trusts in the righteousness of Jesus Christ, God counts that person's belief as righteousness. God counts that person as *being in Christ*, as *being in* the righteousness of Christ.

Note: if a person is not *in Christ*, if he has not been clothed in the righteousness of Christ, then he shall appear naked in the great day of judgment. He shall be ashamed before God and rejected by God.

This is the great counsel, the great advice of the Lord Jesus Christ, His great message to the lukewarm and half-committed church and believers: "Buy of me the white clothing of my righteousness. Putting on my clothing, my righteousness, is the only way you can ever be acceptable to God."

**Therefore, if anyone is in Christ, he is a new creation; the old has gone, the new has come! (2 Cor 5:17)**

**God made him who had no sin to be sin for us, so that in him we might become the righteousness of God. (2 Cor 5:21)**

**And to put on the new self, created to be like God in true righteousness and holiness. (Eph 4:24)**

**For you died, and your life is now hidden with Christ in God. (Col 3:3)**

**And have put on the new self, which is being renewed in knowledge in the image of its Creator. (Col 3:10)**

c.  The church needed to buy eye salve. Remember the city was well known for its medical school that concentrated on treating the eyes with a famous eye salve. Christ is telling them that no matter how much they treat their eyes, they are still blind and in the dark. Why? Because they do not spiritually see the Light of the world, the Lord Jesus Christ Himself. They see only themselves...
    *  their prosperous life and blessings
    *  their good behavior
    *  their good works
    *  their abilities
    *  their wisdom
    *  their religious gifts
    *  their prosperous church

They saw little if any of Christ Himself. They did not see their need for Him, nor did they see what His presence and power could do for them and their church. They were blinded to their own need and to Christ and the great difference He could make in life. The eye salve means the God-given ability to see spiritual truth. They needed to depend upon Christ to give them the ability to see the light of the world.

**In him was life, and that life was the light of men. (John 1:4)**

**When Jesus spoke again to the people, he said, "I am the light of the world. Whoever follows me will never walk in darkness, but will have the light of life." (John 8:12)**

**Then Jesus told them, "You are going to have the light just a little while longer. Walk**

while you have the light, before darkness overtakes you. The man who walks in the dark does not know where he is going. (John 12:35)

The man without the Spirit does not accept the things that come from the Spirit of God, for they are foolishness to him, and he cannot understand them, because they are spiritually discerned. The spiritual man makes judgments about all things, but he himself is not subject to any man's judgment: (1 Cor 2:14-15)

For God, who said, "Let light shine out of darkness," made his light shine in our hearts to give us the light of the knowledge of the glory of God in the face of Christ. (2 Cor 4:6)

For it is light that makes everything visible. This is why it is said: "Wake up, O sleeper, rise from the dead, and Christ will shine on you." (Eph 5:14)

So that you may become blameless and pure, children of God without fault in a crooked and depraved generation, in which you shine like stars in the universe (Phil 2:15)

2. Christ counsels them to be earnest and to repent. Note what Christ says: He loves them. They are lukewarm and indifferent to Him, only half-committed to Him, but He still loves them. The word used for love (philo) means a dear love, a tender, fatherly love. This is the reason He rebukes and chastens the lukewarm and half-committed person. It is not out of anger that Christ tells people they are doing wrong, sinning, coming short, and are doomed. He tells them out of love. They must know they are doing wrong in order to correct their behavior. They must know that judgment lies ahead so that they will do whatever is needed to save themselves. The Lord's rebuke and chastening hand is for one purpose only: Christ loves them and wants them to see their wrong, correct their behavior, and change their lives. He wants people to possess the fullness of life and the hope of eternal life.

Note: the matter is so critical that Christ exhorts them to be *earnest in repenting*. The word earnest means to boil and burn with zeal, sincerity, and earnestness in repenting. It means to burn a path to repent; to get to the matter of repenting immediately. Being lukewarm and half-committed to Christ is so serious a matter that a person must repent immediately. A person cannot afford one minute more before repenting. He is bordering on being *spit out* of the mouth of Christ (v.16).

3. Christ counsels them to *open the door of their heart* and to let Him in. This is one of the most beautiful and meaningful pictures of Christ in all of Scripture. At least five scenes are being pictured.

a. There is the *standing Christ*. He stands at the door. This symbolizes His readiness to enter the life of a person. He is the One who takes the initiative to save man.
   ⇒ He is the One who has walked over and come to man. Man has not come to Him.
   ⇒ He is the One who has approached man. Man has not approached Him.

Jesus Christ stands before the heart of man as the Savior of the world, as loving man so much that He has come into the world to save man. He is the One who has traveled such a great distance from the majesty of heaven down to man's heart.

The LORD is close to the brokenhearted and saves those who are crushed in spirit. (Psa 34:18)

The LORD is near to all who call on him, to all who call on him in truth. (Psa 145:18)

No one has ever gone into heaven except the one who came from heaven—the Son of Man. (John 3:13)

For the bread of God is he who comes down from heaven and gives life to the world." For I have come down from heaven not to do my will but to do the will of him who sent me. (John 6:33, 38)

But here is the bread that comes down from heaven, which a man may eat and not die. I am the living bread that came down from heaven. If anyone eats of this bread, he will live forever. This bread is my flesh, which I will give for the life of the world." (John 6:50-51)

Jesus said to them, "If God were your Father, you would love me, for I came from God and now am here. I have not come on my own; but he sent me. (John 8:42)

b. There is the *knocking Christ*. He stands at the door and knocks. This symbolizes the seeking Christ. Christ has not only come to earth and walked over to man's heart, He knocks upon the heart of man; He actively seeks to enter man's heart. He knocks and knocks at the door of man's heart and He refuses to give up. He keeps on knocking and knocking for man to open up and let Him in. Christ knocks so much that a person has to either open up or deaden his ears to the knock.

"What do you think? If a man owns a hundred sheep, and one of them wanders away, will he not leave the ninety-nine on the hills and go to look for the one that wandered off? (Mat 18:12)

"Suppose one of you has a hundred sheep and loses one of them. Does he not leave the ninety-nine in the open country and go after the lost sheep until he finds it? (Luke 15:4)

"Or suppose a woman has ten silver coins and loses one. Does she not light a lamp, sweep the house and search carefully until she finds it? (Luke 15:8)

For the Son of Man came to seek and to save what was lost." (Luke 19:10)

The next day Jesus decided to leave for Galilee. Finding Philip, he said to him, "Follow me." (John 1:43)

Later Jesus found him at the temple and said to him, "See, you are well again. Stop sinning or something worse may happen to you." (John 5:14)

Jesus heard that they had thrown him out, and when he found him, he said, "Do you believe in the Son of Man?" (John 9:35)

c. There is the *pleading Christ*. He pleads for entrance. This symbolizes the compassion of Christ. He not only knocks, He pleads and begs for man to open His heart. He is merciful and full of compassion. He knows what life should be, for He created life. Therefore, He knows that life must be lived in wholehearted commitment to righteousness or else it is wasted and doomed. He longs for man to have real life, abundant and eternal life. Therefore, He knocks and keeps on knocking at the door of a man's heart, and while He is knocking, He pleads and begs for the man to hear Him.

**Thought 1.** How often people hear the voice of Christ yet they refuse to let Him in! They hear His voice when they hear the Word of God preached and taught or witnessed to by a dynamic minister or some believer or from some tract or Bible literature. But they hardened their ears and pay no attention to the pleading of the Lord's voice.

> **"Come to me, all you who are weary and burdened, and I will give you rest. (Mat 11:28)**
> **He sent his servants to those who had been invited to the banquet to tell them to come, but they refused to come. "Then he sent some more servants and said, 'Tell those who have been invited that I have prepared my dinner: My oxen and fattened cattle have been butchered, and everything is ready. Come to the wedding banquet.' (Mat 22:3-4)**
> **"O Jerusalem, Jerusalem, you who kill the prophets and stone those sent to you, how often I have longed to gather your children together, as a hen gathers her chicks under her wings, but you were not willing. (Mat 23:37)**
> **At the time of the banquet he sent his servant to tell those who had been invited, 'Come, for everything is now ready.' (Luke 14:17)**
> **"I tell you the truth, whoever hears my word and believes him who sent me has eternal life and will not be condemned; he has crossed over from death to life. (John 5:24)**
> **But concerning Israel he says, "All day long I have held out my hands to a disobedient and obstinate people." (Rom 10:21)**
> **No, but the sacrifices of pagans are offered to demons, not to God, and I do not want you to be participants with demons. (1 Cor 10:20)**
> **The Spirit and the bride say, "Come!" And let him who hears say, "Come!" Whoever is thirsty, let him come; and whoever wishes, let him take the free gift of the water of life. (Rev 22:17)**
> **"Come now, let us reason together," says the LORD. "Though your sins are like scarlet, they shall be as white as snow; though they are red as crimson, they shall be like wool. (Isa 1:18)**
> **"Come, all you who are thirsty, come to the waters; and you who have no money, come, buy and eat! Come, buy wine and milk without money and without cost. (Isa 55:1)**

d. There is the *penetrating Christ*. This is the most glorious promise imaginable! Imagine the Spirit of Jesus Christ living within the heart and life and body of a person. When a person hears His voice and opens his heart, Christ enters; He *penetrates* the life of the person. This symbolizes the life changing presence and power of the living Christ. When He enters and penetrates a person's life, He causes the most radical changes imaginable.

⇒ He causes the person to be *born again*.

> **In reply Jesus declared, "I tell you the truth, no one can see the kingdom of God unless he is born again." "How can a man be born when he is old?" Nicodemus asked. "Surely he cannot enter a second time into his mother's womb to be born!" Jesus answered, "I tell you the truth, no one can enter the kingdom of God unless he is born of water and the Spirit. (John 3:3-5)**

⇒ He makes a *new creation* out of the person.

> **Therefore, if anyone is in Christ, he is a new creation; the old has gone, the new has come! (2 Cor 5:17)**

⇒ He makes a *new person, a new self* out of the person.

> **And to put on the new self, created to be like God in true righteousness and holiness. (Eph 4:24)**
> **And have put on the new self, which is being renewed in knowledge in the image of its Creator. (Col 3:10)**

⇒ He changes the person's perishable nature into an *imperishable nature*.

> **For you have been born again, not of perishable seed, but of imperishable, through the living and enduring word of God. (1 Pet 1:23)**

⇒ He gives the person a new *divine nature*, the very nature of God Himself.

> **Through these he has given us his very great and precious promises, so that through them you may participate in the divine nature and escape the corruption in the world caused by evil desires. (2 Pet 1:4)**

e. There is the *companion Christ*. This symbolizes fellowship. When Jesus Christ enters and penetrates a person's heart, He lives forever within the life of the person. He is *always present* with the person...

⇒ looking after and caring for him.
⇒ talking and sharing with him.
⇒ leading and guiding him.
⇒ strengthening and empowering him.
⇒ providing for and meeting his needs.
⇒ maneuvering and working all things out for good for him.
⇒ furnishing and filling him with love, joy, and peace.

When Jesus Christ enters a life there is no good thing whatsoever that is kept from the person.

He has the richest fellowship possible, fellowship and communion with the Son of God Himself. And the person has it forever and ever.

They asked each other, "Were not our hearts burning within us while he talked with us on the road and opened the Scriptures to us?" (Luke 24:32)

I in them and you in me. May they be brought to complete unity to let the world know that you sent me and have loved them even as you have loved me. (John 17:23)

God, who has called you into fellowship with his Son Jesus Christ our Lord, is faithful. (1 Cor 1:9)

Don't you know that you yourselves are God's temple and that God's Spirit lives in you? (1 Cor 3:16)

Do you not know that your body is a temple of the Holy Spirit, who is in you, whom you have received from God? You are not your own; You were bought at a price. Therefore honor God with your body. (1 Cor 6:19-20)

I have been crucified with Christ and I no longer live, but Christ lives in me. The life I live in the body, I live by faith in the Son of God, who loved me and gave himself for me. (Gal 2:20)

But the fruit of the Spirit is love, joy, peace, patience, kindness, goodness, faithfulness, Gentleness and self-control. Against such things there is no law. (Gal 5:22-23)

So that Christ may dwell in your hearts through faith. And I pray that you, being rooted and established in love, May have power, together with all the saints, to grasp how wide and long and high and deep is the love of Christ, And to know this love that surpasses knowledge—that you may be filled to the measure of all the fullness of God. (Eph 3:17-19)

To them God has chosen to make known among the Gentiles the glorious riches of this mystery, which is Christ in you, the hope of glory. (Col 1:27)

**6** (3:21-22) **Overcomers—Promise**: there is the promise to the overcomers. The promise is glorious! The overcomer shall sit upon the throne of Christ and of God. The person who overcomes the lukewarmness and half-hearted commitment to Christ, who repents and turns his life over to Christ, shall sit upon the throne of Christ and of God. What does this mean?

- That we shall rule and reign with Christ forever and ever.
- That we shall be assigned certain duties in the new heavens and earth, given the responsibility to oversee and manage the universe for Christ (Mt.25:21, 23; Lk.19:17, 19).
- That we shall rule and oversee the work and duties of angels (1 Cor.6:2-3).

It means that we shall rule as kings with Christ throughout the whole universe and for all of eternity (see note, *Rewards*—Rev.14:13 for a complete list of the rewards of believers. Also see note—Rev.21:24-27.)

**CHAPTER 4**

**VISION TWO, 4:1-16:21**

**III. THE PICTURE OF THINGS HEREAFER, 4:1-5:14**

**A. The Throne of God: The Focal Point of History, 4:1-11**

**1 John is given the vision**
a. Sees an open door in heaven
b. Hears a commanding voice
c. Is called to "Come up here": To see things that must take place
d. Is in the Spirit at once
e. Sees the astounding sight of God sitting upon His throne

**2 The One on the throne**
a. His position: Sitting—as God
b. His description: Indescribable

**3 The twenty-four elders**[DS1]
a. Were seated upon thrones that surrounded God's throne
b. Were clothed in white
c. Wore crowns of gold

**4 The awesomeness of the throne**
a. Lightning, rumblings, and peals of thunder

After this I looked, and there before me was a door standing open in heaven. And the voice I had first heard speaking to me like a trumpet said, "Come up here, and I will show you what must take place after this." 2 At once I was in the Spirit, and there before me was a throne in heaven with someone sitting on it. 3 And the one who sat there had the appearance of jasper and carnelian. A rainbow, resembling an emerald, encircled the throne. 4 Surrounding the throne were twenty-four other thrones, and seated on them were twenty-four elders. They were dressed in white and had crowns of gold on their heads. 5 From the throne came flashes of lightning, rumblings and peals of thunder. Before the throne, seven lamps

were blazing. These are the seven spirits of God. 6 Also before the throne there was what looked like a sea of glass, clear as crystal. In the center, around the throne, were four living creatures, and they were covered with eyes, in front and in back. 7 The first living creature was like a lion, the second was like an ox, the third had a face like a man, the fourth was like a flying eagle. 8 Each of the four living creatures had six wings and was covered with eyes all around, even under his wings. Day and night they never stop saying: "Holy, holy, holy is the Lord God Almighty, who was, and is, and is to come." 9 Whenever the living creatures give glory, honor and thanks to him who sits on the throne and who lives for ever and ever, 10 The twenty-four elders fall down before him who sits on the throne, and worship him who lives for ever and ever. They lay their crowns before the throne and say: 11 "You are worthy, our Lord and God, to receive glory and honor and power, for you created all things, and by your will they were created and have their being."

b. Seven blazing lamps: the seven spirits of God
c. A sea of crystal

**5 The four living creatures who surround the throne of God**
a. Their position: Nearest to God—surrounding His throne
b. Their description

c. Their function: To glorify & honor God

**6 The function of the elders**
a. To show subservience
b. To worship
c. To show the supreme worthiness of the Lord

d. To praise

---

**VISION TWO, 4:1-16:21**

# DIVISION III

## THE PICTURE OF THINGS HEREAFTER, 4:1-5:14

### A. The Throne of God: The Focal Point of History, 4:1-11

(4:1-11) **Introduction—Vision—Revelation, Outlined—End of the World**: this begins a new vision, the second great vision given to John the Apostle. The Lord's personal message to the individual churches is now over. He has told them who He is, pointed out their failures, and warned and counseled them to correct their failures. He has also given them the great promises of heaven if they will only overcome.

Now it is time for the churches to see the future events that are coming upon the earth. It is time for the churches to know that *Jesus Christ is coming back to earth. He is going to end the world and establish the kingdom of God* forever and ever in a new heavens and earth. Remember the brief outline of the Revelation given by John:

> **"Write, therefore, what you have seen, what is now and what will take place later. (Rev 1:19)**

⇒ "What you have seen" (the vision of the glorified Christ).
⇒ "What is now" (the churches upon earth, their state and condition and the Lord's personal message to them).
⇒ "What will take place later" (the future events that are to happen at the end of the world and throughout eternity).

The present passage, this vision of John, begins the future events. "What will take place later" is now revealed. And note how much God reveals to us, nineteen great chapters—an enormous amount of detail about coming events (chapters 4-22).

In this vision two great things are seen: first, the throne of God is seen. Second, God Himself is seen holding a book which contains the destiny of the world in the end times. However the book is sealed, and no one is found worthy to open and reveal the contents of the book. This discourages John, for the possibility of seeing the destiny of the world had excited him. But just as John despairs, One steps forward who is worthy to open the book. That Person is the Lamb of God, the Lamb slain before the foundation of the earth, Jesus Christ Himself.

Now to the present passage: the throne of God. John is transported into heaven and the very first thing that he sees is the throne of God. He sees God Himself seated upon His great throne.

1. John is given the vision (v.1-2).
2. The One on the throne (v.2-3).
3. The twenty-four elders (v.4).
4. The awesomeness of the throne (v.5-6).
5. The four living creatures who surround the throne of God (v.6-9).
6. The function of the elders (v.10-11).

**1** (4:1-2) **Heaven—Door, Spiritual—Vision**: John is given the vision. Five quick things happened to John .

1. He saw a door opened in heaven. What he was about to see was coming from heaven, from God Himself. The future events were not of his own imagination. They were to be of God, of the very Word of God itself.

**Thought 1.** This means we can trust the events written down in Revelation. They will happen as recorded. It is the Word of God.

**Thought 2.** There are three *doors* mentioned in Revelation.
1) There is the *open door* for evangelism and missions, the door which God opens to the churches for bearing witness to the glorious gospel of the Lord Jesus Christ. It is the opportunity that God opens for them to carry the gospel to their neighbors, communities, cities, states, and countries and world—even to the uttermost part of the earth.

I know your deeds. See, I have placed before you an open door that no one can shut. I know that you have little strength, yet you have kept my word and have not denied my name. (Rev 3:8)
But you will receive power when the Holy Spirit comes on you; and you will be my witnesses in Jerusalem, and in all Judea and Samaria, and to the ends of the earth." (Acts 1:8)

2) There is the *door of the human heart*. When believers carry the message of the gospel to their neighbors, it is then up to the individual person to open the door of his heart and receive the gospel. The decision is the neighbor's. Every person has a door that has to be opened before Christ will enter—the door of his heart.

Here I am! I stand at the door and knock. If anyone hears my voice and opens the door, I will come in and eat with him, and he with me. (Rev 3:20)

3) There is the *door of revelation*. Once a person has opened the door of his heart to Christ, Christ reveals the glorious things of Himself, of God, of heaven, and of this world. In addition, Christ

reveals some of the events that are to take place as history unfolds itself—some of the events that surround the return of the Lord Jesus Christ and the end time.

**After this I looked, and there before me was a door standing open in heaven. And the voice I had first heard speaking to me like a trumpet said, "Come up here, and I will show you what must take place after this." (Rev 4:1)**
**We have not received the spirit of the world but the Spirit who is from God, that we may understand what God has freely given us. This is what we speak, not in words taught us by human wisdom but in words taught by the Spirit, expressing spiritual truths in spiritual words. The man without the Spirit does not accept the things that come from the Spirit of God, for they are foolishness to him, and he cannot understand them, because they are spiritually discerned. (1 Cor 2:12-14)**

2. John heard a commanding voice, the very same voice he had heard in the first vision (Rev.1:10).

3. John was called to *come up here* into heaven. Note why! The reason is clearly stated: to see future events, things that *must* take place. The word *must* is a most important word. The events of world history are not by chance. They do not simply happen. They are of God, of His will—things that must happen. God works them out. They are according to His divine will. God is sovereign. He rules over the world. History is in His hands and under His ultimate control.

4. John was immediately *in the Spirit*: he was having a deep, intense spiritual experience with God; he was in an ecstatic state with his mind and spirit taken up and above this earth into heaven.

5. John saw the most astounding sight imaginable: God and the throne of God. John emphatically declares that He saw God sitting on the throne of God.

**Thought 1.** The picture being dramatized is this: the throne in heaven, God's throne, is the throne above all thrones. It is the supreme seat of honor and majesty, of sovereignty and power. God is the supreme Majesty of the universe, the One who controls and holds all the events of history in His hands. He is the *Supreme Authority* over all the world and the coming events of the end time. No person can cause the events to take place but Him. The Lord Jesus Christ is returning to earth and the events of the end time are going to happen. But they are going to happen because of Him and because of Him alone. And note: the throne is "in heaven." That is, the events are set forever. God rules and reigns forever. There will never be an end to His rule. (This is great security to the believer. God has promised to deliver and keep the believer from the hour of trial, the great tribulation [cp. Rev.3:10]).

**2** (4:2-3) **God, Described**: there is the sight of God sitting upon the great throne of God. Note an astounding thing. The appearance of the One on the throne is so glorious and majestic that He is indescribable. No human shape or form can describe Him. God is described in terms of light, the dazzling light of the most precious gems and jewels of that day.

He is seen in all of His brilliance and dazzling splendor (Ps.104:2; 1 Tim.6:16; 1 Jn.1:5; cp. Jn.12:35-36).

The jewels chosen to describe God proclaim a marvelous message to the hearer. They were considered the most brilliant and the most valued, precious, and desired gems on earth. Thus God is seen and described as the most brilliant and valued, precious, and desired Being—a Being of indescribable glory and splendor.

⇒ The countenance of God shone like a jasper stone. The stone referred to was different from the jasper stone of today. The idea is that the stone was some sort of translucent crystal through which light was shining. It was shining so brightly that it was apparently like the concentrated light of a laser. This represents the penetrating perfection and purity of God.

⇒ The carnelian stone was a fiery red stone and it represents the justice of God.

⇒ The rainbow that surrounded the throne looked like emerald green. This represents the mercy of God and the new covenant of grace given to man by God. (Cp. the promise of mercy made to Noah. Cp. Gen.9:11-17.)

**Thought 1.** Note this: the throne of God covers the whole scope of salvation.

⇒ There is God in all of His perfection and purity. And there is man who comes short of God's perfection and purity, short of God's glory.

> **For all have sinned and fall short of the glory of God, (Rom 3:23)**

⇒ There is God's justice and judgment. Man, being short of God's perfection and purity, cannot live with God. God can allow only perfection into His presence. If He allowed sin and unrighteousness to live in His presence, they would contaminate heaven; heaven would no longer be heaven. Therefore, God must execute judgment upon sin and unrighteousness.

⇒ There is God's mercy and grace. God loves man; therefore, He sent His Son to bear the sins of man. His Son actually took the sins of man upon Himself and bore the guilt of judgment against them. Therefore, man can now be free of sin. He can become acceptable to God if he will accept the sacrifice of Christ for his sins. God has had mercy upon man.

All of this is seen in the throne of God, the whole scope of human history, of the glorious salvation God has planned for man. The throne of God and God Himself declares that He is perfect and pure and just and yet full of mercy and grace. Note how all this is exactly what man needs: he needs perfection, and he needs justice to be executed upon the evil and unrighteousness of this earth. He needs to receive mercy and grace so that he can live forever in perfection.

This is the light of God, the very light that man needs. It is the penetrating light that is gloriously reflected from the throne and presence of God. God is light and in Him is no darkness at all.

> **He wraps himself in light as with a garment; he stretches out the heavens like a tent (Psa 104:2)**

> Who alone is immortal and who lives in unapproachable light, whom no one has seen or can see. To him be honor and might forever. Amen. (1 Tim 6:16)

> This is the message we have heard from him and declare to you: God is light; in him there is no darkness at all. (1 John 1:5)

> Then Jesus told them, "You are going to have the light just a little while longer. Walk while you have the light, before darkness overtakes you. The man who walks in the dark does not know where he is going. Put your trust in the light while you have it, so that you may become sons of light." When he had finished speaking, Jesus left and hid himself from them. (John 12:35-36)

**3** (4:4) **Elders of Revelation**: there is the sight of twenty-four elders sitting around the throne of God. Note what is said about the elders.

1. They are seated upon thrones that surround God's throne. This shows that they...

- are near God, being honored with His presence.
- are resting in God, being fulfilled, complete, and satisfied.
- are enthroned with God, that is, they are given a permanent place in His presence forever and ever.

2. They are clothed in white. This means that they are dressed in the purity and holiness of God and of Christ. There is no imperfection in them at all (see note, pt.1b—Rev.3:18-20 for more discussion).

3. They have crowns of gold on their heads. This means that they hold positions of authority; that they are given some duty and responsibility to oversee for God; that they serve God by overseeing some rule and domain; and that others serve under them. Simply stated, they rule and reign for God, serving Him by managing some vast rule and domain of the universe.

---

**DEEPER STUDY # 1**

(4:4) **Elders of Revelation**: Who are the elders of revelation? Note three points.

1. Opinions vary and they differ drastically. When all the views are considered, the strongest arguments boil down to three major thoughts.

a. They are thought to be the twelve patriarchs and the twelve apostles combined—the heads of the believers, of the church of both the Old and New Testament. That is, they are thought to be the heads and representatives of all the believers of both the Old and New Testament. The reasons for holding this position are as follows:

⇒ The patriarchs' names are on the twelve gates of the New Jerusalem and the apostles' names are on the foundations (Rev.21:12, 14).

⇒ A strong argument for this position is their song which proclaims that the Lamb "has purchased men for God." They call themselves purchased ones (Rev.5:9, Textus, Receptus, the Greek text used for the KJV. However, this is disputed. See note—Rev.5:9.)

⇒ They are numbered and crowned, whereas spirits and angels are never specifically numbered or crowned in Scripture.

⇒ Everything about the elders is said to be a promise to believers: the thrones, the white clothing, and the crowns.

b. They are thought to be angelic beings, a council of angelic beings surrounding God (1 Ki.22:19; Ps.89:7; Is.24:23). The reasons for holding this position are as follows:

⇒ The angels are said to be organized in special ranks or orders. The various ranks are bound to have leaders or elders responsible for overseeing each of the ranks (Ro.8:38; Eph.3:10; Col.1:16). Angels are clothed in white (Mt.28:3; Mk.16:5; Jn.20:12; Acts 1:10).

⇒ Thrones are ascribed to angelic beings, and it is assumed that if thrones are, then angels must be wearing crowns, at least some higher ranking angels must be. However, crowns are never said to be worn by angels (Ro.8:38; Eph.3:10; Col.1:16). The angels are related more to the four living creatures and their function—the function of surrounding the throne of God and of worshipping and serving Him—than are the redeemed saints. The picture of the elders is always associated with the four living creatures (Rev.5:8; 8:3; 7:9-11, 13-14; 11:16-18; 14:1-3; 19:1-4).

⇒ A council of angelic beings are said to surround the throne of God in the Old Testament (Ps.89:7; Is.24:23; 1 Ki.22:19).

⇒ Angels are more likely to offer up the prayers of believers to God than some elder believers from among the saints of God (Rev.5:8).

⇒ An angel is more likely to reveal future events to John during his vision than is an elder believer. This happens later on in the vision of John (Rev.7:13-14).

⇒ Twenty-four angels are more likely to serve as the counterpart to the elders of Israel (Ex.24:11).

⇒ Twenty-four angels are more likely to serve as the counterpart of twenty-four orders of priests than are believers. The earthly pattern of heavenly things is more likely to be a pattern of angels than of believers (1 Chron.24).

⇒ The visions of the beings surrounding the throne of God is this: there is the great innumerable multitude of believers, then the angels, then the elders, and then the four living creatures. The point is that the elders are listed with angelic beings in contrast to the redeemed (cp. Rev.7:9-11; 19:1-4).

c. In the Old Testament there were thousands of priests. Of course, they all could not come together at the same time to serve in the temple. Thus King David, divided the priests into twenty-four groups, each group to serve two weeks at a time (1 Chron.24). One thing needs to be noted. When the twenty-four priests met in the temple precincts to serve their two week ministry, the whole priestly house was represented. Therefore, the elders in heaven are said to be the symbolic representatives of *all the redeemed of the Lord.*

⇒ The crowns and white robes are promised to the faithful (Rev.2:10; 3:4).

⇒ The thrones of authority and responsibility are promised to the disciples (Mt.19:27-30).

2. All the Scriptures that mention the elders are these.
   a. The elders sit on thrones surrounding the throne of God.

> **Surrounding the throne were twenty-four other thrones, and seated on them were twenty-four elders. They were dressed in white and had crowns of gold on their heads. (Rev 4:4)**
>
> **And they sang a new song before the throne and before the four living creatures and the elders. No one could learn the song except the 144,000 who had been redeemed from the earth. (Rev 14:3)**
>
> **The twenty-four elders and the four living creatures fell down and worshiped God, who was seated on the throne. And they cried: "Amen, Hallelujah!" (Rev 19:4)**

b. The elders cast their crowns before the throne of God.

> **The twenty-four elders fall down before him who sits on the throne, and worship him who lives for ever and ever. They lay their crowns before the throne and say: (Rev 4:10)**

c. The elders worship God.

> **Whenever the living creatures give glory, honor and thanks to him who sits on the throne and who lives for ever and ever, The twenty-four elders fall down before him who sits on the throne, and worship him who lives for ever and ever. They lay their crowns before the throne and say: "You are worthy, our Lord and God, to receive glory and honor and power, for you created all things, and by your will they were created and have their being." (Rev 4:9-11)**
>
> **And when he had taken it, the four living creatures and the twenty-four elders fell down before the Lamb. Each one had a harp and they were holding golden bowls full of incense, which are the prayers of the saints. And they sang a new song: "You are worthy to take the scroll and to open its seals, because you were slain, and with your blood you purchased men for God from every tribe and language and people and nation. You have made them to be a kingdom and priests to serve our God, and they will reign on the earth." Then I looked and heard the voice of many angels, numbering thousands upon thousands, and ten thousand times ten thousand. They encircled the throne and the living creatures and the elders. (Rev 5:8-11)**
>
> **The four living creatures said, "Amen," and the elders fell down and worshiped. (Rev 5:14)**
>
> **All the angels were standing around the throne and around the elders and the four living creatures. They fell down on their faces before the throne and worshiped God, (Rev 7:11)**

**And the twenty-four elders, who were seated on their thrones before God, fell on their faces and worshiped God, (Rev 11:16)**

**And they sang a new song before the throne and before the four living creatures and the elders. No one could learn the song except the 144,000 who had been redeemed from the earth. (Rev 14:3)**

**The twenty-four elders and the four living creatures fell down and worshiped God, who was seated on the throne. And they cried: "Amen, Hallelujah!" (Rev 19:4)**

d. One elder encourages John when he weeps.

**Then one of the elders said to me, "Do not weep! See, the Lion of the tribe of Judah, the Root of David, has triumphed. He is able to open the scroll and its seven seals." (Rev 5:5)**

e. One elder brings the progress of saints to God.

**Then I saw a Lamb, looking as if it had been slain, standing in the center of the throne, encircled by the four living creatures and the elders. He had seven horns and seven eyes, which are the seven spirits of God sent out into all the earth. (Rev 5:6)**

f. One elder explains part of the vision to John.

**Then one of the elders said to me, "Do not weep! See, the Lion of the tribe of Judah, the Root of David, has triumphed. He is able to open the scroll and its seven seals." (Rev 5:5)**
**Then one of the elders asked me, "These in white robes—who are they, and where did they come from?" I answered, "Sir, you know." And he said, "These are they who have come out of the great tribulation; they have washed their robes and made them white in the blood of the Lamb. (Rev 7:13-14)**

3. Note two significant points.
   a. The elders are mentioned right along with God, Christ, the living creatures, angels, and with the redeemed believers who are already in heaven. They are set apart or distinct and different from each of these. Therefore, if the elders are angels as some believe, they are the leaders or elders of the angels. If they are believers, then they must be leaders or elders from among believers.
   b. John nowhere says who the elders are. He only speaks of them as part of the vast array of heavenly beings who worship and serve our God and His Son, the Lord Jesus Christ.

(Remember: the purpose of *The Preacher's Outline and Sermon Bible* is to present only what the Scripture says, not to give personal opinions. The beat of our heart is to be true to the Word of God and to let the Word speak for itself. This we do to the best of our ability. We leave the declarations of denominational and theological positions up to the individual minister of God and to those who feel called to make such declarations. Our call with *The Preacher's Outline and Sermon Bible* is *only* to outline the Scripture and to develop the points of the outline to the best of our ability. Our prayer is that this approach will help you to get into the Word of God more and more and help you to expound the Word more and more to God's dear people.)

**4** (4:5-6) **God, Throne of—Throne**: there is the awesomeness of the throne. Three things are now added to the throne of God to show how awesome the presence of God is.

1. There is God's voice which is so commanding that it sounds like a combination of lightning, rumblings and peals of thunder (v.5). This shows us just how majestic and awesome the voice of God is. His voice flashes and thunders the great pronouncements of God. The very will of God is sounded forth from the throne of God with the *speed of lightning* and with the *awesomeness of thunder*. And His will is done. The events of history take place as He has ordered. This particular sight of God's majestic pronouncements is a scene of the coming judgment. The dreadful storm is about to break loose on the earth be-neath.

2. The seven torches of burning, blazing fire are a symbol of the Holy Spirit in all of His fullness and completeness (v.5. See notes—Rev.1:4; 3:1 for more discussion.)

3. There is a sea of glass stretching out before the throne (v.6a). The sea "looks like a transparent glassy sea, as if of crystal" (The Amplified New Testament).

⇒ The elders of Israel saw a similar sight.

**And saw the God of Israel. Under his feet was something like a pavement made of sapphire, clear as the sky itself. (Exo 24:10)**

⇒ Ezekiel himself saw a similar sight.

**Spread out above the heads of the living creatures was what looked like an expanse, sparkling like ice, and awesome. Above the expanse over their heads was what looked like a throne of sapphire, and high above on the throne was a figure like that of a man. (Ezek 1:22, 26)**

⇒ God had instructed the temple to have a brazen sea stretched out before it, and remember: the tabernacle and temple were shadows of real things in heaven.

**He made the Sea of cast metal, circular in shape, measuring ten cubits from rim to rim and five cubits high. It took a line of thirty cubits to measure around it. (1 Ki 7:23)**

The sea of glass symbolizes at least three things.
   a. The glassy sea shows us the value and preciousness of God's presence. In the old days it was almost impossible to make pure glass. Pure glass that was as clear as crystal was considered to be as valuable and precious as gold.

**Neither gold nor crystal can compare with it, nor can it be had for jewels of gold. (Job 28:17)**

b. The glassy sea shows us how clearly God is able to see everything that is out before His throne. It stands for His omniscience and penetrating vision into all things. Nothing is hid from Him who is upon the throne of heaven.

c. The glassy sea shows us the spectacular purity of God, as clear and pure as perfect glass and crystal. The glassy sea shows us how far away God is from the impurities of a contaminated world. He is as far away as a sea made of pure glass and pure crystal.

**5** (4:6-9) **Creature of Revelation, The Four**: there are the four living creatures who surround the throne of God. Note three things about them.

1. First is their position. They are the closest beings to God. They are the angelic beings who are posted in the middle of each side of the throne. They are the guardians of God's throne and of His holy presence (cp. Rev.4:6; 5:6; 14:3).

2. Note their description.
⇒ They are always found near the throne of God (Rev.4:6; 5:6; 14:3).
⇒ They have six wings and are full of eyes (Rev.4:6, 8).
⇒ Their function has to do with the holiness and wrath of God (Rev.6:1, 7; 15:7).
⇒ They declare the holiness of God day and night and never cease to declare His holiness (Rev.4:8).

Who are these living beings who are privileged to be in God's presence day and night, and to declare His majestic holiness? These beings who never have to leave God's presence, not even for a moment? Who would be so honored as to have this glorious privilege?

Undoubtedly, they are beings who were created for this very purpose. They seem to be the same beings as the cherubim seen in Ezekiel's vision (Ezk.10:4) and the seraphim seen in Isaiah's vision (Is.6:1-3). Note that John chooses certain animals on earth to describe certain characteristics that he notices.
⇒ One being was like a lion: this symbolizes supremacy
⇒ One being was like an ox (calf): this symbolizes strength.
⇒ One being was like a man: this symbolizes intelligence.
⇒ One being was like an eagle: this symbolizes swiftness.

3. Note their function: to glorify and honor God day and night. The living creatures show us two things about God.

First, they show us the supremacy, strength, intelligence, and swiftness of God. They stand for all that God is.

Second, they show us that all of nature owes its worship to God, both animals and man. They picture all the beings of nature standing before God and praising Him. All the world, both animal and man, are represented in the four living beings as they worship God day and night, crying out to Him, "Holy, holy, holy is the Lord God Almighty, who was, and is, and is to come" (v.8).
⇒ All the world is to praise God for His holiness.

> For it is written: "Be holy, because I am holy." (1 Pet 1:16)
> Exalt the LORD our God and worship at his holy mountain, for the LORD our God is holy. (Psa 99:9)

> And they were calling to one another: "Holy, holy, holy is the LORD Almighty; the whole earth is full of his glory." (Isa 6:3)
> Who will not fear you, O Lord, and bring glory to your name? For you alone are holy. All nations will come and worship before you, for your righteous acts have been revealed." (Rev 15:4)
> I am the LORD who brought you up out of Egypt to be your God; therefore be holy, because I am holy. (Lev 11:45)

⇒ All the world is to praise God for His sovereignty and omnipotence.

> "I know that you can do all things; no plan of yours can be thwarted. (Job 42:2)
> Our God is in heaven; he does whatever pleases him. (Psa 115:3)
> Yes, and from ancient days I am he. No one can deliver out of my hand. When I act, who can reverse [hinder] it?" (Isa 43:13)
> Jesus looked at them and said, "With man this is impossible, but with God all things are possible." (Mat 19:26)
> Now to him who is able to establish you by my gospel and the proclamation of Jesus Christ, according to the revelation of the mystery hidden for long ages past, (Rom 16:25)

⇒ All the world is to praise God for His eternal existence.

> I lift my hand to heaven and declare: As surely as I live forever, (Deu 32:40)
> The eternal God is your refuge, and underneath are the everlasting arms. He will drive out your enemy before you, saying, 'Destroy him!' (Deu 33:27)
> Your name, O LORD, endures forever, your renown, O LORD, through all generations. (Psa 135:13)
> But do not forget this one thing, dear friends: With the Lord a day is like a thousand years, and a thousand years are like a day. (2 Pet 3:8)
> "I am the Alpha and the Omega," says the Lord God, "who is, and who was, and who is to come, the Almighty." (Rev 1:8)

**Thought 1.** What an indictment against man! How little we praise and worship God—truly praise and worship Him. Imagine! There are four beings who have been created to worship God day and night, never to cease from worshipping Him. Four beings who cry out day and night the glorious praise: "Holy, holy, holy is the Lord God Almighty, who was, and is, and is to come" (v.8).

**6** (4:10-11) **Elders of Revelation, Twenty-Four**: there is the function of the twenty-four elders. Their function is fourfold.

1. They show subjection and subservience. They fall down before the throne of God. They yield all they are and have to Him.

> **Thought 1.** What a lesson for us! How we must learn how great God is—that He dwells in such glory and majesty, dominion, and power that we owe Him our lives and our all.

> > Therefore, I urge you, brothers, in view of God's mercy, to offer your bodies as living sacrifices, holy and pleasing to God—this is your spiritual act of worship. Do not conform any longer to the pattern of this world, but be transformed by the renewing of your mind. Then you will be able to test and approve what God's will is—his good, pleasing and perfect will. (Rom 12:1-2)
> > Do you not know that your body is a temple of the Holy Spirit, who is in you, whom you have received from God? You are not your own; You were bought at a price. Therefore honor God with your body. (1 Cor 6:19-20)
> > And God is able to make all grace abound to you, so that in all things at all times, having all that you need, you will abound in every good work. (2 Cor 9:8)
> > How can I repay the LORD for all his goodness to me? (Psa 116:12)

2. They worship God as the eternal God.

> **Thought 1.** He alone is our hope for living forever. If we fail to worship Him and to worship Him in truth, then we shall miss eternal life.

> > Come, let us bow down in worship, let us kneel before the LORD our Maker; (Psa 95:6)
> > Worship the LORD in the splendor of his holiness; tremble before him, all the earth. (Psa 96:9)
> > Jesus said to him, "Away from me, Satan! For it is written: 'Worship the Lord your God, and serve him only.'" (Mat 4:10)
> > God is spirit, and his worshipers must worship in spirit and in truth." (John 4:24)
> > He said in a loud voice, "Fear God and give him glory, because the hour of his judgment has come. Worship him who made the heavens, the earth, the sea and the springs of water." (Rev 14:7)

> > But he said to me, "Do not do it! I am a fellow servant with you and with your brothers the prophets and of all who keep the words of this book. Worship God!" (Rev 22:9)

3. They show the supreme worthiness of the Lord. They lay their crowns before the Lord. The Lord has given the right to rule with him by overseeing certain domains throughout the universe. But in true humility and thankfulness, the elders cast their crowns down before Him. Why? To show that He alone is worthy and they are acknowledging the truth forever and ever.

> > I call to the LORD, who is worthy of praise, and I am saved from my enemies. (2 Sam 22:4)
> > "You are worthy, our Lord and God, to receive glory and honor and power, for you created all things, and by your will they were created and have their being." (Rev 4:11)
> > In a loud voice they sang: "Worthy is the Lamb, who was slain, to receive power and wealth and wisdom and strength and honor and glory and praise!" (Rev 5:12)

4. They vocally declare His worthiness, and they praise Him as the Lord God of the universe and of creation. The Greek actually reads "You are worthy, our Lord and our God" (ho kurios kai ho Theos hemon). This means that God is supreme; He is the first Being of the universe. He is the glorious Creator of all things. He is the One who created all things by His will.

> > In the beginning God created the heavens and the earth. (Gen 1:1)
> > You alone are the LORD. You made the heavens, even the highest heavens, and all their starry host, the earth and all that is on it, the seas and all that is in them. You give life to everything, and the multitudes of heaven worship you. (Neh 9:6)
> > He spreads out the northern skies over empty space; he suspends the earth over nothing. (Job 26:7)
> > In the beginning you laid the foundations of the earth, and the heavens are the work of your hands. (Psa 102:25)
> > "Men, why are you doing this? We too are only men, human like you. We are bringing you good news, telling you to turn from these worthless things to the living God, who made heaven and earth and sea and everything in them. (Acts 14:15)
> > By faith we understand that the universe was formed at God's command, so that what is seen was not made out of what was visible. (Heb 11:3)

| | CHAPTER 5 | 2 And I saw a mighty angel proclaiming in a loud voice, "Who is worthy to break the seals and open the scroll?" | 2 **The search for one worthy to open the Book of Destiny** |
|---|---|---|---|
| | **B. The Book of Destiny Is Sealed: The Future of the World, 5:1-4** | | a. The search proclaimed by an angel |
| | | 3 But no one in heaven or on earth or under the earth could open the scroll or even look inside it. | b. The search fails |
| **1 The book or scroll itself** | Then I saw in the right hand of him who sat on the throne a scroll with writing on both sides and sealed with seven seals. | | |
| a. Is in God's right hand | | | |
| b. Is written on the front & back | | 4 I wept and wept because no one was found who was worthy to open the scroll or look inside. | c. The prophet weeps |
| c. Is sealed with seven seals | | | d. The contents of the book are sealed |

# DIVISION III

## THE PICTURE OF THINGS HEREAFTER, 4:1-5:14

## B. The Book of Destiny Is Sealed: The Future of the World, 5:1-4

(5:1-4) **Introduction**: there should be no break between chapters four and five. The same scene of God's throne is being covered. God is seen sitting upon His throne and holding a sealed book in His right hand. Note again, the book is sealed. It has never been opened. The importance of the sealed book cannot be over-emphasized. The book is the key to understanding the rest of Revelation. The book or scroll is the official document of the last days of human history, the climactic events of the universe. The world's future is about to be unfolded before one's very eyes (cp. Rev.1:1) (Note: a person might want to combine this outline and the next if he has time in his teaching session.)

1. The book itself (v.1).
2. The search for one worthy to open the Book of Destiny (v.2-4).

**1** (5:1) **Destiny, Book of**: there is the book itself.

1. John sees God holding the book in the palm of His right hand. The picture is this: God is extending the book outward, poised to hand it to someone if a person can be found worthy enough to open it. The fact that God Himself is holding the book in His right hand shows us several things:

⇒ God is the supreme Authority over the end of the world. He governs all the events of history both upon the earth and throughout the universe. God holds the future in His hands, the destiny of the world.

> **Now to the King eternal, immortal, invisible, the only God, be honor and glory for ever and ever. Amen. (1 Tim 1:17)**
> **Then I heard what sounded like a great multitude, like the roar of rushing waters and like loud peals of thunder, shouting: "Hallelujah! For our Lord God Almighty reigns. (Rev 19:6)**
> **The LORD will reign for ever and ever." (Exo 15:18)**

⇒ God is ready to carry out and execute the events. He is ready for the end time to begin, ready for the end of the world to be launched. It is simply a matter of finding someone worthy to carry out and oversee the events for God.

2. The book is written on both the front and back of the pages. The book was actually a roll or a scroll. Remember:

back then, there were no printing presses or books as we know them. They wrote on small sheets of paper (papyrus) about ten inches by eight inches, close to the size of our eleven by eight and one half inch sheets. If a large amount of writing was to be done, they joined sheets together. When the writing was completed, they rolled the sheets up and tied some thread or ribbon around the roll. This is what is meant by the book being sealed. They seldom wrote on the back side, for whatever was written on the back side would be exposed when the last sheet was rolled up and tied.

Again, note that the book or scroll held by God *was written* on both the front and back. This shows us...

• that the events of the end time are many and that it will take some time, a great deal of time, for all of them to take place.

• that God is going to reveal a great deal about the end time to man. When? As soon as He can find someone worthy enough to open the book.

3. The book is sealed with seven seals. This shows us three things.

a. The seven seals show us that the book is the last will and testament of God. In the Roman world a man's will had to be witnessed by seven persons, and each attached his own personal seal to one of the threads of the document. The will could be opened only when the recipient came to claim the will. This book in God's right hand may mean that it is His last will for the earth; the book contains what He wills for those who have rejected and cursed Him and what He wills for those who have accepted and worshipped Him. The book is His last will and testament for the consummation of the world.

b. The seven seals show us that the book is large; it has a great deal of material in it. It has so much that seven seals are required to bind and hold it together. Again, this means...

• that there are a lot of events that are included in the end time; that many events are to take place.

• that God is going to reveal much to man as soon as someone is found worthy enough to open this book.

c. The seven seals also show us the secrecy of the book. God has sealed the book with seven seals in order to keep the events of the end time from being known. They are not to be known by man until God

Himself is ready to reveal them. Man can never figure out the events, not by his own intellect.

**Oh, the depth of the riches of the wisdom and knowledge of God! How unsearchable his judgments, and his paths beyond tracing out! (Rom 11:33)**

**2** (5:2-4) **Destiny, Book of**: there is the search for one worthy to open the book. Note four significant facts.

1. John saw a strong angel—an angel so strong that he could shout throughout the universe and be heard by all in both heaven and earth. He shouted out the most penetrating question of human history: "Who is worthy to break the seals and open the scroll?" This shows us how supreme and majestic God really is. He is so far above all creatures—even the creatures in heaven as well as those on earth—that a search has to be conducted to find someone who is worthy to approach Him and carry out His will.

2. The search fails. There just is no being any place that is worthy to approach God and to execute His will throughout the universe.

   a. No person in heaven was found worthy to open the book. Imagine! The glorious angels, the seraphim and cherubim, the four living creatures privileged to surround the throne of God, the twenty four elders, all the redeemed—no being in heaven was worthy enough to approach God and open the book.

   b. No person on earth was found worthy to open the book: no statesman, no educator, no scientist, no minister, no prophet, no astrologer, no magician.

   c. No person under the earth: no person from among the dead—as great as some have been in past history—no person from the past was found worthy to open the book.

**No, we speak of God's secret wisdom, a wisdom that has been hidden and that God destined for our glory before time began. None of the rulers of this age understood it, for if they had, they would not have crucified the Lord of glory. (1 Cor 2:7-8)**

**The man without the Spirit does not accept the things that come from the Spirit of God, for they are foolishness to him, and he cannot understand them, because they are spiritually discerned. (1 Cor 2:14)**

**The god of this age has blinded the minds of unbelievers, so that they cannot see the light of the gospel of the glory of Christ, who is the image of God. (2 Cor 4:4)**

**They are darkened in their understanding and separated from the life of God because of the ignorance that is in them due to the hardening of their hearts. (Eph 4:18)**

3. The search fails, and John breaks down and cries bitterly. Why? There were two reasons. Because John saw something that he had never seen before:

   ⇒ John saw the greatness of God, the supreme majesty and glory of God, how far superior God is to all living creatures.

There was not a single person or being any place that could be found worthy to approach God and open the book and carry out the events of human history. All creatures were too short of God's glory—all creatures, both of heaven and earth were so far short of God's glory and majesty they just could not approach God, not apart from His glorious mercy and grace. As stated, John saw as never before the greatness of God, the glory and majesty, the dominion and power of God, how high and how far superior God is to all creatures. God broke John in humility and with a sense of his own unworthiness. John wept bitterly at his own unworthiness before God who is so high and lifted up.

**"I baptize you with water for repentance. But after me will come one who is more powerful than I, whose sandals I am not fit to carry. He will baptize you with the Holy Spirit and with fire. (Mat 3:11)**

**The centurion replied, "Lord, I do not deserve to have you come under my roof. But just say the word, and my servant will be healed. (Mat 8:8)**

**And anyone who does not take his cross and follow me is not worthy of me. (Mat 10:38)**

**Produce fruit in keeping with repentance. And do not begin to say to yourselves, 'We have Abraham as our father.' For I tell you that out of these stones God can raise up children for Abraham. (Luke 3:8)**

**I am no longer worthy to be called your son; make me like one of your hired men.' "The son said to him, 'Father, I have sinned against heaven and against you. I am no longer worthy to be called your son.' (Luke 15:19, 21)**

**"I tell you the truth," he said, "this poor widow has put in more than all the others. (Luke 21:3)**

But John wept for another reason as well: he was not going to be able to see the future of the world, the events of the end time. The promise had been made to him that he would see these things that "will take place later," but now he was not going to see them. And why? Because there was no person worthy to approach God and open the book. He and all the other beings of heaven and earth were too far short of God to understand and execute the will of God for the end time.

**Be always on the watch, and pray that you may be able to escape all that is about to happen, and that you may be able to stand before the Son of Man." (Luke 21:36)**

**Jesus replied, "You do not realize now what I am doing, but later you will understand." (John 13:7)**

**"I have much more to say to you, more than you can now bear. (John 16:12)**

**Now we see but a poor reflection as in a mirror; then we shall see face to face. Now I know in part; then I shall know fully, even as I am fully known. (1 Cor 13:12)**

4. The reason no person is worthy to open this book is because of its contents. The book is the destiny of the world—what is to happen in the end time at the end of the world. Chapters 6-21 show this clearly. It is the book of redemption (cp. Lk.21:28; Ro.8:22-23; Eph.1:13-14). God's people are to be redeemed and the evil and corrupt people are to be overthrown and judged. Human history and all

matter throughout the universe—all that is corrupt, deteriorating, decaying, and dying—is to be overthrown and consumed. And a new earth and a new heaven are to be created. All the redeemed are to inherit and inhabit the new earth and heavens. This is both the fate and the redemption of the world. This is history written before it happens. Therefore, the person who opens this book must be a person who can grasp exactly what the book is saying, and then he must be able to carry out God's will and execute the events. The person must have the very mind and power of God. Who can execute and rule over the events of the end time? There is only one such Person: the Son of God Himself, the Lord Jesus Christ. Christ and Christ alone is worthy to open the book. This is the book of redemption, the book of historical optimism. The same book is referred to in Daniel 12:8-9 and Ezekiel 2:9-10. The message of this book is now prophesied as the seals are broken and the events of the last days are seen. Note the size and thickness of this particular scroll. It takes seven seals to bind it. All that is in the rest of Revelation is contained therein.

Note also, the book is in God's hand. History is in God's hand. He is in charge. He has a plan, a purpose for the universe. Who is worthy to carry out this plan, this purpose? Who can rule and reign over these events? The idea is that Christ and Christ alone is worthy.

**Thought 1.** Note that the same book is referred to by Ezekiel and Daniel.

> **Then I looked, and I saw a hand stretched out to me. In it was a scroll, Which he unrolled before me. On both sides of it were written words of lament and mourning and woe. (Ezek 2:9-10)**
> **I heard, but I did not understand. So I asked, "My lord, what will the outcome of all this be?" He replied, "Go your way, Daniel, because the words are closed up and sealed until the time of the end. (Dan 12:8-9)**

**Thought 2.** Note three significant lessons for us.
1) The book is in God's hand. He is in charge of human history, and He has a definite plan and purpose for the universe. The fear of the *bomb*, an *unstable economy*, the *environment*, the *drugs*, the *criminal society*, and the other *massive problems* of the world seem to have no answer. But God does: He is going to bring history to a climax and establish righteousness throughout all the earth. The believer is to be the most optimistic person on earth.

> **In my Father's house are many rooms; if it were not so, I would have told you. I am going there to prepare a place for you. And if I go and prepare a place for you, I will come back and take you to be with me that you also may be where I am. (John 14:2-3)**
> **It teaches us to say "No" to ungodliness and worldly passions, and to live self-controlled, upright and godly lives in this present age, While we wait for the blessed hope—the glorious appearing of our great God and Savior, Jesus Christ, (Titus 2:12-13)**

> **Dear friends, now we are children of God, and what we will be has not yet been made known. But we know that when he appears, we shall be like him, for we shall see him as he is. (1 John 3:2)**

2) We should all bow in utter humility and dependency upon God, for He is higher above us than even the outer reaches of space. His glory is set above the heavens. We are nothing before Him; consequently, we should live in the reverence and fear and worship of Him, praising Him day and night while we have breath.

> **Come, let us bow down in worship, let us kneel before the LORD our Maker; (Psa 95:6)**
> **Worship the LORD in the splendor of his holiness; tremble before him, all the earth. (Psa 96:9)**
> **Jesus said to him, "Away from me, Satan! For it is written: 'Worship the Lord your God, and serve him only.'" (Mat 4:10)**
> **God is spirit, and his worshipers must worship in spirit and in truth." (John 4:24)**
> **He said in a loud voice, "Fear God and give him glory, because the hour of his judgment has come. Worship him who made the heavens, the earth, the sea and the springs of water." (Rev 14:7)**
> **But he said to me, "Do not do it! I am a fellow servant with you and with your brothers the prophets and of all who keep the words of this book. Worship God!" (Rev 22:9)**

3) We should pay close attention to the book of Revelation, study and live in its message. It is the revelation of God's will for the end time, the events that are yet to take place throughout the universe.

> **[The mystery of God] which was not made known to men in other generations as it has now been revealed by the Spirit to God's holy apostles and prophets. (Eph 3:5)**
> **Do your best to present yourself to God as one approved, a workman who does not need to be ashamed and who correctly handles the word of truth. (2 Tim 2:15)**
> **All Scripture is God-breathed and is useful for teaching, rebuking, correcting and training in righteousness, (2 Tim 3:16)**
> **Like newborn babies, crave pure spiritual milk, so that by it you may grow up in your salvation, Now that you have tasted that the Lord is good. (1 Pet 2:2-3)**
> **Now the Bereans were of more noble character than the Thessalonians, for they received the message with great eagerness and examined the Scriptures every day to see if what Paul said was true. (Acts 17:11)**
> **"Now I commit you to God and to the word of his grace, which can build you up and give you an inheritance among all those who are sanctified. (Acts 20:32)**

| | | | |
|---|---|---|---|
| | **C. The Book of Destiny Is Opened: The Lamb Alone Is Worthy to Open the Book, 5:5-14** | because you were slain, and with your blood you purchased men for God from every tribe and language and people and nation. | 1) Because He was slain for man & has redeemed man |
| **1 The glorious announcement: God has intervened & sent One worthy to open the book** <br> a. The Lion of Judah <br> b. The Root of David <br> c. The one who has prevailed | 5 Then one of the elders said to me, "Do not weep! See, the Lion of the tribe of Judah, the Root of David, has triumphed. He is able to open the scroll and its seven seals." | 10 You have made them to be a kingdom and priests to serve our God, and they will reign on the earth." <br> 11 Then I looked and heard the voice of many angels, | 2) Because of His universal salvation <br> 3) Because of His great gift of royalty <br><br> **4 The majestic worship of Christ by the angels** <br> a. Their outer circle |
| **2 The supreme moment: The first sight of Christ in heaven** <br> a. His position <br> b. His redemption: He is the Lamb of God <br> c. His power: He has seven horns <br> d. His knowledge: He has seven eyes <br> e. His destiny & sovereignty: He took the book | 6 Then I saw a Lamb, looking as if it had been slain, standing in the center of the throne, encircled by the four living creatures and the elders. He had seven horns and seven eyes, which are the seven spirits of God sent out into all the earth. <br> 7 He came and took the scroll from the right hand of him who sat on the throne. | numbering thousands upon thousands, and ten thousand times ten thousand. They encircled the throne and the living creatures and the elders. <br> 12 In a loud voice they sang: "Worthy is the Lamb, who was slain, to receive power and wealth and wisdom and strength and honor and glory and praise!" | b. Their great number <br><br> c. Their song <br> 1) His power <br> 2) His wealth <br> 3) His wisdom <br> 4) His strength <br> 5) His honor & glory <br> 6) His praise |
| **3 The majestic worship of Christ by the four living creatures & the elders** <br> a. They fall down & play harps, praising Him <br><br> b. They offer the prayers of saints <br><br> c. They sing a new song praising Him for His worthiness | 8 And when he had taken it, the four living creatures and the twenty-four elders fell down before the Lamb. Each one had a harp and they were holding golden bowls full of incense, which are the prayers of the saints. <br> 9 And they sang a new song: "You are worthy to take the scroll and to open its seals, | 13 Then I heard every creature in heaven and on earth and under the earth and on the sea, and all that is in them, singing: "To him who sits on the throne and to the Lamb be praise and honor and glory and power, for ever and ever!" <br> 14 The four living creatures said, "Amen," and the elders fell down and worshiped. | **5 The majestic worship of Christ by the whole universe** <br> a. All creatures worship both God & Christ <br><br> b. The four living creatures say "Amen" <br> c. The elders fall down & worship the eternal God |

# DIVISION III

## THE PICTURE OF THINGS HEREAFTER, 4:1-5:14

### C. The Book of Destiny Is Opened: The Lamb Alone Is Worthy to Open the Book, 5:5-14

(5:5-14) **Introduction**: this is a most dramatic moment. Remember, John is having a vision, and his mind or spirit has been transported above earth into heaven. Therefore, everything he is experiencing is bound to be dramatic. But this moment must be the most dramatic of all: he is about to get his very first glimpse of Jesus Christ Himself. He is about to see the exalted Lord.

The background is this: God is holding the Book of Destiny in His right hand. A search has been conducted throughout the whole universe for someone worthy enough to open the book. But no one is worthy; there is no one good enough to open it. John is heartbroken and is weeping bitterly, for God is ready to reveal the secrets of the end time to man. But no person can be found to open the book and to oversee the climactic events of the end time. The situation looks hopeless. But then all of a sudden one of the heavenly elders steps forth and announces that someone has been found to open the Book of Destiny. There is one Person who is worthy. This is the great subject of this passage: the *Book of Destiny is opened—the Lamb alone is worthy*.

1. The glorious announcement: God has intervened and sent One worthy to open the book (v.5).
2. The supreme moment: the first sight of Christ in heaven (v.6-7).
3. The majestic worship by the four living creatures and the elders (v.8-10).

4. The majestic worship by the angels (v.11-12).
5. The majestic worship by the whole universe (v.13-14).

**1** (5:5) **Jesus Christ, Names and Titles—Lion of Judah—Root of David**: there is the glorious announcement—God has intervened. He Himself has sent One worthy to open the Book of Destiny. Who is He?

1. He is the "Lion of Judah." This is a title of the Messiah. The symbol of the lion shows that He is the strongest and most powerful member of the tribe of Israel. Judah was the strongest tribe of Israel, the strongest by far. Therefore way back in history, God had prophesied through Jacob that his own son Judah would be a "lion's whelp" (young cub). If Judah himself was only a young cub, then the Messiah Himself must be like the King of beasts, the lion. Very simply, the prophecy predicted that the coming Messiah would possess the strength and power of a lion, the king of beasts. Who then is worthy to open the book? Jesus Christ, the lion of Judah, the all powerful Messiah and King. He and He alone is worthy enough to take the book and carry out the events of the end time.

> **You are a lion's cub, O Judah; you return from the prey, my son. Like a lion he crouches and lies down, like a lioness—who dares to rouse him? The scepter will not**

depart from Judah, nor the ruler's staff from between his feet, until he comes to whom it belongs and the obedience of the nations is his. (Gen 49:9-10)

2. He is the "Root of David." The Messiah was to be of the household of David, of the root and seed of Jesse, of his family tree, of his blood, of his stem. Who then is worthy to open the book? The prophesied Son of David, the Messiah and King of the world. He and He alone is worthy to take the book and carry out the events of the end time.

A shoot will come up from the stump of Jesse; from his roots a Branch will bear fruit. (Isa 11:1)

3. He is the One who has prevailed and conquered and won the victory; therefore, He is able to open the Book of Destiny. Over what has He prevailed? What is it that He has conquered?

He is able to open the scroll and its seven seals." (Rev 5:5)

⇒ He has conquered sin.

In him we have redemption through his blood, the forgiveness of sins, in accordance with the riches of God's grace (Eph 1:7)
The Son is the radiance of God's glory and the exact representation of his being, sustaining all things by his powerful word. After he had provided purification for sins, he sat down at the right hand of the Majesty in heaven. (Heb 1:3)
He himself bore our sins in his body on the tree, so that we might die to sins and live for righteousness; by his wounds you have been healed. (1 Pet 2:24)
For Christ died for sins once for all, the righteous for the unrighteous, to bring you to God. He was put to death in the body but made alive by the Spirit, (1 Pet 3:18)

⇒ He has conquered death.

For he must reign until he has put all his enemies under his feet. The last enemy to be destroyed is death. (1 Cor 15:25-26)
But it has now been revealed through the appearing of our Savior, Christ Jesus, who has destroyed death and has brought life and immortality to light through the gospel. (2 Tim 1:10)
Since the children have flesh and blood, he too shared in their humanity so that by his death he might destroy him who holds the power of death—that is, the devil— And free those who all their lives were held in slavery by their fear of death. (Heb 2:14-15)

⇒ He has conquered this evil world.

"I have told you these things, so that in me you may have peace. In this world you will have trouble. But take heart! I have overcome the world." (John 16:33)

Who gave himself for our sins to rescue us from the present evil age, according to the will of our God and Father, (Gal 1:4)

⇒ He has conquered Satan and all other evil forces.

"Or again, how can anyone enter a strong man's house and carry off his possessions unless he first ties up the strong man? Then he can rob his house. (Mat 12:29)
He replied, "I saw Satan fall like lightning from heaven. (Luke 10:18)
Now is the time for judgment on this world; now the prince of this world will be driven out. (John 12:31)
I will not speak with you much longer, for the prince of this world is coming. He has no hold on me, (John 14:30)
And in regard to judgment, because the prince of this world now stands condemned. (John 16:11)
For David did not ascend to heaven, and yet he said, "'The Lord said to my Lord: "Sit at my right hand Until I make your enemies a footstool for your feet."' (Acts 2:34-35)
And having disarmed the powers and authorities, he made a public spectacle of them, triumphing over them by the cross. (Col 2:15; cp. Heb 2.14-15)

⇒ He has conquered all dominion, authority and power.

Then the end will come, when he hands over the kingdom to God the Father after he has destroyed all dominion, authority and power. (1 Cor 15:24)

⇒ He has conquered hell.

"I tell you the truth, whoever hears my word and believes him who sent me has eternal life and will not be condemned; he has crossed over from death to life. (John 5:24)
Who is he that condemns? Christ Jesus, who died—more than that, who was raised to life—is at the right hand of God and is also interceding for us. Who shall separate us from the love of Christ? Shall trouble or hardship or persecution or famine or nakedness or danger or sword? As it is written: "For your sake we face death all day long; we are considered as sheep to be slaughtered." No, in all these things we are more than conquerors through him who loved us. For I am convinced that neither death nor life, neither angels nor demons, neither the present nor the future, nor any powers, Neither height nor depth, nor anything else in all creation, will be able to separate us from the love of God that is in Christ Jesus our Lord. (Rom 8:34-39)
I am the Living One; I was dead, and behold I am alive for ever and ever! And I hold the keys of death and Hades. (Rev 1:18)

**2** (5:6-7) **Jesus Christ, Person—Lamb of God**: there is the supreme moment, the first sight of Jesus Christ in heaven. John had seen Christ in his first vision, but Christ was standing in the midst of the churches. But now the supreme moment arrives—the moment when John catches his first sight of the glorified Son of God in heaven. The sight was bound to be the most spectacular sight ever seen in human history, for God was letting a man see His Son at the throne of God. He was showing why His Son is worthy to rule and reign over the universe. When John caught his first glimpse of Christ, he immediately noticed five things.

1. Jesus Christ is the center of the heavenly scene.
    ⇒ He was right before the throne of God, joining God at the very throne of God itself.
    ⇒ Then the four living beings surround Him.
    ⇒ Then come the circle of elders.

Jesus Christ is the very center and focus of attention: every eye and thought is upon Him. He is the centerpiece of God's throne room, the central figure on the stage of universal history, the history of both heaven and earth.

2. Jesus Christ is the sacrificial Lamb of God who has been slain. The picture of Jesus Christ as the Lamb of God is seen throughout Scripture.

Scripture declares that Jesus Christ is the Lamb of God who died for our sins.
    ⇒ The Lamb of God was symbolized in the Passover. The lamb was sacrificed so that the judgment of God could pass over the people.

**Tell the whole community of Israel that on the tenth day of this month each man is to take a lamb for his family, one for each household. (Exo 12:3)**

    ⇒ Isaiah had said that the Messiah was to bear our sins by being led like a lamb to the slaughter.

**We all, like sheep, have gone astray, each of us has turned to his own way; and the LORD has laid on him the iniquity of us all. He was oppressed and afflicted, yet he did not open his mouth; he was led like a lamb to the slaughter, and as a sheep before her shearers is silent, so he did not open his mouth. (Isa 53:6-7)**

    ⇒ John the Baptist declared Jesus to be the Lamb of God who takes away the sin of the world.

**The next day John saw Jesus coming toward him and said, "Look, the Lamb of God, who takes away the sin of the world! (John 1:29)**
**When he saw Jesus passing by, he said, "Look, the Lamb of God!" (John 1:36)**

    ⇒ Peter had said that persons are redeemed by the precious blood of Christ, a lamb without blemish or defect.

**For you know that it was not with perishable things such as silver or gold that you were redeemed from the empty way of life handed down to you from your forefathers, But with the precious blood of Christ, a lamb without blemish or defect. (1 Pet 1:18-19)**

Note this: A.T. Robertson, the Greek scholar, points out that the word for *lamb* throughout the New Testament is *ho amnos*. But throughout Revelation John uses another word *arnion*, and he uses the word twenty-nine times for the crucified Christ. The difference is this: the word chosen by John stresses the slaughter, suffering, pain, agony, and humiliation of Christ. And *all the suffering* is still seen in heaven. As Robertson says: "The Lamb is now alive, but...with the marks of the sacrifice" (*Word Pictures In The New Testament*, Vol.6, p.334).

The point is this: Jesus Christ is the perfect sacrifice for our sins. He lived a sinless life when He was upon earth; He was the Ideal and Perfect Man. Therefore, whatever Jesus Christ did as the Perfect and Ideal Man, it could stand for and cover us. When He died for our sins, He died as the ideal and perfect sacrifice. His sacrifice for our sins was perfectly acceptable to God. Therefore, His sacrifice for sin stands for and covers us.

What happens is this: when we believe in Jesus Christ, God takes our faith and counts it as the sacrifice of Christ. God counts the sacrifice of Christ for us. This means that we are free from sin. We stand sinless before God, acceptable to Him—all because Jesus Christ, the Lamb of God, removed our sins from us. We are cleansed from sin by the sacrifice of Christ. We are made perfectly righteous by the sacrifice of Christ. Jesus Christ is the Lamb of God who has taken away our sin and clothed us in the white robes of righteousness before God.

This is the reason Jesus Christ stands in the center stage of heaven. But even in heaven He stands as the One who has loved and given Himself for us; He stands as the Lamb who was slain as the *perfect sacrifice* for our sins.

**He did not enter by means of the blood of goats and calves; but he entered the Most Holy Place once for all by his own blood, having obtained eternal redemption. The blood of goats and bulls and the ashes of a heifer sprinkled on those who are ceremonially unclean sanctify them so that they are outwardly clean. How much more, then, will the blood of Christ, who through the eternal Spirit offered himself unblemished to God, cleanse our consciences from acts that lead to death, so that we may serve the living God! (Heb 9:12-14)**
**Day after day every priest stands and performs his religious duties; again and again he offers the same sacrifices, which can never take away sins. But when this priest had offered for all time one sacrifice for sins, he sat down at the right hand of God. Since that time he waits for his enemies to be made his footstool, (Heb 10:11-13)**
**He himself bore our sins in his body on the tree, so that we might die to sins and live for righteousness; by his wounds you have been healed. (1 Pet 2:24)**
**For Christ died for sins once for all, the righteous for the unrighteous, to bring you to God. He was put to death in the body but made alive by the Spirit, (1 Pet 3:18)**

3. Jesus Christ is the omnipotent power of the universe. Remember that the number seven in the Bible means completeness, fullness, and perfection. Jesus Christ is seen with *seven horns* which symbolizes complete and perfect strength

and power. He stands in heaven as the supreme power and force of the universe.

> **Then Jesus came to them and said, "All authority in heaven and on earth has been given to me. (Mat 28:18)**
>
> **No one takes it [my life] from me, but I lay it down of my own accord. I have authority to lay it down and authority to take it up again. This command I received from my Father." (John 10:18)**
>
> **For you granted him authority over all people that he might give eternal life to all those you have given him. (John 17:2)**
>
> **And who through the Spirit of holiness was declared with power to be the Son of God by his resurrection from the dead: Jesus Christ our Lord. (Rom 1:4)**
>
> **For by him all things were created: things in heaven and on earth, visible and invisible, whether thrones or powers or rulers or authorities; all things were created by him and for him. He is before all things, and in him all things hold together. (Col 1:16-17)**
>
> **In the past God spoke to our forefathers through the prophets at many times and in various ways, But in these last days he has spoken to us by his Son, whom he appointed heir of all things, and through whom he made the universe. The Son is the radiance of God's glory and the exact representation of his being, sustaining all things by his powerful word. After he had provided purification for sins, he sat down at the right hand of the Majesty in heaven. (Heb 1:1-3)**

4. Jesus Christ is the supreme intelligence of the universe. The *seven eyes* symbolize complete and perfect knowledge, intelligence, and wisdom. He is omniscient; He knows all and sees all. Absolutely nothing escapes His sight and knowledge. Note: this is a symbol of the seven spirits of God which is the Holy Spirit (see notes—Rev.1:4; 3:1 for discussion). In the person of the Holy Spirit, Jesus Christ is everywhere, seeing and knowing all.

> **He did not need man's testimony about man, for he knew what was in a man. (John 2:25)**
>
> **Then they prayed, "Lord, you know everyone's heart. Show us which of these two you have chosen (Acts 1:24)**
>
> **In whom are hidden all the treasures of wisdom and knowledge. (Col 2:3)**
>
> **The Spirit of the LORD will rest on him— the Spirit of wisdom and of understanding, the Spirit of counsel and of power, the Spirit of knowledge and of the fear of the LORD— (Isa 11:2)**
>
> **No one will offer food to comfort those who mourn for the dead—not even for a father or a mother—nor will anyone give them a drink to console them. (Jer 16:7)**

5. Jesus Christ is sovereign. He alone walks over and takes the Book of Destiny out of the hand of God. He and He alone is worthy to execute and carry out the events of the end time. This is simply a graphic way of saying what is said in the very first verse of Revelation.

> **The revelation of Jesus Christ, which God gave him to show his servants what must soon take place. He made it known by sending his angel to his servant John, (Rev 1:1)**

**3** (5:8-10) **Worship of Christ**: there is the majestic worship by the four living creatures and the elders. As soon as Jesus Christ takes the book out of the hand of God, all of heaven and earth break loose in a song of praise. And note there are three waves of praise sung to Christ.

⇒ There is the praise of the four living creatures and of the elders who surround the throne of God.

⇒ Then there is the wave of praise from the numberless host of angels, ten thousands times ten thousands, and thousands of thousands of them. The idea is that the number is so large that man and his computers could not count the number.

⇒ Then there is the majestic worship of all creatures in both heaven and earth, and under the earth in the graves, and in the seas. All of creation—every being ever created—breaks loose in a chorus of praise to the Lord and to the Lamb of God who sits upon the throne (Jesus Christ).

The present note covers the praise of the four living creatures and the elders who immediately surround the Lord Jesus Christ and the throne of God. Note three things about their worship.

1. They fall down before Christ, the Lamb of God, and play harps. Remember: the harp was the usual instrument used to sing the Psalms of praise to our Lord (cp. Ps.33:2; 98:5; 147:7).

2. They offer up golden bowls of incense to the Lord which is the symbol of the prayers of believers (saints).

> **Thought 1.** Just think of this: the very beings closest to God offer up our prayers to Christ for us. The heavenly host is concerned over our welfare even as the Lord is. They long for us to be helped through the trials and temptations of life even more than we long to be delivered through them. What a precious truth.

3. They sing a new song focused upon the worthiness of Christ. Remember: God had just held out the Book of Destiny and the shattering call had just pierced the air for someone worthy to step forth and to take the book. Someone was needed to open the book and carry out the events upon earth. But no one was found worthy. Not even those who surround the very throne of God, the four living creatures and elders, were worthy. Only one Person could step forward: the Lamb of God Himself, the Lord Jesus Christ. This is the scene here: when the living creatures and elders see the Lamb of God step forward and take the book from God, they fall down in worship and adoration and sing a song to Him, a song that has never been sung before.

> **And they sang a new song: "You are worthy to take the scroll and to open its seals, because you were slain, and with your blood you purchased men for God from every tribe and language and people and nation. You have made them to be a kingdom and priests to serve our God, and they will reign on the earth." (Rev 5:9-10)**

Note that they praise Christ for four things.

    a. They praise Him because He was slain for man and has redeemed or "purchased men for God" (v.9). They praise Christ because He died for the sins of man and has set man free from sin and death and the punishment to come. (See note 2, pt.2—Rev.5:6-7. Also see note—Rev.1:5-6 for more discussion.)

> **Since we have now been justified by his blood, how much more shall we be saved from God's wrath through him! (Rom 5:9)**
> **Christ redeemed us from the curse of the law by becoming a curse for us, for it is written: "Cursed is everyone who is hung on a tree." (Gal 3:13)**
> **In him we have redemption through his blood, the forgiveness of sins, in accordance with the riches of God's grace (Eph 1:7)**
> **In whom we have redemption, the forgiveness of sins. (Col 1:14)**
> **Who gave himself for us to redeem us from all wickedness and to purify for himself a people that are his very own, eager to do what is good. (Titus 2:14)**
> **He did not enter by means of the blood of goats and calves; but he entered the Most Holy Place once for all by his own blood, having obtained eternal redemption. (Heb 9:12)**
> **For you know that it was not with perishable things such as silver or gold that you were redeemed from the empty way of life handed down to you from your forefathers, But with the precious blood of Christ, a lamb without blemish or defect. (1 Pet 1:18-19)**

    b. They praise Him because of His universal salvation (v.9). No person is beyond His reach. He saves people from every tribe and language and race and nation. There is no prejudice or discrimination with Christ, no favorites and no partiality. He loves every person: male and female, poor and rich, black and white, yellow and red, ignorant and wise. Christ saves all who will come from every corner of the earth. Those who surround Christ and the throne of God shout their praise to Christ for His universal salvation.

> **And all mankind will see God's salvation.'" (Luke 3:6)**
> **For, "Everyone who calls on the name of the Lord will be saved." (Rom 10:13)**
> **Who wants all men to be saved and to come to a knowledge of the truth. (1 Tim 2:4)**
> **For the grace of God that brings salvation has appeared to all men. It teaches us to say "No" to ungodliness and worldly passions, and to live self-controlled, upright and godly lives in this present age, (Titus 2:11-12)**
> **The Lord is not slow in keeping his promise, as some understand slowness. He is patient with you, not wanting anyone to perish, but everyone to come to repentance. (2 Pet 3:9)**

> **Here I am! I stand at the door and knock. If anyone hears my voice and opens the door, I will come in and eat with him, and he with me. (Rev 3:20)**

    c. They praise Christ because He has given believers the great gift of royalty (v.10). He makes them a kingdom and priests and note: they shall rule on the earth serving the Lord Jesus Christ forever and ever as kings and priests. (See note—Rev.14:13; 21:24-27 for complete list of rewards.)

> **"His master replied, 'Well done, good and faithful servant! You have been faithful with a few things; I will put you in charge of many things. Come and share your master's happiness!' (Mat 25:23)**
> **You are those who have stood by me in my trials. And I confer on you a kingdom, just as my Father conferred one on me, (Luke 22:28-29)**
> **The Spirit himself testifies with our spirit that we are God's children. Now if we are children, then we are heirs—heirs of God and co-heirs with Christ, if indeed we share in his sufferings in order that we may also share in his glory. (Rom 8:16-17)**
> **And from Jesus Christ, who is the faithful witness, the firstborn from the dead, and the ruler of the kings of the earth. To him who loves us and has freed us from our sins by his blood, And has made us to be a kingdom and priests to serve his God and Father—to him be glory and power for ever and ever! Amen. (Rev 1:5-6)**
> **I saw thrones on which were seated those who had been given authority to judge. And I saw the souls of those who had been beheaded because of their testimony for Jesus and because of the word of God. They had not worshiped the beast or his image and had not received his mark on their foreheads or their hands. They came to life and reigned with Christ a thousand years. (Rev 20:4)**
> **Those who are wise will shine like the brightness of the heavens, and those who lead many to righteousness, like the stars for ever and ever. (Dan 12:3)**

**4** (5:11-12) **Worship—Angels:** there is the majestic worship by the angels. Note three facts about the angels.

    1. They are the center circle of the praise chorus.

    2. Their number is astounding: an *innumerable number* is what Scripture is declaring.

    3. Their song includes seven points.

        a. They praise Christ for His power. He is omnipotent: He possesses all power. He is able to open God's Book of Destiny and to carry out and execute God's will throughout the universe. He is able to carry out the events of history and the events of the end time. He is the sovereign Ruler of the universe.

> **Then Jesus came to them and said, "All authority in heaven and on earth has been given to me. (Mat 28:18)**

For you granted him authority over all people that he might give eternal life to all those you have given him. (John 17:2)

And who through the Spirit of holiness was declared with power to be the Son of God by his resurrection from the dead: Jesus Christ our Lord. (Rom 1:4)

But to those whom God has called, both Jews and Greeks, Christ the power of God and the wisdom of God. (1 Cor 1:24)

Now to him who is able to do immeasurably more than all we ask or imagine, according to his power that is at work within us, (Eph 3:20)

b. They praise Christ for His riches. He possesses the wealth to meet any need throughout the universe, any need that we or any other creature may have.

Or do you show contempt for the riches of his kindness, tolerance and patience, not realizing that God's kindness leads you toward repentance? (Rom 2:4)

For you know the grace of our Lord Jesus Christ, that though he was rich, yet for your sakes he became poor, so that you through his poverty might become rich. (2 Cor 8:9)

In him we have redemption through his blood, the forgiveness of sins, in accordance with the riches of God's grace (Eph 1:7)

In order that in the coming ages he might show the incomparable riches of his grace, expressed in his kindness to us in Christ Jesus. (Eph 2:7)

Although I am less than the least of all God's people, this grace was given me: to preach to the Gentiles the unsearchable riches of Christ, (Eph 3:8)

And my God will meet all your needs according to his glorious riches in Christ Jesus. (Phil 4:19)

c. They praise Christ for His wisdom. He is omniscient, seeing and knowing all. He knows all about God and heaven, and all about us and our world with all its temptations and trials. He can, therefore, carry out the will of God laid out in the Book of Destiny, and He can help us through all the trials and temptations of life.

It is because of him that you are in Christ Jesus, who has become for us wisdom from God—that is, our righteousness, holiness and redemption. (1 Cor 1:30)

For we do not have a high priest who is unable to sympathize with our weaknesses, but we have one who has been tempted in every way, just as we are—yet was without sin. Let us then approach the throne of grace with confidence, so that we may receive mercy and find grace to help us in our time of need. (Heb 4:15-16)

The LORD is my strength and my shield; my heart trusts in him, and I am helped. My heart leaps for joy and I will give thanks to him in song. (Psa 28:7)

Yet I am poor and needy; may the Lord think of me. You are my help and my deliverer; O my God, do not delay. (Psa 40:17)

So do not fear, for I am with you; do not be dismayed, for I am your God. I will strengthen you and help you; I will uphold you with my righteous right hand. (Isa 41:10)

d. They praise Him for His strength. No one nor any thing can stand against Him, not even for a moment unless He allows it. He has infinite strength, the very strength of God Himself. All He has to do is speak the Word and His will is done. Therefore, He can carry out the events in the Book of Destiny, and he can meet our every need.

Jesus looked at them and said, "With man this is impossible, but with God all things are possible." (Mat 19:26)

For nothing is impossible with God." (Luke 1:37)

No temptation has seized you except what is common to man. And God is faithful; he will not let you be tempted beyond what you can bear. But when you are tempted, he will also provide a way out so that you can stand up under it. (1 Cor 10:13)

Now to him who is able to do immeasurably more than all we ask or imagine, according to his power that is at work within us, (Eph 3:20)

The Lord will rescue me from every evil attack and will bring me safely to his heavenly kingdom. To him be glory for ever and ever. Amen. (2 Tim 4:18)

To him who is able to keep you from falling and to present you before his glorious presence without fault and with great joy— To the only God our Savior be glory, majesty, power and authority, through Jesus Christ our Lord, before all ages, now and forevermore! Amen. (Jude 1:24-25)

"I know that you can do all things; no plan of yours can be thwarted. (Job 42:2)

Our God is in heaven; he does whatever pleases him. (Psa 115:3)

So do not fear, for I am with you; do not be dismayed, for I am your God. I will strengthen you and help you; I will uphold you with my righteous right hand. (Isa 41:10)

Yes, and from ancient days I am he. No one can deliver out of my hand. When I act, who can reverse it?" (Isa 43:13)

e. They praise Him for His honor. He is the Son of God possessing the very nature of God, the eternal and sovereign Majesty, the Creator and Sustainer of the universe. He is the One appointed to open the Book of Destiny and to execute its events throughout the universe. Therefore, He is the One who is to be honored by all.

Therefore God exalted him to the highest place and gave him the name that is above every name, That at the name of

Jesus every knee should bow, in heaven and on earth and under the earth, And every tongue confess that Jesus Christ is Lord, to the glory of God the Father. (Phil 2:9-11)

Let us rejoice and be glad and give him glory! For the wedding of the Lamb has come, and his bride has made herself ready. (Rev 19:7)

Glorify the LORD with me; let us exalt his name together. (Psa 34:3)

Let them exalt him in the assembly of the people and praise him in the council of the elders. (Psa 107:32)

f. They praise Him for His glory. As stated, He is the supreme Glory and Majesty of the universe, so glorious that His glory shines brighter than the sun to give light in the spiritual world or dimension. His own glory is the light of heaven. In Him is no flaw or defect whatsoever. Therefore, He and He alone is worthy to open the Book of Destiny and to carry out the will of God throughout the universe. He and He alone is due all the glory of the universe.

In the same way, let your light shine before men, that they may see your good deeds and praise your Father in heaven. (Mat 5:16)

This is to my Father's glory, that you bear much fruit, showing yourselves to be my disciples. (John 15:8)

So that with one heart and mouth you may glorify the God and Father of our Lord Jesus Christ. (Rom 15:6)

Do you not know that your body is a temple of the Holy Spirit, who is in you, whom you have received from God? You are not your own; You were bought at a price. Therefore honor God with your body. (1 Cor 6:19-20)

Ascribe to the LORD the glory due his name; worship the LORD in the splendor of his holiness. (Psa 29:2)

Be exalted, O God, above the heavens; let your glory be over all the earth. (Psa 57:5)

g. They praise Him for His blessing. He deserves all the blessing or praise that heaven and earth can give, for He has blessed all. He has given life and all the good things of life to all creatures. All blessings have come from Him. Therefore, all the blessings that heaven and earth can give are due Him.

Giving thanks to the Father, who has qualified you to share in the inheritance of the saints in the kingdom of light. (Col 1:12)

Let the peace of Christ rule in your hearts, since as members of one body you were called to peace. And be thankful. (Col 3:15)

Give thanks in all circumstances, for this is God's will for you in Christ Jesus. (1 Th 5:18)

When you have eaten and are satisfied, praise the LORD your God for the good land he has given you. (Deu 8:10)

Enter his gates with thanksgiving and his courts with praise; give thanks to him and praise his name. (Psa 100:4)

O LORD, you are my God; I will exalt you and praise your name, for in perfect faithfulness you have done marvelous things, things planned long ago. (Isa 25:1)

**5** (5:13-14) **Worship**: there is the majestic worship by the whole universe. After each group of created beings has sung their chorus of praise, then all of creation—every being and creature who has ever lived in both heaven and earth—shall break forth in one chorus of praise to both God and Christ. What shall they praise God and Christ for?
⇒ for their praise
⇒ for their honor
⇒ for their glory
⇒ for their power

Then the four living creatures shall shout "Amen." And the elders shall fall down and worship the Lord Jesus Christ who lives forever and ever.

Never has there been a chorus of worship as will be seen in the glorious day of redemption when all creation shall praise Him who is our Lord and Savior, even the Son of God Himself. And remember why:
⇒ because He is worthy to step forward and take the Book of Destiny out of the hand of God.
⇒ because He is worthy to rule and reign over all history, both now and in the last days and throughout all of eternity, world without end.

So that with one heart and mouth you may glorify the God and Father of our Lord Jesus Christ. (Rom 15:6)

You were bought at a price. Therefore honor God with your body. (1 Cor 6:20)

We pray this so that the name of our Lord Jesus may be glorified in you, and you in him, according to the grace of our God and the Lord Jesus Christ. (2 Th 1:12)

He said in a loud voice, "Fear God and give him glory, because the hour of his judgment has come. Worship him who made the heavens, the earth, the sea and the springs of water." (Rev 14:7)

**CHAPTER 6**

**IV. THE SEVEN SEAL JUDGMENTS: EVENTS PRECEDING THE GREAT TRIBULA- TION, 6:1-7:17**

**A. The Lamb Breaks the First Four Seals of the Book of Destiny: The Appearance of the Antichrist & His Power, 6:1-8**

**1  The 1st Seal: A white horse & rider**

a. He possesses a bow
b. He is given a crown
c. His purpose: He goes forth to conquer

**2  The 2nd Seal: A red horse & rider**

a. He is given power & a large sword

I watched as the Lamb opened the first of the seven seals. Then I heard one of the four living creatures say in a voice like thunder, "Come!" 2 I looked, and there before me was a white horse! Its rider held a bow, and he was given a crown, and he rode out as a conqueror bent on conquest. 3 When the Lamb opened the second seal, I heard the second living creature say, "Come!" 4 Then another horse came out, a fiery red one. Its rider was given power to take peace from the earth and to make men slay each other. To him was given a large sword. 5 When the Lamb opened the third seal, I heard the third living creature say, "Come!" I looked, and there before me was a black horse! Its rider was holding a pair of scales in his hand. 6 Then I heard what sounded like a voice among the four living creatures, saying, "A quart of wheat for a day's wages, and three quarts of barley for a day's wages, and do not damage the oil and the wine!" 7 When the Lamb opened the fourth seal, I heard the voice of the fourth living creature say, "Come!" 8 I looked, and there before me was a pale horse! Its rider was named Death, and Hades was following close behind him. They were given power over a fourth of the earth to kill by sword, famine and plague, and by the wild beasts of the earth.

b. He removes peace & causes killing or war

**3  The 3rd Seal: A black horse & rider**

a. He possesses a set of scales
b. He causes famine & scarcity
c. He controls food distribution, but he protects the rich (oil & wine)

**4  The 4th Seal: A pale horse & rider**

a. He has the name of Death
b. He is followed by Hades
c. He is given one fourth of the earth to kill by war & famine

# DIVISION IV

## THE SEVEN SEAL JUDGMENTS: EVENTS PRECEDING THE GREAT TRIBULATION, 6:1-7:17

### A. The Lamb Breaks the First Four Seals of the Book of Destiny: The Appearance of the Antichrist and His Power, 6:1-8

(6:1-7:17) **DIVISION OVERVIEW: End Time**: the dramatic moment has arrived. God's book—the Book of Destiny, the great book of history, the book that spells out what is to happen in the end time—is now to be opened. But note: the Lamb does not open the scroll at this point. He merely breaks the seals. And the events of the seals are not the end of history itself. They are the events which immediately precede the end. The seals of a book have to be broken before the book itself is opened. The seals are preliminary to opening the book. This is exactly what Christ Himself said. Remember the apostles had asked Christ two questions: When would the temple be destroyed, and what would be the sign of His coming and of the end of the world (cp. Mt.24:3)?

⇒ Christ answered by giving nine signs, and He called this period of history "the beginning of "birth pains" or "leg of sorrows" (Mt.24:5-14, esp. v.8). After He had given the nine signs, He said "then shall the end come" (Mt.24:14).

Note that it was after the nine signs, after the *"beginning of birth pains" or "the beginning of sorrows"* that Christ said the end would come. By the end He meant what He Himself called the *great distress or the great tribulation* that is coming upon the earth in the end time. (The following chart will perhaps help us see what our Lord predicted and what is now beginning to happen in the book of Revelation.)

### THE END TIME

| *The Words of Christ* | | *The Book of Revelation* |
|---|---|---|
| • The beginning of birth pains or of sorrows: birth pains, preliminary trouble and evil in society and nature, yet world evangelism continues (Mt.24:5-14). | ...corresponds to | ...The Seven Seals (Rev.6:1-17) |
| • "The Great Distress or the great Tribulation": unparalleled trials (Mt.24:15-28). | ...corresponds to | ...The Seven Trumpets, the bowls, and the beast (Rev.8:1-18:24). |
| • "The Son of Man coming" | ...corresponds to | ...The Final Triumph of Christ (Rev.19:1-22:21). |

Note the clear and astounding similarity between what our Lord said and the book of Revelation. The very similarity shows the *mind of God* revealing these things. This should make every person, believer and unbeliever alike, stand in stark amazement and bow before Him who alone can save us and give us life eternal.

⇒ There is a similarity between "the beginning of birth pains [sorrows]" (Mt.24:5-14) and the seals of Revelation (Rev.6:1-17). The end of the world *will not come all at once.* The future will be filled with wars, natural disasters, persecutions, and the claims of false deliverers (messiahs). And at the very end there will be an increase and intensification of the signs. But this is not all. There is to be a terrible sign: the appearance of the rider on the white horse (see note—Rev.6:2), "the abomination that cause desolation (NIV), the abomination of desolation" (AV), "the desolating sacrilege" (RSV), "the man of lawlessness" (2 Th.2:3), the "little horn" (Dan.7), the antichrist. This person will afflict the people of God beyond imagination. (See note—Rev.11:7.)

⇒ There seems to be a similarity between "the great tribulation" spoken of by Christ and the seven trumpets, the seven bowl judgments, and the beast covered by Revelation.

⇒ Others point to a great similarity between "the beast" (antichrist) pictured time and again in Revelation and "the abomination that causes desolation" spoken of by Christ (see DEEPER STUDY # 1,2— Mt.24:1-31; note—Rev.11:7).

This distinction is extremely important in understanding the book of Revelation. Why? Because our Lord Himself said the same thing. In essence He has told us how to outline and look at Revelation. Therefore we are most wise to follow the outline of the end times that He has given us. In the final analysis it is better to be *simple minded* and to follow what He has said than to be *wise* and strike out on our own and end up adding something to His Word that displeases Him (cp. Rev.22:18-19). We reverence and fear Him. We want to be acceptable to our wonderful Lord, and during these latter years, more than anything else in all the world, we want to show our love for Him by obeying Him and following His Word to the utmost. For this reason, we shall approach the Revelation as our Lord predicted the end time. (See outline and notes—Mt.24:1-51; 25:1-46 for more discussion.)

**(6:1-8) Introduction**: the dramatic moment has now come. The seals that bind God's book are now to be broken. One by one they shall be broken. Amazingly, as the seals are broken, the most astounding thing happens. What is written under the seals of the book leaps off its pages and acts out the events of the future for John and the heavenly host. They actually see what appears to be a picture or a movie of the end time. This is important to note, for John and the heavenly host are not reading the book. They are witnessing the events of the end time.

The first four seal judgments seem to be a description of the antichrist gaining control over the nations of the earth. He will do it by waging war (the red horse), by gaining control over the economy (the black horse), and by having his opponents put to death (the pale horse). In the next outline and passage, when we look at the fifth seal, we will see that it reveals what will happen to the souls of Christian martyrs who are slain by the antichrist. The sixth seal will show God's wrath being stirred and being prepared to move in

judgment against the antichrist. The seventh seal is the seal that brings forth the "great tribulation," the terrible period of God's judgment.

In the Scripture before us the Lamb of God, the Lord Jesus Christ Himself, breaks the first four seals. When He does, one of the four living creatures who surrounds the throne of God thunders forth the command: "come forth." And when He thunders His command, the terrible scene of some end time event thunders across the scene of world history.

1. The first seal: a white horse and rider (v.1-2).
2. The second seal: a red horse and rider (v.3-4).
3. The third seal: a black horse and rider (v.5-6).
4. The fourth seal: a pale horse and rider (v.7-8).

**1** (6:1-2) **Antichrist—Four Horsemen**: the first seal is the thundering appearance of a *white horse and its rider*. Who is this rider? His identity is widely disputed, but the conclusion of most commentators is that he is one of two persons.

1. One view is that he symbolizes the victorious Christ Himself or either the victorious proclamation of the gospel. It is argued that the color *white* is always associated with Christ throughout Revelation. In addition, the rider is said to be crowned. Therefore, this rider must be Christ Himself.

Others argue, however, that Christ cannot be commanded by heavenly creatures; therefore, it cannot be Christ Himself. Hence, the horseman must be the conquest of the Word of God as prophesied by Christ (Mk.13:10).

2. The second major view is that the rider is conquest in general, the antichrist in particular.

⇒ He is the deceiver; therefore, he appears in *white* (Mt.24:5; 2 Th.2:11).

⇒ The crown he wears is different from the crown worn by Christ in Rev.19. It is the crown of the conqueror (stephenos) not the royal crown of a king (diadema).

⇒ The bow symbolizes conquest. In the Old Testament it is always the symbol of military power (Ps.46:9; Hos.1:5).

⇒ It is further argued that to be consistent one must relate this horseman to the other three. The four present a picture of the *four horsemen of the Apocalypse* that are to descend upon the earth in the latter days with terrifying destruction.

In one's interpretation, it is extremely important to note this: when the rider appears upon the scene, he *already possesses a bow*. But *the crown is given* to him. After it is given, then he goes forth to conquer. This points strongly to a counterfeit Christ. Note three facts:

⇒ First, this rider has a bow. Christ possesses no bow; a weapon of war is not a part of His being.

⇒ Second, this rider is given a crown. Christ is not given a crown. One has to say that Christ has been crowned throughout all of eternity or else at His ascension.

⇒ Third, this rider sets out to conquer. There is no specific point of time at which Christ set forth to conquer the hearts of men. He has always been about the mission of salvation. Conquering men's hearts will continue to be His mission until the day of judgment appears. Thus, there is no point from which He has to move to conquer; He is conquering souls even as He has always been conquering souls. But this is not true with this rider. This horseman who sets out to conquer is one who already possesses a bow and is given a crown at some point in time. From that point, he *goes forth* to conquer. (Cp. The Little Horn of Dan.7; The Man of Sin and the Beast and the Ruler of the Restored Roman Empire of Rev.13; the Abomination of Desolation of Mt.24:15.)

The strongest arguments seem to point toward the white rider being the antichrist. How is the antichrist going to conquer the world? Scripture tells us that it is going to be through deception. Because of the sins and evil of people, because people have chosen to go the way of sin and evil, the antichrist is going to be able to deceive them.

> **And then the lawless one will be revealed, whom the Lord Jesus will overthrow with the breath of his mouth and destroy by the splendor of his coming. The coming of the lawless one will be in accordance with the work of Satan displayed in all kinds of counterfeit miracles, signs and wonders, And in every sort of evil that deceives those who are perishing. They perish because they refused to love the truth and so be saved. (2 Th 2:8-10)**

People do not receive the love of the truth about the Lord Jesus Christ; people could care less about God's salvation; therefore, God is going to judge the world. The beginning of His judgment is going to be His allowing the antichrist to come upon the world scene. God is going to allow men to be deceived because they have rejected the love of the truth. They have rejected and cursed Him and His glorious salvation revealed in His Son, the Lord Jesus Christ. Therefore, God is going to send a strong deception upon the earth, the very deception for which men long, a strong world ruler who seemingly can solve the world's problems and bring utopia to earth. And men are going to give their kingdoms to him; that is, they are going to sign treaties and agreements that will allow him to rule over their nations and lives.

> **For this reason God sends them a powerful delusion so that they will believe the lie (2 Th 2:11)**
> **For God has put it into their hearts to accomplish his purpose by agreeing to give the beast their power to rule, until God's words are fulfilled. (Rev 17:17)**

**Thought 1.** What could cause men to turn the government of the world over to one man? Christ Himself told us. (Note that all of this is given by Christ in Matthew 24:1f.)

⇒ A world that is full of false messiahs claiming that they have the answers to life will prepare the way for the antichrist. But their claims are false; therefore, they leave the human heart empty and hopeless. When the heart is empty and hopeless, it will turn to a person (the antichrist) who promises utopia, that is, heaven upon earth.

> **For many will come in my name, claiming, 'I am the Christ, 'and will deceive many. (Mat 24:5)**

⇒ A world that is full of violence, wars, and rumors of war will prepare the way for the antichrist. Millions of lives, homes, families, and all else will destroyed. A devastated people will turn to any leader who can bring peace and restoration.

> **You will hear of wars and rumors of wars, but see to it that you are not alarmed. Such things must happen, but the end is still to come. Nation will rise against nation, and kingdom against kingdom. (Mat 24:6-7)**

⇒ A world that is rocked with natural disaster after natural disaster will prepare the way for the antichrist. Disaster after disaster will cause people to quake in fear. Fear will drive people to a world leader who can promise and provide economic and medical help and aid.

> **There will be famines and earthquakes in various places. Nation will rise against nation, and kingdom against kingdom. (Mat 24:7b)**

⇒ A world that is torn apart religiously will prepare the way for the antichrist. Severe religious persecution and terrible apostasy and betrayal will sweep the earth. There will be division within the ranks of religion and families and between neighbors sweeping the earth in the end time. This will cause people to turn for help in bringing peace between religions.

> **"Then you will be handed over to be persecuted and put to death, and you will be hated by all nations because of me. At that time many will turn away from the faith and will betray and hate each other, (Mat 24:9-10)**

⇒ A world that is full of false religion and false preachers will prepare the way for the antichrist. False religion will leave the heart hungry for something real; therefore, they will be ripe for the promises of the antichrist.

> **And many false prophets will appear and deceive many people. (Mat 24:11)**

⇒ A world that falls further and further away from God, that experiences increasing sin (sin that just grows and grows) and a love that grows cold will prepare the way for the antichrist. People will be begging for help in dealing with lawlessness, drunkenness, drugs, occults, crime, and on and on. They will look toward anyone who can bring true care, affection, and love back into society.

> **Because of the increase of wickedness, the love of most will grow cold, (Mat 24:12)**

**2** (6:3-4) **Antichrist—Four Horsemen**: the second seal is the thundering appearance of a *red horse and its rider*. Who is this rider? He is the rider who has power to take peace from the earth so that men will kill each other. He is the rider who is given a *large* sword. He is the rider...

- of strife
- of violence
- of assault
- of division
- of abuse
- of anger

- of hate
- of uprising
- of murder
- of insurrection
- of war
- of bloodshed

He is the rider who divides race against race, class against class, neighbor against neighbor, employee against employer, husband against wife, religion against religion, and nation against nation. He is the rider who takes peace from the earth and causes every kind of division he can. He is the rider who destroys every human relationship that he can.

Now who is the rider upon the horse? John does not say, but note these facts:

⇒ The last days will bring terrible days of evil.

**But mark this: There will be terrible times in the last days. People will be lovers of themselves, lovers of money, boastful, proud, abusive, disobedient to their parents, ungrateful, unholy, Without love, unforgiving, slanderous, without self-control, brutal, not lovers of the good, (2 Tim 3:1-3)**

⇒ The last days will bring terrible days of wars and rumors of wars.

**You will hear of wars and rumors of wars, but see to it that you are not alarmed. Such things must happen, but the end is still to come. Nation will rise against nation, and kingdom against kingdom. There will be famines and earthquakes in various places. (Mat 24:6-7)**

⇒ The devil himself is called "an enormous red dragon."

**Then another sign appeared in heaven: an enormous red dragon with seven heads and ten horns and seven crowns on his heads. (Rev 12:3)**

⇒ The devil is a murderer and a great liar and deceiver and has been from the beginning.

**You belong to your father, the devil, and you want to carry out your father's desire. He was a murderer from the beginning, not holding to the truth, for there is no truth in him. When he lies, he speaks his native language, for he is a liar and the father of lies. (John 8:44)**

⇒ The antichrist who will be the supreme representative of the devil upon earth will become a mass murderer and use the sword against both God's people and those who oppose him. This is one way that he brings the world into subjection under his government.

**He was given power to make war against the saints and to conquer them. And he was given authority over every tribe, people, language and nation. All inhabitants of the earth will worship the beast—all whose names have not been written in the book of life belonging to the Lamb that was slain**

**from the creation of the world. (Rev 13:7-8; cp. Rev.17:15-18)**

**While people are saying, "Peace and safety," destruction will come on them suddenly, as labor pains on a pregnant woman, and they will not escape. (1 Th 5:3)**

Now, who is the rider upon the red horse? We can say that he either represents the lack of peace the antichrist and his government bring to the world or else he is the antichrist himself. To say one is to say the other. When the antichrist and his government appear upon the world scene of human history, he will bring peace and safety for a while. But then there will be a break in his peaceful behavior: he and his government will explosively destroy the peace of the world. This will take place right before the *great distress or the great tribulation* takes place. It is the increased world violence that Christ predicted for the end time, right before the *great tribulation*.

**You will hear of wars and rumors of wars, but see to it that you are not alarmed. Such things must happen, but the end is still to come. Nation will rise against nation, and kingdom against kingdom. There will be famines and earthquakes in various places. (Mat 24:6-7)**

**3** (6:5-6) **Antichrist—Four Horsemen**: the third seal is the thundering appearance of a *black horse and its rider*. This rider also seems to be the antichrist and his power to control the economy and distribution of food. Food will be rationed in the end time. Remember there will be more wars and conflicts and violence raging all over the world during the end time than ever before. The result of war is often famine, and the end time will be no different. The only difference is that the famine will be far more severe and involve far more people. The end times will see an intensification of all the terrible sufferings known to man.

1. The rider of the black horse (the antichrist) has a set of scales to measure out the wheat. Wheat or barley was the basic food for people in John's day. The rider caused famine and scarcity. Note that it took...
   - a "a day's wages" (denarius) to buy a quart of wheat.
   - a day's wages to buy three quarts of barley.

Imagine working and earning only enough money to buy what food was needed for that day! What would a person do about feeding his family and providing the other necessities of life such as housing, heat, clothing, and transportation? This will be the situation in the end time, *right before the great distress or the great tribulation* is to take place.

2. The rider controls food distribution. This is probably one way that he gains and holds control over the world, at least for a season. The idea is that food will be strictly controlled. But note: there will be plenty of oil and wine. How could oil and wine which come from trees and vines be available when wheat and barley are scarce and shriveled up with a draught? From stockpiles and from the fact that trees and vines have roots more deeply in the ground than crops. They can usually survive and produce more through a draught than crops. Also, trees will produce for years without being cared for. War will keep men from growing crops, but trees will keep on producing without much attention. Oil and wine were luxury items in the ancient world. As is true

in most famines, the wealthy will have food, the poor will not.

The end time will be marked by famine after famine all over the world. It will take all a man can do just to survive.

> **You will hear of wars and rumors of wars, but see to it that you are not alarmed. Such things must happen, but the end is still to come. Nation will rise against nation, and kingdom against kingdom. There will be famines and earthquakes in various places. (Mat 24:6-7)**
>
> **Those killed by the sword are better off than those who die of famine; racked with hunger, they waste away for lack of food from the field. (Lam 4:9)**
>
> **Our skin is hot as an oven, feverish from hunger. (Lam 5:10)**

**4** (6:7-8) **Antichrist—Four Horsemen**: the fourth seal is the thundering appearance of a *pale horse and its rider*. The Amplified New Testament translates the word *pale* as "ashy pale horse [black and blue as if made so by bruising]." Remember: this is not yet the end of time. This horseman, just as the other three, is to appear before the end time. But what happens under his attack causes such devastation that it boggles and weakens the mind. Note: this rider also seems to represent the terrible devastation caused by the antichrist and his government or the antichrist himself. Two significant facts are given about him.

1. The rider (antichrist) has a name, that of Death; and sitting right behind him is Hades or hell, the realm of the dead. His very name announces that some terrible devastation is about to be set loose upon the earth.

2. The rider (antichrist) is given power to cause unbelievable pain and suffering: he is personally responsible for killing one fourth of the people on earth. Unbelievable! How can one rider possibly kill one fourth of the people? A number that would equal over one billion today? There are four ways.

⇒ The sword can help to kill that many people. That is, war and genocide, by deliberately setting a policy to destroy certain races or groups of people.

> **Thought 1.** All it would take is someone like Hitler to launch a larger war, perhaps an atomic war upon earth. Or someone like Hitler to launch a worldwide holocaust or a Stalin to create a worldwide Siberia where millions upon millions of people were killed (see note—Mt.24:6-7 for more discussion).

⇒ Hunger and starvation can help to kill that many people. That is, the rider can starve people and cause famine due to war and the rationing of food.

> **Thought 2.** Reports tell us that while we slept last night there were about 40,000 children alone who starved to death. Imagine! In the twentieth and twenty first century 40,000 children starve to death

every day! Yet think of all the money we have in our pockets, and of the money so many are banking. Tens of thousands starving to death and we have the money and the resources to keep it from happening. But out of selfishness and greed, we hoard. If so much death from starvation occurs when we could stop it but don't, how many would be dying from starvation due to the kind of world war we would see in the modern world? How much of the earth would be scorched and unfit for farming? How savage and lawless would people become if they were starving and saw someone with a little food? (See note—Mt.24:7 for more discussion.)

⇒ Pestilence can help to kill that many people: that is, germ warfare and the diseases that result from the unsanitary conditions of refugee and concentration camps and from war and genocide. (See note, pt.2— Mt.24:7 for more discussion.)

> **Thought 3.** Think of the outcome of disease that will occur when the next war breaks out: the unsanitary conditions and the outbreak of both old and new diseases such as we witnessed with the venereal diseases, flu epidemics, small pox, polio, measles, aids, and diphtheria. And there will be little if any medical supplies.

⇒ Wild beasts will help to kill that many people. That is, due to war and the transplanting of people, billions of people, especially children, will be homeless. This rider is responsible for exposing people to the beasts of the forests and jungles who will be just as hungry and insane from the lack of food as people will be.

> **You will hear of wars and rumors of wars, but see to it that you are not alarmed. Such things must happen, but the end is still to come. Nation will rise against nation, and kingdom against kingdom. There will be famines and earthquakes in various places. (Mat 24:6-7)**

> **Thought 4.** The picture of the four horsemen of the Apocalypse is not a pretty picture; nevertheless, any thinking and honest person knows that it is a real possibility with the weapons of war that exist today. The truth is: Holy Scripture says that it is going to happen. It will happen right before the events of the end time are to be launched by God. But as terrible as the four horsemen events are, they are not the worst judgments that are to take place upon earth. The worst will still lie ahead when the end time itself is launched. These judgments are just the seal judgments. The end time judgments are called the *trumpet judgments* and the *bowl judgments*. May God help us to turn to the Lord Jesus Christ for salvation before the end comes.

| | **B. The Lamb Breaks the Fifth Seal: The Slain Martyrs, 6:9-11** | voice, "How long, Sovereign Lord, holy and true, until you judge the inhabitants of the earth and avenge our blood?" 11 Then each of them was | |
|---|---|---|---|
| 1 They are under the altar | 9 When he opened the fifth seal, I saw under the altar the souls of those who had been slain because of the word of God and the testimony they had maintained. | given a white robe, and they were told to wait a little longer, until the number of their fellow servants and brothers who were to be killed as they had been was completed. | 4 They are given white robes<br>5 They are assured of justice |
| 2 They are slain for God's Word & testimony | | | |
| 3 They are crying for justice | 10 They called out in a loud | | |

# DIVISION IV

## THE SEVEN SEAL JUDGMENTS: EVENTS PRECEDING THE GREAT TRIBULATION, 6:1-7:17

### B. The Lamb Breaks the Fifth Seal: The Slain Martyrs, 6:9-11

(6:9-11) **Introduction**: the dramatic moment has arrived. God's book—the Book of Destiny, the great book of history, the book that spells out the future of the world—is now being opened. There is only one Person worthy enough to open it—the Son of God, the Lord Jesus Christ Himself. The book is so important and secretive, it contains such important subjects, that God has had seven seals tied around it for all of eternity. No one has ever seen the contents of the book; no one has ever seen the events that are to happen at the end of the world. But now, in the most dramatic of moments, Jesus Christ has stepped forward to the throne of God and taken the book out of God's extended hand. Standing around the throne with pounding hearts burning with anticipation were all the heavenly host and John the apostle to whom God was giving this vision. Then the most astounding thing happened. When Jesus Christ began to break the seals in order to open the book—when He broke the first seal, out from under the seal leaped a horseman. What was written in the book was actually leaping off its pages and being acted out before John and the heavenly host. It was like a dramatic book of pictures or of a movie of the future, of the events that are to happen in the end time.

But note a significant fact: Christ has not yet opened the book or scroll; He is merely breaking the seals. What John and heaven are witnessing are the events that are to happen right before the end time, the period of history that Jesus Christ called "the beginning of birth pains" or "the beginning of sorrows." Again, the events of the seals are preliminary to the end time. They are coming upon the earth *before the end time*. They have to be broken—their breaking open has to take place before the book and its events can be seen. Four seals were broken in the previous passage. When they were, the four horsemen of the Apocalypse leaped forth and executed their wrath upon the world. Now it is time for the dramatic breaking of the fifth seal, time for another astounding event to leap across the scene of world history.

1. They are under the alter (v.9).
2. They are slain for God's Word and testimony (v.9).
3. They are crying for justice (v.10).
4. They are given white robes (v.11).
5. They are assured of justice (v.11).

**1** (6:9) **Fifth Seal—Martyrs—Altar, Heavenly**: the Lamb of God, the Lord Jesus Christ, breaks the fifth seal. When He does, the souls of all the martyrs of the world are seen under the altar of God. This could be a picture of all the martyrs who have died for the Lord Jesus Christ down through the ages. It tells us where their souls are. But note: this particular reference is probably to the martyrs of the end time. The fact that they cry out for justice against those who killed them and that judgment falls in the sixth seal points to the reference being to the end time martyrs. But what John and the heavenly host see is probably the souls of all martyrs, for the souls of all are no doubt living together before God. This is a most precious thought: the martyrs of God are very special to God, and because of their strong testimony and sacrifice for Him, they hold a very special place before Him.

The slain martyrs are under the altar. Remember what Scripture teaches about the tabernacle: the furnishings of the tabernacle were only patterns of the worship center in heaven (cp. Ex.25:8-9, 40; Num.8:4; Heb.8:5; 9:23). This means that there is a perfected altar of sacrifice in the throne room of heaven. What is the altar of sacrifice or what is called in the Bible the altar of burnt offering or brazen altar? (See note and DEEPER STUDY # 1—Heb.9:11-14; cp. Ex.39:39.) It was the altar where the animals were sacrificed. The blood was poured out at the foot of the altar, symbolizing that the animal was being sacrificed for the person offering it.

This is the picture here: the lives of the martyrs, their blood, has been sacrificed and poured out for God. The martyrs have offered their lives up for God, paid the supreme price and literally sacrificed all they were for God. They offered up their lives upon the altar of sacrifice for God. Therefore, in heaven the martyrs have a very special place before God: they stand at the foot of the altar. They are a group of believers who are given a very special place near to God for all of eternity.

**Thought 1.** There is a strong lesson in this for all believers of all ages. God has a very special place for those who are faithful until death, a place that is close and dear to His heart and throne. This should stir us to be faithful every minute of every day. What a precious and heartwarming thought! To be close to God, close to His throne and presence, serving Him throughout all of eternity and then laying down one's life for Him.

> For whoever wants to save his life will lose it, but whoever loses his life for me will find it. (Mat 16:25)
> Then he said to them all: "If anyone would come after me, he must deny himself and take up his cross daily and follow me. (Luke 9:23)

Therefore, I urge you, brothers, in view of God's mercy, to offer your bodies as living sacrifices, holy and pleasing to God—this is your spiritual act of worship. Do not conform any longer to the pattern of this world, but be transformed by the renewing of your mind. Then you will be able to test and approve what God's will is—his good, pleasing and perfect will. (Rom 12:1-2)

Do you not know that your body is a temple of the Holy Spirit, who is in you, whom you have received from God? You are not your own; You were bought at a price. Therefore honor God with your body. (1 Cor 6:19-20)

But even if I am being poured out like a drink offering on the sacrifice and service coming from your faith, I am glad and rejoice with all of you. (Phil 2:17)

**2** (6:9) **Martyrs—Witnessing—Word of God**: the slain martyrs are slain for God's Word and for the testimony they had borne for Christ. There are two things here.

1. They were slain for the Word of God. In the last days of human history some people will still love Christ and still believe the Holy Scriptures. They will love the Word of God...

- believe it
- live by it
- read it
- study it
- witness to it
- teach it
- preach it
- pray over it

Because of this, the world will react against the Word of God and kill believers. Why?

⇒ The world will react because God's Word demands that a person give his first loyalty to Jesus Christ. In the end time under the antichrist, the peoples of the world will be required to give their first loyalty to the state. The government will demand loyalty to the state first, then the people can have freedom of religion and worship whatever god they wish. The state will develop the idea of what could be called a *state religion*, something close to what exists in some states today. Believers, of course, can only give their first loyalty to Christ; therefore, they will be killed, for they cannot deny the Word of God.

Having brought the apostles, they made them appear before the Sanhedrin to be questioned by the high priest. "We gave you strict orders not to teach in this name," he said. "Yet you have filled Jerusalem with your teaching and are determined to make us guilty of this man's blood." Peter and the other apostles replied: "We must obey God rather than men! (Acts 5:27-29)

⇒ The world will react because God's Word demands that a person live a pure and righteous life. In the end time people will be as they have always been: unwilling to give up the reins to their lives. They will continue to rebel against God, to do what they want, their own thing, instead of living like God says to live. But in the end time rebellion against God will be intensified. People will...

- reject God more
- curse God more
- deny God more
- ignore God more
- neglect God more
- disobey God more
- disbelieve God more

The point is this: the world in the end time will reject God's Word. The world and its government will demand that believers give their first allegiance to the state and that they keep quiet about the righteousness proclaimed in Scripture. The government will be like so many governments that deny a personal God and have a law against worshipping a personal God. The state will be atheistic and exalt itself as god.

Now the Bereans were of more noble character than the Thessalonians, for they received the message with great eagerness and examined the Scriptures every day to see if what Paul said was true. (Acts 17:11)

And we also thank God continually because, when you received the word of God, which you heard from us, you accepted it not as the word of men, but as it actually is, the word of God, which is at work in you who believe. (1 Th 2:13)

All Scripture is God-breathed and is useful for teaching, rebuking, correcting and training in righteousness, (2 Tim 3:16)

Therefore, get rid of all moral filth and the evil that is so prevalent and humbly accept the word planted in you, which can save you. Do not merely listen to the word, and so deceive yourselves. Do what it says. Anyone who listens to the word but does not do what it says is like a man who looks at his face in a mirror And, after looking at himself, goes away and immediately forgets what he looks like. But the man who looks intently into the perfect law that gives freedom, and continues to do this, not forgetting what he has heard, but doing it—he will be blessed in what he does. (James 1:21-25)

2. They were slain for the testimony they had borne concerning Jesus Christ. The martyrs will believe that Jesus Christ is the Son of God, the Savior of the world. They will believe that God loved the world so much that He sent His Son to save the world. But the world rejects Jesus Christ, His deity, that He is the Son of God. The world is willing to accept that Jesus Christ was a great religious and moral teacher but no more than that. In the end time the world's rejection of Christ as the Son of God will be intensified so much that they will kill all those who proclaim Christ to be the Son of God, the Savior of the world.

The believers of the end time will be martyred because they refuse to deny Christ. They will not deny their Savior and Lord, the Son of God Himself. (Cp. Rev.1:9; 12:11, 17; 19:10; 20:4 for other references where martyrs died for their testimony for Christ.)

Who is the liar? It is the man who denies that Jesus is the Christ. Such a man is the antichrist—he denies the Father and the Son. No one who denies the Son has the Father; whoever acknowledges the Son has the Father also. (1 John 2:22-23)

This is how you can recognize the Spirit of God: Every spirit that acknowledges that Jesus Christ has come in the flesh is from God, But every spirit that does not acknowledge Jesus is not from God. This is the spirit of the antichrist, which you have heard is coming and even now is already in the world. (1 John 4:2-3)

Anyone who believes in the Son of God has this testimony in his heart. Anyone who does not believe God has made him out to be a liar, because he has not believed the testimony God has given about his Son. And this is the testimony: God has given us eternal life, and this life is in his Son. He who has the Son has life; he who does not have the Son of God does not have life. I write these things to you who believe in the name of the Son of God so that you may know that you have eternal life. (1 John 5:10-13)

**Thought 1.** The altar is mentioned throughout Revelation (Rev.8:3, 5; 13; 11:1; 14:18; 16:7. In 8:3, 5 the altar would be the altar of incense.)

**3** (6:10) **Martyrs—Justice:** the slain martyrs cry out for justice. Note two facts.

1. They address God as the *Sovereign Lord, holy and true.*

  a. The Word used here for "Lord" (despotes) means Master or Sovereign. God is the supreme Master and Sovereign of the universe. Therefore, all prayer is to be directed to Him, for all lives belong to Him, the lives of the martyrs and the lives of their persecutors.

  b. God is holy, completely set apart from all other beings in the universe. He deserves to look upon nothing but righteousness and purity and holiness. The martyrs want all sin and evil erased so that God will not be disobeyed any more by unholy living. Therefore, they address Him as the Sovereign and holy Lord.

  c. God is true to His Word and promises. Therefore, He is the One who is to execute justice and bring all things to a climax in the end time. He is the One who has to stop all the evil and terrible things done by men. If justice is to be executed upon earth, He is the One who has to do it. Therefore, martyrs address God as the Sovereign Lord, holy and true.

2. The martyrs cry out for justice and for vengeance against their persecutors. This is shocking, that believers in heaven would seek vengeance against men upon earth instead of loving them and longing for them to be saved. Is this an accurate picture? No, it is not. This is not what the martyrs are doing. Their cry is a cry for vindication of the Word of God and of Christ, not a cry for vengeance. Note exactly what they are saying: they are crying out for God to avenge *their blood.* Why was their blood spilt? Why were they killed? Because the persecutors *rebelled against the Word of God and against Jesus Christ as the Son of God.* This is that for which the martyrs are crying, for vindication, not for vengeance. They are crying out for God...

• to stop the injustice against His Word and against His Son, the Lord Jesus Christ.
• to stop the injustice against His own glory and justice.

• to stop the injustice of sin and evil against Himself.
• to stop the injustice of unrighteousness and to bring righteousness to the universe.

They were, in essence, praying for God's kingdom to come upon earth. Their Lord had taught them to pray both "your kingdom come" as well as "forgive those who do evil against you."

Remember this as well: no one suffers the hell and wrath of sin any more than a martyr. A martyr has endured the greatest wrath and hell that sin can cast against a person: it is the fire and wrath of sin that kills him. Therefore, the martyr above all others knows how terrible sin insults and rages against God. When a martyr reaches heaven and sees the Lord and the Father and all the glory and majesty of heaven, and then begins to share with the Lord, the martyr is bound to cry out:

They called out in a loud voice, "How long, Sovereign Lord, holy and true, until you judge the inhabitants of the earth and avenge our blood?" (Rev 6:10)

How long will the enemy mock you, O God? Will the foe revile your name forever? (Psa 74:10)

How long, O LORD? Will you be angry forever? How long will your jealousy burn like fire? Pour out your wrath on the nations that do not acknowledge you, on the kingdoms that do not call on your name; (Psa 79:5-6)

How long will the wicked, O LORD, how long will the wicked be jubilant? They pour out arrogant words; all the evildoers are full of boasting. (Psa 94:3-4)

**4** (6:11) **Martyrs—White Robes:** the slain martyrs are given white robes. The white robes stand for purity and righteousness. Believers are made pure and righteous in the righteousness of Jesus Christ. These martyrs are wearing the robes that all believers upon the earth will wear, the white robes of the righteousness of Jesus Christ. (See note, pt.1—Rev.3:18-20 for more discussion.)

**5** (6:11) **Martyrs—Justice:** the slain martyrs are assured of justice.

1. Note a glorious thing: the martyrs are said to be *waiting* or *resting* in heaven.

  ⇒ They are resting in the peace of Christ, free from all struggle.

There remains, then, a Sabbath-rest for the people of God; (Heb 4:9)

Then each of them was given a white robe, and they were told to wait a little longer, until the number of their fellow servants and brothers who were to be killed as they had been was completed. (Rev 6:11)

  ⇒ They are resting from all their exhausting labor upon earth.

Then I heard a voice from heaven say, "Write: Blessed are the dead who die in the Lord from now on." "Yes," says the Spirit, "they will rest from their labor, for their deeds will follow them." (Rev 14:13)

⇒ They are resting from the wicked of the earth.

> There the wicked cease from turmoil, and there the weary are at rest. (Job 3:17)

⇒ They are resting from all the trials and temptations of life; they are to be freed from all tears and sorrow and crying and pain and death.

> He will wipe every tear from their eyes. There will be no more death or mourning or crying or pain, for the old order of things has passed away." (Rev 21:4)

⇒ They are resting in the perfection of a new life, even in the righteousness of Jesus Christ.

> Therefore, if anyone is in Christ, he is a new creation; the old has gone, the new has come! (2 Cor 5:17)
> God made him who had no sin to be sin for us, so that in him we might become the righteousness of God. (2 Cor 5:21)
> And to put on the new self, created to be like God in true righteousness and holiness. (Eph 4:24)
> He who was seated on the throne said, "I am making everything new!" Then he said, "Write this down, for these words are trustworthy and true." (Rev 21:5)

> Those who walk uprightly enter into peace; they find rest as they lie in death. (Isa 57:2)

2. Note what the Lord tells the martyrs: it will still be a little while before the end of the world comes. The question is not whether or not the end will ever come. It *is coming*. It is just that it is not yet time. There is still to be more witness borne to the world. The name of Jesus Christ has not been proclaimed enough to the world, not yet. And some believers are still to be martyred for the name of Christ. The number of martyrs are not yet fulfilled. The place for martyrs in heaven is not yet filled. More believers must be sold out to Christ and on fire proclaiming His salvation; more believers must die for His testimony before the end comes.

**Thought 1.** What a dynamic challenge for us! To be on fire for God and to be proclaiming Jesus Christ! We must not fear; we must be willing to witness for Him even if it means that we must die for Him and His cause of eternal salvation.

> So do not be ashamed to testify about our Lord, or ashamed of me his prisoner. But join with me in suffering for the gospel, by the power of God, (2 Tim 1:8)
> Bear in mind that our Lord's patience means salvation, just as our dear brother Paul also wrote you with the wisdom that God gave him. (2 Pet 3:15)
> But you will receive power when the Holy Spirit comes on you; and you will be my witnesses in Jerusalem, and in all Judea and Samaria, and to the ends of the earth." (Acts 1:8)
> For we cannot help speaking about what we have seen and heard." (Acts 4:20)

| | C. The Lamb Breaks the Sixth Seal: The Great Day of God's Wrath Begins—The Universe Will Be Shattered, 6:12-17 | scroll, rolling up, and every mountain and island was removed from its place. | & the mountains & islands will be removed |
|---|---|---|---|
| | | 15 Then the kings of the earth, the princes, the generals, the rich, the mighty, and every slave and every free man hid in caves and among the rocks of the mountains. | 2 The effects of God's wrath upon people<br>a. Great fear will grip all the unbelievers upon earth |
| 1 The effects of God's wrath upon the universe<br>a. A great earthquake<br>b. The sun & moon will be blackened & eclipsed & the stars or meteorites will shower the earth | 12 I watched as he opened the sixth seal. There was a great earthquake. The sun turned black like sackcloth made of goat hair, the whole moon turned blood red,<br>13 And the stars in the sky fell to earth, as late figs drop from a fig tree when shaken by a strong wind. | 16 They called to the mountains and the rocks, "Fall on us and hide us from the face of him who sits on the throne and from the wrath of the Lamb!<br>17 For the great day of their wrath has come, and who can | b. All unbelievers will cry for death<br>3 The reason for the catastrophes & the panic of men<br>a. The face of God<br>b. The Lamb's wrath<br>c. The great day of wrath & judgment has come |
| c. The heavens will disappear | 14 The sky receded like a | stand?" | d. The judgment of all |

# DIVISION IV

## THE SEVEN SEAL JUDGMENTS: EVENTS PRECEDING THE GREAT TRIBULATION, 6:1-7:17

### C. The Lamb Breaks the Sixth Seal: The Great Day of God's Wrath Begins—The Universe Will Be Shattered, 6:12-17

(6:12-17) **Introduction**: the sixth seal is now broken and the great day of God's wrath begins. The universe is shattered; both heaven and earth feel the judgment of natural catastrophes. But remember: this is still not the end of the world; it is still not the final judgment. The seals of the Book of Destiny have to be broken before the book can be read. Therefore, the seal judgments are events that are to happen right before the end begins. Here is the beginning of God's wrath against the violence, hatred, and rebellion of a corrupt and evil world.

1. The effects of God's wrath upon the universe (v.12-14)
2. The effects of God's wrath upon people (v.15-16).
3. The reason for the catastrophes and the panic of men (v.16-17).

**1** (6:12-14) **Judgment—Universe—World**: there are the effects of God's judgment upon the universe.

1. There will be a great earthquake. Note the word *great*. This will be no ordinary earthquake. The idea is that it will be beyond anything ever known to man. Imagine the destruction of property, the loss of life, the fear gripping the hearts of people, and the further damage caused by the aftershocks of the earthquake.

⇒ Jesus Christ Himself predicted there would be more earthquakes in the latter days than ever before.

**Nation will rise against nation, and kingdom against kingdom. There will be famines and earthquakes in various places. (Mat 24:7)**

⇒ Revelation mentions three great earthquakes.

**I watched as he opened the sixth seal. There was a great earthquake. The sun turned black like sackcloth made of goat hair, the whole moon turned blood red, (Rev 6:12)**

**At that very hour there was a severe earthquake and a tenth of the city collapsed. Seven thousand people were killed in the earthquake, and the survivors were terrified and gave glory to the God of heaven. (Rev 11:13)**

**The seventh angel poured out his bowl into the air, and out of the temple came a loud voice from the throne, saying, "It is done!" Then there came flashes of lightning, rumblings, peals of thunder and a severe earthquake. No earthquake like it has ever occurred since man has been on earth, so tremendous was the quake. The great city split into three parts, and the cities of the nations collapsed. God remembered Babylon the Great and gave her the cup filled with the wine of the fury of his wrath. (Rev 16:17-19)**

⇒ The Old Testament predicted earthquakes in the end time.

**In my zeal and fiery wrath I declare that at that time there shall be a great earthquake in the land of Israel. (Ezek 38:19)**

**I looked at the mountains, and they were quaking; all the hills were swaying. (Jer 4:24)**

**"Will not the land tremble for this, and all who live in it mourn? The whole land will rise like the Nile; it will be stirred up and then sink like the river of Egypt. (Amos 8:8)**

**Before them the earth shakes, the sky trembles, the sun and moon are darkened, and the stars no longer shine. (Joel 2:10)**

**"This is what the LORD Almighty says: 'In a little while I will once more shake the heavens and the earth, the sea and the dry land. (Hag 2:6)**

2. The sun and moon will be eclipsed and blackened and stars or meteorites will shower the earth. Very practically there are times when such astronomical happenings occur now.

⇒ The heavenly bodies are sometimes darkened by such catastrophes as volcanic eruptions, wind storms, and smoke from fires. Of course whatever darkens the sun hides the light of the moon and stars from earth.

⇒ Stars or meteorites of varying sizes fall from outer space to earth quite often.

Is this what is meant by these passages or is there to be *unbelievable disorder* inflicted upon some of the stars above, disorder causing massive explosions and fireworks and hurling meteorites throughout space—a volcanic eruption in the heavens that affects all the universe? There is no way to know. All we know is that there is going to be a severe intensification of astronomical happenings, and they will begin right before the end time comes.

Scripture declares emphatically that these events will occur during the end times. (Note: the stars fall to earth only two times: here when the sixth seal is broken [Rev.6:13], and after the tribulation when Christ returns to earth [Mt.24:29-31]).

⇒ Astronomical happenings will occur right before the end time.

**And the stars in the sky fell to earth, as late figs drop from a fig tree when shaken by a strong wind. (Rev 6:13)**

⇒ Astronomical happenings occur during the tribulation.

**The fourth angel sounded his trumpet, and a third of the sun was struck, a third of the moon, and a third of the stars, so that a third of them turned dark. A third of the day was without light, and also a third of the night. (Rev 8:12)**

**When he opened the Abyss, smoke rose from it like the smoke from a gigantic furnace. The sun and sky were darkened by the smoke from the Abyss. (Rev 9:2)**

**The fifth angel poured out his bowl on the throne of the beast, and his kingdom was plunged into darkness. Men gnawed their tongues in agony (Rev 16:10)**

⇒ Astronomical happenings will occur right after the tribulation when the day of the Lord comes.

**"Immediately after the distress of those days "'the sun will be darkened, and the moon will not give its light; the stars will fall from the sky, and the heavenly bodies will be shaken.' (Mat 24:29)**

**See, the day of the LORD is coming—a cruel day, with wrath and fierce anger— to make the land desolate and destroy the sinners within it. The stars of heaven and their constellations will not show their light. The rising sun will be darkened and the moon will not give its light. I will punish the world for its evil, the wicked for their sins. I will put an end to the arrogance of the haughty and will humble the pride of the ruthless. (Isa 13:9-11)**

**In that day the LORD will punish the powers in the heavens above and the kings on the earth below. They will be herded together like prisoners bound in a dungeon; they will be shut up in prison and be punished after many days. The moon will be abashed, the sun ashamed; for the LORD Almighty will reign on Mount Zion and in Jerusalem, and before its elders, gloriously. (Isa 24:21-23)**

**When I snuff you out, I will cover the heavens and darken their stars; I will cover the sun with a cloud, and the moon will not give its light. All the shining lights in the heavens I will darken over you; I will bring darkness over your land, declares the Sovereign LORD. (Ezek 32:7-8)**

**I will show wonders in the heavens and on the earth, blood and fire and billows of smoke. The sun will be turned to darkness and the moon to blood before the coming of the great and dreadful day of the LORD. (Joel 2:30-31)**

**The sun and moon will be darkened, and the stars no longer shine. The LORD will roar from Zion and thunder from Jerusalem; the earth and the sky will tremble. But the LORD will be a refuge for his people, a stronghold for the people of Israel. (Joel 3:15-16)**

3. The heavens will disappear and the mountains and the hills will be moved out of their place. What does this mean? Note that men are so frightened that they cry for the mountains and rocks to fall upon them. This is a prophetic way to describe the devastation of the astronomical happenings and the great earthquake and meteorites falling to earth.

**All the stars of the heavens will be dissolved and the sky rolled up like a scroll; all the starry host will fall like withered leaves from the vine, like shriveled figs from the fig tree. (Isa 34:4)**

**In the beginning you laid the foundations of the earth, and the heavens are the work of your hands. They will perish, but you remain; they will all wear out like a garment. Like clothing you will change them and they will be discarded. (Psa 102:25-26)**

**I looked at the mountains, and they were quaking; all the hills were swaying. (Jer 4:24)**

**The mountains quake before him and the hills melt away. The earth trembles at his presence, the world and all who live in it. (Nahum 1:5)**

**2** (6:15-16) **Judgment—Universe—World**: there are the effects of God's judgment upon people. Note two significant things.

1. Great fear will grip all unbelievers upon earth. Note the list of those who fear:

⇒ The kings and rulers of the earth will fear.
⇒ The great and powerful of the earth will fear.
⇒ The rich and wealthy of the earth will fear.
⇒ The military chiefs of the earth will fear.
⇒ The mighty and the strong of the earth will fear.
⇒ The slave and insignificant of the earth will fear.
⇒ The free and independent of the earth will fear.

Every unbeliever upon earth will be stricken with terror, a maddening terror. They will be so frightened that panic will sweep the earth. No one is going to escape the judgment of God, and they all know it. And there is no partiality with God; God has no favorites. The world of unbelievers will quake in terror and fright before the unusual events happening in outer space and upon earth. There will be a sense, an awareness, a consciousness that the judgment of God is looming right over the horizon. The very atmosphere of the earth will be heavy with the feeling that the end is at hand.

**Wail, for the day of the LORD is near; it will come like destruction from the Almighty. Terror will seize them, pain and anguish will grip them; they will writhe like a woman in labor. They will look aghast at each other, their faces aflame. (Isa 13:6, 8)**
**"The great day of the LORD is near— near and coming quickly. Listen! The cry on the day of the LORD will be bitter, the shouting of the warrior there. (Zep 1:14)**
**Blow the trumpet in Zion; sound the alarm on my holy hill. Let all who live in the land tremble, for the day of the LORD is coming. It is close at hand— (Joel 2:1)**

2. All unbelievers will cry for death. The terror and fright will be so maddening that the world will panic. People will be madly rushing about to hide in the secret dens and rocks of the earth, begging to die and to be annihilated in order to keep from having to face God's eternal judgment.

**Then "'they will say to the mountains, "Fall on us!" And to the hills, "Cover us!"'" (Luke 23:30)**
**Men will flee to caves in the rocks and to holes in the ground from dread of the LORD and the splendor of his majesty, when he rises to shake the earth. (Isa 2:19)**
**The LORD thunders at the head of his army; his forces are beyond number, and mighty are those who obey his command. The day of the LORD is great; it is dreadful. Who can endure it? (Joel 2:11)**
**The high places of wickedness will be destroyed— it is the sin of Israel. Thorns and thistles will grow up and cover their altars. Then they will say to the mountains,**

**"Cover us!" And to the hills, "Fall on us!" (Hosea 10:8)**

**3** (6-17) **Day of the Lord—Judgment**: there is the reason for the catastrophes throughout the universe and for the panic of men—the great day of God's wrath is at hand. What is the great day of God's wrath? These two verses tell us.

⇒ It is the day when all unbelievers must stand before the face of God who sits upon the throne of the universe.
⇒ It is the day when all unbelievers must face the wrath of the Lamb; the day when they must face the Son of God Himself, the Lord Jesus Christ whom they have rejected, denied, cursed, disobeyed, disbelieved, ignored, and neglected.
⇒ It is the great day of His wrath, the very day that His wrath is to fall, the very day that every unbeliever must face Him.
⇒ It is the day when no unbeliever shall stand, the day when all unbelievers shall crumble and be subjected to the humiliation of eternal guilt, condemnation, and punishment.

John Walvoord puts it in simple and striking words:

"The Day of the Lord is a period of time in which God will deal with wicked men directly and dramatically in fearful judgment. Today a man may be a blasphemer of God, an atheist, can denounce God and teach bad doctrine. Seemingly God does nothing about it. But the day designated in Scripture as 'the day of the Lord' is coming when God will punish human sin, and He will deal in wrath and in judgment with a Christ-rejecting world. One thing we are sure of, that God in His own way will bring every soul into judgment" (*The Thessalonian Epistles*. Grand Rapids, MI: Zondervan, 1967, p.76).

But remember: this is a picture of what will be happening right before the Day of the Lord comes. It has not yet come. The end time has not yet happened. This event—the catastrophe in the heavens and on earth and the fright and panic that strikes people with maddening terror—all this is right before the end times begin. This is just the breaking of the seals of God's book on the destiny of the world. The events within the pages of the book—the worst judgments—are yet to come.

**Thought 1.** The message to all people everywhere is twofold:

1) All unbelievers will stand face to face with God on the great day of His wrath, and the day is right over the horizon.

⇒ The wrath of God is coming upon the rich and the powerful who thought they were self-sufficient.
⇒ The wrath of God is coming upon the religious who thought they could be good enough and do enough good to be acceptable to God.
⇒ The wrath of God is coming upon the poor who thought they were too insignificant or else thought their oppression would cause God to look upon them with mercy.

⇒ The wrath of God is coming upon the intelligent who thought they were too knowledgeable to believe in Christ.

⇒ The wrath of God is coming upon the scientist and technician because they thought they had progressed so far they could disprove God.

2) We must trust Jesus Christ and escape the great day of God's wrath.

**There is a judge for the one who rejects me and does not accept my words; that very word which I spoke will condemn him at the last day. (John 12:48)**

**But because of your stubbornness and your unrepentant heart, you are storing up wrath against yourself for the day of God's wrath, when his righteous judgment will be revealed. (Rom 2:5)**

**For the great day of their wrath has come, and who can stand?" (Rev 6:17)**

**The eyes of the arrogant man will be humbled and the pride of men brought low; the LORD alone will be exalted in that day. The LORD Almighty has a day in store for all the proud and lofty, for all that is exalted (and they will be humbled), (Isa 2:11-12)**

**See, the day of the LORD is coming —a cruel day, with wrath and fierce anger— to make the land desolate and destroy the sinners within it. The stars of heaven and their constellations will not show their light. The rising sun will be darkened and the moon will not give its light. I will punish the world for its evil, the wicked for their sins. I will put an end to the arrogance of the haughty and will humble the pride of the ruthless. (Isa 13:9-11)**

**"The great day of the LORD is near— near and coming quickly. Listen! The cry on the day of the LORD will be bitter, the shouting of the warrior there. That day will be a day of wrath, a day of distress and anguish, a day of trouble and ruin, a day of darkness and gloom, a day of clouds and blackness, A day of trumpet and battle cry against the fortified cities and against the corner towers. (Zep 1:14-16)**

**"Surely the day is coming; it will burn like a furnace. All the arrogant and every evildoer will be stubble, and that day that is coming will set them on fire," says the LORD Almighty. "Not a root or a branch will be left to them. (Mal 4:1)**

| | CHAPTER 7 | the sea or the trees until we put a seal on the foreheads of the servants of our God." | |
|---|---|---|---|
| | **D. The Fate of Believers in the Great Tribulation (Part I): A Remnant of 144,000 From Israel Will Be Saved, 7:1-8** | 4 Then I heard the number of those who were sealed: 144,000 from all the tribes of Israel. | **3 God will give the wonderful counsel to seal 144,000 Jews from all the tribes of Israel** |
| **1 The winds of judgment are in the hands of God & His angels, not in the hands of evil** | After this I saw four angels standing at the four corners of the earth, holding back the four winds of the earth to prevent any wind from blowing on the land or on the sea or on any tree. 2 Then I saw another angel coming up from the east, having the seal of the living God. He called out in a loud voice to the four angels who had been given power to harm the land and the sea: 3 "Do not harm the land or | 5 From the tribe of Judah 12,000 were sealed, from the tribe of Reuben 12,000, from the tribe of Gad 12,000, 6 From the tribe of Asher 12,000, from the tribe of Naphtali 12,000, from the tribe of Manasseh 12,000, 7 From the tribe of Simeon 12,000, from the tribe of Levi 12,000, from the tribe of Issachar 12,000, 8 From the tribe of Zebulun 12,000, from the tribe of Joseph 12,000, from the tribe of Benjamin 12,000. | |
| **2 God will give the most wonderful command: To delay the judgments until God's people can be sealed** | | | |

# DIVISION IV

## THE SEVEN SEAL JUDGMENTS: EVENTS PRECEDING THE GREAT TRIBULATION, 6:1-7:17

### D. The Fate of Believers in the Great Tribulation (Part I): A Remnant of 144,000 From Israel Will Be Saved, 7:1-8

(7:1-8) **Introduction**: Jesus Christ is holding the great book of God in His hands, the Book of Destiny, the book that tells what is to happen at the end of the world. The book is so important and so secretive that God has it bound with seven seals until it is time for it to be opened. Remember: the events have not yet happened upon earth. They are things that are to happen in the end time. But God has given us a glimpse into the things. Why? To warn us to turn to His Son. Christ alone can save us from the judgment to come. Therefore, we must follow Him ever so diligently while we walk upon earth. This glimpse into the great book of God, into the destiny of the world, is given to us in this great book of Revelation. We have just seen Jesus Christ break open six of the seals that bind the book. To our horror, when He broke them open, the four horsemen of the Apocalypse were seen storming across the face of the earth with their terror and devastation. We have seen how the four horsemen represent the wars and killing, famine and pestilence, hunger and starvation, death and hell that the antichrist will unleash upon the earth. We have seen how evil will mass together every force of demonic power it can in order to make a final assault upon the earth. And we have seen that the destructive devastation will kill one fourth of the world's population. Shocking! One fourth of the population will be killed by the catastrophic devastation of evil unleashed upon the earth. But to our horror, this is not all. God's great book declares this is just the *beginning of birth pains [sorrows] and woes*. But this terrible devastation, as horrible as it is, is nothing compared to what is yet to come. When all the judgments have fallen, the earth and the world shall be utterly destroyed. How it is to happen will be seen when the seventh seal is broken open. When the seventh seal is broken, the seven seal judgments are over; the period of history that will be known as the *beginning of birth pains [sorrows] and woes* will be finished. But the *great tribulation* itself will be launched by the seventh seal..

- the *great tribulation* that will witness the shattering blast of seven trumpets of judgment.
- the *great tribulation* that will witness the wrath of seven bowls of judgment poured out upon the earth.

Now, for a critical question: Will anyone be saved through such terrible days? Can anyone survive such terrible happenings? As Scripture itself has just asked:

**For the great day of their wrath has come, and who can stand?" (Rev 6:17)**

Can anyone stand? Will anyone turn to the Lord and be delivered through this terrible time? Yes! There is to be a remnant of Israel saved: 144,000 Jews shall be saved.

1. The winds of judgment are in the hands of God and His angels, not in the hands of evil (v.1-2).
2. God will give the most wonderful command: to delay the judgments until God's people can be sealed (v.2-3).
3. God will give the wonderful counsel to seal 144,000 Jews from all the tribes of Israel (v.4-8).

**1** (7:1-2) **End Time—Israel—Jews—Salvation**: the winds of judgment are in the hands of God and His angels, not in the hands of evil. This is a most wonderful truth, and it is exactly what is being declared here. Four angels stand at the four corners of the earth holding the four winds of judgment so that they cannot blow upon the earth. "The four corners of the earth are the four main points of the compass: north, south, east, and west" (Lehman Strauss. *The Book of the Revelation*. Neptune, NJ: Loizeaux Brothers, 1964, p.170). The picture is that God is in control of the whole earth, of every direction upon earth. And He is merciful. He has not unleashed His avenging angels of wrath upon earth, not yet. In mercy He has chosen to wait a little while longer.

**Thought 1.** This is a most comforting thought: to know that judgment is in the hands of God; to know that it is God Himself who is to execute judgment. It is comforting because of what Jesus Christ has done for us. Just think! Every person has the privilege of escaping judgment. No person has to stand before the face of God at the throne of judgment. Every person can be saved and delivered from condemnation by receiving the Lord Jesus Christ as his Lord and Savior.

But note: the winds of judgment are to be unleashed upon the earth. Every person will face these awful times unless he has surrendered his life to Christ. And then most tragic of all, he will have to face the eternal judgment and condemnation from the presence of God forever.

> **"When the Son of Man comes in his glory, and all the angels with him, he will sit on his throne in heavenly glory. All the nations will be gathered before him, and he will separate the people one from another as a shepherd separates the sheep from the goats. (Mat 25:31-32)**
>
> **By the same word the present heavens and earth are reserved for fire, being kept for the day of judgment and destruction of ungodly men. (2 Pet 3:7)**
>
> **And I saw the dead, great and small, standing before the throne, and books were opened. Another book was opened, which is the book of life. The dead were judged according to what they had done as recorded in the books. The sea gave up the dead that were in it, and death and Hades gave up the dead that were in them, and each person was judged according to what he had done. Then death and Hades were thrown into the lake of fire. The lake of fire is the second death. If anyone's name was not found written in the book of life, he was thrown into the lake of fire. (Rev 20:12-15)**

**2** (7:2-3) **Seal—Israel, Salvation of**: God will give the most wonderful command. The command will be to delay the judgments of the great tribulation until all the servants of God can be sealed. The *seal* means the mark of possession, authority, power, protection, and preservation.

⇒ In ancient times a king's ring was his seal. He would stamp the mark of his ring upon all official documents showing their possession, authority, and power. This is certainly part of the meaning here. The 144,000 will be sealed—protected and preserved—by God (cp. Gen. 41:42; Esther 3:10; 8:2; Dan.6:17; Mt.27:66).

> **They were told not to harm the grass of the earth or any plant or tree, but only those people who did not have the seal of God on their foreheads. (Rev 9:4)**
>
> **Then I looked, and there before me was the Lamb, standing on Mount Zion, and with him 144,000 who had his name and his Father's name written on their foreheads. (Rev 14:1)**
>
> **They will see his face, and his name will be on their foreheads. (Rev 22:4)**

> **"Do not harm the land or the sea or the trees until we put a seal on the foreheads of the servants of our God." (Rev 7:3)**
>
> **And said to him, "Go throughout the city of Jerusalem and put a mark on the foreheads of those who grieve and lament over all the detestable things that are done in it." (Ezek 9:4)**

⇒ In the New Testament the believer is sealed with the Spirit of God; that is, the Holy Spirit seals and guarantees that the believer belongs to God. The presence of the Holy Spirit living within the heart and life of the believer is his seal and his guarantee that he will escape the judgment of God and live eternally with God.

> **Who is a deposit guaranteeing our inheritance until the redemption of those who are God's possession—to the praise of his glory. (Eph 1:14)**
>
> **Set his seal of ownership on us, and put his Spirit in our hearts as a deposit, guaranteeing what is to come. (2 Cor 1:22)**
>
> **Now it is God who has made us for this very purpose and has given us the Spirit as a deposit, guaranteeing what is to come. (2 Cor 5:5)**

In contrast to the seal of God upon His servants, the lawless and rebellious followers of the beast (the antichrist) will bear his mark or seal (Rev.16:2). God will seal His servants to identify them and to assure their protection from the wrath and destruction coming upon the earth. Remember: God does not condemn His followers. His followers escape the judgment of God. The judgment and destruction from God's hands fall only on "those men which have not the seal of God on their foreheads." This is clearly stated in Revelation.

⇒ The demonic forces that are to be unleashed upon earth will not touch God's people.

> **They were told not to harm the grass of the earth or any plant or tree, but only those people who did not have the seal of God on their foreheads. (Rev 9:4)**

⇒ The bowl judgment of sores will not touch God's people. Judgment is poured out only upon those who have the mark of the beast.

> **The first angel went and poured out his bowl on the land, and ugly and painful sores broke out on the people who had the mark of the beast and worshiped his image. (Rev 16:2)**

This should not seem strange to us, that God will judge the unbelievers who follow the antichrist and not judge believers. As stated, God does not condemn His people; He condemns and judges unbelievers. And the judgments of the great tribulation are to be upon an evil and apostate world. A good example is Moses and the plagues of Israel. Remember the event: the ten plagues, as terrible and devastating as they were, fell upon all the Egyptians; but they did not afflict the believers among Israel. The true believers were *sealed* from the plagues.

However, it should be remembered that believers will be persecuted and slaughtered by the antichrist during the last three and a half years of his reign, that is, during the great tribulation (cp. Rev.7:14). The believers of the end time will not suffer the judgments of God upon the apostate world, but they will suffer the persecution of the antichrist.

> **The Lord is not slow in keeping his promise, as some understand slowness. He is patient with you, not wanting anyone to perish, but everyone to come to repentance. (2 Pet 3:9)**
>
> **Enoch, the seventh from Adam, prophesied about these men: "See, the Lord is coming with thousands upon thousands of his holy ones To judge everyone, and to convict all the ungodly of all the ungodly acts they have done in the ungodly way, and of all the harsh words ungodly sinners have spoken against him." (Jude 1:14-15)**
>
> **And that you, O Lord, are loving. Surely you will reward each person according to what he has done. (Psa 62:12)**
>
> **"I the LORD search the heart and examine the mind, to reward a man according to his conduct, according to what his deeds deserve." (Jer 17:10)**

**Thought 1.** God gives the most wonderful promises to genuine believers. No believer will ever be judged and condemned to death and hell. There is nothing, absolutely nothing, that can separate a genuine believer from the love of God.

> **"For God so loved the world that he gave his one and only Son, that whoever believes in him shall not perish but have eternal life. (John 3:16)**
>
> **"I tell you the truth, whoever hears my word and believes him who sent me has eternal life and will not be condemned; he has crossed over from death to life. (John 5:24)**
>
> **But God demonstrates his own love for us in this: While we were still sinners, Christ died for us. Since we have now been justified by his blood, how much more shall we be saved from God's wrath through him! For if, when we were God's enemies, we were reconciled to him through the death of his Son, how much more, having been reconciled, shall we be saved through his life! (Rom 5:8-10)**
>
> **Who shall separate us from the love of Christ? Shall trouble or hardship or persecution or famine or nakedness or danger or sword? As it is written: "For your sake we face death all day long; we are considered as sheep to be slaughtered." No, in all these things we are more than conquerors through him who loved us. For I am convinced that neither death nor life, neither angels nor demons, neither the present nor the future, nor any powers, Neither height nor depth, nor anything else in all creation, will be able to separate us from the love of**

> **God that is in Christ Jesus our Lord. (Rom 8:35-39)**
>
> **How great is the love the Father has lavished on us, that we should be called children of God! And that is what we are! The reason the world does not know us is that it did not know him. (1 John 3:1)**

**3** (7:4-8) **Israel—Salvation**: God will give the wonderful counsel to seal 144,000 Jewish believers. And note: there will be 12,000 from each of the twelve tribes. This is exactly what this passage says. This is clear indication that Israel will be saved in the end time. This is exactly what Christ revealed to Paul. (See outline and notes—Romans chapters 9-11 where the problem of Israel is dealt with. Especially see outline and notes, *Restoration of Israel and Its Surety*—Ro.11:25-36.)

This passage should be taken at its face value, that is, that 144,000 Jews will be converted during the great distress or the great tribulation. There are several strong reasons for this.

1. This passage says that 144,000 Jews will be converted. This is the very subject of chapter seven: to show who is to be saved during the tribulation. The answer is that both Jews and Gentiles will be saved, some 144,000 Jews and an innumerable number of Gentiles (v.9-17 of the next outline). This is described in the simplest and plainest of terms.

2. The 144,000 are apparently a special body of Jewish believers who are dedicated to serve the Lord Jesus Christ totally and wholly during the tribulation of the last days. Note three things that Revelation says about them. (See notes—Rev.14:4-5 for more discussion.)

 a. They are pure, that is, they kept themselves pure, undefiled by women. The days of the end time will be filled with horror after horror. The worst holocaust the world has ever witnessed will be launched by the antichrist and millions will be killed. A special commitment will be needed to stand up for Christ. Apparently, these 144,000 form a *special body of believers* who vow and commit their lives to the end to never deny Christ. They apparently take a special vow to be the encouragers and ministers to the believers and to the others who will be so severely attacked and persecuted by the antichrist. (The vow and commitment the 144,000 will take will be somewhat like the vow the Pharisees took when they first formed to stand against Antiochus Epiphanes. See DEEPER STUDY # 3, *Pharisees*—Acts 23:8.)

> **Because of the present crisis, I think that it is good for you to remain as you are. Are you married? Do not seek a divorce. Are you unmarried? Do not look for a wife. (1 Cor 7:26-27)**
>
> **These are those who did not defile themselves with women, for they kept themselves pure. They follow the Lamb wherever he goes. They were purchased from among men and offered as firstfruits to God and the Lamb. No lie was found in their mouths; they are blameless. (Rev 14:4-5)**

 b. They are called the servants of our God, followers of the Lamb wherever he goes They are a body of believers who give themselves to serve God while ungodliness and evil are raging in the end time.

They will be ministering, witnessing, and encouraging the believers and the Jews who are having to flee into the wilderness and hiding places of the world to escape the holocaust. The 144,000 will have a great part to play in the turning of Israel to Christ, their true Messiah, in the end time.

> **"Do not harm the land or the sea or the trees until we put a seal on the foreheads of the servants of our God." (Rev 7:3)**

c. They are said to be purchased, redeemed from among men (Jewish men), and offered as first-fruits to God and Christ. This simply means that they will be the first Jews to be saved in the tribulation.

> **These are those who did not defile themselves with women, for they kept themselves pure. They follow the Lamb wherever he goes. They were purchased from among men and offered as firstfruits to God and the Lamb. (Rev 14:4)**

3. This is undoubtedly part of the restoration of Israel. Christ clearly revealed that Israel was to be saved in the end time. (See outline and notes—Romans chapters 9-11; especially chapter eleven.)

> **God did not reject his people, whom he foreknew. Don't you know what the Scripture says in the passage about Elijah—how he appealed to God against Israel: (Rom 11:2)**
>
> **For if their rejection is the reconciliation of the world, what will their acceptance be but life from the dead? (Rom 11:15)**
>
> **And if they [Israel] do not persist in unbelief, they will be grafted in, for God is able to graft them in again. After all, if you [Gentile believers] were cut out of an olive tree that is wild by nature, and contrary to nature were grafted into a cultivated olive tree, how much more readily will these, the natural branches, be grafted into their own olive tree! (Rom 11:23-24)**
>
> **I do not want you to be ignorant of this mystery, brothers, so that you may not be conceited: Israel has experienced a hardening in part until the full number of the Gentiles has come in. And so all Israel will be saved, as it is written: "The deliverer will come from Zion; he will turn godlessness away from Jacob. (Rom 11:25-26)**

| | | |
|---|---|---|
| | **E. The Fate of Believers in the Great Tribulation (Part II): A Countless Number of People Will Be Saved, 7:9-17** | and strength be to our God for ever and ever. Amen!" |
| **1 Their origin: Everywhere**<br>a. All nations & tribes<br>b. All peoples & languages | 9 After this I looked and there before me was a great multitude that no one could count, from every nation, tribe, people and language, standing before the throne and in front of the Lamb. They were wearing white robes and were holding palm branches in their hands. | 13 Then one of the elders asked me, "These in white robes—who are they, and where did they come from?"<br>14 I answered, "Sir, you know." And he said, "These are they who have come out of the great tribulation; they have washed their robes and made them white in the blood of the Lamb. |
| **2 Their glorious position**<br>a. Before the throne & the Lamb<br>b. Clothed in white<br>c. Holding palm branches<br>d. Shouting praise for their salvation | 10 And they cried out in a loud voice: "Salvation belongs to our God, who sits on the throne, and to the Lamb." | 15 Therefore, "they are before the throne of God and serve him day and night in his temple; and he who sits on the throne will spread his tent over them. |
| **3 Their glorious companions**<br>a. The companions' identity: The angels, the elders, the four creatures<br>b. The function of the companions: To praise God for saving believers out of the tribulation | 11 All the angels were standing around the throne and around the elders and the four living creatures. They fell down on their faces before the throne and worshiped God,<br>12 Saying: "Amen! Praise and glory and wisdom and thanks and honor and power | 16 Never again will they hunger; never again will they thirst. The sun will not beat upon them, nor any scorching heat.<br>17 For the Lamb at the center of the throne will be their shepherd; he will lead them to springs of living water. And God will wipe away every tear from their eyes." |

| |
|---|
| **4 Their identity: An elder asks John for the people's identity**<br>a. They are people out of the great tribulation<br>b. They have washed their robes in the Lamb's blood |
| **5 Their function: To serve God continuously** |
| **6 Their blessings: Bliss**<br>a. They will have God's presence—forever<br>b. They will have their physical needs met<br>c. They will be protected<br>d. They will have their spiritual needs met<br>e. They will be led to the fountain of life<br>f. Their sorrow will be wiped away |

# DIVISION IV

## THE SEVEN SEAL JUDGMENTS: EVENTS PRECEDING THE GREAT TRIBULATION, 6:1-7:17

### E. The Fate of Believers in the Great Tribulation (Part II): A Countless Number of People Will Be Saved, 7:9-17

(7:9-17) **Introduction**: Who shall be saved during the awful tribulation coming upon earth? The terrible tribulation is coming in the end time, right before the end of the world. The time will be so terrible that one fourth of the earth's population will be destroyed by war, famine, pestilence, hunger, and starvation. It will be a time so terrible that the Bible calls it the period of Death and Hades (Hell). But remember this is just the beginning. There is to be a time of so much horror and fright that it can only be called the *great tribulation*. When it comes there will be no end to the destruction and loss of life.

The important question is this: Is there any hope? Is there any way that people can be saved during this period of great tribulation? Yes! There will be a countless multitude of believers saved.

1. Their origin: everywhere (v.9).
2. Their glorious position (v.9-10).
3. Their glorious companions (v.11-12).
4. Their identity: An elder asks John for the multitudes' identity (v.13-14).
5. Their function: To serve God continuously (v.15).
6. Their blessings: bliss (v.15-17).

**1** (7:9) **Salvation—Saved, The**: there is the origin of the countless numbers. Who are they? They are people from everywhere (cp. Rev.5:9).

⇒ From all nations: all, not just some; not even most, but from all nations.

⇒ From all tribes: there will not be a tribe from any place on earth left out. All tribes will have some people within them who will be saved in the great tribulation.

⇒ From all peoples: there will not be a people who will not have some saved from their number.

⇒ From all languages: there will not be a language from which there will not be some saved.

During the *great tribulation* there will be people who will turn to Christ by the millions. As terrible as the birth pains or sorrows and woes will be, the destruction and devastation will apparently stir people by the teeming millions to turn to Christ. This is glorious news: it means that the greatest revival in the history of the world will take place during the tribulation coming upon earth. Just imagine: "a great multitude that no one could count"—teeming millions standing before the throne of God in heaven. And as we shall see in a few moments, they come out of the terrible tribulation upon earth. There will be people saved during those awful days.

**Thought 1.** This means a most glorious thing: God never shuts the door against anyone who wills to give his heart and life to His Son, the Lord Jesus Christ.

**I say to you that many will come from the east and the west, and will take their places at the feast with Abraham, Isaac and Jacob in the kingdom of heaven. (Mat 8:11)**

For, "Everyone who calls on the name of the Lord will be saved." (Rom 10:13)

Who wants all men to be saved and to come to a knowledge of the truth. (1 Tim 2:4)

And they sang a new song: "You are worthy to take the scroll and to open its seals, because you were slain, and with your blood you purchased men for God from every tribe and language and people and nation. (Rev 5:9)

After this I looked and there before me was a great multitude that no one could count, from every nation, tribe, people and language, standing before the throne and in front of the Lamb. They were wearing white robes and were holding palm branches in their hands. (Rev 7:9)

These are those who did not defile themselves with women, for they kept themselves pure. They follow the Lamb wherever he goes. They were purchased from among men and offered as firstfruits to God and the Lamb. No lie was found in their mouths; they are blameless. (Rev 14:4-5)

Then I heard what sounded like a great multitude, like the roar of rushing waters and like loud peals of thunder, shouting: "Hallelujah! For our Lord God Almighty reigns. Let us rejoice and be glad and give him glory! For the wedding of the Lamb has come, and his bride has made herself ready. (Rev 19:6-7)

**2** (7:9-10) **Saved, The—Throne, God's**: there is the glorious position of the countless multitude. Note the four facts given about them.

1. They stand before the throne of God and before the Lamb, the Lord Jesus Christ. They have the most glorious of privileges:
⇒ to be near God and Christ
⇒ to be face to face with God and Christ
⇒ to be honored with the very presence of God and Christ
⇒ to know God and Christ in all Their fullness and being

2. They are clothed with white robes. This means they have been made pure and free from all the blemishes of sin and from all the corruption of the world—all by the righteousness of Jesus Christ. It means they have been perfected and stand before God perfected. The white robe of righteousness is...
• a sign of righteousness through Christ
• a sign of being made free from the defilement and smut of sin through Christ
• a sign of the victory over sin, death, and judgment through Christ
• a sign of being perfected forever through Christ
• a sign of being a heavenly creature, of having the glorious privilege of living forever in the presence of God through Christ.

3. They hold palm branches in their hands. The palms are symbols of celebration, triumph, victory, deliverance, and joy. The redeemed before God celebrate their triumph over the terrible tribulation and the sin, evil, death, and corruption of the world.
⇒ They celebrate their victory in Christ.
⇒ They celebrate their deliverance in Christ.
⇒ They celebrate their joy in Christ.

4. They shout praises for their salvation. Note what it is that they shout:

And they cried out in a loud voice: "Salvation belongs to our God, who sits on the throne, and to the Lamb." (Rev 7:10)

They praise God for salvation. They praise God...
• because God has saved and delivered them through the great trials upon earth.
• because God has given them the power to believe and to endure to the end.
• because God has accepted them.
• because God has given them the glorious privilege of His presence.
• because God has completed their salvation, perfected them forever and ever with His glory.

**Thought 1.** William Barclay has a statement about this point that is a dynamic challenge to us. His words should stir us to endure any trial or temptation, no matter how severe:

"God is the great saviour, the great rescuer, the great deliverer of His people, And the deliverance which God gives is the greatest deliverance of all, for it is not the deliverance of escape; it is the deliverance of conquest. It is not the deliverance which saves a man from trouble it is the deliverance which brings a man triumphantly through trouble. It does not make life easy, but it certainly makes life great. It is not part of the Christian hope to look for a life in which a man is saved from all trouble and distress; the Christian hope is that a man in Christ can endure any kind of trouble and distress, and remain erect all through them, and come out to glory on the other side" (*The Revelation of John*, Vol.2. "The Daily Study Bible." Philadelphia, PA: The Westminster Press, 1959, p.32).

**"For God so loved the world that he gave his one and only Son, that whoever believes in him shall not perish but have eternal life. (John 3:16)**

For the wages of sin is death, but the gift of God is eternal life in Christ Jesus our Lord. (Rom 6:23)

He who did not spare his own Son, but gave him up for us all—how will he not also, along with him, graciously give us all things? (Rom 8:32)

Thanks be to God for his indescribable gift! (2 Cor 9:15)

For it is by grace you have been saved, through faith—and this not from yourselves, it is the gift of God— (Eph 2:8)

For the grace of God that brings salvation has appeared to all men. It teaches us to say "No" to ungodliness and worldly passions, and to live self-controlled, upright** and godly lives in this present age, (Titus 2:11-12)

Through Jesus, therefore, let us continually offer to God a sacrifice of praise—the fruit of lips that confess his name. (Heb 13:15)

But you are a chosen people, a royal priesthood, a holy nation, a people belonging to God, that you may declare the praises of him who called you out of darkness into his wonderful light. (1 Pet 2:9)

**3** (7:11-12) **Angels—Elders—Four Living Creatures**: there are the companions of the countless multitude. This is a picture of all those who stand before the throne of God with the numberless multitude. It is the picture of wave after wave of different beings standing in circles before the throne of God.

⇒ The outer circle is the angels. Note that they surround or encircle the throne.

⇒ Next come the twenty-four elders.

⇒ Then there are the four living creatures who stand at the four corners of the throne.

⇒ Finally, as we have seen, there is the countless multitude of believers who stand face to face with the throne of God and the Lamb.

The countless multitude has just sung their praises to God for His great salvation. When they do, the rest of the heavenly beings fall down before the throne on their faces and worship God.

1. They praise God for His *praise*. Every good and perfect gift comes from God. These heavenly beings acknowledge this fact and praise God's name for it.

2. They praise God for His *glory*. God is glorious, the most glorious Person in all the universe. He is so glorious that His glory outshines the sun. It is the light of His glory that will provide the light of heaven. God is to be praised for the perfection of His glory. But note: God shares His glory with His creatures. Every creature in heaven is given and perfected in glory. God is to be praised for the gift of His glory as well as for His own glory.

3. They praise God for His *wisdom*. God is the *Supreme and Majestic Intelligence* of the universe. He is omniscient, possessing all intelligence and perfect intelligence. It is God who planned creation and all the worlds and creatures of all dimensions whoever they are. It is God who planned salvation and redemption through His Son, the Lord Jesus Christ. It is God who has the knowledge to work all things out for good. He is to be praised for His wisdom.

4. They offer thanksgiving to God. They thank Him for creation, life, salvation, redemption, and for everything else. Again, they know that every good and perfect gift came from Him.

5. They praise God for His *honor*. God is the Supreme and Majestic Being of the universe. There is none like Him. In addition, God is faithful and true. He never fails to keep His Word and promises nor to do what is best. He is the perfection of honor and truth and trustworthiness. Therefore, God's honor is praised.

6. They praise God for His *power*. God is the Supreme and Majestic Force of the universe. He is the Force that created the universe and that sustains and holds it together and that is moving it toward its destined end. In addition, God is the Supreme Force that works out the salvation and redemption of man and that works out all things for good to those who love Him. He is the Supreme Power who oversees our lives and delivers us from evil, death, and corruption. Therefore, God is praised for His power.

7. They praise God for His *strength*. God is strong; He never tires or becomes weary. There is no weakness in Him whatever. God is so strong that He is always able to help any of His creatures. Anyone can approach God anytime for strength and receive His help. God never fails; He possesses perfect strength and shall possess it forever and ever. Therefore, God's strength is praised.

**Thought 1.** The praise of heavenly beings is an example for us. Scripture is clear: we are always to be thanking and praising God.

Through Jesus, therefore, let us continually offer to God a sacrifice of praise—the fruit of lips that confess his name. (Heb 13:15)

But you are a chosen people, a royal priesthood, a holy nation, a people belonging to God, that you may declare the praises of him who called you out of darkness into his wonderful light. (1 Pet 2:9)

You were bought at a price. Therefore honor God with your body. (1 Cor 6:20)

Giving thanks to the Father, who has qualified you to share in the inheritance of the saints in the kingdom of light. (Col 1:12)

Let the peace of Christ rule in your hearts, since as members of one body you were called to peace. And be thankful. (Col 3:15)

Give thanks in all circumstances, for this is God's will for you in Christ Jesus. (1 Th 5:18)

Sing praises to the LORD, enthroned in Zion; proclaim among the nations what he has done. (Psa 9:11)

May the peoples praise you, O God; may all the peoples praise you. (Psa 67:3)

**4** (7:13-14) **Tribulation, Great—Believers—White Robes—Martyrs**: there is the identity of the countless numbers. Note that the countless people have not yet been identified. Now they are. John is stunned by the sight and praise of the heavenly scene. He just stands there in stark amazement and stone silence, unable to think. To stir him, one of the elders walks over and asks John who the countless people are. Of course, John does not know, but the elder does. He was only arousing John out of his stunned state of mind. John does all he can do; he simply replies, "Sir, you know who they are." It is then that the elder tells John what he is witnessing. Remember: this scene has not yet happened. God is giving John a vision of things that are to happen in the future. The day is coming when a countless number, apparently millions, will stand before God having just entered heaven. Who are they? Two things are said about them.

1. They are *believers* out of the great tribulation. Shocking! But a great multitude, which no man could number—millions of believers—will die from the holocaust in the great tribulation.

Note: this is exactly what Scripture says. There will be millions of believers in the great tribulation, a mass of believers that no man can number. The devastation and destruction taking place will cause millions from all over the world to turn to Christ.

Now observe closely: they are in heaven, not on earth. This means that the antichrist has killed them. He has launched an all out attack against Christ, attempting to wipe the believer from off the face of the earth. This is clearly described by Scripture.

⇒ Daniel predicted this terrible time of trouble.

> **"At that time Michael, the great prince who protects your people, will arise. There will be a time of distress such as has not happened from the beginning of nations until then. But at that time your people—everyone whose name is found written in the book—will be delivered. (Dan 12:1)**

⇒ Jesus Christ foretold that the *great distress, the great tribulation* was coming upon the earth.

> **For then there will be great distress, unequaled from the beginning of the world until now—and never to be equaled again. If those days had not been cut short, no one would survive, but for the sake of the elect those days will be shortened. (Mat 24:21-22)**

⇒ Paul described the attacks of the antichrist against Christ and all religions.

> **Don't let anyone deceive you in any way, for that day will not come until the rebellion occurs and the man of lawlessness is revealed, the man doomed to destruction. He will oppose and will exalt himself over everything that is called God or is worshiped, so that he sets himself up in God's temple, proclaiming himself to be God. (2 Th 2:3-4)**

⇒ John says that the antichrist will actually make war against the saints (believers) of God.

> **He was given power to make war against the saints and to conquer them. And he was given authority over every tribe, people, language and nation. (Rev 13:7)**

⇒ John says that the purpose of the antichrist is to set up the worship of the state as the first loyalty of the citizens of the world. (This will be the means the government will use to hold the people together under one government.)

> **He was given power to give breath to the image of the first beast, so that it could speak and cause all who refused to worship the image to be killed. (Rev 13:15)**

The point is this: in the *great tribulation* the government of the antichrist will launch an all out attack against Christ and His followers. (The attack will also be against all people who have a strong religious faith, including Jews, Moslems, Hindus, and others.) A believer will have to deny Christ or else be put to death. Millions—all those who are true believers—will refuse. They will refuse for the same reason any true believer would refuse: because they love the Lord with all their heart, and because they have the glorious hope of living with Christ forever and ever, worshipping and serving Him in perfection throughout all of eternity.

2. They are those who have washed their robes white. How? In the blood of the Lamb. The clothing of all heavenly beings is colored white. White stands for purity and perfection. It means that the person has no spot of sin, evil, or corruption in him. He is clean and pure from all defilement and sin and imperfection. Therefore, white stands for perfection, for sinless perfection, for perfect righteousness.

But note a critical fact: no person upon earth is sinless, righteous, perfect, pure, or incorruptible. Every person sins, and every person is corruptible. We all die and end up in the grave. How then did these martyrs—the believers of the countless multitude—get white robes? This verse tells us:

> **They have washed their robes and made them white in the blood of the Lamb. (Rev 7:14. See note, pt.2, Lamb of God—Rev.5:6-7 for discussion and verses.)**

**5** (7:15) **Believers, Redeemed—Heaven**: there is the function of the countless multitude. They serve God continually, day and night. The temple here means the very presence of God, the most holy place in all the universe, heaven itself. It means to have direct access into the presence of God anytime, anyplace. The picture is this:

⇒ Believers will be perfected so that they never tire or become weary or need sleep. They will be able to serve and work continuously day and night.

⇒ Believers will serve God: they will be ruling and reigning throughout the universe, overseeing the new heavens and earth for Christ.

> **Jesus said to them, "I tell you the truth, at the renewal of all things, when the Son of Man sits on his glorious throne, you who have followed me will also sit on twelve thrones, judging the twelve tribes of Israel. (Mat 19:28)**
>
> **"His master replied, 'Well done, good and faithful servant! You have been faithful with a few things; I will put you in charge of many things. Come and share your master's happiness!' (Mat 25:23)**
>
> **The Lord answered, "Who then is the faithful and wise manager, whom the master puts in charge of his servants to give them their food allowance at the proper time? It will be good for that servant whom the master finds doing so when he returns. I tell you the truth, he will put him in charge of all his possessions. (Luke 12:42-44)**
>
> **"'Well done, my good servant!' his master replied. 'Because you have been trustworthy in a very small matter, take charge of ten cities.' "His master answered, 'You take charge of five cities.' (Luke 19:17, 19)**
>
> **Now if we are children, then we are heirs—heirs of God and co-heirs with Christ, if indeed we share in his sufferings in order that we may also share in his glory. (Rom 8:17)**
>
> **If we endure, we will also reign with him. If we disown him, he will also disown us; (2 Tim 2:12)**

Do you not know that the saints will judge the world? And if you are to judge the world, are you not competent to judge trivial cases? Do you not know that we will judge angels? How much more the things of this life! (1 Cor 6:2-3)

And from Jesus Christ, who is the faithful witness, the firstborn from the dead, and the ruler of the kings of the earth. To him who loves us and has freed us from our sins by his blood, (Rev 1:5)

You have made them to be a kingdom and priests to serve our God, and they will reign on the earth." (Rev 5:10)

**6** (7:15-17) **Believers—Rewards—Heaven:** there are the blessings and bliss of the countless multitude.

1. They will have the living presence of God with them forever.
   ⇒ The presence of God will actually be manifested to the believer unceasingly. God will be dwelling, living, moving, and having His being in the believer in an unbroken communion and fellowship.

2. They will have all their physical needs met. Hunger and thirst stand for all the physical necessities of life that they lacked when upon earth. Many of these dear believers will suffer terribly. They will be placed in extermination camps by the antichrist and his government. They will be starved to death. Some will be forced to flee their homes and belongings. They will starve to death while trying to scratch food out of the forests. The picture of how a war-torn, persecuted people suffering starvation and thirst is well known to the modern world. Such scenes are often seen on television. But in heaven the believers will have all their needs met.

3. They will be protected. This is the symbol of the sun and heat. The prison and labor camps of a persecuted and war-torn people is the picture here. The picture would also include the homeless who have to wander about exposed to the elements of nature. Scorching heat and frigid cold will take the lives of many. But in heaven, they will be protected from all enemies, even from the sun and heat.

4. They will have all their spiritual needs met. The Lamb of God Himself shall shepherd the believers. He will feed them and meet all their needs. This refers to spiritual needs, the needs of the soul for life, love, joy, peace, security, completeness, fullness, assurance, and confidence. Christ will feed the soul of the believer. (cp. Ps.23:1f.).

5. They will have the leadership and direction of the Lord to guide them. There will never be another mistake or misstep taken. The Lamb of God Himself will give direction and guidance. He will assign the responsibilities and tell believers exactly what to oversee for Him, and they will joyfully do it. Serving Christ, being directed and guided by Him, will be like drinking from the fountain of living water.

6. They will have all sorrow wiped away from their eyes. Note by whom: God Himself shall wipe every tear from their eyes. In heaven believers shall never again suffer, not even a single pain or hurt. They shall be perfected forever.

Blessed are those who hunger and thirst for righteousness, for they will be filled. (Mat 5:6)

But whoever drinks the water I give him will never thirst. Indeed, the water I give him will become in him a spring of water welling up to eternal life." (John 4:14)

Then Jesus declared, "I am the bread of life. He who comes to me will never go hungry, and he who believes in me will never be thirsty. (John 6:35)

"Do not let your hearts be troubled. Trust in God ; trust also in me. In my Father's house are many rooms; if it were not so, I would have told you. I am going there to prepare a place for you. And if I go and prepare a place for you, I will come back and take you to be with me that you also may be where I am. (John 14:1-3)

For our light and momentary troubles are achieving for us an eternal glory that far outweighs them all. (2 Cor 4:17)

Now there is in store for me the crown of righteousness, which the Lord, the righteous Judge, will award to me on that day—and not only to me, but also to all who have longed for his appearing. (2 Tim 4:8)

Praise be to the God and Father of our Lord Jesus Christ! In his great mercy he has given us new birth into a living hope through the resurrection of Jesus Christ from the dead, And into an inheritance that can never perish, spoil or fade—kept in heaven for you, (1 Pet 1:3-4)

Dear friends, do not be surprised at the painful trial you are suffering, as though something strange were happening to you. But rejoice that you participate in the sufferings of Christ, so that you may be overjoyed when his glory is revealed. (1 Pet 4:12-13)

Cast all your anxiety on him because he cares for you. (1 Pet 5:7)

He will wipe every tear from their eyes. There will be no more death or mourning or crying or pain, for the old order of things has passed away." (Rev 21:4)

They will neither hunger nor thirst, nor will the desert heat or the sun beat upon them. He who has compassion on them will guide them and lead them beside springs of water. (Isa 49:10)

| | CHAPTER 8 | pets. | given seven trumpets (specific judgments) |
|---|---|---|---|
| | V. THE SEVEN TRUMPET JUDGMENTS: EVENTS DURING THE GREAT TRIBULATION, 8:1-11:19 | 3 Another angel, who had a golden censer, came and stood at the altar. He was given much incense to offer, with the prayers of all the saints, on the golden altar before the throne. | b. There is a golden censer with the prayers of saints |
| | A. The Breaking of the Seventh Seal: Awesome Preparation for Judgment, 8:1-5 | 4 The smoke of the incense, together with the prayers of the saints, went up before God from the angel's hand. | |
| 1 Picture 1: A shattering silence | When he opened the seventh seal, there was silence in heaven for about half an hour. | 5 Then the angel took the censer, filled it with fire from the altar, and hurled it on the earth; and there came peals of thunder, rumblings, flashes of lightning and an earthquake. | 3 Picture 3: The signs of the coming judgment begin upon earth |
| 2 Picture 2: The instruments of judgment<br>a. There are seven angels | 2 And I saw the seven angels who stand before God, and to them were given seven trum- | | |

# DIVISION V

## THE SEVEN TRUMPET JUDGMENTS: EVENTS DURING THE GREAT TRIBULATION, 8:1-11:19

### A. The Breaking of the Seventh Seal: Awesome Preparation for Judgment, 8:1-5

(8:1-5) **Introduction**: remember what we have just seen. God has just handed Jesus Christ the great *Book of Destiny*, the book that tells about the end of the world. The book was so full and so secretive that it was bound with seven seals. When Christ began to break the seals, the most unusual thing happened. A picture, a movie-like scene, began to be played out before John and the heavenly host. What they saw was the horror and the terrible things that are to happen at the end of the world.

⇒ The first four seals showed the four horsemen of the apocalypse storming over the face of the earth. These four horsemen represented the havoc that shall be wrought upon the earth by the antichrist. They show his gaining control of the world through war, famine, and economic controls. The events are characteristic of most ages, but they are to be intensified in the tribulation at the end of the world.

⇒ The fifth seal (Rev.6:9) showed the martyrs who were slaughtered by the antichrist while he gained control of much of the earth and its economy (Rev.6:6).

⇒ The sixth seal showed the rumblings of God's judgment being prepared and simply says, "the great day of their wrath has come," the very threshold of the great tribulation (Rev.6:12f).

Now we come to the seventh seal. But before we discuss it, remember that the seals of a scroll are not part of the scroll. They are merely ribbons or some cord or tape that is wrapped around the scroll or book to hold it together. They have to be broken to open the book. The point is this: the seal judgments are events that happen before the end time itself, before the events of the book itself are ever seen. The seal judgments are the events that happen before the *great tribulation* itself takes place. This is exactly what Christ said:

⇒ Christ called the preliminary events "the *beginning of birth pains*" "*the beginning of sorrows or woes*" (Mt.24:8. See outline and notes—Mt. 24:1-14.)

⇒ Christ called the most terrible events of the last days the "*great distress*" or "*the great tribula-*

*tion*" (Mt.24:21. See outline and notes—Mt.24:15-28.)

Now, it is time for the seventh seal to be broken. When it is broken, there is seen the awesome preparation for judgment.

1. Picture 1: a shattering silence (v.1).
2. Picture 2: the instruments of judgment (v.2-4).
3. Picture 3: the signs of the coming judgment begin upon earth (v.5).

**1** (8:1) **Seal Judgments**: when the seventh seal is broken, there is the picture of a shattering silence. This was the silence of awe and of reverence before God, fearing what may be coming forth. The heavenly host had seen so much that they were stricken numb with silence. When the seventh seal is broken, nothing happens. There is stillness, complete and absolute stillness. Christ stands there in stone silence. He does not move or speak. Neither does anyone else. They dare not, for the Lord says nothing, and the seal has produced no event. As stated, the silence is a silence of awe and reverence before God, fearing what might be coming forth. It was a silence of suspense and trembling anticipation, expecting some terrible judgment to burst across the scene of human history. Note that the silence lasts about one half hour.

> **I make known the end from the beginning, from ancient times, what is still to come. I say: My purpose will stand, and I will do all that I please. (Isa 46:10)**
> **Therefore the prudent man keeps quiet in such times, for the times are evil. (Amos 5:13)**
> **But the LORD is in his holy temple; let all the earth be silent before him." (Hab 2:20)**
> **Be still before the LORD, all mankind, because he has roused himself from his holy dwelling." (Zec 2:13)**

**2** (8:2-4) **Trumpet Judgments**: there is the picture of the instruments of justice and judgment. Note two instruments of judgment.

1. There are seven angels who suddenly lurch out from the Book of Destiny and immediately take their place before God. God hands them seven trumpets. Again note this: the seven angels come forth when the seventh seal is broken. Picture the scene:

⇒ Picture the heavenly host surrounding the throne of God.

⇒ Picture all the spectacular scenes, horror, and suffering that have been witnessed.

⇒ Picture the breaking of the seventh seal and the stone silence for thirty minutes—stone silence.

⇒ Then bursting into view are seven mighty angels taking their place before the throne of God. Picture them standing there tall, broad, and erect. The power they possess is clearly seen in their very persons.

The heavenly host knows something: when God hands these mighty messengers seven trumpets, the judgments about to take place will be coming directly from God Himself. Trumpets always symbolize God intervention into human history. God is about to move against the godless and evil society of earth. This is critical to note, for God does not condemn and punish His followers. The judgments of God are to fall only upon the unbelievers of the world, only upon those who have followed the antichrist, only those who have the mark of the beast.

> **They were told not to harm the grass of the earth or any plant or tree, but only those people who did not have the seal of God on their foreheads. (Rev 9:4)**
>
> **The first angel went and poured out his bowl on the land, and ugly and painful sores broke out on the people who had the mark of the beast and worshiped his image. (Rev 16:2)**
>
> **Then men will say, "Surely the righteous still are rewarded; surely there is a God who judges the earth." (Psa 58:11)**

**Thought 1.** George Ladd makes a statement that we must always remember about the judgment of God:

> "The wrath of God is not merely judicial; it also embodies a merciful purpose. It is designed to drive men to their knees by harsh experiences while the time for decision remains, before it is too late. This is hinted at in several passages.
>
> "After the sixth trumpet, we read, 'The rest of mankind, who were not killed by these plagues, did not repent of the works of their hands nor give up worshipping demons and idols' (9:20) ...When men are confronted by the...wrath of God in judgment, they should be humbled in repentance and turn from their wickedness to worship the God of heaven.
>
> "The same note resounds in connection with the bowls of wrath. After the fifth bowl, we read that men 'cursed the God of heaven for their pain and sores and did not repent of their deeds' (16:10). If it

were possible to drive men to repentance, the plagues of the trumpets and bowls would do so" (*The Revelation of John.* Grand Rapids, MI: Eerdmans, 1972, p.124).

**Thought 2.** William Barclay gives three purposes for the blowing of a trumpet that are worthy of our note:

> "It can sound the alarm. It can waken from sleep or warn of danger. And God is always sounding His warnings in the ears of men.
>
> "It can be the fanfare which announces the arrival of royalty. It is a fitting symbol to express the invasion of time by the King of eternity.
>
> "It can be the summons to battle. And God is always summoning His people to take sides in the strife of truth with falsehood, and to become soldiers of the King of kings" (*The Revelation of John*, Vol.2, p.52).

2. The second instrument of judgment is the prayers of all the saints or believers. Note that these are the prayers of *all* the saints. Some were in heaven and some were still on earth. All had suffered and some were still suffering the savage persecution of the antichrist and his government. Remember how savage the persecution will be: literally millions, numberless multitudes will be killed (Rev.7:9-17). Believers will be crying out to God day and night for deliverance, for justice, for vindication—for the hand of such cruelty to be dealt with either by conversion or removal, and to be dealt with speedily.

The point is this: the day is coming when God is going to answer the prayers of His dear people. He is going to cast His judgment against the antichrist and his government and all those who have followed him. All who have opposed God are going to suffer judgment, the most horrible judgment imaginable, all who have stood against God...

• by ridiculing and mocking His people
• by cursing and abusing His people
• by attacking and striking His people
• by arresting and imprisoning His people
• by condemning and killing His people

All who have rebelled against Jesus Christ—rejected, denied, cursed, ignored, neglected, disobeyed, and disbelieved Him—all shall be judged. The judgment of God is about to fall upon the earth. They who have been so cruel and inhumane shall now suffer the most horrible punishment imaginable. And the punishment shall come from Him who is just and righteous as well as love. God is going to hear and answer the prayers of His dear people, His followers who suffered so much at the hands of a godless society that chose to follow the savagery of the antichrist.

> **"So I say to you: Ask and it will be given to you; seek and you will find; knock and the door will be opened to you. (Luke 11:9)**
>
> **If you remain in me and my words remain in you, ask whatever you wish, and it will be given you. (John 15:7)**
>
> **And receive from him anything we ask, because we obey his commands and do what pleases him. (1 John 3:22)**

He will call upon me, and I will answer him; I will be with him in trouble, I will deliver him and honor him. (Psa 91:15)

Before they call I will answer; while they are still speaking I will hear. (Isa 65:24)

'Call to me and I will answer you and tell you great and unsearchable things you do not know.' (Jer 33:3)

This third I will bring into the fire; I will refine them like silver and test them like gold. They will call on my name and I will answer them; I will say, 'They are my people,' and they will say, 'The LORD is our God.'" (Zec 13:9)

**3** (8:5) **Judgment**: there are the signs of the coming judgment beginning upon earth. Note the verse.

> **Then the angel took the censer, filled it with fire from the altar, and hurled it on the earth; and there came peals of thunder, rumblings, flashes of lightning and an earthquake. (Rev 8:5)**

The angel takes fire from the altar, and note where he puts it: he mixes it in with the prayers of the suffering saints. Their prayers for vindication and justice and the fire of God's holy wrath are mixed together. Why? To be cast upon the earth. The day is coming when God will be ready to judge the godless society of the earth; He will be ready to avenge His name and the faith of His dear people who have been treated so savagely. The justice of God will strike out in wrath against the ungodly and evil of the earth.

Note this: the angel casts both the fire and prayers of the saints upon the earth. When he does, all the voices upon earth begin to wonder and question, for there is...

- an enormous increase of violent thunderstorms with their thunderings and lightnings.
- an enormous increase of earthquakes.

The ungodly millions upon earth know that something is about to happen, something terrible. And it is: the judgment of God is about to fall upon the ungodly of the world. The *great tribulation* is now being launched.

> **But I tell you, it will be more bearable for Tyre and Sidon on the day of judgment than for you. (Mat 11:22)**

And if any place will not welcome you or listen to you, shake the dust off your feet when you leave, as a testimony against them." (Mark 6:11)

Enoch, the seventh from Adam, prophesied about these men: "See, the Lord is coming with thousands upon thousands of his holy ones To judge everyone, and to convict all the ungodly of all the ungodly acts they have done in the ungodly way, and of all the harsh words ungodly sinners have spoken against him." (Jude 1:14-15)

Look, he is coming with the clouds, and every eye will see him, even those who pierced him; and all the peoples of the earth will mourn because of him. So shall it be! Amen. (Rev 1:7)

The fear of the LORD is pure, enduring forever. The ordinances of the LORD are sure and altogether righteous. (Psa 19:9)

They will sing before the LORD, for he comes, he comes to judge the earth. He will judge the world in righteousness and the peoples in his truth. (Psa 96:13)

**Thought 1.** Scripture plainly declares that God is going execute judgment upon this corruptible world and the ungodly.

> **Enoch, the seventh from Adam, prophesied about these men: "See, the Lord is coming with thousands upon thousands of his holy ones (Jude 1:14)**
>
> **For he has set a day when he will judge the world with justice by the man he has appointed. He has given proof of this to all men by raising him from the dead." (Acts 17:31)**
>
> **The wrath of God is being revealed from heaven against all the godlessness and wickedness of men who suppress the truth by their wickedness, (Rom 1:18)**
>
> **They will sing before the LORD, for he comes, he comes to judge the earth. He will judge the world in righteousness and the peoples in his truth. (Psa 96:13)**

| | B. The Blast of the First Four Trumpets: Natural Catastrophes, 8:6-12 | 9 A third of the living creatures in the sea died, and a third of the ships were destroyed. | d. Turns one third of the sea to blood red |
|---|---|---|---|
| | | | e. Destroys one third of the sea life & one third of the ships |
| 1 The 1st trumpet: A fierce storm | 6 Then the seven angels who had the seven trumpets prepared to sound them. | 10 The third angel sounded his trumpet, and a great star, blazing like a torch, fell from the sky on a third of the rivers and on the springs of water— | 3 The 3rd trumpet: A meteoric mass |
| a. Includes hail & fire mixed with blood | 7 The first angel sounded his trumpet, and there came hail and fire mixed with blood, and it was hurled down upon the earth. A third of the earth was burned up, a third of the trees were burned up, and all the green grass was burned up. | 11 The name of the star is Wormwood. A third of the waters turned bitter, and many people died from the waters that had become bitter. | a. Affects one third of the water systems |
| b. Destroys one third of the vegetation | | | b. Is named Wormwood |
| | | | c. Contaminates one third of the waters—killing many |
| 2 The 2nd trumpet: A massive volcanic explosion | 8 The second angel sounded his trumpet, and something like a huge mountain, all ablaze, was thrown into the sea. A third of the sea turned into blood, | 12 The fourth angel sounded his trumpet, and a third of the sun was struck, a third of the moon, and a third of the stars, so that a third of them turned dark. A third of the day was without light, and also a third of the night. | 4 The 4th trumpet: An astronomical eclipse |
| a. Is a mass of rock as large as a mountain | | | a. Darkens one third of the heavenly bodies |
| b. Is still a fire | | | |
| c. Is thrown into the sea | | | b. Affects day & night |

# DIVISION V

## THE SEVEN TRUMPET JUDGMENTS: EVENTS DURING THE GREAT TRIBULATION, 8:1-11:19

### B. The Blast of the First Four Trumpets: Natural Catastrophes, 8:6-12

(8:6-12) **Introduction**: the great trumpet judgments will be blown upon the earth. Remember: this will be the judgment of God upon a world that will slaughter the innocent and curse God; a world of ungodly and evil people who will reject, deny, and rebel against Jesus Christ. This is the judgment of God against a world that will launch the worst holocaust in the history of the world; that will slaughter millions of believers who refuse to deny Jesus Christ and to accept the mark of the antichrist. God's judgment will be trumpeted across the face of the earth. Judgment will fall upon the mean, the ungodly, and the evil of the world.

Note: the seven angels will prepare to sound forth the trumpet blast of their judgments. This passage deals with the first four trumpet judgments. The judgments will focus upon natural catastrophes, both upon the earth and upon the heavenly bodies. The purpose of these natural disasters will be to bring people to repentance.

1. The first trumpet: a fierce storm (v.6-7).
2. The second trumpet: a massive volcanic explosion (v.8-9).
3. The third trumpet: a meteoric mass (v.10-11).
4. The fourth trumpet: an astronomical eclipse (v.12).

**1** (8:6-7) **Trumpet Judgments—Judgment**: there will be the blast of the first trumpet judgment, that of a fierce storm. Remember the terrifying disturbances that will be taking place in outer space and upon earth in the latter days. The universe and the laws of nature will be swaying: enormous and violent disturbances will be taking place all throughout the universe. We saw this under the seal judgments.

> I watched as he opened the sixth seal. There was a great earthquake. The sun turned black like sackcloth made of goat hair, the whole moon turned blood red, And the stars in the sky fell to earth, as late figs drop from a fig tree when shaken by a strong wind. The sky receded like a scroll, rolling up, and every mountain and island was removed from its place. (Rev 6:12-14)

These cosmic disturbances will cause utter chaos in the earth's weather. A violent storm will brew someplace on the earth, a storm more violent than any storm ever seen before. The storm will rain hail that looks like fire mingled with blood. The reddish color will no doubt be a mixture of sand blown up into the clouds by some of the most fierce winds ever seen by man. Note the force of the winds. The storm will be so strong that its winds will carry it across one third of the earth—strong enough to destroy and devastate one third of the vegetation (grass and trees). Think of the enormous destruction and utter devastation:

⇒ the destroyed crops and food supply for both man and animal
⇒ the interrupted agricultural rotation through lack of seed and ability to plant again
⇒ the shortage of food
⇒ the dry, desert lands that will result from the destruction of trees

One third of the vegetation of the earth will be destroyed in this judgment. Why? Because the end of the world will be at hand. God will begin to judge the *ungodly* and the *evil* of this earth. It will be time for people to know that God is truly God, and that He is to be obeyed or else people will be judged and punished. This judgment will be a warning: people must repent or even worse judgments will come.

⇒ This judgment will be similar to the plagues upon Egypt by Moses.

> When Moses stretched out his staff toward the sky, the LORD sent thunder and hail, and lightning flashed down to the ground. So the LORD rained hail on the land of Egypt; Hail fell and lightning flashed back and forth. It was the worst storm in all the land of

Egypt since it had become a nation. (Exo 9:23-24)

⇒ This judgment will be similar to the storm upon the enemies of Joshua and Israel.

As they fled before Israel on the road down from Beth Horon to Azekah, the LORD hurled large hailstones down on them from the sky, and more of them died from the hailstones than were killed by the swords of the Israelites. (Josh 10:11)

⇒ Other Biblical references to hail storms are as follows.

The LORD thundered from heaven; the voice of the Most High resounded. (Psa 18:13)

See, the Lord has one who is powerful and strong. Like a hailstorm and a destructive wind, like a driving rain and a flooding downpour, he will throw it forcefully to the ground. (Isa 28:2)

Therefore tell those who cover it with whitewash that it is going to fall. Rain will come in torrents, and I will send hailstones hurtling down, and violent winds will burst forth. (Ezek 13:11)

The first angel sounded his trumpet, and there came hail and fire mixed with blood, and it was hurled down upon the earth. A third of the earth was burned up, a third of the trees were burned up, and all the green grass was burned up. (Rev 8:7)

**2** (8:8-9) **Trumpet Judgments**: there will be the blast of the second trumpet judgment. This will probably be some unparalleled volcanic explosion either from underneath the sea or else close to the sea. The explosion will apparently be as forceful as an atomic explosion, forceful enough to explode a mass of rock as large as a mountain into some ocean. Note these facts:
   ⇒ The explosion will be so forceful that the mass of rock flying upward is so large that it looks like a great mountain.
   ⇒ The explosive mass will still be ablaze when it hits the earth.
   ⇒ The explosive mass will be thrown into one of the seas.
   ⇒ One third of that particular sea will turn blood red.
   ⇒ One third of the sea life of that sea will be destroyed.
   ⇒ One third of the ships in that particular ocean will be destroyed.

Again, picture the shortage of sea life for food, the devastation to the fishing industry and businesses, the interruption of shipping commerce and trade, the financial loss because of the destroyed ships and their cargo. Commerce and food supply will be crippled worldwide by the blast of the first and second trumpets.
   ⇒ The destruction of fish will be similar to the plague upon Egypt.

Moses and Aaron did just as the LORD had commanded. He raised his staff in the presence of Pharaoh and his officials and struck the water of the Nile, and all the water was changed into blood. The fish in the Nile died, and the river smelled so bad that the Egyptians could not drink its water. Blood was everywhere in Egypt. (Exo 7:20-21)

Hear the word of the LORD, you Israelites, because the LORD has a charge to bring against you who live in the land: "There is no faithfulness, no love, no acknowledgment of God in the land. There is only cursing, lying and murder, stealing and adultery; they break all bounds, and bloodshed follows bloodshed. Because of this the land mourns, and all who live in it waste away; the beasts of the field and the birds of the air and the fish of the sea are dying. (Hosea 4:1-3)

The LORD Almighty has a day in store for all the proud and lofty, for all that is exalted, For every trading ship and every stately vessel. (Isa 2:12, 16)

⇒ The judgment of God was predicted centuries ago.

"I will sweep away everything from the face of the earth," declares the LORD. "I will sweep away both men and animals; I will sweep away the birds of the air and the fish of the sea. The wicked will have only heaps of rubble when I cut off man from the face of the earth," declares the LORD. (Zep 1:2-3)

He turned their waters into blood, causing their fish to die. (Psa 105:29)

**3** (8:10-11) **Trumpet Judgments**: there will be the blast of the third trumpet judgment, that of a meteoric mass. This will apparently be some huge meteor that explodes before it hits the earth. It will scatter over one third of the world. The balls and particles that fall into the rivers and springs of water will drastically affect the water systems in that part of the world. It will actually poison the water, and before men become aware of it, many will die from drinking the water. Because of the bitter taste of the water, the star is called Wormwood. Wormwood is a plant that is very bitter. Think of the effect of this meteoric mass upon the earth:
   ⇒ the shortage of water
   ⇒ the thirst among people
   ⇒ the panic because of thirst
   ⇒ the mobilization of emergency aid needed to get water to one third of the earth
   ⇒ the sheer terror, fright, and agony burning at the minds of people because of these three judgments

But remember upon whom the judgments will be falling: upon the ungodly and the evil of the earth, upon the antichrist and his government and followers, upon those who have literally slain millions of God's people upon the earth, upon those who have abused, mocked, cursed, beaten, imprisoned and killed the followers of God's Son, the Lord Jesus Christ.

117

**Thought 1.** Note how the bitterness of Wormwood is used in Scripture.

1) Wormwood became a symbol of idolatry because of its bitterness. Idolatry is a bitter taste for God to swallow; therefore, He will give the idolater the *bitterness or wormwood of judgment.*

> The LORD said, "It is because they have forsaken my law, which I set before them; they have not obeyed me or followed my law. Instead, they have followed the stubbornness of their hearts; they have followed the Baals, as their fathers taught them." Therefore, this is what the LORD Almighty, the God of Israel, says: "See, I will make this people eat bitter food and drink poisoned water. (Jer 9:13-15)

2) Wormwood is used to symbolize the bitterness that an immoral person brings into one's life.

> For the lips of an adulteress drip honey, and her speech is smoother than oil; But in the end she is bitter as gall, sharp as a double-edged sword. Her feet go down to death; her steps lead straight to the grave. (Prov 5:3-5)

3) Wormwood is used to symbolize the way people dismiss and treat God with disdain.

> Make sure there is no man or woman, clan or tribe among you today whose heart turns away from the LORD our God to go and worship the gods of those nations; make sure there is no root among you that produces such bitter poison. (Deu 29:18)
> The LORD said, "It is because they have forsaken my law, which I set before them; they have not obeyed me or followed my law. Instead, they have followed the stubbornness of their hearts; they have followed the Baals, as their fathers taught them." Therefore, this is what the LORD Almighty, the God of Israel, says: "See, I will make this people eat bitter food and drink poisoned water. (Jer 9:13-15)
> Therefore, this is what the LORD Almighty says concerning the prophets: "I will make them eat bitter food and drink poisoned water, because from the prophets of Jerusalem ungodliness has spread throughout the land." (Jer 23:15)
> Seek the LORD and live, or he will sweep through the house of Joseph like a fire; it will devour, and Bethel will have no one to quench it. You who turn justice into bitterness and cast righteousness to the ground (Amos 5:6-7)

**4** (8:12) **Trumpet Judgments**: there will be the blast of the fourth trumpet judgment, that of some astronomical eclipse. Some kind of unusual eclipse is going to happen in the heavens.

> Before them the earth shakes, the sky trembles, the sun and moon are darkened, and the stars no longer shine. (Joel 2:10)
> "In that day," declares the Sovereign LORD, "I will make the sun go down at noon and darken the earth in broad daylight. (Amos 8:9)

Just what Scripture is saying here is difficult to understand. It seems that one of three things is meant.

⇒ That one third of the sun, moon, and stars will be eclipsed.

⇒ That there will be an eclipse that will blacken out one third of the day; that is, there will be one third less light.

⇒ That there will be no light whatsoever for a third of the night; that is, the moon will be eclipsed for one third of each night.

Whatever is meant, the event will be a judgment, a plague of God's. He will be behind the event, striking fear in the *ungodly* and *evil* of this world. God will have two purposes: to lead men to repent and, if they refuse, to judge them for all the evil and ungodly acts against His name and His people.

The picture is this: God has had enough. It is time to stop all the evil and murderous behavior of people. He is ready to end the world and send Christ back to earth to establish righteousness upon earth forever. But He still wants to reach as many as He can. In mass, the world has rejected Him and His people; and they have set a course of genocide, attempting to wipe all believers off the face of the earth. The antichrist and his followers have launched a holocaust that has slaughtered millions. Therefore, God is now moving in judgment by throwing the forces of nature out of course. He is getting ready to destroy the earth and begin anew; but in the meantime, He offers the opportunity of repentance to any who will turn from their sin to His beloved Son, the Lord Jesus Christ.

⇒ This judgment will be similar to the plague of darkness cast upon Egypt by Moses.

> Then the LORD said to Moses, "Stretch out your hand toward the sky so that darkness will spread over Egypt— darkness that can be felt." So Moses stretched out his hand toward the sky, and total darkness covered all Egypt for three days. No one could see anyone else or leave his place for three days. Yet all the Israelites had light in the places where they lived. (Exo 10:21-23)

⇒ One such astronomical event has already happened in the seal judgments.

> I watched as he opened the sixth seal. There was a great earthquake. The sun turned black like sackcloth made of goat hair, the whole moon turned blood red, And the stars in the sky fell to earth, as late figs drop from a fig tree when shaken by a strong wind. The sky receded like a scroll, rolling up, and every mountain and island was removed from its place. (Rev 6:12-14)

⇒ Other Scriptures predict such astronomical events for the latter days.

> Before them the earth shakes, the sky trembles, the sun and moon are darkened, and the stars no longer shine. (Joel 2:10)

> "In that day," declares the Sovereign LORD, "I will make the sun go down at noon and darken the earth in broad daylight. (Amos 8:9)

⇒ Jesus Christ predicted such astronomical events for the latter days.

> "There will be signs in the sun, moon and stars. On the earth, nations will be in anguish and perplexity at the roaring and tossing of the sea. Men will faint from terror, apprehensive of what is coming on the world, for the heavenly bodies will be shaken. At that time they will see the Son of Man coming in a cloud with power and great glory. When these things begin to take place, stand up and lift up your heads, because your redemption is drawing near." (Luke 21:25-28)

| | | |
|---|---|---|
| | **C. The Blast of the Fifth Trumpet: A Demonic-like Locust Plague Upon the Ungodly & Evil, 8:13-9:11** | seal of God on their foreheads. |
| | | the seal of God |
| **1 The blast of judgment is now to be far more severe**<br>a. To be against man himself (the ungodly, v.4)<br>b. To be very severe: A triple judgment | 13 As I watched, I heard an eagle that was flying in midair call out in a loud voice: "Woe! Woe! Woe to the inhabitants of the earth, because of the trumpet blasts about to be sounded by the other three angels!" | 5 They were not given power to kill them, but only to torture them for five months. And the agony they suffered was like that of the sting of a scorpion when it strikes a man.<br>6 During those days men will seek death, but will not find it; they will long to die, but death will elude them. |
| | | d. They are not to kill people, only torment them |
| | | e. The result: People are to be so weary of torture that they desire to die |
| **2 The unnamed star or person**<br>a. He had fallen from heaven<br>b. He is given the key to the bottomless pit—the Abyss<br>**3 The bottomless pit or abyss is opened** | **CHAPTER 9**<br><br>The fifth angel sounded his trumpet, and I saw a star that had fallen from the sky to the earth. The star was given the key to the shaft of the Abyss.<br>2 When he opened the Abyss, smoke rose from it like the smoke from a gigantic furnace. The sun and sky were darkened by the smoke from the Abyss. | 7 The locusts looked like horses prepared for battle. On their heads they wore something like crowns of gold, and their faces resembled human faces.<br>8 Their hair was like women's hair, and their teeth were like lions' teeth.<br>9 They had breastplates like breastplates of iron, and the sound of their wings was like the thundering of many horses and chariots rushing into battle. |
| | | **5 The locusts have a horrifying appearance & power**<br>a. Like war horses: Attack<br>b. Gold crowns: Successful<br>c. Men's faces: Intelligence<br>d. Women's hair: Beauty to seduce<br>e. Lion's teeth: Devouring<br>f. Breastplates: Indestructible<br>g. Sound of wings: Frightening<br>h. Stinging tails: Demonic torture |
| **4 The locusts from the Abyss are sent to inflict unbearable punishment**<br>a. They are given scorpion-like power<br>b. They are restrained from destroying nature<br>c. They are to afflict only people who do not have | 3 And out of the smoke locusts came down upon the earth and were given power like that of scorpions of the earth.<br>4 They were told not to harm the grass of the earth or any plant or tree, but only those people who did not have the | 10 They had tails and stings like scorpions, and in their tails they had power to torment people for five months.<br>11 They had as king over them the angel of the Abyss, whose name in Hebrew is Abaddon, and in Greek, Apollyon. | 
| | | **6 The king of the locusts is identified**<br>a. Abaddon (Hebrew): Destruction Apollyon (Greek): Destroyer |

# DIVISION V

## THE SEVEN TRUMPET JUDGMENTS: EVENTS DURING THE GREAT TRIBULATION, 8:1-11:19

### C. The Blast of the Fifth Trumpet: A Demonic-like Locust Plague Upon the Ungodly and Evil, 8:13-9:11

(8:13-9:11) **Introduction**: the worst holocaust the world has ever seen will be taking place. Millions of believers will be slaughtered by the antichrist's godless society and government. The godless government will insist that the people's first loyalty belongs to the state. The antichrist will set up the state as a god and demand total allegiance. He will do what so many governments do today and have always done: demand that people focus upon the government and recognize it as the great provider and protector of society. He and his government will declare the age-old philosophy of the supreme state, that the government alone can meet the needs of people and bring utopia to them. Those who refuse to give the government their first loyalty will be hunted down, imprisoned and executed. Take just a moment and think about all the governments over the earth that hold to the supremacy of the state and deny God and disallow freedom of worship. When the antichrist comes to power, he will exalt the government and its leader worldwide.

But this is only a fraction of what will be happening in the end time. The great tribulation will have just begun, and every person on earth who puts God first will be slaughtered. As stated, millions of believers will have already died in the worst holocaust in world history. It is because of this and all

the other terrible sins and evils of a godless society that God decides to judge and end the world.

What we have seen thus far is this: the great tribulation has now begun. The great Book of God has now been opened, the Book of Destiny, the book that reveals what is to happen in the end time. God's judgment upon the ungodly and the evil of this world has begun to fall. Four trumpet judgments have blasted the earth with natural disaster after natural disaster. The destruction and devastation upon earth has been unparalleled.

⇒ One third of the vegetation has been destroyed.

⇒ One third of some sea has been polluted and a third of the sea life has died.

⇒ One third of the water systems of the world have been polluted by a meteoric mass from heaven falling upon earth.

⇒ One third of day and night has been affected because of astronomical happenings throughout space.

Now, we come to the blast of the fifth trumpet judgment: a demonic-like locust plague upon the ungodly and evil of the earth.

1. The blast of judgment is now to be far more severe (v.13).
2. The unnamed star or person (Ch.9:1).
3. The bottomless pit or abyss is opened (v.2).
4. The locusts from the abyss are sent to inflict unbearable punishment (v.3-6).
5. The locusts have a horrifying appearance and power (v.7-10).
6. The king of the locusts is identified (v.11).

**1** (8:13) **Judgment**: the trumpet blast of the fifth judgment will be far more severe than the other judgments. The other four trumpet judgments were directed against the earth itself and involved natural catastrophes. Now the judgments will be directed against the ungodly and evil of this earth. It will not affect those who refuse to give their allegiance to the antichrist, who refuse the mark of the beast (Rev.9:4). Remember: God will seal His followers; he will protect believers so that His judgments do not fall upon them. His judgments will be for the ungodly and the evil, not for those who have trusted His Son. Of course, as in every generation, believers will be martyred at the hands of ungodly men. But believers will not suffer the judgments of God. They will be protected even as Israel was protected during the Egyptian plagues under Moses. (See note—Rev.7:2-3.)

Note that an eagle flys through the midst of heaven. The idea is that it soars in the height of the sky, right at the zenith of the noonday sun. Why? So that all can see him and hear his voice cry out a threefold woe upon the ungodly of the earth. This, of course, is symbolic language stressing the strength, swiftness, and certainty of the judgments. An eagle is strong and swift, and when it swoops down upon its prey, judgment is certain. The eagle is a symbol of vengeance (cp. Dt.28:49; Hos.8:1; Hab.1:8). (A.T. Robertson. *Word Pictures In The New Testament*, Vol.6, p.360.)

> **Thought 1.** None of the ungodly and evil of the world will escape the judgment of God. God is *just and righteous* as well as love, perfect in justice and righteousness. Therefore, *perfect justice* is to be executed upon the ungodly and evil. They are to reap *exactly* what they have sown. God Himself will execute justice and righteousness in the trumpet judgments. This is the fifth trumpet blasting its judgment upon the ungodly of the earth. This is the beginning of the *great tribulation* that is coming upon the earth. This is what the great Book of God, the Book of Destiny, reveals. But remember: as just stated, God is loving as well as just. Therefore, any person who repents and turns to God's Son, the Lord Jesus Christ, can still be saved, no matter how ungodly he has lived.

**2** (9:1) **Satan—Angels, Fallen—Abyss—Bottomless Pit**: there will be the unnamed star or person. A star is said to fall from heaven. What is this star? It is a person. The word *star* is used in its symbolic way to refer to a person of fame or of high position. Who is this person? Note these facts.

⇒ He is said to be a star "fallen" (peptokota) from heaven to earth. This is past tense; it means that he was already fallen when God gave him the key to the bottomless pit.

⇒ Christ said that He saw Satan fall from heaven.

> **He replied, "I saw Satan fall like lightning from heaven. (Luke 10:18)**

⇒ Scripture gives a glimpse into the fall of Satan. He was apparently the highest arch-angel created by God. But he did what every person has done, began to look at himself and choose to go his own way. Therefore, God had to do what he has to do with everyone of us when we reject and rebel against Him: God had to cast Satan out of heaven, out of His holy presence.

> **How you have fallen from heaven, O morning star, son of the dawn! You have been cast down to the earth, you who once laid low the nations! You said in your heart, "I will ascend to heaven; I will raise my throne above the stars of God; I will sit enthroned on the mount of assembly, on the utmost heights of the sacred mountain. I will ascend above the tops of the clouds; I will make myself like the Most High." But you are brought down to the grave, to the depths of the pit. (Isa 14:12-15)**

⇒ He is given the keys to the bottomless pit, that is, the Abyss, the place where Scripture says the demons and devils are kept. (This is discussed in the next note.)

The point is this: in comparing Scripture with Scripture, this fallen star or angel seems to be Satan himself. If he is not Satan, then he is probably some high ranking fallen angel in the spirit world. Presently Jesus Christ has the keys to the bottomless pit, but He gives them to Satan and allows Satan to afflict the earth with his hordes of demons. Why? So that the world of evil men can reap what they have sown. However, note that God restrains and limits his evil destruction even as He does in our day and time (cp. Mt.8:29; Lk.8:31; Rev.1:18; 3:7; cp. Rev.20:11-15).

**3** (9:2) **Abyss—Bottomless Pit**: there will be the bottomless pit or Abyss. It will be opened by the fallen angel of Satan. What is the abyss or bottomless pit? It is the place where *evil spirits and demons* are kept until the end of the world. (See DEEPER STUDY # 1, *Hell*—1 Pt.3:19-20 for all the prisons or compartments of hell.) Their final doom will be Gehenna or the lake of fire, the place where all those who have rebelled against God are to be condemned (Rev.20:10, 14-15). Note what happens when this fallen angel opens the Abyss: smoke arises out of the pit, smoke that is just like the smoke of a great furnace. The smoke in the atmosphere became so heavy and thick that the sun was darkened. This symbolizes what will happen to the ungodly and evil:

⇒ The darkness of the underworld will attack them.

⇒ They will have the breath of life suffocated out of them by trouble after trouble.

⇒ They will experience horror after horror arising out of the bottomless pit, the Abyss.

> **And they [evil spirits] begged him repeatedly not to order them to go into the Abyss. (Luke 8:31)**
> **The fifth angel sounded his trumpet, and I saw a star that had fallen from the sky to the earth. The star was given the key to the shaft of the Abyss. When he opened the Abyss, smoke rose from it like the smoke from a gigantic**

furnace. The sun and sky were darkened by the smoke from the Abyss. And out of the smoke locusts came down upon the earth and were given power like that of scorpions of the earth. They had as king over them the angel of the Abyss, whose name in Hebrew is Abaddon, and in Greek, Apollyon. (Rev 9:1-3, 11)

Now when they have finished their testimony, the beast that comes up from the Abyss will attack them, and overpower and kill them. (Rev 11:7)

The beast, which you saw, once was, now is not, and will come up out of the Abyss and go to his destruction. The inhabitants of the earth whose names have not been written in the book of life from the creation of the world will be astonished when they see the beast, because he once was, now is not, and yet will come. (Rev 17:8)

And I saw an angel coming down out of heaven, having the key to the Abyss and holding in his hand a great chain. He seized the dragon, that ancient serpent, who is the devil, or Satan, and bound him for a thousand years. (Rev 20:1-2)

**4** (9:3-6) **Evil Spirits—Judgment**: there will be the locust-like demons from the Abyss. They will be sent to inflict unbearable punishment upon the ungodly. Why are these demons called locusts? Because locusts are a symbol of God's anger against the ungodly and evil of the world (Ex.10:13; Joel 1:4). Note five facts about the judgment of these locust-like demons.

1. The locust-like demons will be given scorpion-like power (v.3). The scorpion strikes its victim with its tail; its sting is in its tail. It has a poisonous fluid that it injects into the wound of its victim. The sting is not fatal, but it causes terrible suffering.

What is being said is this: in the great tribulation demons with scorpion-like power will be set loose from the bottomless pit.

Remember: the world and the laws of nature are being so radically affected that one natural disaster after another will be occurring all over the world. There will be a shortage of food, water, and the basic essentials of life. Animals will be scurrying about even as men are, frantically searching for food. There is, of course, even the possibility of some bizarre animal mutation resulting from all the natural changes and scientific experimentation in the latter days. The point is this: we know better than to laugh at such prospects today because of what science is doing with the genes and basic elements of life. Indescribable monstrosities are very possible today.

But note: this is a judgment from God. It is not something man brings on himself. God may allow the evil spirits to use something man has developed, but God's judgment will be behind it all. Evil spirits, the demons from the bottomless pit, will be loosed and given scorpion-like power to afflict the ungodly and evil of this world. Note: they do not kill people; they only afflict and torture people. The demons will torture everyone in their paths just like the locusts of the field.

2. The locust-like demons will be restrained from damaging nature (v.4). This shows that they will not be real earthly locusts, for locusts feed upon vegetation.

3. The locust-like demons are to afflict only people who do not have the seal of God (v.4). God will seal His people during the great tribulation. His people will be protected from suffering the judgments cast upon the ungodly and evil of this world. Many believers will be afflicted and die at the hands of the antichrist, but not a single believer will be touched by the judgment of God. God's wrath falls only upon unbelievers. This has always been true and it always will be (see notes—Rev.7:2-3; 8:13 for more discussion).

4. The locust-like demons will not kill people, only torture them (v.5). This is critical to note. This fact alone seems to point to the demonic force being some locust-like animal that actually sweeps the earth, an animal that stings people with some poison venom that tortures but does not kill its victims. This may seem cruel, but we must always keep in mind what is happening: the ungodly and evil of the last days will launch a holocaust upon the world far beyond anything anyone could have ever imagined. They will literally torture and slaughter millions. Therefore, as God has always said, a man reaps what he sows. Consequently, the ungodly and evil of the end times will be punished with an equal judgment, a torture equal to the torture they have inflicted. (See DEEPER STUDY # 1, *Judicial Judgment of God*—Jn.12:39-41; note—Ro.1:24.)

Note that the torment is to last five months. The idea is a continuous attack: the locust-like demons are to continuously attack the ungodly for five long months. But even during this awful judgment God shows mercy and is going to give man a chance to repent (cp. v.20-21). As always, most will refuse, but God will still offer His mercy because He loves and longs for man to be saved and to know the glories of heaven and eternal life.

5. The result of the torment upon people will be so agonizing and the pain so excruciating that people will beg for death (v.6). But they will not die. Remember: most people lack the courage to commit suicide. They wish to die, but they do not have the courage to go ahead and take their own lives. The scene of the last days is that people will be so afflicted with torment that they will wish to die, but they cannot. The affliction is not strong enough to kill them, and they are unable to gather up enough courage to kill themselves. Death is out of their reach. They must suffer the torture of God's judgment.

⇒ Jeremiah predicted that men would suffer so much that they would crave death.

> Wherever I banish them, all the survivors of this evil nation will prefer death to life, declares the LORD Almighty.' (Jer 8:3)

⇒ Other Scriptures talk about the despair and hopelessness of men in affliction.

> To those who long for death that does not come, who search for it more than for hidden treasure, (Job 3:21)
> Even then you frighten me with dreams and terrify me with visions, So that I prefer strangling and death, rather than this body of mine. (Job 7:14-15)
> "I loathe my very life; therefore I will give free rein to my complaint and

speak out in the bitterness of my soul. (Job 10:1)

You brought us into prison and laid burdens on our backs. (Psa 66:11)

We are consumed by your anger and terrified by your indignation. (Psa 90:7)

For I eat ashes as my food and mingle my drink with tears Because of your great wrath, for you have taken me up and thrown me aside. (Psa 102:9-10)

The sinners in Zion are terrified; trembling grips the godless: "Who of us can dwell with the consuming fire? Who of us can dwell with everlasting burning?" (Isa 33:14)

**5** (9:7-10) **Evil Spirits—Judgment**: there will be the appearance and power of the locust-like demons. Eight descriptions are given. The point being made is the terrifying appearance and power of the demonic forces of the end time. Man must beware and prepare. He must prepare by receiving Jesus Christ as his Savior so that he may escape the demonic hoard that is to come in the last days.

1. The demonic locusts are like horses prepared for battle: *posed and ready to attack*. This could also mean that they will be larger than the average size locusts (cp. Joel 2:4).

2. The demonic locusts will have heads that look like they are crowned with gold: this symbolizes that they will have *authority* to afflict men. They will be as *conquerors and be successful* in their attacks.

3 The demonic locusts will appear to have the faces of men: this symbolizes the *determination and intelligence* of men. They will be set like flint in their attacks and have the intelligence to attack and inflict damage with their scorpion like poison.

4. The demonic locusts will have hair like hair of women: beauty to seduce and ensnare, to help them to seem innocent and harmless at first. This may mean long antennae to help them in their attack and escape.

5. The demonic locusts will have teeth as a lion: ferocious, fierce, devouring, and cruel (cp. Joel 1:6).

6. The demonic locusts will have breastplates as of iron: indestructible, protected, and defended. People will be helpless in killing them.

7. The demonic locusts will have wings that sound like many chariots rushing into battle: frightening and overwhelming. There will be a sense of hopelessness in defending against them (cp. Joel 2:4-5).

8. The demonic locusts will have stinging tails like scorpions: demonic torture.

**Thought 1.** When the end of the world approaches, there will be far more demonic forces at work than ever before. The intensification staggers the human mind. But God loves us and wants us to escape the fangs of the devil and the demonic hordes. Therefore, He warns us about what is coming. We must escape the coming judgments which are to be blasted against the ungodly and evil of the last days. God has made a way for us to escape. What is that way? The Lord Jesus Christ, the Son of God Himself. We must receive Jesus Christ as our Lord and Savior, casting ourselves totally upon Him.

How shall we escape if we ignore such a great salvation? This salvation, which was first announced by the Lord, was confirmed to us by those who heard him. (Heb 2:3)

While people are saying, "Peace and safety," destruction will come on them suddenly, as labor pains on a pregnant woman, and they will not escape. (1 Th 5:3)

Be sure of this: The wicked will not go unpunished, but those who are righteous will go free. (Prov 11:21)

Therefore this is what the LORD says: 'I will bring on them a disaster they cannot escape. Although they cry out to me, I will not listen to them. (Jer 11:11)

Woe to you who long for the day of the LORD! Why do you long for the day of the LORD? That day will be darkness, not light. It will be as though a man fled from a lion only to meet a bear, as though he entered his house and rested his hand on the wall only to have a snake bite him. (Amos 5:18-19)

**6** (9:11) **Evil Spirits—Satan—Angels, Fallen**: there will be the king of the demonic locusts. Four things are said about him.

1. He is an *angel*: a creature of enormous beauty and strength.

2. He is *the angel of the Abyss*: a fallen angel. He was once an angel of heaven, a servant of God; but now he is an angel of the underworld, of sin and evil and of all ungodliness and unrighteousness.

3. He is the king, the ruler and governor, over the Abyss. Note: there are various levels of authority and power and rule in the spiritual world just as there are in this world. This fallen angel rules over the power of darkness. It is under his command and authority.

4. He has both a Greek and an Hebrew name. His Hebrew name is Abaddon which means *destruction*, and his Greek name is Apollyon which means *destroyer*. What better name could there be to describe this ruler of the demonic locusts? No creature and no force leaves behind any more destruction than that of the ferocious locust. Who is this fallen angel? Again, it has to be either Satan himself or one of his commanding angels.

**Thought 1.** Note a critical fact: the enemy of man is the spiritual force that lies behind this world, a force that the Bible calls Satan. We only deceive ourselves if we do not cast ourselves upon the power and salvation of Jesus Christ. Jesus Christ delivers us from the grip of this evil force and person who leads us into evil and dooms us to death. Jesus Christ, the very Son of God Himself, has defeated Satan in order to deliver us from the grip of Satan and his power of sin and death.

When anyone hears the message about the kingdom and does not understand it, the evil one comes and snatches away what was sown in his heart. This is the seed sown along the path. (Mat 13:19)

You belong to your father, the devil, and you want to carry out your father's desire. He was a murderer from the beginning, not holding to the truth, for there is no truth in him. When he lies, he speaks his native language, for he is a liar and the father of lies. (John 8:44)

Now is the time for judgment on this world; now the prince of this world [Satan] will be driven out. (John 12:31)

I will not speak with you much longer, for the prince of this world [Satan] is coming. He has no hold on me, (John 14:30)

And even if our gospel is veiled, it is veiled to those who are perishing. The god of this age has blinded the minds of unbelievers, so that they cannot see the light of the gospel of the glory of Christ, who is the image of God. (2 Cor 4:3-4)

In which you used to live when you followed the ways of this world and of the ruler of the kingdom of the air [Satan], the spirit who is now at work in those who are disobedient. (Eph 2:2)

For our struggle is not against flesh and blood, but against the rulers, against the authorities, against the powers of this dark world and against the spiritual forces of evil in the heavenly realms. (Eph 6:12)

And having disarmed the powers and authorities, he made a public spectacle of them, triumphing over them by the cross. (Col 2:15)

Since the children have flesh and blood, he too shared in their humanity so that by his death he might destroy him who holds the power of death—that is, the devil— And free those who all their lives were held in slavery by their fear of death. (Heb 2:14-15)

Be self-controlled and alert. Your enemy the devil prowls around like a roaring lion looking for someone to devour. (1 Pet 5:8)

He who does what is sinful is of the devil, because the devil has been sinning from the beginning. The reason the Son of God appeared was to destroy the devil's work. (1 John 3:8)

| | D. The Blast of the Sixth Trumpet: Demonic-like Military Horsemen, 9:12-21 | this: Their breastplates were fiery red, dark blue, and yellow as sulfur. The heads of the horses resembled the heads of lions, and out of their mouths came fire, smoke and sulfur. | c. The horses 1) Have heads like lions: Ferocious & devouring |
|---|---|---|---|
| 1 More woes lie ahead | 12 The first woe is past; two other woes are yet to come. | 18 A third of mankind was killed by the three plagues of fire, smoke and sulfur that came out of their mouths. | 2) Have mouths spitting fire: Hellish nature |
| 2 The four fallen angels are set loose<br>a. At the command of a voice from the altar<br><br>b. Were bound at the Euphrates River | 13 The sixth angel sounded his trumpet, and I heard a voice coming from the horns of the golden altar that is before God.<br>14 It said to the sixth angel who had the trumpet, "Release the four angels who are bound at the great river Euphrates." | 19 The power of the horses was in their mouths and in their tails; for their tails were like snakes, having heads with which they inflict injury. | 3) Kill one third of the ungodly & evil<br>4) Their power is in their mouth, head, and snake-like tails: Torture & death |
| c. Were prepared to destroy one third of humanity | 15 And the four angels who had been kept ready for this very hour and day and month and year were released to kill a third of mankind. | 20 The rest of mankind that were not killed by these plagues still did not repent of the work of their hands; they did not stop worshiping demons, and idols of gold, silver, bronze, stone and wood—idols that cannot see or hear or walk. | 4 The judgment has a purpose: To lead people to repentance<br>a. The survivors do not repent<br>b. The repentance needed |
| 3 The military horsemen & their demonic horses appear<br>a. Their number: 200 million<br>b. The riders: Have breastplates that are indestructible | 16 The number of the mounted troops was two hundred million. I heard their number.<br>17 The horses and riders I saw in my vision looked like | 21 Nor did they repent of their murders, their magic arts, their sexual immorality or their thefts. | |

# DIVISION V

## THE SEVEN TRUMPET JUDGMENTS: EVENTS DURING THE GREAT TRIBULATION, 8:1-11:19

### D. The Blast of the Sixth Trumpet: Demonic-like Military Horsemen, 9:12-21

(9:12-21) **Introduction**: the trumpet blast of judgment is going to fall upon the earth, upon the ungodly and evil of this world. We have seen this in the first four trumpet blasts that fell upon nature. Horrifying and catastrophic events destroyed one third of the vegetation, water supply, sea life, and the shipping and fishing commerce of the world. Scientists warn us all the time about the possibility of such horrors unless the environment is protected. Such a horrible time is coming. But note: in the first four trumpet judgments, man himself will not be afflicted, not on a massive scale. That is, man's body will not be attacked; his body will not suffer any massive ill effects from the catastrophes. But after the natural disasters the ungodly and evil of the world will be judged. The last three trumpet judgments will be directed against them personally, and millions will be afflicted and destroyed. They are going to reap what they have sown. They have sown terrible ungodliness; therefore, they are to reap the punishment of their evil. And the punishment is to be so severe, it can only be called a prolonged period of woe. The last three trumpet judgments are the *woe judgments*, the judgments directed against the ungodly and evil of this world. The first woe judgment was seen in the former passage, the blast of a demonic-like plague of locusts. The demonic locusts could only torture men, not kill them. But now the sixth trumpet blasts forth its judgment, and another horde of demons come forth. This time, however, there is a difference. These are military demons, and they shall take their toll upon human life. An astronomical number of the ungodly and evil of the world will die under the judgment of God's righteous hand in this *woe* judgment. This is the judgment of the demonic military horsemen.

1. More woes lie ahead (v.12).
2. The four fallen angels are set loose (v.13-15).
3. The military horsemen and demonic horses appear (v.16-19).
4. The judgment has a purpose: to lead people to repentance (v.20-21).

**1** (9:12) **Judgment—Woe**: more *woes* lie ahead. There is to be catastrophic destruction and devastation in the *great tribulation* that is coming upon the earth. It will be such a terrible time that it can only be described as a period of *woe*, that is, of extreme grief, distress, suffering, affliction, and calamity. The *woe judgments* of God are the trumpet judgments that zero in on afflicting the bodies of the ungodly. One woe has already been covered, the demonic-like locusts. Two more woe judgments are yet to fall upon the evil people of the world.

**2** (9:13-15) **Angels, Fallen—Judgment**: there are the four fallen angels set loose. Three facts are given about their being loosed.

1. They are set loose by a command coming from the golden altar. This is the altar of incense where the prayers of God's people are kept (cp. Rev.6:9-10; 8:3-4). This symbolizes a significant fact: God launches this judgment especially to vindicate the millions who will be slaughtered in the holocaust of the antichrist. God is going to be perfectly just. He is going to execute perfect justice against the antichrist and his followers who have slaughtered millions. They too

shall be slain by the judgment of God. The very prayers of the golden altar cry out for the name of God to be vindicated against those who laughed, mocked, rejected, denied, disbelieved, disobeyed, and cursed God. God is going to hear these prayers.

2. The four released angels are bound at the great river Euphrates. Note the definite article used: *the*. The four fallen angels are four specific angels. As will be seen in a few moments, they will be four angels of high military rank.

Why would the angels come from the Euphrates? Scripture does not say, but two reasons seem likely.

⇒ The head or spring of the Euphrates river flowed out of the garden of Eden. It was there, of course, where Satan first tempted and overthrew man. The first sin that resulted in the fallen human race took place at the head of the Euphrates river. It was also there that the first murder took place and it was in the region of the Euphrates that the first organized rebellion against God took place. (All this is pointed out by the excellent Bible expositor, Lehman Strauss. *The Book of the Revelation*, p.194).

⇒ The Euphrates was the western boundary of the promised land that God promised to Abraham.

Therefore, beyond the Euphrates can be looked upon as the outer reaches of the earth, as the place where the spiritual enemies of man are kept. As William Barclay says:

"The angels, therefore, come from the distant lands, from the strange and alien and hostile places, from these very parts of the world from which the Assyrians and the Babyloni-ans had in time past descended with destruction upon Israel. So, then, the angels come from the quarter from which disaster had in ancient times come upon God's people Israel....The four angels are Angels of Punishment; they come from the part of the world from which death and disaster and slavery had so often come" (*The Revelation of John*, Vol.2, p.64).

3. The four fallen angels were loosed and they prepared to execute a judgment upon the earth: the judgment of slaying one third of the ungodly and evil population of the world. Remember why: because the billions upon earth will follow and give their total allegiance and support to the antichrist and the policies of his government. One of the major policies will be the holocaust launched against the believers of the world. Literally millions will be slaughtered. Simply stated, God will not be able to take the diabolical evil of ungodly people any more. He will allow His justice to finally be executed and demonstrated: the diabolical, the ungodly and evil, shall reap the slaughter they have inflicted upon others.

4. Note one other fact: God has already set the time for this judgment. There is an exact year, month, day, and even hour that this judgment is to fall upon the ungodly and evil. The hour is already fixed.

**3** (9:16-19) **Judgment—Angels, Fallen**: there are the military horsemen and their demonic horses. Five things are said about this demonic horde.

1. There will be an army of two hundred million. Imagine an army of two hundred million demonic spirits let loose upon the earth. This will be the army that the four fallen angels will command, an army such as the world has never seen before.

2. The riders will have breastplates. The breastplates are "fiery red, dark blue, and yellow as sulfur (NIV), fiery red and sapphire blue and sulfur (brimstone) yellow" (The Amplified New Testament). The breastplate symbolizes that they will be indestructible, protected and defended as they go to war against the ungodly of the world. Man will not be able to stop them.

3. The horses will be horrible and add terror upon terror on the ungodly.

⇒ They will have heads like lions: ferocious, fierce, devouring, cruel, and consuming.

⇒ They will have mouths that spit out fire: a hellish and fiery nature; a vengeful, angry, and wrathful nature (cp. Rev.14:10; 19:20; 21:8).

⇒ They will kill one third of the ungodly and evil upon earth. How? By the plague of fire, smoke, and brimstone. (Note: the weapons used by this demonic army are not given. But observe how fire, smoke, and brimstone sounds like an atomic explosion. We must, however, keep in mind that this slaughter is being masterminded by evil spirits and demonic forces—all being executed under God's will as a judgment upon the ungodly and evil of the world.)

⇒ Their power is in their mouths, heads, and tails. The head symbolizes intelligence; the mouth symbolizes deceptive speech and a hunger to consume and to destroy; and the snake-like tails symbolize poisonous strikes and deadly wounds.

**Thought 1.** The picture of the great tribulation is a picture of horror heaped upon horror. It is a frightful and fearful scene. But note: with what we know about the possibility of atomic destruction, environmental devastation, and the possibility of some monstrous gene mutation—the judgments of God's book can no longer be doubted. Not if God is really God, and not if He is truly just, and not if some diabolical leader arises (as they have in the past) who launches a holocaust against God's people. God is bound to execute justice if some demon of a person slaughters millions and millions of His people, and if the whole world gives its support. It is this that will cause the antichrist to differ from all former world leaders who have killed millions. They had only limited support. But in the last days, the antichrist will have the support of most of the ungodly and evil people of the earth.

**4** (9:20-21) **Judgment**: there is the purpose for the judgment—repentance. Two significant points are now made.

1. The ungodly and evil survivors of the earth still do not repent and turn to God. Two thirds of the population will survive, not because they deserve to survive but because God is merciful. God is always merciful even in the midst of judgment. He will give the ungodly of the earth another chance to repent, speaking to them through the judgments, but they will not repent.

**Thought 1.** Lehman Strauss makes an excellent point about this fact:

"God has never delighted in the death of the wicked. In the midst of His visitations of severest judgments, He delights to be gracious to the guilty. But alas, the death of one billion people in the earth, with the accompanying grief and the confusion which must follow such a disaster, finds the residue of people not willing to repent. Such is the human heart, deceitful above all things and desperately wicked. After two world wars, and one hundred lesser wars in the past fifty years, the world is more wicked than ever. Instead of repentance, sin increases" (*The Book of the Revelation*, p.196).

2. There will be several gross sins for which the ungodly need to repent. And remember: there will be an enormous increase and intensification of the evils in the end time.

   a. There will be an increase in the worship of evil spirits and the worship of idols. Actually, the devils are said to be behind the worship of idols. Just think about how much worship of evil spirits and idols is going on today. How much is going on in the cities of the world at any given moment? Scripture actually declares that the worship of all gods except the Son of God, the Lord Jesus Christ, is the worship of an evil spirit or idol. In fact, Scripture even declares that covetousness is idolatry. Why? Because a person has set his heart on something other than God Himself, and man owes his first allegiance to God.

   Note that no idol can see, hear, or walk; and how true this is. They cannot answer a single prayer, give a single ounce of strength, lift a single finger to help, save a single hair, extend life a single minute, carry a person one single inch toward heaven. They cannot arouse one single moment of acceptance out of God nor give one moment of eternal life to a person. An idol is lifeless. It can do nothing for man. But note: the evil spirits behind the idols can damage and destroy a person's soul forever. It will be this that will cause so much idolatry and worship of evil spirits in the last days. The antichrist will demand the worship of the state. There will apparently be laws passed demanding that a person give his first loyalty to the state, much as we see in some nations today and have seen in past history. The worship of the state, of course, aids a government in keeping control of its people. This is the worst kind of idolatry, for a person has to submit to the state or else he is usually imprisoned and executed. In the government of the antichrist, people will be executed for not giving their first loyalty to the state.

   God hates idolatry and demands in no uncertain terms that man turn away from his idolatry and from the worship of evil spirits.

   **No, but the sacrifices of pagans are offered to demons, not to God, and I do not want you to be participants with demons. (1 Cor 10:20)**

   **Dear children, keep yourselves from idols. (1 John 5:21)**

   **The rest of mankind that were not killed by these plagues still did not repent of the work of their hands; they did not stop worshiping demons, and idols of gold, silver, bronze, stone and wood—idols that cannot see or hear or walk. (Rev 9:20)**

   **"You shall not make for yourself an idol in the form of anything in heaven above or on the earth beneath or in the waters below. (Exo 20:4)**

   **"'Do not make idols or set up an image or a sacred stone for yourselves, and do not place a carved stone in your land to bow down before it. I am the LORD your God. (Lev 26:1)**

   **The images of their gods you are to burn in the fire. Do not covet the silver and gold on them, and do not take it for yourselves, or you will be ensnared by it, for it is detestable to the LORD your God. (Deu 7:25)**

   **Be careful, or you will be enticed to turn away and worship other gods and bow down to them. (Deu 11:16)**

   **"I am the LORD; that is my name! I will not give my glory to another or my praise to idols. (Isa 42:8)**

   **They must no longer offer any of their sacrifices to the goat idols to whom they prostitute themselves. This is to be a lasting ordinance for them and for the generations to come.' (Lev 17:7)**

   **They made him jealous with their foreign gods and angered him with their detestable idols. They sacrificed to demons, which are not God— gods they had not known, gods that recently appeared, gods your fathers did not fear. (Deu 32:16-17)**

   **They worshiped their idols, which became a snare to them. They sacrificed their sons and their daughters to demons. They shed innocent blood, the blood of their sons and daughters, whom they sacrificed to the idols of Canaan, and the land was desecrated by their blood. They defiled themselves by what they did; by their deeds [imaginations] they prostituted themselves. (Psa 106:36-39)**

   b. There will be an increase in the sin of *murder*. Remember all the martyrs John saw in heaven, the countless multitude of believers slaughtered by the antichrist and his government and followers. The martyrs were so many that "no one could count [them]" (Rev.7:9). Believers will be slaughtered all over the world—from all nations and tribes and languages and people. Just think of the holocaust that will take place—not even a single tribe of the earth, not where a believer exists, escapes the attempt of the antichrist and the world to stamp out the followers of the Lord Jesus Christ. The antichrist will have his followers all over the world and they will support his murderous moves against the believers of the Lord Jesus Christ.

   **At that time many will turn away from the faith and will betray and hate each other, (Mat 24:10)**

   ⇒ Note: this is undoubtedly the difference between the holocaust of the past and the holocaust of the antichrist. In the past the diabolical leaders like Hitler and Stalin had only a number of people who supported their murderous genocide; the antichrist will have worldwide support. The fact that it is world-wide and that it is launched against all the followers of God's Son will trigger God's decision to go ahead and move in His final judgment.

The point is this: murder will be one of the great sins of the antichrist and his followers. It is a sin for which the ungodly and evil must repent or face the terrible judgments of the end time and of eternity.

**"You have heard that it was said to the people long ago, 'Do not murder, and anyone who murders will be subject to judgment.' But I tell you that anyone who is angry with his brother will be subject to judgment. Again, anyone who says to his brother, 'Raca,' is answerable to the Sanhedrin. But anyone who says, 'You fool!' will be in danger of the fire of hell. (Mat 5:21-22)**

**"Which ones?" The man inquired. Jesus replied, "'Do not murder, do not commit adultery, do not steal, do not give false testimony, (Mat 19:18)**

**If you suffer, it should not be as a murderer or thief or any other kind of criminal, or even as a meddler. (1 Pet 4:15)**

**Anyone who hates his brother is a murderer, and you know that no murderer has eternal life in him. (1 John 3:15)**

**"You shall not murder. (Exo 20:13)**

c. There will be an increase in the sin of magical arts or sorcery (pharmakon). Note that the Greek word is close to the spelling of the English word *pharmacy*, that is, a place that handles drugs. Magical arts or sorcery includes all kinds of witchcraft, the use of drugs or of evil spirits to gain control over the lives of others or over one's own life. In the present context it would include all forms of sorcery including astrology, palm reading, séances, fortune telling, crystals, and other forms of witchcraft.

**Saul died because he was unfaithful to the LORD; he did not keep the word of the LORD and even consulted a medium for guidance, (1 Chr 10:13)**

**When men tell you to consult mediums and spiritists, who whisper and mutter, should not a people inquire of their God? Why consult the dead on behalf of the living? To the law and to the testimony! If they do not speak according to this word, they have no light of dawn. (Isa 8:19-20)**

**I will destroy your witchcraft and you will no longer cast spells. (Micah 5:12)**

**Idolatry and witchcraft; hatred, discord, jealousy, fits of rage, selfish ambition, dissensions, factions (Gal 5:20)**

d. There will be an increase in immorality (porneias): a broad word including all forms of immoral and sexual acts. It is pre-marital sex and adultery; it is abnormal sex, all kinds of sexual vice.

**Flee from sexual immorality. All other sins a man commits are outside his body, but he who sins sexually sins against his own body. (1 Cor 6:18)**

**But among you there must not be even a hint of sexual immorality, or of any kind of impurity, or of greed, because these are improper for God's holy people. (Eph 5:3)**

**Put to death, therefore, whatever belongs to your earthly nature: sexual immorality, impurity, lust, evil desires and greed, which is idolatry. (Col 3:5)**

e. There will be an increase in thefts (klemmaton): to cheat and steal; to take wrongfully from another person, either legally or illegally.

**"You shall not steal. (Exo 20:15)**

**"'Do not steal. "'Do not lie. "'Do not deceive one another. (Lev 19:11)**

**He who has been stealing must steal no longer, but must work, doing something useful with his own hands, that he may have something to share with those in need. (Eph 4:28)**

**And not to steal from them, but to show that they can be fully trusted, so that in every way they will make the teaching about God our Savior attractive. (Titus 2:10)**

**CHAPTER 10**

**E. The Great Announcement of the Final Triumph Over Evil (Part I): The Little Book, 10:1-11**

**1 The mighty messenger of the great announcement**
a. Was clothed with a cloud
b. Had a rainbow upon his head
c. Had a face like the sun
d. Had legs like fiery pillars
e. Held the little book
f. Set his feet upon the sea & the land

g. Called forth seven thundering judgments
h. A voice stops John from revealing the message of the seven thunders

**2 The declaration & oath of the great announcement**

a. He wraps the great

Then I saw another mighty angel coming down from heaven. He was robed in a cloud, with a rainbow above his head; his face was like the sun, and his legs were like fiery pillars.
2 He was holding a little scroll, which lay open in his hand. He planted his right foot on the sea and his left foot on the land,
3 And he gave a loud shout like the roar of a lion. When he shouted, the voices of the seven thunders spoke.
4 And when the seven thunders spoke, I was about to write; but I heard a voice from heaven say, "Seal up what the seven thunders have said and do not write it down."
5 Then the angel I had seen standing on the sea and on the land raised his right hand to heaven.
6 And he swore by him who

lives for ever and ever, who created the heavens and all that is in them, the earth and all that is in it, and the sea and all that is in it, and said, "There will be no more delay!
7 But in the days when the seventh angel is about to sound his trumpet, the mystery of God will be accomplished, just as he announced to his servants the prophets."
8 Then the voice that I had heard from heaven spoke to me once more: "Go, take the scroll that lies open in the hand of the angel who is standing on the sea and on the land."
9 So I went to the angel and asked him to give me the little scroll. He said to me, "Take it and eat it. It will turn your stomach sour, but in your mouth it will be as sweet as honey."
10 I took the little scroll from the angel's hand and ate it. It tasted as sweet as honey in my mouth, but when I had eaten it, my stomach turned sour.
11 Then I was told, "You must prophesy again about many peoples, nations, languages and kings."

announcement with the most solemn of oaths
b. The great announcement: There shall no longer be a delay—the mystery of God is to be finished
 1) In the days of the 7th angel & trumpet
 2) The mystery prophesied to God's prophets

**3 The sour & sweet taste of the great announcement**
a. John is commanded to go to the angel & take the open book

b. John is commanded by the angel to take & eat the book: The message of the book is sour & sweet

 1) John's obedience
 2) Result: Is both sweet & sour

c. John is commanded to proclaim the message of the book to the world

# DIVISION V

## THE SEVEN TRUMPET JUDGMENTS: EVENTS DURING THE GREAT TRIBULATION, 8:1-11:19

## E. The Great Announcement of the Final Triumph Over Evil (Part I): The Little Book, 10:1-11

(10:1-11) **Introduction**: six trumpet judgments have been blasted across the face of the earth. The earth has been hit with...

- industry and shipping commerce.
- a meteoric mass that contaminated one third of the water supply.
- an astronomical eclipse that temporarily wiped out one third of the daylight.
- a demonic-like locust attack that caused unbearable torture upon the ungodly of the earth.
- a second demonic-like military attack that killed one third of the ungodly and evil of the earth.

It is now time for the seventh trumpet judgment to blast forth. But before it does, so much horror and destruction has hit the earth that the human heart cries out, "Is there no hope? Is the earth doomed? Is it to be a dead planet? Is it to be nothing more than a ball of molten lava floating through space like so many other dead planets and stars? Is all life to be destroyed? Is this the pessimistic and hopeless future of the earth?" No! A thousand no's! All the destruction and devastation will take place upon earth, but there is to be a final triumph over evil and destruction. This is the great an-

nouncement of this passage. God's eternal plan for salvation and for a new heavens and earth will be consummated.

⇒ All the prophets of doomsday are wrong. God is going to save all who will give their lives to Him, and He is going to make a new heavens and earth that will be perfect and last forever and ever.

⇒ All the prophets of humanism (man is his own god) are wrong. The earth is going to suffer convulsive and catastrophic horrors. The earth and its time are running down, and man himself cannot stop the process.

But this is the glorious message of these next four passages (chapters ten and eleven). God is going to conquer evil. This is the great announcement of the final triumph over evil.

1. The mighty messenger of the great announcement (v.1-4).
2. The declaration and oath of the great announcement (v.5-7).
3. The sour and sweet taste of the great announcement (v.8-11).

**1** (10:1-4) **Angel—Salvation—Jesus Christ**: first, there is the mighty angel or messenger of the great announcement. This angel was apparently the mightiest of God's messengers. Remember: the word angel means messenger. Note how mighty he is.

⇒ The messenger came down from heaven. He came from the very presence and throne of God Himself, from the most exalted place. This tells us that he is the very highest of beings. The great announcement he was about to make was the announcement straight from the throne of God itself.

⇒ The messenger was robed in a cloud: this symbolizes a majestic, glorious, and heavenly appearance. Just as the heavens are clothed with the majesty and glory of clouds, so this angel was clothed. He was clothed in the cloud of the majesty and glory of heaven. The great announcement he was about to make was coming from the majesty and glory of heaven.

⇒ The messenger had a rainbow above his head: this symbolizes the glory and mercy of God. This is seen in that a rainbow is part of the glory of the throne of God (Ezk.1:28), and it was the sign of God's mercy shown to Noah (Gen.9:12-13). Therefore, the glory of God and the mercy of God are seen in this angel. The great announcement he was about to make was to be a message of glory and mercy.

⇒ The messenger had a face that shone like the sun. This symbolizes the light, luster, brightness, brilliance, and splendor of the messenger. The great announcement of the messenger was to be the message of enormous light, luster, and splendor.

⇒ The messenger had feet like fiery pillars. This symbolizes the holiness, purity, righteousness, and strength of the messenger. The great announcement of the messenger was to be the strong pillar of God's holiness, purity, and righteousness to earth.

⇒ The messenger held a little scroll or book that was open. What is the book? Verse eleven says that it is the message that must be proclaimed to the world. What is that message? The Word of God, the Holy Scriptures, both the love and grace and the judgment and woe of God. The great announcement of the messenger was to be the message of God's Word, in particular the message of Revelation.

⇒ The messenger planted his feet upon the sea and the land. This symbolizes the gigantic size, strength, and power of the messenger. He was claiming both sea and land, the whole world for God. The great announcement of the messenger was a message that was to involve the whole universe.

⇒ The messenger had a voice that roared like a lion. This symbolizes the voice of God, the very voice of the lion of Judah, Christ Himself (Rev.5:5; Joel 3:16; Hos.11:10). The great announcement was to be the very message of God Himself.

⇒ The messenger called forth seven thundering voices. The number seven symbolizes completeness, fulfillment and finality. Thunder symbolizes the power and strength of God's voice. The great announcement of the messenger will be the message of completeness and fulfillment and of finality. And the seven thunders of God's voice have the power to complete and fulfill and finalize all things.

⇒ But note: a voice from heaven stops John from revealing the message of the seven thunders. The voice tells John to seal up whatever it was that the seven thunders said.

The point is this: a great announcement is to be made to the earth, an announcement so great that the mightiest of messengers is sent from heaven to deliver it. The very might of this messenger shows that the great announcement must be heard by all. The awesome importance of the great announcement is clearly seen by glancing at what the mighty messenger shows us. He shows us that the great announcement...

• comes straight from the throne of God itself.
• comes straight from the majesty and glory of heaven.
• is a message of glory and mercy.
• is a message of enormous light, luster, and splendor.
• is to be the strong pillar of God's holiness, purity, and righteousness upon earth.
• is to be the message of God's Word.
• is to be a message that involves the whole universe.
• is to be the message of God Himself.
• is to be the completion, fulfillment, and finalization of all things.

**Thought 1.** Who is this mighty angel or messenger? Some commentators say that it is Christ Himself. Others say that it is one of the mightiest of angels in heaven. The description given can easily fit Christ or one of the mighty angels, and the meaning of the passage is not changed by holding to either position. However, note this: the messenger calls the two witnesses of chapter eleven, "my two witnesses" (Rev.11:3). This points toward the angel being Christ Himself.

**2** (10:5-7) **Salvation—Majesty of God—Redemption**: second, there is the declaration and oath of the great announcement. Note how spectacular this moment is, yet how meaningful. The mighty angel, so huge in size and majestic in being that he straddles the whole earth with one foot upon the sea and one foot upon the earth, lifts up his hand toward heaven and wraps the great announcement in the most solemn of oaths. He swears by God Himself:

⇒ "By him who lives forever and ever."
⇒ "Who created the heavens and all that is in them."
⇒ "Who created the earth and all that is in it."
⇒ "Who created the sea and all that is in it."

Once the solemn oath has been taken, then the great announcement is made. What is it? That time shall be no more. The delay of the end will be no more. The consummation of all things is at hand. When? When all the catastrophes have happened—all the horror that *Revelation* covers up to this point—when they have all happened—then the voice and trumpet of the seventh angel will blast forth and the very last events of human history will take place. God is going to confront the ungodly and the evil of the world for the last time, and He is going to destroy them and establish righteousness in the earth forever and ever.

Note what the angel declares: this climax of human history is the mystery of God, the very same mystery and message that has been declared by the prophets. The ungodly and evil of the world should have accepted the message of the prophets, but they chose to go their own way. They committed all kinds of evil and violent deeds upon earth. Therefore, after the first six trumpet judgments take place upon earth, God is going to launch the last events of human history:

⇒ The antichrist, the great world leader who brought peace and so much hope to the world while the world was suffering so much catastrophe, is going to turn against the world.

⇒ The Lord God, the Lord Jesus Christ Himself, is going to launch His last judgment upon the earth and destroy both the antichrist and his followers—all the ungodly and evil upon earth.

⇒ The Lord Jesus Christ is going to establish His kingdom and righteousness upon earth and reign for one thousand years.

⇒ The Lord Jesus Christ is going to create a new heavens and earth that will last forever and ever.

The seventh trumpet is going to bring forth the last events of human history. Time will soon be no more, not like man has known it, not after the events of the seventh trumpet. When the events of the seventh trumpet have taken place, then the mystery of God will be finalized. The glorious salvation and redemption of the whole universe will then take place. This is the great announcement. There is hope for the world. We can be optimistic and look forward to the most glorious salvation imaginable. God is going to save all who will let Him; and in addition, He is going to create a new heavens and a new earth that will last for ever and ever.

I consider that our present sufferings are not worth comparing with the glory that will be revealed in us. The creation waits in eager expectation for the sons of God to be revealed. For the creation was subjected to frustration, not by its own choice, but by the will of the one who subjected it, in hope That the creation itself will be liberated from its bondage to decay and brought into the glorious freedom of the children of God. We know that the whole creation has been groaning as in the pains of childbirth right up to the present time. (Rom 8:18-22)

All these people were still living by faith when they died. They did not receive the things promised; they only saw them and welcomed them from a distance. And they admitted that they were aliens and strangers on earth. People who say such things show that they are looking for a country of their own. If they had been thinking of the country they had left, they would have had opportunity to return. Instead, they were longing for a better country—a heavenly one. Therefore God is not ashamed to be called their God, for he has prepared a city for them. (Heb 11:13-16)

But the day of the Lord will come like a thief. The heavens will disappear with a roar; the elements will be destroyed by fire, and the earth and everything in it will be laid bare. Since everything will be destroyed in this way, what kind of people ought you to be? You ought to live holy and godly lives [behavior] as you look forward to the day of God and speed its coming. That day will bring about the destruction of the heavens by fire, and the elements will melt in the heat. But in keeping with his promise we are looking forward to a new heaven and a new earth, the home of righteousness. (2 Pet 3:10-13)

Then I saw a new heaven and a new earth, for the first heaven and the first earth had passed away, and there was no longer any sea. I saw the Holy City, the new Jerusalem, coming down out of heaven from God, prepared as a bride beautifully dressed for her husband. And I heard a loud voice from the throne saying, "Now the dwelling of God is with men, and he will live with them. They will be his people, and God himself will be with them and be their God. He will wipe every tear from their eyes. There will be no more death or mourning or crying or pain, for the old order of things has passed away." He who was seated on the throne said, "I am making everything new!" Then he said, "Write this down, for these words are trustworthy and true." (Rev 21:1-5)

"Behold, I will create new heavens and a new earth. The former things will not be remembered, nor will they come to mind. (Isa 65:17)

"As the new heavens and the new earth that I make will endure before me," declares the LORD, "so will your name and descendants endure. (Isa 66:22)

**3** (10:8-11) **Scroll—Book of Revelation, Little:** third, there is the bitter and sweet taste of the great announcement. Note three significant points.

1. John is commanded by the voice of heaven to go over and take the little scroll or book from the mighty angel.

**Thought 1.** There are two lessons for us in this.
1) The Word of God is never just handed to us; it is never forced upon us. If we are to receive its message, we have to go over to the book shelf, table, or drawer and take it and study it.
2) God commands us to go over and take the Word of God and study its messages.

Now the Bereans were of more noble character than the Thessalonians, for they received the message with great eagerness and examined the Scriptures every day to see if what Paul said was true. (Acts 17:11)

"Now I commit you to God and to the word of his grace, which can build you up and give you an inheritance among all those who are sanctified. (Acts 20:32)

Do your best to present yourself to God as one approved, a workman who does not need to be ashamed and who correctly handles the word of truth. (2 Tim 2:15)

All Scripture is God-breathed and is useful for teaching, rebuking, correcting and training in righteousness, (2 Tim 3:16)

Like newborn babies, crave pure spiritual milk, so that by it you may grow up in your salvation, Now that you have tasted that the Lord is good. (1 Pet 2:2-3)

2. John is commanded to take and eat and consume the little scroll or book. This he does, and when he does, the message of the book is both sweet and sour. What does this mean? It means that the Word of God contains...
- both sin and forgiveness
- both death and life
- both judgment and salvation
- both damnation and deliverance
- both heaviness and joy
- both hell and heaven
- both bondage and freedom
- both destruction and a new world
- both corruption and perfection

When John saw the truth of the world, its evil and corruption and the coming judgment upon it, he tasted the sourness, the bitterness of God's Word. When he saw the righteousness and perfection and the salvation that is coming to the world, he tasted the sweetness of God's Word.
⇒ Ezekiel had a similar experience.

> Then I looked, and I saw a hand stretched out to me. In it was a scroll, Which he unrolled before me. On both sides of it were written words of lament and mourning and woe. And he said to me, "Son of man, eat what is before you, eat this scroll; then go and speak to the house of Israel." So I opened my mouth, and he gave me the scroll to eat. Then he said to me, "Son of man, eat this scroll I am giving you and fill your stomach with it." So I ate it, and it tasted as sweet as honey in my mouth. He then said to me: "Son of man, go now to the house of Israel and speak my words to them. (Ezek 2:9-3:4)

⇒ The people of Isaiah's days did not want to hear the truth of their evil.

> Go now, write it on a tablet for them, inscribe it on a scroll, that for the days to come it may be an everlasting witness. These are rebellious people, deceitful children, children unwilling to listen to the Lord's instruction. They say to the seers, "See no more visions!" And to the prophets, "Give us no more visions of what is right! Tell us pleasant things, prophesy illusions. Leave this way, get off this path, and stop confronting us with the Holy One of Israel!" (Isa 30:8-11)

Pleasant words are sweet, but if they are false their end leads to death.

> Pleasant words are a honeycomb, sweet to the soul and healing to the bones. There is a way that seems right to a man, but in the end it leads to death. (Prov 16:24-25)

3. John is recommissioned: he is to proclaim the Word of God to the whole world. He is to proclaim the sour as well as the sweet, the judgments that are coming as well as the salvation that is coming. The final days of human history are coming, are about to begin—the days of the seventh trumpet. The days are to include some judgments beyond anything ever experienced before: these judgments and the glorious promise of a new world are both to be proclaimed by John. He is to hold nothing back. He is to proclaim the full message of God's book, His Holy Word.

**Thought 1.** Every minister and teacher of God's Word is called to proclaim both the sweet and sour of God's Word, both the grace and judgment of God. And the minister and teacher is to be faithful to his call: he is to proclaim the judgment of God as well as the grace of God. He must hold nothing back. The truth must be proclaimed, for the eternal fate of people is at stake.

> "Go, stand in the temple courts," he said, "and tell the people the full message of this new life." (Acts 5:20)
> These, then, are the things you should teach. Encourage and rebuke with all authority. Do not let anyone despise you. (Titus 2:15)
> But the LORD said to me, "Do not say, 'I am only a child.' You must go to everyone I send you to and say whatever I command you. (Jer 1:7)
> "Get yourself ready! Stand up and say to them whatever I command you. Do not be terrified by them, or I will terrify you before them. (Jer 1:17)
> You must speak my words to them, whether they listen or fail to listen, for they are rebellious. (Ezek 2:7)
> "Son of man, I have made you a watchman for the house of Israel; so hear the word I speak and give them warning from me. (Ezek 3:17)

**CHAPTER 11**

**F. The Final Triumph Over Evil (Part II): The Great Destruction of Israel & Jerusalem, 11:1-2**

1 **The great destruction of Israel: Her temple, worship, & people**

2 **The great destruction of Jerusalem & the Jews for three & one half years**

I was given a reed like a measuring rod and was told, "Go and measure the temple of God and the altar, and count the worshipers there. 2 But exclude the outer court; do not measure it, because it has been given to the Gentiles. They will trample on the holy city for 42 months.

# DIVISION V

## THE SEVEN TRUMPET JUDGMENTS: EVENTS DURING THE GREAT TRIBULATION, 8:1-11:19

### F. The Final Triumph Over Evil (Part II): The Great Destruction of Israel and Jerusalem, 11:1-2

(11:1-2) **Introduction**: this is one of the most important and one of the most exciting chapters in Revelation. There are at least five reasons why this is true (note: it is part of the message of the *little scroll or book* that John is to declare):

⇒ It points to the rebuilding and destruction of the temple in Jerusalem.

⇒ It shows the destruction of Jerusalem by the Gentiles.

⇒ It ties in with the prophecies of our Lord and of Scripture about the end time and the antichrist.

⇒ It covers the great salvation of Israel and the coming kingdom of God. It gives a glimpse as to how Israel will be saved and how God will conquer the evil, corruptions, and kingdoms of this world and set up His own kingdom

⇒ It is a summary, an overview of the rest of the book. It foreshadows and pictures the things that are yet to come in the book of *Revelation*.

The great Greek scholar A.T. Robertson says that no matter how a person interprets this passage, there are three clear points: "the chastisement of Jerusalem or Israel (verses 1 and 2), the mission of the two witnesses (verses 3-12), the rescue of the remnant (verse 13)" (*Word Pictures In The New Testament*, Vol.6, p.376). The remnant, of course, refers to Jews who truly believe that Jesus Christ is the Messiah.

The subject of this whole chapter, Chapter eleven, could be *The Great Salvation of Israel and the Coming Kingdom of God*. The first part, this particular Scripture and outline, is *The Great Destruction of Israel*. (Cp. Ezk.40:3, 6; Zech.2:1; Amos 7:7-9.)

1. The great destruction of Israel: her temple, worship, and people (v.1).
2. The great destruction of Jerusalem and the Jews for three and one half years (v.2).

**1** (11:1) **Israel—Temple—Gentiles**: there is the great judgment of Israel, of her temple, worship [altar], people, and city. John is instructed to take a rod and measure the

temple, its altar and the people who worship there. The words *rod* and *measure* are used in the Bible in two ways.

⇒ The rod can be used to measure a building for construction or for restoration, or it can be used to measure a place for preservation or protection (cp. Zech.2:1-5).

This is a possible meaning here. God could be saying that He wants the true worshippers of Israel preserved and protected while the antichrist and Gentile nations trod Jerusalem underfoot (v.2). He could be saying that He wants a remnant of Jewish believers saved, protected, and preserved during the great tribulation (cp. Romans chapters 9-11).

⇒ The word *rod* can mean to measure a place for destruction and punishment or correction and chastening (2 Sam.7:14; 8:2; 2 Kings 21:13; Is.34:11; Lam.2:8).

This too is a possible meaning here. God could be saying that He wants the temple and the Jewish people measured for judgment and correction; that in the last days they must be judged along with everyone else because of their unbelief, denial, rejection, and blasphemy against God's Son, the Lord Jesus Christ.

Which of the two meanings is meant here? Before an answer is given, several facts need to be considered.

1. Scripture says that the antichrist is to actually walk into the temple and demand that the world give their first loyalty to him and the state.

⇒ Jesus Christ Himself said that the antichrist would actually stand in the *holy place* of the Jews (their temple) and make this proclamation. (Remember Jerusalem is looked upon by several major world religions as being one of the religious centers of the world [religions such as Judaism, Islam, and Christianity]. No better place could be chosen to launch the worship of the state, especially when an attempt will be made to wipe out all Christian believers.)

**"So when you see standing in the holy place 'the abomination that causes**

desolation,' spoken of through the prophet Daniel—let the reader understand— (Mat 24:15. See notes, Antichrist—Mt.24:15 for more discussion. Cp. Dan.9:24-27; 11:31; 2:11.)

⇒ Second Thessalonians says that the antichrist will set himself up in God's temple declaring that he is god, that is, that he and the state can meet the needs of man and bring utopia to the world.

**Don't let anyone deceive you in any way, for that day will not come until the rebellion occurs and the man of lawlessness is revealed, the man doomed to destruction. He will oppose and will exalt himself over everything that is called God or is worshiped, so that he sets himself up in God's temple, proclaiming himself to be God. (2 Th 2:3-4)**

These Scriptures clearly say that the antichrist is going to appear in the temple, even in the very holy place of the temple. This means that the Jews must rebuild the temple in Jerusalem before this event can ever happen. The temple was destroyed in 70 A.D.

2. There are five temples mentioned in Scripture that need to be noted at this point.
⇒ Solomon's temple (1 Ki.7:1f): destroyed by Nebuchadnezar in 587 B.C.
⇒ Zerubbabel's temple (Ezra 3:12): he rebuilt the temple after the Babylonian captivity, but it was desecrated and dedicated to the god of Jupiter by Antiochus Epiphanes in 168-170 B.C.
⇒ Herod's temple (Jn.2:20): this was the temple that existed in the days of our Lord and was so well known to Him. It was destroyed by Titus in 70 A.D.
⇒ There are two future temples yet to be built.
⇒ The temple of the tribulation, the one to be rebuilt during the first three and one half years of the antichrist (2 Th.2:4; Rev.11:2).
⇒ The temple of the millennium, the temple of our Lord (Acts 15:16; Ezk. chapters 40-43).

3. Now, note what John is told to do. He is instructed to take the rod and measure the temple, the altar, and the worshippers. If we say that God means for him to mark the Jews in order to preserve and save them, then this means one of two things.
⇒ That the temple and its worshippers will be saved and preserved and not destroyed by the antichrist. In light of the above passages and the attacks of the antichrist against all that is called God, this is difficult to see (cp. 2 Th.2:4).
⇒ That this is a symbolic passage; that there will not necessarily be a true temple rebuilt; that what God means is to mark the true Jewish worshippers for protection and for preservation. There is a serious problem with this position. It is very difficult to say that the temple, the altar, and the people are not real things, but rather symbols. This is especially true when Jerusalem is so strongly pointed to as a real place, the place "where...their Lord was crucified" (Rev.11:8).

For these reasons and others that would just take too long to go into at this point, it seems best to see God telling John to measure the temple for judgment and correction. The

Jews are just as guilty as the Gentiles in rejecting God's Son, the Lord Jesus Christ. They are just as guilty as most others in rebelling against the Lord...
• rejecting Him
• disbelieving Him
• cursing Him
• neglecting Him
• denying Him
• disobeying Him
• ignoring Him
• blaspheming Him

Therefore, God has to judge them just as He has to judge all the ungodly and evil of this world. God has no favorites and shows no partiality. All the ungodly and evil are to be judged in the last days including the ungodly and evil of the Jews. Therefore, the Jews with their temple and their city will be trodden underfoot by the antichrist just as so many others will be.

**Thought 1.** Any person who does not approach God through the Lord Jesus Christ is worshipping a false god. There is only one true and living God and that is the Father of our Lord Jesus Christ. A worshipper may be a Jew or a Gentile—it does not matter—he must worship God through the Lord Jesus Christ or else his worship is false. This is the reason God marks the Jewish temple and worship for destruction. He is judging and condemning false worship. Once the temple is destroyed in the end time—very, very soon—the self-righteous spirit of the Jews will be broken and they will turn to the Lord Jesus Christ and many thousands will be saved. But until they do, the unbelieving Jews are marked for judgment just as all other unbelievers are.

**"Not everyone who says to me, 'Lord, Lord,' will enter the kingdom of heaven, but only he who does the will of my Father who is in heaven. (Mat 7:21)**
**"'These people honor me with their lips, but their hearts are far from me. They worship me in vain; their teachings are but rules taught by men.'" (Mat 15:8-9)**
**He replied, "Isaiah was right when he prophesied about you hypocrites; as it is written: "'These people honor me with their lips, but their hearts are far from me. (Mark 7:6)**
**For there is one God and one mediator between God and men, the man Christ Jesus, (1 Tim 2:5)**
**They claim to know God, but by their actions they deny him. They are detestable, disobedient and unfit for doing anything good. (Titus 1:16)**
**But the ministry Jesus has received is as superior to theirs as the covenant of which he is mediator is superior to the old one, and it is founded on better promises. (Heb 8:6)**
**For Christ did not enter a man-made sanctuary that was only a copy of the true one; he entered heaven itself, now to appear for us in God's presence. (Heb 9:24)**
**For this reason Christ is the mediator of a new covenant, that those who are called may receive the promised eternal inheritance—now that he has died as a ransom to set them free from the sins committed under the first covenant. (Heb 9:15)**

**To Jesus the mediator of a new covenant, and to the sprinkled blood that speaks a better word than the blood of Abel. (Heb 12:24)**

**My dear children, I write this to you so that you will not sin. But if anybody does sin, we have one who speaks to the Father in our defense—Jesus Christ, the Righteous One. (1 John 2:1)**

**2** (11:2) **Israel—Temple—Gentile Court—Jerusalem—Gentiles**: there is the trampling underfoot or destruction of Jerusalem and the Jews for three and one half years. Note several points.

1. The court of the Gentiles and the city of Jerusalem are not measured or maked for judgment. The court of the Gentiles was the outside courtyard of the temple. The temple was divided into four courts, all surrounding a center building or shrine called the Most Holy Place or Holy of Holies. The courts moving out away from the Holy Place were...

- the court of the priests (where the altar of the burnt offering stood).
- the court of Israel or of Jewish men.
- the court of the women.

These were the inner courts, the temple proper, the worship center for Jews only. No Gentile was ever allowed within these court barriers. Surrounding these courts for Jewish worshippers was a huge outer court, the court of the Gentiles. This was the only court the proselytes and interested persons were allowed to enter.

Why would the Gentile court and the city of Jerusalem not be measured for judgment? Because they will already be under the antichrist and his government. The government of Israel and the other governments of the world will have already submitted to the rule of the antichrist. There will already be a one world government. But this will not be the case with true Jewish worshippers, nor with true Christian believers, nor some other strong worhsippers of other religions. The antichrist will have a problem securing the loyalty of people all around the world who have strong faith. Strong Jewish worshippers will do what they have always done: refuse to buckle under to any Gentile ruler. This passage, verses one and two, is a prophecy: the temple will be destroyed and Jewish worhsippers will be persecuted. The antichrist is going to attack them with a vengeance never before seen in the history of the world. Of course, as has already been seen, he is also going to attack Christian believers (Rev.7:9f) and all other persons of strong faith (2 Th.2:4. Cp. Rev.13:1-18; Mt.24:15; Dan.11:40-45; 12:7.)

2. Forty two months (three and one half years) is the set time that the antichrist and his terrible persecutions will be unleashed upon the world.

⇒ This will be the time that the holy city will be oppressed: forty-two months (Rev.11:2).
⇒ This will be the time that the two witnesses will bear testimony to Israel and to the world: a thousand two hundred and sixty days (Rev.11:3).
⇒ This will be the time that the woman in the desert will be preserved: a thousand two hundred and sixty days (Rev.12:6, 14).
⇒ This will be the time that the beast will be allowed to blaspheme God: forty two months (Rev.13:5).

3. Scripture teaches that the antichrist will rule for a seven year period. Both Christ and Daniel say this. Christ says that the *abomination that causes desolation* (the antichrist) will launch the worst tribulation the world has ever known (Mt. 24:15, 21). In His own words, the signs that occur up until the abomination that causes desolation are called "the beginning of birth pains" or "the beginning of sorrows" (Mt. 24:8); and the trials after the abomination that causes desolation takes place are called "great tribulation," tribulations so great that they are unparalleled in history (Mt.24:21). Daniel also gives a division of time just as Christ does.

**He [the prince] will confirm a covenant with many for one 'seven.' In the middle of the 'seven' he will put an end...abomina-tion that causes desolation," (Dan 9:27)**

"In the middle of the seven" (Daniel's seventieth week) definitely points to a period of time (one week) that is divided into two parts. Now note these factors.

a. Daniel was dealing with the "seventieth week," the *end* of his seventy week prophecy. Two facts tell us that Daniel was also dealing with the *end time* just as Christ was: (1) the fact that Christ was dealing with the end of Jerusalem and the end of the world and, (2) the fact that Christ said He was elaborating on Daniel's prophecy.

b. Daniel said that what begins the second half of his seventieth week is "the abomination that causes desolation" or the prince who causes "abominable idols" (H.C. Leupold. *Exposition of Daniel*. Grand Rapids, MI: Baker, 1969, p.434).

The words of Christ should be carefully noted: "So when you see standing in the holy place 'the abomination that causes desolation,' spoken of through the prophet Daniel...." (Mat 24:15). Christ was about to elaborate and explain in more detail what Daniel prophesied. Thus Christ explained that the first half of Daniel's week would consist of signs which were "the beginning of birth pains [sorrows]" (Mt.24:8; cp. Mt.24:5-14), and the last half of Daniel's week would consist of unparalleled trials of "great tribulation." The second half of the week would be launched by "the abomination that causes desolation, by his "standing in the holy place" (Mt. 24:15, 21).

Another matter that needs to be looked at is the time frame of the end time (the seventieth week) as predicted by Christ and Daniel.

Scripture refers to the length in these words (see notes—Rev.11:2; 12:6).

"Time, times, and half a time" (Dan.7:25; 12:7).
"1260 days" (Rev.12:6).
"42 months" (Rev.11:2; 13:5-6).

Based upon the days and months given in the *Book of Revelation*, if Daniel's time equals one year, then his words, "Time [1 year], times [2 years], and half a time [1/2 year]" are equal to 3 1/2 years. Daniel stated that the abomination that desolation shall be executed "in the middle of the 'seven.'" that is, after three and one half years. It is assumed that Christ's words "the beginning of birth pains" (that is, the first half of the week) are also three and one half years. Thus in combining the two periods of time (3 1/2 years each), the length of the last days or end time is said to be a literal seven years. Based upon the words of Revelation the prophecy of Christ can be charted as follows.

## THE END OF THE WORLD

| Seeing the Sign of the<br>Abomination that causes Desolation<br>*In the Middle of the Time or Years*<br>(Mt.24:15) | | Seeing the<br>*Son of Man Coming*<br>(Mt.24:29-30) |
|---|---|---|
| 3½ years<br>Signs which are<br>"The beginning of birth<br>pains" or "the beginning<br>of sorrows" (Mt.24:8) | 3½ years<br>Unparalleled trials of<br>"the great distress" or the<br>great tribulation" (Mt.24:21) | "His angels...gather<br>His elect"<br>(Mt.24:31) |

4. In summary, all this points to a period of three and one half years of great satanic power in the world. Particular emphasis is laid upon the final days of the antichrist, a period known as the *great tribulation*. It is in the last three and one half years of his rule that the antichrist will launch the worst tribulation the world has ever known. In the present passage he will trample underfoot the Jewish people and create a holocaust such as the world has never seen. (See outline and DEEPER STUDY # 1—Mt.24:15 for more discussion.)

**Thought 1.** God judges sin and unbelief. He always judges the ungodly and evil, even if they are religious and declare that they are righteous. This is what God is doing in the end time: judging the idolaters, sorcerers, murderers, immoral, and thieves of the world. This is the reason God is going to judge Israel in the end time. They are as guilty as all other people of the world. But note: there is a limit to the judgment. It will last only three and one half years. God will stop the judgment and have mercy upon all those who will turn to Him for mercy.

**LORD, I have heard of your fame; I stand in awe of your deeds, O LORD. Renew them in our day, in our time make them known; in wrath remember mercy. (Hab 3:2)**

**Thought 2.** It will be seen in the next passage that God uses the suffering of the Jewish people to ripen them for the gospel and the glorification of His name. This persecution is but the first step to prepare them for the coming salvation.

**Thought 3.** Note the words "the Gentiles" (v.2). This refers to what is called the *"times of the Gentiles."* In order to have a complete picture, note these facts.
1) The "times of the Gentiles" was launched with the Babylonians under Nebuchadnezar (2 Chron.36:1-31).
2) The "times of the Gentiles" will end at the climax of human history when Jesus Christ returns in great glory and power and destroys the antichrist and his government and followers (Rev.19:11-21; Lk.21:24).

| | | |
|---|---|---|
| | **G. The Final Triumph Over Evil (Part III): The Two Witnesses—How Israel Turns to God, 11:3-13** | is figuratively called Sodom and Egypt, where also their Lord was crucified. | made a spectacle before the world<br>1) In apostate Jerusalem<br>2) Viewed by the world |

**1 They are God's witnesses**
  a. They are sent forth by God
  b. They are sent forth for a set time
  c. They are sent forth as prophets
  d. They will have their needs met by God

**2 They will have great power**
  a. As Elijah did

  b. As Moses did

**3 They are persecuted & martyred by the beast**[DS1]
  a. They are assassinated by the beast, the antichrist: He comes out of the abyss, the bottomless pit
  b. Their dead bodies are

3 And I will give power to my two witnesses, and they will prophesy for 1,260 days, clothed in sackcloth."
4 These are the two olive trees and the two lampstands that stand before the Lord of the earth.
5 If anyone tries to harm them, fire comes from their mouths and devours their enemies. This is how anyone who wants to harm them must die.
6 These men have power to shut up the sky so that it will not rain during the time they are prophesying; and they have power to turn the waters into blood and to strike the earth with every kind of plague as often as they want.
7 Now when they have finished their testimony, the beast that comes up from the Abyss will attack them, and overpower and kill them.
8 Their bodies will lie in the street of the great city, which

is figuratively called Sodom and Egypt, where also their Lord was crucified.
9 For three and a half days men from every people, tribe, language and nation will gaze on their bodies and refuse them burial.
10 The inhabitants of the earth will gloat over them and will celebrate by sending each other gifts, because these two prophets had tormented those who live on the earth.
11 But after the three and a half days a breath of life from God entered them, and they stood on their feet, and terror struck those who saw them.
12 Then they heard a loud voice from heaven saying to them, "Come up here." And they went up to heaven in a cloud, while their enemies looked on.
13 At that very hour there was a severe earthquake and a tenth of the city collapsed. Seven thousand people were killed in the earthquake, and the survivors were terrified and gave glory to the God of heaven.

made a spectacle before the world
  1) In apostate Jerusalem
  2) Viewed by the world

  3) Mocked by the world

**4 They are resurrected by God's breath**
  a. They stand upon their feet
  b. They strike fear in the observers
  c. They are caught up to heaven
    1) By God's command

    2) Before all enemies
**5 They are vindicated**
  a. By God's judgment: An (Mt.24:31) earthquake

  b. By those remaining: They glorify God

# DIVISION V

## THE SEVEN TRUMPET JUDGMENTS: EVENTS DURING THE GREAT TRIBULATION, 8:1-11:19

## G. The Final Triumph Over Evil (Part III): The Two Witnesses—How Israel Turns to God, 11:3-13

(11:3-13) **Introduction**: what we have just seen in Revelation is horrifying. The terrible prophecy about the antichrist is going to take place.
  ⇒ The prophecy by our Lord: "So when you see standing in the holy place 'the abomination that causes desolation,' spoken of through the prophet Daniel—let the reader understand—" (Mt. 24:15).
  ⇒ The prophecy predicted by Paul: "[The antichrist] He will oppose and will exalt himself over everything that is called God or is worshiped, so that he sets himself up in God's temple, proclaiming himself to be God." (2 Th.2:4).

The antichrist will turn against all who call upon God and who refuse to bow down before the state and give the state their first allegiance. The antichrist will destroy Jerusalem and the temple, and will launch the worst holocaust the world has ever seen. As has been seen in previous passages, the holocaust will be launched against all true believers and followers of the Lord Jesus Christ. It will also be launched against the followers of other religions who have strong faith including the Jews, Moslems, Hindus, and others. Millions upon millions, a countless number, will be slaughtered (Rev.7:9-17). But it will also be launched against the Jews

and Israel as a nation. The anti-christ will utterly destroy Jerusalem and its temple. He will hotly pursue the Jews and attempt to trample the Jewish people underfoot (Rev.11:1-2).

But note: this present passage shows us a most wonderful thing. God will not forsake the Jew. Despite the Jews' unbelief and rebellion against God's Son as the Messiah—despite their denial of the Lord Jesus Christ—God still loves the Jew. He loves them...
  • for Abraham's sake
  • for Jacob's sake
  • for David's sake
  • for Paul's sake
  • for Peter's sake

God still loves Israel. He still loves the Jew—for the sake of the nation's fathers and for the sake of all true believers who founded the nation for God and followed the Lord Jesus Christ (Ro.11:28; cp. Ro.11:16). Because of God's great love and because of the godly people of Israel, God is going to turn Israel. God is going to save Israel. This present passage shows how part of the turning is going to take place. God is going to send Israel two great witnesses. This is part of the message that John saw in the little book handed to him (Rev.10:10-11). This is the glorious message of Israel's salvation: the message that two great witnesses will be sent to bear testimony to Israel and to the world. These two great messengers will proclaim the salvation that is in God's Son, the Lord Jesus Christ.

1. They are God's witnesses (v.3-4).
2. They will have great power (v.5-6).
3. They are persecuted and martyred by the beast (v.7-10).
4. They are resurrected by God's breath (v.11-12).
5. They are vindicated (v.13).

**1** (11:3-4) **Witnesses—Ministers—Call**: the two witnesses are God's witnesses.

1. They will be sent forth by God. God says, "I will give power to my two witnesses." It is God who calls, gifts, commissions, and empowers them.

2. They will be sent forth for a set time, only for three and one half years. This means that they are raised up only for the *great tribulation period* of history (see note, pt.2—Rev.11:2 for discussion).

3. They will be sent forth as true prophets who condemn sin and proclaim the salvation that is in Christ Jesus the Lord. This is shown by the dress mentioned, that of sackcloth. This was the dress worn by the prophets of old. The point of the dress is to show that their message will be straightforward and pull no punches. It will be a message against the sins of the Jews and of the world, a condemning message. But note: they will also be proclaiming the Lord Jesus Christ as the Savior of the world. This is shown by the statement made about them: they are assassinated in the city where "*their* Lord was crucified" (v.8). They are going to be proclaiming that the only hope and salvation of this world is found in God's Son, the Lord Jesus Christ. They will, of course, be condemning the unbelief and denial of Christ as the Messiah, the unbelief and denial that has characterized the Jews down through the centuries.

4. They will have their needs met by God (v.4). Note that they will be like two olive trees and two lampstands standing before the God of the earth. This is a reference to two great Old Testament witnesses for God, Joshua and Zerubbabel (cp. Zech. chapters 4-5). The point is that the God of the whole earth will meet their needs:

⇒ God will make them as strong and fruitful as two olive trees.
⇒ God will make their witness to shine forth as the light of two lampstands.

**Thought 1.** These same four things can be said about every true minister sent forth by God. This should never be forgotten.

1) It is God who sends forth the minister: God calls, gifts, commissions, and empowers the minister to bear witness for Him, and when God does, the minister must bear a strong witness.
2) It is God who sends forth the minister to certain ministries and for set periods of time.
3) It is God who sends forth the minister as a prophet to preach against the sin and corruption of this world and to proclaim the salvation that is in Christ Jesus our Lord.
4) It is God who supplies the minister, who gives him fruit and gives him a strong witness, a witness that shines as the light of the lampstand.

> You did not choose me, but I chose you and appointed you to go and bear fruit—fruit that will last. Then the Father will give you whatever you ask in my name. (John 15:16)

> But the Lord said to Ananias, "Go! This man is my chosen instrument to carry my name before the Gentiles and their kings and before the people of Israel. (Acts 9:15)

> 'Now get up and stand on your feet. I have appeared to you to appoint you as a servant and as a witness of what you have seen of me and what I will show you. (Acts 26:16)

> That God was reconciling the world to himself in Christ, not counting men's sins against them. And he has committed to us the message of reconciliation. We are therefore Christ's ambassadors, as though God were making his appeal through us. We implore you on Christ's behalf: Be reconciled to God. (2 Cor 5:19-20)

> Then I heard the voice of the Lord saying, "Whom shall I send? And who will go for us?" And I said, "Here am I. Send me!" (Isa 6:8)

> "'On that day,' declares the LORD Almighty, 'I will take you, my servant Zerubbabel son of Shealtiel,' declares the LORD, 'and I will make you like my signet ring, for I have chosen you,' declares the LORD Almighty." (Hag 2:23)

**2** (11:5-6) **Ministers—Power**: the two witnesses possess great power. Their power will be the same as that of Elijah and Moses.

⇒ They will have the power of the fire of Elijah. Note where the fire comes from: their mouths. This probably means the fire and power of their words and preaching. They will have so much influence and power from God that the antichrist and leaders will hesitate killing them. Their preaching will apparently stir conviction and cause many to turn to God.
⇒ They will have the power to perform miracles within nature: to cause it to rain and not to rain as Elijah did (cp. 2 Ki.1:9f; 17:1f); to strike the earth with plagues such as Moses did (cp. Ex.7:14f).

The point is this: their power is given to them by God. And in the end time, supernatural power will be needed to protect their lives. Remember all the catastrophes that are taking place upon earth and the horror of the holocaust that has been launched by the antichrist. These two witnesses will need enough power and influence to keep the leaders of the world from assassinating them until God's purpose is completed. This is the reason for their unusual, miraculous power.

**Thought 1.** When God calls a minister, God empowers him. God will give him whatever power he needs to complete his task. What the minister must do is learn to call upon God for more and more power and trust God for it and then act upon it.

> But you will receive power when the Holy Spirit comes on you; and you will be my witnesses in Jerusalem, and in all Judea and Samaria, and to the ends of the earth." (Acts 1:8)

> With great power the apostles continued to testify to the resurrection of the Lord Jesus, and much grace was upon them all. (Acts 4:33)

My message and my preaching were not with wise and persuasive words, but with a demonstration of the Spirit's power, (1 Cor 2:4)

I pray that out of his glorious riches he may strengthen you with power through his Spirit in your inner being, (Eph 3:16)

Now to him who is able to do immeasurably more than all we ask or imagine, according to his power that is at work within us, (Eph 3:20)

Because our gospel came to you not simply with words, but also with power, with the Holy Spirit and with deep conviction. You know how we lived among you for your sake. (1 Th 1:5)

For God did not give us a spirit of timidity, but a spirit of power, of love and of self-discipline. (2 Tim 1:7)

**Thought 2.** Who are the two witnesses? There are many different ideas.

⇒ Some say the passage is an allegory symbolizing the law and the prophets; others say the law and the gospel; others say the 144,000 converted Jews (Rev.7:1f); others say the church; and others continue on and on with more ideas.

⇒ Some say that the two witnesses are actual persons, and some even identify them saying that they will be Enoch and Elijah or Elijah and Moses sent back to earth.

It is difficult to see how the two witnesses could be anything other than two men. There are just too many specific statements made about them that point toward human personality, statements that could never be applied to the church or to other things without really twisting this passage.

⇒ George Ladd says:

"The description of the two witnesses and the character of their ministry is given in such detail that it seems more likely that John conceived of these two witnesses as two actual historical...personages who will be sent to Israel to bring about her conversion" (*The Revelation of John*, p.154).

⇒ William Barclay says:

"But the picture of the two witnesses is so clear and so definite that it does not seem to be only an allegory; it seems to refer to definite persons" (*The Revelation of John*, Vol.2, p.86).

⇒ Lehman Strauss says:

"The two witnesses are not the law and the gospel, or the Old Testament and the New Testament. They speak. They have mouths. They are heard, handled, and hated. They are individuals, for after their martyrdom John sees their 'dead bodies' ([Rev.]11:9). By no stretch of the imagination can we regard these witnesses as other than real persons" (*The Book of the Revelation*, p.211).

Who are they? If they are two persons, then who are they? Scripture does not say. But note that traits of their ministry are just like those of Elijah and Moses. This, of course, does not mean that these two great prophets have to come back to earth. It only means that the same kind of spirit that existed in these two great men will dwell in the two witnesses. The two great witnesses of the end time will have the spirit of Elijah and Moses. Remember: this is exactly what Jesus Christ said about Elijah, the Messiah's forerunner. But Jesus said that John the Baptist was His forerunner, that Scripture was speaking about the spirit of Elijah returning, that the forerunner would have the very same kind of spirit that Elijah had (cp. Mt.11:13-14). It is much more natural and Biblical to say the same thing here: that the two witnesses in the end time will be two men with the same kind of spirit that Moses and Elijah had.

**3** (11:7-10) **Antichrist—Beast of Revelation**: the two witnesses are persecuted and martyred by the beast, that is, the antichrist. (See outlines and notes, *Antichrist*—Rev.11:7; 13:1-10; note and DEEPER STUDY # 1—Mt.24:15; note—2 Th.2:4-9 for discussion.) Note that this is the first mention of the beast or antichrist by name in the book of Revelation. And note what the very first information is: his origin, the fact that he will come from the devil himself, from the Abyss, from the bottomless pit of hell. (See note, *Abyss—Bottomless Pit*—Rev.9:2.) The idea is that he will be a murdering tyrant just like the devil (cp. Jn.7:44), and his desire will be to assassinate the two witnesses. But he will not touch them until they have finished their testimony. God will protect them. However, the antichrist will war against them; that is, he will plot and do all he can to discredit their witness. But as soon as their testimony is finished, after three and one half years (v.3), the antichrist will be successful; he will assassinate them.

What then happens shows how effective their message will have been. Many throughout the world, especially the leaders, will hate them. Their deaths will become an international affair. The leaders will leave their bodies lying in the streets of Jerusalem for three days. Note how Scripture graphically describes the event:

**For three and a half days men from every people, tribe, language and nation will gaze on their bodies and refuse them burial. The inhabitants of the earth will gloat over them and will celebrate by sending each other gifts, because these two prophets had tormented those who live on the earth. (Rev 11:9-10)**

The idea is that the whole world will witness the scene. This, of course, points toward international reporting of the event by some kind of media or television. Note that gifts will be exchanged among people because they are so pleased to see these two witnesses assassinated. This could be pointing to a political plot by the antichrist and a professional assassin. The gifts would be the payoff of the assassins. It is difficult to see what the gifts would be if they are not political payoffs from the antichrist to the leaders of some government for having assassinated the two witnesses.

The point of the verses is the political intrigue of the antichrist and other government leaders (v.7-10). They kill these two great servants of God, and they have so much political power that they can kill two preachers with worldwide influence and leave their bodies in the streets for three days (v.8-9). Just picture a few of the greatest religious leaders in the world today. Then imagine some world leader murdering them and having so much power that he could leave their bodies lying in the streets for three days. This gives some idea of the enormous power the antichrist will have.

Note one other significant fact: Jerusalem is called Sodom and Egypt. This is describing the spiritual condition of Jerusalem in the end time.

⇒ Jerusalem will be as Sodom: a city of worldliness, immorality, and shameful sin; a city who would not receive the messengers of God (cp. Gen.19:4f).

⇒ Jerusalem will be as Egypt: a nation that enslaved and killed God's people (Ex.1:7f).

## DEEPER STUDY # 1

(11:7) **Beast, The—Antichrist**: Who is the antichrist, the beast (11:7)? Scripture never really uses the term *the antichrist* to refer to the great "man of lawlessness" who is to appear in the end time. It does refer to false teachers as antichrists (1 Jn.2:22). However, down through the centuries, believers have always referred to the coming "man of lawlessness" as *the antichrist*. Why? Because he is to stand so opposed to Christ and fiercely persecute believers. He will be the very embodiment of evil against Christ and against the followers of Christ. He will be the one man who will be so against Christ that he can actually be called *the antichrist*.

Now who is the antichrist? Scripture tells us, and what Scripture reveals is fascinating yet horrifying. When we look back over human history and think about some of the evil men who have terrorized and massacred millions, it is utterly frightening. Think of the Neros, Hitlers, and Stalins of human history. And then think what would have happened if they had been dictators of the whole world. The death of millions would have soared to tens and tens of millions. Such is the picture of horror and havoc to be wrought by the world leader, the antichrist. His horror will be so frightening that one of his names is simply *the beast*. Note what Scripture calls him.

⇒ He is the *abomination that causes desolation* prophesied by Christ:

> "So when you see standing in the holy place 'the abomination that causes desolation,' spoken of through the prophet Daniel—let the reader understand— (Mat 24:15)

⇒ He is the *man of lawlessness* prophesied by Paul:

> Don't let anyone deceive you in any way, for that day will not come until the rebellion occurs and the man of lawlessness is revealed, the man doomed to destruction. He will oppose and will exalt himself over everything that is called God or is worshiped, so that he sets himself up in God's temple, proclaiming himself to be God. (2 Th 2:3-4)

⇒ He is the *little horn* prophesied by Daniel

> He will speak against the Most High and oppress his saints and try to change the set times and the laws. The saints will be handed over to him for a time, times and half a time. (Dan 7:25; cp. Dan.7:8)

⇒ He is the very embodiment of Satan himself, the man of lawlessness who comes out of the Abyss, out of the bottomless pit of hell itself.

> Four great beasts, each different from the others, came up out of the sea. (Dan 7:3)
>
> "After that, in my vision at night I looked, and there before me was a fourth beast—terrifying and frightening and very powerful. It had large iron teeth; it crushed and devoured its victims and trampled underfoot whatever was left. It was different from all the former beasts, and it had ten horns.
> "While I was thinking about the horns, there before me was another horn, a little one, which came up among them; and three of the first horns were uprooted before it. This horn had eyes like the eyes of a man and a mouth that spoke boastfully. (Dan 7:7-8)
>
> The beast, which you saw, once was, now is not, and will come up out of the Abyss and go to his destruction. The inhabitants of the earth whose names have not been written in the book of life from the creation of the world will be astonished when they see the beast, because he once was, now is not, and yet will come. (Rev 17:8)

⇒ He is the world ruler who will make war against God's people and slaughter them.

> I also wanted to know about the ten horns on its head and about the other horn that came up, before which three of them fell—the horn that looked more imposing than the others and that had eyes and a mouth that spoke boastfully. As I watched, this horn was waging war against the saints and defeating them, (Dan 7:20-21)
>
> He will speak against the Most High and oppress his saints and try to change the set times and the laws. The saints will be handed over to him for a time, times and half a time. (Dan 7:25)
>
> After this I looked and there before me was a great multitude that no one could count, from every nation, tribe, people and language, standing before the throne and in front of the Lamb. They were wearing white robes and were holding palm branches in their hands. Then one of the elders asked me, "These in white robes—who are they, and where did they come from?" I answered, "Sir, you know." And he said, "These are they who have come out of the great tribulation; they have washed their robes and made them white in the blood of the Lamb. (Rev 7:9, 13-14)

⇒ He is the world ruler who will conquer the world.

> "He gave me this explanation: 'The fourth beast is a fourth kingdom that

will appear on earth. It will be different from all the other kingdoms and will devour the whole earth, trampling it down and crushing it. (Dan 7:23)

"The ten horns you saw are ten kings who have not yet received a kingdom, but who for one hour will receive authority as kings along with the beast. They have one purpose and will give their power and authority to the beast. (Rev 17:12-13)

**Thought 1.** William Barlcay describes him well:

"Just as the Christ is the Holy One and the Anointed King of God, so Antichrist is the Unholy One and King of all evil. Just as the Christ, the Messiah, is the incarnation of God and goodness, so Antichrist is the incarnation of the Devil and of evil. Just as the Christ is the champion of God, so Antichrist is the champion of every force in the universe which is opposed to God" (*The Revelation of John*, Vol.2, p.70).

**4** (11:11-12) **Witnesses of Revelation, Two**: the two witnesses are resurrected and caught up to heaven. This will be one of many spectacular events of the last days. The breath of God will be breathed into the dead bodies of these two slain witnesses. They will stand to their feet, and when they do, fear will strike the hearts of all those who see them. How many will see them? Will the whole world witness their resurrection as they had witnessed their dead bodies lying in the streets? Will the cameras of the media be zeroing in on them when they arise? We are not told, but the idea being conveyed seems to be that the whole world will not see them arise, but many Jews seem to be affected by what happens (v.13). Whatever the case, imagine the amazement when the two witnesses begin to ascend up into heaven. The sight is bound to make an enormous impact upon those who witness it.

**Thought 1.** Note how this parallels the resurrection and ascension of our Lord and symbolizes what is to happen to believers when Jesus Christ comes. Every believer has the glorious hope of being raised and meeting the Lord in the air.

That all may honor the Son just as they honor the Father. He who does not honor the Son does not honor the Father, who sent him. (John 5:23)

For my Father's will is that everyone who looks to the Son and believes in him shall have eternal life, and I will raise him up at the last day." (John 6:40)

Jesus said to her, "I am the resurrection and the life. He who believes in me will live, even though he dies; (John 11:25)

In my Father's house are many rooms; if it were not so, I would have told you. I am going there to prepare a place for you. And if I go and prepare a place for you, I will come back and take you to be with me that you also may be where I am. (John 14:2-3)

For the Lord himself will come down from heaven, with a loud command, with the voice of the archangel and with the trumpet call of God, and the dead in Christ will rise first. After that, we who are still alive and are left will be caught up together with them in the clouds to meet the Lord in the air. And so we will be with the Lord forever. Therefore encourage each other with these words. (1 Th 4:16-18)

**5** (11:13) **Witnesses—Israel, Salvation**: the two witnesses receive a great vindication. There will be a great earthquake that will kill seven thousand persons. Then the most wonderful thing will happen: the rest of the Jews in Jerusalem become fearful and give glory to the God of heaven. This points strongly to the conversion of the Jews, certainly to a great number of them repenting and giving *true* glory to God. Note exactly what happened: "the survivors were terrified, and gave glory to the God of heaven." George Ladd points out that when this phrase is used in Revelation and other Scriptures, it suggests true repentance (*The Revelation of John*, p.159f).

He said in a loud voice, "Fear God and give him glory, because the hour of his judgment has come. Worship him who made the heavens, the earth, the sea and the springs of water." (Rev 14:7)

Who will not fear you, O Lord, and bring glory to your name? For you alone are holy. All nations will come and worship before you, for your righteous acts have been revealed." (Rev 15:4)

They were seared by the intense heat and they cursed the name of God, who had control over these plagues, but they refused to repent and glorify him. (Rev 16:9)

Let us rejoice and be glad and give him glory! For the wedding of the Lamb has come, and his bride has made herself ready. (Rev 19:7)

The nations will walk by its light, and the kings of the earth will bring their splendor into it. (Rev 21:24)

Live such good lives among the pagans that, though they accuse you of doing wrong, they may see your good deeds and glorify God on the day he visits us. (1 Pet 2:12)

Then Joshua said to Achan, "My son, give glory to the LORD, the God of Israel, and give him the praise. Tell me what you have done; do not hide it from me." (Josh 7:19)

Let them give glory to the LORD and proclaim his praise in the islands. (Isa 42:12)

Give glory to the LORD your God before he brings the darkness, before your feet stumble on the darkening hills. You hope for light, but he will turn it to thick darkness and change it to deep gloom. (Jer 13:16)

This is either the salvation of Israel or one of the great movements toward salvation that the Jews will experience in the end time. This is the fulfillment or part of the fulfillment prophesied by Paul: that "all Israel will be saved." (Rom.11:26)

⇒ George Ladd has an excellent comment on this:

> "Because of these mighty acts of God in the end time, the Jewish people will repent of their sins and give glory to the true God. Previously they have not glorified God; they had crucified his Messiah and rejected his prophets. But now they repent of their disobedience and glorify God" (*The Revelation of John*, p.159f).

⇒ William Barclay says:

> "The great interest of this passage lies in the fact that the unbelievers were won by the sacrificial death of the witnesses and by God's vindication of them" (*The Revelation of John*, Vol.2, p.88).

⇒ Robertson quotes H.B. Swete as saying:

> "A general movement toward Christianity, induced by fear or despair—a prediction fulfilled more than once in...history" (*Word Pictures In The New Testament*, Vol.6, p.384).

**Thought 1.** The great need today is for men to fear God, to fear His judgment so much that they will turn from sin, repent, and give glory to Him.

His mercy extends to those who fear him, from generation to generation. (Luke 1:50)

But accepts men from every nation who fear him and do what is right. (Acts 10:35)

So that with one heart and mouth you may glorify the God and Father of our Lord Jesus Christ. (Rom 15:6)

You were bought at a price. Therefore honor God with your body. (1 Cor 6:20)

Through Jesus, therefore, let us continually offer to God a sacrifice of praise—the fruit of lips that confess his name. (Heb 13:15)

And now, O Israel, what does the LORD your God ask of you but to fear the LORD your God, to walk in all his ways, to love him, to serve the LORD your God with all your heart and with all your soul, (Deu 10:12)

You who fear the LORD, praise him! All you descendants of Jacob, honor him! Revere him, all you descendants of Israel! (Psa 22:23)

Who, then, is the man that fears the LORD? He will instruct him in the way chosen for him. (Psa 25:12)

How great is your goodness, which you have stored up for those who fear you, which you bestow in the sight of men on those who take refuge in you. (Psa 31:19)

| | | | | |
|---|---|---|---|---|
| | **H. The Final Triumph Over Evil (Part IV): An Overall Picture of Things to Come, 11:14-19** | to you, Lord God Almighty, the One who is and who was, because you have taken your great power and have begun to reign. | | c. For taking supreme authority |
| **1 The third woe comes quickly; that is, the seventh trumpet is the third woe** | 14 The second woe has passed; the third woe is coming soon. | 18 The nations were angry; and your wrath has come. The time has come for judging the dead, and for reward- | **4** | **Scene 3: The nations make a final rebellion & are destroyed** <br> a. The nations rebel <br> b. The wrath of God falls |
| | 15 The seventh angel sounded his trumpet, and there were loud voices in heaven, which said: "The kingdom of | ing your servants the prophets and your saints and those who reverence your name, both small and great— and | | c. The dead are judged <br> d. The godly are rewarded |
| **2 Scene 1: This world becomes God's kingdom** | the world has become the kingdom of our Lord and of his Christ, and he will reign for ever and ever." | for destroying those who destroy the earth." | **5** | e. The destroyers are destroyed <br> **Scene 4: God's temple is to be opened** |
| | 16 And the twenty-four elders, who were seated on | 19 Then God's temple in heaven was opened, and within his temple was seen | | a. God's covenant & promises are seen to be true |
| **3 Scene 2: The Lord God Almighty is acclaimed** <br> a. By the elders | their thrones before God, fell on their faces and worshiped God, | the ark of his covenant. And there came flashes of lightning, rumblings, peals of | | b. God's majesty is experienced |
| b. As the eternal God | 17 Saying: "We give thanks | thunder, an earthquake and a great hailstorm. | | |

# DIVISION V

## THE SEVEN TRUMPET JUDGMENTS: EVENTS DURING THE GREAT TRIBULATION, 8:1-11:19

## H. The Final Triumph Over Evil (Part IV): An Overall Picture of Things to Come, 11:14-19

(11:14-19) **Introduction**: the end time will be a period of horror and tragedy. The world and its people will go through great tribulation, tribulation such as the world has never before seen. Scene after scene of catastrophe and horror have already been seen. Imagine what John was going through. He was having to look upon these scenes and be an eyewitness of these horrors. This is the reason here and there throughout Revelation we have seen Christ give John a scene of hope and of the glory that is to come. This is what the present passage is all about. John once again needs to be lifted up and encouraged. Therefore, God gives him a broad overview of what is yet to come; John sees in sketch form the glory with the horror. This is the overall picture of things to come.

1. The third woe comes quickly; that is, the seventh trumpet is the third woe (v.14-15).
2. Scene 1: this world becomes God's kingdom (v.15).
3. Scene 2: the Lord God Almighty is acclaimed (v.16-17).
4. Scene 3: the nations make a final rebellion and are destroyed (v.18).
5. Scene 4: God's temple is to be opened (v.19).

**1** (11:14-15) **Woe—Trumpet Judgments**: the third woe will come quickly. By woe is meant a period of extreme grief, distress, suffering, affliction, and calamity. Remember: there are to be only three woes.

⇒ The first woe will be the demonic locust-like creatures that sweep the earth and torment people (Rev.8:13-9:11).
⇒ The second woe will be demonic military horse-like creatures that sweep the earth, and kill one third of the ungodly and evil population (Rev.9:12-21).
⇒ The third woe is the seventh trumpet, the judgments that result from the blast of the seventh trumpet.

But note when the seventh trumpet blasts there is no judgment and there is no woe that comes forth. Why? Because there are some things that need to be seen before the judgments actually take place. The judgments and woe of the seventh trumpet are actually the seven bowl judgments; that is, the seventh trumpet will blast forth seven more judgments, and these will be far worse than any of the judgments cast upon the earth. In fact, the bowl judgments will bring the climax of human history and the end of time as we know it.

But first, as stated, there are some things that we need to see and understand. And the first thing is most interesting: it is an overview of the events that are yet to take place in the Revelation. The present passage leaps ahead and shows us in a broad summary what is to happen over the next ten chapters of this great book. God prepared John's heart for the terrible events that were yet to be revealed to him, prepared him by showing that God would triumph over evil and establish His kingdom forever. God gave John and gives us five scenes of what is yet to come.

**2** (11:15) **Kingdom of God—World**: scene one—the kingdom of the world has become the kingdom of our Lord and of His Christ. The Greek tense is past tense, the kingdom of the world has become the Lord's kingdom. The scene jumps over all of history and shows our God and His Christ ruling over the whole world. All the kingdoms of this world are done away with, and all the people upon earth live and work as citizens of God's kingdom. Presently, in our day and time, human governments involve...

• Authority and rule and reign: some earthly authorities and rulers are good and some are bad.
• Laws: earthly laws favor some people and treat others unjustly.

- Work: some have jobs and others do not have jobs.
- Economies: some earthly economies are healthy and others are bad.
- Protection: some earthly governments protect their citizens, others abuse and enslave them.
- Provision: some earthly governments provide for their citizens and help their citizens provide for themselves and others do not.
- Services: some earthly governments provide good services for their people such as roads, sewage, water, jobs, and health care or else they provide poor service.

The point is this: earthly governments are imperfect and weak and are unable to bring utopia to man. Earthly governments are flooded with the poor, hungry, homeless, sick, selfish, rich, proud, and all the other evils and imperfections that enslave the citizens of this world. Earthly governments focus upon this earth and all the pleasures and possessions of this earth and upon war and conflict. This will be especially true in the end time under the antichrist. The world will be engulfed in sin and evil, selfishness and greed, war and conflict. But this is not the end: this is the glorious message of this point. The kingdoms of this world are going to become the kingdom of our God and His Christ. God is going to reign over the world, bringing heaven to this universe. When? During the millennium. The millennium simply means the period of time, a period of one thousand years, that Jesus Christ is to return to this earth and rule over the nations and people of the earth.

**Thought 1.** Just think! Utopia is coming to earth. Peace and prosperity are coming. There will no longer be hunger, thirst, homelessness, disease, war, murder, nor any of the other evils upon earth. But note: utopia will only come when Jesus Christ returns to rule the earth. Man fails and fails miserably in his attempts to clean up the world and to establish peace. But God loves man and loves him dearly. Therefore, He is going to help man. God is going to send His dear Son back to earth to establish peace and prosperity for all. God is going to do for man what man has so miserably failed to do. This is the glorious promise of this passage.

Then I heard a loud voice in heaven say: "Now have come the salvation and the power and the kingdom of our God, and the authority of his Christ. For the accuser of our brothers, who accuses them before our God day and night, has been hurled down. (Rev 12:10)

Then I heard what sounded like a great multitude, like the roar of rushing waters and like loud peals of thunder, shouting: "Hallelujah! For our Lord God Almighty reigns. (Rev 19:6)

On his robe and on his thigh he has this name written: KING OF KINGS AND LORD OF LORDS. (Rev 19:16)

I saw thrones on which were seated those who had been given authority to judge. And I saw the souls of those who had been beheaded because of their testimony for Jesus and because of the word of God. They had not worshiped the beast or his image and had not received his mark on their foreheads or their hands. They came to life and reigned with Christ a thousand years. This is the first resurrection. Blessed and holy are those who have part in the first resurrection. The second death has no power over them, but they will be priests of God and of Christ and will reign with him for a thousand years. (Rev 20:4-6)

He will be great and will be called the Son of the Most High. The Lord God will give him the throne of his father David, And he will reign over the house of Jacob forever; his kingdom will never end." (Luke 1:32-33)

"In the time of those kings, the God of heaven will set up a kingdom that will never be destroyed, nor will it be left to another people. It will crush all those kingdoms and bring them to an end, but it will itself endure forever. (Dan 2:44)

How great are his signs, how mighty his wonders! His kingdom is an eternal kingdom; his dominion endures from generation to generation. (Dan 4:3)

At the end of that time, I, Nebuchadnezzar, raised my eyes toward heaven, and my sanity was restored. Then I praised the Most High; I honored and glorified him who lives forever. His dominion is an eternal dominion; his kingdom endures from generation to generation. (Dan 4:34)

"I issue a decree that in every part of my kingdom people must fear and reverence the God of Daniel. "For he is the living God and he endures forever; his kingdom will not be destroyed, his dominion will never end. (Dan 6:26)

"In my vision at night I looked, and there before me was one like a son of man, coming with the clouds of heaven. He approached the Ancient of Days and was led into his presence. He was given authority, glory and sovereign power; all peoples, nations and men of every language worshiped him. His dominion is an everlasting dominion that will not pass away, and his kingdom is one that will never be destroyed. (Dan 7:13-14)

**3** (11:16-17) **God, Praise:** scene two—the Lord God Almighty is acclaimed. As soon as the angel gave a glimpse into the future that showed the victory of God, the twenty four elders fell on their faces before God. They worshipped and praised Him for three things.

1. They praised God as the Lord God Almighty.
   ⇒ Lord: He deserved to be the Lord and Master, the Ruler over all lives.
   ⇒ God: He was the Creator and Maker of all, and He was the only one who deserved to be worshipped.
   ⇒ Almighty: He was omnipotent, that is, all powerful. He can do anything, and He will always be able to execute His will.

2. They praised Him as the Lord God who "is and who was." That is, He is eternal. He is the One existing now, who was always existing, and is to always exist. The Lord

God possesses life forever and ever. Therefore, He is able to give life to whom He wills.

3. They praised Him for taking His great power back from the world and beginning to reign in His rightful place. God has allowed Satan to have access to the world and to man. And, most unfortunately, man has chosen to follow Satan instead of God. But not all people. Some people have done exactly what God was after: freely chosen to believe and follow Him—freely chosen to love God supremely. The result has been a world inhabited by a mass of people who deny and ignore God, with only a few people who choose to focus upon God. And the inevitable has happened: the selfishness and greed and lust that grips people who focus only upon self has consumed the world. The world is wrecked with so much sin and evil that problems have become so mammoth that they are now beyond solving.

But note: God is going to solve them. This is the declaration of the praise of the twenty four elders. They have just witnessed the scene of the future, the scene where God has just taken back His power over the world from Satan. They have witnessed the rule of God's love and righteousness upon earth.

> You will be with child and give birth to a son, and you are to give him the name Jesus. He will be great and will be called the Son of the Most High. The Lord God will give him the throne of his father David, And he will reign over the house of Jacob forever; his kingdom will never end." (Luke 1:31-33)
>
> Now to the King eternal, immortal, invisible, the only God, be honor and glory for ever and ever. Amen. (1 Tim 1:17)
>
> And sang the song of Moses the servant of God and the song of the Lamb: "Great and marvelous are your deeds, Lord God Almighty. Just and true are your ways, King of the ages. (Rev 15:3)
>
> Then I heard what sounded like a great multitude, like the roar of rushing waters and like loud peals of thunder, shouting: "Hallelujah! For our Lord God Almighty reigns. (Rev 19:6)
>
> The LORD will reign for ever and ever." (Exo 15:18)
>
> And said: "O LORD, God of our fathers, are you not the God who is in heaven? You rule over all the kingdoms of the nations. Power and might are in your hand, and no one can withstand you. (2 Chr 20:6)
>
> Who is he, this King of glory? The LORD Almighty— he is the King of glory. *Selah* (Psa 24:10)

**4** (11:18) **Satan, Final Rebellion**: scene 3—the nations of the world will make a final rebellion against God and will be destroyed and face the eternal judgment of God. Note five points.

1. There will be the final rebellion of the nations against the Lord Jesus Christ at the end of the millennium (the thousand year rule of Christ upon earth). The devil and his followers are going to try to defeat Christ and His followers in a last ditch battle upon earth. Remember: Christ will be ruling upon earth for one thousand years, and that is a long, long time. Over the period of the thousand years, people will do what people so often do now: become dull and lethargic to Christ and His power and to His call and will. Therefore when Satan is loosed to tempt and lead them, many will attempt to overthrow Christ and His followers.

The result will be quick and catastrophic for the ungodly nations and people of this earth.

> When the thousand years are over, Satan will be released from his prison And will go out to deceive the nations in the four corners of the earth—Gog and Magog—to gather them for battle. In number they are like the sand on the seashore. They marched across the breadth of the earth and surrounded the camp of God's people, the city he loves. But fire came down from heaven and devoured them. And the devil, who deceived them, was thrown into the lake of burning sulfur, where the beast and the false prophet had been thrown. They will be tormented day and night for ever and ever. (Rev 20:7-10)

2. The wrath of God will fall.

> Whoever believes in the Son has eternal life, but whoever rejects the Son will not see life, for God's wrath remains on him." (John 3:36)
>
> The wrath of God is being revealed from heaven against all the godlessness and wickedness of men who suppress the truth by their wickedness, (Rom 1:18)
>
> But for those who are self-seeking and who reject the truth and follow evil, there will be wrath and anger. (Rom 2:8)
>
> Let no one deceive you with empty words, for because of such things God's wrath comes on those who are disobedient. (Eph 5:6)
>
> Kiss the Son, lest he be angry and you be destroyed in your way, for his wrath can flare up in a moment. Blessed are all who take refuge in him. (Psa 2:12)

3. The dead will be judged.

> "When the Son of Man comes in his glory, and all the angels with him, he will sit on his throne in heavenly glory. All the nations will be gathered before him, and he will separate the people one from another as a shepherd separates the sheep from the goats. (Mat 25:31-32)
>
> Just as man is destined to die once, and after that to face judgment, (Heb 9:27)
>
> If this is so, then the Lord knows how to rescue godly men from trials and to hold the unrighteous for the day of judgment, while continuing their punishment. (2 Pet 2:9)
>
> By the same word the present heavens and earth are reserved for fire, being kept for the day of judgment and destruction of ungodly men. (2 Pet 3:7)
>
> In this way, love is made complete among us so that we will have confidence on the day of judgment, because in this world we are like him. (1 John 4:17)

Enoch, the seventh from Adam, prophesied about these men: "See, the Lord is coming with thousands upon thousands of his holy ones To judge everyone, and to convict all the ungodly of all the ungodly acts they have done in the ungodly way, and of all the harsh words ungodly sinners have spoken against him." (Jude 1:14-15)

4. The godly will be rewarded, that is, the believers, the prophets, and those who fear God's name.

"Blessed are you when people insult you, persecute you and falsely say all kinds of evil against you because of me. Rejoice and be glad, because great is your reward in heaven, for in the same way they persecuted the prophets who were before you. (Mat 5:11-12)
And if anyone gives even a cup of cold water to one of these little ones because he is my disciple, I tell you the truth, he will certainly not lose his reward." (Mat 10:42)
"His master replied, 'Well done, good and faithful servant! You have been faithful with a few things; I will put you in charge of many things. Come and share your master's happiness!' (Mat 25:23)
But love your enemies, do good to them, and lend to them without expecting to get anything back. Then your reward will be great, and you will be sons of the Most High, because he is kind to the ungrateful and wicked. (Luke 6:35)
Because you know that the Lord will reward everyone for whatever good he does, whether he is slave or free. (Eph 6:8)
Blessed are all who take refuge in him. (Psa 2:12)

5. The destroyers of human life will have their own lives destroyed.

And give relief to you who are troubled, and to us as well. This will happen when the Lord Jesus is revealed from heaven in blazing fire with his powerful angels. He will punish those who do not know God and do not obey the gospel of our Lord Jesus. They will be punished with everlasting destruction and shut out from the presence of the Lord and from the majesty of his power (2 Th 1:7-9)
These men are springs without water and mists driven by a storm. Blackest darkness is reserved for them. (2 Pet 2:17)
Enoch, the seventh from Adam, prophesied about these men: "See, the Lord is coming with thousands upon thousands of his holy ones To judge everyone, and to convict all the ungodly of all the ungodly acts they have done in the ungodly way, and of all the harsh words ungodly sinners have spoken against him." (Jude 1:14-15)
Then I saw a great white throne and him who was seated on it. Earth and sky fled from his presence, and there was no place for them. And I saw the dead, great

and small, standing before the throne, and books were opened. Another book was opened, which is the book of life. The dead were judged according to what they had done as recorded in the books. The sea gave up the dead that were in it, and death and Hades gave up the dead that were in them, and each person was judged according to what he had done. Then death and Hades were thrown into the lake of fire. The lake of fire is the second death. If anyone's name was not found written in the book of life, he was thrown into the lake of fire. (Rev 20:11-15)

**Thought 1.** This is a strong warning to us all, a warning that must be heeded and heeded now or else we shall be eternally doomed.
1) A person must not join those who rebel against God. If he rebels against God, then he must face God as a rebel who stands opposed to God and who fights against the kingdom of God.
2) The wrath of God is going to fall against all who rebel against God.
3) The dead will face God. All the dead, every single person who has lived or ever will live—all shall stand face to face with God.
4) The godly will be rewarded. All who fear God's name will be greatly rewarded.
5) The ungodly and evil will be destroyed. All who destroy human life—their own lives or the lives of others—shall be destroyed.

**5** (11:19) **Temple of God**: scene four—God's temple will be opened. This is the picture of eternity. God will dwell with His own in His temple—in all the universe. His promises will then be known to be true, and His majesty will be experienced. (See outlines and notes—Rev.21:1-22:5. See DEEPER STUDY # 3, pt.3-4—Mt.19:23-24.)
1. There is a heavenly temple after which the earthly temple and tabernacle were patterned. Scripture clearly says this.

The cherubim are to have their wings spread upward, overshadowing the cover with them. The cherubim are to face each other, looking toward the cover. (Exo 25:20)
It was necessary, then, for the copies of the heavenly things to be purified with these sacrifices, but the heavenly things themselves with better sacrifices than these. (Heb 9:23)

This is a wonderful thing, for it means that our earthly worship is patterned after the heavenly worship. However, we must never forget that the eternal, the new heavens and earth, will have no temple in them. Lehman Strauss states this well.

"When the New Jerusalem comes down from Heaven, it is called 'the holy city' (Revelation 21:2), and John states expressly, 'I saw no temple there' (21:22). When the scenes in chapter 21 are fulfilled there will be no need for a temple as a place of worship. If all were holy on earth now, there would be no need for a place of worship. Jesus said, 'God is Spirit: and they that worship Him must worship Him in spirit and in truth' (John 4:24). True worship is a matter of the heart" (*The Book of the Revelation*, p.225).

2. There is another interpretation of this passage that needs to be noted. William Barclay states it well:

> "The Temple is opened; but there is more than that. The Ark of the Covenant is seen. Now the Ark of the Covenant was in the Holy of Holies, the inside of which no ordinary person had ever seen, and into which even the High Priest went only on the Day of Atonement. This vision involves the opening up of the Temple and even the opening up of the Holy of Holies. This can have only one meaning; it must mean that now the glory of God is going to be fully displayed. That which was secret is going to be revealed; that which no man has seen is going to be opened to the sight of men. The full glory of God is going to burst upon men.

> "Why the special reference to the Ark of the Covenant? This is to remind people of God's special covenant with His own people. Originally that covenant had been with the people Israel; but the new covenant is the covenant in Jesus Christ with all of every nation who love and who believe in Jesus. This means that in the full display of God's glory, in the destruction of God's enemies, God will remember His covenant and God will be true to His own. Whatever the terror and whatever the destruction to come, God will not break the covenant that He made with His people and will not be false to His promises.

> "So this picture is a picture of the coming of the full glory of God, which is a terrifying threat to the enemies of God, but an uplifting promise to the people of God's covenant" (*The Revelation of John*, Vol.2, p.89f).

| | CHAPTER 12 | 2 She was pregnant and cried out in pain as she was about to give birth. | b. Her cry: For deliverance |
|---|---|---|---|
| | **VI. THE SEVENTH TRUMPET IN DETAIL (PART I): TWO SPIRITUAL WONDERS STRUGGLING BEHIND THE GREAT TRIBULATION, 12:1-17** | 3 Then another sign appeared in heaven: an enormous red dragon with seven heads and ten horns and seven crowns on his heads. | **2 The second character: A great red dragon—Satan** a. His description |
| | | 4 His tail swept a third of the stars out of the sky and flung them to the earth. The dragon stood in front of the woman who was about to give birth, so that he might devour her child the moment it was born. | b. His power |
| | **A. The Central Characters in the Great Tribulation, 12:1-5** | | c. His aim: To devour the child |
| **1 The first character: A woman with child** a. Her description | **A** great and wondrous sign appeared in heaven: a woman clothed with the sun, with the moon under her feet and a crown of twelve stars on her head. | 5 She gave birth to a son, a male child, who will rule all the nations with an iron scepter. And her child was snatched up to God and to his throne. | **3 The main character: A man child—Jesus** a. His purpose: To rule b. His ascension: To be exalted |

# DIVISION VI

## THE SEVENTH TRUMPET IN DETAIL (PART I): TWO SPIRITUAL WONDERS STRUGGLING BEHIND THE GREAT TRIBULATION, 12:1-17

### A. The Central Characters in the Great Tribulation, 12:1-5

(12:1-5) **Introduction**: this is one of the most revealing and fascinating chapters in all the Bible. It rolls back the curtain between earth and heaven and shows what lies behind all the sin and evil and all the conflict and struggle of this world. It reveals a great *spiritual struggle* occurring behind the scenes of this world. And in the last days that spiritual struggle will be more intense than ever. The conflict will be so intense that the struggle waged upon earth is called by our Lord the *great tribulation*. By *great* He meant the most intense and terrible tribulation the world has ever seen. But why does the world suffer tribulation? Why does there have to be tribulation upon earth? And why will there be such intense and terrible tribulation in the end time? This passage tells us: it shows us the great *spiritual warfare* that is waged behind the scenes of this world, the great spiritual warfare that is being fought for the souls of men. There are three principle characters who have been involved in the spiritual warfare. These characters are the subject of this first passage.

1. The first character: a woman with child (v.1-2).
2. The second character: a great red dragon—Satan (v.3-4).
3. The main character: a man child—Jesus (v.5).

**1** (12:1-2) **Israel**: there is the first character in the great tribulation—a woman with child. Note how the woman bursts upon the scene. She is said to be a "wondrous sign" or "wonder" (semeion). Note also that she is in heaven. This means that she is the heavenly representative of some earthly people. Who is the woman on earth, what people does she represent?

1. This woman is not identified, but it is clear who she is.
   a. She is clothed with the sun, with the moon under her feet and a crown of twelve stars on her. This refers back to the Old Testament to a dream that Joseph had:

> Then he had another dream, and he told it to his brothers. "Listen," he said, "I had another dream, and this time the sun and moon and eleven stars were bowing down to me." When he told his father as well as his brothers, his father rebuked him and said, "What is this dream you had? Will your mother and I and your brothers actually come and bow down to the ground before you?" His brothers were jealous of him, but his father kept the matter in mind. (Gen 37:9-11)

Note that Jacob understood exactly what Joseph meant: the sun represented the father Jacob, the moon the mother, and the twelve stars the brothers. The dream was a picture of Israel; Joseph was dreaming that Israel would be saved from destruction through him.

   b. She is pregnant and the child is pictured as being born (v.2, 5). Note what is said about the child.

> She gave birth to a son, a male child, who will rule all the nations with an iron scepter. And her child was snatched up to God and to his throne. (Rev 12:5)

This clearly refers to Jesus Christ. He and He alone was born to rule all nations (cp. Ps.2:9), and He alone was exalted to the throne of God. As stated, this is a clear reference to Jesus Christ.

2. Now who is this woman? There are three main positions about who she is.
   a. Some say she is Mary, the mother of Jesus. But there are just too many supernatural things said about this woman for her to be an earthly or human being.

b. Some say she is the church. But this is difficult to see, for the church did not give birth to Christ. On the contrary, Christ gave birth to the church.

c. Some say she is the ideal Zion, the ideal Jerusalem, the ideal Israel, the chosen people, the community of God from which Christ came. These say the mother represents all the true people of God, those before Jesus came and those after He came. Paul actually speaks of the Jerusalem which is above, who is the mother of the people of God on earth (Gal.4:26). This position is a possible identification of the woman. But again, this position does not fill all the things said about the woman, not as well as Israel itself does.

d. Some say that the woman represents Israel, the very people who gave birth to Jesus Christ. This seems to be the clearest identification of the woman. As we progress through the passage, we will see that everything said about this woman fits Israel just like a glove.

⇒ Paul himself said that Jesus Christ came out of Israel (Ro.9:5).

⇒ Isaiah prophesied that Israel would have labor pains and bring forth a male child (Is.66:7-8).

**2** (12:3-4) **Satan—Dragon**: there is the second character in the great tribulation—an enormous dragon, that is, the devil. Note that the dragon is also said to be a *sign* in heaven. Three significant things need to be discussed about this sign.

1. There is the description and authority of the dragon or devil. The description is entirely different from what most people think. When people think of the devil, they picture a fiery red serpent-like creature with two horns and a long pointed tail who holds a pitchfork in his hand. But this is a total misconception, a far cry from the truth. When Scripture speaks of Satan as a dragon, it is referring to the evil work he does, not to his looks or appearance. Scripture says that Satan is the highest and most glorious being ever created by God, that his being is so magnificent that he shines like the sun and actually possesses glory just like God. Note what this verse says about his description, and remember: this is not picturing what he looks like. It is describing his authority and power.

⇒ Satan has seven heads: seven is the number of completeness and fullness. Satan is complete in intelligence; he has full knowledge. He is not omniscient, of course, but his knowledge is complete and full.

⇒ Satan has seven crowns: this symbolizes authority, rule, and dominion—a crowned ruler who has a kingdom that he rules over. Scripture clearly says that Satan is a crowned ruler and that his authority is well beyond anything that man ever thinks.

⇒ Satan has ten horns: this symbolizes great power, but power that pierces, rips, and tears—all in the most ferocious and vicious way. It symbolizes that he uses his head and authority in an evil way.

⇒ Satan is the *god of this world* who blinds men's minds.

> **The god of this age has blinded the minds of unbelievers, so that they cannot see the light of the gospel of the glory of Christ, who is the image of God. (2 Cor 4:4)**

⇒ Satan is the *prince of this world*.

> **Now is the time for judgment on this world; now the prince of this world will be driven out. (John 12:31)**
> **I will not speak with you much longer, for the prince of this world is coming. He has no hold on me, (John 14:30)**
> **And in regard to judgment, because the prince of this world now stands condemned. (John 16:11)**

⇒ Satan is the *ruler of the kingdom of the air*.

> **In which you used to live when you followed the ways of this world and of the ruler of the kingdom of the air, the spirit who is now at work in those who are disobedient. (Eph 2:2)**

⇒ Satan is the king of a kingdom.

> **If Satan drives out Satan, he is divided against himself. How then can his kingdom stand? (Mat 12:26)**
> **Again, the devil took him to a very high mountain and showed him all the kingdoms of the world and their splendor. "All this I will give you," he said, "if you will bow down and worship me." (Mat 4:8-9)**

⇒ Satan has his grip upon the whole world.

> **We know that we are children of God, and that the whole world is under the control of the evil one. (1 John 5:19)**

2. There is the origin of the dragon or devil. This statement is telling where Satan came from. This is clearly seen in the Greek tenses of the statement. Note the two statements in the Greek:

⇒ His tail "sweeps" (surei, present tense) a third part of heaven. That is, Satan pulls and drags a third of the stars (angels) of heaven.

⇒ He "flung" (ebalen) them down or threw them down. This is past tense; that is, it tells us what Satan did long ago.

The point is this: today, in the present moment, Satan has authority over one third of the stars or angels of heaven. How? Because in the past he flung them down with himself. Now note two points.

a. Where were Satan and the angels flung down from? Heaven. They were the stars of heaven, but they were cast down from heaven. Eons ago, sometime before man ever began, God created an angel, the highest and most glorious being ever created.

⇒ His name is *Lucifer* which means *star of the morning*.

⇒ He was the *anointed cherub who covered* the very throne of God itself. He was the angel put in charge of the glory of God's very own throne.

But something happened: he did what so many people do. He began to look at himself, and he began to want to live like he wanted instead of like

God wanted. He wanted to do his own thing instead of doing like God said. Therefore, he rebelled against God, and in his rebellion he led one third of the angelic beings with him. Consequently, God had no choice but to cast him down from his exalted position in heaven. From what we can glean from Scripture this is what happened to Lucifer, how he became the devil, the arch-enemy of God (see Deeper Study # 1—Rev.12:9; Deeper Study # 1—2 Cor.4:4; note—1 Pt.5:8 for more discussion).

> **How you have fallen from heaven, O morning star, son of the dawn! You have been cast down to the earth, you who once laid low the nations! You said in your heart, "I will ascend to heaven; I will raise my throne above the stars of God; I will sit enthroned on the mount of assembly, on the utmost heights of the sacred mountain. I will ascend above the tops of the clouds; I will make myself like the Most High." But you are brought down to the grave, to the depths of the pit. (Isa 14:12-15)**

> **The word of the LORD came to me: "Son of man, take up a lament concerning the king of Tyre and say to him: 'This is what the Sovereign LORD says: "'You were the model of perfection, full of wisdom and perfect in beauty. You were in Eden, the garden of God; every precious stone adorned you: ruby, topaz and emerald, chrysolite, onyx and jasper, sapphire, turquoise and beryl. Your settings and mountings were made of gold; on the day you were created they were prepared. You were anointed as a guardian cherub, for so I ordained you. You were on the holy mount of God; you walked among the fiery stones. You were blameless in your ways from the day you were created till wickedness was found in you. Through your widespread trade you were filled with violence, and you sinned. So I drove you in disgrace from the mount of God, and I expelled you, O guardian cherub, from among the fiery stones. Your heart became proud on account of your beauty, and you corrupted your wisdom because of your splendor. So I threw you to the earth; I made a spectacle of you before kings. By your many sins and dishonest trade you have desecrated your sanctuaries. So I made a fire come out from you, and it consumed you, and I reduced you to ashes on the ground in the sight of all who were watching. All the nations who knew you are appalled at you; you have come to a horrible end and will be no more.'"** (Ezek 28:11-19)

> **Then another sign appeared in heaven: an enormous red dragon with seven heads and ten horns and seven crowns on his heads. His tail swept a third of the stars out of the sky and flung them to the earth. The dragon stood in front of the woman who was about to give birth, so that he might devour her child the moment it was born. (Rev 12:3-4)**

3. There is the aim of the dragon or devil. Satan's aim is to devour the woman, to destroy Israel. This has always been Satan's aim. Why? Because he is out to get back at God for judging him. He is out to hurt God, to cut the heart of God. And the best way he can do this is to turn the hearts of people away from God and lead them to sin and to follow the way of evil.

Now, go way back in history again, to the time when God promised to send the Savior to the world. When God first promised to send Christ to save the world, Satan knew it. He was listening. He was the *serpent* who had tempted Adam and Eve and led them to sin and hurt God. But God loved Adam and Eve and wanted to save them from sin and death; therefore, God promised to send *the seed*, the Savior of the world, who would crush the head and power of Satan.

> **And I will put enmity between you and the woman, and between your offspring and hers; he will crush your head, and you will strike his heel." (Gen 3:15)**

As stated, Satan heard the promise. Consequently, he was bound to do all he could to delay the coming of the Seed, the Savior. He, of course, knew what we know: no person can stop God's plan and will. But Satan wanted to get as many people as he could to sin and to turn away from God so that God's heart would be cut and hurt. He wanted to delay his own defeat and the crushing of his head as long as he could. This is what is meant by this verse:

> **His tail swept a third of the stars out of the sky and flung them to the earth. The dragon stood in front of the woman who was about to give birth, so that he might devour her child the moment it was born. (Rev 12:4)**

Satan has tried from the very beginning to destroy the seed of the woman. He has been waging war against the *Seed* of God, the Savior of the world, ever since God promised to save the world. The great Baptist preacher W.A. Criswell points this out by tracing some of the attempts of the devil throughout the Bible (*Expository Sermon On Revelation*, Vol.4. Grand Rapids, MI: Zondervan, 1969, p.86-87). For clarity, the attempts are put in chart form by us.

| *The Seed or Line Through Whom the Promised Seed Was to Come* | *The Strategies of Satan to Destroy the Seed or Devour the Child and God's Great Deliverance* |
|---|---|
| ⇒ There was the line of Abel, Adam's Son. | ⇒ Satan led Cain to kill Abel, but God gave Adam another son, Seth (Gen.4:1f). |
| ⇒ There was the early line of the godly seed. | ⇒ Satan led the godly line to mix with the ungodly and led them into such vile wickedness that God had to destroy the earth. But God raised up Noah (Gen.6:5f). |
| ⇒ There was the line of Abraham, Isaac, and Jacob. | ⇒ Satan led Esau to threaten to kill his brother, Jacob. But God protected Jacob (Gen.27:41f). |
| ⇒ There was the line of the children of Israel. | ⇒ Satan led Pharaoh to attempt to kill all the male babies of Israel. But God saved Moses (Ex.1:8f). |
| ⇒ There was the line of David. | ⇒ Satan led son after son of David into sin and to murder and disqualify themselves. But God always kept at least one son of David alive (2 Sam. 13f). |
| ⇒ There was the line of the sons of David. | |
| ⇒ There was the line of Jehosophat's sons. | ⇒ Satan led Jehoram, one of Jehosophat's sons, to kill all his brothers. But God caused sons to be born to Jehoram to carry on the line (2 Chron.21:1f). |
| ⇒ There was the line of Ahaziah. | ⇒ Satan led an enemy to come in and kill all the sons but one—Ahaziah (2 Ki.8:25f). |
| | ⇒ Satan led Jehu to kill Ahaziah, and the queen's mother, Athaliah, took over the throne and killed all the sons. But God led the wife of the high priest to save one small baby, Joash. At this point the line of the promised seed rested in the saving of this little baby's life (2 Ki.9:11f). |
| ⇒ There was the line of the chosen people. | ⇒ Satan led King Ahasuerus to exterminate all of God's people. But God gave him a most restless and frightening night of sleep. The king, therefore, spared the chosen line (Esther). |
| ⇒ There was the line of the Promised Seed, Jesus Himself, at His birth. | ⇒ Satan led King Herod to slay all the babies in Bethlehem in an attempt to kill the promised child. But God warned Joseph and told Joseph to flee with the child (Mt.2:1f). |
| ⇒ There was the line of the Promised Seed, Jesus Himself, at his temptation. | ⇒ Satan tempted Jesus to cast Himself down from the pinnacle of the temple, to secure the loyalty and worship of the people by the spectacular instead of the cross. But Jesus chose God's way, the way of the cross, instead of Satan's way (Mt.4:1f). |
| ⇒ There was the line of the Promised Seed, Jesus Himself, at his hometown, Nazareth. | ⇒ Satan led the citizens of Nazareth to try to cast Jesus off the cliff of a hill, but Jesus escaped (Lk.4:29). |
| ⇒ There was the line of the Promised Seed, Jesus Himself, in facing the religionists. | ⇒ Satan led the religionists to hate Jesus and to plot is death time and again (Jn.7:1f). But Jesus escaped time and again. |
| ⇒ There was the line of the Promised Seed, Jesus Himself, on the cross. | ⇒ Satan led the world to put Jesus on the cross and to kill Him. But God raised Jesus from the dead (Jn.19:1f). |

This is how Satan has attempted to hurt God, by doing all he could to devour the woman, the line of Israel. He did all he could to keep the Savior, the Lord Jesus Christ, from being born. Now that Christ has come, Satan does all he can to turn people away from judgment to come. Even when people do repent and turn to follow Christ, Satan does all he can to turn the followers of the Lord away from Him.

This is the battle, the combat, the struggle that is going on behind the scenes in the spiritual world. And the war will wage on and on until the world ends. The point of the present passage in Revelation is to show how the struggle will intensify in the *great tribulation*. During the *great*

*tribulation* Satan will use all the resources that he has to destroy the "seed of the woman," the followers of the Lord Jesus Christ. He will do all he can to cut and hurt the heart of God. God is not willing that a single soul perish; therefore, when Satan is successful in turning and destroying one person, the heart of God is cut and hurt as deeply as a cut can pierce.

**Thought 1.** Note: although the present passage is dealing primarily with the great tribulation, the same spiritual struggle is waged in every generation of history. Satan is out to turn every person he can away from God. He wants people to follow him instead of God. He wants the obedience of people instead of people giving their obedience and loyalty to God.

**3** (12:5) **Jesus Christ**: there is the third character in the great tribulation, Jesus Christ Himself. Note two points.

1. Jesus Christ was born or sent into the world to rule the world. He was sent by God to bring godliness and righteousness to earth, to use an iron scepter of judgment in order to get rid of sin and ungodliness in the world.

   a. This He did, of course, by the cross. Upon the cross Jesus Christ made it possible for men to be forgiven their sins and to stand before God, to stand before God free of sin. He did this by bearing the sins of men upon Himself when He died on the cross. He took the sins and the punishment of sins upon Himself. Therefore, man can now be free of sin and acceptable to God. Jesus Christ judged sin, condemned it upon the cross. Therefore, we can say that the rod of iron was used first of all upon Satan when Jesus Christ died upon the cross. Jesus Christ judged and destroyed the power of Satan.

> **Now is the time for judgment on this world; now the prince of this world will be driven out. (John 12:31)**
>
> **Since the children have flesh and blood, he too shared in their humanity so that by his death he might destroy him who holds the power of death—that is, the devil— (Heb 2:14)**
>
> **And having disarmed the powers and authorities, he made a public spectacle of them, triumphing over them by the cross. (Col 2:15)**
>
> **He who does what is sinful is of the devil, because the devil has been sinning from the beginning. The reason the Son of God appeared was to destroy the devil's work. (1 John 3:8)**

   b. Jesus Christ will also use the iron scepter against the nations of the world—against all the ungodly and evil of the world—in the end time. Jesus Christ shall rule all nations and bring righteousness and godliness to this earth by exerting all the authority and discipline of God needed. He shall bring the kingdom of God to earth.

> **You will rule them with an iron scepter; you will dash them to pieces like pottery." (Psa 2:9)**
>
> **'He will rule them with an iron scepter; he will dash them to pieces like pottery' — just as I have received authority from my Father. (Rev 2:27)**
>
> **Out of his mouth comes a sharp sword with which to strike down the nations. "He will rule them with an iron scepter." He treads the winepress of the fury of the wrath of God Almighty. (Rev 19:15)**

2. Jesus Christ ascended and was exalted to the throne of God. This is proof that He shall rule and reign and bring righteousness to the earth.

> **But from now on, the Son of Man will be seated at the right hand of the mighty God." (Luke 22:69)**
>
> **And who through the Spirit of holiness was declared with power to be the Son of God by his resurrection from the dead: Jesus Christ our Lord. (Rom 1:4)**
>
> **Which he exerted in Christ when he raised him from the dead and seated him at his right hand in the heavenly realms, (Eph 1:20)**
>
> **Therefore God exalted him to the highest place and gave him the name that is above every name, That at the name of Jesus every knee should bow, in heaven and on earth and under the earth, And every tongue confess that Jesus Christ is Lord, to the glory of God the Father. (Phil 2:9-11)**
>
> **Who has gone into heaven and is at God's right hand—with angels, authorities and powers in submission to him. (1 Pet 3:22)**
>
> **For to us a child is born, to us a son is given, and the government will be on his shoulders. And he will be called Wonderful Counselor, Mighty God, Everlasting Father, Prince of Peace. Of the increase of his government and peace there will be no end. He will reign on David's throne and over his kingdom, establishing and upholding it with justice and righteousness from that time on and forever. The zeal of the LORD Almighty will accomplish this. (Isa 9:6-7)**

B. **The Mighty Spiritual Struggle Behind the Great Tribulation, 12:6-17**

1 **The woman flees for her life**
 a. To a place prepared by God
 b. For three & one half years
2 **The great war over Israel & God's people is fought in heaven**
 a. The forces
  1) Michael & his angels
  2) Satan & his angels
 b. The outcome
  1) Satan will be defeated
  2) Satan will be barred from heaven

  3) Satan^DS1 & his angels will be cast out of heaven
3 **The glorious victory & salvation are won**
 a. The victory: Salvation

 b. The result: Satan can no longer accuse believers before God

 c. The weapons used
  1) The Lamb's blood
  2) The believers' testimony

6 The woman fled into the desert to a place prepared for her by God, where she might be taken care of for 1,260 days.
7 And there was war in heaven. Michael and his angels fought against the dragon, and the dragon and his angels fought back.
8 But he was not strong enough, and they lost their place in heaven.
9 The great dragon was hurled down—that ancient serpent called the devil, or Satan, who leads the whole world astray. He was hurled to the earth, and his angels with him.
10 Then I heard a loud voice in heaven say: "Now have come the salvation and the power and the kingdom of our God, and the authority of his Christ. For the accuser of our brothers, who accuses them before our God day and night, has been hurled down.
11 They overcame him by the blood of the Lamb and by the word of their testimony; they did not love their lives

so much as to shrink from death.
12 Therefore rejoice, you heavens and you who dwell in them! But woe to the earth and the sea, because the devil has gone down to you! He is filled with fury, because he knows that his time is short."
13 When the dragon saw that he had been hurled to the earth, he pursued the woman who had given birth to the male child.
14 The woman was given the two wings of a great eagle, so that she might fly to the place prepared for her in the desert, where she would be taken care of for a time, times and half a time, out of the serpent's reach.
15 Then from his mouth the serpent spewed water like a river, to overtake the woman and sweep her away with the torrent.
16 But the earth helped the woman by opening its mouth and swallowing the river that the dragon had spewed out of his mouth.
17 Then the dragon was enraged at the woman and went off to make war against the rest of her offspring—those who obey God's commandments and hold to the testimony of Jesus.

  3) The believers' loyalty
4 **The warning to earth is given**
 a. Because the devil is angered over his defeat
 b. Because the devil has not yet been destroyed; he has a little time left
5 **The dragon launches an attack upon the woman**
 a. The severe persecution

 b. The startling deliverance by the wings of a powerful eagle
  1) To her place of safety
  2) Kept for three & one half years

 c. The serpent's attempt to flood the woman: Uses every means

 d. The earth's enormous help

 e. The open attack upon the remaining seed

# DIVISION VI

## THE SEVENTH TRUMPET IN DETAIL (PART I): TWO SPIRITUAL WONDERS STRUGGLING BEHIND THE GREAT TRIBULATION, 12:1-17

### B. The Mighty Spiritual Struggle Behind the Great Tribulation, 12:6-17

(12:6-17) **Introduction**: the curtain has been rolled back between earth and heaven, and we have seen a mighty spiritual conflict going on behind all the ungodliness and evil of this world. We have seen that the dragon, the devil, is out to hurt and cut the heart of God. He does this by turning people away from Christ and leading them to destroy their lives by following evil. The Revelation has shown us this: the rampage of the devil against God will intensify in the end time, especially during the *tribulation*. This is the weighty discussion of this passage: *the spiritual struggle behind the great tribulation—the dragon's (Satan's) attacks against the woman (Israel).*

1. The woman flees for her life (v.6).
2. The great war over Israel and God's people is fought in heaven (v.7-9).
3. The glorious victory and salvation are won (v.10-11).
4. The warning to earth is given (v.12).
5. The dragon launches an attack upon the woman (v.13-17).

**1** (12:6) **Israel—Tribulation, Great**: the woman flees for her life. This is the picture of the terrible holocaust of the end time. We know this because of the thousand two hundred and sixty days (three and one half years) mentioned. This is the period always referred to as the *great tribulation* (see note, pt.2-4—Rev.11:2 for more discussion). The woman, Israel, is going to be severely persecuted by the antichrist in the end time. The Jews are going to have to flee for their lives, flee to the wilderness of the mountains, hills, and forests—to every hiding place they can find. However we must always keep in mind that the holocaust is going to be launched against the Gentile believers of the end time as well. There will literally be millions—a numberless number—of Gentile believers slaughtered right along with the Jews (cp. Rev.7:9). All believers and Israel, the Old Testament people of God, will be fleeing to every corner of wilderness in the world, seeking any place they can to hide.

Note the wonderful promise: God has a place for His people to hide. God is going to save a remnant of believers. He is going to use this persecution to turn even more Jews to His Son, who is the true Messiah, even the Lord Jesus Christ.

> God did not reject his people, whom he foreknew. Don't you know what the Scripture says in the passage about Elijah—how he appealed to God against Israel: (Rom 11:2)
>
> For if their rejection is the reconciliation of the world, what will their acceptance be but life from the dead? (Rom 11:15)
>
> And if they [Israel] do not persist in unbelief, they will be grafted in, for God is able to graft them in again. After all, if you [Gentile believers] were cut out of an olive tree that is wild by nature, and contrary to nature were grafted into a cultivated olive tree [Israel], how much more readily will these, the natural branches, be grafted into their own olive tree! (Rom 11:23-24)
>
> I do not want you to be ignorant of this mystery, brothers, so that you may not be conceited: Israel has experienced a hardening in part until the full number of the Gentiles has come in. And so all Israel will be saved, as it is written: "The deliverer will come from Zion; he will turn godlessness away from Jacob. (Rom 11:25-26)
>
> That is why I am suffering as I am. Yet I am not ashamed, because I know whom I have believed, and am convinced that he is able to guard what I have entrusted to him for that day. (2 Tim 1:12)
>
> When he had fled from Saul into the cave. Have mercy on me, O God, have mercy on me, for in you my soul takes refuge. I will take refuge in the shadow of your wings until the disaster has passed. (Psa 57:1)
>
> Indeed, he who watches over Israel will neither slumber nor sleep. (Psa 121:4)
>
> You have been a refuge for the poor, a refuge for the needy in his distress, a shelter from the storm and a shade from the heat. For the breath of the ruthless is like a storm driving against a wall (Isa 25:4)
>
> But now, this is what the LORD says— he who created you, O Jacob, he who formed you, O Israel: "Fear not, for I have redeemed you; I have summoned you by name; you are mine. When you pass through the waters, I will be with you; and when you pass through the rivers, they will not sweep over you. When you walk through the fire, you will not be burned; the flames will not set you ablaze. (Isa 43:1-2)

**2** (12:7-9) **Satan—Tribulation, Great—End Time**: the great war over Israel and God's people is to be fought in heaven. The mighty struggle for the believer's soul occurs in the spiritual realm, the spiritual world or dimension of being. This is the picture of these three verses. The intense struggle for the souls of Israel and the believers in the end time will be occurring in the spiritual world. Remember: Israel and the believers are having to flee for their lives from the worst holocaust the world has ever seen. It has been launched by the antichrist, the one man who embodies the very evil of the devil himself. These verses show us what lies behind this terrible holocaust, what is causing the terrible attack against Israel and the believers.

1. The forces of the spiritual struggle are Michael and his angels and Satan and his fallen angels. Note several things.

   a. Scripture teaches that God has assigned angels to look after and to minister to believers.

   > Are not all angels ministering spirits sent to serve those who will inherit salvation? (Heb 1:14. See DEEPER STUDY # 1— Heb.1:4-14 for more discussion.)

   b. Scripture teaches there are ranks and orders of angels, that there are various levels of authority among angels. They rule as powers over the spiritual world. This is true among both good and evil angels.

   > For I am convinced that neither death nor life, neither angels nor demons, neither the present nor the future, nor any powers, Neither height nor depth, nor anything else in all creation, will be able to separate us from the love of God that is in Christ Jesus our Lord. (Rom 8:38-39)
   >
   > [Christ is] far above all rule and authority, power and dominion, and every title that can be given, not only in the present age but also in the one to come. (Eph 1:21)
   >
   > His intent [purpose] was that now, through the church, the manifold wisdom of God should be made known to the rulers and authorities in the heavenly realms, (Eph 3:10)
   >
   > For our struggle is not against flesh and blood, but against the rulers, against the authorities, against the powers of this dark world and against the spiritual forces of evil in the heavenly realms. (Eph 6:12)
   >
   > For by him all things were created: things in heaven and on earth, visible and invisible, whether thrones or powers or rulers or authorities; all things were created by him and for him. (Col 1:16)
   >
   > And you have been given fullness in Christ, who is the head over every power and authority. (Col 2:10)
   >
   > And having disarmed the powers and authorities, he made a public spectacle of them, triumphing over them by the cross. (Col 2:15)

   c. Michael is one of the archangels who serves God. In Scripture he is presented as being above all the other angels. He seems to be the prime administrator of God (Dan.10:21; 12:1, 7-12; 1 Th.4:16; Jude 9) He is also pictured as the guardian angel of God's people. He struggles against the fallen angels who seek control over the nations and people of the earth (Dan.10:13, 21; 12:1; cp. Dan. chapters 10-12).

2. A spiritual war will be fought in the end time between the spiritual forces of good and evil. Satan and his angels will attempt to do what they have always tried to do: stamp out Israel and the followers of Christ. But there will be one difference: verse twelve tells us what it is. Satan "knows that

he his time is short." God will be ready to end human history. Therefore, Satan will attack both Israel and the believers as never before. He will literally try to wipe out every Jew and believer that he can. Why? Because every one who is killed will never be able to accept Christ nor bear testimony and lead anyone else to Christ. God will hurt and be cut that much more because more people will be lost and never became true worshippers of God.

But note what the glorious outcome of the battle will be. Satan and his fallen angels will be *defeated* and cast out of heaven once for all. After this event—when this battle takes place in the *great tribulation*—Satan will never again have access into heaven. He will never again accuse a believer before God.

Remember: Satan is said to presently have access to heavenly places and to God (Lk.10:18; Eph.6:12; Job 1:6f). But this will be the final battle between evil and good. This is the picture being painted by Revelation. After this battle, Satan will be defeated forever.

> Now I have come to explain to you what will happen to your people in the future, for the vision concerns a time yet to come." (Dan 10:14)
>
> "At that time Michael, the great prince who protects your people, will arise. There will be a time of distress such as has not happened from the beginning of nations until then. But at that time your people—everyone whose name is found written in the book—will be delivered. (Dan 12:1)

**Thought 1.** In all the graphic description of the above we must remember what will be happening upon earth. Israel and believers will be suffering the worst horror of evil ever launched upon earth: the holocaust of the antichrist. He will be doing all he can to eliminate every Jew and believer from the face of the earth. Why? All because of the dragon, that ancient serpent, called the devil and Satan. (See DEEPER STUDY # 1, *Satan*—Rev.12:9 for more discussion.)

---

**DEEPER STUDY # 1**

(12:9) **Satan**: Satan is called "the great dragon...that ancient serpent." His name is *Lucifer*. He was probably one of the highest angels ever created by God, but he fell because of selfishness and pride (Is.14:12; cp. 1 Tim.3:6. See note—Rev.12:3-4; DEEPER STUDY # 1—2 Cor.4:4; notes—2 Cor.11:13-15; 1 Pt.5:8.) He is "an angel of light" with such deceptive and seductive power that even some ministers follow him, ministers who "masquerade as servants of righteousness" (2 Cor.11:14-15). Throughout Scripture Satan is described as follows:

1. He is "the god of this world" who blinds men's minds (2 Cor.4:4).
2. He is "the prince of this world" (Jn.12:31; 14:20; 16:11) and "the ruler of the kingdom of the air" (Eph.2:2; 6:12).
3. He is Satan, which means the adversary (1 Chron.21:1; Job 1:6; 2:1-6; Zech.3:1;Mt.4:10; Mk.1:13; Lk.4:8; Jn.13:27; Acts 5:3; 26:18; Ro.16:20).
4. He is the devil, which means the slanderer (Mt.4:1, 5, 8, 11; Lk.4:2-6, 13; 1 Pt.5:8; Rev.20:2).
5. He is the deceiver of the whole world (2 Cor.11:3; Rev.12:9).

6. He is the tempter (Mt.4:3; 1 Th.3:5).
7. He is the evil one (Mt.6:13; 13:19, 38).
8. He is the father of lies (Jn.8:44).
9. He is the accuser of our brothers (Rev.12:10).
10. He is a murderer (Jn.8:44).
11. He is called Beelzebub (Mt.12:24; Mk.3:22; Lk.11:15).
12. He is called Belial (2 Cor.6:15).
13. He is called Abaddon (Rev.9:11).
14. He is called the angel of the Abyss or bottomless pit (Rev.9:11).
15. He is called Apollyon (Rev.9:11).
16. He is called the enemy (Mt.13:39).
17. He is called the gates of Hades (hell) (Mt.16:18).
18. He is called an enormous red dragon (Rev.12:3).
19. He is called a lying spirit (1 Ki.22:22).
20. He is called that ancient serpent (Rev.12:9; 20:2; cp. Gen.3:4, 14; 2 Cor.11:3).
21. He is called the dominion of darkness (Col.1:13).
22. He called the prince of devils (Mt.12:24).
23. He is called the ruler of this dark world (Eph.6:12).
24. He is called the spirit who is now at work in those who are disobedient (Eph.2:2).
25. He is called the evil spirit (Mt.12:43).

(See notes—Lk.22:3; DEEPER STUDY # 1—2 Cor.4:4; note—Col.2:15; note and DEEPER STUDY # 1—Jas.4:7; notes—1 Pt.5:8; Rev.12:3-4 for more discussion.)

Satan's purpose in making war against God is twofold.

1. Satan's purpose is power and worship, to receive as much of the power and worship of the universe as possible (Is.14:12-17; Ezk.28:11-17). He goes about this in three ways.

⇒ He opposes and disturbs God's work in the world (Is.14:12-17; Ezk.28:11-17; Job 1:6; 2:1-6; Mt.4:10; Mk.1:13; Lk.4:8; Rev.12:7-9).

⇒ He discourages believers through various strategies (see notes—Lk.22:31; Eph.6:10-12).

⇒ He arouses God's justice against people by leading people to sin and to deny and rebel against God. And when they do, God's justice has to act and judge people to the fate of their choice: that of living with Satan eternally (see note—Mt.12:25-26; Jn.13:31-32).

2. Satan's purpose is to hurt and cut the heart of God. Why? Because God has judged and condemned him for rebelling against God. Therefore, Satan does all he can to get back at God. The best way he can do this is to turn the hearts of people away from God and lead them to sin and to follow the way of evil. (See notes, pt.3—Rev.12:3-4; pt.2—Rev.12:7-9; pt.2—Rev.12:10-11 for more discussion.)

However, Christ has broken Satan's power by two acts (see notes—Jn.12:31-32; 16:11; 8:44; Col.2:15).

1. By never giving in to the devil's temptation (Mt.4:1-11) and by never sinning (2 Cor.5:21). Christ overcame sin. He was righteous; He was perfect.

2. By destroying the devil's power of death. Christ was not held by physical or spiritual death (Heb.2:14-15). He arose and ascended to God's right hand.

It is for this reason that the Bible says "the one who is in you is greater than the one who is in the world" (1 Jn.4:4); and again, "If God is for us, who can be against us?" (Ro.8:31).

**3** (12:10-11) **Salvation—Victory—Heavenly Praise**: the glorious victory and salvation are won by Christ. Note three facts.

1. A loud voice in heaven will shout out that the victory and salvation are now won—once-for-all. Who will this voice be? God's people. We know this because the voice refers to "our brothers." Note what the voice will declare:

⇒ The great salvation of our God: God will be ready to launch the glorious day of salvation, the day of redemption, to bring every person who has ever trusted him into eternity. God will be ready to save the whole world, making a new heavens and earth. The final triumph of salvation will be ready to take place.

⇒ The great strength of God will have just been demonstrated. Satan will have been defeated and cast out of heaven.

⇒ The great kingdom of our God will now be ready to be established forever and ever.

⇒ The power of God's Christ and Messiah will be proven. Every true believer will now live with God forever, worshipping and serving Him—all because of the power of God's Messiah.

> **For the kingdom of God is not a matter of talk but of power. (1 Cor 4:20)**
>
> **Saying: "We give thanks to you, Lord God Almighty, the One who is and who was, because you have taken your great power and have begun to reign. (Rev 11:17)**
>
> **Then I heard what sounded like a great multitude, like the roar of rushing waters and like loud peals of thunder, shouting: "Hallelujah! For our Lord God Almighty reigns. (Rev 19:6)**

2. The result of God's salvation will be glorious: Satan will be barred from heaven. He will no longer be able to accuse believers before God. Scripture teaches that Satan takes the sins of believers and throws them up into God's face. He points out every failure of a believer. Why? As stated before, to hurt and cut God. God gave His Son to die for the sins of men. Therefore, every time a believer sins, the devil reminds God...

• that the death of His Son was wasted and useless; it was not worth the price if believers are going to trample the blood of Christ underfoot.

• that the believers' love for Christ and God is hypocritical and shameful.

• that the believer could care less about God and Christ: he does not care enough to obey God. If he did, the believer would not sin.

• that the believer is not worth all the pain and hurt; that God should go ahead and wipe out the human race.

On and on we could go, but the point is the accusation of Satan against believers. But note: Satan will be thrown out of heaven. He will never again be able to appear before God and cut God by the sins and failures of believers.

> **Then he showed me Joshua the high priest standing before the angel of the LORD, and Satan standing at his right side to accuse him. (Zec 3:1)**
>
> **One day the angels came to present themselves before the LORD, and Satan also came with them. (Job 1:6)**

3. The weapons used to gain the victory over Satan will be threefold. Remember these are the very weapons that Michael and the angels will use in the battle with Satan (v.7-9). Michael and the angels will protect Israel and the believers in the end time, and a remnant of Israel and of Gentiles will be saved. How?

a. By the blood of the Lamb, of the Lord Jesus Christ (see note, pt.2—Rev.5:6-7).

b. By the word of their testimony, that is, by proclaiming the Word of God and by continuing to confess the Lord Jesus Christ as their Lord and Savior.

> **For we cannot help speaking about what we have seen and heard." (Acts 4:20)**
>
> **So do not be ashamed to testify about our Lord, or ashamed of me his prisoner. But join with me in suffering for the gospel, by the power of God, (2 Tim 1:8)**
>
> **But in your hearts set apart Christ as Lord. Always be prepared to give an answer to everyone who asks you to give the reason for the hope that you have. But do this with gentleness and respect, (1 Pet 3:15)**

c. By being loyal to Christ even to death. Note: many will die, millions in fact. But they shall live eternally. They shall never taste death. Quicker than the blink of an eye God shall transfer them to heaven into His very presence. But remember why: because they were loyal; they stood fast in Christ and refused to deny Him.

> **For whoever wants to save his life will lose it, but whoever loses his life for me will find it. (Mat 16:25)**
>
> **Then he said to them all: "If anyone would come after me, he must deny himself and take up his cross daily and follow me. (Luke 9:23)**
>
> **"If anyone comes to me and does not hate his father and mother, his wife and children, his brothers and sisters—yes, even his own life—he cannot be my disciple. And anyone who does not carry his cross and follow me cannot be my disciple. (Luke 14:26-27)**
>
> **"I tell you the truth," Jesus said to them, "no one who has left home or wife or brothers or parents or children for the sake of the kingdom of God Will fail to receive many times as much in this age and, in the age to come, eternal life." (Luke 18:29-30)**
>
> **Therefore, my dear brothers, stand firm. Let nothing move you. Always give yourselves fully to the work of the Lord, because you know that your labor in the Lord is not in vain. (1 Cor 15:58)**
>
> **The Lord will rescue me from every evil attack and will bring me safely to his heavenly kingdom. To him be glory for ever and ever. Amen. (2 Tim 4:18)**

**Thought 1.** The only way we can ever conquer Satan is to use these same three weapons.

1) We must be covered by the blood of the Lamb and we must claim the blood of the Lamb.

2) We must have a strong testimony for Christ, strongly proclaim the Word of God and

continue to confess the Lord Jesus Christ as our Lord and Savior.

3) We must be loyal to Christ even to death (Mt.10:22).

**4** (12:12) **Warning—Satan:** the warning to earth is given. Satan will be hurled, cast down to earth, and he will have one more chance to wreck and destroy all he can. Remember two things:

⇒ First, the rise of the antichrist is a judgment of God upon earth and its people. Why? Because of people's ungodliness, evil, idolatry, murder, sorcery, immorality, and thievery. In the end time evil will grow worse and worse. Therefore God will let man run wild with their evil, have their own way; and in the end, men will turn to a world leader who promises utopia upon earth, the antichrist himself.

⇒ Second, Satan has been hurled out of heaven. In the *great tribulation* Satan is a defeated foe, but he will not be destroyed—not yet. God is going to judge the world through him.

This is what is being pictured in this verse. When Satan is cast out of heaven, he knows he has but a brief time. Therefore, he stirs up the antichrist to create the worst devastation ever seen upon earth.

**5** (12:13-17) **Satan—Israel—Believers:** the dragon, the devil, will launch a terrible attack against the woman. Four points are given.

1. Satan will severely persecute the woman, Israel, and all believers who refuse to deny Christ. There will be a holocaust unparalleled in human history. Through the antichrist, Satan will launch an attempt to literally wipe the Jews and believers from off the face of the earth. The world will witness not a local or national holocaust but a world-wide slaughter. All over the world...

- the knock on the door by the secret police will be heard by frightened Jews and believers hovered in the corners of their homes.
- the arrests and jailing will be efficient and quick and will include children as well as adults.
- the boxcars will roll once again as they have so often in history, packing Jews and believers together like herded cattle.
- the execution camps will be restored and the executions will be quick and efficient.

2. The woman (Israel) and the believers will be delivered by the wings of an eagle. This is simply a picture of the delivering arms of God. This does not mean, of course, that no Jew and no believer will be killed. The exact opposite is true: the antichrist will slaughter millions, more by far than any other holocaust ever launched in history (cp. Rev.7:4, 9). God will give His dear people the wings of an eagle to deliver some on home to heaven and others to safety upon earth. Note that the persecution will continue for three and one half years (cp. v.6).

> 'You yourselves have seen what I did to Egypt, and how I carried you on eagles' wings and brought you to myself. (Exo 19:4)
> Like an eagle that stirs up its nest and hovers over its young, that spreads its wings to catch them and carries them on its pin-

ions. The LORD alone led him; no foreign god was with him. (Deu 32:11-12)

3. The serpent, the devil, will attempt to flood Israel and believers with tribulation after tribulation. The idea is an onrushing flood of trouble and persecution, attempt after attempt, horror after horror.

> The cords of death entangled me; the torrents of destruction overwhelmed me. (Psa 18:4)
> Therefore let everyone who is godly pray to you while you may be found; surely when the mighty waters rise, they will not reach him. (Psa 32:6)
> The flood would have engulfed us, the torrent would have swept over us, (Psa 124:4)
> But now, this is what the LORD says— he who created you, O Jacob, he who formed you, O Israel: "Fear not, for I have redeemed you; I have summoned you by name; you are mine. When you pass through the waters, I will be with you; and when you pass through the rivers, they will not sweep over you. When you walk through the fire, you will not be burned; the flames will not set you ablaze. (Isa 43:1-2)

4. There will be enormous help coming from the earth. God is going to use the earth to swallow up the flooding waters or attacks, of the devil and his antichrist. This probably means one or both of the following:

⇒ The devastations, natural catastrophes, of God's judgments upon the earth will distract and require the attention of the antichrist. The catastrophes, natural suffering of the earth, will save a remnant of Israel and believers. Remember the enormous destruction upon earth that has already happened due to the seal and trumpet judgments (see outline and notes—Rev.6:3-8; 6:12-17; 8:6-9:11; 8:6-12; 8:13-9:11; 9:12-21). There will also be nations who do not go along with the policies of the antichrist and they will give refuge to the Jews and believers who escape to their shores.

⇒ The dragon will launch an attack upon the rest of the woman's seed. This probably refers to the devil and his antichrist launching a more aggressive attack against the Jews and believers who did not flee to other parts of the earth for safety (nations or barren and destroyed parts). Again, remember that vast areas of the earth will be barren due to the natural catastrophes or judgments of God. This could be what is meant by the wilderness areas to which so many flee. In this day, when travel is so easy and with spy satellites and airplanes and helicopters, the wilderness has to mean either huge areas of vast wastelands or else nations that will be sympathetic to the persecuted believers. But not all will flee. Therefore, the antichrist will turn against those who remain behind with more animosity than ever.

**Thought 1.** The attacks of Satan have always been devastating, devastating in that his attacks destroy human lives. We must, therefore, stand fast in Christ and proclaim the victory of Christ over the devil. People can be saved through Jesus Christ alone. Therefore, the glorious message of salvation in Christ must be proclaimed to every man, woman, and child on earth. Jesus Christ is their only hope of deliverance from the destruction of Satan.

But I am afraid that just as Eve was deceived by the serpent's cunning, your minds may somehow be led astray from your sincere and pure devotion to Christ. (2 Cor 11:3)

Finally, be strong in the Lord and in his mighty power. Put on the full armor of God so that you can take your stand against the devil's schemes. (Eph 6:10-11)

Since the children have flesh and blood, he too shared in their humanity so that by his death he might destroy him who holds the power of death—that is, the devil—and free those who all their lives were held in slavery by their fear of death. (Heb 2:14-15)

Submit yourselves, then, to God. Resist the devil, and he will flee from you. (James 4:7)

Be self-controlled and alert. Your enemy the devil prowls around like a roaring lion looking for someone to devour. Resist him, standing firm in the faith, because you know that your brothers throughout the world are undergoing the same kind of sufferings. (1 Pet 5:8-9)

CHAPTER 13

VII.THE SEVENTH
   TRUMPET IN
   DETAIL (PART II):
   THE WAR OF THE
   DRAGON UPON THE
   EARTH, 13:1-18

A. The Attack Through the
   First Beast: A Political
   Ruler, 13:1-10

1 His origin: The sea
2 His great political power
   a. Heads: Wisdom
   b. Horns: Confederated
      power
   c. Crowns: Ruling authority
   d. Blasphemous name:
      Claims divine authority
   e. Combined world em-
      pires*DS1*

3 His dramatic rise to power
   a. Through an alliance with
      the dragon, Satan
   b. Through a healing from a
      mortal wound

4 His means of securing
   world government

And the dragon stood on the shore of the sea. And I saw a beast coming out of the sea. He had ten horns and seven heads, with ten crowns on his horns, and on each head a blasphemous name.
2 The beast I saw resembled a leopard, but had feet like those of a bear and a mouth like that of a lion. The dragon gave the beast his power and his throne and great authority.
3 One of the heads of the beast seemed to have had a fatal wound, but the fatal wound had been healed. The whole world was astonished and followed the beast.
4 Men worshiped the dragon because he had given authority to the beast, and they also worshiped the beast and asked, "Who is like the beast? Who can make war against him?"
5 The beast was given a mouth to utter proud words and blasphemies and to exercise his authority for forty-two months.
6 He opened his mouth to blaspheme God, and to slander his name and his dwelling place and those who live in heaven.
7 He was given power to make war against the saints and to conquer them. And he was given authority over every tribe, people, language and nation.
8 All inhabitants of the earth will worship the beast—all whose names have not been written in the book of life belonging to the Lamb that was slain from the creation of the world.
9 He who has an ear, let him hear.
10 If anyone is to go into captivity, into captivity he will go. If anyone is to be killed with the sword, with the sword he will be killed. This calls for patient endurance and faithfulness on the part of the saints.

a. Through the worldly &
   ungodly living of people
b. Through personal ability
   & appeal
c. Through military strength
d. Through speech, oratory,
   & blasphemy
e. Through spiritual & supernatural (satanic) power
   for three & one half years
f. Through world atheism &
   humanism

g. Through religious persecution

h. Through conquering
   many nations

i. Through imperial worship

5 His adversaries: The
   genuinely saved
   a. Are secure in the Lamb's
      Book of Life

   b. Are the hearers

   c. Are to accept God's
      will—even captivity
   d. Are not to defend the
      faith by force
   e. Are to be steadfast &
      loyal

# DIVISION VII

## THE SEVENTH TRUMPET IN DETAIL (PART II):
## THE WAR OF THE DRAGON UPON THE EARTH, 13:1-18

### A.  The Attack Through the First Beast: A Political Ruler, 13:1-10

(13:1-10) **Introduction**: this chapter is the key to the whole book of Revelation. It covers the antichrist, the terrible world ruler who is going to arise in the end time and embody the depth and terror of evil. If a person understands this chapter, then he will understand the great book of *Revelation*. To understand the antichrist is to understand...

- how and why the end time will be swept with so much evil and horror.
- how and why the judgments of God will fall upon the ungodly and evil of the end time, fall with terrible severity.
- how and why God will end the world when He does.
- how and why such glorious promises are given to Israel and the believers who follow Him in the end time.
- how and why so many of the Old Testament prophecies are fulfilled in the end time.

This is the chapter that discusses the two terrible rulers that are to arise in the end time, the antichrist and his cohort, the worldwide religious leader who will help the antichrist gain and maintain control over the world. Their rule will be so savage and cruel that the Scripture calls them beasts. They will launch the most terrorizing holocaust ever witnessed by the world. Literally millions of people—a numberless number—will be slaughtered, not only in one or several nations but all over the world. The murder and evil will be so terrible that God just will not take the evil of man any longer. The antichrist will not only bring the world to the brink of disaster, he will cross the brink and cause the utter destruction of the world as we know it. Under the antichrist, the world will be utterly decimated and destroyed.

Remember what has just happened (chapter 12). Revelation has just given us a glimpse into the spiritual world, shown us what lies behind the sin and evil of this earth. It has shown us this: there is a great spiritual evil fighting to lead man away from God, struggling to get people to live ungodly and evil lives. But in the end time this spiritual evil—the dragon, that ancient serpent, the devil and Satan—is going to be cast down to earth. When he is, he knows that he has only a short time left before God dooms him for eternity. Therefore, he is going to unleash a wrath and fury beyond anything the world has ever known. In the last days the devil is going to launch a campaign of evil and terror unparalleled in human history—such horror that it staggers the imagination. How is Satan going to do this? Through a world leader—a leader who will gain control of the world just as any other leader gains control of a nation. Who is that leader? *The antichrist.* Satan is going to raise up a man who will be the very embodiment of evil—everything that Satan wants a man to be This is the warning about the terrible antichrist. This is the passage that tells us about the political leader of the end time, the leader who will rule over the whole world, the antichrist.

1. His origin: the sea (v.1).
2. His great political power (v.1-2).
3. His dramatic rise to power (v.2-3).
4. His means of securing world government (v.4-8).
5. His adversaries: the genuinely saved (v.8-10).

**1** (13:1) **Antichrist**: there is the origin of the beast or antichrist. He arises up "out of the sea." This is explained in Rev.17:15 where the *waters* are said to be "peoples, multitudes, nations and languages." The antichrist arises from among the people. Remember the terrible things that will be taking place upon earth...

- the increase in world violence, conflict, terrorist activities, wars and rumors of wars.
- the increase in natural catastrophes such as famines, earthquakes, and diseases. (See notes— Rev.6:3-8; 6:12-17; 8:6-12; 8:13-9:11; 9:12-21.)

The people and nations will be clamoring for a leader who can offer them hope and help. The antichrist will see their restlessness and political turbulence and give the people the hope they crave.

> **Oh, the raging of many nations—they rage like the raging sea! Oh, the uproar of the peoples—they roar like the roaring of great waters! Although the peoples roar like the roar of surging waters, when he rebukes them they flee far away, driven before the wind like chaff on the hills, like tumbleweed before a gale. In the evening, sudden terror! Before the morning, they are gone! This is the portion of those who loot us, the lot of those who plunder us. (Isa 17:12-14)**
>
> **But the wicked are like the tossing sea, which cannot rest, whose waves cast up mire and mud. "There is no peace," says my God, "for the wicked." (Isa 57:20-21)**

**2** (13:1-2) **Antichrist**: there is the great political power of the beast or antichrist. Everything said about the antichrist is symbolic of the enormous political power that he will gain.

1. The antichrist will have seven heads. This means at least two things.
   a. The antichrist will have enormous ability, a most unusual genius. The number seven in the Bible means complete and full. The antichrist will be full of ability. He will be a supernatural genius, possessing complete knowledge and wisdom. He will be able to think, plan, act, respond, and react to situations quicker and more efficiently than any man has ever been able to do. Think how far a person could go in political circles and in gaining power if he had what we might term perfect ability—if he was full of knowledge, understanding, and wisdom. He would be head and shoulders above all others,

able to maneuver and manipulate power and people as no man has ever been able to do. Think of the greatest leader who has ever lived and compare the antichrist to him: the antichrist will have seven times the ability of that leader; the antichrist will have full and complete ability.

   b. The seven heads and ten horns also refer to the ten nations he will rule over. In the beginning there will be ten nations, but he will take over or be given the power and rule of three, which leaves seven. The heads of these seven will most likely surrender their governments to his rule. Therefore, the beast or antichrist has the power of seven heads, seven heads of state. (See DEEPER STUDY # 1—Rev.13:2 for chart and full explanation of this point.)

2. The antichrist will have ten horns. This is the same number of horns that the dragon (devil) had. This again points to the antichrist being the representative or embodiment of the devil upon earth. The horns mean power, and the fact that there are ten horns means a confederated power of ten nations. He will be the political head over ten nations. Horns, of course, pierce, rip, and tear in the most fierce and vicious way. The picture is that of a confederation of ten nations that will be frightening and strike terror in the hearts of the world.

3. The antichrist wears ten crowns upon his ten horns. Crowns, of course, mean authority and power: he will be the leader and ruler of these ten nations. He will hold the reigns of power and authority over the confederation of ten nations, nations that are pictured as so frightening that they are called the *horns of beasts*, horns that are able to rip and tear open the heart and bodies of other nations and people.

4. The antichrist will have ten blasphemous names on his seven heads. This means that his blasphemy against God and believers and against the people of the world will be complete. He will be the very fulfillment and embodiment of blasphemy.

   ⇒ He will be the *abomination that causes desolation* who will stand in the very *holy place* of the temple in Jerusalem and blaspheme the name of God. He will demand that people give their first loyalty to the state.

> **"So when you see standing in the holy place 'the abomination that causes desolation,' spoken of through the prophet Daniel—let the reader understand— (Mat 24:15)**

   ⇒ He will be the *man of lawlessness* who opposes all religions, everything that is called God or is worshipped.

> **He will oppose and will exalt himself over everything that is called God or is worshiped, so that he sets himself up in God's temple, proclaiming himself to be God. (2 Th 2:4)**

   ⇒ He will speak great and boastful and terrible words against the Most High.

> **He will speak against the Most High and oppress his saints and try to change the set times and the laws. The saints will be handed over to him for a time, times and half a time. (Dan 7:25)**

⇒ He will demand that all worship him and his state.

**Men worshiped the dragon [Satan] because he had given authority to the beast [antichrist] , and they also worshiped the beast and asked, "Who is like the beast? Who can make war against him?" (Rev 13:4)**

5. The antichrist will combine and embody three of the world's most powerful empires, that is, empires that had conquered and controlled most of the known world of their day. This is what is meant by his being like three animals: the leopard, bear, and lion. The picture being painted is that he will embody all the desire and lust for power, all the characteristics and traits of these three empires. Imagine! Take all the lust for power that existed within three of the greatest empires to rule the known world and combine that lust for power in one leader and government. The intensity of so much *lust for power* will be such a driving force that it will reek havoc and horror all over the world. No nation will be spared from the fright and terror of such a drive and lust for power. Who are the three empires that will be wrapped up in the beast? Note that the antichrist is said...

- to look like a leopard
- to have feet like a bear
- to have a mouth like a lion

What world empires do these animals represent? And what are the traits that will characterize the anti-christ? (See Deeper Study # 1—Rev.13:2 for chart and discussion.)

**DEEPER STUDY # 1**
**(13:2) Antichrist—Daniel, Visions of—End Time—Rome, Revived Roman Empire**: the antichrist will possess the characteristics and traits of three world empires and he shall arise from a fourth and possess those characteristics as well. What four empires—world empires—will be wrapped up in him? The visions of Daniel will tell us. The following chart shows us how the visions in Daniel match John's vision in Revelation. They are both talking about the end time and the power the antichrist and his government will have in the end time. Note how Daniel definitely says that the first government empire is the empire of Babylon. It is only natural, therefore, to understand the following empires as the next four worldwide empires to appear in history. This will become clear as the visions are studied in the following chart. Note four significant points.

## 1) THERE ARE THE VISIONS OR DREAMS IN DANIEL THAT MATCH THE VISION OF JOHN IN REVELATION

| *There Was Nebuchadnezzar's Dream of the Large Statue* | *There was Daniel's Dream of the Four Beasts* | *There was John's Vision of the Combined World Empire of the Antichrist* |
|---|---|---|
| Note the four metals of the Large Statue:<br>⇒ gold<br>⇒ silver<br>⇒ bronze<br>⇒ iron | Note the four great beasts:<br>⇒ lion<br>⇒ bear<br>⇒ leopard<br>⇒ a beast—dreadful, terrible, and strong | Note the four great beasts:<br>⇒ leopard<br>⇒ bear<br>⇒ lion<br>⇒ the beast of the antichrist who combines all the others |
| **"You looked, O king, and there before you stood a large statue—an enormous, dazzling statue, awesome in appearance. The head of the statue was made of pure gold, its chest and arms of silver, its belly and thighs of bronze, its legs of iron, its feet partly of iron and partly of baked clay. (Dan 2:31-33)** | **In the first year of Belshazzar king of Babylon, Daniel had a dream, and visions passed through his mind as he was lying on his bed. He wrote down the substance of his dream. Daniel said: "In my vision at night I looked, and there before me were the four winds of heaven churning up the great sea. Four great beasts, each different from the others, came up out of the sea. (Dan 7:1-3)** | **And the dragon stood on the shore of the sea. And I saw a beast coming out of the sea. He had ten horns and seven heads, with ten crowns on his horns, and on each head a blasphemous name. The beast I saw resembled a leopard, but had feet like those of a bear and a mouth like that of a lion. The dragon gave the beast his power and his throne and great authority. (Rev 13:1-2)** |

## 2) THERE IS THE INTERPRETATION OF THE IMAGE AND THE FOUR BEASTS IN DANIEL THAT MATCH THE COMBINED WORLD EMPIRES OF THE ANTICHRIST

| *The Interpretation of the Image* | *The Interpretation of the Four Beasts* | *The Interpretation of the Combined World Empires of the Antichrist* |
|---|---|---|
| The head of gold is the first world empire: Babylon under Nebuchadnezzar. | The lion is the first world empire: Babylon. | The antichrist will combine the traits of the lion: Babylon. |
| **"This was the dream, and now we will interpret it to the king. You, O king, are the king of kings. The God of heaven has given you dominion and power and might and glory; In your hands he has placed mankind and the beasts of the field and the birds of the air. Wherever they live, he has made you ruler over them all. You are that head of gold. (Dan 2:36-38)** | **"The first was like a lion, and it had the wings of an eagle. I watched until its wings were torn off and it was lifted from the ground so that it stood on two feet like a man, and the heart of a man was given to it. (Dan 7:4)** | **And I saw a beast coming out of the sea...[it had] a mouth like that of a lion. (Rev 13:1-2)** |
| The silver is the second world empire: Medo-Persia (cp. Dan.8:20). | The bear is the second world empire: Medo-Persia. | The antichrist will combine the traits of the bear: Medo-Persia. |
| **In your hands he has placed mankind and the beasts of the field and the birds of the air. (Dan 2:38a)** | **"And there before me was a second beast, which looked like a bear. It was raised up on one of its sides, and it had three ribs in its mouth between its teeth. It was told, 'Get up and eat your fill of flesh!' (Dan 7:5; cp. Dan.8:20)** | **And I saw a beast coming out of the sea...[it] had feet like those of a bear. (Rev 13:1-2)** |
| The bronze is the third world empire: Greece (cp. Dan.8:21). | The leopard is the third world empire: Greece (cp. Dan.8:21-22; 10:20; 11:2-4). | The antichrist will combine the traits of the leopard: Greece. |
| **Next, a third kingdom, one of bronze, will rule over the whole earth. (Dan 2:39b)** | **"After that, I looked, and there before me was another beast, one that looked like a leopard. And on its back it had four wings like those of a bird. This beast had four heads, and it was given authority to rule. (Dan 7:6)** | **And I saw a beast coming out of the sea...[it] resembled a leopard. (Rev 13:1-2)** |
| The iron is the fourth world empire: Rome (cp. Dan.9:26). | The dreadful, terrible, and strong beast is the fourth world empire: Rome (cp. Dan.7:23-24; 9:26). | The antichrist will be as the iron and the terrible beast with the ten horns, that is, Rome. He will combine all the traits of Rome. |
| **Finally, there will be a fourth kingdom, strong as iron—for iron breaks and smashes everything—[all other kingdoms] and as iron breaks things to pieces, so it will crush and break all the others [kingdoms]. (Dan 2:40)** | **"After that, in my vision at night I looked, and there before me was a fourth beast—terrifying and frightening and very powerful. It had large iron teeth; it crushed and devoured its victims and trampled underfoot whatever was left. It was different from all the former beasts, and it had ten horns. (Dan 7:7)** | **And the dragon stood on the shore of the sea. And I saw a beast coming out of the sea. He had ten horns and seven heads, with ten crowns on his horns, and on each head a blasphemous name. (Rev 13:1)** |

## 3) THERE IS THE INTERPRETATION OF THE TEN TOES OF THE IMAGE AND OF THE TEN HORNS OF THE FOURTH BEAST THAT MATCH THE COMBINED WORLD EMPIRE OF THE ANTICHRIST

*The Interpretation of the Ten Toes of the Image*

The ten toes are part iron and part clay. They cannot mix; the Roman empire falls apart. But it is part iron, so certain parts of it can survive and revive.

**Just as you saw that the feet and toes were partly of baked clay and partly of iron, so this will be a divided kingdom; yet it will have some of the strength of iron in it, even as you saw iron mixed with clay. As the toes were partly iron and partly clay, so this kingdom will be partly strong and partly brittle. And just as you saw the iron mixed with baked clay, so the people will be a mixture and will not remain united, any more than iron mixes with clay. (Dan 2:41-43)**

The idea is that certain elements and traits of the Roman empire will survive. Then later on in history the traits will revive with the seed of man. But these elements and traits will not mix to bring the perfect world or government.

*The Interpretation of the Ten Horns of the Dreadful, Terrible, and Strong Beast*

The ten horns give rise to a little horn that conquers and rules three of the ten horns. The little horn is a man who arises to power by conquering these three nations.

**"While I was thinking about the horns, there before me was another horn, a little one, which came up among them; and three of the first horns were uprooted before it. This horn had eyes like the eyes of a man and a mouth that spoke boastfully. (Dan 7:8)**

The idea is that a leader will arise from a "little horn," a small nation, and conquer three nations. Then the other seven nations will willingly submit to him and join him in his blasphemy of God and mankind.

*The Interpretation of the Dreadful, Terrible, and Strong Beast of Revelation*

The antichrist will have seven heads and ten horns and ten crowns, and seven heads that will be full of blasphemy.

**And the dragon stood on the shore of the sea. And I saw a beast coming out of the sea. He had ten horns and seven heads, with ten crowns on his horns, and on each head a blasphemous name. (Rev 13:1)**

The idea is that the antichrist will be the head of seven heads or governments, that he will have ten horns, the power of ten governments. He will have conquered three governments himself (Dan.7:8). All seven heads of state and the ten governments under him will blaspheme the name of God.

## 4) THERE ARE THE TRAITS OF THE METALS, OF THE IMAGE, AND OF THE FOUR BEASTS THAT MATCH THE COMBINED TRAITS OF THE ANTICHRIST

*The Traits of the Metals of the Image or of Its Empires*

Gold:
  ⇒ is valuable and desired

  ⇒ has a high luster that attracts & appeals to man

  ⇒ is extremely inactive, that is, it is unaffected by nature: air, heat, and moisture

  ⇒ hold's heat and electricity; it is a volatile energy when pressed

...which means that...

...which means that...

...which means that...

...which means that...

*The Antichrist Will Combine All the Traits of the Four Empires*

  ⇒ the antichrist will be desired by the world.

  ⇒ the antichrist will be attractive and appealing to the world.

  ⇒ the antichrist will be unfeeling and unaffected by the sufferings of the environment and of people.

  ⇒ the antichrist will be volatile, wrathful, vengeful.

**Silver:**
- ⇒ is malleable and easily beaten into all shapes and forms
- ⇒ is easily tarnished
- ⇒ is the most superior of all metals in *conducting* heat and electricity

...which means that...

...which means that...

...which means that...

- ⇒ The antichrist will have great ability to compromise and give and take
- ⇒ The antichrist will be easily corrupted.
- ⇒ The antichrist will be a strong commentator, able to pass on his ideas and wrath to others.

**Bronze:**
- ⇒ harder than most common alloys (except steel)
- ⇒ strongly resistant (often used in bearings, fittings, etc.)

...which means that...

...which means that...

- ⇒ He will be hard and indifferent to others.
- ⇒ He will resist and stand against opponents, strongly so.

**Iron:**
- ⇒ is easily magnetized
- ⇒ is easily combined with other metals

...which means that...

...which means that...

- ⇒ He will have a magnetic appeal; people and nations will willingly follow him.
- ⇒ He will be able to combine others into a confederation of states, one world government.

### The Traits of the Four Beasts

| The lion. | The antichrist will have a mouth like a lion: |
|---|---|
| | ⇒ A ferocious roar that will sweep worldwide and will shout blasphemies that will strike fear in both nations and people |
| | ⇒ Sharp teeth that will drive deep into the flesh of the world, tearing, chewing, and eating up the nations and peoples of the world |
| The bear. | The antichrist will have feet like a bear: |
| | ⇒ Big and tough feet that will cover a large area and pursue its prey of people and nations without giving up |
| | ⇒ Strong claws that grip the prey of nations and people without letting them go and possessing the power to rip them apart |
| The leopard. | The antichrist will have a body like a leopard: |
| | ⇒ Sleek and beautiful and attractive, a nature that appeals to the nations and people of the world. |
| | ⇒ Full of spots that symbolize an evil, sneaky, ferocious, and wild nature |
| The dreadful and terrible and strong beast. | The antichrist will combine all the traits of the old Roman empire. |

**3** (13:2-3) **Antichrist**: there is the dramatic rise to power by the antichrist. There will be two reasons for this dramatic rise.

1. The dragon, that is, supernatural spiritual forces, will *be at work. That great spiritual force, Satan himself, is going* to propel the antichrist into power. The antichrist is going to be willing to give himself completely over to this world, completely over to secular and humanistic society. He will give himself over to seeking the power, fame, wealth, possessions, and pleasures of this world. He is going to give himself completely to doing all the evil imaginable. But note: there will be a vast difference

between his evil and the evil of other men. When we do evil, we do it on a personal and small scale, or if we are a world leader on a larger national basis. The worst examples of secularism, worldliness, and evil ever witnessed have been *mad leaders* such as Hitler and Stalin. But the worldliness and evil of the antichrist will be intensified; it will be far worse. His evil will blow across the face of many more nations and people. His evil will cover the world. Just imagine a Hitler or a Stalin with the power to launch their evil all over the world. How will one man ever get that much power? We will see the details in a later note. But behind the scenes, behind what people can see with the naked eye, there lies Satan. Satan is going to embody the man. The man, the antichrist, is going to make an alliance with the devil. He is going to give himself totally over to do the works of Satan. He is going to be so committed to evil that Scripture says that he will actually came out of the "Abyss or bottomless pit," which means that he will either come from Satan himself or else be filled with an evil spirit straight out of the Abyss. Remember: this was pointed out earlier (Rev.11:7). Note that Satan is going to do these things for the antichrist.

    a. Satan will give the antichrist his power
- ⇒ the power of inner strength and energy and spirit
- ⇒ the power of personality
- ⇒ the power of ability, persuasion, and influence
- ⇒ the power of force and might

    b. Satan will give the antichrist his seat, that is, his throne, his government. Satan will give the antichrist just what he offered Christ: the governments of the world (cp. Mt.4:8-10).

    c. Satan will give the antichrist his authority; that is, he will give him complete authority, dictatorial rule and command and influence. He will give the antichrist the greatest power and rule ever known in the world.

2. The antichrist will be healed from a mortal wound. It is important to see what is being said here. The mortal wound to the antichrist is mentioned three times in this chapter and also elsewhere in Revelation.

> **One of the heads of the beast seemed to have had a fatal wound, but the fatal wound had been healed. The whole world was astonished and followed the beast. (Rev 13:3)**
>
> **He exercised all the authority of the first beast on his behalf, and made the earth and its inhabitants worship the first beast, whose fatal wound had been healed. (Rev 13:12)**
>
> **Because of the signs he was given power to do on behalf of the first beast, he deceived the inhabitants of the earth. He ordered them to set up an image in honor of the beast who was wounded by the sword and yet lived. (Rev 13:14)**
>
> **The beast, which you saw, once was, now is not, and will come up out of the Abyss and go to his destruction. The inhabitants of the earth whose names have not been written in the book of life from the creation of the world will be astonished when they see the beast, because he once was, now is not, and yet will come. (Rev 17:8)**

> **The beast who once was, and now is not, is an eighth king. He belongs to the seven and is going to his destruction. (Rev 17:11)**

There are three possible interpretations of this.

    a. The death of the beast refers to the political death of the Roman empire. Remember the Roman empire was the beast who had feet of iron and clay mixed. But the iron empire could not last because it had clay mixed in with it. Therefore, it was doomed to crumble and be divided. However, the iron continues on; that is, some of the traits and elements continue on in the world. Therefore in the end time, the old Roman empire will be revived and the spirit of Rome will dominate the world once again.

    b. The antichrist will actually be the return of some evil ruler who has lived in past history. The devil will raise him up and send him back to earth (cp. Rev.17:11).

    c. The mortal wound is an assassination attempt or some accident that happens to the antichrist, probably at the beginning of his rule. The false prophet (the second beast) performs a miracle and heals the antichrist. Remember: the false prophet will have the power to perform some outstanding miracles. It will be these miracles that will help him to gain credibility and the support of the masses of the world. This possibility sounds reasonable in light of what is said about the false prophet.

> **Because of the signs he was given power to do on behalf of the first beast, he deceived the inhabitants of the earth. He ordered them to set up an image in honor of the beast who was wounded by the sword and yet lived. (Rev 13:14)**

Now, which of these interpretations is correct? It is difficult to see how either one could be true without the other. A government has to have a leader, and a leader has to have a government. Daniel's prophecy definitely says that the antichrist is going to arise from the crumbled Roman empire and combine the traits of it and the other worldwide governments of ancient history. This is clearly pointed out in the visions of the image and the beast, and it is clearly pointed out in this vision of John when it is compared with Daniel. Again, a quick study of the chart shows this (see DEEPER STUDY # 1—Rev.13:2). And as stated, the healing of the antichrist from a mortal would seems to be what Scripture is saying (Rev.13:14).

The antichrist is to rule over the final government of the earth. Man's dream of a one world government will become a reality. But the government will have a leader, one man who will be emperor, king, or president, whatever the world will call him. Note that Scripture also points this out.

    ⇒ The antichrist will be thrown into the lake of fire. Nations and empires are not thrown into the fiery lake, people are.

> **But the beast was captured, and with him the false prophet who had performed the miraculous signs on his behalf. With these signs he had deluded those who had received the mark of the beast and worshiped his image. The two of them were thrown alive into the fiery lake of burning sulfur. (Rev 19:20)**

⇒ The antichrist is said to be a man.

> **Don't let anyone deceive you in any way, for that day will not come until the rebellion occurs and the man of lawlessness is revealed, the man doomed to destruction. (2 Th 2:3)**

⇒ The antichrist will stand in the temple of God in Jerusalem and proclaim himself as God. A nation cannot do this; only a man can do this.

> **"So when you see standing in the holy place 'the abomination that causes desolation,' spoken of through the prophet Daniel—let the reader understand— (Mat 24:15)**
> **He will oppose and will exalt himself over everything that is called God or is worshiped, so that he sets himself up in God's temple, proclaiming himself to be God. (2 Th 2:4)**

⇒ The antichrist will come as a false leader even as other antichrists have come as false leaders.

> **Dear children, this is the last hour; and as you have heard that the antichrist is coming, even now many antichrists have come. This is how we know it is the last hour. (1 John 2:18)**

We could go on and on with the Scriptures showing how they pile evidence upon evidence that the antichrist will be a man and not only a revival of great empires of the past. As stated earlier, the great empires will be revived and embodied or combined into one political government. But that government will be headed up and led by one leader or one head of state, the head of state whom the Bible calls the antichrist.

**4** (13:4-8) **Antichrist—World—End Time:** there is the means of securing world government. There are nine methods listed in this passage that the antichrist will use.

1. The antichrist will secure power because of the worldly and ungodly living of people (v.4). Note the statement about the people who live in the end time: "they worshiped the dragon," that is, the devil. To worship the devil means to walk in the *way of sin and evil and ungodliness*, not just what modern man calls devil worship and witchcraft. In the last days people will become more and more sinful, worldly, evil, and ungodly. They will become more and more secular and humanistic.

> **The rest of mankind that were not killed by these plagues still did not repent of the work of their hands; they did not stop worshiping demons, and idols of gold, silver, bronze, stone and wood—idols that cannot see or hear or walk. Nor did they repent of their murders, their magic arts, their sexual immorality or their thefts. (Rev 9:20-21)**
> **But mark this: There will be terrible times in the last days. People will be lovers of themselves, lovers of money, boastful, proud, abusive, disobedient to their parents, ungrateful, unholy, Without love, unforgiv-**
> **ing, slanderous, without self-control, brutal, not lovers of the good, Treacherous, rash, conceited, lovers of pleasure rather than lovers of God— Having a form of godliness but denying its power. Have nothing to do with them. (2 Tim 3:1-5)**
> **While evil men and impostors will go from bad to worse, deceiving and being deceived. (2 Tim 3:13)**

2. The antichrist will secure power by personal ability and appeal (v. 4b). They worship the beast and say "who is like the beast?" By worship is meant loyalty and allegiance. The antichrist will...
- be full of knowledge
- be an unusual genius
- be intelligent
- have unbelievable insight
- be magnetic
- have supreme charisma
- be a wonder to behold in ability and appeal

Remember: the world will be undergoing catastrophic disaster after disaster such as earthquakes and famine. In addition, there will be an enormous increase and intensification of wars and rumors of wars, military brush fires, uprisings, and terrorists attacks. On top of this will be the increasing sin and evil, drugs and immoralities raging across the world. The last days are anything but a pleasant picture. But the truth has to be faced, and we can see the trend by the way the societies of the world are deteriorating. Even the world leaders recognize their inability to stop the onrushing mad trend of lawlessness. Therefore, sometime in the future, when a certain leader comes upon the scene, and he has the answer to some of the problems, the people of the world will be ready to listen. They will exclaim: "Who is like this man." They will readily give their allegiance and loyalty to him. There will be a movement among the citizenry of the world toward him even as the citizens of Europe moved toward a more democratic government in the 1990's. The citizens will demand that their government leaders listen and follow this man who seems to have the answers.

⇒ All the world will wonder and be amazed and admire the beast.

> **One of the heads of the beast seemed to have had a fatal wound, but the fatal wound had been healed. The whole world was astonished and followed the beast. (Rev 13:3)**

⇒ He will be full of ability and understanding.

> **And the dragon stood on the shore of the sea. And I saw a beast coming out of the sea. He had ten horns and seven heads, with ten crowns on his horns, and on each head a blasphemous name. (Rev 13:1) (The number seven means complete ability and wisdom.)**
> **"In the latter part of their reign, when rebels have become completely wicked, a stern-faced king, a master of intrigue, will arise. (Dan 8:23)**

3. The antichrist will secure power by military and economic strength (v.4). At first when he enters upon the world scene, he and his government will conquer three nations and he will completely absorb those three nations into his. Then

seven others will subject to his rule and government peacefully. He will then be powerful, a mighty government with which the rest of the world has to contend. He will be so powerful that the Scriptures describe him as a beast with seven heads (governments) and ten horns (nations) over which he rules. The governments over which he rules will be some of the nations of the Middle East and of Europe and their great reservoirs of wealth. The nations under his control will be so wealthy and militarily strong that people will ask: "Who can make war against him?" Who is able to stop him militarily?

> **"While I was thinking about the horns, there before me was another horn, a little one, which came up among them; and three of the first horns were uprooted before it. This horn had eyes like the eyes of a man and a mouth that spoke boastfully. (Dan 7:8)**

The antichrist will apparently have under his authority the strongest military machine the world has ever known. And people will know it. Therefore, nation after nation will give their allegiance and loyalty to him. They will peacefully surrender to him. Keep in mind other prophecies that tell us that he will be able to bring peace and safety to the earth for a while. Few, if any, will be able to make war or to rebel under the control of his government.

⇒ Other nations will fear him.

> **"Who is like the beast? Who can make war against him?" (Rev 13:4)**

⇒ He will control enormous amounts of money and wealth.

> **Instead of them, he will honor a god of fortresses; a god unknown to his fathers he will honor with gold and silver, with precious stones and costly gifts. He will gain control of the treasures of gold and silver and all the riches of Egypt, with the Libyans and Nubians in submission. (Dan 11:38, 43)**

⇒ He can set up rulers and leaders as he likes.

> **"The ten horns you saw are ten kings who have not yet received a kingdom, but who for one hour will receive authority as kings along with the beast. They have one purpose and will give their power and authority to the beast. They will make war against the Lamb, but the Lamb will overcome them because he is Lord of lords and King of kings—and with him will be his called, chosen and faithful followers." Then the angel said to me, "The waters you saw, where the prostitute sits, are peoples, multitudes, nations and languages. The beast and the ten horns you saw will hate the prostitute. They will bring her to ruin and leave her naked; they will eat her flesh and burn her with fire. For God has put it into their hearts to accomplish his purpose by agreeing to give the beast their power to rule, until God's words are fulfilled. (Rev 17:12-17)**

> **He will attack the mightiest fortresses with the help of a foreign god and will greatly honor those who acknowledge him. He will make them rulers over many people and will distribute the land at a price. (Dan 11:39)**

4. The antichrist will secure power through speech, oratory, persuasion, and blasphemy (v.5). He will have a mouth that can speak great things. He will offer hope to a world that is facing catastrophe after catastrophe and that is crumbling under unsolved problems of drug addiction, alcoholism, famine, disease, homelessness, terrorist actions, and war. He will be able to bring peace and come up with some solutions to some of the problems. He will appear to be the savior of mankind. Remember: he will be strong enough militarily to bring peace to the smaller nations of the world that are so often suffering uprisings and terrorists actions. And he will be extremely wealthy, ruling so many nations with wealth that he can help solve some of the economic problems of the world mentioned above.

> **Instead of them, he will honor a god of fortresses; a god unknown to his fathers he will honor with gold and silver, with precious stones and costly gifts. (Dan 11:38)**
> **He will gain control of the treasures of gold and silver and all the riches of Egypt, with the Libyans and Nubians in submission. (Dan 11:43)**

5. The antichrist will secure power for three and one half years (v.5). He will be able to offer the world peace and prosperity for three and one half years. But note: his power is not his own. It is a given power, a power given to him by Satan.

> **[Power was given to him] for forty-two months (Rev.13:5b).**

6. The antichrist will secure power through atheism and humanism (v.6). He will reject and deny God, and openly blaspheme God. And he will do it in the famous Jewish temple (to be rebuilt) in the most famous religious city of the world, Jerusalem. The thing to note is his atheistic and humanistic belief. He will live and proclaim what man wants to hear in a scientific and technological world, a world that wants all the pleasure and possessions it can experience. He will push the philosophy of man and the state, that man and the state are the ultimate in life—that man can solve his own problems. And many in the world will applaud what he is able to achieve in peace and in the economy of the world. They will gladly follow him in his idolatrous worship of the state and blasphemy of God. (See pts.2,3—Rev.18:2-7 for more discussion.)

> **He will speak against the Most High and oppress his saints and try to change the set times and the laws. The saints will be handed over to him for a time, times and half a time. (Dan 7:25)**
> **"The king will do as he pleases. He will exalt and magnify himself above every god and will say unheard-of things against the God of gods. He will be successful until the time of wrath is completed, for what has been determined must take place. (Dan 11:36)**

167

He opened his mouth to blaspheme God, and to slander his name and his dwelling place and those who live in heaven. (Rev 13:6)

7. The antichrist will secure power through religious persecution (v.7. See notes—Rev.7:13-14; 11:1; 11:2; 11:3-13 for discussion.)

He will oppose and will exalt himself over everything that is called God or is worshiped, so that he sets himself up in God's temple, proclaiming himself to be God. (2 Th 2:4)

After this I looked and there before me was a great multitude that no one could count, from every nation, tribe, people and language, standing before the throne and in front of the Lamb. They were wearing white robes and were holding palm branches in their hands. Then one of the elders asked me, "These in white robes—who are they, and where did they come from?" I answered, "Sir, you know." And he said, "These are they who have come out of the great tribulation [martyred by the antichrist]; they have washed their robes and made them white in the blood of the Lamb. (Rev 7:9; 13-14)

Then I heard a voice from heaven say, "Write: Blessed are the dead who die in the Lord from now on." "Yes," says the Spirit, "they will rest from their labor, for their deeds will follow them." (Rev 14:13)

And I saw what looked like a sea of glass mixed with fire and, standing beside the sea, those who had been victorious over the beast and his image and over the number of his name. They held harps given them by God And sang the song of Moses the servant of God and the song of the Lamb: "Great and marvelous are your deeds, Lord God Almighty. Just and true are your ways, King of the ages. Who will not fear you, O Lord, and bring glory to your name? For you alone are holy. All nations will come and worship before you, for your righteous acts have been revealed." (Rev 15:2-4)

As I watched, this horn was waging war against the saints and defeating them, (Dan 7:21)

He will confirm a covenant with many for one 'seven.' In the middle of the 'seven' he will put an end to sacrifice and offering. And on a wing of the temple he will set up an abomination that causes desolation, until the end that is decreed is poured out on him." (Dan 9:27)

And in the first year of Darius the Mede, I took my stand to support and protect him.) "Now then, I tell you the truth: Three more kings will appear in Persia, and then a fourth, who will be far richer than all the others. When he has gained power by his wealth, he will stir up everyone against the kingdom of Greece. (Dan 11:1-2)

"One from her family line will arise to take her place. He will attack the forces of the king of the North and enter his fortress; he will fight against them and be victorious. (Dan 11:7)

The man clothed in linen, who was above the waters of the river, lifted his right hand and his left hand toward heaven, and I heard him swear by him who lives forever, saying, "It will be for a time, times and half a time. When the power of the holy people has been finally broken, all these things will be completed." (Dan 12:7)

He was given power to make war against the saints and to conquer them. And he was given authority over every tribe, people, language and nation. (Rev 13:7)

He was given power to give breath to the image of the first beast, so that it could speak and cause all who refused to worship the image to be killed. (Rev 13:15)

8. The antichrist will secure power through conquering many nations (v.7). He shall be able to extend his power over every tribe and people and language and nation. Note the word *every*. How will he gain world authority? Some by war and military might, but most nations will most likely follow willingly and peacefully—offer their allegiance and loyalty—to a government...
- that can definitely protect them and assure peace.
- that can help them with great economic aid.

**Thought 1.** America's ability to do this is one example. Many nations willingly follow and are loyal to this great nation for these very reasons. However, in the end time, the picture is that the antichrist will offer to do even more. Keep in mind that he will control many of the nations of the Middle East and of Europe—nations that are so rich, both in oil and other products and resources. Remember also: oil is an absolute essential to all the economies of the world. Nations and people will do anything for oil and its wealth. This is certainly one way the antichrist could demand and gain control over the nations and peoples of the earth. This is especially true if he was to appear benevolent and to offer peace and aid to a world devastated by natural disasters, social ills, and human suffering.

"While I was thinking about the horns, there before me was another horn, a little one [the antichrist], which came up among them; and three of the first horns were uprooted before it. This horn had eyes like the eyes of a man and a mouth that spoke boastfully. (Dan 7:8)

He will also invade the Beautiful Land. Many countries will fall, but Edom, Moab and the leaders of Ammon will be delivered from his hand. He will extend his power over many countries; Egypt will not escape. (Dan 11:41-42; cp. Ezk. chapters 38-39)

He was given power to make war against the saints and to conquer them. And he was given authority over every tribe, people, language and nation. (Rev 13:7)

9. The antichrist will secure power through imperial worship (v.8a). All the ungodly and evil people upon earth

shall worship him. This points toward worship of the state in the end time. Just think of the vast numbers of people with so many different languages and cultures involved in a world government. Some unifying principle, some common spirit, will be needed to hold the people together. This principle, this spirit, will be wrapped up in the government and leader of the government (the antichrist). Remember: he and his government will bring peace and economic help to the world, and will have solutions to some of the problems raging within society. The antichrist and his government will be represented, honored, and worshipped far more than any emperor of Rome or any Hitler, Mussolini, or any other leader in past history. It will be a small step from the honor of the people over to being idolized by the people. In order to keep and hold the world together, the antichrist and his government will institute the same thing the old Roman empire did: the worship of the state. Every citizen will be required to honor and give his first loyalty and allegiance to the state. The people may possibly be allowed to worship their own gods as well, but the state will demand the first loyalty. Keep in mind that the state (the antichrist) will be the central thing to the people of the world, the very thing that brought them peace and prosperity. The antichrist, of course, sits at the top of the state and all attention focuses upon him as the *god* of might and provision.

Remember: the worship of the state will probably be launched in the middle of the tribulation period. At that time, the antichrist will enter Jerusalem and march into the temple and declare that he and his state are to be the first objects of worship (gods). Whatever the case and whatever happens, Scripture definitely says that the antichrist will be worshipped, that is, given the first loyalty by the people of the earth. (See note—Rev.13:13-17 for more discussion.)

> **"So when you see standing in the holy place 'the abomination that causes desolation,' spoken of through the prophet Daniel—let the reader understand— (Mat 24:15)**
> **He will oppose and will exalt himself over everything that is called God or is worshiped, so that he sets himself up in God's temple, proclaiming himself to be God. (2 Th 2:4)**
> **Men worshiped the dragon because he had given authority to the beast, and they also worshiped the beast and asked, "Who is like the beast? Who can make war against him?" (Rev 13:4)**
> **All inhabitants of the earth will worship the beast—all whose names have not been written in the book of life belonging to the Lamb that was slain from the creation of the world. (Rev 13:8)**
> **Therefore rejoice, you heavens and you who dwell in them! But woe to the earth and the sea, because the devil has gone down to you! He is filled with fury, because he knows that his time is short." The woman was given the two wings of a great eagle, so that she might fly to the place prepared for her in the desert, where she would be taken care of for a time, times and half a time, out of the serpent's reach. (Rev 12:12, 14)**
> **A third angel followed them and said in a loud voice: "If anyone worships the beast and his image and receives his mark on the forehead or on the hand, He, too, will drink**

> **of the wine of God's fury, which has been poured full strength into the cup of his wrath. He will be tormented with burning sulfur in the presence of the holy angels and of the Lamb. And the smoke of their torment rises for ever and ever. There is no rest day or night for those who worship the beast and his image, or for anyone who receives the mark of his name." (Rev 14:9-11)**
> **The first angel went and poured out his bowl on the land, and ugly and painful sores broke out on the people who had the mark of the beast and worshiped his image. (Rev 16:2)**
> **"The king will do as he pleases. He will exalt and magnify himself above every god and will say unheard-of things against the God of gods. He will be successful until the time of wrath is completed, for what has been determined must take place. (Dan 11:36)**

**5** (13:8-10) **Antichrist**: there are the adversaries of the antichrist, the true believers. True believers will not worship the antichrist. Every believer can be loyal and can support his government fully, one hundred per cent. But no true believer can give his first loyalty to anyone other than to God. Therefore, true believers will not worship the antichrist nor his state. Note four statements made about the believers, the adversaries to the antichrist.

1. They are secure in the Lamb's book of life (see notes, pt.2b—Rev.3:4-6; 5:6-7.)
2. They are the hearers of this message, the people who heed the warning of the judgment to come and who repent and turn to the Lord Jesus Christ.
3. They are the ones who know that God truly judges the evil and ungodly. The true believer knows...
   - that if he leads others into captivity (whether of sin or prison), he himself shall be led into captivity.
   - that if he murders, he shall be judged by God and put to death eternally.

The true believer knows that God judges and that His judgment is just—that we reap exactly what we sow. Therefore, the true believer repents of sin and turns to follow God. True believers are the ones who will be the adversaries to the antichrist.

4. The true believer is steadfast and loyal to the faith. The true believer will be easily known in the end time. He will be the person standing fast for Christ. There will be droves denying Christ, but there will also be millions turning to him, an innumerable number (Rev.7:9). The Spirit of God will be as active as He has ever been. He will infuse believers with the strength to stand fast for Christ. As a result millions will be martyred in the worst holocaust in human history. The scene will be both tragic and glorious at the same time. For many will be giving one of the strongest testimonies ever given for Christ: they will be suffering persecution, but standing fast in their faith for Christ.

> **All men will hate you because of me, but he who stands firm to the end will be saved. (Mat 10:22)**
> **Therefore, my dear brothers, stand firm. Let nothing move you. Always give yourselves fully to the work of the Lord,**

because you know that your labor in the Lord is not in vain. (1 Cor 15:58)

Blessed is the man who perseveres under trial, because when he has stood the test, he will receive the crown of life that God has promised to those who love him. (James 1:12)

Therefore, prepare your minds for action; be self-controlled; set your hope fully on the grace to be given you when Jesus Christ is revealed. (1 Pet 1:13)

For it is commendable if a man bears up under the pain of unjust suffering because he is conscious of God. (1 Pet 2:19)

Be self-controlled and alert. Your enemy the devil prowls around like a roaring lion looking for someone to devour. Resist him, standing firm in the faith, because you know that your brothers throughout the world are undergoing the same kind of sufferings. (1 Pet 5:8-9)

Therefore, dear friends, since you already know this, be on your guard so that you may not be carried away by the error of lawless men and fall from your secure position. (2 Pet 3:17)

I am coming soon. Hold on to what you have, so that no one will take your crown. (Rev 3:11)

| Outline | Scripture |
|---|---|
| | **B. The Attack Through the Second Beast: A False Prophet, 13:11-18** |
| **1 His origin & description**<br>a. Comes out of the earth<br>b. Appears to be a lamb<br>c. Speaks as a dragon | 11 Then I saw another beast, coming out of the earth. He had two horns like a lamb, but he spoke like a dragon. |
| **2 His objective: To secure the loyalty & allegiance of the world for the antichrist & his state** | 12 He exercised all the authority of the first beast on his behalf, and made the earth and its inhabitants worship the first beast, whose fatal wound had been healed. |
| **3 His means of securing loyalty & devotion**<br>a. Through the deception of great miraculous signs, especially with fire | 13 And he performed great and miraculous signs, even causing fire to come down from heaven to earth in full view of men. |
| b. Through universal religion<br>1) Centered around an image of the beast | 14 Because of the signs he was given power to do on behalf of the first beast, he deceived the inhabitants of the earth. He ordered them to set up an image in honor of the beast who was wounded by the sword and yet lived. |
| 2) Centered around some supernatural power that enables the image to speak<br>c. Through religious persecution | 15 He was given power to give breath to the image of the first beast, so that it could speak and cause all who refused to worship the image to be killed. |
| d. Through economic control over the world | 16 He also forced everyone, small and great, rich and poor, free and slave, to receive a mark on his right hand or on his forehead,<br>17 So that no one could buy or sell unless he had the mark, which is the name of the beast or the number of his name. |
| **4 His number, 666**<br>a. The number of the beast<br>b. The number of a man | 18 This calls for wisdom. If anyone has insight, let him calculate the number of the beast, for it is man's number. His number is 666. |

# DIVISION VII

## THE SEVENTH TRUMPET IN DETAIL (PART II): THE WAR OF THE DRAGON UPON THE EARTH, 13:1-18

### B. The Attack Through the Second Beast: A False Prophet, 13:11-18

(13:11-18) **Introduction**: zeal, devotion, allegiance, loyalty, dedication—there is a desire within man to commit his life to something. Every person, no matter who he is, must have something that interests and motivates him, something that stirs him to arise in the morning and function and move and act throughout the day—something about which he can speak with excitement and commitment. It may be a job, family, school, sport, girlfriend, car, house, land, money, or power. Man has to have something to drive and motivate him, something to which he can devote himself and give his loyalty.

The great problem facing a world government—the government that will embrace every nation and people on earth, the government of the antichrist—is this: How do you get everyone on earth to be loyal to the government? Think of all the tribes, languages, peoples, and nations upon earth.

⇒ What can bring them all together?
⇒ What can be used to bind their loyalty and allegiance to the state?
⇒ What unifying principle, what unifying spirit can be found to focus the support of the people for the government?

This will be the problem facing the antichrist and his government in the end time. But remember the chaotic mess of the world in the last days: there will be natural disaster after natural disaster. Earthquakes, violent storms, and famine will be sweeping the earth in record numbers unparalleled in human history. There will be diseases and pestilences unheard of. In addition, nation after nation will be wrecked with war and rumors of war and violent overthrowing of governments and terrorist actions. Then there is the sinful and evil behavior of man. There will be an enormous increase in drugs, assaults, murders, rapes, immorality, divorce, stealing, witchcraft, and on and on. The world will be in a chaotic upheaval. There will be a social crisis all over the world. People will be frantic for some answers, for some leader to appear on the scene who can help and bring some order.

There will be such a man—the beast, the antichrist. This was the discussion of the former passage. But note this passage: the antichrist is going to have help. There is a second beast, a beast who is going to help the antichrist find the unifying principle to hold the loyalty of the people. This second beast will understand the spirit of man, that man must have something to which he can be devoted, something to which he can be attached. The second beast will give the antichrist that something, that devotion—the very thing that will hold the people of the world together. This second beast will become the worldwide spokesman and propaganda chief for the antichrist. He will become the right hand man of the antichrist. This is the second beast that will attack the earth and its people in the last days, the false prophet.

1. His origin and description (v.11).
2. His objective: to secure the loyalty and allegiance of the world for the antichrist and his state (v.12).
3. His means of securing loyalty and devotion (v.13-17).
4. His number, 666 (v.18).

**1** (13:11) **Prophet of Revelation, False—Beast of Revelation, Second**: there is the origin and description of the second beast.

1. He comes out of the earth. This means that he comes out from among the common people of the earth. He will be from among the masses, yet he will hold a high office and be the second most powerful man in the government of the last days. This will, of course, give him a strong identity with the masses of the earth. It will help him wield influence and secure their support for the programs of the antichrist and his government.

2. He appears to be a lamb, for he only has two horns like a little lamb. No person is ever afraid of a little lamb.

There is nothing about this beast that seems wild or evil. The little lamb symbolizes at least three things.

    a. This beast will appear innocent, harmless, mild, meek, attractive, and lovable. Most people will be attracted to him; no one will fear him. There will be absolutely nothing about his appearance to frighten anyone. People will be pulled to him and want to touch and embrace him just as onlookers feel pulled toward a little lamb.

    b. This beast will appear to be a follower of the Lord Jesus Christ, the Lamb of God. He will appear to be one of God's little lambs or sheep. That is, he will be a religious leader. Just like a lamb, he will appear to be religiously clean, free from evil and violence and wrong and ungodliness. He will appear to represent the Lord Jesus Christ and peace and love and joy. People will think that he can do no wrong, or at least not any serious wrong.

    c. This beast will speak as a dragon. His voice is going to betray him. What he has to say will reveal that he is not a prophet of God, but a false prophet.

      ⇒ He will not be teaching God's Word, but the word of the antichrist and state.

      ⇒ He will not be speaking the truth; he will be speaking a lie.

      ⇒ He will not be the spokesman for God, but the spokesman for the government of the antichrist.

      ⇒ He will not be speaking for people to support God, but for people to support the civil power.

      ⇒ He will not be promoting the Lord Jesus Christ; he will be promoting the policies of the antichrist.

The second beast will become the spokesman, the great motivator of the masses for the antichrist. He will be the person who will come up with the unifying principle, the motivational spirit that will hold the loyalty of the people to the antichrist and his state.

Note this: we know that he will be a religious leader, for after this passage he is called the *false prophet* whenever he is mentioned (Rev.16:13; 19:20; 20:10). Keep this in mind: he will hold the second highest position of authority in the world. The antichrist will promote him to be second in command, to be the chief executive officer of the government. But note his origin and background: he comes from religion, from Christianity itself. He is a prophet, a priest, a minister who professes to be a follower and teacher of the Lord Jesus Christ.

> **For such people are not serving our Lord Christ, but their own appetites. By smooth talk and flattery they deceive the minds of naive people. (Rom 16:18)**
>
> **For such men are false apostles, deceitful workmen, masquerading as apostles of Christ. And no wonder, for Satan himself masquerades as an angel of light. It is not surprising, then, if his servants masquerade as servants of righteousness. Their end will be what their actions deserve. (2 Cor 11:13-15)**
>
> **But mark this: There will be terrible times in the last days. People will be lovers of themselves, lovers of money, boastful, proud, abusive, disobedient to their parents, ungrateful, unholy, Having a form of godliness but denying its power. Have nothing to do with them. While evil men and impostors**

> **will go from bad to worse, deceiving and being deceived. (2 Tim 3:1-2, 5, 13)**
>
> **Many deceivers, who do not acknowledge Jesus Christ as coming in the flesh, have gone out into the world. Any such person is the deceiver and the antichrist. (2 John 1:7)**

**2** (13:12) **Prophet of Revelation, False—Beast of Revelation, Second**: there is the objective of the second beast or false prophet. His objective is to secure the devotion, loyalty, and allegiance of the world to the antichrist and his government. Note two most significant points.

1. This second beast will exercise all the power of the antichrist. The antichrist will give the false prophet the right to speak and act for him. When he speaks and acts, he will do it with the full authority and power of the throne. He will be the chief executive officer of the antichrist, the second in command, the chief of staff, the full representative of the antichrist.

2. But remember: this beast is a prophet, a prominent religious leader. He comes from the root of Christianity and from the church. He is either a minister or a priest. He will represent the Lamb of God, the Lord Jesus Christ. But the antichrist notices him and entices him to use his religious *position and influence* for the state. This means a significant thing. It means that the false prophet...

• will hold some high position in religion.

• will be very influential and probably already known by many in the world.

• will be very charismatic, able to effectively speak and communicate with people face to face, in meetings and in mass, over television and radio or whatever visual and sound media will exist in that day. This would be the only conceivable way he could mobilize support from around the world.

Now, what is the objective of the false prophet? To secure the devotion, loyalty, and allegiance to the antichrist and his state. As stated in the introduction, the end time government will have to come up with some way to hold the support of the people of the world, people with so many diverse backgrounds and cultures, needs and wants. This will be the objective of this beast, of the false prophet. He will become a part of the civil government, of the state itself...

• He will use his high office in religion to rally people to support the antichrist and the state.

• He will focus worship, that is, the devotion and loyalty of people upon the antichrist and his state.

• He will do what he can to lead people to be loyal and devoted to the state and its leader, the antichrist.

This may seem repetitive, but it is essential to see the objective of the false prophet. In the end time, the government and its leader, the antichrist, will have to solve the problem about how to hold the support of so many diverse people throughout the world. A worldwide religion—one great spirit focused upon the government and its leader—will be the answer. Everyone in the world will be expected to give his first loyalty and allegiance to the state and the antichrist. Everyone's second loyalty and allegiance may perhaps be given to any religion of their choice, but their first loyalty will have to be to the state and its leader, the state and leader that has brought peace to the world and provided so much for the people of the world.

**3** (13:13-17) **Prophet of Revelation, False—Beast of Revelation, Second**: there is the means of securing the loyalty and devotion of the people of the earth. The false prophet will use four things to secure the people's loyalty.

1. The false prophet will deceive people with great miraculous signs, especially with fire (v.13). The false prophet will face a problem: How can he possibly convince the masses of the world that God will understand their act of showing loyalty and allegiance to the state? That God would approve an occasional act of worship and expression of devotion to the state and its leader? There will be only one way: the false prophet must prove that he is truly of God, that he has the approval of God in preparing the new worship. How can he prove his credentials, prove that he and his proposal for a new worship are of God? By signs, miraculous signs. Remember: the two great witnesses of God—the witnesses who will be in Jerusalem preaching the gospel—will be able to work miracles and to call fire down from heaven. The idea is that this miracle will cause people to fear them long enough to keep the government from killing them, at least for three and one half years (Rev.11:3-13). This miracle will be duplicated by the false prophet. The devil will empower the false prophet to duplicate the miracle. People will then think that the false prophet is a true prophet, as much a prophet of God as the two witnesses in Jerusalem. Just what the miracle involves is never said, but the idea is that it will be awe-inspiring and assure the people of the earth that the false prophet is definitely a prophet of God and is speaking for God. Therefore, whatever he suggests must be acceptable to God. Think how believable he will be if the mortal wound to the antichrist (some assassination attempt) is actually healed by the false prophet (Rev.13:3). To the masses of the world both the antichrist and the false prophet will look like the next thing to God Himself. The masses will be ready to follow the declaration of the false prophet, ready to worship or occasionally to show their support and loyalty to the antichrist and the state.

The point is this: the false prophet will prove that he and his declarations are *ex cathedra*, of God, by performing miracles. This is one way he will deceive and gather the support of the world's masses.

2. The false prophet will use universal religion to secure the loyalty of the people (v.14-15). This is what the Scripture has been building up to, the worship of the antichrist and his state. We must remember that the worship of the state and its leader is not a far-fetched idea. In every generation there are dictators and leaders of government who insist upon the first loyalty and allegiance of the nation's citizens. Religion is subjected to the state and expected to support the state totally or else it and its followers are persecuted and often killed. Of course, each of these is on a small scale compared to the whole world; nevertheless, they provide a small scale example of what the end time world government will do under the antichrist.

An even better example is the old Roman empire. Rome instituted the worship of the state and emperor as the unifying principle to hold the people of the vast empire together. William Barclay has an excellent discussion of this that shows how easily the situation can arise. This is especially true in light of the fact that it has already been done on somewhat of a worldwide scale. The leaders of the end time government will certainly not be ignorant of history. They will know exactly what Rome did, and the history lesson will not fall on deaf ears. In fact, Scripture teaches that the government of the end time will be a revival of the old Roman government; that is, the end time government will have many of the traits and characteristics of the old Roman empire.

But more important than any of these factors, there will be one thing above all others that will stir a universal worship of the antichrist and his state. What is it? The peace and economic recovery the antichrist will bring to the earth. The political unrest and economic crises and chaotic mess of the world in the end time will be ready-made for a leader with some answers. As stated in the introduction to this passage (what is said in the introduction to this outline is being repeated here because of its importance to this note):

> "Remember the chaotic mess of the world in the last days. There will be natural disaster after natural disaster: earthquakes, violent storms, and famine will be sweeping the earth in record numbers, unparalleled in human history. There will be diseases and pestilences unheard of. In addition, nation after nation will be wrecked with war and rumors of war and violent overthrowing of governments and terrorist actions. Then there is the sinful and evil behavior of man. There will be an enormous increase in drugs, assaults, murders, rapes, immorality, divorce, stealing witchcraft, and on and on. The world will be in a chaotic upheaval. There will be a social crisis all over the world. People will be frantic for some answers, for some leader to appear on the scene who can help and bring some order."

The antichrist will be that man. Remember how he arose from a small nation, from the East. He conquers three nations and then seven willingly come under his rule. He will at long last bring peace to that area of the world and possess enormous wealth and one of the largest military machines the world has ever seen. Somehow, some way, he will be able to propose some solutions to some of the problems of the world and to offer peace; and he will be made the supreme chief of some organization that has enormous influence. From that post he will be able to maneuver and make power plays to secure more and more power. And all the time his idea and program for world peace and economic prosperity will be succeeding. He will be so successful that people will begin to say: "Who is like the beast? Who is able to match him or to oppose him?" (cp. Rev.13:3). The point is this: the antichrist will bring peace and prosperity to the earth, and the people will be thankful and hold him in the highest of honor and esteem. They will be willing to follow his policies and programs.

Now, note something: note how all this focuses upon the antichrist and his government, upon who he is and what he can do for the people and the world. This alone borders on adulation and worship. It is close to what he and the state will want: the constant and permanent loyalty of the people to the state. The government and antichrist will have to seal the loyalty of the people; they will have to come up with some way to assure the people's continued support.

This is where the second beast comes in; this is where the idea of the universal religion enters. All the antichrist and the state need is for the people to show every so often that they do support and give their first loyalty to the state. Rome had the people make only one act of worship a year, and when they bowed in worship to the state before some local authority, the people were given a certificate to show that they so honored the state. Now with this as background to show us how it can easily happen in the end time, note two points.

a. The universal worship will center around an image to the beast. The false prophet will suggest that the people of the world make an image of the beast. Note two Scriptures, the first from Christ Himself:

"So when you see standing in the holy place 'the abomination that causes desolation,' spoken of through the prophet Daniel—let the reader understand— (Mat 24:15)

Don't let anyone deceive you in any way, for that day will not come until the rebellion occurs and the man of lawlessness is revealed, the man doomed to destruction. He will oppose and will exalt himself over everything that is called God or is worshiped, so that he sets himself up in God's temple, proclaiming himself to be God. (2 Th 2:3-4)

The temple of God is the temple of the Jews at Jerusalem. It is prophesied that it will be rebuilt in the end time. The false prophet will convince the people...

- that the world has been blessed with the peace and economic recovery wrought by the antichrist.
- that the antichrist is the one who is bringing the utopian kingdom to earth, the utopian society where there is going to be perfect peace; and he is the one who is solving the problems of society and providing plenty of food and housing and jobs for everyone.
- that every one needs to show their support and loyalty to the utopian state that the antichrist has wrought.
- that the only way to keep the movement going and continuing is for everyone to honor the state and give their first loyalty and allegiance to the state.
- that the best way to show one's loyalty is to have an image of the state (symbolized in its leader, the antichrist) in the great religious center of the world, and then on a local basis to have everyone express their loyalty (worship) to the state before some state authority. Of course, the person would receive some certificate showing that he had expressed his first loyalty to the antichrist and his government.

The false prophet will have to convince the world and its masses that a state religion—symbolized in the leader of the state—is the best way to keep the utopian state continuing. And he will be successful, for this passage says that the prophecy of Christ given above will come about. The false prophet will set up the image to the beast of the antichrist and his government, and he will set it up in the temple of God.

He was given power to give breath to the image of the first beast, so that it could speak and cause all who refused to worship the image to be killed. (Rev 13:15)
A third angel followed them and said in a loud voice: "If anyone worships the beast and his image and receives his mark on the forehead or on the hand, He, too, will drink

of the wine of God's fury, which has been poured full strength into the cup of his wrath. He will be tormented with burning sulfur in the presence of the holy angels and of the Lamb. And the smoke of their torment rises for ever and ever. There is no rest day or night for those who worship the beast and his image, or for anyone who receives the mark of his name." (Rev 14:9-11)

And I saw what looked like a sea of glass mixed with fire and, standing beside the sea, those who had been victorious over the beast and his image and over the number of his name. They held harps given them by God (Rev 15:2)

The first angel went and poured out his bowl on the land, and ugly and painful sores broke out on the people who had the mark of the beast and worshiped his image. (Rev 16:2)

But the beast was captured, and with him the false prophet who had performed the miraculous signs on his behalf. With these signs he had deluded those who had received the mark of the beast and worshiped his image. The two of them were thrown alive into the fiery lake of burning sulfur. (Rev 19:20)

I saw thrones on which were seated those who had been given authority to judge. And I saw the souls of those who had been beheaded because of their testimony for Jesus and because of the word of God. They had not worshiped the beast or his image and had not received his mark on their foreheads or their hands. They came to life and reigned with Christ a thousand years. (Rev 20:4)

b. But note a second thing as well: the universal worship will center around some supernatural power that will enable the beast to speak (v.15). Just as there are all kinds of shrines and places where miracles are supposed to have happened today, there will be a spectacular miracle in the end time. Satan will cause a miracle to happen; some people, worshipping in the shrine built to the antichrist, will hear the image speak or else it will speak periodically. Remember: the end times will be a day of mass deception and counterfeit religion for the ungodly and evil of this world. God is going to allow the world to be deceived and deluded as part of the judgment for their ungodliness and evil.

And in every sort of evil that deceives those who are perishing. They perish because they refused to love the truth and be saved. For this reason God sends them a powerful delusion so that they will believe the lie (2 Th 2:10-11)

3. The false prophet will use religious persecution to secure loyalty to the antichrist and the state (v.15b). Very simply, anyone who does not worship the state and the beast or antichrist will be slaughtered. Of course, no believer can confess loyalty to a person or government above God. The true believer can be loyal to his government, one hundred percent loyal, but he cannot put anything above God, not even the state. Therefore, the worst holocaust ever known to

man will take place in the end time. True believers and all other people who have strong religious faith—including Jews, Moslems, Hindus, and others—will be slaughtered in the holocaust of the antichrist. (See outline and notes—Rev.7:9-17; 11:1; 11:2; 11:3-13.)

> **After this I looked and there before me was a great multitude that no one could count, from every nation, tribe, people and language, standing before the throne and in front of the Lamb. They were wearing white robes and were holding palm branches in their hands. Then one of the elders asked me, "These in white robes—who are they, and where did they come from?" I answered, "Sir, you know." And he said, "These are they who have come out of the great tribulation; they have washed their robes and made them white in the blood of the Lamb. (Rev 7:9, 13-14)**
>
> **He was given power to make war against the saints and to conquer them. And he was given authority over every tribe, people, language and nation. (Rev 13:7)**
>
> **Then I heard a voice from heaven say, "Write: Blessed are the dead who die in the Lord from now on." "Yes," says the Spirit, "they will rest from their labor, for their deeds will follow them." (Rev 14:13)**
>
> **And I saw what looked like a sea of glass mixed with fire and, standing beside the sea, those who had been victorious over the beast and his image and over the number of his name. They held harps given them by God And sang the song of Moses the servant of God and the song of the Lamb: "Great and marvelous are your deeds, Lord God Almighty. Just and true are your ways, King of the ages. (Rev 15:2-3)**
>
> **I saw thrones on which were seated those who had been given authority to judge. And I saw the souls of those who had been beheaded because of their testimony for Jesus and because of the word of God. They had not worshiped the beast or his image and had not received his mark on their foreheads or their hands. They came to life and reigned with Christ a thousand years. (Rev 20:4)**

4. The false prophet will use economic controls to secure loyalty to the antichrist and the state (v.16-17). The Scripture is self-explanatory. There will be some mark placed upon the head or forearm of people to show that they are loyal to the state. Food and supplies and other purchases—the whole economy—will be based upon this mark. A person must have the mark to buy anything. If he does not, then he is a traitor to the state and antichrist. The person will have no choice: he either gives his first loyalty to the state or else be killed or starved to death or be forced to flee to the wildernesses of the world for safety and survival. Many believers, of course, will do the latter, and God will keep a remnant alive as a testimony to his name. (See note—Rev.12:6; 12:13-17 for more discussion.)

> **A third angel followed them and said in a loud voice: "If anyone worships the beast and his image and receives his mark on the forehead or on the hand, he, too, will drink of the wine of God's fury, which has been poured full strength into the cup of his wrath. He will be tormented with burning sulfur in the presence of the holy angels and of the Lamb. And the smoke of their torment rises for ever and ever. There is no rest day or night for those who worship the beast and his image, or for anyone who receives the mark of his name." (Rev 14:9-11)**
>
> **The first angel went and poured out his bowl on the land, and ugly and painful sores broke out on the people who had the mark of the beast and worshiped his image. (Rev 16:2)**
>
> **I saw thrones on which were seated those who had been given authority to judge. And I saw the souls of those who had been beheaded because of their testimony for Jesus and because of the word of God. They had not worshiped the beast or his image and had not received his mark on their foreheads or their hands. They came to life and reigned with Christ a thousand years. (Rev 20:4)**

**4** (13:18) **Antichrist:** there is the number of the beast or antichrist. It is the infamous number that is more well known in literature than any other number: 666. What does it mean? No one knows. Scripture does not say what it means. All we know is what Scripture says: "for the number is that of a man." In Scripture the perfect number is seven. Therefore, since man's number is six, that means that man is incomplete and short of God's glory, short of God's perfection. *The number of the beast* is the same, and the spiritual man is to count it such. The beast is not God—far from it. He, too, is mere man, short of the triune God. His days are numbered; he will do what all other human leaders have done—die and pass on to face the eternal judgment of God.

> **Thought 1.** This is critical: we must never forget that all men—no matter how great they may be nor how much they may do for us—will die. And they will all face the judgment of God. This will be true of the most powerful of all leaders, the antichrist of the end time. How critical it is for every man to be prepared to stand up for Christ when the end comes.

| | | heaven like the roar of rushing waters and like a loud peal of thunder. The sound I heard was like that of harpists playing their harps. | **voice of God** a. As rushing waters: Satisfying b. As thunder: Awesome c. As harps: Calming |
|---|---|---|---|
| | **CHAPTER 14** **VIII. THE SEVENTH TRUMPET IN DETAIL (PART III): THE VICTORY OF THE LAMB IS ASSURED, 14:1-20** | 3 And they sang a new song before the throne and before the four living creatures and the elders. No one could learn the song except the 144,000 who had been redeemed from the earth. | 4 **They will be uniquely privileged before all other beings** |
| | **A. Assurance 1: The Redeemed Will Be With Jesus, 14:1-5** | 4 These are those who did not defile themselves with women, for they kept themselves pure. They follow the Lamb wherever he goes. They were purchased from among men and offered as firstfruits to God and the Lamb. | 5 **They will be clearly identified** a. The pure b. The followers of the Lamb c. The ones sacrificed to God |
| 1 | **They will be with Jesus** | Then I looked, and there before me was the Lamb, standing on Mount Zion, and with him 144,000 who had his name and his Father's name written on their foreheads. | |
| 2 | **They will be sealed with God's name** | | d. The truthful |
| 3 | **They will hear the very** | 2 And I heard a sound from | mouths; they are blameless. e. The blameless |

# DIVISION VIII

## THE SEVENTH TRUMPET IN DETAIL (PART III): THE VICTORY OF THE LAMB IS ASSURED, 14:1-20

### A.  Assurance 1: The Redeemed Will Be with Jesus, 14:1-5

(14:1-5) **Introduction**: the last days of world history are going to be terrible days, days of horror. The dragon of the underworld, that ancient serpent who is called the devil and Satan, is going to unleash the fury of his wrath upon earth. He is going to send forth his own spirit and enter into one man and use that man to offer the utopian state to the world. He is going to empower that man, the antichrist, to bring peace and prosperity to the earth, and Satan is going to build up all the hope that man has ever had for a utopian world. Man is going to place all his hope in this one world ruler, and the antichrist is going to fulfill man's hope and longing.

⇒ He is going to give the world peace, worldwide peace.

⇒ He is going to move the world toward economic prosperity, toward jobs and a livelihood for everyone.

⇒ He is going to propose programs for the hungry, homeless, and diseased, and for the other problems of the world—propose programs that will work to some degree.

⇒ He is going to have some solutions for the problems of drugs, alcoholism, and the other devastating ills of society.

⇒ He is going to have a program to help the people tragically affected by the natural catastrophes that will be devastating the earth during the end time.

But then the terrifying horror will happen: he will turn against millions upon earth, against all those who have strong religious faith: the Jews, Christians, Moslems, Hindus, and all the others. He and his state will launch the worst holocaust the world has ever witnessed. He will slaughter any who do not give their first loyalty and allegiance to the state and its leader, the antichrist himself.

This is what the great book of Revelation has just shown us, the terrifying picture of the antichrist and his chief executive officer, the false prophet. These two beasts will bring such horror to the people of the end time that the evil explodes the human mind.

Note this: John the apostle, the one to whom Jesus Christ was giving this vision, needed relief from such horrors; and so do we, the readers. The human mind and heart can take only so many pictures of tragedy before it needs an infusion of hope. This is what chapter fourteen of the Revelation is: it is a picture of victory. The victory of the Lamb of God, of the Lord Jesus Christ, is assured. In rapid fire, John is given seven visions, visions that show the glorious triumph that lies ahead for those who follow the Lord Jesus Christ and endure to the end. The first vision of triumph concerns the redeemed. The redeemed are seen as victorious. They are seen with Jesus their Lord. Remember: John is seeing these things as though they already existed. He is looking at the future triumph.

1. They will be with Jesus (v.1).
2. They will be sealed with God's name (v.1).
3. They will hear the very voice of God (v.2).
4. They will be uniquely privileged before all other beings (v.3).
5. They will be clearly identified (v.4-5).

**1** (14:1) **Heaven**: the redeemed will be seen with Jesus. The Lamb is Jesus Christ, our Lord and Savior, the One whom all true believers love and adore and long to be with. He is the Lamb who was slain for our sins, the Lamb who took all our sins upon Himself and died for them, the Lamb who sacrificed Himself for us so that we might be acceptable to God (see note—Rev.5:6-7 for more discussion).

Note where He stands: on Mount Zion. Mount Zion was another name for Jerusalem. It has always been used to refer to heaven itself, to the heavenly Jerusalem. Here Mount Zion means the heavenly city of God, heaven itself. These dear believers are seen with the Lord Jesus Christ in heaven. They are right next to their Lord and Savior, the Lamb of

God who was slain for them, slain so that they might have the right to live in heaven. How they love Him, and how wonderfully they are privileged to be right next to Him.

Now note who is with Him: the one hundred and forty four thousand Jews who had taken a vow to stand up for Christ, the Christian Jews who had not denied Him during the holocaust of the antichrist. Their commitment will be rewarded: they will be with the Lamb, the Lord Jesus Christ.

> **Then the righteous will shine like the sun in the kingdom of their Father. He who has ears, let him hear. (Mat 13:43)**
>
> **Now if we are children, then we are heirs—heirs of God and co-heirs with Christ, if indeed we share in his sufferings in order that we may also share in his glory. (Rom 8:17)**
>
> **Who, by the power that enables him to bring everything under his control, will transform our lowly bodies so that they will be like his glorious body. (Phil 3:21)**
>
> **When Christ, who is your life, appears, then you also will appear with him in glory. (Col 3:4)**
>
> **There will be no more night. They will not need the light of a lamp or the light of the sun, for the Lord God will give them light. And they will reign for ever and ever. (Rev 22:5)**
>
> **Jesus answered him, "I tell you the truth, today you will be with me in paradise." (Luke 23:43)**
>
> **Whoever serves me must follow me; and where I am, my servant also will be. My Father will honor the one who serves me. (John 12:26)**
>
> **In my Father's house are many rooms; if it were not so, I would have told you. I am going there to prepare a place for you. And if I go and prepare a place for you, I will come back and take you to be with me that you also may be where I am. (John 14:2-3)**
>
> **"Father, I want those you have given me to be with me where I am, and to see my glory, the glory you have given me because you loved me before the creation of the world. (John 17:24)**
>
> **For I am already being poured out like a drink offering, and the time has come for my departure. I have fought the good fight, I have finished the race, I have kept the faith. Now there is in store for me the crown of righteousness, which the Lord, the righteous Judge, will award to me on that day— and not only to me, but also to all who have longed for his appearing. (2 Tim 4:6-8)**

**2** (14:1) **Sealed:** the redeemed will be sealed with God's name, with the name of the Lamb's Father. This tells us why they will be in heaven: they will be identified with Christ and God. They will refuse to take the seal of the antichrist (see note—Rev.13:13-17). They will make a vow to serve God and to take His seal. Therefore, they will have nothing to do with the seal of the antichrist (see note, *Seal—* Rev.7:2-3 for discussion and verses).

**Thought 1.** There are many antichrists in the world now, many false teachers, who deny that the Lord Jesus Christ is the Son of God (cp. 1 Jn.2:18-23; 4:2-3). We must guard against these antichrists, these false teachers. We must believe in the Lamb of God, in the Lord Jesus Christ, the very Son of God who came to take away the sins of the world. We must become identified with both the Lamb and His Father. We must be sealed with God's name, with the name of the Lamb's Father. Note this: the Lamb has a Father, the true and living God, the only true and living God there is.

**3** (14:2) **Voice, of God:** the redeemed will hear the voice of God. Imagine having the glorious privilege to hear the voice of God! It will be the most wonderful privilege imaginable, and it will be the privilege of the 144,000 Jewish servants who will be faithful to Christ and to the dear believers in the tribulation.

1. The voice of God is like the sound of *rushing waters*: forceful and mighty, as powerful as the sound of many Niagara Falls or of many rushing and mountainous waves of the sea. Yet the many waters can also be the quieting, comforting, and peaceful rippling of many creeks. When we hear the voice of God we know that it is Him speaking, for it will be both powerful and comforting at the same time.

2. The voice of God is like the sound of thunder: deep, rumbling, arousing, stirring, and distinctive. When He speaks, we will be aroused and stirred from what we are doing. His voice will demand full attention.

> **Thought 1.** What a lesson for us today. How we should be listening to the voice of God in His Word. His Word is just as powerful as His voice will be when we get to heaven. The problem is this: we are not listening to His Word, not nearly as much as we should be.

3. The voice of God is like the sound of many harps: restful, calming, soothing, relaxing, and fulfilling. Soft music does this for us, and God's voice is just like soft music: it can calm our hearts in the most troublesome of times. And oh how the voice of God will need to be heard in the tribulation!

The point is this: the 144,000 will be rewarded with the voice of God. They will have the glorious privilege of hearing the voice of God.

**4** (14:3) **Heavenly Song:** the redeemed will be uniquely privileged. They will have a song of victory to sing before all the heavenly host. But note: the words of the song are not here or anywhere else given. We will not know the words until the glorious *day of redemption* comes. However, what a glorious privilege! To have a special song to sing and present to all the beings of heaven. The Jews who receive the Lord Jesus Christ and vow to be the servants of God during the *great tribulation* will be given a special song of victory. They shall triumph over the antichrist and his holocaust and over evil and death. They shall live forevermore in the presence of our God and Savior, the Lord Jesus Christ. When they arrive in heaven victorious and triumphant, they will have something to sing about: the glorious victory given them in Jesus Christ our Lord.

> **I will praise you, O LORD, with all my heart; I will tell of all your wonders. (Psa 9:1)**
>
> **Praise the LORD with the harp; make music to him on the ten-stringed lyre. (Psa 33:2)**

May the peoples praise you, O God; may all the peoples praise you. (Psa 67:3)

Come, let us sing for joy to the LORD; let us shout aloud to the Rock of our salvation. (Psa 95:1)

Through Jesus, therefore, let us continually offer to God a sacrifice of praise—the fruit of lips that confess his name. (Heb 13:15)

But you are a chosen people, a royal priesthood, a holy nation, a people belonging to God, that you may declare the praises of him who called you out of darkness into his wonderful light. (1 Pet 2:9)

**5** (14:4-5) **Jews, Redeemed**: the redeemed will be clearly identified. Who are the 144,000 Jews? They were seen earlier in Revelation (see outline and notes—Rev.7:1-8). Note what is said about them here.

1. They will be virgins: they will never marry. The days of the end time will be filled with horror after horror: the worst holocaust the world has ever witnessed will be launched by the antichrist and millions will be killed. A special commitment will be needed to stand up for Christ. Apparently, these 144,000 form a body of believers who vow and commit their lives to never deny Christ. They apparently take a special vow to be the ministers to the people who will be so severely attacked and persecuted by the antichrist.

We who are strong ought to bear with the failings of the weak and not to please ourselves. (Rom 15:1)

Peter said to him, "We have left everything to follow you!" (Mark 10:28)

After this, Jesus went out and saw a tax collector by the name of Levi sitting at his tax booth. "Follow me," Jesus said to him, And Levi got up, left everything and followed him. (Luke 5:27-28)

In the same way, any of you who does not give up everything he has cannot be my disciple. (Luke 14:33)

"I tell you the truth," Jesus said to them, "no one who has left home or wife or brothers or parents or children for the sake of the kingdom of God Will fail to receive many times as much in this age and, in the age to come, eternal life." (Luke 18:29-30)

What is more, I consider everything a loss compared to the surpassing greatness of knowing Christ Jesus my Lord, for whose sake I have lost all things. I consider them rubbish, that I may gain Christ (Phil 3:8)

2. They will be followers of the Lamb: wholly committed to Jesus Christ and separated from the sin and evil of this world, that is, from the lust of the flesh, the lust of the eyes, and from the pride of life (the boasting of what a person has and does). They will be redeemed and ministers of God who will follow the leadership of the Lord's Spirit: they will go throughout the wildernesses and hiding places of this earth to minister to the millions trying to escape the holocaust of the antichrist. They will follow the Lamb, the Lord Jesus Christ, no matter where He leads and no matter how difficult the call and ministry may be. They will sell out completely to the Lord Jesus Christ.

**Thought 1.** What a dynamic lesson on commitment! How desperately we need to be just as committed as these dear servants of the Lord will be!

Then he said to them all: "If anyone would come after me, he must deny himself and take up his cross daily and follow me. (Luke 9:23)

"If anyone comes to me and does not hate his father and mother, his wife and children, his brothers and sisters—yes, even his own life—he cannot be my disciple. And anyone who does not carry his cross and follow me cannot be my disciple. (Luke 14:26-27)

My sheep listen to my voice; I know them, and they follow me. (John 10:27)

Whoever serves me must follow me; and where I am, my servant also will be. My Father will honor the one who serves me. (John 12:26)

For if you live according to the sinful nature, you will die; but if by the Spirit you put to death the misdeeds of the body, you will live, (Rom 8:13)

Those who belong to Christ Jesus have crucified the sinful nature with its passions and desires. (Gal 5:24)

So then, just as you received Christ Jesus as Lord, continue to live in him, (Col 2:6)

To this you were called, because Christ suffered for you, leaving you an example, that you should follow in his steps. (1 Pet 2:21)

Whoever claims to live in him must walk as Jesus did. (1 John 2:6)

3. They will be the redeemed from among men, the first fruits to God and the Lamb. This simply means that they will be the first Jews to be saved in the tribulation.

4. They will be truthful, never lying or telling a falsehood. Apparently this will be part of the vow the group of believers will take. It will be easy in the days of the antichrist to simply lie and say that one will give his first loyalty to the antichrist and his state and then to continue on worshipping God in the secret of one's home. But this is a lie, and the 144,000 will take a vow to never lie.

**Thought 1.** This is a day of untruthfulness, lying, and deception. Practically everyone lies and deceives:
- ⇒ husbands and wives and children
- ⇒ employers and employees
- ⇒ students and teachers
- ⇒ neighbors and friends
- ⇒ rulers and leaders
- ⇒ the educated and the uneducated
- ⇒ ministers and laymen
- ⇒ politicians and citizens

The call of the day is for truthfulness—a commitment to the truth. We desperately need real men and real women who will make a vow to be truthful and never to lie or deceive.

You belong to your father, the devil, and you want to carry out your father's desire. He was a murderer from the beginning, not holding to the truth, for there is no truth in him. When he lies, he speaks his native language, for he is a liar and the father of lies. (John 8:44)

"He committed no sin, and no deceit was found in his mouth." (1 Pet 2:22)

Who is the liar? It is the man who denies that Jesus is the Christ. Such a man is the antichrist—he denies the Father and the Son. (1 John 2:22)

Blessed is the man whose sin the LORD does not count against him and in whose spirit is no deceit. (Psa 32:2)

He was assigned a grave with the wicked, and with the rich in his death, though he had done no violence, nor was any deceit in his mouth. (Isa 53:9)

The remnant of Israel will do no wrong; they will speak no lies, nor will deceit be found in their mouths. They will eat and lie down and no one will make them afraid." (Zep 3:13)

5. They will be blameless: unspotted, undefiled, unpolluted, and without blemish before God. They will commit and set their lives completely apart unto God.

**Thought 1.** Just imagine being blameless before God—living such a life that one would be totally unspotted, undefiled, unpolluted, and without blemish. What a challenge! How desperately real men and real women are needed today—men and women so strong that they will commit themselves to being blameless before God and the world.

Do not offer the parts of your body to sin, as instruments of wickedness, but rather offer yourselves to God, as those who have been brought from death to life; and offer the parts of your body to him as instruments of righteousness. (Rom 6:13)

Therefore, I urge you, brothers, in view of God's mercy, to offer your bodies as living sacrifices, holy and pleasing to God—this is your spiritual act of worship. Do not conform any longer to the pattern of this world, but be transformed by the renewing of your mind. Then you will be able to test and approve what God's will is—his good, pleasing and perfect will. (Rom 12:1-2)

Do you not know that your body is a temple of the Holy Spirit, who is in you, whom you have received from God? You are not your own; You were bought at a price. Therefore honor God with your body. (1 Cor 6:19-20)

"Therefore come out from them and be separate, says the Lord. Touch no unclean thing, and I will receive you." "I will be a Father to you, and you will be my sons and daughters, says the Lord Almighty." (2 Cor 6:17-18)

For he chose us in him before the creation of the world to be holy and blameless in his sight. In love (Eph 1:4)

For you know that it was not with perishable things such as silver or gold that you were redeemed from the empty way of life handed down to you from your forefathers, But with the precious blood of Christ, a lamb without blemish or defect. (1 Pet 1:18-19)

| | B. Assurance 2: The Gospel Will Be Preached to the Whole World, 14:6-7 |
|---|---|
| 1 The messenger: An angel will have the eternal gospel to give to the whole earth | 6 Then I saw another angel flying in midair, and he had the eternal gospel to proclaim to those who live on the earth—to every nation, tribe, language and people. |
| 2 The points of the message<br>a. Fear God: Judgment has come<br>b. Worship God: He is the Creator | 7 He said in a loud voice, "Fear God and give him glory, because the hour of his judgment has come. Worship him who made the heavens, the earth, the sea and the springs of water." |

# DIVISION VIII

## THE SEVENTH TRUMPET IN DETAIL (PART III): THE VICTORY OF THE LAMB IS ASSURED, 14:1-20

### B. Assurance 2: The Gospel Will be Preached to the Whole World, 14:6-7

(14:6-7) **Introduction**: the Lord Jesus Christ is going to be victorious over the world. He will triumph over evil and bring righteousness and godliness to earth. The kingdom of God will reign upon earth. How do we know this for sure? Because the Scripture reveals it to us. This is the purpose of this great chapter: to show us that the victory of the Lord Jesus Christ over this world and its ungodliness is assured. In rapid fire Christ gives John seven visions revealing the triumph of Christ. In the first vision the redeemed were seen with Jesus (Rev.14:15). Now, in the next six visions John hears six of the most glorious announcements. The announcements proclaim six events that stagger the human mind, but the events will take place. John, the true witness of God, has already seen the events and their outcome. Christ Himself revealed the events to John. They have already been announced by heaven; they are set and fixed to happen. These glorious events will take place. We can know and be assured that Jesus Christ is going to triumph. The victory of the Lamb is assured. This is the second great assurance given to believers: the gospel will be preached to the whole world.

1. The messenger: an angel will have the eternal gospel to give to the whole earth (v.6).
2. The points of the message (v.7).

**1** (14:6) **Gospel—End Time—World Evangelism**: the messenger who will have the gospel will be an angel. Does this mean that he will have the gospel to preach himself or that he will have the gospel to give to believers to preach? Or is this just a picture that the gospel will be preached throughout the whole world in the end time? Christ Himself, when He was on earth, predicted the evangelization of the whole world (Mt.24:14). There are those who think that evil will be so rampant in the end time and that believers will be on the run so much from the holocaust of the antichrist that they will not be able to preach and spread the Word. They think that God will have to change His method of getting the gospel out to the world, change it by going back to using angels just like He did in the Old Testament period of history (cp. Lk.2:10f; Heb.2:2). There are others who think that this is a vision symbolizing the preaching of the gospel to the world. Whatever the case, remember this: God's people and the Jews are going to be scattered all over the earth, hid-

ing and scratching for food wherever they can. They will have to be fleeing in order get away from the holocaust of the antichrist. But God's people, His true servants, always share the gospel wherever they are to whomever they feel they can trust. Remember also that the earth will help to hide and feed the Jews and the followers of Christ just as they have in every holocaust. Not every unbeliever is hardhearted even in the end time (Rev.12:16). The Jewish servants, the 144,000 who have committed themselves to minister to God's people, will certainly be witnessing. They will no doubt be moving out into the wilderness areas and hiding places of the world themselves. That will be where God's people, the Jews, will be. And that is the only place the 144,000 Jewish servants will probably be safe. Also remember that civilization and the population are going to be shrunk much smaller than what they are now. There will be vast devastation upon the earth and whole areas of the earth will become uninhabitable, totally unsuitable for human life (see outline and notes—Rev.6:7-8; 6:12-17; 8:6-12; 9:12-21). In addition to all this, think of the witnessing that will be going on among the countless multitude of Gentiles that will be converted throughout the tribulation of the end time. God's people, His true followers, are never silent. They always talk about and share Christ among one another and to those who befriend and help them. And one thing is sure: when so many earthly horrors and supernatural catastrophes and events are taking place in the end time, no believer will keep silent, not when he is with other believers and people who are kind enough to help hide him from the holocaust.

The point is this: there will be witnessing in the last days. The glorious gospel will be proclaimed by God's people. And if they for some unknown reason hush, God will proclaim the gospel of His Son through angels. As Jesus Himself said to the religionists of His day: if the people keep silent, then the very stones themselves will cry out (Lk.19:40).

**Thought 1.** The gospel must be proclaimed to the whole earth. Not a single place must be missed. It must be proclaimed to every nation, tribe, language, and people.

**Therefore go and make disciples of all nations, baptizing them in the name of the Father and of the Son and of the Holy**

Spirit, And teaching them to obey everything I have commanded you. And surely I am with you always, to the very end of the age." (Mat 28:19-20)

He said to them, "Go into all the world and preach the good news to all creation. (Mark 16:15)

But you will receive power when the Holy Spirit comes on you; and you will be my witnesses in Jerusalem, and in all Judea and Samaria, and to the ends of the earth." (Acts 1:8)

We proclaim him [Christ], admonishing and teaching everyone with all wisdom, so that we may present everyone perfect in Christ. (Col 1:28)

For we cannot help speaking about what we have seen and heard." (Acts 4:20)

So do not be ashamed to testify about our Lord, or ashamed of me his prisoner. But join with me in suffering for the gospel, by the power of God, (2 Tim 1:8)

But in your hearts set apart Christ as Lord. Always be prepared to give an answer to everyone who asks you to give the reason for the hope that you have. But do this with gentleness and respect, (1 Pet 3:15)

But if I say, "I will not mention him or speak any more in his name," his word is in my heart like a fire, a fire shut up in my bones. I am weary of holding it in; indeed, I cannot. (Jer 20:9)

**2** (14:7) **Evangelism—Witnessing—End Time—Gospel**: there are the points of the message. They are twofold. Note this: they are the very subjects that would be flooding the minds and conversations of people in the midst of the holocaust and the catastrophic judgments that will be destroying so much of the earth: fear God, for judgment is come. Worship God the Creator—repent, turn from the worship of sin and of the antichrist and worship God. This is not a different gospel. To *fear God* and at the same to *give Him glory* clearly implies repentance, true repentance. There is *no glory* ever acceptable to God other than the glory of a truly repentant heart. (See note—Rev.11:13 for more discussion.)

1. There will be the message to fear God.

**Thought 1.** Few people fear God. This is what God calls the *day of grace*, the day when He reaches out for people in love. But the day of His judgment is coming. This is the very message of Revelation. Therefore, we must fear God even in this day of grace and love. God tolerates our rebellion and denial of Him only for now, only to give us a chance to be saved and to escape the coming judgment. But this chance is going to soon pass. We must, therefore, repent and fear God and do what the next point says, "Worship Him."

**Do not be afraid of those who kill the body but cannot kill the soul. Rather, be afraid of the One who can destroy both soul and body in hell. (Mat 10:28)**

**His mercy extends to those who fear him, from generation to generation. (Luke 1:50)**

**Granted. But they [Israel] were broken off because of unbelief, and you stand by faith. Do not be arrogant, but be afraid. (Rom 11:20)**

**Since you call on a Father who judges each man's work impartially, live your lives as strangers here in reverent fear. (1 Pet 1:17)**

**And now, O Israel, what does the LORD your God ask of you but to fear the LORD your God, to walk in all his ways, to love him, to serve the LORD your God with all your heart and with all your soul, (Deu 10:12)**

**"Now fear the LORD and serve him with all faithfulness. Throw away the gods your forefathers worshiped beyond the River and in Egypt, and serve the LORD. (Josh 24:14)**

**How great is your goodness, which you have stored up for those who fear you, which you bestow in the sight of men on those who take refuge in you. (Psa 31:19)**

**Now all has been heard; here is the conclusion of the matter: Fear God and keep his commandments, for this is the whole *duty* of man. (Eccl 12:13)**

2. There will be the message to worship God.

**Jesus said to him, "Away from me, Satan! For it is written: 'Worship the Lord your God, and serve him only.'" (Mat 4:10)**

**Jesus declared, "Believe me, woman, a time is coming when you will worship the Father neither on this mountain nor in Jerusalem. (John 4:21)**

**He said in a loud voice, "Fear God and give him glory, because the hour of his judgment has come. Worship him who made the heavens, the earth, the sea and the springs of water." (Rev 14:7)**

**Ascribe to the LORD the glory due his name. Bring an offering and come before him; worship the LORD in the splendor of his holiness. (1 Chr 16:29)**

**Ascribe to the LORD the glory due his name; worship the LORD in the splendor of his holiness. (Psa 29:2)**

**Come, let us bow down in worship, let us kneel before the LORD our Maker; (Psa 95:6)**

**Worship the LORD in the splendor of his holiness; tremble before him, all the earth. (Psa 96:9)**

| | C. Assurance 3: Babylon, the Godless State & Religion, Will Fall, 14:8 |
|---|---|
| 1 The fall announced<br>2 The reason why Babylon will be destroyed: It will be the capital of an apostate civilization | 8 A second angel followed and said, "Fallen! Fallen is Babylon the Great, which made all the nations drink the maddening wine of her adulteries." |

# DIVISION VIII

## THE SEVENTH TRUMPET IN DETAIL (PART III)
## THE VICTORY OF THE LAMB IS ASSURED, 14:1-20

### C. Assurance 3: Babylon, the Godless State and Religion, Will Fall, 14:8

(14:8) **Introduction**: Jesus Christ is going to triumph over the godless society and corrupt religion of this world. No matter the government and religion, if the government and religion are godless and corrupt, they are going to be judged and doomed. The wrath of God is going to fall upon them, and they will be crushed as the dust of the earth. This is the third great assurance given to the godly people of this earth: Babylon will fall.

1. The fall announced (v.8).
2. The reason why Babylon will be destroyed: it will be the capital of an apostate civilization (v.8).

**1** (14:8 **Babylon—Civilization—World Government, Corrupt**: the fall is announced—Babylon is fallen. In the Old Testament Babylon was the great enemy of Israel (cp. Is.21:9; Jer.50:2; 51:8). Because of this, the very name of Babylon came to stand for...

- a corrupt political system that stood against God.
- a corrupt economic system that stood against God.
- a corrupt religion that stood against God.

Babylon symbolized the political, economic, and religious center of a godless society. It was a society—nation or government or religion—that defied God. Here in the Revelation Babylon stands for the city of the antichrist, the capital of the world: it stands for the political and economic system which he establishes. But it also stands for the religious capital or system of the second beast, the apostate and universal state and religion which he sets up before the whole world. (See outlines and notes—Rev. chapters 17 and 18. This is seen in these two chapters.) Both the corrupt political and religious systems of the end time will be destroyed once for all *in the end time*.

> Look, here comes a man in a chariot with a team of horses. And he gives back the answer: 'Babylon has fallen, has fallen! All the images of its gods lie shattered on the ground!'" (Isa 21:9)
>
> "Announce and proclaim among the nations, lift up a banner and proclaim it; keep nothing back, but say, 'Babylon will be captured; Bel will be put to shame, Marduk filled with terror. Her images will be put to shame and her idols filled with terror.' (Jer 50:2)
>
> The noise of battle is in the land, the noise of great destruction! How broken and

> shattered is the hammer of the whole earth! How desolate is Babylon among the nations! I set a trap for you, O Babylon, and you were caught before you knew it; you were found and captured because you opposed the LORD. The LORD has opened his arsenal and brought out the weapons of his wrath, for the Sovereign LORD Almighty has work to do in the land of the Babylonians. (Jer 50:22-25)
>
> Babylon will suddenly fall and be broken. Wail over her! Get balm for her pain; perhaps she can be healed. (Jer 51:8)
>
> With a mighty voice he shouted: "Fallen! Fallen is Babylon the Great! She has become a home for demons and a haunt for every evil spirit, a haunt for every unclean and detestable bird. (Rev 18:2)

**2** (14:8) **Babylon—Judgment—Wrath**: there is the reason why Babylon will be destroyed. Why will the political and religious system of the world be destroyed in the end time? Is not a one-world government and religion a good thing? Will not the dream of men for a one-world government and religion bring the *kingdom of utopia* to earth? This verse says that Babylon will be destroyed for one reason: she will make all nations drink of the wine of her fornication. The picture is twofold.

1. Babylon, the end time government, will be like a prostitute who entices men into bed with her by giving them wine and getting them so intoxicated that they can no longer resist her seduction.

The end time government will be just like the prostitute: Babylon will seduce and entice the governments of the world to join her in her corruption. What will the corruption be? (See note—Rev.9:20-21 for discussion.)

a. There will be the corruption of idolatry. The state will push the secular and humanistic society, the fact that man and his government are the answer to the utopian society and world. Therefore, the antichrist and his government will set up the state as the first loyalty of a person.

> For since the creation of the world God's invisible qualities—his eternal power and divine nature—have been clearly seen, being understood from what has been made, so that men are without excuse. For although they knew God, they neither glorified

him as God nor gave thanks to him, but their thinking became futile and their foolish hearts were darkened. Although they claimed to be wise, they became fools They exchanged the truth of God for a lie, and worshiped and served created things rather than the Creator—who is forever praised. Amen. (Rom 1:20-22, 25)

The rest of mankind that were not killed by these plagues still did not repent of the work of their hands; they did not stop worshiping demons, and idols of gold, silver, bronze, stone and wood—idols that cannot see or hear or walk. (Rev 9:20)

No, but the sacrifices of pagans are offered to demons, not to God, and I do not want you to be participants with demons. (1 Cor 10:20)

Dear children, keep yourselves from idols. (1 John 5:21)

"You shall not make for yourself an idol in the form of anything in heaven above or on the earth beneath or in the waters below. (Exo 20:4)

"'Do not make idols or set up an image or a sacred stone for yourselves, and do not place a carved stone in your land to bow down before it. I am the LORD your God. (Lev 26:1)

The images of their gods you are to burn in the fire. Do not covet the silver and gold on them, and do not take it for yourselves, or you will be ensnared by it, for it is detestable to the LORD your God. (Deu 7:25)

Be careful, or you will be enticed to turn away and worship other gods and bow down to them. (Deu 11:16)

"I am the LORD; that is my name! I will not give my glory to another or my praise to idols. (Isa 42:8)

They must no longer offer any of their sacrifices to the goat idols to whom they prostitute themselves. This is to be a lasting ordinance for them and for the generations to come.' (Lev 17:7)

They made him jealous with their foreign gods and angered him with their detestable idols. They sacrificed to demons, which are not God— gods they had not known, gods that recently appeared, gods your fathers did not fear. (Deu 32:16-17)

They worshiped their idols, which became a snare to them. They sacrificed their sons and their daughters to demons. They shed innocent blood, the blood of their sons and daughters, whom they sacrificed to the idols of Canaan, and the land was desecrated by their blood. They defiled themselves by what they did; by their deeds they prostituted themselves. (Psa 106:36-39)

b. There will be the corruption of murder. A spirit of senseless murder and lawlessness will be sweeping the earth; in addition, there will be the slaughtering of millions who will refuse to place the state before God.

Nor did they repent of their murders, their magic arts, their sexual immorality or their thefts. (Rev 9:21)

"You shall not murder. (Exo 20:13)

"You have heard that it was said to the people long ago, 'Do not murder, and anyone who murders will be subject to judgment.' But I tell you that anyone who is angry with his brother will be subject to judgment. Again, anyone who says to his brother, 'Raca, ' is answerable to the Sanhedrin. But anyone who says, 'You fool!' will be in danger of the fire of hell. (Mat 5:21-22)

"Which ones?" The man inquired. Jesus replied, "'Do not murder, do not commit adultery, do not steal, do not give false testimony, (Mat 19:18)

If you suffer, it should not be as a murderer or thief or any other kind of criminal, or even as a meddler. (1 Pet 4:15)

Anyone who hates his brother is a murderer, and you know that no murderer has eternal life in him. (1 John 3:15)

c. There will be the corruption by magical arts or sorcery: the interest and the governing of life by the horoscope, astrology, witchcraft, and demons in this world.

Nor did they repent of their murders, their magic arts, their sexual immorality or their thefts. (Rev 9:21)

Saul died because he was unfaithful to the LORD; he did not keep the word of the LORD and even consulted a medium for guidance, (1 Chr 10:13)

When men tell you to consult mediums and spiritists, who whisper and mutter, should not a people inquire of their God? Why consult the dead on behalf of the living? To the law and to the testimony! If they do not speak according to this word, they have no light of dawn. (Isa 8:19-20)

I will destroy your witchcraft and you will no longer cast spells. (Micah 5:12)

Idolatry and witchcraft; hatred, discord, jealousy, fits of rage, selfish ambition, dissensions, factions (Gal 5:20)

d. There will be the corruption by sexual immorality: the immorality of the end times will run wild, even more so than today.

Nor did they repent of their murders, their magic arts, their sexual immorality or their thefts. (Rev 9:21)

Flee from sexual immorality. All other sins a man commits are outside his body, but he who sins sexually sins against his own body. (1 Cor 6:18)

But among you there must not be even a hint of sexual immorality, or of any kind of impurity, or of greed, because these are improper for God's holy people. (Eph 5:3)

Put to death, therefore, whatever belongs to your earthly nature: sexual immorality, impurity, lust, evil desires and greed, which is idolatry. (Col 3:5)

e. There will be the corruption of thefts: stealing in both high and low places, in the shops and in the workplaces, from neighbors, and from employers will be running wild.

> Nor did they repent of their murders, their magic arts, their sexual immorality or their thefts. (Rev 9:21)
>
> "You shall not steal. (Exo 20:15)
>
> "'Do not steal. "'Do not lie. "'Do not deceive one another. (Lev 19:11)
>
> He who has been stealing must steal no longer, but must work, doing something useful with his own hands, that he may have something to share with those in need. (Eph 4:28)
>
> And not to steal from them, but to show that they can be fully trusted, so that in every way they will make the teaching about God our Savior attractive. (Titus 2:10)

The last days will be corrupt and evil and murderous days, and it will be because of the godless and secular society and government of the antichrist. This is the reason the one-world government will be destroyed. Man's heart is evil and secular and will remain evil until he allows the Son of God, the Lord Jesus Christ, to create his heart anew and make him a new creature.

2. Note a second picture: there is the picture of wrath. Babylon, the godless society of the antichrist, will seduce the world to drink the *maddening wine of her adulteries*. This means that she thinks her wine leads to pleasure, to the utopian state, to the glorious one-world government and religion that men have always dreamed about. But the government and religion of the end time will be discussed: they will lead to wrath, the wrath of God. The justice and fury of God is going to fall upon the whoredom of Babylon, the godless society of the antichrist. All the ungodly and evil people and nations of the world who follow him will suffer the wrath and fury of God.

> "When the Son of Man comes in his glory, and all the angels with him, he will sit on his throne in heavenly glory. All the na-tions will be gathered before him, and he will separate the people one from another as a shepherd separates the sheep from the goats. (Mat 25:31-32)
>
> Whoever believes in the Son has eternal life, but whoever rejects the Son will not see life, for God's wrath remains on him." (John 3:36)
>
> The wrath of God is being revealed from heaven against all the godlessness and wickedness of men who suppress the truth by their wickedness, (Rom 1:18)
>
> But for those who are self-seeking and who reject the truth and follow evil, there will be wrath and anger. (Rom 2:8)
>
> Let no one deceive you with empty words, for because of such things God's wrath comes on those who are disobedient. (Eph 5:6)
>
> By the same word the present heavens and earth are reserved for fire, being kept for the day of judgment and destruction of ungodly men. (2 Pet 3:7)
>
> Enoch, the seventh from Adam, prophesied about these men: "See, the Lord is coming with thousands upon thousands of his holy ones To judge everyone, and to convict all the ungodly of all the ungodly acts they have done in the ungodly way, and of all the harsh words ungodly sinners have spoken against him." (Jude 1:14-15)
>
> Let his own eyes see his destruction; let him drink of the wrath of the Almighty. (Job 21:20)
>
> In the hand of the LORD is a cup full of foaming wine mixed with spices; he pours it out, and all the wicked of the earth drink it down to its very dregs. (Psa 75:8)
>
> Awake, awake! Rise up, O Jerusalem, you who have drunk from the hand of the LORD the cup of his wrath, you who have drained to its dregs the goblet that makes men stagger. (Isa 51:17)
>
> So I took the cup from the Lord's hand and made all the nations to whom he sent me drink it: (Jer 25:17)

| | D. Assurance 4: Justice Will Be Executed, 14:9-12 | sulfur in the presence of the holy angels and of the Lamb.<br>11 And the smoke of their torment rises for ever and ever. There is no rest day or night for those who worship the beast and his image, or for anyone who receives the mark of his name." | of angels & of Christ<br>d. Tormented for ever and ever & have no rest day or night |
|---|---|---|---|
| 1 **The person to be judged: Any person who follows the beast & receives the beast's mark** | 9 A third angel followed them and said in a loud voice: "If anyone worships the beast and his image and receives his mark on the forehead or on the hand, | | |
| 2 **The judgment**<br>a. God's fury—wrath<br>b. Tormented with burning sulfur<br>c. Tormented in the presence | 10 He, too, will drink of the wine of God's fury, which has been poured full strength into the cup of his wrath. He will be tormented with burning | 12 This calls for patient endurance on the part of the saints who obey God's commandments and remain faithful to Jesus. | 3 **The person who escapes judgment**<br>a. Keeps God's commandments<br>b. Keeps the faith of Jesus |

# DIVISION VIII

## THE SEVENTH TRUMPET IN DETAIL (PART III): THE VICTORY OF THE LAMB IS ASSURED, 14:1-20

### D. Assurance 4: Justice Will Be Executed, 14:9-12

(14:9-12) **Introduction**: this is a terrifying passage, one of the most horrible pictures in all the Word of God. It is the picture of the anger and wrath of God against the ungodly and evil of this world. Those who do not repent and turn to God in the end time will have the wrath of God fall upon them. Those who are not moved by the sufferings and testimonies of God's people—the millions who will be dying as martyrs for Christ—who are not moved to repent, will suffer the wrath of God. This is the third great assurance: justice will triumph. True justice will be executed upon earth. All the ungodliness and evil and all the injustices of this earth committed against God and man shall be corrected. True justice will be executed against all the ungodly and evil of this earth.

1. The person to be judged: any person who follows the beast and receives the beast's mark (v.9).
2. The judgment (v.10-11).
3. The person who escapes judgment (v.12).

**1** (14:9) **Judgment—Mark of the Beast**: there are the persons to be judged. The judgment of God is going to fall upon all those who follow the beast and receive the mark of the beast (see notes, pt.4—Rev.13:13-17; 13:18 for discussion). This mark will show that a person gives his first loyalty and allegiance to the state and secular society and its leader, the antichrist. The person who declares his allegiance, who worships and puts the state and secular society before God—that is the person who will receive the mark of the beast. He is the person who will be saying to God...

- that God is second.
- that the state and its leader are more important than God.
- that the state and its leader can do more for man than God.
- that society needs to focus upon the state and its leader, not God.
- that the state and earthly leaders are the hope of man, not God.

Note how this belief runs through society today. In fact it is a common belief that runs through every generation. There are always multitudes who believe that man can control his own destiny, that what is important is good government, good education, good medicine, good social services, and on and on. All of these are necessary and we should dil-

igently labor to have the best of everything. But these are not the end of life. They can only make life comfortable and perhaps extend life for a little more time. They cannot help us beyond this life. Only God can. Government and good services are not the savior of man, God is. Man is not a god, capable of bringing the perfect society to earth; God alone is God. This does not mean that we should not work to have the best society we can. It means that while we work for the good of society, we honor and worship and trust God. This is where so many fail today and have failed in the past and will fail in the end time. The people of the end time will be making the same gross mistake so many in our generation are making; they will worship man and government, look to man and government instead of to God. The difference is this: in order to hold the masses of people together in the end time, the government will officially insist that the first loyalty of its citizens be to the state. Religion will be subjected to the state. The end result will be the massive slaughter and holocaust of all who refuse. This is the reason the wrath of God will fall upon the people of the end time.

**2** (14:10-11) **Judgment—God, Wrath of—Hell**: there is the judgment. Four things are said about the judgment of God.

1. The ungodly and evil will drink the fury and wrath of God.

> **He, too, will drink of the wine of God's fury, which has been poured full strength into the cup of his wrath. He will be tormented with burning sulfur in the presence of the holy angels and of the Lamb. (Rev 14:10)**

When thinking of the judgment of God, we must never forget a significant fact: God must keep heaven perfect. When He creates the new heavens and earth, He has to exclude and shut out all those...

- who have cursed, denied, disbelieved, and rejected Him.
- who are hostile and who are enemies of Him and His righteousness.
- who do not want His control and restraint upon their lives.

- who reject the righteousness of God's Son and do not let it cover them; who refuse to believe that Christ is the sinless Son of God who died for their sins.

God has no choice but to keep all these out of heaven. Remember something else as well: God has given man every chance; He has done everything that can be done to reach out and save man. He has sent man prophet after prophet and given man His Word. And most of all, He has given the world His own Son to save man. But man continues to reject and deny and even curse His Son. When the world does this to God's Son, the only Son He has, what kind of attitude can we expect God to have in the day of judgment? Soft and tender? Or angry and wrathful? We must never forget that God is not only love (perfect love) but He is also just (perfect justice). Just as His love has to be perfectly demonstrated toward man (by giving His own Son to die for man), so His justice has to be perfectly demonstrated. There has to come a day when God shows His perfect love to all those who trusted Him by making a new and perfect heavens and earth. But when that day comes, He has to be just and exclude all the ungodly and evil. If He were not just, then the new heavens and earth would be corrupted by the ungodly and evil. God is perfect love; therefore, He is going to give the believer a new world in which dwells perfect righteousness and love and joy and peace. But to do this, the ungodly and evil of the earth must be judged and separated and shut out. God will execute perfect justice: wrath and anger will fall upon the ungodly and evil of this world.

⇒ The ungodly will *drink* the cup of God's fury: that is, the fury of God will be drunk and will permeate their whole being, move throughout their whole body. It will be thorough and all inclusive. Not a part of the ungodly's being, not a moment of the ungodly's time will be free from the fury of God.

⇒ The ungodly will drink the cup of God's fury without any mixture. Nothing else will be mixed with His fury, no love, no feelings of sympathy, no regret, no compassion. The full fury of God will fall upon the ungodly.

⇒ The ungodly will suffer a double portion of God's judgment: the cup of His fury and the cup of His wrath. Note the verse carefully: both the fury and wrath of God will be served in the awful day of judgment.

**Whoever believes in the Son has eternal life, but whoever rejects the Son will not see life, for God's wrath remains on him." (John 3:36)**

**The wrath of God is being revealed from heaven against all the godlessness and wickedness of men who suppress the truth by their wickedness, (Rom 1:18)**

**But for those who are self-seeking and who reject the truth and follow evil, there will be wrath and anger. (Rom 2:8)**

**Let no one deceive you with empty words, for because of such things God's wrath comes on those who are disobedient. (Eph 5:6)**

**A second angel followed and said, "Fallen! Fallen is Babylon the Great, which made all the nations drink the maddening wine of her adulteries."** (Rev 14:8)

**In the hand of the LORD is a cup full of foaming wine mixed with spices; he pours it out, and all the wicked of the earth drink it down to its very dregs. (Psa 75:8)**

**This is what the LORD says: "If those who do not deserve to drink the cup must drink it, why should you go unpunished? You will not go unpunished, but must drink it. (Jer 49:12)**

2. The ungodly and evil will be tormented with fire and burning sulfur. This is a probably a picture of Sodom and Gomorrah.

**He, too, will drink of the wine of God's fury, which has been poured full strength into the cup of his wrath. He will be tormented with burning sulfur in the presence of the holy angels and of the Lamb. (Rev 14:10)**

**By the time Lot reached Zoar, the sun had risen over the land. Then the LORD rained down burning sulfur on Sodom and Gomorrah—from the LORD out of the heavens. (Gen 19:23-24)**

This is undoubtedly the most terrorizing judgment that has ever fallen upon the earth up to this time. Men sometimes scoff at the idea of a coming judgment, and they doubt that two cities were ever destroyed as Scripture says that Sodom and Gomorrah were. But several hundred years after the event, the Lord Himself confirmed the fact, and He declared that the same fire and burning sulfur were going to fall upon the ungodly and evil in the day of judgment.

**I tell you the truth, it will be more bearable for Sodom and Gomorrah on the day of judgment than for that town. (Mat 10:15)**

**But I tell you that it will be more bearable for Sodom on the day of judgment than for you." (Mat 11:24)**

**I tell you, it will be more bearable on that day for Sodom than for that town. (Luke 10:12)**

**But the day Lot left Sodom, fire and sulfur rained down from heaven and destroyed them all. (Luke 17:29)**

Fire and burning sulfur is the picture of the hot flaming molten lava that flows from the mouth of a volcano that has erupted. It is a terrible thought to think that a person would *choose* to spend eternity suffering as though he was caught in the bed of fire and burning sulfur.

**Thought 1.** This is a horrible picture, and it is not a pleasant thought, but we must always remember two things:

1) These are not the words of a preacher. They are the words and warnings of Scripture. Scripture is honest and true; therefore, if there is truly a place that is like suffering in fire and burning sulfur, then Scripture will tell us. This must never be overlooked: Scripture does tell us. Therefore, part of the judgment of hell will be just like suffering in fire and burning sulfur.

2) Today, right now, is the day of God's love and grace. Therefore, we must cast ourselves upon God's love. We must heed the warning of fire and burning sulfur and repent and turn to God.

**But the beast was captured, and with him the false prophet who had performed the miraculous signs on his behalf. With these signs he had deluded those who had received the mark of the beast and worshiped his image. The two of them were thrown alive into the fiery lake of burning sulfur. (Rev 19:20)**

**And the devil, who deceived them, was thrown into the lake of burning sulfur, where the beast and the false prophet had been thrown. They will be tormented day and night for ever and ever. (Rev 20:10)**

**But the cowardly, the unbelieving, the vile, the murderers, the sexually immoral, those who practice magic arts, the idolaters and all liars—their place will be in the fiery lake of burning sulfur. This is the second death." (Rev 21:8)**

**Then the LORD rained down burning sulfur on Sodom and Gomorrah—from the LORD out of the heavens. (Gen 19:24)**

**I will execute judgment upon him with plague and bloodshed; I will pour down torrents of rain, hailstones and burning sulfur on him and on his troops and on the many nations with him. (Ezek 38:22)**

3. The ungodly and evil will be tormented in the presence of the holy angels and Christ.

**He will be tormented with burning sulfur in the presence of the holy angels and of the Lamb. (Rev 14:10)**

Christ will give the order to cast unbelievers into hell and the holy angels will carry out the orders. Christ will be there and every eye of all unbelievers will see Him. Why? So that He will be vindicated as the Son of God. The vast, vast majority of the human race denies, curses, and rejects Jesus Christ as the Son of God. They insist that He was either mistaken or a liar and deceiver or insane by claiming to be the Son of God. But in the great day of judgment, that horrible day, all the terrible things the ungodly and evil have done against Him—they shall all know that He is exactly who He claimed to be:

⇒ the Son of the living God, the true Messiah who had come to save them all—everyone of them.

⇒ the Son of God who now stands as the Judge of the world to rid the universe of all the ungodly and evil.

⇒ the exalted Lord who is bringing godliness and righteousness to the universe.

**"At that time the sign of the Son of Man will appear in the sky, and all the nations of the earth will mourn. They will see the Son of Man coming on the clouds of the sky, with power and great glory. (Mat 24:30)**

**"When the Son of Man comes in his glory, and all the angels with him, he will sit on his throne in heavenly glory.**

**All the nations will be gathered before him, and he will separate the people one from another as a shepherd separates the sheep from the goats. (Mat 25:31-32)**

**And give relief to you who are troubled, and to us as well. This will happen when the Lord Jesus is revealed from heaven in blazing fire with his powerful angels. He will punish those who do not know God and do not obey the gospel of our Lord Jesus. (2 Th 1:7-8)**

**Enoch, the seventh from Adam, prophesied about these men: "See, the Lord is coming with thousands upon thousands of his holy ones (Jude 1:14)**

**Look, he is coming with the clouds, and every eye will see him, even those who pierced him; and all the peoples of the earth will mourn because of him. So shall it be! Amen. (Rev 1:7)**

4. The ungodly and evil will be tormented forever and ever.

**And the smoke of their torment rises for ever and ever. (Rev 14:11)**

The picture is that of duration, of how long a person will have to stay in hell. Note the picture: it is that of punishment, torment, agony, and misery; that of wrenching and twisting in pain and suffering—that of never being relieved, of never having peace or rest, not even for a single night or day. There is no peace in hell; there is no rest in hell. There is only torment and horror, unbroken punishment and suffering. The agony and misery, the pain and suffering of the fire and burning sulfur never ends. The smoke of their torment ascends up *forever and ever*. The torment of the ungodly and evil will never end.

**Thought 1.** We must all face this one fact: if Jesus Christ is truly the Son of God and if Scripture is truly the Scripture of God, then we are doomed to eternal punishment if we reject Jesus Christ. This is the teaching both of Jesus Christ and of Scripture. A great day of separation is coming, a day when all those who believe in Jesus Christ will be separated from those who have denied, disbelieved, and cursed God and Christ. The unbeliever is not going to live in the same world that the believer will live in. The person who truly believes in Christ is going to live in a world with God. The person who rejects God is going to live in a world apart from God, a world that Christ and Scripture call hell. And hell is a world of everlasting punishment.

**"Then he will say to those on his left, 'Depart from me, you who are cursed, into the eternal fire prepared for the devil and his angels. "Then they will go away to eternal punishment, but the righteous to eternal life." (Mat 25:41, 46)**

**And if your eye causes you to sin, pluck it out. It is better for you to enter the kingdom of God with one eye than to have two eyes and be thrown into hell, Where "'their worm does not die, and the fire is not quenched.' (Mark 9:47-48)**

His winnowing fork is in his hand, and he will clear his threshing floor, gathering his wheat into the barn and burning up the chaff with unquenchable fire." (Mat 3:12)

The Son of Man will send out his angels, and they will weed out of his kingdom everything that causes sin and all who do evil. They will throw them into the fiery furnace, where there will be weeping and gnashing of teeth. (Mat 13:41-42)

If your hand or your foot causes you to sin cut it off and throw it away. It is better for you to enter life maimed or crippled than to have two hands or two feet and be thrown into eternal fire. (Mat 18:8)

He, too, will drink of the wine of God's fury, which has been poured full strength into the cup of his wrath. He will be tormented with burning sulfur in the presence of the holy angels and of the Lamb. (Rev 14:10)

And the devil, who deceived them, was thrown into the lake of burning sulfur, where the beast and the false prophet had been thrown. They will be tormented day and night for ever and ever. (Rev 20:10)

If anyone's name was not found written in the book of life, he was thrown into the lake of fire. (Rev 20:15)

But the cowardly, the unbelieving, the vile, the murderers, the sexually immoral, those who practice magic arts, the idolaters and all liars—their place will be in the fiery lake of burning sulfur. This is the second death." (Rev 21:8)

The sinners in Zion are terrified; trembling grips the godless: "Who of us can dwell with the consuming fire? Who of us can dwell with everlasting burning?" (Isa 33:14)

"And they will go out and look upon the dead bodies of those who rebelled against me; their worm will not die, nor will their fire be quenched, and they will be loathsome to all mankind." (Isa 66:24)

**3** (14:12) **Judgment, Escape From—Believers**: there is the person who escapes the judgment of God. Three things are said about the person who escapes the judgment of God.

1. He is a saint who endures. The word *saint* means to be set apart and separated unto God. It means that a person has separated himself from the world and set his life apart unto God. It means that he dedicates and commits his life, *all he is and has*, to God. But note: the true saint is a person who endures. Once he has made a commitment to God, if he is sincere, he endures. He continues to live a life...

- that is separated from the world.
- that is set apart and committed to God.

In the last days, during the *great tribulation*, believers will face terrible times. They will have to deny Christ and accept the mark of the beast or else face death. If they endure for Christ—if they are sincere in believing that heaven is real and that Christ loves them—then they will escape the judgment of God. But only those who endure, who truly set their lives apart unto God, only those will escape the coming judgment.

All men will hate you because of me, but he who stands firm to the end will be saved. (Mat 10:22)

"As the Father has loved me, so have I loved you. Now remain in my love. (John 15:9)

Therefore, I urge you, brothers, in view of God's mercy, to offer your bodies as living sacrifices, holy and pleasing to God—this is your spiritual act of worship. Do not conform any longer to the pattern of this world, but be transformed by the renewing of your mind. Then you will be able to test and approve what God's will is—his good, pleasing and perfect will. (Rom 12:1-2)

Therefore, my dear brothers, stand firm. Let nothing move you. Always give yourselves fully to the work of the Lord, because you know that your labor in the Lord is not in vain. (1 Cor 15:58)

"Therefore come out from them and be separate, says the Lord. Touch no unclean thing, and I will receive you." "I will be a Father to you, and you will be my sons and daughters, says the Lord Almighty." (2 Cor 6:17-18)

You need to persevere so that when you have done the will of God, you will receive what he has promised. (Heb 10:36)

Blessed is the man who perseveres under trial, because when he has stood the test, he will receive the crown of life that God has promised to those who love him. (James 1:12)

Therefore, prepare your minds for action; be self-controlled; set your hope fully on the grace to be given you when Jesus Christ is revealed. (1 Pet 1:13)

Be self-controlled and alert. Your enemy the devil prowls around like a roaring lion looking for someone to devour. Resist him, standing firm in the faith, because you know that your brothers throughout the world are undergoing the same kind of sufferings. (1 Pet 5:8-9)

Therefore, dear friends, since you already know this, be on your guard so that you may not be carried away by the error of lawless men and fall from your secure position. (2 Pet 3:17)

Do not love the world or anything in the world. If anyone loves the world, the love of the Father is not in him. For everything in the world—the cravings of sinful man, the lust of his eyes and the boasting of what he has and does—comes not from the Father but from the world. (1 John 2:15-16)

2. He obeys God's commandments. He believes God and he loves God; therefore, he obeys God. The proof that he loves God is seen in his obedience.

⇒ He loves God enough to want to please God.
⇒ He loves God enough to want God's approval.
⇒ He loves God enough to want God to accept him.

The person pleases God by doing what God says. He receives God's approval and acceptance by obeying God. Therefore, he dedicates his life to obey God's commandments. He refuses to accept the mark of the beast; he rejects the beast and follows God. Therefore, he will escape the coming judgment.

"Not everyone who says to me, 'Lord, Lord,' will enter the kingdom of heaven, but only he who does the will of my Father who is in heaven. (Mat 7:21)

"Therefore everyone who hears these words of mine and puts them into practice is like a wise man who built his house on the rock. The rain came down, the streams rose, and the winds blew and beat against that house; yet it did not fall, because it had its foundation on the rock. But everyone who hears these words of mine and does not put them into practice is like a foolish man who built his house on sand. The rain came down, the streams rose, and the winds blew and beat against that house, and it fell with a great crash." (Mat 7:24-27)

Jesus replied, "If anyone loves me, he will obey my teaching. My Father will love him, and we will come to him and make our home with him. (John 14:23)

If you obey my commands, you will remain in my love, just as I have obeyed my Father's commands and remain in his love. You are my friends if you do what I command. (John 15:10, 14)

Peter and the other apostles replied: "We must obey God rather than men! (Acts 5:29)

"Blessed are those who wash their robes, that they may have the right to the tree of life and may go through the gates into the city. (Rev 22:14)

3. He remains faithful to Jesus. He believes in Jesus Christ, that Jesus Christ is the Son of God who died for his sins. The believer has, therefore, dedicated his life to follow Jesus Christ. He has cast himself upon and put his faith in Jesus Christ. He has cast his life and destiny into the hands of Christ, not into the hands of the antichrist and his government. Therefore, he will escape the coming judgment of God.

That everyone who believes in him may have eternal life. (John 3:15)

"I tell you the truth, whoever hears my word and believes him who sent me has eternal life and will not be condemned; he has crossed over from death to life. (John 5:24)

Jesus said to her, "I am the resurrection and the life. He who believes in me will live, even though he dies; (John 11:25)

But these are written that you may believe that Jesus is the Christ, the Son of God, and that by believing you may have life in his name. (John 20:31)

For everyone born of God overcomes the world. This is the victory that has overcome the world, even our faith. Who is it that overcomes the world? Only he who believes that Jesus is the Son of God. (1 John 5:4-5)

That if you confess with your mouth, "Jesus is Lord," and believe in your heart that God raised him from the dead, you will be saved. For it is with your heart that you believe and are justified, and it is with your mouth that you confess and are saved. (Rom 10:9-10)

| | E. Assurance 5: The Dead Will Be at Rest & Rewarded, 14:13 |
|---|---|
| 1 **Their identity: The dead who are in the Lord** | 13 Then I heard a voice from heaven say, "Write: Blessed are the dead who die in the Lord from now on." "Yes," says the Spirit, "they will rest from their labor, for their deeds will follow them." |
| 2 **Their reward** a. Rest from earthly labors | |
| b. Heavenly work to do for Christ | |

# DIVISION VIII

## THE SEVENTH TRUMPET IN DETAIL (PART III): THE VICTORY OF THE LAMB IS ASSURED, 14:1-20

### E.  Assurance 5: The Dead Will Be at Rest and Rewarded, 14:13

(14:13) **Introduction**: every one of us will die. The day is coming when we will no longer exist here on earth. We will be gone forever. Believers know this: this is the very reason they are willing to separate themselves from the world and to live for Christ. It is the reason they are willing to give all they are and have to Christ and His mission. It is the reason believers do not live in sin, but struggle and fight to conquer the sins and temptations of this life. This is the reason they refuse to deny Christ; the reason they suffer the persecutions of this world, the ridicule, abuse, mockery, strange looks, sneers, isolation, cursing, and sometimes imprisonment and death. Believers know they have a date with death just as all other persons do. Therefore, they give their lives to Jesus Christ. Why? Because Jesus Christ is the Savior and Lord of the world. Jesus Christ and Jesus Christ alone has died for our sins, and He alone can free us from sin. He alone can free us from sin and make us acceptable to God. Jesus Christ alone can give us the right to live forever. Therefore, believers commit their lives to follow Christ. Consequently, they have the most glorious hope; God gives them the greatest promise imaginable. God declares that they shall live forever. This is the fifth great assurance: *the dead shall be at rest and be rewarded by the Lord Jesus Christ.*

1. Their identity: the dead who are in the Lord (v.13).
2. Their reward (v.13).

**1** (14:13) **Death—In Christ—Heaven—Eternal Life:** there are the dead who die *in the Lord.* What does it mean to *die in the Lord?* It means that a person *lived in the Lord* when he was on earth. It means that when he was living, he believed in the Lord Jesus Christ and followed after the Lord with all his heart and life. Therefore when he faced death, he was *in the Lord*: he died *being in the Lord.*

Note this: when a person *truly believes in Christ*, God *places and positions* him *in Christ*, in all that Christ is. Christ lived and died and arose, so to be in Christ means that a person lives, dies, and arises in Christ. The person who believes in Jesus Christ is identified with Christ: that is, he is counted and considered to be "in Christ," reckoned and credited as being "in Christ."

Spelled out in a little more detail, when a person believes *in* Christ, God places and positions the believer "in" Christ. The believer's faith actually causes God to identify the believer *with Christ*, to count the believer...

- as having lived *in* Christ when Christ lived upon earth. Therefore, the believer is counted sinless and righteous because Christ was sinless and righteous.
- as having died *in* Christ. Therefore, the believer never has to die (Jn.3:16). The penalty and condemnation of his sins are already paid for in the death of Christ.
- as having been raised *in* Christ. Therefore, the believer has received the *new life* of Christ. Just as Christ had a new life after His resurrection, even so the believer receives the *new life* of Christ when he believes in Christ. (See outline and notes—Ro.6:2-5. Also see notes and DEEPER STUDY # 2—Ro.4:22; 5:1; 6:14-15.)

To be *in Christ* means that a believer walks and lives in Christ day-by-day. It means that he does not "walk after the flesh, but after the Spirit" (Ro.8:1, 4). It means that denying ungodliness and worldly lusts, he should live soberly, righteously, and godly, in this present world (Tit.2:12). It means that he bears the fruit of the Spirit (Gal.5:22-23). It means that he abides *in* Christ, that he becomes as connected and attached to Christ...

- as members of the body are connected and attached to each other (1 Cor.12:12-27).
- as the branch is connected and attached to the vine (Jn.15:4-7).

From this it is clearly seen that a person who is *in the Lord* lives day by day for the Lord. Therefore, when the day comes that he is to die, he does what he did the day before: he lives for the Lord right on through death. He lives for the Lord while dying. The day of death is but another day for *living in the Lord.* He is *in the Lord* whether living or dying. Therefore, when he dies the most wonderful thing happens to the believer: he never tastes nor experiences death. When the moment comes that he is to pass from this world into the next world, quicker than the eye can blink God transfers him into heaven, into the very presence of the throne of God.

Note one other significant fact: the person who dies in the Lord is declared *blessed*: "Blessed are the dead who die in the Lord." This is the declaration of Scripture.

> **If we live, we live to the Lord; and if we die, we die to the Lord. So, whether we live or die, we belong to the Lord. (Rom 14:8)**
>
> **We are confident, I say, and would prefer to be away from the body and at home with the Lord. (2 Cor 5:8)**
>
> **For to me, to live is Christ and to die is gain. (Phil 1:21)**

He who has an ear, let him hear what the Spirit says to the churches. To him who overcomes, I will give the right to eat from the tree of life, which is in the paradise of God. (Rev 2:7)

Therefore, "they are before the throne of God and serve him day and night in his temple; and he who sits on the throne will spread his tent over them. (Rev 7:15)

"Blessed are those who wash their robes, that they may have the right to the tree of life and may go through the gates into the city. (Rev 22:14)

Even though I walk through the valley of the shadow of death, I will fear no evil, for you are with me; your rod and your staff, they comfort me. (Psa 23:4)

Precious in the sight of the LORD is the death of his saints. (Psa 116:15)

When calamity comes, the wicked are brought down, but even in death the righteous have a refuge. (Prov 14:32)

For the Lord himself will come down from heaven, with a loud command, with the voice of the archangel and with the trumpet call of God, and the dead in Christ will rise first. After that, we who are still alive and are left will be caught up together with them in the clouds to meet the Lord in the air. And so we will be with the Lord forever. Therefore encourage each other with these words. (1 Th 4:16-18)

**2** (14:13)          **Death—Rewards—Believers—Heaven— Eternal Life**: there are the rewards of those who *die in the Lord*. Two great rewards are mentioned.

1. There is the reward of rest from earthly labor. The picture is that of work, labor, and toil; of strenuous work and exhausting labor and fatiguing toil. It is being under pressure, being under so much pressure it is like being in a boiler; of being tense, of being gripped in a vice of tension. The picture is that of laboring so much that one is utterly exhausted and worn out.

⇒ This is the way the believer is to labor in witnessing and ministering for Christ.
⇒ This is the way the believer is to stand up against all the temptations and trials of this life.
⇒ This is the way the believers of the end time are to stand up for Christ and refuse to follow the beast and to
⇒ accept his mark.

When a person is this faithful for Christ, when he is truly *in the Lord*, truly living for the Lord, then he dies in the Lord. And the Lord takes him home to heaven and gives him rest from his labor and toil and exhaustion. But note what the word "rest" (*anapaesontai*) means. It means to be refreshed, revitalized, restirred, recharged, and rejuvenated. It means to be free of all temptations and trials, to be comforted and relaxed while being refreshed and recharged. When we get to heaven, we will be free from all the temptations and trials and labors of this earth. We will also be perfected in body, free from ever getting tired, from aching muscles and headaches and heavy eyes; free from ever becoming exhausted and weary again. We will be perfected: we will live in a perfect society of godliness and righteous-

ness forever and ever. In that glorious day we will rest from all our labors and struggles in this corruptible world.

There the wicked cease from turmoil, and there the weary are at rest. (Job 3:17)

And give relief to you who are troubled, and to us as well. This will happen when the Lord Jesus is revealed from heaven in blazing fire with his powerful angels. (2 Th 1:7)

There remains, then, a Sabbath-rest for the people of God; (Heb 4:9)

Then I heard a voice from heaven say, "Write: Blessed are the dead who die in the Lord from now on." "Yes," says the Spirit, "they will rest from their labor, for their deeds will follow them." (Rev 14:13)

Then the righteous will shine like the sun in the kingdom of their Father. He who has ears, let him hear. (Mat 13:43)

For our light and momentary troubles are achieving for us an eternal glory that far outweighs them all. (2 Cor 4:17)

But our citizenship is in heaven. And we eagerly await a Savior from there, the Lord Jesus Christ, Who, by the power that enables him to bring everything under his control, will transform our lowly bodies so that they will be like his glorious body. (Phil 3:20-21)

When Christ, who is your life, appears, then you also will appear with him in glory. (Col 3:4)

Therefore I endure everything for the sake of the elect, that they too may obtain the salvation that is in Christ Jesus, with eternal glory. (2 Tim 2:10)

2. There is the reward of heavenly work to do. Heaven is not going to be inactivity like so many people think:
⇒ It will not be floating around on a fluffy cloud playing a harp. This would be no way to spend eternity.
⇒ It will not be standing around singing the praises of God all the time. No doubt there will be an unbroken consciousness of God's presence and an unbroken fellowship and communion with Him. But standing around and doing nothing but singing and praising the Lord and doing that on and on and on forever and ever would be no way to spend eternity. Our Lord is worthy of more than just words and music.

Heaven is going to be full of both *worship and service*, and we stress that it will be *service* because of the tendency to ignore the fact. Remember two significant things:
a. Heaven is another dimension of being, another world, the spiritual world which is the real and permanent world. It is the physical world and dimension that is corruptible, that ages, decays, deteriorates, and passes away. The real and permanent world, the spiritual world and dimension, is incorruptible. Therefore, God is going to destroy the heavens and the earth and make a new heavens and earth. He is going to transform the universe into the spiritual dimension of being, into the permanent and incorruptible dimension. This earth and the heavens—all the universe—will be transformed into the spiritual world, into the permanent, incor-

ruptible, and eternal world, into the spiritual dimension of being, the world that lasts forever and ever (cp. 2 Pt.3:10-13). Therefore, when we work and serve Christ in the new heavens and earth, we will never tire nor become exhausted. We will be able to work and serve Christ forever without ever feeling pressure, tension, headaches, or sleepy.

b. Genuine believers are to be made kings and priests in heaven. We are going to rule and reign with Christ, rule and reign under the leadership, direction, and supervision of Christ. Jesus Christ and Scripture make this perfectly clear. Believers shall be rewarded with work to do and be made responsible for position and rule. (See note, pt.2b— Rev.19:7-8 for more discussion.)

**Rewards Dealing with our Nature or State of Being**

⇒ Being adopted, receiving the full rights of sons of God (Gal.4:4-7; 1 Jn.3:1).
⇒ Being made blameless and harmless (Ph.2:15).
⇒ Being given eternal life (Jn.3:16; 1 Tim.6:19).
⇒ Being given lasting possessions (Heb.10:34).
⇒ Being given a glorious body (Ph.3:11, 21; 1 Cor.15:42-44).
⇒ Being given eternal glory and honor and peace (Ro.2:10).
⇒ Being given eternal rest and peace (Heb.4:9; Rev.14:13).
⇒ Being given the blessings of the Lord (Pr.10:22).
⇒ Being given the knowledge of Christ Jesus (Ph.3:8).
⇒ Being given enduring wealth and prosperity (Pr.8:18).
⇒ Being made priests (Rev.20:6).

⇒ Being given a crown that will last forever (1 Cor.9:25).
⇒ Being given a crown of righteousness (2 Tim.4:8).
⇒ Being given a crown of life (Jas.1:12).
⇒ Being given a crown of glory (1 Pt.5:4).

**Rewards Dealing with Work or Position or Rule**

⇒ Being made exalted beings (Rev.7:9-12).
⇒ Being placed in charge of many things (Mt.25:23).
⇒ Being given the Kingdom of God (Jas.2:5; Mt.25:34).
⇒ Being given a position or rule and authority (Lk.12:42-44; Lk.22:28-29; 1 Cor.6:2-3).
⇒ Being given eternal responsibility and joy (Mt.25:21, 23).
⇒ Being given rule and authority over cities (Lk.19:17, 19).
⇒ Being given thrones and the privilege of reigning forever (Rev.20:4; 22:5).
⇒ Being given the privilege of surrounding the throne of God (Rev.7:9-13; 20:4).
⇒ Being made priests (Rev.20:6).
⇒ Being made kings (Rev.1:5; 5:10).

**Rewards Dealing with our Inheritance or Wealth**

⇒ Being made an heir of God (Ro.8:16-17; Tit.3:7).
⇒ Being given an incorruptible inheritance that can never perish, spoil or fade (1 Pt.1:3-4).
⇒ Being given the blessings of the Lord (Pr.10:22).
⇒ Being given enduring wealth and prosperity (Pr.8:18).
⇒ Being given unsearchable riches (Eph.3:8).
⇒ Being given treasures in heaven (Mt.19:21; Lk.12:33).

| | F. Assurance 6: The Glorious Harvest of the Godly Will Take Place, 14:14-16 |
|---|---|
| **1  The harvester: The Son of Man**<br> a. In a white cloud<br><br><br><br> b. Wears a gold crown<br> c. Has a sharp sickle | 14 I looked, and there before me was a white cloud, and seated on the cloud was one "like a son of man" with a crown of gold on his head and a sharp sickle in his hand. |
| **2  The harvest of the earth**<br> a. The angelic cry: The harvest is ripe<br><br><br><br><br><br> b. The harvesting | 15 Then another angel came out of the temple and called in a loud voice to him who was sitting on the cloud, "Take your sickle and reap, because the time to reap has come, for the harvest of the earth is ripe."<br>16 So he who was seated on the cloud swung his sickle over the earth, and the earth was harvested. |

# DIVISION VIII

## THE SEVENTH TRUMPET IN DETAIL (PART III): THE VICTORY OF THE LAMB IS ASSURED, 14:1-20

### F.  Assurance 6: The Glorious Harvest of the Godly Will Take Place, 14:14-16

(14:14-16) **Introduction**: Jesus Christ is going to be victorious over all the ungodly and evil of this world. This is the great announcement of the two angels in this passage. Jesus Christ is going to triumph. In the last days of human history, He is coming back, and He is going to harvest the earth. He is going to reap those who believe in Him and take them on to heaven with Him. But He is going to judge the ungodly and evil of this earth. Christ and His followers will be vindicated: the world will see and know that Christ is truly the Son of God who came to earth to save man. The world is going to know...

- that He was well worth forsaking the world and its pleasures and possessions for.
- that He was well worth following and standing up for.
- that He was well worth even dying for.
- that He was well worth denying oneself for.
- that He was well worth sacrificing everything for.
- that He was well worth suffering persecution for.

When Jesus Christ returns in judgment, the world will know that He is exactly who He claimed to be: the Son of God, the Lord and Majesty of the universe. But it will be too late. He is returning in judgment. He came the first time in mercy and grace to save people. But now, the next time, He returns in glory and majesty to judge the earth. This is the scene of this passage. This is the sixth great assurance to believers: *the day of harvest is coming.* The Lord God is going to reap the earth. The believers are going to be taken home to heaven to live with God and Christ forever. And all the ungodly and evil are to be judged and shut out from God's presence. There is to be a perfect world in which nothing reigns but godliness and righteousness. God is going to create a new heavens and earth, and believers are to have the glorious privilege of living there with God forever and ever. This is the scene of this passage: *the great day of earth's* *harvest, the glorious harvest of God's dear people, the harvest of the earth will take place.*

1. The harvester: the Son of Man (v.14).
2. The harvest of the earth (v.15-16).

**1** (14:14) **Jesus—Jesus Christ, Return**: there is the harvester of the earth, the Son of Man Himself. The Son of Man is Jesus Christ. Jesus Christ is not only what an ordinary man is, a son of man; Jesus Christ is what every man ought to be, the Son of Man Himself. When He came to earth, He suffered through all the temptations and trials of life just as all men do. But there was one vast difference: Jesus Christ never sinned. He was sinless. Therefore, He is the Ideal Man, the Representative Man, the Perfect Man, the embodiment of everything a man ought to be. Jesus Christ is the perfect picture of a man. Everything that God wants a man to be is seen perfectly in Jesus Christ.

The title also stresses the Ideal Servant of man. When Jesus Christ came to earth, He loved and cared for the poor, the broken-hearted, the captive, the blind, the bruised, the outcast, the bereaved. Jesus Christ is the perfect and ideal example of concern and caring. He secured and set an example of how every person ought to serve others.

But note: people do not believe this. They do not believe that God sent His Son into the world to save them. People reject Jesus Christ as the sinless Son of God, as the perfect Son of Man, as the ideal of what all sons of men should be. Some are willing to accept Him as a great teacher and religious leader, but they rebel against, deny, and even curse Him as the Son of Man. This is the reason Jesus Christ is going to return to earth as the Son of Man: to vindicate exactly who He is. The world is going to know that the Man Jesus, the carpenter from Nazareth, is the very One whom God sent to set the pattern for all men, the pattern of how we should live and minister to others. God sent His Son Jesus to be *the Son of Man* for all men. And when He returns, all men will know it, for He shall return as *the Son of Man.*

Now, note how He will return.

1. Jesus Christ shall return in a white cloud: white symbolizes the purity of heaven. He will be coming...

- from the world of purity and godliness.
- in the purity and godliness of heaven.
- to bring purity and godliness to the whole universe.

2. Jesus Christ shall return wearing a gold crown. Gold symbolizes value and preciousness, and the crown symbolizes royalty, rule, dominion, and sovereignty. Jesus Christ is coming to take His rightful place in the world, to conquer all the ungodliness and evil of the world and to bring the rule and reign of God to the universe. Nothing could be any more precious nor of any more value than the rule of God upon earth. Life in God's new heavens and earth will be the most precious and valuable experience imaginable.

3. Jesus Christ shall return with a sharp sickle in His hand. The sickle is a sharp tool with a long knife-like edge used to harvest the grain of the fields. This is a picture of judgment. In the end time when Jesus Christ returns, He will be returning with the sickle in His hand. He will be returning to judge the world.

> **If anyone is ashamed of me and my words in this adulterous and sinful generation, the Son of Man will be ashamed of him when he comes in his Father's glory with the holy angels." (Mark 8:38)**
>
> **For as the Father has life in himself, so he has granted the Son to have life in himself. And he has given him authority to judge because he is the Son of Man. (John 5:26-27)**
>
> **"Look," he said, "I see heaven open and the Son of Man standing at the right hand of God." (Acts 7:56)**
>
> **For he has set a day when he will judge the world with justice by the man he has appointed. He has given proof of this to all men by raising him from the dead." (Acts 17:31)**
>
> **And give relief to you who are troubled, and to us as well. This will happen when the Lord Jesus is revealed from heaven in blazing fire with his powerful angels. He will punish those who do not know God and do not obey the gospel of our Lord Jesus. (2 Th 1:7-8)**
>
> **Enoch, the seventh from Adam, prophesied about these men: "See, the Lord is coming with thousands upon thousands of his holy ones To judge everyone, and to convict all the ungodly of all the ungodly acts they have done in the ungodly way, and of all the harsh words ungodly sinners have spoken against him." (Jude 1:14-15)**
>
> **Look, he is coming with the clouds, and every eye will see him, even those who pierced him; and all the peoples of the earth will mourn because of him. So shall it be! Amen. (Rev 1:7)**

**2** (14:15-16) **Judgment—Jesus Christ, Return**: there is the harvest of the earth, the separation of believers from the ungodly and evil of the earth. The scene is spectacular and

awesome: there is Jesus Christ hovering over the earth with a sickle in His hand, and in a moment's time every eye sees Him. The sight is wonderful and glorious to believers, for it means that the great day of their redemption has come. But it means fear and horror to unbelievers, for it means that the great day of God's wrath has come to fall upon them. Note two significant things.

1. First, note that the harvest of the earth will be ripe. Another angel comes out of the temple of God, that is, out of heaven itself. This means that he comes from the very presence of God and is bringing the very message of God. What he has to say is from God Himself. What is the message? The harvest of the earth is ripe. The time for God's Son, the Son of Man, to reap has come. Therefore, the shout of the angel is, "Take *your* sickle and reap!"

Note that the reference is to Christ Himself. It is time for Him to reap *His harvest*, those who belong to Him. It is time for Him to separate His own followers from the ungodly and evil and to take His followers to be with Him. Keep in mind that this is speaking of the end time, right before the world is to end. The believers, the followers of Christ upon earth during those days, will have suffered enough at the hands of the antichrist and a godless world. The heart of Christ—as much as He longs for all persons to be saved, as much as He may wish to continue to be patient so that one more person might be saved—can take no more. He cannot bear the ungodliness and evil against His people and against Himself any longer. It is time, time for the great day of *His harvest*, time to reap the fruit He has borne, time to take His dear servants home to heaven, His dear servants who have borne so much trial and so many temptations.

2. Second, note that the harvest takes place (v.16). Jesus Christ "swings his sickle over the earth; and the earth was harvested." The believers are harvested; they are taken out of the world and away from its ungodliness and evil. They are harvested to be with Christ forever and ever. They are delivered and freed from all the toil and sufferings of this earth. Never again will a believer...

- suffer due to the mistreatment of an ungodly person.
- suffer due to hunger or cold or heat.
- suffer due to disease or accident.
- suffer due to toil and exhaustion.
- suffer due to temptation and trial.
- suffer due to sin and ungodliness and evil and death.

Never again will the believer suffer a single tear. The believers of the end time, those dear people who trust and stand for Christ against the antichrist and his godless society—all believers are going to be harvested and taken home to heaven to be with Christ forever and ever. Christ is going to join us together: us and all of our dear loved ones who have gone before and all of the tribulation saints. Jesus Christ is going to take us all and form one great massive society with which He is going to populate the new heavens and earth. We—all believers of all time—are to be the citizens of the new heavens and earth. We are to be the *servants* of God and Christ, the servants who oversee the operation of the universe for God.

Now note: this is the picture of the believers of the end time being harvested. This is the picture of their being taken up from off the earth and taken into the shelter of heaven, taken out of the stormy and violent weather of a godless world. This is the picture of the wheat being separated from the tares, the picture of the Son of Man reaping His harvest, His fruit, His people. This is exactly what Christ and Scripture say.

Let both grow together until the harvest. At that time I will tell the harvesters: First collect the weeds and tie them in bundles to be burned; then gather the wheat and bring it into my barn.'" (Mat 13:30)

This is how it will be at the end of the age. The angels will come and separate the wicked from the righteous (Mat 13:49)

All the nations will be gathered before him, and he will separate the people one from another as a shepherd separates the sheep from the goats. (Mat 25:32)

His winnowing fork is in his hand to clear his threshing floor and to gather the wheat into his barn, but he will burn up the chaff with unquenchable fire." (Luke 3:17)

And besides all this, between us and you a great chasm has been fixed, so that those who want to go from here to you cannot, nor can anyone cross over from there to us.' (Luke 16:26)

Misfortune pursues the sinner, but prosperity is the reward of the righteous. (Prov 13:21)

| | | G. Assurance 7: The Terrible Harvest of the Ungodly Will Take Place, 14:17-20 | clusters of grapes from the earth's vine, because its grapes are ripe." | 2) Cries out for judgment to begin |
|---|---|---|---|---|
| | | | 19 The angel swung his sickle on the earth, gathered its grapes and threw them into the great winepress of God's wrath. | b. The terror of God's wrath |
| **1** | **The harvester: A great angel** a. Comes out of the temple b. Has a sharp sickle | 17 Another angel came out of the temple in heaven, and he too had a sharp sickle. | | |
| **2** | **The terror of the harvest of the ungodly** a. The terror of the angelic cry 1) Has the power of the fire of judgment | 18 Still another angel, who had charge of the fire, came from the altar and called in a loud voice to him who had the sharp sickle, "Take your sharp sickle and gather the | 20 They were trampled in the winepress outside the city, and blood flowed out of the press, rising as high as the horses' bridles for a distance of 1,600 stadia. | **3** | **The terror of Armageddon, the place where the wrath of God falls** a. Outside the city (Jerusalem) b. A horrifying judgment: Complete & thorough |

# DIVISION VIII

## THE SEVENTH TRUMPET IN DETAIL (PART III): THE VICTORY OF THE LAMB IS ASSURED, 14:1-20

## G.  Assurance 7: The Terrible Harvest of the Ungodly Will Take Place, 14:17-20

(14:17-20) **Introduction**: the great day of earth's harvest is coming, the harvest of the ungodly and evil of this world. Jesus Christ is going to judge all the ungodly and evil of this world. Not a single person will escape. And He is going to judge them in wrath, not in love. The day is coming when the world will be ripe for judgment, a day when ungodliness and evil will be cut totally loose and run rampant upon earth. Horrors of lawlessness and evil and murder will run so wild that Christ cannot take it anymore. The people of the world will be engulfed in idolatry, murder, sorcery, immorality, and stealing. They will be materialistic and worldly, atheistic and God-rejecting: there will be no hope whatsoever that they will ever change and turn to God. There is coming a time when the situation upon earth is utterly hopeless and helpless. When that day comes, then comes the *great tribulation* of the earth. And in the end of that *great tribulation*, in the very last day of world history, Jesus Christ shall reap the earth. The last passage looked at the reaping of the godly. This passage looks at the reaping of the ungodly and evil of this world. This is *the great day of earth's harvest; the terrible harvest of the ungodly and evil of this world will take place.*

1. The harvester: a great angel (v.17).
2. The terror of the harvest of the ungodly (v.18-19).
3. The terror of Armageddon, the place where the wrath of God falls (v.20).

**1** (14:17) **Judgment—Ungodly—End Time**: there is the harvester, a great angel.

⇒ He comes out of the temple of God. This means he is from heaven, from God, from the very presence of God and on a special mission for God.
⇒ He holds a sharp sickle in his hand, the threshing tool of the farmer or vineyard keeper.

**2** (14:18-19) **Judgment—Ungodly—Unbelievers**: there is the terror of the harvest of the ungodly.

1. There will be the terror of the angelic cry. This is a second angel, but he does not come from God's presence. He comes from the altar of incense, that is, from the altar where the prayers of God's people are kept, and where the martyred saints of Christ are stationed in heaven. Remember: there have been millions of believers martyred down through the centuries, and there will be millions more martyred in the end time. Through all of their suffering they

were praying for the same thing for which we pray: for God's kingdom to come to earth, for righteousness and justice and love to rule upon earth. When this angel appears, he symbolizes that these prayers of God's people are about to be answered. The Lord Jesus Christ is now ready to rid the world of all the ungodly and evil. Note two things.

a. The angel has the power of fire. This means that the fire of God's judgment is to be cast upon the earth and all unbelievers are to be consumed.
b. The angel cries out for judgment to begin. Note how the ungodly and evil of the earth are said to be clusters of grapes hanging on the vine of the earth. There are two vines in the earth: the vine of Jesus Christ and the vine of the world.

⇒ Jesus Christ said that He is the vine and His followers are the branches.

> **"I am the vine; you are the branches. If a man remains in me and I in him, he will bear much fruit; apart from me you can do nothing. (John 15:5)**

⇒ This passage also says that the earth has a vine, a vine of worldliness and ungodliness and evil, a vine that will reach its full growth in the end time in the antichrist and his followers.

> **Still another angel, who had charge of the fire, came from the altar and called in a loud voice to him who had the sharp sickle, "Take your sharp sickle and gather the clusters of grapes from the earth's vine, because its grapes are ripe." (Rev 14:18)**

**Thought 1.** A person chooses upon which vine he will hang. He chooses which cluster of grapes he wishes to be a part: the followers of Jesus Christ or the followers of the world and of the antichrist, the followers of righteousness or the followers of the ungodly and evil.

> **As soon as the grain is ripe, he puts the sickle to it, because the harvest has come." (Mark 4:29)**
> **Multitudes, multitudes in the valley of decision! For the day of the LORD is near in the valley of decision. (Joel 3:14)**

**For he says, "In the time of my favor I heard you, and in the day of salvation I helped you." I tell you, now is the time of God's favor, now is the day of salvation. (2 Cor 6:2)**

2. There will be the time of God's wrath. This is a frightening picture of terror and horror, of the terrible judgment to come.

**The angel swung his sickle on the earth, gathered its grapes and threw them into the great winepress of God's wrath. (Rev 14:19)**

The angel lifts the sickle high into the air and with the swift stroke of God's omnipotent power, he swings the sickle of eternal judgment into the earth. The vine of the earth is cut, all the ungodly and evil of the earth are...

- cut down and gathered together.
- cast into the winepress of God's wrath.

What is the winepress of God's wrath? The winepress was a trough usually made out of either stone or brick that was placed over a large vat. The grapes off the vine were placed into the trough. People would trample the grapes and the juice would flow through holes in the bottom of the trough into the vat underneath.

This is a graphic picture of the wrath of God. God's wrath will be like the trampling of grapes underfoot. The picture is that of no mercy, no compromise, and no grace. The picture is twofold.

a. The trampling of the grapes was deliberate. It was purposeful. It was to get the juice out of the grapes not to save the grapes. There was no love, no compassion, no feelings for the grapes. The grapes were to be trampled underfoot. This will be the wrath of God. God's wrath will be deliberate and purposeful. It will be to execute perfect justice upon the ungodly and evil of this world. There will be no love, no compassion, no mercy, no feelings extended out in the terrible day of the harvest of the earth. All persons, every single one of us, will stand before God who is perfectly just, who in His perfection of justice must execute justice upon all persons. All the ungodly and evil of this world will be cast into the winepress of God's wrath and trampled underfoot without any compassion or mercy.

b. The trampling of the grapes was thorough. The clusters of grapes were trampled and trampled until every single grape was crushed. So shall the wrath of God be. God's wrath will be thorough. Not a single person shall escape the wrath of God. All the ungodly and evil of this world shall be placed in the winepress of God's holy wrath. God's wrath will execute perfect justice. God will be totally unlike man: He will show no partiality, no favoritism, and no discrimination. God will see that all persons receive exactly what they deserve, exactly what their works were upon earth. God will see that every unjust and ungodly and evil act against God and others is repaid—measured out exactly on the basis of what each person did. God's wrath will be *perfect retribution*. No ungodly person will be judged for anything that he did not do. But he will be judged for what he did do. The ungodly and evil are guilty: they never trusted Jesus Christ to bear the guilt of their ungodliness and evil for them.

Therefore, they must bear the guilt themselves; they must suffer the wrath of God. And the wrath of God is going to trample underfoot all the ungodly and evil of this world.

**The angel swung his sickle on the earth, gathered its grapes and threw them into the great winepress of God's wrath. (Rev 14:19)**
**Out of his mouth comes a sharp sword with which to strike down the nations. "He will rule them with an iron scepter." He treads the winepress of the fury of the wrath of God Almighty. (Rev 19:15)**
**Whoever believes in the Son has eternal life, but whoever rejects the Son will not see life, for God's wrath remains on him." (John 3:36)**
**The wrath of God is being revealed from heaven against all the godlessness and wickedness of men who suppress the truth by their wickedness, (Rom 1:18)**
**But for those who are self-seeking and who reject the truth and follow evil, there will be wrath and anger. (Rom 2:8)**
**Let no one deceive you with empty words, for because of such things God's wrath comes on those who are disobedient. (Eph 5:6)**
**By the same word the present heavens and earth are reserved for fire, being kept for the day of judgment and destruction of ungodly men. (2 Pet 3:7)**
**Enoch, the seventh from Adam, prophesied about these men: "See, the Lord is coming with thousands upon thousands of his holy ones To judge everyone, and to convict all the ungodly of all the ungodly acts they have done in the ungodly way, and of all the harsh words ungodly sinners have spoken against him." (Jude 1:14-15)**
**Kiss the Son, lest he be angry and you be destroyed in your way, for his wrath can flare up in a moment. Blessed are all who take refuge in him. (Psa 2:12)**
**"I have trodden the winepress alone; from the nations no one was with me. I trampled them in my anger and trod them down in my wrath; their blood spattered my garments, and I stained all my clothing. (Isa 63:3)**

**3** (14:20) **Armageddon—Judgment**: there is the terror of Armageddon, the place where the wrath of God is to fall. Note two significant points.

1. The winepress of God's judgment is trampled down *"outside the city." "The city"* always refers to Jerusalem. This is a reference to what the Bible and believers call...

- the great battle of Armageddon
- the great day of the Lord
- the final battle of human history
- the judgment of God upon the ungodly and evil of this world
- the end of Satan's rule upon earth

This is a picture of the armed forces of the world gathering outside Jerusalem under the leadership of the antichrist. They are there in all their earthly glory and might, or so they think. While there, the midnight hour of judgment strikes. The time for God's eternal judgment and wrath to fall comes, and the quickest defeat in human history occurs against the greatest army every amassed by man. The antichrist and the armies of his military might are destroyed by the very Word of the Lord's mouth and by the glory of His appearance. Second Thessalonians graphically describes the scene (see note—2 Th.2:8).

2. Note what the horrifying scene will look like: blood will flow out of the winepress of God's wrath and the blood will be as deep as two feet in some places. The distance that the blood will flow is said to be about 184 miles—about the length of Palestine. The picture being painted is that of a *thorough judgment*. The army of the ungodly in all their glory and might will be immediately and thoroughly destroyed by the winepress of God's wrath. (See notes—Rev.16:12-16; 19:17-21 for more discussion.)

⇒ Isaiah graphically pictures the scene.

> Who is this coming from Edom, from Bozrah, with his garments stained crimson? Who is this, robed in splendor, striding forward in the greatness of his strength? "It is I, speaking in righteousness, mighty to save." Why are your garments red, like those of one treading the winepress? "I have trodden the winepress alone; from the nations no one was with me. I trampled them in my anger and trod them down in my wrath; their blood spattered my garments, and I stained all my clothing. For the day of vengeance was in my heart, and the year of my redemption has come. I looked, but there was no one to help, I was appalled that no one gave support; so my own arm worked salvation for me, and my own wrath sustained me. I trampled the nations in my anger; in my wrath I made them drunk and poured their blood on the ground." (Isa 63:1-6)

⇒ Joel graphically pictures the scene.

> Proclaim this among the nations: Prepare for war! Rouse the warriors! Let all the fighting men draw near and attack. Beat your plowshares into swords and your pruning hooks into spears. Let the weakling say, 'I am strong!' Come quickly, all you nations from every side, and assemble there. Bring down your warriors, O LORD! 'Let the nations be roused; let them advance into the Valley of Jehoshaphat, for there I will sit to judge all the nations on every side. Swing the sickle, for the harvest is ripe. Come, trample the grapes, for the winepress is full and the vats overflow— so great is their wickedness!' Multitudes, multitudes in the valley of decision! For the day of the LORD is near in the valley of decision. The sun and moon will be darkened, and the stars no longer shine. The LORD will roar from Zion and thunder from Jerusalem; the earth and the sky will tremble. But the LORD will be a refuge for his people, a stronghold for the people of Israel. 'Then you will know that I, the LORD your God, dwell in Zion, my holy hill. Jerusalem will be holy; never again will foreigners invade her. (Joel 3:9-17)

⇒ The Revelation graphically pictures the scene.

> He is dressed in a robe dipped in blood, and his name is the Word of God. The armies of heaven were following him, riding on white horses and dressed in fine linen, white and clean. Out of his mouth comes a sharp sword with which to strike down the nations. "He will rule them with an iron scepter." He treads the winepress of the fury of the wrath of God Almighty. On his robe and on his thigh he has this name written: KING OF KINGS AND LORD OF LORDS. And I saw an angel standing in the sun, who cried in a loud voice to all the birds flying in midair, "Come, gather together for the great supper of God, So that you may eat the flesh of kings, generals, and mighty men, of horses and their riders, and the flesh of all people, free and slave, small and great." Then I saw the beast [antichrist] and the kings of the earth and their armies gathered together to make war against the rider on the horse and his army. But the beast was captured, and with him the false prophet who had performed the miraculous signs on his behalf. With these signs he had deluded those who had received the mark of the beast and worshiped his image. The two of them were thrown alive into the fiery lake of burning sulfur. The rest of them were killed with the sword that came out of the mouth of the rider on the horse, and all the birds gorged themselves on their flesh. (Rev 19:13-21)

⇒ Second Thessalonians graphically describes the scene.

> And then the lawless one will be revealed, whom the Lord Jesus will overthrow with the breath of his mouth [His Word] and destroy by the splendor of his coming [His glory]. The coming of the lawless one will be in accordance with the work of Satan displayed in all kinds of counterfeit miracles, signs and wonders, And in every sort of evil that deceives those who are perishing. They perish because they refused to love the truth and so be saved. For this reason God sends them a powerful delusion so that they will believe the lie And so that all will be condemned who have not believed the truth but have delighted in wickedness. (2 Th 2:8-12)

CHAPTER 15

IX. THE SEVENTH TRUM-
PET IN DETAIL (PART
IV): THE THIRD
GREAT WONDER,
THE SEVEN BOWL
JUDGMENTS, 15:1-
16:21

A. The Heavenly Prepara-
tion for Judgment, 15:1-8

1 **The sign of judgment in heaven**

2 **The reason for the judgment: Believers will be martyred by the beast or antichrist**
a. Will be before the throne of God on the sea of glass
b. Will be victorious over the antichrist
c. Will be given harps: Rest & praise
d. Will sing the songs of victory
  1) To the Almighty God: For His works

I saw in heaven another great and marvelous sign: seven angels with the seven last plagues—last, because with them God's wrath is completed.
2 And I saw what looked like a sea of glass mixed with fire and, standing beside the sea, those who had been victorious over the beast and his image and over the number of his name. They held harps given them by God
3 And sang the song of Moses the servant of God and the song of the Lamb: "Great and marvelous are your deeds, Lord God Almighty. Just and true are your ways, King of the ages.
4 Who will not fear you, O Lord, and bring glory to your name? For you alone are holy. All nations will come and worship before you, for your righteous acts have been revealed."
5 After this I looked and in heaven the temple, that is, the tabernacle of the Testimony, was opened.
6 Out of the temple came the seven angels with the seven plagues. They were dressed in clean, shining linen and wore golden sashes around their chests.
7 Then one of the four living creatures gave to the seven angels seven golden bowls filled with the wrath of God, who lives for ever and ever.
8 And the temple was filled with smoke from the glory of God and from his power, and no one could enter the temple until the seven plagues of the seven angels were completed.

  2) To the King of saints or nations: To the truth & justice of His ways
  3) To the Lord: To the fear & glory of His name
  4) To the holy & righteous God: For all nations shall worship Him

3 **The judgment of God will be sent forth**
a. The door to God's presence is opened
b. The seven angels come out from God's presence with the seven plagues

c. The seven angels are given seven bowls of judgment

d. The door of heaven & of salvation is closed

# DIVISION IX

## THE SEVENTH TRUMPET IN DETAIL (PART IV): THE THIRD GREAT WONDER, THE SEVEN BOWL JUDGMENTS, 15:1-16:21

### A. The Heavenly Preparation for Judgment, 15:1-8

(15:1-8) **Introduction**: Revelation reveals that there is to be a terrible time coming upon the earth in the end time, a time so terrible that Christ Himself described it as the *great distress or the great tribulation* (Mt.24:21). Revelation uses some descriptive language to describe this period of time. It calls the judgments of the period trumpet judgments, picturing the blast of trumpets. There have been seven trumpet judgments altogether. But when the seventh trumpet blasted an amazing thing happened. There was no blast of judgment, not immediately. Instead an over-all picture of the end time was blown forth:

⇒ There was a picture of Israel being chosen as the nation through which God would send His Son into the world, the picture of Jesus Christ coming to the earth as the Savior of the world (Rev.12:1-5).
⇒ There was the picture of the dragon, that ancient serpent, who is called the devil and Satan, working to get men to be ungodly and evil—all because he wants to cut and hurt the heart of God (Rev.12:6-17).
⇒ There was the picture of the antichrist and of his right hand man coming upon the earth, the picture of how they will gain and consolidate power over the whole earth and launch the worst holocaust the world has ever seen (Rev.13:1-18).
⇒ There was the glorious picture of the very end of the world when Jesus Christ triumphs over all the ungodly and evil of this world, the picture of Jesus Christ harvesting the earth, of His taking be-

lievers to heaven with Him and judging unbelievers (Rev.14:1-20).

Now, the seventh trumpet blasts forth its judgments. And the judgments come fast and furious. Why? Because they are the very last judgments. God has decided to end human history. He has decided to stop all the ungodliness and evil of the earth. He can no longer take the rebellion, denial, cursing, immorality, stealing, drunkenness, sorcery (magical acts), and murder of man. Therefore, Jesus Christ will destroy all the ungodly and evil of this world and do it quickly. Remember: the whole tribulation period will last seven years. It will be divided into two periods: the first period will be three and one half years and is called *the beginning of birth pains or the beginning of sorrows*. The last period will also be three and one half years and is called *the great tribulation*.

⇒ When the tribulation begins, during the first three and one half years, there will be seven seal judgments that will take place upon earth (Rev.6:1-7:17).
⇒ When the *great tribulation* itself begins, the final three and one half years, there will be seven trumpet judgments that will take place upon earth (Rev.8:1-14:20).
⇒ Then, at the very end of the tribulation period, there will be seven more judgments, the seven bowl judgments. The bowl judgments will end human history as we know it.

This passage is the heavenly preparation for judgment. This is the preparation that will be made for the launch of the judgments that will end all the ungodliness and evil of man upon earth.

1. The sign of judgment in heaven (v.1).
2. The reason for the judgment: believers will be martyred by the beast or antichrist (v.2-4).
3. The judgment of God will be sent forth (v.5-8).

**1** (15:1) **Heaven—Wrath, God's**: there is the sign of God's judgment in heaven. The scene in heaven strikes reverence in the human heart. Note: the scene in heaven is said to be a sign:

⇒ a sign that is great and awesome
⇒ a sign of seven mighty angels or messengers prepared to go forth for God
⇒ a sign of seven plagues that are said to be the *last plagues*
⇒ a sign of God's wrath

This awesome sign in heaven is intended to stir people to bow before God who is *just*. God is love, but God is also just. And His justice is ready to be executed upon earth. His wrath against all the ungodly and evil upon this earth is ready to fall. God is ready to clean up the earth and to bring the reign of godliness and righteousness, love and joy, peace and glory. Therefore, man must prepare: repent and get ready before it is too late.

> **And saying, "Repent, for the kingdom of heaven is near." (Mat 3:2)**
> **I tell you, no! But unless you repent, you too will all perish. (Luke 13:3)**
> **Repent of this wickedness and pray to the Lord. Perhaps he will forgive you for having such a thought in your heart. (Acts 8:22)**
> **Let the wicked forsake his way and the evil man his thoughts. Let him turn to the LORD, and he will have mercy on him, and to our God, for he will freely pardon. (Isa 55:7)**

**2** (15:2-4) **End Time—Believers**: there is the reason for the judgment. Believers will be slaughtered by the beast or antichrist. This explains why the wrath of God is going to fall upon the earth in the last days. The beast, the antichrist, will launch the worst holocaust the world has ever seen. Literally millions of believers will be slaughtered during his rule upon earth. These verses show these dear believers in heaven. Note four things about them.

1. The martyred believers will be on the sea of glass that stretches out before the throne of God itself (cp. Rev.4:6). Note that the glass is mingled with fire. This symbolizes...

- the *fire of persecution* these dear believers went through.
- the *fire of judgment* that is about to fall upon the ungodly and evil of the earth.

2. The martyred believers will be victorious over the antichrist. They...

- will not worship his image (Rev.13:15).
- will not receive his mark (Rev.13:16-17).
- will not receive the number of his name, the number of 666 (Rev.13:18).

True believers in the end time will not follow the antichrist. They will refuse to worship the state and its leader.

Therefore, the leader and his government will prosecute and kill the believers as revolutionaries against the government. Remember, the holocaust will not cover just a local nation or even several nations as all genocides have in the past. The holocaust of the end time will be *worldwide*. There will be millions more than ever before slaughtered in the most cruel and savage ways imaginable. They will be slaughtered because they are falsely accused of being enemies of the state. The result will be that God can take it no more. He is going to step in and stop the foolishness and evil of men. He is going to stop the evil rule of man upon this earth.

3. The martyred believers will possess harps. The harps are symbols of being soothed and given rest and of praising and worshipping God. God will soothe the hurt and pain of the martyred believers and give them rest, and they will praise and worship Him.

4. The martyred believers will sing two great songs of victory: the song of the Lamb and the song of Moses that was sung by the children of Israel when they crossed the Red Sea (Ex.15:1-19). Note what they sing.

a. They sing to the Almighty God, praising His works.

> **And [they] sang the song of Moses the servant of God and the song of the Lamb: "Great and marvelous are your deeds, Lord God Almighty. (Rev 15:3a)**

b. They sing to the King of the ages, to the justice and truth of His ways.

> **Just and true are your ways, King of the ages. (Rev 15:3b)**

c. They sing to the Lord, to the fear and glory of His name.

> **Who will not fear you, O Lord, and bring glory to your name? (Rev 15:4a)**

d. They sing to the holy and just God, for all nations shall come and worship Him because He is going to judge the earth.

> **For you alone are holy. All nations will come and worship before you, for your righteous acts have been revealed." (Rev. 4b). (Note that the millennial reign of Christ is being referred to in this statement of praise.)**

**Thought 1.** The persons who stand up for Jesus Christ against the temptations and trials of this life are the persons who will be in heaven. But to be in heaven we must stand up for Christ. We must never accept the marks of this world or be identified among the number of unbelievers. We must be diligent and bear only the marks of Christ.

> **All men will hate you because of me, but he who stands firm to the end will be saved. (Mat 10:22)**
> **Therefore, my dear brothers, stand firm. Let nothing move you. Always give yourselves fully to the work of the Lord, because you know that your labor in the Lord is not in vain. (1 Cor 15:58)**
> **Blessed is the man who perseveres under trial, because when he has stood the test, he will receive the crown of life that God has**

promised to those who love him. (James 1:12)

Therefore, dear friends, since you already know this, be on your guard so that you may not be carried away by the error of lawless men and fall from your secure position. (2 Pet 3:17)

For everyone born of God overcomes the world. This is the victory that has overcome the world, even our faith. Who is it that overcomes the world? Only he who believes that Jesus is the Son of God. (1 John 5:4-5)

He who has an ear, let him hear what the Spirit says to the churches. To him who overcomes, I will give the right to eat from the tree of life, which is in the paradise of God. (Rev 2:7)

To him who overcomes and does my will to the end, I will give authority over the nations— (Rev 2:26)

He who overcomes will, like them, be dressed in white. I will never blot out his name from the book of life, but will acknowledge his name before my Father and his angels. (Rev 3:5)

Him who overcomes I will make a pillar in the temple of my God. Never again will he leave it. I will write on him the name of my God and the name of the city of my God, the new Jerusalem, which is coming down out of heaven from my God; and I will also write on him my new name. (Rev 3:12)

To him who overcomes, I will give the right to sit with me on my throne, just as I overcame and sat down with my Father on his throne. (Rev 3:21)

He who overcomes will inherit all this, and I will be his God and he will be my son. (Rev 21:7)

**3** (15:5-8) **Judgment—Wrath, of God:** there will be the judgment of God sent forth. Note four things.

1. The door to the "tabernacle of the Testimony" is opened up (v.5). The "tabernacle of the Testimony" refers to the inner sanctuary of the tabernacle in the Old Testament, that is, to the *Holy of Holies* or the *Most Holy Place*. The picture is this: the judgment of God will come from the *Most Holy Place*, from the very presence and heart of God Himself. His presence and heart will have been violated and polluted enough by sin and evil. Therefore, His presence and heart will be vindicated. God Himself will send forth His final judgment upon the antichrist and his ungodly followers.

2. The seven angels come out from the *Most Holy Place*, out from God's own presence, and they are awesome creatures (v.6). The scene is terrifying, for...

- they hold the seven plagues in their hands.
- they are dressed in pure and white—clean and shining—linen, the symbol of the *holiness of heaven*. God's holiness, His righteousness, and His justice are now to be exercised and brought to this world, to rule and reign throughout the whole earth.
- they have gold belts, the symbol of royalty and authority and power. God has the right and power as the Sovereign King of the universe to execute justice.

3. The seven angels are given seven gold bowls that are fitted with the wrath of God (v.7). The idea of bowls is that there is no lid or covering on the bowls. They will be poured out upon the earth quickly and efficiently. And every effort to stop the judgment and wrath of God will only result in their being splashed or spilt upon the antagonist. That is, nothing will be able to stop the bowl judgments of God. God will be ready to stop the ungodly and evil of this world. And note: He has the right to judge the world. He is the One who lives forever and ever. He and He alone is God. Therefore, His wrath is going to fall upon all who have refused to drink the cup of His salvation.

⇒ There is the cup of salvation.

> **I will lift up the cup of salvation and call on the name of the LORD. (Psa 116:13)**

⇒ There is the cup of wrath and judgment.

> **In the hand of the LORD is a cup full of foaming wine mixed with spices; he pours it out, and all the wicked of the earth drink it down to its very dregs. (Psa 75:8)**

4. The door to the temple of God, to heaven and salvation, will be closed. No one will be able to enter heaven any longer, not until the seven judgments are completed. This is a terrifying thought. When the final judgments begin to fall in the last days, the grace of God will be withdrawn and prayer for mercy will do no good. The door to heaven and salvation will be closed. The judgment of God will be falling upon the antichrist and his ungodly and evil followers. Note how descriptive the scene is pictured: the glory and power of God which shines brighter than the sun itself becomes so furious and hot that smoke begins to arise from their energy. The glory and power of God are energized and flexed to consume the evil of this earth. And no man will be able to enter the temple of God's presence and stop it. It will be too late.

> **Whoever believes in the Son has eternal life, but whoever rejects the Son will not see life, for God's wrath remains on him." (John 3:36)**

> **The wrath of God is being revealed from heaven against all the godlessness and wickedness of men who suppress the truth by their wickedness, (Rom 1:18)**

> **But for those who are self-seeking and who reject the truth and follow evil, there will be wrath and anger. (Rom 2:8)**

> **Let no one deceive you with empty words, for because of such things God's wrath comes on those who are disobedient. (Eph 5:6)**

> **Kiss the Son, lest he be angry and you be destroyed in your way, for his wrath can flare up in a moment. Blessed are all who take refuge in him. (Psa 2:12)**

> **"You have covered yourself with anger and pursued us; you have slain without pity. You have covered yourself with a cloud so that no prayer can get through. (Lam 3:43-44)**

## CHAPTER 16

**B. The Pouring Out of the Bowl Judgments, 16:1-21**

| Outline | Scripture |
|---|---|
| **1 A great voice crying, Go pour out the wrath of God upon the earth** | Then I heard a loud voice from the temple saying to the seven angels, "Go, pour out the seven bowls of God's wrath on the earth." |
| **2 The 1st Bowl: Upon the earth**<br>a. The judgment: Ulcerous sores<br>b. The object: Worshippers of the beast | 2 The first angel went and poured out his bowl on the land, and ugly and painful sores broke out on the people who had the mark of the beast and worshiped his image. |
| **3 The 2nd Bowl: Upon the sea**<br>a. The judgment: The sea becomes as blood<br>b. The object: All sea creatures | 3 The second angel poured out his bowl on the sea, and it turned into blood like that of a dead man, and every living thing in the sea died. |
| **4 The 3rd Bowl: Upon fresh waters**<br>a. The judgment: The waters become as blood<br>b. The object: An unjust, murderous world<br>c. The reason: God executes justice<br><br>1) Because of murder<br><br><br>2) Because God is true & just | 4 The third angel poured out his bowl on the rivers and springs of water, and they became blood.<br>5 Then I heard the angel in charge of the waters say: "You are just in these judgments, you who are and who were, the Holy One, because you have so judged;<br>6 For they have shed the blood of your saints and prophets, and you have given them blood to drink as they deserve."<br>7 And I heard the altar respond: "Yes, Lord God Almighty, true and just are your judgments." |
| **5 The 4th Bowl: Upon the sun**<br>a. The judgment: A scorching heat<br>b. The object: Rebellious & hardened men<br>c. The reaction: Men blame God; they curse & do not repent | 8 The fourth angel poured out his bowl on the sun, and the sun was given power to scorch people with fire.<br>9 They were seared by the intense heat and they cursed the name of God, who had control over these plagues, but they refused to repent and glorify him. |
| **6 The 5th Bowl: Upon the beast's throne or kingdom**<br>a. The judgment: A thick darkness & agony<br>b. The object: The beast & the ungodly<br>c. The reaction: Men | 10 The fifth angel poured out his bowl on the throne of the beast, and his kingdom was plunged into darkness. Men gnawed their tongues in agony<br>11 And cursed the God of heaven because of their pains and their sores, but they re- |
| blame God; they curse & do not repent | fused to repent of what they had done. |
| **7 The 6th Bowl: Upon the Euphrates River**<br>a. The judgment: The Euphrates dried up<br>b. The reason: To allow a great confederated army to cross<br>c. The source or moving spirit behind the confederation: Evil spirits<br><br>d. The day of the event: The great day of God, the Almighty<br><br>e. The great warning of God to His people: Stay awake<br><br><br>f. The place of the great battle: Armageddon | 12 The sixth angel poured out his bowl on the great river Euphrates, and its water was dried up to prepare the way for the kings from the East.<br>13 Then I saw three evil spirits that looked like frogs; they came out of the mouth of the dragon, out of the mouth of the beast and out of the mouth of the false prophet.<br>14 They are spirits of demons performing miraculous signs, and they go out to the kings of the whole world, to gather them for the battle on the great day of God Almighty.<br>15 "Behold, I come like a thief! Blessed is he who stays awake and keeps his clothes with him, so that he may not go naked and be shamefully exposed."<br>16 Then they gathered the kings together to the place that in Hebrew is called Armageddon. |
| **8 The 7th Bowl: In the air**<br>a. God's thundering announcement: It is done<br><br>b. The phenomena of God's glory: Nature breaks loose with violent storms, & a great earthquake completely destroys the godless world & its cities<br><br>1) The just wrath upon Babylon<br><br>2) The breakup of the earth<br><br>3) The great hail storm<br><br>c. The reaction: Men blame God; they curse & do not repent | 17 The seventh angel poured out his bowl into the air, and out of the temple came a loud voice from the throne, saying, "It is done!"<br>18 Then there came flashes of lightning, rumblings, peals of thunder and a severe earthquake. No earthquake like it has ever occurred since man has been on earth, so tremendous was the quake.<br>19 The great city split into three parts, and the cities of the nations collapsed. God remembered Babylon the Great and gave her the cup filled with the wine of the fury of his wrath.<br>20 Every island fled away and the mountains could not be found.<br>21 From the sky huge hailstones of about a hundred pounds each fell upon men. And they cursed God on account of the plague of hail, because the plague was so terrible. |

# DIVISION IX

## THE SEVENTH TRUMPET IN DETAIL (PART IV): THE THIRD GREAT WONDER, THE SEVEN BOWL JUDGMENTS, 15:1-16:21

### B. The Pouring Out of the Bowl Judgments, 16:1-21

(16:1-21) **Introduction**: judgment is coming to this earth, terrifying judgment, judgment of such horror that it staggers human imagination. When? At the end of the world, right at the close of the period of history that the Bible calls the *great tribulation*. There are three terrifying judgments during the last days of human history.

⇒ There will be the seven seal judgments. These will be preliminary judgments, judgments that take place before the great tribulation. They occur during a period of time that Christ called the *beginning of woes*.

⇒ There will be the seven trumpet judgments that take place during the days of the *great tribulation* period.

⇒ There will be the bowl judgments of this passage. As stated, the bowl judgments take place right at the very end of the world, at the very end of the *great tribulation*.

There is to be one terrifying difference between the horrors of the bowl judgments and the other judgments. The seal judgments and the trumpet judgments will be limited judgments, but not the bowl judgments. The bowl judgments are total. Complete and final devastation will fall upon the ungodly and evil of this world under the bowl judgments. The bowl judgments will stop and end man's ungodly and evil ways upon earth.

1. A great voice crying, Go pour out the wrath of God upon the earth (v.1).
2. The 1st Bowl: upon the earth (v.2).
3. The 2nd Bowl: upon the sea (v.3).
4. The 3rd Bowl: upon fresh waters (v.4-7).
5. The 4th Bowl: upon the sun (v.8-9).
6. The 5th Bowl: upon the beast's seat, throne, or kingdom (v.10-11).
7. The 6th Bowl: upon the Euphrates River (v.12-16).
8. The 7th Bowl: in the air (v.17-21).

**1** (16:1) **Voice of God**: there is a great voice shouting out, "Go, pour out the wrath of God upon the earth." This voice must be the voice of God. God alone could give the order to end world history. Note that it is the wrath of God being poured upon the earth. This immediately tells us several things:

⇒ That God is just and righteous. Therefore, we can have confidence that God will right all the wrongs and injustices upon earth.

⇒ That God loves and cares for the earth. He will not allow ungodliness and evil to continue on and on without being stopped.

**2** (16:2) **Judgment—Bowl**: there is the first bowl judgment. It is poured out upon the earth. What is the judgment? Some kind of ulcerous sore. People will be afflicted with some kind of festering, cancerous sore. The idea is...

• that the sores will be harmful and malignant, open and foul; painful and putrefying, ugly and repulsive, humiliating and embarrassing.

• that the sores will cause agony and torture, giving no rest during the day or night.

• that the sores will be incurable and that there will be no relief from the pain.

But note a significant fact: the judgment is poured out only upon the antichrist and his followers, only upon the people who receive the mark of the beast and worship him and his government.

**Thought 1.** Note that the ulcerous sores are something like the judgment of boils that fell upon the Egyptians (Ex.9:8-11; cp. Dt.28:35).

**3** (16:3) **Judgment—Bowl**: there is the second bowl judgment. It is poured out on *the sea*. This probably points to the Mediterranean sea and not to all the oceans of the world. If it meant all the oceans, little human life of any kind could survive. This is especially true in the next judgment. We must always remember that the center of the antichrist's power will be in the Middle East or in some nation of Europe that was part of the old Roman Empire. Therefore, the concentration of judgments will probably be there. The sea will become infected with some kind of blood red contamination and all sea life within it will be killed. Imagine the sight of all sea life washing ashore along the coastlines of the sea, the smell and sight of death everywhere.

⇒ Imagine all the fishing industries and commercial outlets bankrupted and the effect upon the economy. It is all in the process of being destroyed because of the terrible evil of the ungodly of the world.

(Note: many commentators feel this does refer to all the seas of the world, and that the next judgment refers to all the fresh waters of the earth.)

**Thought 1.** There is an example of this in the *red tide* that sometimes strikes the coastlines of the world. When the red tide strikes, it pollutes the water, sometimes for mile after mile. The pollution is sometimes so bad that millions of fish and other sea life are destroyed. Fishing and harvesting of sea life for food are affected for months and sometimes years when the red tide strikes a body of water

The point is this: the red tide shows us that the sea can be contaminated. In the end time God *is going to contaminate the sea*, the whole sea. It is going to be destroyed.

**4** (16:4-7) **Judgment—Bowl**: there is the third bowl judgment. It is poured out on the fresh waters where the antichrist and his followers are concentrated. Again, this must be the meaning. Everyone on earth would die from this if there were no fresh water to drink, die within just a few days. This is the very same judgment that fell upon the sea. But just think for a moment: the effects of fresh water pollution will be much more devastating upon the antichrist and his followers. There will be little water available throughout the Middle East and Europe where his power is concentrated...

• little water for drinking

• no water for washing and bathing

Just think of the water and food that will have to be transported and airlifted into the Middle East and Europe from other parts of the world. As we shall see in a moment, the armed forces will no doubt be supplied first.

Now note something: these judgments are predictions about what is going to happen in the end time. Therefore, there are always people who hear about the judgments and question them because they do not fit in with their idea of God. To them God is too loving and kind to ever do such a thing as pour His wrath out on earth. But note: Jesus Christ knew that there would be objections to these judgments. Therefore, right here in the midst of the third judgment,

Jesus Christ reminds John and all others why God is going to pour out His wrath on the earth and destroy it. What is the reason? Why would God destroy the earth and punish people? For two reasons.

1. First, because of the mass murder that will be launched in the end time (v.16). The antichrist and his followers will launch the most terrible holocaust ever witnessed by the world. Every believer and every Jew and every person who remains loyal to his religion—all who refuse to worship the state and its leader in the end time—they will all be slaughtered. There will be millions heaped upon millions of people slaughtered by the most cruel and inhuman methods imaginable.

2. Second, because God is true and righteous; He is just (v.7). Therefore, in the end time God will be confronted with such horrifying evil that He can no longer take the ungodly and evil of people. God will reach a point when His love for the godly people of the earth and for righteousness cannot take the murderous ways and rejection of people any more. When the holocaust is launched worldwide, He is going to punish the evil doers and end the world.

⇒ They imprisoned and tortured millions; therefore, God is going to punish them with an equal punishment, that of cancerous sores.

⇒ They murdered and shed the blood of millions. Therefore, God is going to punish the evil by allowing a bloody red substance to pollute the sea and the fresh water of the earth.

Note that an angel declares the true and righteous judgment of God. The angel declares that God is perfectly just, that He executes exactly what the ungodly and evil deserve.

> By myself I can do nothing; I judge only as I hear, and my judgment is just, for I seek not to please myself but him who sent me. (John 5:30)
> Now we know that God's judgment against those who do such things is based on truth. (Rom 2:2)
> Like your name, O God, your praise reaches to the ends of the earth; your right hand is filled with righteousness. (Psa 48:10)
> The LORD works righteousness and justice for all the oppressed. (Psa 103:6)
> Righteous are you, O LORD, and your laws are right. (Psa 119:137)
> The LORD is righteous in all his ways and loving toward all he has made. (Psa 145:17)
> Declare what is to be, present it— let them take counsel together. Who foretold this long ago, who declared it from the distant past? Was it not I, the LORD? And there is no God apart from me, a righteous God and a Savior; there is none but me. (Isa 45:21)

**Thought 1.** The rivers of Egypt were polluted by God with some kind of blood red pollution (Ex.7:17-25).

**5** (16:8-9) **Judgment—Bowl**: there is the fourth bowl judgment. It is poured out on the sun. Severe heat and radiation from the sun are going to scorch the ungodly and evil of this earth. There will be a heat wave unlike anything the earth has ever known. The sun will burn and scorch people with a blazing, fierce heat. They will be in misery and tor-

mented and will fret and groan and be miserable. The idea is that the weather will be so hot that it will be like burning in a hot oven.

Note: the ungodly will still not repent. They will do what unbelievers have usually done when things go bad: curse and blaspheme the name of God. It may be the hitting of one's fingers with a hammer or an accident in a car—no matter what it is, the response of the unbeliever is usually to curse and blaspheme. And in the end time it will be no different. The ungodly and evil will not repent any more than they do today. They will only curse the name of God.

> "You stiff-necked people, with uncircumcised hearts and ears! You are just like your fathers: You always resist the Holy Spirit! (Acts 7:51)
> So I told you, but you would not listen. You rebelled against the Lord's command and in your arrogance you marched up into the hill country. (Deu 1:43)
> Although the LORD sent prophets to the people to bring them back to him, and though they testified against them, they would not listen. (2 Chr 24:19)
> They turned their backs to me and not their faces; though I taught them again and again, they would not listen or respond to discipline. (Jer 32:33)
> "We will not listen to the message you have spoken to us in the name of the LORD! (Jer 44:16)
> "But they refused to pay attention; stubbornly they turned their backs and stopped up their ears. (Zec 7:11)

**6** (16:10-11) **Judgment—Bowl**: there is the fifth bowl judgment. It is poured out on the throne of the antichrist. The whole kingdom of the antichrist and his followers will be full of darkness. This is not referring to spiritual darkness, but to some phenomena that blots out the light and heat of the day. Note: this is a drastic change from the scorching light and heat of the fourth judgment. Some darkness, some thick, heavy pitch black darkness will fall upon the whole kingdom of the antichrist, upon him and all who follow him. Note: this judgment seems to exclude the nations who are not actively included in the antichrist's kingdom. Remember: there will be many nations cooperating with the antichrist but who are not actively included in his kingdom, not in the plotting of his murderous evil. They are, of course, guilty by association, guilty because they have formed an alliance with the antichrist. But they are apparently spared some of the judgments because they are not quite as guilty. However, their armies will be destroyed and their governments and cities utterly destroyed at Armageddon— all because they are ungodly and evil in so many other ways. (However, please note: again, this judgment—in fact, all the bowl judgments—could be worldwide. All the world to some degree will be cooperating with the antichrist. He will be sitting at the head of some world organization like the United Nations or the European Common Market. Therefore, the seat and kingdom of the antichrist could refer to the whole world.)

⇒ Joel predicted this heavy, black darkness.

> Blow the trumpet in Zion; sound the alarm on my holy hill. Let all who live in the land tremble, for the day of

204

the LORD is coming. It is close at hand— A day of darkness and gloom, a day of clouds and blackness. Like dawn spreading across the mountains a large and mighty army comes, such as never was of old nor ever will be in ages to come. (Joel 2:1-2)

⇒ Christ predicted that the sun and all other light would be darkened, stricken with pitch black darkness.

"Immediately after the distress of those days "'the sun will be darkened, and the moon will not give its light; the stars will fall from the sky, and the heavenly bodies will be shaken.' (Mat 24:29)

The suffering will be excruciating and gnawing. The suffering of the sores, thirst, filth, and smell of water pollution, scorching heat, and now pitch black darkness will cause the antichrist and his followers to curse and blaspheme more and more. Note that the torment will be so painful and unbearable that they will be gnawing their tongue (v.10). But they will still not repent of their ungodly and evil deeds. They will only become more and more stubborn and hardened in their wickedness and rebellion against God.

**Thought 1.** Thick, heavy, pitch black darkness was also one of the judgments to fall upon Egypt (Ex.10:21-23).

**7** (16:12-16) **Judgment—Bowl**: there is the sixth bowl judgment. It is poured out upon the Euphrates River (cp. Rev.9:13-21). Note verse sixteen quickly: the purpose of this sixth judgment is to prepare the nations and armies of the world for the great battle of Armageddon.

**Then they gathered the kings [the nations] together to the place that in Hebrew is called Armageddon. (Rev 16:16)**

It is a judgment of deception, not of affliction. Armageddon is the last great war of the earth which will be instigated by the antichrist and his government. Note six facts in this sixth bowl judgment.

1. The judgment dries up the great Euphrates River. The Euphrates is the longest and by far the most important river of western Asia. It is 1780 miles long and ranges from 300 to 1200 yards wide. Its depth ranges from about 10 to 30 feet. From the Persian Gulf inland it can be navigated by small vessels for about 1200 miles. How could a river of such enormous size ever be dried up? Today, of course, man can build huge lakes, rivers, and canals such as the Panama Canal. Man can also divert huge lakes and rivers. Remember this: in the end time natural disasters will be increasingly striking the earth. Whole areas of the world will be devastated by the forces of nature going wild. Just how the great Euphrates River will be dried up—by man or by some devastation of nature—is not known. But Scripture clearly says that the waters of the river will be dried up. (Cp. Rev.6:1-8; 6:12-17; 8:6-12; 8:13-9:11; 9:12-21; 13:11-18.)

2. The reason for the drying up of the Euphrates is to allow a great armed confederation of nations to form and march against Israel and to exterminate the Jews. (See notes—Rev.14:20; 19:17-21 for more discussion.) Note: this

confederation is called the kings of the east. Remember two things:

   a. No matter how sophisticated weapons get, it takes a soldier to set foot on a land to conquer it.

   b. A foot soldier is needed to conquer a nation when the conquerors want to preserve the land. Atomic weapons would only destroy the land and make it unusable for decades. In the end time the nations or kings of the east will want to preserve Palestine for its land and enormous wealth. Therefore, they will march against it with foot soldiers and weapons that will preserve the land itself. God will apparently help the advancement of the troops by seeing that the great Euphrates River is dried up when the march begins. The point is this: when the antichrist and the confederation of nations under his power begin to march against Israel, the other nations of the world apparently become edgy and nervous. The reason may be...

• the fear of a military move to conquer the world by beginning in Palestine.

• the resources of the Middle East and the threat to those resources (such as oil).

• the insanity of exterminating a whole people and nation like the Jews.

**The sixth angel poured out his bowl on the great river Euphrates, and its water was dried up to prepare the way for the kings from the East. (Rev 16:12; cp. Ezk. chapters 38-39)**

**"In the time of those kings, the God of heaven will set up a kingdom that will never be destroyed, nor will it be left to another people. It will crush all those kingdoms and bring them to an end, but it will itself endure forever. (Dan 2:44; cp. Dan. 7:19-27)**

**He will judge between the nations and will settle disputes for many peoples. They will beat their swords into plowshares and their spears into pruning hooks. Nation will not take up sword against nation, nor will they train for war anymore. (Isa 2:4)**

**But with righteousness he will judge the needy, with justice he will give decisions for the poor of the earth. He will strike the earth with the rod of his mouth; with the breath of his lips he will slay the wicked. (Isa 11:4)**

**Proclaim this among the nations: Prepare for war! Rouse the warriors! Let all the fighting men draw near and attack. Beat your plowshares into swords and your pruning hooks into spears. Let the weakling say, 'I am strong!' Come quickly, all you nations from every side, and assemble there. Bring down your warriors, O LORD! 'Let the nations be roused; let them advance into the Valley of Jehoshaphat, for there I will sit to judge all the nations on every side. Swing the sickle, for the harvest is ripe. Come, trample the grapes, for the winepress is full and the vats overflow— so great is their wickedness!' Multitudes, multitudes in the valley of decision! For the day of the LORD is near in the valley of decision. The sun and moon will be darkened, and the stars no longer shine. The LORD will roar from**

Zion and thunder from Jerusalem; the earth and the sky will tremble. But the LORD will be a refuge for his people, a stronghold for the people of Israel. (Joel 3:9-16)

Therefore wait for me," declares the LORD, "for the day I will stand up to testify. I have decided to assemble the nations, to gather the kingdoms and to pour out my wrath on them— all my fierce anger. The whole world will be consumed by the fire of my jealous anger. (Zep 3:8)

I will take away the chariots from Ephraim and the war-horses from Jerusalem, and the battle bow will be broken. He will proclaim peace to the nations. His rule will extend from sea to sea and from the River to the ends of the earth. (Zec 9:10)

On that day I will set out to destroy all the nations that attack Jerusalem. (Zec 12:9; cp. Zech.12:1-9)

3. There is the source or spirit behind the confederation of nations. Note: this verse says that all the nations of the earth are going to be involved in the great battle of Armageddon.

⇒ The kings from the east: all the nations east of Palestine, apparently involving the Arabs, China, and all the other eastern nations. These will probably be headed up by the antichrist.
⇒ The kings from the north: all the nations north of Palestine including Russia.
⇒ The kings from the south: all nations south of Palestine including the nations of Africa.
⇒ The kings from the west: all the nations west of Palestine including a western alliance and involving some of the European nations and probably including America and other nations of the Americas and Canada.

Armies will gather from every nation with each taking sides to protect its own interest. As stated, the point of conflict may be oil in the Middle East or the utter insanity of the antichrist to exterminate a whole people like the Jews, or it may be some other interest that we know nothing about yet. The point to see is this: in the last days all the nations of the world will converge upon the Middle East and be stationed within the borders of Palestine at Megiddo. Each of the nations will join forces with two or more sides. They will be there to protect their own national interests in the Middle East and Palestine.

Note what is behind the whole scene: evil spirits. Evil spirits are giving power to the mouth of the antichrist and his false prophet. This means the power to influence and deceive the leaders of other nations. The evil spirits will give the two leaders supernatural power to inspire their confederation to march and conquer Palestine. All the other nations will march to protect their interest in the region (perhaps oil). The description of the evil spirits as frogs symbolizes the ability to leap and spread the deception from the dragon (the devil) to the antichrist and to his false prophet or executive officer and then to each of the nations. The picture is that of the demons working miracles. What kind of miracles? Scripture does not say, but the idea is that of...

• *deceptive dreams* of glory
• *glorious triumphs* and visions of grandeur

• *setting passions aflame* and of striking fear within the heart, and arousing bitterness and hate among nations.

The result of the evil spirits is the gathering together of all the armies of the world to the place in Palestine called Armageddon or the valley and mountain of Megiddo. This is the great valley that runs through the middle of Palestine from the Mediterranean Sea to the Jordan River. It is about 200 miles long and ten miles wide.

The great dragon was hurled down— that ancient serpent called the devil, or Satan, who leads the whole world astray. He was hurled to the earth, and his angels with him. (Rev 12:9)

Then I saw three evil spirits that looked like frogs; they came out of the mouth of the dragon, out of the mouth of the beast and out of the mouth of the false prophet. They are spirits of demons performing miraculous signs, and they go out to the kings of the whole world, to gather them for the battle on the great day of God Almighty. (Rev 16:13-14)

4. There is the day of Armageddon. The day when all this will happen is called by Scripture "the great day of God, the Almighty" (NASB). This is the day the armies of the world will be destroyed, all the ungodly and evil of this world. It is the day when Jesus Christ will return to rule and reign over the earth. When all the armies are gathered together for battle then Jesus Christ will consummate this age of grace. Time and history as we know it will be no more. Godliness and righteousness will be brought to earth by the Lord Jesus Christ Himself.

5. There is the great warning of Christ to the people of the earth: watch and be prepared. Only those who have kept themselves unspotted from the worldliness of this earth and from following the antichrist will escape the terrible judgment coming. A person must be clothed in the white garment of the Lord's righteousness. The person must trust and diligently seek the righteousness of Jesus Christ or else he will be found naked and stripped of the white garment of the Lord's righteousness.

Note: Jesus Christ says He is returning to earth as a thief, totally unexpected. Just when He is coming back for the believers of the tribulation period is not known—not by anyone. Therefore, all must watch and be prepared.

6. The place of the great battle is called Armageddon or the great valley of Megiddo in Palestine. (See outline and notes—Rev.19:17-21 for more discussion.)

"Therefore keep watch, because you do not know the day or the hour. (Mat 25:13)

It will be good for those servants whose master finds them watching when he comes. I tell you the truth, he will dress himself to serve, will have them recline at the table and will come and wait on them. (Luke 12:37)

You are all sons of the light and sons of the day. We do not belong to the night or to the darkness. So then, let us not be like others, who are asleep, but let us be alert and self-controlled. (1 Th 5:5-6)

I am coming soon. Hold on to what you have, so that no one will take your crown. (Rev 3:11)

> **"Behold, I come like a thief! Blessed is he who stays awake and keeps his clothes with him, so that he may not go naked and be shamefully exposed." (Rev 16:15)**

**8** (16:17-21) **Judgment—Bowl**: there is the seventh bowl judgment. It is poured out into the air or atmosphere. The very air that man breathes is affected; it is poisoned. The very breath of life is taken from him. Note three points.

1. God's thundering voice announces, "It is done." The judgment upon all the ungodly and evil armies of this world is seen consummated: all the armies of the ungodly and evil nations are wiped out by the judgment of God.

2. Nature breaks loose in the most terrifying devastation and horror imaginable. The most awesome and spectacular display of the power and glory of God is launched. There will be violent storms and a *worldwide catastrophic earthquake*. Imagine an earthquake that will violently affect the whole world. The Amplified New Testament states it well:

> **Then there came flashes of lightning, rumblings, peals of thunder and a severe earthquake. No earthquake like it has ever occurred since man has been on earth, so tremendous was the quake. (Rev 16:18)**

a. The great city of Jerusalem will be shaken by the earthquake and divided into three parts, that is, ut-terly destroyed. Babylon, the capital of the anti-christ, will collapse and be broken up into three parts (v.19). That is, it will be utterly destroyed.

b. There will be whole cities throughout the nations of the world that will collapse into utter ruin (v.19). There will be devastation, destruction, horror, injury, death, and mass confusion.

c. The great world capital, Babylon, will be remembered by God, and He will especially pour upon her the cup and fierceness of His wrath (v.19).

d. Much of the earth will literally break up: some islands and mountains will disappear (v.20).

e. The storms will rain great hail storms out of heaven weighing up to one hundred pounds (v.21).

3. There is the reaction of the ungodly and evil survivors around the world. They still blame and curse God, and still do not repent. We would expect repentance, but the ungodly and evil of the last days will be as hard and stubborn as the ungodly and evil are today.

> **And the dragon stood on the shore of the sea. And I saw a beast coming out of the sea. He had ten horns and seven heads, with ten crowns on his horns, and on each head a blasphemous name. (Rev 13:1)**
>
> **And cursed the God of heaven because of their pains and their sores, but they refused to repent of what they had done. (Rev 16:11)**

| | | away in the Spirit into a desert. There I saw a woman sitting on a scarlet beast that was covered with blasphemous names and had seven heads and ten horns. | ceive its power from the beast or antichrist |
|---|---|---|---|
| | **CHAPTER 17** | | a. Has the color of scarlet |
| | **VISION THREE, 17:1-20:15** | | b. Has the blasphemous names |
| | **X. THE JUDGMENT OF BOTH RELIGIOUS BABYLON & POLITICAL BABYLON, 17:1-18:24** | 4 The woman was dressed in purple and scarlet, and was glittering with gold, precious stones and pearls. She held a golden cup in her hand, filled with abominable things and the filth of her adulteries. | c. Has seven heads & ten horns |
| | | | 6 **Religious Babylon will have a rich appearance but will be corrupt** |
| | **A. The Description of Religious Babylon, of False Religion, 17:1-6** | | a. Outwardly: Luxurious wealth |
| | | | b. Inwardly: Corrupt idolatry |
| 1 **An angel approaches John** | One of the seven angels who had the seven bowls came and said to me, "Come, I will show you the punishment of the great prostitute, who sits on many waters. | 5 This title was written on her forehead: MYSTERY BABYLON THE GREAT THE MOTHER OF PROSTITUTES AND OF THE ABOMINATIONS OF THE EARTH. | 7 **Religious Babylon will have a striking name** |
| a. Commands John: Come | | | a. Mystery, Babylon the Great |
| b. Promises to show the judgment of Babylon | | | b. The mother of prostitutes |
| 2 **Religious Babylon is a great prostitute** | | | |
| 3 **Religious Babylon sits on many waters—peoples, v.1** | 2 With her the kings of the earth committed adultery and the inhabitants of the earth were intoxicated with the wine of her adulteries." | 6 I saw that the woman was drunk with the blood of the saints, the blood of those who bore testimony to Jesus. When I saw her, I was greatly astonished. | 8 **Religious Babylon will be prejudiced & have fierce power** |
| 4 **Religious Babylon will be supported by the nations of the world** | | | |
| 5 **Religious Babylon will re-** | 3 Then the angel carried me | | |

## VISION THREE, 17:1-20:15

# DIVISION X

## THE JUDGMENT OF BOTH RELIGIOUS BABYLON AND POLITICAL BABYLON, 17:1-18:24

### A. The Description of Religious Babylon, of False Religion, 17:1-6

(17:1-18:24) **DIVISION OVERVIEW: Babylon**: Jesus Christ is coming back to this earth. He is coming to bring righteousness to this earth. But before He can come and establish righteousness in the earth a few things have to be done.

⇒ All the godless and evil armies of this earth have to be destroyed. This we have just seen in the former chapter (Revelation Chapter 16).

⇒ All the false religion in this world has to be destroyed. This is the discussion of the present chapter (Revelation Chapter 17).

⇒ All the godless politics and governments and social systems of this world have to be destroyed. This will be the discussion of the next chapter (Revelation Chapter 18).

When these three things are done, then the ungodly and evil of this earth will be removed and Jesus Christ can come to earth and set up His kingdom of righteousness. As stated, the armies were destroyed in the former chapter. Now, God shows us how both false religion and the godless governments and politics of this world will be destroyed.

Note one thing: false religion and godless government have always been upon the earth, and they will be until the end time. In the end time the antichrist and the false prophet will institute a one-world religion, the worship of the state and its leader, the antichrist himself. All the evil that has ever been embodied in false religion will show its ugly head in the end time. False religion and godless government will be at their height, but they will also be at their lowest and most evil. It is this false religion and godless government of the end time, the worship of the state and the antichrist, that is the discussion of the present passage. But we must keep this in mind: all false religion and godless governments are embodied in the government and false religion of the end time. All godless government and false religion will be judged and wiped from off the face of the earth by the judgment of God. This is the great subject of this passage: *the judgment of godless government and false religion, of what the Scripture calls political and religious Babylon.*

(17:1-6) **Introduction**: false religion has done more to doom people than any other single thing. How? By its deception. False religion promises life, salvation, peace, security, and hope in some kind of life hereafter. But if it is false, it is a lie, total deception. This will be the great tragedy of false Babylon, of false religion in the end time. It will doom people by the millions, doom them for eternity. This is the reason this particular chapter is given in Revelation: to warn us about false religion and to warn us of religious Babylon, the false religion that is going to sweep the earth in the end time.

1. An angel approaches John (v.1).
2. Religious Babylon is a great prostitute (v.1).
3. Religious Babylon sits on many waters, that is, peoples (v.1).
4. Religious Babylon will be supported by the nations of the world (v.2).
5. Religious Babylon will receive its power from the beast or antichrist (v.3).
6. Religious Babylon will have a rich appearance but will be corrupt (v.4).
7. Religious Babylon will have a striking name (v.5).
8. Religious Babylon will be prejudiced and have fierce power (v.6).

**1** (17:1) **Religion, False—Babylon**: an angel approaches John. Remember John is having a vision of the last days of human history. He has just been shown the great devastation of the last war, Armageddon, and of the catastrophic destruction of the great cities of the earth. He is standing there in utter shock and stone silence just as anyone else would be. But then all of a sudden one of the seven angels goes over to John. This is one of the seven angels who had poured the wrath of God upon the earth. The angel tells John to "come here, and I will show you the future judgment of false religion in the earth." John walks over and sees one of the most amazing sights a person could ever witness: the description and judgment of false religion in the world.

**2** (17:1) **Religion, False—Babylon**: religious Babylon (false religion) is a great prostitute. In the Bible, prostitution stands for false gods, false worship, false religion, and false devotion. It stands for idolatry. It stands for worshipping something other than God Himself, other than the only true and living God. This is the picture of religious Babylon. It is a false religion, the worship of an idol. A person commits spiritual prostitution...

- when he imagines what God is like and follows his own thoughts about God rather than what Scripture reveals God to be.
- when he follows an earthly religion and its rituals, ceremonies, and teaching instead of following Jesus Christ as revealed in the Scripture.
- when he molds and makes an image and worships it.

Spiritual prostitution means to follow a false religion and worship, the worship of a false god. This is the picture of religious Babylon. The religion of the end time will be a false religion, the worship of an idol and not of God Himself.

> **Although they claimed to be wise, they became fools And exchanged the glory of the immortal God for images made to look like mortal man and birds and animals and reptiles. (Rom 1:22-23)**
> **The Spirit clearly says that in later times some will abandon the faith and follow deceiving spirits and things taught by demons. (1 Tim 4:1)**
> **Having a form of godliness but denying its power. Have nothing to do with them. (2 Tim 3:5)**
> **Dear children, keep yourselves from idols. (1 John 5:21)**
> **Be careful, or you will be enticed to turn away and worship other gods and bow down to them. (Deu 11:16)**
> **"I am the LORD; that is my name! I will not give my glory to another or my praise to idols. (Isa 42:8)**
> **"Gather together and come; assemble, you fugitives from the nations. Ignorant are those who carry about idols of wood, who pray to gods that cannot save. (Isa 45:20)**

**3** (17:1) **Deception—Religion, False**: religious Babylon (false religion) sits on *many waters*, that is, people and nations. What this means is explained in verse fifteen:

> **Then the angel said to me, "The waters you saw, where the prostitute sits, are peoples, multitudes, nations and languages. (Rev 17:15)**

The picture is that religious Babylon will fill the earth: many races and multitudes and nations and languages will be caught up in the worship of the false religion.

> **Thought 1.** As just stated, millions will be caught up in the false religion of the end time. But think about today: think about how many millions are following a false religion and worshipping idols around the world. But even closer to home: think how many profess Christ and yet do not believe or teach Christ and the Word of God.

**4** (17:2) **Religion, False**: religious Babylon (false religion) will be supported by the kings, that is, by the nations and governments of the world. The governments of the world will encourage the worship of religious Babylon. This is, of course, referring to the worship of the state or government and secular society of the antichrist. (see note—Rev.13:13-17 for discussion. This is an important note to see how religious Babylon gains and maintains power in the end time and becomes *the worldwide* religion.) Religious Babylon will seduce the world with the wine of her false teaching. She will entice the peoples of the earth to worship the antichrist and his government and secular society.

Remember: the argument for worshipping the state and secular society will be strong. The antichrist and his government will bring peace and economic recovery to the earth. He will also provide massive aid to help the nations and peoples of the earth during the natural disasters that are increasingly striking the earth (see outlines and notes—Rev.6:1-8; 6:12-17; 8:6-12; 8:13-9:11; 9:12-21; 13:11-18 for more discussion). Whole areas of the earth will be devastated by the forces of nature going wild. The world and its people will be begging for help from some leader who has some answers. And the antichrist will be the one person and government that will have the answers, at least for a while. Therefore, the world will turn to him and his state for help and leadership. Many of the leaders and governments of the world will support his idea of a state religion in order to keep the masses of the world loyal to the state. The leaders of many nations will be convinced that the way to keep people supporting the government is this: lead the people to worship the government and to look to the government to meet the needs of society. The leaders will make the government or state the focus of attention, the center around which all life revolves. The government or state will become the god and man will become its servant. (Cp. communism or any other socialist or dictatorial state that is totally focused upon the government.)

The point is this: in the end time there will be a worldwide religion, a religion of the state. There will be a religious Babylon, a false religion that will try to seduce all the peoples of the earth into its control. The false religion will have the support of the kings and leaders of the world.

> **Thought 1.** How many people prefer to belong to a religion or church that allows worldliness, that does not teach and preach separation?

> **Therefore, I urge you, brothers, in view of God's mercy, to offer your bodies**

as living sacrifices, holy and pleasing to God—this is your spiritual act of worship. Do not conform any longer to the pattern of this world, but be transformed by the renewing of your mind. Then you will be able to test and approve what God's will is—his good, pleasing and perfect will. (Rom 12:1-2)

"Therefore come out from them and be separate, says the Lord. Touch no unclean thing, and I will receive you." "I will be a Father to you, and you will be my sons and daughters, says the Lord Almighty." (2 Cor 6:17-18)

Do not love the world or anything in the world. If anyone loves the world, the love of the Father is not in him. For everything in the world—the cravings of sinful man, the lust of his eyes and the boasting of what he has and does—comes not from the Father but from the world. (1 John 2:15-16)

**Thought 2.** Many governments support major religions because of the good the religions do. Religion helps the state in promoting law and order, loyalty to the state, peace, morality, and discipline.

**5** (17:3) **Religious Babylon—Religion, False**: religious Babylon or the false religion of the state will receive its power from the beast, that is, from the antichrist. The false religion in the end time will be supported by the antichrist and his government (see note—Rev.13:12 for discussion). Note three facts.

1. Religious Babylon sits upon a scarlet beast. *Sitting* means that the false religion is supported and dependent upon the state.

2. The scarlet beast is the antichrist. It is he who is covered with names that blaspheme God. This means that all the heads or governments under his authority blaspheme and rebel against God. The false religion will actually represent blasphemous governments. It will not be a religion at all; it will be the worship of the state itself.

3. The beast with seven heads and ten horns is the antichrist. The seven heads are the seven nations that will voluntarily surrender to the control of the antichrist. He will have conquered three nations. The three conquered nations and the seven nations who voluntarily subject to his control give the antichrist the power of ten horns or nations. That is, the ten horns refer to ten powerful nations that will be under his control (see notes—Rev.13:1-2). He will have the power of the ten nations to support him in enforcing the state religion (see note—Rev.13:1).

The false religion will be dependent upon the power of the antichrist and the governments under his control. It will be the power of these governments that will hold the false religion up before the world. The nations under the control of the antichrist will be the primary nations preaching the false religion of Babylon, that is, the worship of the state.

**Thought 1.** There are many who try to mix religion with the world. They base their religion and morals upon their desires, upon what they want to do out in the world. Their religion is determined by their desires for the world. The world and its possessions and pleasures are put first, and then whatever religion is needed to salve their consciences is accepted.

Do you not know that your body is a temple of the Holy Spirit, who is in you, whom you have received from God? You are not your own; You were bought at a price. Therefore honor God with your body. (1 Cor 6:19-20)

"Be careful, or your hearts will be weighed down with dissipation, drunkenness and the anxieties of life, and that day will close on you unexpectedly like a trap. (Luke 21:34)

Set your minds on things above, not on earthly things. (Col 3:2)

It teaches us to say "No" to ungodliness and worldly passions, and to live self-controlled, upright and godly lives in this present age, (Titus 2:12)

You adulterous people, don't you know that friendship with the world is hatred toward God? Anyone who chooses to be a friend of the world becomes an enemy of God. (James 4:4)

**6** (17:4) **Religion, False**: the wealth and corruption of religious Babylon (false religion) in the end time will be tragic.

1. The false religion of the end time will be extremely wealthy. This is what is meant by the purple and scarlet clothing and the gold and precious stones and pearls.

**Thought 1.** Imagine a religion that is wealthy in the possessions of this world while so many in the world are in such desperate need! There are 40,000 children who die from hunger every day, and that is only the children who die from starvation. This 40,000 does not include the adults. And remember: in the end time the needs will be far greater among the millions suffering from the devastation of the catastrophes that will be hitting the earth and from the holocaust launched by the antichrist. Yet, the religion of the day will be wealthy and will even be hoarding its wealth. What a lesson to all believers and churches!

Jesus answered, "If you want to be perfect, go, sell your possessions and give to the poor, and you will have treasure in heaven. Then come, follow me." (Mat 19:21)

Then he said to them all: "If anyone would come after me, he must deny himself and take up his cross daily and follow me. (Luke 9:23)

In the same way, any of you who does not give up everything he has cannot be my disciple. (Luke 14:33)

"I tell you the truth," Jesus said to them, "no one who has left home or wife or brothers or parents or children for the sake of the kingdom of God Will fail to receive many times as much in this age and, in the age to come, eternal life." (Luke 18:29-30)

2. The false religion of the end time will be corrupt. It will offer a cup to help the people of the world, but the cup is filled with abominable things and filth. That is, what the false religion offers is idolatry, a polluted and corrupt worship.

**Thought 1.** All false religions feed people nothing but abominable things and filth. The teachings and doctrines of false religion are disgusting and repulsive. Imagine being fed filth and abominable things. This is what Scripture says we eat if we feast upon false religion.

> They claim to know God, but by their actions they deny him. They are detestable, disobedient and unfit for doing anything good. (Titus 1:16)
> But there were also false prophets among the people, just as there will be false teachers among you. They will secretly introduce destructive heresies, even denying the sovereign Lord who bought them— bringing swift destruction on themselves. Many will follow their shameful ways and will bring the way of truth into disrepute. (2 Pet 2:1-2)
> Dear children, keep yourselves from idols. (1 John 5:21)
> Be careful, or you will be enticed to turn away and worship other gods and bow down to them. (Deu 11:16)

**7** (17:5) **Religion, False—Babylon, Religious:** the name of religious Babylon or false religion in the end time is striking.

> This title was written on her forehead: **MYSTERY BABYLON THE GREAT THE MOTHER OF PROSTITUTES AND OF THE ABOMINATIONS OF THE EARTH.** (Rev 17:5)

1. The name of religious Babylon, false religion, is a mystery. That is, the fact that false religion is false is not known to all people. Many do not know that they are worshipping a false religion. The fact has to be revealed to them.

**Thought 1.** How true this is! Think how many millions are worshipping a false god or a false Christ, a Christ that differs entirely from the Christ revealed by the Word of God.

2. Religious Babylon will be the *mother* of many false religions and abominations upon the earth. She gives rise to many false teachings and deceptions, to many corruptions in the worship of God. This tells us who religious Babylon is. It goes back to the building of the *tower of Babel* in the Old Testament. Under a leader named Nimrod, man decided to build the *ideal state or utopia.* Man turned away from God and set out to make himself secure by building a tower straight up to heaven. That is, he sought security, provision, and help from other men rather than from God. He joined hands with other people in trying to build the perfect and ideal world by their own efforts and without God. They omitted God altogether; they left God totally out of the picture. Note: the tower of Babel is the founding of the city of *Babylon,* the very first time the word *Babylon* is mentioned in the Bible. Thereafter, Babylon came to mean...

- either godless religion (cp. Is.1:21; Jer.2:20; 3:1; Ezk.16:15; Hos.2:5; 3:3; 4:15).
- or godless government and society (Is.23:17; Nah.3:4).

The point is this: religious Babylon stands for all false religion. It stands for all the religions that seek after heaven or utopia or the perfect life...

- by man's own works and self effort.
- by man's own goodness and self righteousness.
- by man's own rituals and ceremonies.
- by man's own ideas of God and worship of God.
- by man's own religion and benevolent services.
- by man's own government and state.
- by man's own community and society.

In essence religious Babylon is the mother of all false religion. But there will be one major difference with the end time religion: man's dream for a one-world government and a one-world religion will become a reality. All the evil and wrong that exist in false religion will be combined into one religion in the end time, and it will sweep and consume the world. Religious Babylon will spread her abominable things and filth over all the world under one worldwide state religion. The religion will probably be eclectic, that is, assimilate enough of the major religions of the world to satisfy the great mass of people (cp. Rev.13:13f; 17:5, 15). The apostate religion will become symbolized in the very city of which its center is established—Babylon.

**Thought 1.** The only way to achieve utopia or heaven is through Jesus Christ, not by our own efforts. We should labor and labor diligently to build the best world and society we can, but with God, not without God.

> But seek first his kingdom and his righteousness, and all these things will be given to you as well. (Mat 6:33)
> For, "Everyone who calls on the name of the Lord will be saved." (Rom 10:13)
> For it is by grace you have been saved, through faith—and this not from yourselves, it is the gift of God— Not by works, so that no one can boast. For we are God's workmanship, created in Christ Jesus to do good works, which God prepared in advance for us to do. (Eph 2:8-10)
> Cast all your anxiety on him because he cares for you. (1 Pet 5:7)
> Through the blessing of the upright a city is exalted, but by the mouth of the wicked it is destroyed. (Prov 11:11)
> Righteousness exalts a nation, but sin is a disgrace to any people. (Prov 14:34)

**8** (17:6) **Religion, False—Babylon, Religious:** the religious power and bigotry of religious Babylon (false religion) in the end time will be fierce. The false religion will be the leader in launching the holocaust for the antichrist. Literally millions upon millions—a countless multitude— will be persecuted and killed because they refuse to worship the state and its leader, the antichrist. Note: many of the martyrs will be the followers of Jesus Christ. (See notes— Rev.6:9-11; 7:9-17; 13:13-17 for discussion.)

> "Be on your guard against men; they will hand you over to the local councils and flog you in their synagogues. On my account you will be brought before governors and kings as witnesses to them and to the Gentiles. (Mat 10:17-18)

"Then you will be handed over to be persecuted and put to death, and you will be hated by all nations because of me. At that time many will turn away from the faith and will betray and hate each other, (Mat 24:9-10)

"But before all this, they will lay hands on you and persecute you. They will deliver you to synagogues and prisons, and you will be brought before kings and governors, and all on account of my name. (Luke 21:12)

Remember the words I spoke to you: 'No servant is greater than his master.' If they persecuted me, they will persecute you also. If they obeyed my teaching, they will obey yours also. They will treat you this way because of my name, for they do not know the One who sent me. (John 15:20-21)

They will put you out of the synagogue; in fact, a time is coming when anyone who kills you will think he is offering a service to God. They will do such things because they have not known the Father or me. (John 16:2-3)

In fact, everyone who wants to live a godly life in Christ Jesus will be persecuted, (2 Tim 3:12)

Do not be afraid of what you are about to suffer. I tell you, the devil will put some of you in prison to test you, and you will suffer persecution for ten days. Be faithful, even to the point of death, and I will give you the crown of life. (Rev 2:10)

**B. The Power Behind Religious Babylon, Behind False Religion: The Beast or Antichrist, 17:7-18**

1 The mystery & details given

2 The source of the power of religious Babylon: The beast or antichrist

  a. The greatness of the beast or antichrist

    1) His earthly power

    2) His supernatural power

    3) His end or doom

    4) His impact

  b. The power of the beast or antichrist^DS1

    1) Understood only by spiritual believers

    2) His earthly power

    3) His supernatural power

    4) His great rule & dominion

  c. The terrible purpose of the beast or antichrist

3 The destruction of religious Babylon or false religion

  a. Religious Babylon (false religion) will gain enormous power

  b. Religious Babylon (false religion) will be utterly destroyed by the antichrist & his state

  c. Religious Babylon (false religion) will be utterly destroyed because of God

7 Then the angel said to me: "Why are you astonished? I will explain to you the mystery of the woman and of the beast she rides, which has the seven heads and ten horns. 8 The beast, which you saw, once was, now is not, and will come up out of the Abyss and go to his destruction. The inhabitants of the earth whose names have not been written in the book of life from the creation of the world will be astonished when they see the beast, because he once was, now is not, and yet will come. 9 "This calls for a mind with wisdom. The seven heads are seven hills on which the woman sits. 10 They are also seven kings. Five have fallen, one is, the other has not yet come; but when he does come, he must remain for a little while. 11 The beast who once was, and now is not, is an eighth king. He belongs to the seven and is going to his destruction 12 "The ten horns you saw are ten kings who have not yet received a kingdom, but who for one hour will receive authority as kings along with the beast. 13 They have one purpose and will give their power and authority to the beast. 14 They will make war against the Lamb, but the Lamb will overcome them because he is Lord of lords and King of kings—and with him will be his called, chosen and faithful followers." 15 Then the angel said to me, "The waters you saw, where the prostitute sits, are peoples, multitudes, nations and languages. 16 The beast and the ten horns you saw will hate the prostitute. They will bring her to ruin and leave her naked; they will eat her flesh and burn her with fire. 17 For God has put it into their hearts to accomplish his purpose by agreeing to give the beast their power to rule, until God's words are fulfilled. 18 The woman you saw is the great city that rules over the kings of the earth."

# DIVISION X

## THE JUDGMENT OF BOTH RELIGIOUS BABYLON AND POLITICAL BABYLON, 17:1-18:24

### B. The Power Behind Religious Babylon, Behind False Religion: The Beast or Antichrist, 17:7-18

(17:7-18) **Introduction**: in the end time Jesus Christ will be coming back to earth again. He will be coming back to establish righteousness in the earth. He will bring about the perfect and ideal society and government and the pure worship and service of God. But before He does this, He has to destroy all the ungodly and evil of this world. Righteousness cannot exist with ungodliness and evil. This also means that all false religion has to be destroyed as well. This is the subject of this passage, the destruction of religious Babylon, of false religion in the world. Remember: there will be a worldwide religion in the end time, the worship of the state and its leader, the antichrist. Everyone will be required by law to give his first loyalty to the state or else face death. This worldwide religion, this worship of the government and its leader, is what is meant by *religious Babylon*. The first part of the discussion is covered in the former passage (Rev.17:1-6). Because of the length of the discussion it has been divided into two parts. The present passage is *the judgment of religious Babylon, of false religion* (Part 2).

  1. The mystery and details are given (v.7).

  2. The source of the power of religious Babylon: the beast or antichrist (v.7-14).

  3. The destruction of religious Babylon or false religion (v.15-18).

**1** (17:7) **Religion, False**: religious Babylon, that is false religion, is a *mystery*. How a body of people can claim to believe and follow God and yet honor and put leaders, governments, states, doctrines, and rituals above God is a mystery. It is hypocrisy; it is counterfeit and false religion. How a body of people can claim to believe and follow God and yet slaughter millions of people because the people do not believe as they do is a mystery. It is hypocrisy, counterfeit, and false religion.

    Yet this is just what John witnessed. He saw a picture of what false religion will be like in the last days of world history. And the picture was horrifying. The religion of the last days will join hands with the government of the antichrist and the false religion will sweep the world. John saw that most of the world will be seduced by the appeal of false religion, and most will worship the government as the great provider and protector of society. He also witnessed that religious Babylon or the false religion will slaughter millions upon millions of people because they refuse to put the state and secular society before their own religion. He saw that among these millions will be a great multitude of genuine believers. Seeing all this has left John in a state of bewilderment and amazement, wondering how such could ever take place. While he stood there somewhat shocked, the angel stepped forward and told John that he would now reveal the mystery and details of religious Babylon.

**2** (17:7-14) **Antichrist—Religion**: there is the source of the power of religious Babylon, of false religion. In the end time the source of power for false religion will be the beast or the antichrist. (Note: practically all of the facts given in these verses have been covered in former notes. Where this is true, there is no need to repeat the discussion. Therefore, just a brief explanation will be given and then the note where the major discussion can be found.)

1. There is the greatness of the beast that supports false religion, the greatness of the antichrist (v.7b-8).

   a. There is the great earthly power of the antichrist: seven heads and ten horns. The antichrist will have seven heads or seven governments who will willingly subject themselves to his rule. But he will also have the power of ten horns or governments that support him. How? When he himself first comes to power, he will probably march against three governments and conquer them and absorb them into his own rule or nation. Either this or else three governments will form some alliance or confederation with him as their head. These three plus the seven who willingly submit to his rule will give him the power of ten governments. (See DEEPER STUDY # 1, chart, point 3—Rev. 13:2 for more discussion.) Imagine the great earthly power the antichrist will have by ruling over all these nations and empires. The false religion of the end time will have a great power behind it.

   b. There is the great supernatural power of the antichrist: he will be out of the Abyss or bottomless pit, the very incarnation of evil itself or else be indwelt by some powerful evil spirit from the Abyss or bottomless pit. (See notes—Rev.9:2; 11:7-10; pt.1—Rev.13:2-3 for more discussion.)

   c. There is the end or doom of the antichrist: destruction (apoleian). The word means to be destroyed; to lose one's well-being; to be wasted and ruined and given a worthless existence. It does not mean that a person will cease to exist. It means a person will be destroyed and devastated and condemned to a worthless existence. He will suffer waste and loss and ruin forever and ever.

**Thought 1.** No matter how great a person may be, if he does not know Jesus Christ he will face destruction. The antichrist will be a great man in the eyes of the world. He will rule the whole world, but he will be doomed: all because he never gave his life and heart to Jesus Christ. No matter who the person is, if he stands as an enemy of the cross, he shall be destroyed. It does not matter who he is, either within or without the church, he shall suffer utter destruction. Who is an enemy of the cross? The person...

- who rejects the cross of Christ as the only way to God.
- who does not accept the death of Christ as payment for his sins.
- who does not believe that Christ died for him, that is, as the punishment for his transgressions.
- who does not believe that the penalty for his imperfection was borne by Christ on the cross.
- who does not approach God claiming that he is coming by the death of Christ—that is, that he wants God to accept him in the death of Christ.
- who claims that there are other ways to approach God—ways other than the cross of Christ.
- who considers the cross of Christ to be foolishness.
- who opposes and curses Christ and His cross.
- who persecutes and attempts to stamp out Christ and His cross.
- who denies and questions that Christ died for his sins.

"Then they will go away to eternal punishment, but the righteous to eternal life." (Mat 25:46; cp. v.25-45)

But whoever blasphemes against the Holy Spirit will never be forgiven; he is guilty of an eternal sin." (Mark 3:29)

[Christ] his winnowing fork is in his hand to clear his threshing floor and to gather the wheat into his barn, but he will burn up the chaff with unquenchable fire." (Luke 3:17)

But for those who are self-seeking and who reject the truth and follow evil, there will be wrath and anger. There will be trouble and distress for every human being who does evil: first for the Jew, then for the Gentile; (Rom 2:8-9)

And give relief to you who are troubled, and to us as well. This will happen when the Lord Jesus is revealed from heaven in blazing fire with his powerful angels. He will punish those who do not know God and do not obey the gospel of our Lord Jesus. They will be punished with everlasting destruction and shut out from the presence of the Lord and from the majesty of his power (2 Th 1:7-9)

How much more severely do you think a man deserves to be punished who has trampled the Son of God under foot, who has treated as an unholy thing the blood of the covenant that sanctified him, and who has insulted the Spirit of grace? For we know him who said, "It is mine to avenge; I will repay," and again, "The Lord will judge his people." (Heb 10:29-30)

If this is so, then the Lord knows how to rescue godly men from trials and to hold the unrighteous for the day of judgment, while continuing their punishment. (2 Pet 2:9)

If anyone's name was not found written in the book of life, he was thrown into the lake of fire. (Rev 20:15)

But the cowardly, the unbelieving, the vile, the murderers, the sexually immoral, those who practice magic arts, the idolaters and all liars—their place will be in the fiery lake of burning sulfur. This is the second death." (Rev 21:8)

d. The impact of the antichrist: he will amaze the world (see note, pt.2—Rev.13:4-8).

2. There is the power of the beast that supports religious Babylon or false religion (v.9-14). The power is phenomenal. Note four facts.

   a. The beast or antichrist can be understood only by believers who are spiritually minded (v.9ᵃ).

   b. The great earthly power of the antichrist: he sits on seven mountains and embodies seven great kingdoms (v.9ᵇ-10). (See DEEPER STUDY # 1, pt.2—Rev.13:2; DEEPER STUDY # 1—17:9-10 for discussion.)

   c. The great supernatural power of the antichrist (v.10). He will be the full embodiment of evil. The beast or antichrist passes through three stages. He had an existence in the past, but he ceases to exist for a time. Then he is to ascend from the bottomless pit, that is, he is to either be filled with an evil spirit or else be an incarnation of satanic evil beyond anything ever seen before. He is the beast... the eighth [ruler who]...is one of the seven original rulers (v.11). He is to experience two stages of existence, and the second stage will be a full incarnation of evil. He will embody and include all the terrorizing traits of the ancient empires. (See note, pt.2—Rev.13:2-3; cp. Rev. 13:14-17 for more discussion.)

   d. There is the great rule of the antichrist (v.12-13). His ten horns are ten kingdoms. These ten kingdoms will be under the power of the antichrist and form a great alliance with him (v.13). (See notes—Rev.17:7-14; 13:1; also see DEEPER STUDY # 1, chart, pt.3—Rev.13:2.)

3. There is the terrible purpose of the antichrist and his alliance: to war against the Lamb, the Lord Jesus Christ (v.14). (See notes—Rev.7:13-14; 13:2-3; pts.6, 7, 9—Rev.13:4-7; 11:1; 16:12-16 for discussion.)

---

**DEEPER STUDY # 1**

(17:9-10) **Antichrist—End Time**: the seven mountains or seven heads are said by many to refer to Rome. That is, in the end time religious Babylon or false religion will sit in Rome. This is because Rome was known in ancient times as *the city on seven hills*. But note: this is not what John says. He clearly says that the seven heads represent seven kings or governments (v.10). By seven mountains he means that false religion sits upon seven kingdoms or empires that have complete and full rule and power. Note that the seven mountains and seven heads mean seven kings of kingdoms and empires. Note that this is what Scripture says.

> **"This calls for a mind with wisdom. The seven heads are seven hills on which the woman sits. They are also seven kings. Five have fallen, one is, the other has not yet come; but when he does come, he must remain for a little while. (Rev 17:9-10)**

Who are these kings or kingdoms or empires? There are numerous ideas, but Scripture does not identify these kings. The best way to discover who they are is to look back through the Old Testament and note the kings or empires that *opposed God's people*. When this is done, the following empires *seem* to be the most logical answer.

   ⇒ Five of the kings or empires are fallen. That is, they no longer exist. These seem to be Egypt, Assyria, Babylon, Medo-Persia, and Greece.

   ⇒ One of the kingdoms still remains. That is, it still exists and continues to exist down through the centuries. This would be Rome and the traits of Rome that have continued to exist down through the centuries: traits that exist in the ruling bodies and legislatures of governments, in the representative governments and laws of nations, and in the religion of Papal Rome.

   ⇒ One king or kingdom is not yet come. This would refer to a revival of the Roman empire or of many of the nations that were in the old Roman empire. The antichrist would embrace the traits of all the empires and rule over them all. He would be the eighth ruler mentioned in verse eleven.

**3** (17:15-18) **Religion, False—Babylon, Religious**: there is the destruction of religious Babylon. The antichrist and his political alliance turn against the religious movement of Babylon. Remember: religion will be used by the antichrist to gain and hold the loyalty of the masses all over the world. A state religion will be established: every citizen will be forced to give his first loyalty to the state. It will be the state that will give people so much; therefore, the state will expect first loyalty. But note: the antichrist and the government will turn against religion and utterly destroy religion. Note three significant facts.

1. Religious Babylon (false religion) will gain enormous power in the end time (v.15). Religion will sit upon, that is, be supported by, multitudes and nations and languages. The idea is that practically everyone will be worshipping the image of the beast or state in the end time.

2. Religious Babylon (false religion) is utterly destroyed by the antichrist and his alliance (v.16). Why? The answer is given in the above point—power and money.

   ⇒ Just imagine all the money that it costs to keep a worldwide religion going: all the control and personnel needed and offices and other resources to oversee and make sure the citizens do show loyalty to the state.

   ⇒ Just imagine all the wealth that a worldwide religion would possess through contributions and through the property it would hold.

   ⇒ Remember the devastation that is taking place all across the world during the great tribulation, the enormous cost and great sums of money needed to meet the needs of cities and nations.

Once the antichrist and his state have the loyalty of the people committed to the state, they will no longer need the religion. The state will have the loyalty of the people. What it will not have is the money and wealth of the religion. Therefore, it will destroy the religion for its wealth and power. Note exactly what is said.

   ⇒ The state will *hate* religious Babylon: religion will have served its purpose. The state now wants complete end full control of the people and the wealth.

   ⇒ The state will make religious Babylon *desolate*: religion will be robbed of all its monies, wealth, property, and holdings.

   ⇒ The state will strip religious Babylon, make her *naked*: expose her corruptions to public view, showing why the religion must be destroyed.

   ⇒ The state will *eat her flesh*: consume her and take everything that is worthwhile and beneficial for the state. Whatever will benefit the state, the loyalty of the people and the wealth, will be consumed by the state.

⇒ The state will *burn religion with fire*. There will be nothing left but ashes.

3. Religious Babylon will be destroyed because of God. In the final analysis God is the One who will cause false religion to be destroyed. God will plant the idea to destroy religious Babylon within the mind of the antichrist. God will then arouse the ten other governments to support him. And false religion, religious Babylon, will be wiped off the face of the earth once for all.

Note how clearly religious Babylon is identified (v.18). The woman—religious Babylon, the state religion—is the great city that reigns over the leaders of the world. Religion, the false religion, will be the power that gains and holds the loyalty of the people to the state. But once its purpose is achieved—once the people are loyal to the state—there is no more need for the religion. The state will then covet the full power and wealth of religious Babylon and will go after it.

**CHAPTER 18**

**C. The Collapse of Political Babylon, 18:1-24**

**1 There is the great angelic announcement**

**2 The reasons why Babylon will be destroyed**
a. Because of spiritual corruption

b. Because the city will corrupt nations, government leaders, & merchants

c. Because the city will corrupt people & lead them to sin

d. Because the city will take the lead in persecuting God's people

e. Because of self-glory, pride, selfish extravagance, & indulgence

**3 The quickness of Babylon's destruction**

**4 The impact of Babylon's fall**
a. The mourning by the government leaders of the world

b. The mourning by the businessmen & commercial people of the world
1) They will mourn for selfish reasons: Because of the personal loss

After this I saw another angel coming down from heaven. He had great authority, and the earth was illuminated by his splendor.
2 With a mighty voice he shouted: "Fallen! Fallen is Babylon the Great! She has become a home for demons and a haunt for every evil spirit, a haunt for every unclean and detestable bird.
3 For all the nations have drunk the maddening wine of her adulteries. The kings of the earth committed adultery with her, and the merchants of the earth grew rich from her excessive luxuries."
4 Then I heard another voice from heaven say: "Come out of her, my people, so that you will not share in her sins, so that you will not receive any of her plagues;
5 For her sins are piled up to heaven, and God has remembered her crimes.
6 Give back to her as she has given; pay her back double for what she has done. Mix her a double portion from her own cup.
7 Give her as much torture and grief as the glory and luxury she gave herself. In her heart she boasts, 'I sit as queen; I am not a widow, and I will never mourn.'
8 Therefore in one day her plagues will overtake her: death, mourning and famine. She will be consumed by fire, for mighty is the Lord God who judges her.
9 "When the kings of the earth who committed adultery with her and shared her luxury see the smoke of her burning, they will weep and mourn over her.
10 Terrified at her torment, they will stand far off and cry: "'Woe! Woe, O great city, O Babylon, city of power! In one hour your doom has come!'
11 "The merchants of the earth will weep and mourn over her because no one buys their cargoes any more—
12 Cargoes of gold, silver, precious stones and pearls;

fine linen, purple, silk and scarlet cloth; every sort of citron wood, and articles of every kind made of ivory, costly wood, bronze, iron and marble;
13 Cargoes of cinnamon and spice, of incense, myrrh and frankincense, of wine and olive oil, of fine flour and wheat; cattle and sheep; horses and carriages; and bodies and souls of men.
14 "They will say, 'The fruit you longed for is gone from you. All your riches and splendor have vanished, never to be recovered.'
15 The merchants who sold these things and gained their wealth from her will stand far off, terrified at her torment. They will weep and mourn
16 And cry out: "'Woe! Woe, O great city, dressed in fine linen, purple and scarlet, and glittering with gold, precious stones and pearls!
17 In one hour such great wealth has been brought to ruin!' "Every sea captain, and all who travel by ship, the sailors, and all who earn their living from the sea, will stand far off.
18 When they see the smoke of her burning, they will exclaim, 'Was there ever a city like this great city?'
19 They will throw dust on their heads, and with weeping and mourning cry out: "'Woe! Woe, O great city, where all who had ships on the sea became rich through her wealth! In one hour she has been brought to ruin!
20 Rejoice over her, O heaven! Rejoice, saints and apostles and prophets! God has judged her for the way she treated you.'"
21 Then a mighty angel picked up a boulder the size of a large millstone and threw it into the sea, and said: "With such violence the great city of Babylon will be thrown down, never to be found again.
22 The music of harpists and musicians, flute players and trumpeters, will never be heard in you again. No workman of any trade will ever be found in you again. The sound of a millstone will never be heard in you again.

2) They will be terrorized, fearing the effects of her doom

c. The mourning by the shippers or sea captains of the world

1) They will mourn because the city will be the major shipping center for them
2) They will mourn because they will lose their means of wealth

d. The host of heaven will rejoice

**5 The actual destruction of Babylon**
a. Will be violent

b. Will be total

| 6 The reason for Babylon's destruction repeated | 23 The light of a lamp will never shine in you again. The voice of bridegroom and bride will never be heard in you again. Your merchants | By your magic spell all the nations were led astray. | b. Spiritual corruption |
| | | | c. Deception |
| a. Pride: "Great men" | were the world's great men. | 24 In her was found the blood of prophets and of the saints, and of all who have been killed on the earth." | d. Persecution of believers |

# DIVISION X

## THE JUDGMENT OF BOTH RELIGIOUS BABYLON AND POLITICAL BABYLON, 17:1-18:24

### C. The Collapse of Political Babylon, 18:1-24

(18:1-24) **Introduction**: this is the destruction of Babylon, the great capital of the antichrist. (See notes—Rev.14:8 for more discussion.) In the end time Babylon will be what any great capital city is: a great political, commercial, social, and cultural center. In fact, there are two basic ideas as to what Babylon represents in this passage.

⇒ First, some commentators believe that Babylon represents an actual city upon earth. The city is said to be either Rome or else the city of Babylon that will be rebuilt close to where it existed in ancient history. Babylon itself sat somewhere on the Euphrates River at the head of the Persian Gulf. The great preacher W.A. Criswell says that these commentators believe that the whole eastern area will become enormously wealthy with its rich oil reserves. They believe that the nations throughout the whole region will become nations of great commercial influence and power. The area has by far the largest population concentration in the world, a population that demands goods and a booming economy. In addition, the East sits right in the midst of what could become the greatest commercial market in the world: the whole of Europe sits to the north and west, and Africa with its masses sits due west. Then to the east is the vast markets of China, Japan, Australia, Indonesia, the islands of the Pacific and then there is the huge market of the great American continent.

⇒ Second, there are commentators who believe that Babylon represents all the political, commercial, social, and cultural systems of the world. They believe that it symbolizes the godless and secular societies of this world. Again as W.A. Criswell says, Babylon could represent any great city of the world such as Washington, New York, Tokyo, London, Moscow, or Paris. These commentators believe that this chapter is picturing the great destruction of all the godless societies of the end time with their political, commercial and cultural systems. They believe that Babylon is just a symbol of the destruction of the godless government and society all across the world. (*Expository Sermons On Revelation*, Vol.5, p.18f).

Both of these positions make sense, and both can definitely come true. The eastern nations of the world can undoubtedly become some of the wealthiest nations of the world with their vast population and resources (cp. the vast oil reserves and the possibility of the minerals yet to be discovered). Indeed, some nations already have enormous wealth. Worldwide political and commercial power can come when some leader arises who can pull some of the nations into a confederation of cooperating states, some leader like the antichrist or some forerunner before he enters world history.

With this as background, this Scripture declares emphatically that Babylon is going to be destroyed. The great capital city of the world in the end time is going to be destroyed by the Lord Jesus Christ. Remember *chapter sixteen* where the seventh bowl judgment was poured out and all the great cities of the world were crumbled to ashes. This is where Babylon will be destroyed.

> **Then there came flashes of lightning, rumblings, peals of thunder and a severe earthquake. No earthquake like it has ever occurred since man has been on earth, so tremendous was the quake. The great city split into three parts, and the cities of the nations collapsed. God remembered Babylon the Great and gave her the cup filled with the wine of the fury of his wrath. (Rev 16:18-19)**

Note that God Himself will destroy Babylon. It will be God Himself who will pour out the cup of His wrath upon Babylon, that godless city and society who will bring the *great tribulation* to the world. This is the picture of the *collapse of political Babylon*. (See note—Rev.14:8 for more discussion.)

1. There is the great angelic announcement (v.1).
2. The reasons why Babylon will be destroyed (v.2-7).
3. The quickness of Babylon's destruction (v.8).
4. The impact of Babylon's fall (v.9-20).
5. The actual destruction of Babylon (v.21-23).
6. The reason for Babylon's destruction repeated (v.23-24).

**1** (18:1) **Babylon—Government**: there is the great angelic announcement from heaven. A great angel comes down from heaven. He is coming from God Himself, and he is coming with great authority and power. Note his glory: he is so glorious that the light of his glory blazes across the whole earth. This symbolizes that his message and mission are meant for the whole earth. The glory of what he is about to announce is for the ears of the whole world.

**2** (18:2-7) **Babylon—Society—Government**: there are the reasons why Babylon, the capital of the antichrist, will be destroyed. Remember Babylon can also represent godless society. Five reasons are given why God will destroy the city.

1. Babylon will be destroyed because of spiritual corruption (v.2. See note, pt.2—Rev.18:23-24.) Babylon, the great city of the end time, will not look to God. Therefore, it will become...

- the place for devils and their worship.
- the place for every evil spirit.

Note how graphically the picture is painted: it will become the cage for every unclean and hateful bird. The morals and sins of Babylon will run so loose that the city will become a center for every evil and unclean spirit and filth of the underworld.

⇒ Immorality, sexual immorality, adultery, homosexuality, abnormal sex—all forms of immoral behavior will run wild.
⇒ Lying, stealing, and cheating will run rampant.
⇒ Lusting after more and more of the possessions and pleasures of the world will increase greatly.
⇒ Magical arts or sorcery, devil worship, witchcraft, palm readers, fortune tellers, and astrology will be revived and run loose.
⇒ Secularism, materialism, and humanism will dominate the philosophies and behavior of people.

There will be few who will believe and follow Christ and the Word of God. Babylon and society will be spiritually corrupt.

**Thought 1.** Scripture says that there are several spirits that corrupt man.
⇒ The spirit that makes you a slave again.

> **For you did not receive a spirit that makes you a slave again to fear, but you received the Spirit of sonship. And by him we cry, "Abba, Father." (Rom 8:15)**

⇒ The spirit of the world.

> **We have not received the spirit of the world but the Spirit who is from God, that we may understand what God has freely given us. (1 Cor 2:12)**

⇒ The spirit of man.

> **For who among men knows the thoughts of a man except the man's spirit within him? In the same way no one knows the thoughts of God except the Spirit of God. (1 Cor 2:11)**

⇒ The spirit that works in those who are disobedient.

> **In which you used to live when you followed the ways of this world and of the ruler of the kingdom of the air, the spirit who is now at work in those who are disobedient. (Eph 2:2)**

⇒ The spirit of false teaching and preaching.

> **Dear friends, do not believe every spirit, but test the spirits to see whether they are from God, because many false prophets have gone out into the world. (1 John 4:1)**

⇒ The spirit of falsehood.

> **We are from God, and whoever knows God listens to us; but whoever is not from God does not listen to us. This is how we recognize the Spirit of truth and the spirit of falsehood. (1 John 4:6)**

2. Babylon, the great capital city, will be destroyed because the city corrupted nations, kings, and merchants (v.3). The word "adultery" tells us what this means: adultery means *spiritual adultery*, the rejection of God and the turning to other gods. The world of the end time will be days of secularism, humanism, and materialism. Man will worship himself and his secular society. He will focus his life around...

- technology
- science
- education
- pleasures
- recreation
- comforts

Babylon, the capital of the world, will take the lead in the secular society. It will have economic wealth that will literally intoxicate the world. The businessmen and merchants of the world will grow rich because of its wealth. Its wealth will be so vast that it will be able to control nations and leaders and businessmen all over the world.

The point is this: the capital city will use its influence for evil, for secularism and power. The city will manipulate the nations and leaders of the world to follow its own evil purposes. Those evil purposes will be a secular society, a worship of the state and its leader as the answer to the utopian society, that is, to meeting the needs of the people. The city will lead the nations to exterminate the Jews, Christian believers, and the faithful of all other religions who refuse to give their first loyalty to the state. Babylon will be able to seduce the nations and leaders to follow in this evil plot because of its wealth. (See pt.6—Rev.13:4-8 for more discussion.)

> **As it is written: "God's name is blasphemed among the Gentiles because of you." (Rom 2:24)**

**Thought 1.** Even today, if all the nations of the Middle East could be united under one rule, the confederation of power could make enormous demands and manipulate the money of the nations of the world. How? Through its oil. Add to this confederation some of the nations of Europe, of the Old Roman Empire that will be revived, and imagine the wealth and power. It would be mind-boggling—just stagger the imagination.

3. Babylon will be destroyed because the city will corrupt people through secularism (v.4-5). One of the easiest things in the world is to become influenced by secularism. A secular society offers comfort, health, education, possessions, pleasures, time, recreation, culture, and art. It offers all that a person could ever want physically and mentally. But it denies and rejects God. Therefore, the citizens of a secular society are led to focus life upon this world and nothing more. The result is utterly tragic: the citizens go out into eternity lost and doomed. They enter into whatever lies beyond this world unprepared. And Scripture declares that God and eternity lie beyond this world, either an eternity of hell and punishment apart from God or an eternity of life and reward with God. Therefore Babylon, the great city of secular society, will stand guilty of misleading people into sin, into the false belief of secularism and humanism. Note: these sins are said to have reached up to heaven and that God remembers its crimes (v.5).

But mark this: There will be terrible times in the last days. People will be lovers of themselves, lovers of money, boastful, proud, abusive, disobedient to their parents, ungrateful, unholy, (2 Tim 3:1-2)

For the time will come when men will not put up with sound doctrine. Instead, to suit their own desires, they will gather around them a great number of teachers to say what their itching ears want to hear. (2 Tim 4:3)

God saw how corrupt the earth had become, for all the people on earth had corrupted their ways. (Gen 6:12)

Help, LORD, for the godly are no more; the faithful have vanished from among men. (Psa 12:1)

The godly have been swept from the land; not one upright man remains. All men lie in wait to shed blood; each hunts his brother with a net. (Micah 7:2)

4. Babylon will be destroyed because the city will take the lead in persecuting God's people (v.6). Note the words "what she has done." The antichrist and his government of Babylon will launch the worst holocaust the world has ever seen against believers, the Jews, and the religious faithful of the earth. Literally millions will be persecuted and killed in the most inhuman and terrorizing ways imaginable. The wrath of God will fall upon the government and capital that launched this merciless slaughter of human life. And note: the wrath will be double wrath. God will avenge the death of His dear followers, those who truly trust His Son, the Lord Jesus Christ.

5. Babylon will be destroyed because of self-glory, pride, selfish extravagance, and indulgence (v.7). Every good and every perfect gift comes from God. Therefore, the leaders and citizens of Babylon should praise and thank God for the wealth and comforts of their land and nation. And they should use their wealth to help meet the needs of a world that reels under the weight of so many desperate needs. This is exactly what God expects of every leader and people upon earth. Wealth of land and resources are not given for indulgent and extravagant living, nor for self-glorying and boasting. The natural resources and wealth of the earth have been given by God to take care of the needs of man—all men— not for just a few. God will not, above all else, tolerate selfishness, hoarding, indulgence, extravagance, and then glorying in oneself because one has been able to hoard and bank more than someone else. This is the reason Babylon, the godless capital of the last days, will be destroyed. The city will lead the world to glory in the secular society of the state—the technology, science, humanism, and ability of the state to amass and provide wealth to the world. The city will lead the world to boast in the science and technology and efforts of man and his government—to ignore, reject, and deny God. Therefore, the judgment of God will fall and destroy Babylon.

For whoever exalts himself will be humbled, and whoever humbles himself will be exalted. (Mat 23:12)

You say, 'I am rich; I have acquired wealth and do not need a thing.' But you do not realize that you are wretched, pitiful, poor, blind and naked. (Rev 3:17)

Pride goes before destruction, a haughty spirit before a fall. (Prov 16:18)

Haughty eyes and a proud heart, the lamp of the wicked, are sin! (Prov 21:4)

You said in your heart, "I will ascend to heaven; I will raise my throne above the stars of God; I will sit enthroned on the mount of assembly, on the utmost heights of the sacred mountain. I will ascend above the tops of the clouds; I will make myself like the Most High." (Isa 14:13-14)

Though you soar like the eagle and make your nest among the stars, from there I will bring you down," declares the LORD. (Oba 1:4)

**3** (18:8) **Judgment—Babylon**: there is the quickness of Babylon's destruction. It will happen in one day. Actually verse ten says that the city will be destroyed in *one hour*, which is referring to immediate and instantaneous destruction. In one hour's time the plagues of death, mourning, and famine will sweep through the streets of the city, and then it will happen: the city will be utterly destroyed by fire. How? This verse tells us: by the strength of the Lord God who judges us.

**Thought 1.** Note two possibilities.
⇒ The words *death, mourning and famine* may be referring to an immediate plague of some sort hitting the city all at once, some plague that would have the same effects as poisonous gas.
⇒ The one hour destruction by fire may be referring to an immediate destruction like what fell upon Sodom and Gomorrah or to something that is as forceful and explosive as an atomic bomb.

But I tell you, it will be more bearable for Tyre and Sidon on the day of judgment than for you. (Mat 11:22)

"At that time the sign of the Son of Man will appear in the sky, and all the nations of the earth will mourn. They will see the Son of Man coming on the clouds of the sky, with power and great glory. (Mat 24:30)

This is the verdict: Light has come into the world, but men loved darkness instead of light because their deeds were evil. (John 3:19)

And give relief to you who are troubled, and to us as well. This will happen when the Lord Jesus is revealed from heaven in blazing fire with his powerful angels. He will punish those who do not know God and do not obey the gospel of our Lord Jesus. (2 Th 1:7-8)

Just as man is destined to die once, and after that to face judgment, (Heb 9:27)

If this is so, then the Lord knows how to rescue godly men from trials and to hold the unrighteous for the day of judgment, while continuing their punishment. (2 Pet 2:9)

By the same word the present heavens and earth are reserved for fire, being kept for the day of judgment and destruction of ungodly men. (2 Pet 3:7)

Look, he is coming with the clouds, and every eye will see him, even those who pierced him; and all the peoples of the earth will mourn because of him. So shall it be! Amen. (Rev 1:7)

Declare his glory among the nations, his marvelous deeds among all peoples. (Psa 96:3)

I thought in my heart, "God will bring to judgment both the righteous and the wicked, for there will be a time for every activity, a time for every deed." (Eccl 3:17)

**4** (18:9-20) **Judgment—Babylon:** there is the impact of Babylon's fall. The great influence upon the world can be seen by the reaction of the world to the city's destruction.

1. There will be great mourning by the political leaders and governments of the world who are allied with the antichrist (v.9). There will be some nations whose power depends entirely upon the antichrist and his capital, and there will be other nations whose trade with the city will be less, but their economies will still be greatly affected. Remember: the whole world will be undergoing disaster after disaster at this time, and many of the great cities of the world will be destroyed and reduced to ashes (cp. Rev.16:17-21).

⇒ This means that the mourning for Babylon is symbolic of the mourning that will be going on worldwide.

⇒ This also means that the mourning is self-centered. The leaders of the nations know that Babylon could have been an enormous help in rebuilding. They, of course, will not be aware that Christ is returning to rule upon earth.

A greedy man brings trouble to his family, but he who hates bribes will live. (Prov 15:27)

Whoever loves money never has money enough; whoever loves wealth is never satisfied with his income. This too is meaningless. (Eccl 5:10)

Like a partridge that hatches eggs it did not lay is the man who gains riches by unjust means. When his life is half gone, they will desert him, and in the end he will prove to be a fool. (Jer 17:11)

For the love of money is a root of all kinds of evil. Some people, eager for money, have wandered from the faith and pierced themselves with many griefs. (1 Tim 6:10)

Your gold and silver are corroded. Their corrosion will testify against you and eat your flesh like fire. You have hoarded wealth in the last days. (James 5:3)

2. There will be mourning by the businessmen and commercial people of the world (v.11-17a). There will be businesses all over the world that are devastated by the collapse of Babylon and its wealth, and many more businesses and economies will be drastically affected. There are at least thirty kinds of merchandise listed here in Scripture, merchandise that shows how much of a commercial center the city will become. It will be one of the commercial crossroads of the world, one of the trading and financial centers.

Note how this is brought out so clearly by Scripture. The Amplified New Testament describes it well:

"And the rulers and leaders of the earth, who joined her in her immorality [idolatry] and luxuriated with her, will weep and beat their breasts and lament over her when they see the smoke of her conflagration. They will stand a long way off, in terror of her torment, and they will cry, Woe and alas! the great city! the mighty city, Babylon! In one single hour how your doom (judgment) has overtaken you! And earth's businessmen weep and grieve over her, because no one buys their freight (cargo) any more. Their merchandise is of gold, silver, precious stones and pearls; of fine linen, purple, silk and scarlet [stuffs]; all kinds of scented wood, all sorts of articles of ivory, all varieties of objects of costly woods, bronze, iron and marble; of cinnamon, spices, incense, ointment and perfume, and frankincense; of wine and olive oil, fine flour and wheat; of cattle and sheep, horses and conveyances; and of slaves, [that is] the bodies, and souls of men! The ripe fruits and delicacies for which your soul longed have gone from you, and all your luxuries and dainties, your elegance and splendor are lost to you, never again to be recovered or experienced! The dealers who handled these articles, who grew wealthy through their business with her, will stand a long way off, in terror of her doom and torment, weeping and grieving aloud, and saying, Alas, alas for the great city that was robed in fine linen, in purple and scarlet, bedecked and glittering with gold, with precious stones, and with pearls! Because in one [single] hour all the vast wealth has been destroyed - wiped out" (v.9-17a).

Note what it is that the business and commercial people of the world mourn: the loss of so much wealth (v.17a). Note also the reference to slavery. Babylon, the capital of the world, will be enslaving people all over the world. Keep in mind the holocaust that will be launched against the true followers of Christ, the Jews, and other staunch religionists. The picture will be the same as has been true in every holocaust down through history: the souls of men will mean no more than another piece of merchandise or commodity—all to be used for the benefit of the state and the comfort of the supporters of the state.

A flood will carry off his house, rushing waters on the day of God's wrath. (Job 20:28)

For all can see that wise men die; the foolish and the senseless alike perish and leave their wealth to others. (Psa 49:10)

Cast but a glance at riches, and they are gone, for they will surely sprout wings and fly off to the sky like an eagle. (Prov 23:5)

For riches do not endure forever, and a crown is not secure for all generations. (Prov 27:24)

I hated all the things I had toiled for under the sun, because I must leave them to the one who comes after me. (Eccl 2:18)

**Like a partridge that hatches eggs it did not lay is the man who gains riches by unjust means. When his life is half gone, they will desert him, and in the end he will prove to be a fool. (Jer 17:11)**

**For we brought nothing into the world, and we can take nothing out of it. (1 Tim 6:7)**

3. There will be mourning by the shippers or sea captains of the world. As in every major city, most of the merchandise in Babylon will either be shipped in or shipped out in some sort of trade. The city will be a great crossroads for trade, so great that the shipping industry will suffer a devastating blow by the city's destruction. Think of the transport and shipping companies that will be bankrupt by the collapse of such a major commercial center as Babylon. Yet, think about all the cities that will be reduced to ashes when the catastrophic judgment of the end time falls. Remember this was seen in the last bowl judgment. When God's wrath falls upon the godless societies and cities of this world, and cities crumble by the hundreds and thousands, it will take time for the survivors to learn about the worldwide devastation. It will take as much time as it would take if an atomic war broke out and devastated the great cities of the world. The only difference between the destruction of an atomic war and the destruction of the end time is that God Himself is going to launch the destruction in the end time. In fact, He says that He is going to destroy the godless cities by sending a great earthquake (Rev.16:18f).

The point is this: the destruction and the catastrophic effects of the destruction are going to be worldwide. The survivors will have little left of the world they have always known.

**"Do not store up for yourselves treasures on earth, where moth and rust destroy, and where thieves break in and steal. (Mat 6:19)**

**Man is a mere phantom as he goes to and fro: He bustles about, but only in vain; he heaps up wealth, not knowing who will get it. (Psa 39:6)**

**And when your herds and flocks grow large and your silver and gold increase and all you have is multiplied, Then your heart will become proud and you will forget the LORD your God, who brought you out of Egypt, out of the land of slavery. (Deu 8:13-14)**

**Do not trust in extortion or take pride in stolen goods; though your riches increase, do not set your heart on them. (Psa 62:10)**

**A faithful man will be richly blessed, but one eager to get rich will not go unpunished. (Prov 28:20)**

**Then Jesus said to his disciples, "I tell you the truth, it is hard for a rich man to enter the kingdom of heaven. (Mat 19:23)**

**People who want to get rich fall into temptation and a trap and into many foolish and harmful desires that plunge men into ruin and destruction. (1 Tim 6:9)**

4. There will be rejoicing by the heavenly host (v.20). The collapse of godless Babylon means...
* that the ungodliness and evil of this world are being conquered.
* that righteousness is soon to be established among all people.
* that Jesus Christ is to soon come and set up His kingdom upon earth.
* that there will be no more rejection and rebellion allowed by God.
* that God will be worshipped and served by all people upon earth.
* that all of God's people who suffered abuse and persecution will be vindicated.

**Love must be sincere. Hate what is evil; cling to what is good. (Rom 12:9)**

**And give relief to you who are troubled, and to us as well. This will happen when the Lord Jesus is revealed from heaven in blazing fire with his powerful angels. He will punish those who do not know God and do not obey the gospel of our Lord Jesus. They will be punished with everlasting destruction and shut out from the presence of the Lord and from the majesty of his power (2 Th 1:7-9)**

**For we know him who said, "It is mine to avenge; I will repay," and again, "The Lord will judge his people." (Heb 10:30)**

**It is mine to avenge; I will repay. In due time their foot will slip; their day of disaster is near and their doom rushes upon them." (Deu 32:35)**

**O LORD, the God who avenges, O God who avenges, shine forth. (Psa 94:1)**

**I will carry out great vengeance on them and punish them in my wrath. Then they will know that I am the LORD, when I take vengeance on them.'" (Ezek 25:17)**

**I will take vengeance in anger and wrath upon the nations that have not obeyed me." (Micah 5:15)**

**The LORD is a jealous and avenging God; the LORD takes vengeance and is filled with wrath. The LORD takes vengeance on his foes and maintains his wrath against his enemies. (Nahum 1:2)**

**5** (18:21-23) **Babylon—Judgment**: there is the actual destruction of Babylon. Note two points.

1. The destruction will be violent. This is the picture of the mighty angel taking a huge boulder and casting it into the sea. Picture the might and strength of the angel...
* the thrust and velocity of his throw.
* the violent impact of the boulder as it hits the water.
* the violent and immediate disappearance of the boulder.
* the violent waves that begin to rush out from the boulder in every direction.

The violence of the whole scene is clearly pictured. (The catastrophe pictured is similar to that which would happen in an atomic explosion. Cp. Mal.4:1 in the verses below.)

2. The destruction will be total. The boulder disappeared immediately. Babylon, the godless government and city,

will be found no more. The destruction will be swift and violent, and the city will be utterly devastated and reduced to ashes.

"And the sound of harpists and minstrels and flute players and trumpeters shall never again be heard in you, and no skilled artisan of any craft shall ever again be found in you, and the sound of the millstone shall never again be heard in you. And never again shall the light of a lamp shine in you, and the voice of bridegroom and bride shall never be heard in you again" (v.22-23 b, The Amplified New Testament).

The ax is already at the root of the trees, and every tree that does not produce good fruit will be cut down and thrown into the fire." (Luke 3:9)

And give relief to you who are troubled, and to us as well. This will happen when the Lord Jesus is revealed from heaven in blazing fire with his powerful angels. He will punish those who do not know God and do not obey the gospel of our Lord Jesus. They will be punished with everlasting destruction and shut out from the presence of the Lord and from the majesty of his power (2 Th 1:7-9)

Then a mighty angel picked up a boulder the size of a large millstone and threw it into the sea, and said: "With such violence the great city of Babylon will be thrown down, never to be found again. (Rev 18:21)

The LORD is angry with all nations; his wrath is upon all their armies. He will totally destroy them, he will give them over to slaughter. (Isa 34:2)

I will summon all the peoples of the north and my servant Nebuchadnezzar king of Babylon," declares the LORD, "and I will bring them against this land and its inhabitants and against all the surrounding nations. I will completely destroy them and make them an object of horror and scorn, and an everlasting ruin. (Jer 25:9)

"Surely the day is coming; it will burn like a furnace. All the arrogant and every evildoer will be stubble, and that day that is coming will set them on fire," says the LORD Almighty. "Not a root or a branch will be left to them. (Mal 4:1)

**6** (18:23-24) **Babylon—Judgment—Sins**: there are the reasons for Babylon's destruction repeated. These will be just listed here to give an overview. Note: these are the same sins for which God will judge any nation, government, society, or people.

1. There is pride and arrogance.

The light of a lamp will never shine in you again. The voice of bridegroom and bride will never be heard in you again. Your merchants were the world's great men. By your magic spell all the nations were led astray. (Rev 18:23)

Give her as much torture and grief as the glory and luxury she gave herself. In her heart she boasts, 'I sit as queen; I am not a widow, and I will never mourn.' (Rev 18:7)

Babylon, the jewel of kingdoms, the glory of the Babylonians' pride, will be overthrown by God like Sodom and Gomorrah. (Isa 13:19)

You will take up this taunt against the king of Babylon: How the oppressor has come to an end! How his fury has ended! (Isa 14:4)

2. There is magic, sorcery and corruption.

By your magic spell all the nations were led astray. (Rev 18:23)

With a mighty voice he shouted: "Fallen! Fallen is Babylon the Great! She has become a home for demons and a haunt for every evil spirit, a haunt for every unclean and detestable bird. (Rev 18:2)

3. There is deception.

By your magic spell all the nations were led astray. (Rev 18:23)

For all the nations have drunk the maddening wine of her adulteries. The kings of the earth committed adultery with her, and the merchants of the earth grew rich from her excessive luxuries." (Rev 18:3)

4. There is the persecution of believers.

In her was found the blood of prophets and of the saints, and of all who have been killed on the earth." (Rev 18:24)

Give back to her as she has given; pay her back double for what she has done. Mix her a double portion from her own cup. (Rev 18:6)

5. There is the misuse of wealth: selfishly living in luxury, indulgence, and extravagance.

The light of a lamp will never shine in you again. The voice of bridegroom and bride will never be heard in you again. Your merchants were the world's great men. By your magic spell all the nations were led astray. (Rev 18:23; cp. Rev.18:7, 9, 11-17, 19)

The merchants of the earth grew rich from her excessive luxuries." (Rev 18:3b)

6. There is the corruption of people.

By your magic spell all the nations [people] were led astray. (Rev 18:23c)
Then I heard another voice from heaven say: "Come out of her, my people, so that you will not share in her sins, so that you will not receive any of her plagues; (Rev 18:4)

## CHAPTER 19

### XI. THE GREAT WEDDING SUPPER OF THE LAMB, OF THE LORD JESUS CHRIST, 19:1-10

**1 The Wedding Supper will be a supper of glorious praise**
   a. It will be an hallelujah of salvation

   b. It will be an hallelujah of victory

   c. It will be an hallelujah of worship

   d. It will be an hallelujah of God's omnipotent reign

After this I heard what sounded like the roar of a great multitude in heaven shouting: "Hallelujah! Salvation and glory and power belong to our God,
2 For true and just are his judgments. He has condemned the great prostitute who corrupted the earth by her adulteries. He has avenged on her the blood of his servants."
3 And again they shouted: "Hallelujah! The smoke from her goes up for ever and ever."
4 The twenty-four elders and the four living creatures fell down and worshiped God, who was seated on the throne. And they cried: "Amen, Hallelujah!"
5 Then a voice came from the throne, saying: "Praise our God, all you his servants, you who fear him, both small and great!"
6 Then I heard what sounded like a great multitude, like the roar of rushing waters and like loud peals of thunder, shouting: "Hallelujah! For our Lord God Almighty reigns.
7 Let us rejoice and be glad and give him glory! For the wedding of the Lamb has come, and his bride has made herself ready.
8 Fine linen, bright and clean, was given her to wear." (Fine linen stands for the righteous acts of the saints.)
9 Then the angel said to me, "Write: 'Blessed are those who are invited to the wedding supper of the Lamb!'" And he added, "These are the true words of God."
10 At this I fell at his feet to worship him. But he said to me, "Do not do it! I am a fellow servant with you and with your brothers who hold to the testimony of Jesus. Worship God! For the testimony of Jesus is the spirit of prophecy."

**2 The Wedding Supper will focus upon the Lamb**
**3 The Wedding Supper will have a pure & prepared Bride**
   a. The bride, the church, prepares herself
   b. The bride, the church, does righteous deeds

**4 The Wedding Supper will be a blessed & glorious event**
   a. It will be blessed because of all those invited to the supper
   b. It will be blessed because it is for the worship of God alone

# DIVISION XI

## THE GREAT WEDDING SUPPER OF THE LAMB, OF THE LORD JESUS CHRIST, 19:1-10

(19:1-10) **Introduction**: this is the great *Wedding Supper of the Lamb*, of the Lord Jesus Christ Himself. This is the great supper where all of heaven will be present to celebrate the union of Jesus Christ and the believers who have followed Him down through the centuries. Everyone in heaven will be there: God, Christ, believers, and the heavenly host. It is to be the most celebrated and joyful event ever experienced up to that point in history. Why? Because it is the great Wedding Supper of the Lord Jesus Christ Himself, God's very own Son. God has planned a celebration for His Son above and beyond anything we could ever imagine or describe. It is to be the first time that *all the redeemed* of all ages have ever come together *at one time* to honor the Lamb who was slain to redeem the universe. Because of what He has done for man, He is deserving of all the honor and praise possible from all heavenly creatures. To give Him such glorious honor, God has planned the greatest celebration and banquet imaginable, the celebration that He calls the great *Wedding Supper of the Lamb* (v.9).

1. The Wedding Supper will be a supper of glorious praise (v.1-6).
2. The Wedding Supper will focus upon the Lamb (v.7).
3. The Wedding Supper will have a pure and prepared Bride (v.7-8).
4. The Wedding Supper will be a blessed and glorious event (v.9-10).

**1** (19:1-6) **Wedding Supper of the Lamb—Hallelujah—Worship—Praise**: the Wedding Supper is a supper of glorious praise. Everyone in heaven will be praising God and Christ at the great supper. Note that the praise centers around four *hallelujah's* in these verses (v.1, 3, 4, 6). Hallelujah simply means *praise God*. It is taken from two Hebrew words: *halal* which means *praise* and *jah* which is the name of God.

1. The supper will be the *hallelujah of salvation*. This is probably the heavenly host that will be singing forth this hallelujah (cp. Rev.5:11; Heb.12:22).
   a. Salvation belongs to God: He is the One who has wrought salvation for believers and for the earth. The angels have been watching the plan of God for generations as it has unfolded for man's salvation. They were amazed time and again at God's unbelievable mercy and grace to man. They have witnessed the whole scene of temptation and trial, sin and evil—all of the struggle and conflict upon earth and within the soul of man. Standing there at the great *Wedding Supper of the Lamb*, the angels will see the most spectacular sight they have ever witnessed: the completion of God's salvation. Therefore, they will praise God as the God of salvation at the great *Wedding Supper of the Lamb*.

Thanks be to God for his indescribable gift! (2 Cor 9:15)

But you are a chosen people, a royal priesthood, a holy nation, a people belonging to God, that you may declare the praises of him who called you out of darkness into his wonderful light. (1 Pet 2:9)

The salvation of the righteous comes from the LORD; he is their stronghold in time of trouble. (Psa 37:39)

Surely God is my salvation; I will trust and not be afraid. The LORD, the LORD, is my strength and my song; he has become my salvation." (Isa 12:2)

In that day they will say, "Surely this is our God; we trusted in him, and he saved us. This is the LORD, we trusted in him; let us rejoice and be glad in his salvation." (Isa 25:9)

b. Glory belongs to God: He alone possesses glory. All the glory, light, and splendor of heaven and earth flows out from His own Being. The very glory which will be given to believers in the glorious day of salvation will come from God. Therefore, the angels will praise God for His glory at the great Wedding Supper of the Lamb.

So that with one heart and mouth you may glorify the God and Father of our Lord Jesus Christ. (Rom 15:6)

Do you not know that your body is a temple of the Holy Spirit, who is in you, whom you have received from God? You are not your own; You were bought at a price. Therefore honor God with your body. (1 Cor 6:19-20)

You who fear the LORD, praise him! All you descendants of Jacob, honor him! Revere him, all you descendants of Israel! (Psa 22:23)

Who is he, this King of glory? The LORD Almighty— he is the King of glory. Selah (Psa 24:10)

Ascribe to the LORD the glory due his name; worship the LORD in the splendor of his holiness. (Psa 29:2)

c. Power belongs to God: He is the Supreme power in the universe. It is His power that has saved man and the world. Therefore, his power will be praised at the great Wedding Supper of the Lamb.

Wealth and honor come from you; you are the ruler of all things. In your hands are strength and power to exalt and give strength to all. (1 Chr 29:12)

Let them sacrifice thank offerings and tell of his works with songs of joy. (Psa 107:22)

Our God is in heaven; he does whatever pleases him. (Psa 115:3)

All the angels were standing around the throne and around the elders and the four living creatures. They fell down on their faces before the throne and worshiped God, Saying: "Amen! Praise and glory and wisdom and thanks and honor and power and

strength be to our God for ever and ever. Amen!" (Rev 7:11-12)

2. The supper will be filled with the *hallelujah of victory* (v.2-3). The Lord Jesus Christ will triumph over all the ungodly and evil of the earth.

⇒ He will destroy the godless politics of the world and the social, commercial, cultural, and religious systems of the world.

⇒ He will avenge the persecution and abuse of His dear followers upon earth. He will judge and destroy every evil, abusive, and murdering person on earth, treating them in perfect justice, giving them a punishment equal to the suffering they inflicted upon earth.

⇒ He will return to earth and establish righteousness upon earth.

Therefore at the great Wedding Supper of the Lamb, the angels will break out in praise to God for the great victory He has wrought upon earth. His judgments are true and righteous. His judgments are exactly matched to a person's evil. They are perfect, altogether true and righteous. Therefore, the angels will praise God for His glorious victory at the great Wedding Supper of the Lamb.

Therefore God exalted him to the highest place and gave him the name that is above every name, That at the name of Jesus every knee should bow, in heaven and on earth and under the earth, And every tongue confess that Jesus Christ is Lord, to the glory of God the Father. (Phil 2:9-11)

Giving thanks to the Father, who has qualified you to share in the inheritance of the saints in the kingdom of light. (Col 1:12)

Saying: "We give thanks to you, Lord God Almighty, the One who is and who was, because you have taken your great power and have begun to reign. (Rev 11:17)

My tongue will speak of your righteousness and of your praises all day long. (Psa 35:28)

3. The supper will be filled with the hallelujah of worship (v.4). Note that the twenty four elders and four living creatures will offer this worship. They will burst forth in praise to God Himself, saying nothing but "Hallelujah, Hallelujah, Hallelujah...." God is so wonderful that He Himself just deserves praise, not for any particular thing, but just because He is so wonderful. At the great Wedding Supper of the Lamb, those who are closest to the throne of God will burst forth in praising God just for Himself.

Be exalted, O God, above the heavens; let your glory be over all the earth. (Psa 57:5)

Let them exalt him in the assembly of the people and praise him in the council of the elders. (Psa 107:32)

4. The supper will be filled with the *hallelujah of God's omnipotent reign* (v.5-6). A voice will cry out from the throne of God to all the servants of God and to all who fear and reverence Him—cry out for all the heavenly host to praise the Lord our God for His *omnipotent reign*. The Lord our God, the Lord Jesus Christ, is going to reign in sovereign power upon the earth and He is going to reign forever

and ever over the new heavens and earth. And note: He is going to reign in omnipotent power, supreme over all. The prayer of God's people, "Your kingdom come," is about to become a living reality upon earth forever and ever. At the great *Wedding Supper of the Lamb* all of heaven will be stirred to praise the Lord God for His omnipotent reign.

> **For he must reign until he has put all his enemies under his feet. (1 Cor 15:25)**
>
> **Therefore God exalted him to the highest place and gave him the name that is above every name, That at the name of Jesus every knee should bow, in heaven and on earth and under the earth, And every tongue confess that Jesus Christ is Lord, to the glory of God the Father. (Phil 2:9-11)**
>
> **Saying: "We give thanks to you, Lord God Almighty, the One who is and who was, because you have taken your great power and have begun to reign. (Rev 11:17)**
>
> **Then I heard a loud voice in heaven say: "Now have come the salvation and the power and the kingdom of our God, and the authority of his Christ. For the accuser of our brothers, who accuses them before our God day and night, has been hurled down. (Rev 12:10)**
>
> **Then I heard what sounded like a great multitude, like the roar of rushing waters and like loud peals of thunder, shouting: "Hallelujah! For our Lord God Almighty reigns. (Rev 19:6)**
>
> **"I have installed my King on Zion, my holy hill." Ask of me, and I will make the nations your inheritance, the ends of the earth your possession. (Psa 2:6, 8)**
>
> **The LORD reigns, let the earth be glad; let the distant shores rejoice. (Psa 97:1)**
>
> **"The days are coming," declares the LORD, "when I will raise up to David a righteous Branch, a King who will reign wisely and do what is just and right in the land. (Jer 23:5)**
>
> **He was given authority, glory and sovereign power; all peoples, nations and men of every language worshiped him. His dominion is an everlasting dominion that will not pass away, and his kingdom is one that will never be destroyed. (Dan 7:14)**
>
> **And said: "O LORD, God of our fathers, are you not the God who is in heaven? You rule over all the kingdoms of the nations. Power and might are in your hand, and no one can withstand you. (2 Chr 20:6)**

**2** (19:7) **Wedding Supper of the Lamb**: the Wedding Supper will focus upon the Lamb Himself, the Lord Jesus Christ. Note that all attention at the supper is to be focused upon the Lamb. In most weddings and wedding suppers upon earth, the attention is centered upon the bride. But this will not be true at the great Wedding Supper of the Lamb. The Lamb of God, the Lord Jesus Christ Himself, will be the great focus. The reasons are clearly stated:

⇒ It will be the Lamb who will be the cause of our gladness and rejoicing.

⇒ It will be the Lamb who deserves glory. We would not even be there if it were not for Him.

⇒ It is the Lamb for whom the supper is named; it is His supper, the great *Wedding Supper of the Lamb*.

⇒ It is the Lamb who stirred the bride to make herself ready.

**Thought 1.** If Jesus Christ is to be the focus of attention in that day, how much more should He be today? Jesus Christ is deserving of our attention, all of our attention, all of our lives, all of our service, worship, and praise.

> **Then he said to them all: "If anyone would come after me, he must deny himself and take up his cross daily and follow me. (Luke 9:23)**
>
> **"If anyone comes to me and does not hate his father and mother, his wife and children, his brothers and sisters—yes, even his own life—he cannot be my disciple. And anyone who does not carry his cross and follow me cannot be my disciple. (Luke 14:26-27)**
>
> **Therefore, I urge you, brothers, in view of God's mercy, to offer your bodies as living sacrifices, holy and pleasing to God—this is your spiritual act of worship. Do not conform any longer to the pattern of this world, but be transformed by the renewing of your mind. Then you will be able to test and approve what God's will is—his good, pleasing and perfect will. (Rom 12:1-2)**
>
> **Do you not know that your body is a temple of the Holy Spirit, who is in you, whom you have received from God? You are not your own; You were bought at a price. Therefore honor God with your body. (1 Cor 6:19-20)**
>
> **What is more, I consider everything a loss compared to the surpassing greatness of knowing Christ Jesus my Lord, for whose sake I have lost all things. I consider them rubbish, that I may gain Christ (Phil 3:8)**

**3** (19:7-8) **Wedding Supper of the Lamb—Righteousness**: the Wedding Supper will have a pure and prepared bride. Note two significant points.

1. The bride, the church, the followers of the Lord Jesus Christ, prepares herself. How? This includes everything that a believer does to become acceptable to God.

a. A believer prepares himself by receiving the Lamb of God as his Savior. A person will not be acceptable at the Wedding Supper of the Lamb unless he accepts the sacrifice of the Lamb as the sacrifice for his own sins. He has to come to the Lamb in order to enter the supper of the Lamb. If he does not come to the Lamb then he will never enter the supper. If he does not live with the Lamb while on earth, then when the Lamb appears at the supper, the person will not be there. He will be excluded and shut out.

b. A believer prepares himself by following the Lamb. The Lamb, the Lord Jesus Christ, sacrificed Himself to the ultimate degree. He gave up His life totally and died for man. Therefore, man is to sacrifice himself to the ultimate degree. Man is to die to self and live entirely for the Lamb of God. The believer is...

- to work and labor to the point of exhaustion as the Lamb worked and labored.
- to live righteously and godly just as the Lamb lived.

When the believer denies himself totally and takes up his cross daily and follows Jesus Christ, then he prepares himself for the great *Wedding Supper of the Lamb*. The believer has given all his heart and life to Jesus Christ. Therefore, he will be prepared to share in the great Wedding Supper of the Lamb.

2. A believer prepares himself by righteous deeds or acts (v.8). The word "righteous" (dikaiomata) here means righteous deeds or acts. This would mean two things.

a. The believer acts righteously, *does the right thing* when he receives Jesus Christ as his Savior. It is then that God accepts the belief of the person *as righteousness*. God actually takes a person's faith in His Son and *counts his faith as righteousness*. Why? Because the person believes that the sacrifice of the Lamb, the death of the Lord Jesus Christ, was for the sins of the world. The person believes that Jesus Christ died for his sins, as his sacrifice, as his substitute. He believes that the penalty and judgment of his sins have been paid for by Christ. Therefore, he is free of sin and made acceptable to God. God takes his faith and *counts his faith as righteousness*. God counts him righteous in the righteousness of Jesus Christ. This is what is called *imputed* righteousness, righteousness that is given or put to one's account before God. It is a righteousness that is counted and credited to the believer. Therefore, when the believer is ready to attend the great *Wedding Supper of the Lamb*, he will be given the clean and white clothing necessary to enter the supper. Note: the fine clothing is actually said to be the righteousness or righteous deeds of the saints.

Now, this is the first righteous deed that a person is to do. If he does this righteous deed, then he will be accepted into the great Wedding Supper of the Lamb.

b. The believer is also to do other righteous deeds. He is to serve the Lamb of God to the fullest degree possible. Every believer is aware that not all believers do this; not all believers serve God with all their heart, soul, and body. In fact, some believers do little for Christ. Therefore, note verse eight carefully: the bride of Christ—all believers—will be in heaven. They will be accepted and made perfect in the righteousness of Christ. They have robes that are white and pure. But note: when they get ready to attend the great *Wedding Supper of the Lamb*, God will give believers another garment that is made of fine linen that will be bright and clean. What is the other garment? It is...

- the garment of righteous deeds and acts.
- the garment of reward.
- the garment that *shows position and responsibility*.
- the garment that rewards one for faithfulness.

Remember: Christ and Scripture declare emphatically that there will be positions in the new heavens and earth, degrees of labor and service, of responsibility and duty assigned to all of us. The unfaithful and half-faithful will not be assigned as high a position as the faithful; they will not be as greatly rewarded. We shall all be perfected and glorified in heaven, but we will not all rule and reign in equal positions. The whole universe, both heaven and earth, are to be remade, perfected, and made alive. The Lord Jesus Christ is going to have His followers looking after the universe for Him. What and how much we will be assigned to oversee and reign over depends on our faithfulness now. These robes for the great *Wedding Supper* will be the robes of righteous deeds and works—the robes that will show the position of our authority throughout eternity. They will, no doubt, determine where we will be sitting at the great Wedding Supper. (See note, *Reward*—Rev. 14:13 for more discussion and a list of rewards.)

He who stands firm to the end will be saved. (Mat 10:22)

You, then, why do you judge your brother? Or why do you look down on your brother? For we will all stand before God's judgment seat. (Rom 14:10)

For no one can lay any foundation other than the one already laid, which is Jesus Christ. If any man builds on this foundation using gold, silver, costly stones, wood, hay or straw, His work will be shown for what it is, because the Day will bring it to light. It will be revealed with fire, and the fire will test the quality of each man's work. If what he has built survives, he will receive his reward. If it is burned up, he will suffer loss; he himself will be saved, but only as one escaping through the flames. (1 Cor 3:11-15)

Therefore, my dear brothers, stand firm. Let nothing move you. Always give yourselves fully to the work of the Lord, because you know that your labor in the Lord is not in vain. (1 Cor 15:58)

For we must all appear before the judgment seat of Christ, that each one may receive what is due him for the things done while in the body, whether good or bad. (2 Cor 5:10)

Therefore, dear friends, since you already know this, be on your guard so that you may not be carried away by the error of lawless men and fall from your secure position. (2 Pet 3:17)

Those whom I love I rebuke and discipline. So be earnest, and repent. (Rev 3:19)

Do you not say, 'Four months more and then the harvest'? I tell you, open your eyes and look at the fields! They are ripe for harvest. (John 4:35)

**4** (19:9-10) **Wedding Supper of the Lamb**: the Wedding Supper will be a blessed and glorious event, the most glorious event ever held in history. Note two things.

1. The Wedding Supper will be the most blessed celebration in all of history. The idea is *greatly blessed*. Note: there are those who say the guests refer to a separate group other than the bride, that is, the church. But this is unlikely. This is the supper of the Lamb, not of the Lamb and the Bride. The Lamb is the One who has called all guests to the great supper. In fact believers, the bride, comprise some of the major guests at the supper.

The supper will be a blessed event for one reason: all of the heavenly host will be there, all believers and all angelic beings, and both God and Christ. It will be a blessed event, a glorious and spectacular celebration, because everyone is there—all believers are gathered together in the great banquet hall of God—all are gathered together for the *very first time* in history.

**Thought 1.** It stirs the heart to think there will be periodic suppers throughout eternity when Christ will gather us all together for celebration. Imagine all of us being called together from our various duties and kingdoms from all parts of the universe, called together for a great supper celebration. What a glorious thought! May God stir our hearts to serve our Lord ever so diligently, day and night. Being with our Lord and God in heaven and in eternity, in the new heavens and earth—it will all be worth it when we see Jesus.

"Then he sent some more servants and said, 'Tell those who have been invited that I have prepared my dinner: My oxen and fattened cattle have been butchered, and everything is ready. Come to the wedding banquet.' (Mat 22:4)

Jesus replied: "A certain man was preparing a great banquet and invited many guests. (Luke 14:16)

However, as it is written: "No eye has seen, no ear has heard, no mind has conceived what God has prepared for those who love him"— (1 Cor 2:9)

Then the angel said to me, "Write: 'Blessed are those who are invited to the wedding supper of the Lamb!'" And he added, "These are the true words of God." (Rev 19:9)

He who overcomes will inherit all this, and I will be his God and he will be my son. (Rev 21:7)

2. The Wedding Supper will be blessed because it is for the purpose of worshipping God and Him alone. This is clearly illustrated for us by what happened to John. Remember: John was still a human man, not a redeemed man. The Lord was giving him a vision of the end time and its events. John is so caught up in the majestic splendor and celebration of the supper that he falls down at the feet of the great angel to worship him. But the angel tells John not to worship him nor anyone else, but to worship God alone. There are two reasons given for this.

⇒ First, all creatures, even the majestic angels of heaven, are only servants of God. They may be majestic beings, but they are not God.

⇒ Second, Jesus Christ Himself is the One who bears testimony of the truth. Christ and Christ alone possesses and shares the truth. The only truth that the angels and servants have is the truth borne by Christ. Therefore, He and He alone is worthy of worship. No angel or any other creature possesses the truth. Therefore, worship God and God alone.

Jesus said to him, "Away from me, Satan! For it is written: 'Worship the Lord your God, and serve him only.'" (Mat 4:10)

God is spirit, and his worshipers must worship in spirit and in truth." (John 4:24)

He said in a loud voice, "Fear God and give him glory, because the hour of his judgment has come. Worship him who made the heavens, the earth, the sea and the springs of water." (Rev 14:7)

But he said to me, "Do not do it! I am a fellow servant with you and with your brothers the prophets and of all who keep the words of this book. Worship God!" (Rev 22:9)

Ascribe to the LORD the glory due his name. Bring an offering and come before him; worship the LORD in the splendor of his holiness. (1 Chr 16:29)

Come, let us bow down in worship, let us kneel before the LORD our Maker; (Psa 95:6)

Worship the LORD in the splendor of his holiness; tremble before him, all the earth. (Psa 96:9)

| | XII. THE FINAL TRI-UMPH: THE MIL-LENNIUM USHERED IN, 19:11-20:15 | knows but he himself. 13 He is dressed in a robe dipped in blood, and his name is the Word of God. | 3 | The slaughtering Word of God: Clothed in blood |
|---|---|---|---|---|
| | | 14 The armies of heaven were following him, riding on white horses and dressed in fine linen, white and clean. | 4 | The heavenly, warring Leader: Heavenly armies follow |
| | A. The Coming of Christ As Conqueror, 19:11-16 | 15 Out of his mouth comes a sharp sword with which to strike down the nations. "He will rule them with an iron scepter." He treads the wine-press of the fury of the wrath of God Almighty. | 5 | The fierce Conqueror a. He will have a weapon: The sword of His mouth—His Word b. He will strike & rule the nations c. He will execute fierce wrath |
| 1 The conquering Christ a. He will sit on a white horse b. He will judge with justice | 11 I saw heaven standing open and there before me was a white horse, whose rider is called Faithful and True. With justice he judges and makes war. | | | |
| 2 The consuming Prince a. His eyes are as fire b. His head is crowned c. His name is secret | 12 His eyes are like blazing fire, and on his head are many crowns. He has a name written on him that no one | 16 On his robe and on his thigh he has this name writ-ten: KING OF KINGS AND LORD OF LORDS. | 6 | The King of kings & Lord of lords: A revealed name |

# DIVISION XII

## THE FINAL TRIUMPH: THE
## MILLENNIUM USHERED IN, 19:11-20:15

### A. The Coming of Christ As Conqueror, 19:11-16

(19:11-16) **Introduction**: this passage launches the close of human history. This is Armageddon, the final and climactic war upon earth. This is the battle that destroys all the ungodly and evil upon this earth, the battle that ushers in the right-eousness of God upon earth. Shockingly, Jesus Christ Him-self will fight this battle. This is the scene of the present passage, a picture of Jesus Christ that is seldom imagined. It is the picture of Jesus Christ coming to earth as the Con-queror. Note: there is no action in these six verses; they only give us a picture of what Christ will look like when He re-turns to earth as the Warrior and Conqueror of heaven.

1. The conquering Christ (v.11).
2. The consuming Prince (v.12).
3. The slaughtering Word of God: clothed in blood (v.13).
4. The heavenly, warring Leader: heavenly armies follow (v.14).
5. The fierce Conqueror (v.15).
6. The King of kings and Lord of lords: a revealed name (v.16).

**1** (19:11) **Jesus Christ, Names—Titles**: Jesus Christ will be the *conquering Christ* (v.11). This is what the picture of the white horse symbolizes. In ancient times, when a Roman general entered a city as the conqueror, he rode a white stal-lion to celebrate his triumph. The day will come when Jesus Christ returns to this earth as the conqueror. And when He does, man can depend upon two things.

1. Jesus Christ will be the faithful and true Conqueror.
   ⇒ Faithful means that He can be trusted and relied upon to judge every enemy when He comes. He said that He would conquer and judge and con-demn all the ungodly and evil of this world, and His Word can be trusted and relied upon.
   ⇒ True means true as opposed to false. The con-quest and judgment of Jesus Christ will be true. Jesus Christ will mete out exactly what a person deserves, no more and no less. No ungodly and evil person need ever fear that Jesus Christ will be unjust or unfair with him. Every ungodly and

evil person can count on Jesus Christ being true. Jesus Christ will judge a person perfectly, in per-fect justice. A person will reap exactly what he has sown. He will be judged and condemned for exactly what he has done.

2. Jesus Christ will judge and make war upon the earth with justice. His righteousness will be the criteria, the law by which all shall be judged. Any person who does not measure up to the righteousness of Jesus Christ will be con-quered, judged, and condemned exactly where he comes up short.

> **For the Son of Man is going to come in his Father's glory with his angels, and then he will reward each person according to what he has done. (Mat 16:27)**
> **And I saw the dead, great and small, standing before the throne, and books were opened. Another book was opened, which is the book of life. The dead were judged ac-cording to what they had done as recorded in the books. (Rev 20:12)**
> **"Behold, I am coming soon! My reward is with me, and I will give to everyone ac-cording to what he has done. (Rev 22:12)**
> **And that you, O Lord, are loving. Sure-ly you will reward each person according to what he has done. (Psa 62:12)**
> **"I the LORD search the heart and ex-amine the mind, to reward a man according to his conduct, according to what his deeds deserve." (Jer 17:10)**

**2** (19:12) **Jesus Christ, Person**: Jesus Christ will be the *consuming Prince* (v.12).

1. His eyes will be like blazing fire. This symbolizes a piercing, penetrating power. He sees everywhere, even in the dark places and behind closed doors. His eyes search the innermost recesses of the heart. He knows all; He is omnis-cient and He is able to conquer all those who reject Him and do evil.

His body was like chrysolite, his face like lightning, his eyes like flaming torches, his arms and legs like the gleam of burnished bronze, and his voice like the sound of a multitude. (Dan 10:6)

Nothing in all creation is hidden from God's sight. Everything is uncovered and laid bare before the eyes of him to whom we must give account. (Heb 4:13)

"I the LORD search the heart and examine the mind, to reward a man according to his conduct, according to what his deeds deserve." (Jer 17:10)

Can anyone hide in secret places so that I cannot see him?" Declares the LORD. "Do not I fill heaven and earth?" Declares the LORD. (Jer 23:24)

2. He will be wearing many crowns (diadema), that is, the royal crowns of rule and authority over many kingdoms. He is coming to conquer all the kingdoms of the earth.

3. He will have a name written somewhere on His clothing, but He alone knows what the name will be. It is futile to guess what it will be. We will see it in that day.

Therefore God exalted him to the highest place and gave him the name that is above every name, That at the name of Jesus every knee should bow, in heaven and on earth and under the earth, And every tongue confess that Jesus Christ is Lord, to the glory of God the Father. (Phil 2:9-11)

His eyes are like blazing fire, and on his head are many crowns. He has a name written on him that no one knows but he himself. (Rev 19:12)

**3** (19:13) **Jesus Christ, Person**: Jesus Christ will be the *slaughtering Word of God* (v.13). Note that His robe will be dipped in blood. This symbolizes the blood of His enemies, not His own redemptive blood. Jesus Christ is going to conquer and defeat all the ungodly and evil of this earth. Now note a most significant fact: how He is going to do it. By the Word of God. He possesses the power of God's Word. In fact, this is His very name, the Word of God. Therefore, all He has to do is speak the Word and the very power and energy and force of His Word will slaughter the ungodly and evil of the world.

"I have trodden the winepress alone; from the nations no one was with me. I trampled them in my anger and trod them down in my wrath; their blood spattered my garments, and I stained all my clothing. (Isa 63:3)

But with righteousness he will judge the needy, with justice he will give decisions for the poor of the earth. He will strike the earth with the rod of his mouth; with the breath of his lips he will slay the wicked. (Isa 11:4)

For the word of God is living and active. Sharper than any double-edged sword, it penetrates even to dividing soul and spirit, joints and marrow; it judges the thoughts and attitudes of the heart. (Heb 4:12)

**4** (19:14) **Jesus Christ, Person**: Jesus Christ will be the *heavenly, warring Leader* (v.14). Note that the armies of heaven follow Him. Who are they? Note: they will be dressed in "fine linen, white and clean." This is the very same clothing worn by the believers at the Wedding Supper of the Lamb (cp. Rev.19:8). Therefore, the armies will include the believers who have followed Christ the Messiah down through the centuries, both the believers of the Old and New Testament. The armies will include all the redeemed. In addition, the armies will include the multitude of angels that Jesus Christ said He was going to bring with Him when He returned to earth (Mt.25:31).

"When the Son of Man comes in his glory, and all the angels with him, he will sit on his throne in heavenly glory. (Mat 25:31)

And give relief to you who are troubled, and to us as well. This will happen when the Lord Jesus is revealed from heaven in blazing fire with his powerful angels. He will punish those who do not know God and do not obey the gospel of our Lord Jesus. They will be punished with everlasting destruction and shut out from the presence of the Lord and from the majesty of his power (2 Th 1:7-9)

Enoch, the seventh from Adam, prophesied about these men: "See, the Lord is coming with thousands upon thousands of his holy ones To judge everyone, and to convict all the ungodly of all the ungodly acts they have done in the ungodly way, and of all the harsh words ungodly sinners have spoken against him." (Jude 1:14-15)

**5** (19:15) **Jesus Christ, Person**: Jesus Christ will be the *fierce Conqueror*. This is seen in three things.

1. First, He will have a weapon; a sharp sword will proceed out of His mouth. This symbolizes that His weapon will be the power of His Word. The Word of God is the sword of God.

Take the helmet of salvation and the sword of the Spirit, which is the word of God. (Eph 6:17)

For the word of God is living and active. Sharper than any double-edged sword, it penetrates even to dividing soul and spirit, joints and marrow; it judges the thoughts and attitudes of the heart. (Heb 4:12)

But with righteousness he will judge the needy, with justice he will give decisions for the poor of the earth. He will strike the earth with the rod of his mouth; with the breath of his lips he will slay the wicked. (Isa 11:4)

2. Second, He will strike and rule the nations of the earth with an iron scepter. He will conquer and subject them all and take His rightful place as the Sovereign Lord over the earth and all its peoples.

You will rule them with an iron scepter; you will dash them to pieces like pottery." (Psa 2:9)

But with righteousness he will judge the needy, with justice he will give decisions for the poor of the earth. He will strike the earth with the rod of his mouth; with the breath of his lips he will slay the wicked. (Isa 11:4)

3. Third, He will execute the fury of the wrath of God Almighty (see note, pt.2—Rev.14:18-19; also see note—Rev.14:10-11 for discussion and verses).

**6** (19:16) **Jesus Christ, Person**: Jesus Christ will be the King of kings and Lord of lords. He is the *sovereign King and Sovereign Lord* of the universe. No one exists except by His will and no one shall be allowed to be a citizen of His kingdom unless they have His approval. When He comes as conqueror, He is going to banish all those who have not acknowledged and subjected themselves to His sovereignty, who have *not worshipped and served* Him as the greatest of all Kings and Lords.

Which God will bring about in his own time—God, the blessed and only Ruler, the King of kings and Lord of lords, (1 Tim 6:15)

And from Jesus Christ, who is the faithful witness, the firstborn from the dead, and the ruler of the kings of the earth. To him who loves us and has freed us from our sins by his blood, (Rev 1:5)

They will make war against the Lamb, but the Lamb will overcome them because he is Lord of lords and King of kings—and with him will be his called, chosen and faithful followers." (Rev 17:14)

On his robe and on his thigh he has this name written: KING OF KINGS AND LORD OF LORDS. (Rev 19:16)

| | **B. The Great Battle of Armageddon, 19:17-21** | to make war against the rider on the horse and his army. | |
|---|---|---|---|
| **1 The terrifying call to the supper of the great God** | 17 And I saw an angel standing in the sun, who cried in a loud voice to all the birds flying in midair, "Come, gather together for the great supper of God, | 20 But the beast was captured, and with him the false prophet who had performed the miraculous signs on his behalf. With these signs he had deluded those who had received the mark of the | **3 The simple & quick capture of the hostile forces** |
| a. The guests: Birds | | | |
| b. The purpose: To destroy the wicked | 18 So that you may eat the flesh of kings, generals, and mighty men, of horses and their riders, and the flesh of all people, free and slave, small and great." | beast and worshiped his image. The two of them were thrown alive into the fiery lake of burning sulfur. | **4 The grim judgment of the hostile forces: A lake of fire** |
| **2 The mobilizing of the world's forces** | 19 Then I saw the beast and the kings of the earth and their armies gathered together | 21 The rest of them were killed with the sword that came out of the mouth of the rider on the horse, and all the birds gorged themselves on their flesh. | **5 The weapon of victory** |

# DIVISION XII

## THE FINAL TRIUMPH: THE MILLENNIUM USHERED IN, 19:11-20:15

### B. The Great Battle of Armageddon, 19:17-21

(19:17-21) **Introduction**: this is the great battle of Armageddon, the final battle of human history. This is where human history ends, where the Lord Jesus Christ intervenes and stops the madness and evil of humanity. This is where Jesus Christ returns to earth and destroys the ungodly and evil of this world. This is what the Bible and believers call...

- the great day of Jehovah
- the great day of God
- the day
- the day of the Lord
- the final battle of human history
- the judgment of God upon the godless governments of this world
- the end of the devil's rule upon earth
- the supper of the great God
- the great battle of Armageddon

The battle of Armageddon is the intervention of Jesus Christ into world history. It is His returning to earth and destroying all the forces of evil upon earth—once for all. (See outline and notes—Rev.14:20; 16:12-16 for more discussion.)

1. The terrifying call to the supper of the great God (v.17-18).
2. The mobilizing of the world's forces (v.19).
3. The simple and quick, capture of the hostile forces (v.20).
4. The grim judgment of the hostile forces: a lake of fire (v.20).
5. The weapon of victory (v.21).

**1** (19:17-18) **Armageddon**: there will be the terrifying call to the supper of the great God. This supper differs entirely from the *Wedding Supper of the Lamb* which will be for believers. This supper, the *Supper of the Great God* will be for unbelievers and it will be the most terrifying moment in human history.

Note the terrifying preparation for this supper. A mighty angel cries with a loud voice to *all the birds* of the air. He cries for them to gather together for the Supper of the Great God. Why are the birds of the air called together? Because God is going to destroy the godless nations and armies of this world. God is going to slay all the armies of all the nations of the world. God is ending once for all the slaughter of human life upon this earth. Therefore, the angel is calling together all the birds of the air to feast upon the ungodly of this world when they have been slain. Note who it is to be slain and who is to become a feast for the vultures of the air:

- the flesh of captains
- the flesh of mighty men, that is, the powerful
- the flesh of horses
- the flesh of the riders on the horses
- the flesh of all men, both the slaves and the free, both the small and the great

The idea is that all the armies of the world will be destroyed. Every single army will be destroyed by Jesus Christ when He returns in glory.

> **On the mountains of Israel you will fall, you and all your troops and the nations with you. I will give you as food to all kinds of carrion birds and to the wild animals. (Ezek 39:4)**
>
> **"Son of man, this is what the Sovereign LORD says: Call out to every kind of bird and all the wild animals: 'Assemble and come together from all around to the sacrifice I am preparing for you, the great sacrifice on the mountains of Israel. There you will eat flesh and drink blood. You will eat the flesh of mighty men and drink the blood of the princes of the earth as if they were rams and lambs, goats and bulls—all of them fattened animals from Bashan. At the sacrifice I am preparing for you, you will eat fat till you are glutted and drink blood till you are drunk. At my table you will eat your fill of horses and riders, mighty men and soldiers of every kind,' declares the Sovereign LORD. (Ezek 39:17-20)**

**2** (19:19) **Armageddon**: there will be the mobilizing of the world's armies. Note exactly what is said:

> Then I saw the beast and the kings of the earth and their armies gathered together to make war against the rider on the horse and his army. (Rev 19:19)

⇒ The antichrist is there.
⇒ The kings or leaders of the earth are there (probably negotiating and trying to prevent the battle against each other).
⇒ The armies of the nations are there.

How is it humanly possible for so many great armies to gather in one place? And if a war is going to be fought in Palestine, why bother with foot soldiers when the world has so many sophisticated weapons such as missiles and atomic warheads? The reason is simple: armies use foot soldiers when they want to preserve the land and its resources. In the end time this is exactly what will happen. The antichrist will lead his eastern alliance against Palestine to totally exterminate the Jews and to take the whole Middle East with its rich resources for himself. He will march against those who claim to be followers of the Lord Jesus Christ. Remember, the Jews will have been saved at this time. They will have accepted Jesus Christ as their Messiah (see notes—Rev.7:4-8; 11:3-13). This is what is meant by the statement that the antichrist and his armies gather together to fight against Christ. Jesus Christ and His people are one; therefore, to fight against the followers of Jesus Christ is to fight against Christ. The antichrist cannot use atomic weapons, for the weapons would not only destroy the land and its resources but probably cause a retaliatory strike from some of the other nations of the world.

Now, how did all the armies of the world get to Palestine? There are two ways.

1. They got there the same way they would today. If some major army began to march and to claim all the oil of the Middle East for itself, we all know exactly what would happen. The nations of the world would go to protect their interest. The situation in the end time will be caused by some similar circumstance. Standing where we do today, we cannot see into the future to see what will happen in the Middle East to cause all the nations to gather together. All we know is this: they will all be gathered together in Palestine in the end time.

The point is this: when the antichrist and the confederation of nations under his power begin to march against Israel, the other nations of the world apparently become edgy and nervous. The reason may be...

• the fear of a military move to conquer the world beginning in Palestine.
• the resources of the Middle East and the threat to those resources (such as oil).
• the insanity of exterminating a whole people and nation like the Jews.

> The sixth angel poured out his bowl on the great river Euphrates, and its water was dried up to prepare the way for the kings from the East. (Rev 16:12; cp. Ezk. chapters 38-39)
> "In the time of those kings, the God of heaven will set up a kingdom that will never be destroyed, nor will it be left to another people. It will crush all those kingdoms and

bring them to an end, but it will itself endure forever. (Dan 2:44; cp. Dan. 7:19-27)
> He will judge between the nations and will settle disputes for many peoples. They will beat their swords into plowshares and their spears into pruning hooks. Nation will not take up sword against nation, nor will they train for war anymore. (Isa 2:4)
> But with righteousness he will judge the needy, with justice he will give decisions for the poor of the earth. He will strike the earth with the rod of his mouth; with the breath of his lips he will slay the wicked. (Isa 11:4)
> Proclaim this among the nations: Prepare for war! Rouse the warriors! Let all the fighting men draw near and attack. Beat your plowshares into swords and your pruning hooks into spears. Let the weakling say, 'I am strong!' Come quickly, all you nations from every side, and assemble there. Bring down your warriors, O LORD! 'Let the nations be roused; let them advance into the Valley of Jehoshaphat, for there I will sit to judge all the nations on every side. Swing the sickle, for the harvest is ripe. Come, trample the grapes, for the winepress is full and the vats overflow— so great is their wickedness!' Multitudes, multitudes in the valley of decision! For the day of the LORD is near in the valley of decision. The sun and moon will be darkened, and the stars no longer shine. The LORD will roar from Zion and thunder from Jerusalem; the earth and the sky will tremble. But the LORD will be a refuge for his people, a stronghold for the people of Israel. (Joel 3:9-16)
> Therefore wait for me," declares the LORD, "for the day I will stand up to testify. I have decided to assemble the nations, to gather the kingdoms and to pour out my wrath on them— all my fierce anger. The whole world will be consumed by the fire of my jealous anger. (Zep 3:8)
> I will take away the chariots from Ephraim and the war-horses from Jerusalem, and the battle bow will be broken. He will proclaim peace to the nations. His rule will extend from sea to sea and from the River to the ends of the earth. (Zec 9:10)
> On that day I will set out to destroy all the nations that attack Jerusalem. (Zec 12:9; cp. Zech.12:1-9)

2. The armies of the world will gather in Palestine because there is an evil spirit behind the confederation of nations (cp. Rev.16:13-14). This has been discussed in detail earlier, but is being restated here because of its importance in dealing with the *battle of Armageddon*. (See note—Rev.16:12-16.)

Note: this verse says that all the nations and alliances of the earth are going to be involved in the great battle of Armageddon.

⇒ The kings from the east: all the nations east of Palestine, apparently involving the Arabs, China, and all the other eastern nations. These will probably be headed up by the antichrist.

⇒ The kings from the north: all the nations north of Palestine including Russia.

⇒ The kings from the south: all nations south of Palestine including the nations of Africa.

⇒ The kings from the west: all the nations west of Palestine including a western alliance and involving some of the European nations and probably including America and other powerful nations of the Americas and Canada.

Enemies will gather from every nation with each taking sides to protect its own interest. As stated, the point of conflict may be oil in the Middle East, or the utter insanity of the antichrist setting out to exterminate a whole people like the Jews, or it may be some other interest that we know nothing about yet. The point to see is this: in the last days all the nations of the world will converge upon the Middle East and be stationed within the borders of Palestine at Megiddo. Each of the nations will join forces with two or more sides. They will be there to protect their own national interests in the Middle East and Palestine. (Compare the war of Desert Storm, the United Nations' actions against Iraq when Iraq attacked Kuwait in 1990.)

Note what is behind the whole scene: evil spirits. Evil spirits are giving power to the mouth of the antichrist and his false prophet. This means the power to influence and deceive the leaders of other nations. The evil spirits will give the two leaders supernatural power to inspire their confederation to march and conquer Palestine. All the other nations will march to protect their interest in the region (perhaps oil). The description of the evil spirits as frogs symbolizes the ability to leap and spread the deception from the dragon (the devil) to the antichrist and to his false prophet or executive officer and then to each of the nations. The picture is that of the demons working miracles. What kind of miracles? Scripture does not say, but the idea is that of...

- deceptive dreams of glory
- glorious triumphs
- visions of grandeur
- setting passions aflame
- striking fear within the heart and arousing bitterness and hate among nations.

The result of the evil spirits is this: there will be a gathering together of all the armies of the world to the place in Palestine called Armageddon or the valley and mountain of Megiddo. This is the great valley that runs through the middle of Palestine from the Mediterranean Sea to the Jordan River. It is about 200 miles long and ten miles wide.

> **The great dragon was hurled down— that ancient serpent called the devil, or Satan, who leads the whole world astray. He was hurled to the earth, and his angels with him. (Rev 12:9)**
>
> **Then I saw three evil spirits that looked like frogs; they came out of the mouth of the dragon, out of the mouth of the beast and out of the mouth of the false prophet. They are spirits of demons performing miraculous signs, and they go out to the kings of the whole world, to gather them for the battle on the great day of God Almighty. (Rev 16:13-14)**

**3** (19:20) **Armageddon**: there will be the simple and quick capture of the antichrist and the false prophet. Second Thessalonians tells us exactly what will happen to the antichrist.

> **And then the lawless one will be revealed, whom the Lord Jesus will overthrow with the breath of his mouth and destroy by the splendor of his coming. (2 Th 2:8)**

1. The Lord Jesus shall slay the antichrist with the breath of His mouth. What is *the breath of Jesus' mouth*? It is the breath of truth, holiness, and unlimited power. When Jesus speaks, what He says is of God and unstoppable. When He rents the sky to slay the antichrist, there will be no battle, for all the forces of heaven and earth combined would be as non-existent against the Lord God of the universe. Christ will just speak the Word for the antichrist to be slain and the antichrist will be slain. It will be like the blowing of a little breath and the dust particle is removed never to return.

Leon Morris says that the emphasis is the ease with which the Lord will destroy the " 'lawless one', terrible though he will be" (*The Epistles of Paul to the Thessalonians.* "The Tyndale New Testament Commentaries," ed. by RVG Tasker. Grand Rapids, MI: Eerdmans, 1956, p.131).

*The Pulpit Commentary* says, "The words are to be taken literally as a description of the power and irresistible might of Christ at His coming—that the mere breath of His mouth is sufficient to consume the wicked" (*Second Thessalonians.* "The Pulpit Commentary," Vol.21, ed. by HDM Spence and Joseph S. Exell. Grand Rapids, MI: Eerdmans, 1950, p.25f).

> **But with righteousness he will judge the needy, with justice he will give decisions for the poor of the earth. He will strike the earth with the rod of his mouth; with the breath of his lips he will slay the wicked. (Isa 11:4)**

2. The Lord of glory will destroy the antichrist with the splendor of His coming. The word "splendor" (*epiphaneia*) is a very special word. It is a word chosen by the New Testament to refer only to the coming (*parousia*) of the Lord. It is used only five times in all the New Testament, and in every instance it refers to the Lord's coming into the world. It refers once to His first coming (2 Tim.1:10) and four times to His second coming (1 Tim.6:14; 2 Tim.4:1, 8; Tit.2:13). The whole idea of *splendor* is radiance, glory, and light. Someone has pointed out that when Jesus Christ returns to earth, there will be such a spectacular display of glory and splendor that the explosion of every star in the universe could not match the sight of the Lord (source unknown). When Christ first appears, there will apparently be the energizing of a laser beam of glory zeroed in on the antichrist, and he shall be immediately destroyed by the radiance of the Lord's glory and light—quicker than we could blink an eye. Simply by showing Himself, the Lord will destroy the antichrist. Imagine the enormous power of the Lord's glory, a glory so powerful that it will explode the whole universe and remake it into a new heavens and earth. Note: the word "destroy" does not mean to annihilate, but to make inoperative; to make powerless; to end; to put a stop to the evil work of the antichrist.

**4** (19:20) **Lake of Fire**: there is the horrifying judgment of the antichrist and the false prophet. They will both be immediately thrown alive into the fiery lake of burning sulfur. The lake of fire is called either Gehenna or the *Fiery Lake.* This is the place where all those who have rebelled against God are to be cast at the end of the world—all unbelieving men, fallen angels, demons, and the devil. At the final judgment of unbelievers, the lake of fire is the *final* *hell* to which all the wicked shall be judged and condemned, and the judgment of Gehenna is said to be eternal.

> **The Son of Man will send out his angels, and they will weed out of his kingdom everything that causes sin and all who do evil. They will throw them into the fiery furnace, where there will be weeping and gnashing of teeth. (Mat 13:41-42)**

> **If your hand or your foot causes you to sin cut it off and throw it away. It is better for you to enter life maimed or crippled than to have two hands or two feet and be thrown into eternal fire. (Mat 18:8)**

> **And the devil, who deceived them, was thrown into the lake of burning sulfur, where the beast and the false prophet had been thrown. They will be tormented day and night for ever and ever. (Rev 20:10)**

> **"Then he will say to those on his left, 'Depart from me, you who are cursed, into the eternal fire prepared for the devil and his angels. "Then they will go away to eternal punishment, but the righteous to eternal life." (Mat 25:41, 46)**

> **Then I saw a great white throne and him who was seated on it. Earth and sky fled from his presence, and there was no place for them. And I saw the dead, great and small, standing before the throne, and books were opened. Another book was opened, which is the book of life. The dead were judged according to what they had done as recorded in the books. The sea gave up the dead that were in it, and death and Hades gave up the dead that were in them, and each person was judged according to what he had done. Then death and Hades were thrown into the lake of fire. The lake of fire is the second death. If anyone's name was not found written in the book of life, he was thrown into the lake of fire. (Rev 20:11-15)**

> **But the cowardly, the unbelieving, the vile, the murderers, the sexually immoral, those who practice magic arts, the idolaters and all liars—their place will be in the fiery lake of burning sulfur. This is the second death." (Rev 21:8)**

**5** (19:21) **Armageddon**: there is the weapon of the Lord that He uses to slay the armies. What will the weapon be? A sword, the sword of His mouth. Jesus Christ has no physical, material, carnal, or fleshy weapons made of this earth. He does not need them. The only weapon He ever needs is the *sword of His Word*. All He ever has to do is speak the Word and whatever He says is done—immediately, instantaneously, completely, thoroughly, and finally. One blast of the power of His Word is so forceful that it consumes all that stands before Him. Therefore, in the horrifying battle of Armageddon there will not even be a battle fought. The Lord will simply speak the *Word of death*, and every soul of the godless nations and armies present will drop dead. A horrifying sight, but nevertheless it is the declaration of Scripture. And it will all be so tragic—tragic because everyone present could have given their heart and life to Jesus Christ and been saved. Instead they chose to reject, deny, and curse Christ and God, and slaughter literally millions in the worst holocaust the world will have ever seen. Therefore, the Lord Jesus Christ will have no choice. He will have to stop the slaughter and insane evil of the godless of this world. And He will stop it at Armageddon.

> **For the word of God is living and active. Sharper than any double-edged sword, it penetrates even to dividing soul and spirit, joints and marrow; it judges the thoughts and attitudes of the heart. (Heb 4:12)**

> **Take the helmet of salvation and the sword of the Spirit, which is the word of God. (Eph 6:17)**

> **But with righteousness he will judge the needy, with justice he will give decisions for the poor of the earth. He will strike the earth with the rod of his mouth; with the breath of his lips he will slay the wicked. (Isa 11:4)**

| | | ancient serpent, who is the devil, or Satan, and bound him for a thousand years. | **3** | **How long will Satan be removed?** |
|---|---|---|---|---|
| **1** | **Who is going to remove Satan?** | **CHAPTER 20**<br><br>**C. The Great Removal & Binding of Satan, 20:1-3**<br><br>And I saw an angel coming down out of heaven, having the key to the Abyss and holding in his hand a great chain. | 3 He threw him into the Abyss, and locked and sealed it over him, to keep him from deceiving the nations anymore until the thousand years were ended. After that, he must be set free for a short | **4**<br><br>**5** | **Where is Satan to be placed?**<br><br>**Why is Satan to be bound and removed?** |
| **2** | **Who is Satan?** | 2 He seized the dragon, that | time. | **6** | **Will Satan ever be released again?** |

# DIVISION XII

## THE FINAL TRIUMPH: THE MILLENNIUM USHERED IN, 19:11-20:15

### C. The Great Removal and Binding of Satan, 20:1-3

(20:1-3) **Introduction**: Jesus Christ is coming back to earth again in all the glory and majesty of God. He is coming to eliminate all the ungodly and evil from off the earth. He is coming to establish the rule and reign of God upon earth. The earth will be filled with the righteousness of God and know nothing but the righteousness of God. The day is coming when there will be...

- no more sin, evil or unrighteousness upon earth.
- no more rejection, denial or cursing of God or His Son Jesus Christ.
- no more savagery, murder or war.
- no more sickness, disease or ill health.
- no more pain, suffering or death.

The kingdom of God is coming to earth. The earth is going to be like the Garden of Eden once again, except it will be better—better because Jesus Christ, the Son of God Himself, is going to be ruling and governing the affairs of the world.

This is what is known as the Millennium, which simply means one thousand years, the one thousand year rule of Jesus Christ upon the earth. No man, nation, technology or science can ever bring about the perfect earth. Man cannot create perfection. He cannot develop the perfect state and government, the perfect society and culture, or the perfect life and future. Only God can do that. And this is the most wonderful thing: Scripture declares that this is exactly what God is going to do. Scripture proclaims that the Lord Jesus Christ is coming back to earth in power and glory, coming to bring about the perfect state and government, society and culture, life and future. He is coming back in power and glory to bring the kingdom of God to earth, the rule and reign of love, joy, peace, and righteousness. When? Right after the final war of history; right after all the ungodly and evil nations and armies of the world have been eliminated from the earth. This will be done at the great battle of Armageddon. This was the discussion of the previous passage. Now, right after Armageddon, one more thing needs to be done: the spiritual power that lies behind all the ungodliness and evil of this earth, Satan himself, has to be bound. Man can never be free from evil and lawlessness—he can never have a perfect world—until the temptation to do evil is removed from the earth. So long as there is temptation, man will be lawless and do evil. Therefore, Jesus Christ has to remove the possibility of temptation from the earth. The only way this can be done is to remove Satan. This is the glorious news of this passage: *the great removal and binding of Satan*. Note how God answers all the questions we need to know about the removal of evil and Satan from the earth.

1. Who is going to remove Satan (v.1-2a)?

2. Who is Satan (v.2)?
3. How long will Satan be removed (v.2)?
4. Where is Satan to be placed (v.3)?
5. Why is Satan to be bound and removed (v.3)?
6. Will Satan ever be released again (v.3)?

(Remember: the purpose of *The Preacher's Outline & Sermon Bible®* is to *outline the Bible and to simply develop the points of the Scriptural outline*. Our purpose is not to present theological and denominational positions. For this reason we do not get into all the controversy over pre-, mid-, post-, and non- tribulation and millennial positions. As stated, God has called us to outline and develop only what the Scripture says. To the best of our ability we do this. Our daily and consistent prayer for every reader is that *The Preacher's Outline & Sermon Bible®* will help you to understand God's Word better. This is our sole purpose for existing.)

**1** (20:1-2) **Satan**: Who is going to remove Satan from the earth? The angel of God's power. Note that the angel comes directly out of heaven, from God's presence. Remember "angel" (aggelon) means *messenger*. Some messenger from heaven is going to remove Satan from this earth. Some scholars believe this messenger is Jesus Christ. Note that He has "the keys of death and Hades" (Rev.1:18). They believe that Christ would never give those keys to anyone else. Whatever the case, the messenger holds two things in his hands:

⇒ The key to the Abyss or bottomless pit: this means that he has the power to cast Satan into the Abyss, away from the earth.
⇒ A great chain: this means that he has the power to bind Satan and to keep him from tempting and leading people into sin and ungodliness.

**Thought 1.** Think what this means. There is a power great enough to remove Satan and all the evil and sin from this earth. That power is in heaven, the very power of God Himself.

**The God of peace will soon crush Satan under your feet. The grace of our Lord Jesus be with you. (Rom 16:20)**

**2** (20:2) **Satan—Names - Titles**: Who is Satan? His names tell us.

1. He is the dragon: the spiritual power that stirs up the fiery, cruel, and brutal passions of people and governments,

that causes people and governments to behave like beasts and to ravage and destroy people and property.

> The great dragon was hurled down— that ancient serpent called the devil, or Satan, who leads the whole world astray. He was hurled to the earth, and his angels with him. (Rev 12:9)
> He seized the dragon, that ancient serpent, who is the devil, or Satan, and bound him for a thousand years. (Rev 20:2)

2. He is that *ancient serpent*: the spiritual power that deceives, seduces and beguiles people; that leads people into sin and evil; that leads people to disobey, ignore, and neglect God.

> But I am afraid that just as Eve was deceived by the serpent's cunning, your minds may somehow be led astray from your sincere and pure devotion to Christ. (2 Cor 11:3)
> For such men are false apostles, deceitful workmen, masquerading as apostles of Christ. And no wonder, for Satan himself masquerades as an angel of light. It is not surprising, then, if his servants masquerade as servants of righteousness. Their end will be what their actions deserve. (2 Cor 11:13-15)
> "You will not surely die," the serpent said to the woman. So the LORD God said to the serpent, "Because you have done this, "Cursed are you above all the livestock and all the wild animals! You will crawl on your belly and you will eat dust all the days of your life. (Gen 3:4, 14)

3. He is the *devil*: the spiritual power that slanders, lies, and murders by leading people to lie and murder.

> You belong to your father, the devil, and you want to carry out your father's desire. He was a murderer from the beginning, not holding to the truth, for there is no truth in him. When he lies, he speaks his native language, for he is a liar and the father of lies. (John 8:44)
> Be self-controlled and alert. Your enemy the devil prowls around like a roaring lion looking for someone to devour. (1 Pet 5:8)

4. He is *Satan*: the spiritual power that accuses, opposes, and stands as an enemy to God and His followers. Satan leads his followers, the ungodly and evil of this world, to accuse, oppose, and stand against God and believers, even to the point of persecuting and killing them. He is also the main accuser of believers. He is pictured as constantly pointing out the sins and failures of believers to God. He does this in order to cut the heart of God and to arouse God's justice against man.

> Jesus said to him, "Away from me, Satan! For it is written: 'Worship the Lord your God, and serve him only.'" (Mat 4:10)
> As soon as Judas took the bread, Satan entered into him. "What you are about to do, do quickly," Jesus told him, (John 13:27)

> To open their eyes and turn them from darkness to light, and from the power of Satan to God, so that they may receive forgiveness of sins and a place among those who are sanctified by faith in me.' (Acts 26:18)
> The God of peace will soon crush Satan under your feet. The grace of our Lord Jesus be with you. (Rom 16:20)

This is Satan, the spiritual being who lies behind all the ungodliness and evil in the world. This is Satan, the one who has to be bound and removed from the earth before Jesus Christ can bring the perfect government and society to earth. (See notes, *Satan*—Rev.12:3-4; DEEPER STUDY # 1—12:9 for more discussion.)

**3** (20:2) **Satan**: How long will Satan be removed? The time is clearly stated: for one thousand years. This means a most wonderful thing: there is a period of history coming when there will be no more ungodliness and evil running wild upon earth. This is the period of history that is known as the Millennium, the period when the Lord Jesus Christ will come to rule and reign upon this earth as Sovereign Lord. Scripture says the time will be one thousand years. Think how glorious this will be:

⇒ No more war or killing will exist.
⇒ No more assaults or abuse or crimes will go unpunished.
⇒ No more hunger or homelessness or unemployment will exist.
⇒ No more laziness or lethargy or unconcern will be allowed.
⇒ No more drug-pushing or enslavement to drunkenness will be tolerated.

All the wrongs and ills, evil and lawlessness of this earth will be removed. The perfect government and society, utopia and life will be brought to this earth. Righteousness—all things made righteous—will be established upon the earth for one thousand years.

**4** (20:3) **Satan—Abyss—Bottomless Pit**: Where is Satan to be placed for the thousand years? In the Abyss (see note—Rev.9:2 for discussion).

> In that day the LORD will punish the powers in the heavens above and the kings on the earth below. They will be herded together like prisoners bound in a dungeon; they will be shut up in prison and be punished after many days. (Isa 24:21-22)

**5** (20:3) **Satan—Utopia**: Why is Satan to be bound and removed? The reason is clearly stated: so that he cannot deceive people and nations any more. Right now, sin looks good, tastes good, and feels good. Think about the things that look good, feel good, and taste good:

| | |
|---|---|
| ⇒ food | ⇒ clothes |
| ⇒ sex | ⇒ houses |
| ⇒ honor | ⇒ possessions |
| ⇒ recognition | ⇒ stimulation of the flesh |
| ⇒ vehicles | ⇒ popularity |
| ⇒ money | ⇒ position |
| ⇒ pleasure | ⇒ comfort |
| ⇒ power | |

None of these are wrong. They are necessary to life. But the passion and lusting after these things are wrong. Scripture says that Satan and his evil spirits are the ones who arouse these passions to lust within us. Satan is the evil force and power that arouses us...

- to lust after more and more food.
- to lust after another person.
- to lust after power over others.
- to lust after more and more pleasure and possessions.
- to lust after more and more position and money.

Think what society will be like when Jesus Christ comes to bring utopia, the Kingdom of God, to earth. Think about the love, joy, and peace; the self-control, discipline, and personal strength; the cooperation, unity, and oneness; the individuality, assurance, and security; the purpose, meaning, and significance people will have. When Satan is removed there will be no more deception of people or nations. There will only be a society in which there will be no need and no lack. This is the reason Jesus Christ is going to remove Satan: He, the Son of God, wants man to have the privilege of living in the perfect society on this earth and to do so while the earth is in its present created form.

1. Satan will be bound and removed from earth.

> He replied, "I saw Satan fall like lightning from heaven. (Luke 10:18)
> He seized the dragon, that ancient serpent, who is the devil, or Satan, and bound him for a thousand years. He threw him into the Abyss, and locked and sealed it over him, to keep him from deceiving the nations anymore until the thousand years were ended. After that, he must be set free for a short time. (Rev 20:2-3)

2. There is going to be a change in the earth.

> That the creation itself will be liberated from its bondage to decay and brought into the glorious freedom of the children of God. We know that the whole creation has been groaning as in the pains of childbirth right up to the present time. Not only so, but we ourselves, who have the firstfruits of the Spirit, groan inwardly as we wait eagerly for our adoption as sons, the redemption of our bodies. (Rom 8:21-23)
> The desert and the parched land will be glad; the wilderness will rejoice and blossom. Like the crocus, It will burst into bloom; it will rejoice greatly and shout for joy. The glory of Lebanon will be given to it, the splendor of Carmel and Sharon; they will see the glory of the LORD, the splendor of our God. (Isa 35:1-2)

3. There is going to be a change in the animal kingdom.

> The wolf will live with the lamb, the leopard will lie down with the goat, the calf and the lion and the yearling together; and a little child will lead them. The cow will feed with the bear, their young will lie down together, and the lion will eat straw like the ox. The infant will play near the hole of the cobra, and the young child put his hand into the viper's nest. They will neither harm nor destroy on all my holy mountain, for the earth will be full of the knowledge of the LORD as the waters cover the sea. (Isa 11:6-9)

4. There is going to be a change in the aging, sicknesses, and diseases of the body.

> Then will the eyes of the blind be opened and the ears of the deaf unstopped. Then will the lame leap like a deer, and the mute tongue shout for joy. Water will gush forth in the wilderness and streams in the desert. (Isa 35:5-6)

5. There will be plenty upon earth.

> You will have plenty to eat, until you are full, and you will praise the name of the LORD your God, who has worked wonders for you; never again will my people be shamed. Then you will know that I am in Israel, that I am the LORD your God, and that there is no other; never again will my people be shamed. (Joel 2:26-27)
> 'In that day the mountains will drip new wine, and the hills will flow with milk; all the ravines of Judah will run with water. A fountain will flow out of the Lord's house and will water the valley of acacias. (Joel 3:18)

6. There will be peace on earth.

> In that day there will be a highway from Egypt to Assyria. The Assyrians will go to Egypt and the Egyptians to Assyria. The Egyptians and Assyrians will worship together. In that day Israel will be the third, along with Egypt and Assyria, a blessing on the earth. The LORD Almighty will bless them, saying, "Blessed be Egypt my people, Assyria my handiwork, and Israel my inheritance." (Isa 19:23-25)

7. There will be a change in government.

> The seventh angel sounded his trumpet, and there were loud voices in heaven, which said: "The kingdom of the world has become the kingdom of our Lord and of his Christ, and he will reign for ever and ever." (Rev 11:15)
> On that day living water will flow out from Jerusalem, half to the eastern sea and half to the western sea, in summer and in winter. The LORD will be king over the whole earth. On that day there will be one LORD, and his name the only name. (Zec 14:8-9)

8. There will be righteousness and morality and godliness on earth.

> In the last days the mountain of the Lord's temple will be established as chief among the mountains; it will be raised

above the hills, and all nations will stream to it. Many peoples will come and say, "Come, let us go up to the mountain of the LORD, to the house of the God of Jacob. He will teach us his ways, so that we may walk in his paths." The law will go out from Zion, the word of the LORD from Jerusalem. He will judge between the nations and will settle disputes for many peoples. They will beat their swords into plowshares and their spears into pruning hooks. Nation will not take up sword against nation, nor will they train for war anymore. (Isa 2:2-4)

**6** (20:3) **Satan**: Will Satan ever be released again? Scripture says yes, for a little season (see notes—Rev.20:7-10 for discussion).

| | D. The First Resurrection & Millennial Reign of Christ,ᴰˢ¹ 20:4-6 | or their hands. They came to life and reigned with Christ a thousand years. | |
|---|---|---|---|
| 1 The resurrection & rule of believers<br>a. The sight of thrones, rule, & authority<br>b. The sight of a special group: Martyrs | 4 I saw thrones on which were seated those who had been given authority to judge. And I saw the souls of those who had been beheaded because of their testimony for Jesus and because of the word of God. They had not worshiped the beast or his image and had not received his mark on their foreheads | 5 (The rest of the dead did not come to life until the thousand years were ended.) This is the first resurrection.<br>6 Blessed and holy are those who have part in the first resurrection. The second death has no power over them, but they will be priests of God and of Christ and will reign with him for a thousand years. | 2 The resurrection of believers only<br><br>3 The great privilege of resurrected believersᴰˢ² |

# DIVISION XII

## THE FINAL TRIUMPH: THE MILLENNIUM USHERED IN, 19:11-20:15

### D. The First Resurrection and Millennial Reign of Christ, 20:4-6

(20:4-6) **Introduction**: this is one of the most exciting passages of Scripture in all the Word of God for the believer. It is the great millennial reign of the Lord Jesus Christ here on earth. The word millennium simply means one thousand years. When we speak of the Millennium, we mean the one thousand year rule of Jesus Christ on earth. Remember what has just happened in Revelation, the two great events that have just been revealed to us.

First, Jesus Christ is going to return to earth as conqueror, and He is going to destroy the antichrist and all the war machines and armies of the world at Armageddon. There will not be a shot fired at Armageddon. When Jesus Christ appears in the heavens, He will give one blast of His glory and the most powerful laser beam the world has ever known will destroy the armies and nations of the world.

Second, Christ will take Satan and bind and remove him from the earth for one thousand years. For one thousand years Satan will not be able to tempt or deceive people on earth. This does not mean that people cannot sin or do wrong, for man will still have his human nature that comes short of God *by its very nature*. Man will still have choices to make: to follow Christ or not to follow Christ. But with Satan bound and removed, there will be far less evil and ungodliness in the world. And government and society itself will be under the control of Christ Himself. This means...

- that no more war or killing will exist.
- that no more assaults or abuse or crimes will go unpunished.
- that no more hunger or homelessness or unemployment will exist.
- that no more laziness or lethargy or unconcern will be allowed.
- that no pushing of drugs or enslavement to drunkenness will be tolerated.

Now for the present passage: this is the first resurrection and great millennial reign of Jesus Christ upon earth.

1. The resurrection and rule of believers (v.4).
2. The resurrection of believers only (v.5).
3. The great privilege of believers (v.6).

**DEEPER STUDY # 1**
(20:4-6) **Millennial Reign of Jesus Christ—Millennium**: because of the length and large number of verses contained in this footnote, it is being placed last in this outline. This is to keep from losing one's continuity of thought with the

passage here in Revelation. (See DEEPER STUDY # 2, *Millennium—Rev.20:4-6* for discussion.)

**1** (20:4) **Resurrection, The—Rewards**: there is the resurrection and rule of believers. Note three facts.

1. John sees thrones and people sitting upon them with authority to judge and rule. He also sees the millions of believers who were martyred during the tribulation, those who were killed for their witness for Christ and their stand for the Word of God, and those who refused to worship and receive the mark of the antichrist.

Who are the people sitting upon the thrones? John tells us.

⇒ They are those who *live again* or *come to life again* and who reign with Christ (v.4).
⇒ They are those who take part in the first resurrection.

This tells us exactly who the people are: they are believers who have died, the dead believers of all time. Those who rule and reign with Christ in the Millennium will be the believers whose bodies have come back to life again, all the believers who will take part in the first resurrection.

2. Note that John sets the martyrs of the tribulation off as a special group of believers. Why? Probably because they paid the ultimate price for Christ: they died for Him. Their blood especially cries out for vindication and reward. They, among us all, should be rewarded and given the right to rule with Christ.

3. The millennial reign of Jesus Christ is when the believer's glorious rule and reign with Christ begins. Note what John says he saw:

> **I saw thrones on which were seated those who had been given authority to judge. (Rev 20:4)**

The Millennium is when Jesus Christ sets up the organization and arrangement of rule and reign throughout the whole universe. The millennial reign is when Christ gives believers their duties and responsibilities, their assignments and service for eternity. (The assignments and service will most likely be enlarged at the end of the Millennium when He creates the new heavens and earth.) The Millennium is where Christ removes the fallen spiritual beings from power.

This is where Satan and his heavenly host are bound and removed from power.

⇒ Remember the spiritual forces that fight against God and man, the high places that Scripture says they hold.

> For our struggle is not against flesh and blood, but against the rulers, against the authorities, against the powers of this dark world and against the spiritual forces of evil in the heavenly realms. (Eph 6:12)
> For by him all things were created: things in heaven and on earth, visible and invisible, whether thrones or powers or rulers or authorities; all things were created by him and for him. (Col 1:16)

⇒ As stated, this is where Christ dethrones Satan and his heavenly host.

> And I saw an angel coming down out of heaven, having the key to the Abyss and holding in his hand a great chain. He seized the dragon, that ancient serpent, who is the devil, or Satan, and bound him for a thousand years. He threw him into the Abyss, and locked and sealed it over him, to keep him from deceiving the nations anymore until the thousand years were ended. After that, he must be set free for a short time. (Rev 20:1-3)
> In that day the LORD will punish the powers in the heavens above and the kings on the earth below. (Isa 24:21)

This is where Christ reclaims the positions of the powers, the principalities and the high places of rule throughout the universe and exalts believers to those positions. (See note—Rev. 14:13 for more discussion.)

> Do you not know that the saints will judge the world? And if you are to judge the world, are you not competent to judge trivial cases? Do you not know that we will judge angels? How much more the things of this life! (1 Cor 6:2-3)
> And God raised us up with Christ and seated us with him in the heavenly realms in Christ Jesus, In order that in the coming ages he might show the incomparable riches of his grace, expressed in his kindness to us in Christ Jesus. (Eph 2:6-7)
> If we endure, we will also reign with him. If we disown him, he will also disown us; (2 Tim 2:12)

**2** (20:5) **Resurrection, The**: there is the resurrection of believers only. Scripture could not state it any clearer. The millennial reign of Christ will see only the resurrection of believers. The first resurrection is for believers only. Note verse six: it is for those who are blessed and holy and upon whom the second death (eternal death) has no power. The first resurrection will be only of those who are going to live forever. The rest of the dead, the unbelievers, will not "come

to life" until after the thousand years are finished. Note *exactly* what John says he saw:

> I saw thrones on which were seated those who had been given authority to judge. And I saw the souls of those who had been beheaded because of their testimony for Jesus and because of the word of God. They had not worshiped the beast or his image and had not received his mark on their foreheads or their hands. They came to life and reigned with Christ a thousand years. (The rest of the dead did not come to life until the thousand years were ended.) This is the first resurrection. (Rev 20:4-5)

⇒ He saw people sitting upon thrones with the authority to judge or rule (v.4).
⇒ He saw the martyrs of the tribulation (v.4).
⇒ He saw these living again; that is, they were resurrected in the first resurrection (v.4).
⇒ He saw that the rest of the dead, the unbelievers, would not come to life until the thousand years were finished (cp. Rev.20:13).

Note that this is exactly what Scripture says: there are to be one thousand years between the first resurrection of believers and the rest of the dead (the unbelievers, cp. Rev.20:12-15; 21:8).

**3** (20:6) **Millennium**: there is the great privilege of the *resurrected believers* in the Millennium. Again note: this verse is still referring only to the resurrected believers, not to the people who will be upon earth. The resurrected believers will have six glorious privileges in the Millennium.

1. They will be extremely blessed. "Blessed" (makarios) means joy and satisfaction, being complete and fulfilled, secure and peaceful within one's being; having meaning, significance, and purpose.

> **Thought 1.** To be blessed is what men seek. The problem is that they seek it in the things of this earth: position, money, possessions, fame, power, and worldly pleasures. The only true *blessedness* is found in Jesus Christ. He alone can raise up a person in the first resurrection. He alone can give a person the right to rule and reign with Him in His millennial reign.
>
> "Do not store up for yourselves treasures on earth, where moth and rust destroy, and where thieves break in and steal. But store up for yourselves treasures in heaven, where moth and rust do not destroy, and where thieves do not break in and steal. For where your treasure is, there your heart will be also. (Mat 6:19-21)
> "Therefore come out from them and be separate, says the Lord. Touch no unclean thing, and I will receive you." "I will be a Father to you, and you will be my sons and daughters, says the Lord Almighty." (2 Cor 6:17-18)
> Do not love the world or anything in the world. If anyone loves the world, the love of the Father is not in him. For everything in the world—the cravings of sinful man, the lust of his eyes and the boasting of what he

has and does—comes not from the Father but from the world. (1 John 2:15-16)

Then I heard a voice from heaven say, "Write: Blessed are the dead who die in the Lord from now on." "Yes," says the Spirit, "they will rest from their labor, for their deeds will follow them." (Rev 14:13)

"Behold, I come like a thief! Blessed is he who stays awake and keeps his clothes with him, so that he may not go naked and be shamefully exposed." (Rev 16:15)

Then the angel said to me, "Write: 'Blessed are those who are invited to the wedding supper of the Lamb!'" And he added, "These are the true words of God." (Rev 19:9)

2. The resurrected believers will be holy. That is, they will be perfected into the holiness of Christ Himself. They will be perfectly separated from the world and set apart unto God. They will bear the very same nature of Christ Himself, a holy nature, a nature that is perfectly pure.

For those God foreknew he also predestined to be conformed to the likeness of his Son, that he might be the firstborn among many brothers. (Rom 8:29)

But our citizenship is in heaven. And we eagerly await a Savior from there, the Lord Jesus Christ, Who, by the power that enables him to bring everything under his control, will transform our lowly bodies so that they will be like his glorious body. (Phil 3:20-21)

Dear friends, now we are children of God, and what we will be has not yet been made known. But we know that when he appears, we shall be like him, for we shall see him as he is. (1 John 3:2)

3. The resurrected believers will never be touched by the second death. What is the second death? It means a second kind of death. The first death is when we leave this world and pass on into the next world. The second death refers to eternal death, to being separated from God forever. It means to be put into a different place other than where God is. It means to live someplace other than in heaven with God. Scripture clearly tells us what the second death is:

Then death and Hades were thrown into the lake of fire. The lake of fire is the second death. (Rev 20:14)

The second death is being *separated from God* and being cast into the lake of fire. The point is this: resurrected believers will never have to suffer the second death. Despite our depravity and failure and sins upon earth—despite our rebellion and rejection of God for so many years before we surrendered our lives to Jesus Christ—despite what we might deserve—if we have truly surrendered our lives to Jesus Christ, we will never suffer the second death. This will be one of the glorious privileges of the resurrected believer.

The last enemy to be destroyed is death. (1 Cor 15:26)

When the perishable has been clothed with the imperishable, and the mortal with immortality, then the saying that is written

will come true: "Death has been swallowed up in victory." (1 Cor 15:54)

But it has now been revealed through the appearing of our Savior, Christ Jesus, who has destroyed death and has brought life and immortality to light through the gospel. (2 Tim 1:10)

He will wipe every tear from their eyes. There will be no more death or mourning or crying or pain, for the old order of things has passed away." (Rev 21:4)

He will swallow up death forever. The Sovereign LORD will wipe away the tears from all faces; he will remove the disgrace of his people from all the earth. The LORD has spoken. (Isa 25:8)

4. The resurrected believer will serve as a priest of God and of Christ. This means that believers will have the same right that they have upon earth now, the right to enter the presence of God and Christ as needed. There will be no need for a mediator to stand between God and the believer. As stated, it will be just as it is upon earth now, except that we will be standing face to face with God and Christ, whereas now we approach them through prayer and thought.

You also, like living stones, are being built into a spiritual house to be a holy priesthood, offering spiritual sacrifices acceptable to God through Jesus Christ. (1 Pet 2:5)

And has made us to be a kingdom and priests to serve his God and Father—to him be glory and power for ever and ever! Amen. (Rev 1:6)

Blessed and holy are those who have part in the first resurrection. The second death has no power over them, but they will be priests of God and of Christ and will reign with him for a thousand years. (Rev 20:6)

5. The resurrected believer will rule and reign with Christ. (See notes—Rev.14:13 for discussion.)

6. The resurrected believer will serve under the rule of Christ. (See note—Rev.14:13 for discussion.)

**DEEPER STUDY # 2**
(20:4-6) **Jesus Christ, Millennial Reign—Millennium:** this is the only Scripture that tells us how long the millennial reign of Jesus Christ will be (Rev.20:2, 3, 4, 5, 6, 7). Millennium simply means one thousand years or a period of one thousand years. It refers to the coming again of Jesus Christ to earth, some time in the future when He will be returning to reign over the nations and peoples of the earth.

⇒ Here is a quick Scripture reference to show what is meant.

"In my vision at night I looked, and there before me was one like a son of man, coming with the clouds of heaven. He approached the Ancient of Days and was led into his presence. He was given authority, glory and sovereign power; all peoples, nations and men of every language worshiped him. His dominion is an everlasting dominion that will not pass away, and his kingdom

**is one that will never be destroyed. (Dan 7:13-14)**

⇒ Peter definitely said that the Millennium was coming and that it referred to some future time.

**Repent, then, and turn to God, so that your sins may be wiped out, that times of refreshing may come from the Lord, And that he may send the Christ, who has been appointed for you—even Jesus. He must remain in heaven until the time comes for God to restore everything, as he promised long ago through his holy prophets. (Acts 3:19-21)**

Although this is the only mention of one thousand years, the coming of Jesus Christ to rule this earth is mentioned many, many times in Scripture. Many more verses will be given below, but this gives a quick glimpse as to what is meant by the Millennium. The Millennium simply means the rule of Jesus Christ over this earth, over all the nations and peoples of this earth for one thousand years. Why is a Millennium necessary? Why does Jesus Christ not just end everything when He comes back to earth? Why is He coming back and ruling over this earth for one thousand years? There are at least three reasons.

1. The earth must be ruled over by Christ in its present form. Why? Because the earth belongs to Christ; it belongs to Him by right. Jesus Christ created the world and man. But man gave the world to Satan. Man obeyed Satan instead of God. When he did, he brought evil to earth. Therefore, Jesus Christ has to reclaim the earth and bring righteousness to the earth, and He has to do it while the earth is in its present form. To destroy the earth would be giving up this earth and dooming it to destruction; it would mean that God failed with the present earth. Of course, God cannot fail. Therefore, the Lord Jesus Christ must reclaim this earth and rule over it before He moves the world and believers into the perfect world.

2. Why is the Millennium necessary? Because God has to fulfill all the promises to man that are in His Word. But why would God make such promises that could not be fulfilled in sinful man? God knew that man would fail and that the promises would not be able to be fulfilled. So why make the promises? Because God loves man, and He wants to bless man. God would rather create man and have a few who will believe in Him and bless them than not to create man and have no one to bless.

The point is this: in order to bless the few believers upon earth, in order to fulfill God's promises, Jesus Christ has to come back to this earth while it is in its present form. God made some wonderful and great promises all through the Scripture that have not yet been fulfilled, and they cannot be fulfilled without Christ Himself ruling and reigning and bringing them about. Therefore, He is coming back to complete the promises, coming back while the earth is still in its present form.

3. Why is the Millennium necessary? Because God is love, and He wants to see more and more people saved despite the terrible evil of past history and the horrible evil of the end time under the antichrist. God is still merciful. Therefore, in the Millennium God is going to give man the very presence of His Son in His majestic glory ruling and reigning from Jerusalem. God is going to give man his utopia upon earth: peace and prosperity—give man every opportunity in the world to receive Jesus Christ as Lord and Savior. The Millennium is necessary because of the love of God for man, a love that longs for more and more people to be saved.

Now, what will the Millennium be like? A good way to gain some understanding of the Millennium is to ask questions and then to answer the questions by giving Scriptural support. Any minister or lay believer can do the same study that we are doing. It is needed because of so many erroneous ideas going around about the Millennium. We give just a brief study so that the reader will have some idea of what the Millennium will be. Note four questions and points about the Millennium:

1. What are some verses that tell us that Christ is coming back in glory to rule and reign over the earth?

⇒ He shall rule over and govern the nations.

**He will judge between the nations and will settle disputes for many peoples. They will beat their swords into plowshares and their spears into pruning hooks. Nation will not take up sword against nation, nor will they train for war anymore. (Isa 2:4)**

**Of the increase of his government and peace there will be no end. He will reign on David's throne and over his kingdom, establishing and upholding it with justice and righteousness from that time on and forever. The zeal of the LORD Almighty will accomplish this. (Isa 9:7)**

**See, I have made him a witness to the peoples, a leader and commander of the peoples. (Isa 55:4)**

**May the nations be glad and sing for joy, for you rule the peoples justly and guide the nations of the earth. Selah (Psa 67:4)**

**For dominion belongs to the LORD and he rules over the nations. (Psa 22:28)**

⇒ He shall rule and judge the ends of the earth.

**Those who oppose the LORD will be shattered. He will thunder against them from heaven; the LORD will judge the ends of the earth. "He will give strength to his king and exalt the horn of his anointed." (1 Sam 2:10)**

**He will rule from sea to sea and from the River to the ends of the earth. (Psa 72:8)**

**I will take away the chariots from Ephraim and the war-horses from Jerusalem, and the battle bow will be broken. He will proclaim peace to the nations. His rule will extend from sea to sea and from the River to the ends of the earth. (Zec 9:10)**

⇒ He is coming to rule the earth.

**They will sing before the LORD, for he comes, he comes to judge the earth. He will judge the world in righteousness and the peoples in his truth. (Psa 96:13)**

**Let them sing before the LORD, for he comes to judge the earth. He will judge the world in righteousness and the peoples with equity. (Psa 98:9)**

⇒ He shall be made higher than the kings of the earth.

**May his name endure forever; may it continue as long as the sun. All nations will be blessed through him, and they will call him blessed. (Psa 72:17)**

⇒ All nations shall come and see His glory and every knee shall bow.

**By myself I have sworn, my mouth has uttered in all integrity a word that will not be revoked: Before me every knee will bow; by me every tongue will swear. (Isa 45:23)**
**"And I, because of their actions and their imaginations, am about to come and gather all nations and tongues, and they will come and see my glory. (Isa 66:18)**

⇒ He shall be exalted over all rule and authority in this world and in the world to come.

**Far above all rule and authority, power and dominion, and every title that can be given, not only in the present age but also in the one to come. (Eph 1:21)**

⇒ God shall subject the world to come to Christ.

**It is not to angels that he has subjected the world to come, about which we are speaking. But there is a place where someone has testified: "What is man that you are mindful of him, the son of man that you care for him? You made him a little lower than the angels; you crowned him with glory and honor And put everything under his feet." In putting everything under him, God left nothing that is not subject to him. Yet at present we do not see everything subject to him. (Heb 2:5-8)**

⇒ The kingdom of the world will become the kingdom of God.

**The seventh angel sounded his trumpet, and there were loud voices in heaven, which said: "The kingdom of the world has become the kingdom of our Lord and of his Christ, and he will reign for ever and ever." (Rev 11:15)**

⇒ Christ the Stone shall fill and rule the whole earth.

**Then the iron, the clay, the bronze, the silver and the gold were broken to pieces at the same time and became like chaff on a threshing floor in the summer. The wind swept them away without leaving a trace. But the rock that struck the statue became a huge mountain and filled the whole earth. (Dan 2:35)**

⇒ Christ alone has the right to the crown.

**A ruin! A ruin! I will make it a ruin! It will not be restored until he comes to**
whom it rightfully belongs; to him I will give it.' (Ezek 21:27)

⇒ Kings shall bring gifts to Him and serve Him.

**The kings of Tarshish and of distant shores will bring tribute to him; the kings of Sheba and Seba will present him gifts. All kings will bow down to him and all nations will serve him. (Psa 72:10-11)**

⇒ His enemies shall be made His footstool.

**To which of the angels did God ever say, "Sit at my right hand until I make your enemies a footstool for your feet"? (Heb 1:13)**
**Since that time he waits for his enemies to be made his footstool, (Heb 10:13)**
**Until I make your enemies a footstool for your feet." (Luke 20:43)**
**"'The Lord said to my Lord: "Sit at my right hand until I put your enemies under your feet."' (Mat 22:44)**

⇒ The people will obey Him.

**The scepter will not depart from Judah, nor the ruler's staff from between his feet, until he comes to whom it belongs and the obedience of the nations is his. (Gen 49:10)**

⇒ The people shall gather and obey and serve Him.

**The scepter will not depart from Judah, nor the ruler's staff from between his feet, until he comes to whom it belongs and the obedience of the nations is his. (Gen 49:10)**
**He was given authority, glory and sovereign power; all peoples, nations and men of every language worshiped him. His dominion is an everlasting dominion that will not pass away, and his kingdom is one that will never be destroyed. (Dan 7:14)**

⇒ The people will glorify and fear Him.

**Therefore strong peoples will honor you; cities of ruthless nations will revere you. (Isa 25:3)**

⇒ He shall be given the throne of David.

**He will be great and will be called the Son of the Most High. The Lord God will give him the throne of his father David, (Luke 1:32)**

⇒ He shall rule in Zion (Jerusalem) upon His throne.

**"I have installed my King on Zion, my holy hill." (Psa 2:6)**
**It is he who will build the temple of the LORD, and he will be clothed with majesty and will sit and rule on his throne. And he will be a priest on his throne. And there will be harmony between the two.' (Zec 6:13)**

⇒ Jerusalem will be the place of the Lord's throne.

At that time they will call Jerusalem The Throne of the LORD, and all nations will gather in Jerusalem to honor the name of the LORD. No longer will they follow the stubbornness of their evil hearts. (Jer 3:17)

"The days are coming," declares the LORD, "when this city will be rebuilt for me from the Tower of Hananel to the Corner Gate. The measuring line will stretch from there straight to the hill of Gareb and then turn to Goah. (Jer 31:38-39)

"The distance all around will be 18,000 cubits. "And the name of the city from that time on will be: THE LORD IS THERE." (Ezek 48:35)

'Then you will know that I, the LORD your God, dwell in Zion, my holy hill. Jerusalem will be holy; never again will foreigners invade her. (Joel 3:17)

This is what the LORD says: "I will return to Zion and dwell in Jerusalem. Then Jerusalem will be called the City of Truth, and the mountain of the LORD Almighty will be called the Holy Mountain." (Zec 8:3)

⇒ The kingdom of Israel shall be the Lord's.

Deliverers will go up on Mount Zion to govern the mountains of Esau. And the kingdom will be the Lord's. (Oba 1:21)

⇒ The millennial kingdom will be centered in Jerusalem and the Shekinah glory will dwell there.

Then the LORD will create over all of Mount Zion and over those who assemble there a cloud of smoke by day and a glow of flaming fire by night; over all the glory will be a canopy. It will be a shelter and shade from the heat of the day, and a refuge and hiding place from the storm and rain. (Isa 4:5-6)

At that time they will call Jerusalem The Throne of the LORD, and all nations will gather in Jerusalem to honor the name of the LORD. No longer will they follow the stubbornness of their evil hearts. (Jer 3:17)

"The days are coming," declares the LORD, "when this city will be rebuilt for me from the Tower of Hananel to the Corner Gate. The measuring line will stretch from there straight to the hill of Gareb and then turn to Goah. (Jer 31:38-39)

"The distance all around will be 18,000 cubits. "And the name of the city from that time on will be: THE LORD IS THERE." (Ezek 48:35)

'Then you will know that I, the LORD your God, dwell in Zion, my holy hill. Jerusalem will be holy; never again will foreigners [unbelievers] invade her. (Joel 3:17)

The LORD has taken away your punishment, he has turned back your enemy. The LORD, the King of Israel, is with you; never again will you fear any harm. The LORD your God is with you, he is mighty to save. He will take great delight in you, he will quiet you with his love, he will rejoice over you with singing." (Zep 3:15, 17)

This is what the LORD says: "I will return to Zion and dwell in Jerusalem. Then Jerusalem will be called the City of Truth, and the mountain of the LORD Almighty will be called the Holy Mountain." (Zec 8:3)

⇒ He will bring peace and security to the world.

He will judge between the nations and will settle disputes for many peoples. They will beat their swords into plowshares and their spears into pruning hooks. Nation will not take up sword against nation, nor will they train for war anymore. (Isa 2:4)

Of the increase of his government and peace there will be no end. He will reign on David's throne and over his kingdom, establishing and upholding it with justice and righteousness from that time on and forever. The zeal of the LORD Almighty will accomplish this. (Isa 9:7)

The city streets will be filled with boys and girls playing there." (Zec 8:5)

"'In that day each of you will invite his neighbor to sit under his vine and fig tree,' declares the LORD Almighty." (Zec 3:10)

He will judge between many peoples and will settle disputes for strong nations far and wide. They will beat their swords into plowshares and their spears into pruning hooks. Nation will not take up sword against nation, nor will they train for war anymore. (Micah 4:3)

⇒ Christ will begin to reign right after the victory at Armageddon.

Then I heard what sounded like a great multitude, like the roar of rushing waters and like loud peals of thunder, shouting: "Hallelujah! For our Lord God Almighty reigns. (Rev 19:6; cp. Rev.19:11-21)

⇒ He, the seed of Abraham, shall be given the land of Canaan forever.

The LORD appeared to Abram and said, "To your offspring [Christ] I will give this land." So he built an altar there to the LORD, who had appeared to him. (Gen 12:7; cp. Gal.3:16)

All the land that you see I will give to you and your offspring [Christ] forever. (Gen 13:15)

The whole land of Canaan, where you are now an alien, I will give as an everlasting possession to you and your descendants after you; and I will be their God." (Gen 17:8)

"The LORD, the God of heaven, who brought me out of my father's household and my native land and who spoke to me and promised me on oath, saying, 'To your offspring I will give this land'—he will send his angel before you so that you can get a wife for my son from there. (Gen 24:7)

Stay in this land for a while, and I will be with you and will bless you. For to you and your descendants [Christ] I will give all these lands and will confirm the oath I swore to your father Abraham. I will make your descendants as numerous as the stars in the sky and will give them all these lands, and through your offspring all nations on earth will be blessed, (Gen 26:3-4)

May he give you and your descendants the blessing given to Abraham, so that you may take possession of the land where you now live as an alien, the land God gave to Abraham." There above it stood the LORD, and he said: "I am the LORD, the God of your father Abraham and the God of Isaac. I will give you and your descendants the land on which you are lying. (Gen 28:4, 13; cp. Gal.3:16)

The land I gave to Abraham and Isaac I also give to you, and I will give this land to your descendants after you." (Gen 35:12)

And said to me, 'I am going to make you fruitful and will increase your numbers. I will make you a community of peoples, and I will give this land as an everlasting possession to your descendants after you.' (Gen 48:4)

⇒ The whole earth was given to Israel's seed [Christ] forever.

Keep his decrees and commands, which I am giving you today, so that it may go well with you and your children after you and that you may live long in the land the LORD your God gives you for all time. (Deu 4:40)

It was not through law that Abraham and his offspring [Christ] received the promise that he would be heir of the world [the whole world], but through the righteousness that comes by faith. (Rom 4:13)

⇒ The borders of Israel will be enlarged (Ezk.47:13-21; 48:1-7, 10-14, 20-29).
⇒ The city of Jerusalem will be laid out by very exact measurements (Ezk.48:15-19, 30-35).

2. Who is going to be in the Millennium? (See notes above—Rev.20:4; pt.1—Rev.20:7-10 for discussion.)
3. What will life be like in the Millennium?
   a. Life in the Millennium will be blessed.
      ⇒ There will be a covenant or treaty of worldwide peace and security. Imagine one thousand years of peace and security.

"'I will grant peace in the land, and you will lie down and no one will make you afraid. I will remove savage beasts from the land, and the sword will not pass through your country. (Lev 26:6)

In his days Judah will be saved and Israel will live in safety. This is the name by which he will be called: The LORD Our Righteousness. (Jer 23:6)

In that day I will make a covenant for them with the beasts of the field and the birds of the air and the creatures that move along the ground. Bow and sword and battle I will abolish from the land, so that all may lie down in safety. (Hosea 2:18)

He will judge between many peoples and will settle disputes for strong nations far and wide. They will beat their swords into plowshares and their spears into pruning hooks. Nation will not take up sword against nation, nor will they train for war anymore. Every man will sit under his own vine and under his own fig tree, and no one will make them afraid, for the LORD Almighty has spoken. (Micah 4:3-4)

Though the mountains be shaken and the hills be removed, yet my unfailing love for you will not be shaken nor my covenant of peace be removed," says the LORD, who has compassion on you. (Isa 54:10)

No longer will violence be heard in your land, nor ruin or destruction within your borders, but you will call your walls Salvation and your gates Praise. (Isa 60:18)

⇒ There will be no evil done by one nation against another nation.

The remnant of Israel will do no wrong; they will speak no lies, nor will deceit be found in their mouths. They will eat and lie down and no one will make them afraid." (Zep 3:13)

The LORD has taken away your punishment, he has turned back your enemy. The LORD, the King of Israel, is with you; never again will you fear any harm. (Zep 3:15)

⇒ There will be no sickness.

Worship the LORD your God, and his blessing will be on your food and water. I will take away sickness from among you, And none will miscarry or be barren in your land. I will give you a full life span. (Exo 23:25-26)

Then will the eyes of the blind be opened and the ears of the deaf unstopped. Then will the lame leap like a deer, and the mute tongue shout for joy. Water will gush forth in the wilderness and streams in the desert. (Isa 35:5-6)

⇒ There will be a fruitful human population: no more barrenness or miscarriages.

And none will miscarry or be barren in your land. I will give you a full life span. (Exo 23:26)

"'I will look on you with favor and make you fruitful and increase your numbers, and I will keep my covenant with you. (Lev 26:9)

You will be blessed more than any other people; none of your men or women will be childless, nor any of your livestock without young. (Deu 7:14)

The fruit of your womb will be blessed, and the crops of your land and the young of your livestock—the calves of your herds and the lambs of your flocks. The LORD will grant you abundant prosperity—in the fruit of your womb, the young of your livestock and the crops of your ground—in the land he swore to your forefathers to give you. (Deu 28:4, 11)

You have enlarged the nation and increased their joy; they rejoice before you as people rejoice at the harvest, as men rejoice when dividing the plunder. (Isa 9:3)

⇒ There will be bread and water and the necessities of life for everyone on earth.

"The days are coming," declares the LORD, "when the reaper will be overtaken by the plowman and the planter by the one treading grapes. New wine will drip from the mountains and flow from all the hills. I will bring back my exiled people Israel; they will rebuild the ruined cities and live in them. They will plant vineyards and drink their wine; they will make gardens and eat their fruit. (Amos 9:13-14)

Worship the LORD your God, and his blessing will be on your food and water. I will take away sickness from among you, (Exo 23:25)

Your basket and your kneading trough will be blessed. You will be blessed when you come in and blessed when you go out. The LORD will send a blessing on your barns and on everything you put your hand to. The LORD your God will bless you in the land he is giving you. The LORD will open the heavens, the storehouse of his bounty, to send rain on your land in season and to bless all the work of your hands. You will lend to many nations but will borrow from none. (Deu 28:5-6, 8, 12)

Then the LORD your God will make you most prosperous in all the work of your hands and in the fruit of your womb, the young of your livestock and the crops of your land. The LORD will again delight in you and make you prosperous, just as he delighted in your fathers, (Deu 30:9)

He will be like rain falling on a mown field, like showers watering the earth. In his days the righteous will flourish; prosperity will abound till the moon is no more. Let grain abound throughout the land; on the tops of the hills may it sway. Let its fruit flourish like Lebanon; let it thrive like the grass of the field. (Psa 72:6-7, 16)

In that day the Branch of the LORD will be beautiful and glorious, and the fruit of the land will be the pride and glory of the survivors in Israel. (Isa 4:2)

I will bless them and the places surrounding my hill. I will send down showers in season; there will be showers of blessing. The trees of the field will yield their fruit and the ground will yield its crops; the people will be secure in their land. They will know that I am the LORD, when I break the bars of their yoke and rescue them from the hands of those who enslaved them. I will provide for them a land renowned for its crops, and they will no longer be victims of famine in the land or bear the scorn of the nations. (Ezek 34:26-27, 29)

"In that day I will respond," declares the LORD— "I will respond to the skies, and they will respond to the earth; And the earth will respond to the grain, the new wine and oil, and they will respond to Jezreel. (Hosea 2:21-22)

'In that day the mountains will drip new wine, and the hills will flow with milk; all the ravines of Judah will run with water. A fountain will flow out of the Lord's house and will water the valley of acacias. (Joel 3:18)

"The days are coming," declares the LORD, "when the reaper will be overtaken by the plowman and the planter by the one treading grapes. New wine will drip from the mountains and flow from all the hills. (Amos 9:13)

⇒ There will be food and rest for all and no fear of enemies or criminals.

I will tend them in a good pasture, and the mountain heights of Israel will be their grazing land. There they will lie down in good grazing land, and there they will feed in a rich pasture on the mountains of Israel. (Ezek 34:14)

The remnant of Israel will do no wrong; they will speak no lies, nor will deceit be found in their mouths. They will eat and lie down and no one will make them afraid." (Zep 3:13)

On that day they will say to Jerusalem, "Do not fear, O Zion; do not let your hands hang limp. (Zep 3:16)

On the day the LORD gives you relief from suffering and turmoil and cruel bondage, (Isa 14:3)

In righteousness you will be established: Tyranny will be far from you; you will have nothing to fear. Terror will be far removed; it will not come near you. (Isa 54:14)

⇒ There will be long and full life spans.

> And none will miscarry or be barren in your land. I will give you a full life span. (Exo 23:26)
>
> He will swallow up death forever. The Sovereign LORD will wipe away the tears from all faces; he will remove the disgrace of his people from all the earth. The LORD has spoken. (Isa 25:8)
>
> "Never again will there be in it an infant who lives but a few days, or an old man who does not live out his years; he who dies at a hundred will be thought a mere youth; he who fails to reach a hundred will be considered accursed. (Isa 65:20)
>
> This is what the LORD Almighty says: "Once again men and women of ripe old age will sit in the streets of Jerusalem, each with cane in hand because of his age. (Zec 8:4)

⇒ It will be a day of no tears, but of joy and praise.

> He will swallow up death forever. The Sovereign LORD will wipe away the tears from all faces; he will remove the disgrace of his people from all the earth. The LORD has spoken. (Isa 25:8)
>
> And the ransomed of the LORD will return. They will enter Zion with singing; everlasting joy will crown their heads. Gladness and joy will overtake them, and sorrow and sighing will flee away. (Isa 35:10)
>
> The ransomed of the LORD will return. They will enter Zion with singing; everlasting joy will crown their heads. Gladness and joy will overtake them, and sorrow and sighing will flee away. (Isa 51:11)
>
> Sing, O Daughter of Zion; shout aloud, O Israel! Be glad and rejoice with all your heart, O Daughter of Jerusalem! (Zep 3:14)
>
> To him who is able to keep you from falling and to present you before his glorious presence without fault and with great joy— (Jude 1:24)
>
> In that day you will say: "Give thanks to the LORD, call on his name; make known among the nations what he has done, and proclaim that his name is exalted. (Isa 12:4)

⇒ Shame and guilt will be removed.

> On that day you will not be put to shame for all the wrongs you have done to me, because I will remove from this city those who rejoice in their pride. Never again will you be haughty on my holy hill. (Zep 3:11)
>
> You will have plenty to eat, until you are full, and you will praise the name of the LORD your God, who has worked wonders for you; never again will my people be shamed. Then you

will know that I am in Israel, that I am the LORD your God, and that there is no other; never again will my people be shamed. (Joel 2:26-27)

⇒ There will be recognition and honor and a healthy ego and emotions.

> At that time I will deal with all who oppressed you; I will rescue the lame and gather those who have been scattered. I will give them praise and honor in every land where they were put to shame. At that time I will gather you; at that time I will bring you home. I will give you honor and praise among all the peoples of the earth when I restore your fortunes before your very eyes," says the LORD. (Zep 3:19-20)

⇒ Everyone will be a neighbor to everyone else.

> "'In that day each of you will invite his neighbor to sit under his vine and fig tree,' declares the LORD Almighty." (Zec 3:10)

⇒ There will no longer be any slavery.

> "' In that day,' declares the LORD Almighty, 'I will break the [oppressor's] yoke off their necks and will tear off their bonds; no longer will foreigners enslave them. Instead, they will serve the LORD their God and [the descendent, the Lord Jesus Christ of] David their king, whom I will raise up for them. (Jer 30:8-9)

⇒ People will be able to trust the Lord's strong arm.

> My righteousness draws near speedily, my salvation is on the way, and my arm will bring justice to the nations. The islands will look to me and wait in hope for my arm. (Isa 51:5)

⇒ It will be a day of mercy.

> In love a throne will be established; in faithfulness a man will sit on it— one from the house of David— one who in judging seeks justice and speeds the cause of righteousness. (Isa 16:5)

⇒ All things will be restored.

> He must remain in heaven until the time comes for God to restore everything, as he promised long ago through his holy prophets. (Acts 3:21)

⇒ Destroyed cities will be rebuilt. (Remember: most of the major cities of the world will have been destroyed.)

> They will rebuild the ancient ruins and restore the places long devastated; they will renew the ruined cities that

have been devastated for generations. (Isa 61:4)

They will build houses and dwell in them; they will plant vineyards and eat their fruit. (Isa 65:21)

"The days are coming," declares the LORD, "when the reaper will be overtaken by the plowman and the planter by the one treading grapes. New wine will drip from the mountains and flow from all the hills. I will bring back my exiled people Israel; they will rebuild the ruined cities and live in them. They will plant vineyards and drink their wine; they will make gardens and eat their fruit. (Amos 9:13-14)

⇒ All animals will live in peace. There will be no savagery.

The wolf and the lamb will feed together, and the lion will eat straw like the ox, but dust will be the serpent's food. They will neither harm nor destroy on all my holy mountain," says the LORD. (Isa 65:25)

⇒ Israel will be established as a nation forever.

This is what the LORD says, he who appoints the sun to shine by day, who decrees the moon and stars to shine by night, who stirs up the sea so that its waves roar— the LORD Almighty is his name: "Only if these decrees vanish from my sight," declares the LORD, "will the descendants of Israel ever cease to be a nation before me." This is what the LORD says: "Only if the heavens above can be measured and the foundations of the earth below be searched out will I reject all the descendants of Israel because of all they have done," declares the LORD. (Jer 31:35-37)

⇒ The Gentiles receive the inheritance and blessings of Israel.

You are to allot it as an inheritance for yourselves and for the aliens who have settled among you and who have children. You are to consider them as native-born Israelites; along with you they are to be allotted an inheritance among the tribes of Israel. In whatever tribe the alien settles, there you are to give him his inheritance," declares the Sovereign LORD. (Ezek 47:22-23)

The nobles of the nations assemble as the people of the God of Abraham, for the kings of the earth belong to God; he is greatly exalted. (Psa 47:9)

⇒ The feast of Tabernacles will be celebrated on a yearly basis.

Then the survivors from all the nations that have attacked Jerusalem will go up year after year to worship the King, the LORD Almighty, and to celebrate the Feast of Tabernacles. (Zec 14:16; cp. Ex.23:16. See note—Jn.7:37 for discussion.)

b. Life in the Millennium will be governed by righteousness.

⇒ Christ is going to judge the earth with righteousness and truth.

The God of Israel spoke, the Rock of Israel said to me: 'When one rules over men in righteousness, when he rules in the fear of God, He is like the light of morning at sunrise on a cloudless morning, like the brightness after rain that brings the grass from the earth.' (2 Sam 23:3-4)

May the nations be glad and sing for joy, for you rule the peoples justly and guide the nations of the earth. Selah (Psa 67:4)

They will sing before the LORD, for he comes, he comes to judge the earth. He will judge the world in righteousness and the peoples in his truth. (Psa 96:13)

Let them sing before the LORD, for he comes to judge the earth. He will judge the world in righteousness and the peoples with equity. (Psa 98:9)

In love a throne will be established; in faithfulness a man will sit on it— one from the house of David— one who in judging seeks justice and speeds the cause of righteousness. (Isa 16:5)

"The days are coming," declares the LORD, "when I will raise up to David a righteous Branch, a King who will reign wisely and do what is just and right in the land. (Jer 23:5)

"'In those days and at that time I will make a righteous Branch sprout from David's line; he will do what is just and right in the land. (Jer 33:15)

⇒ Christ is going to appoint a kingdom to the apostles.

And I confer on you a kingdom, just as my Father conferred one on me, (Luke 22:29)

⇒ Christ will prevent evil from being done by one nation to another nation.

The remnant of Israel will do no wrong; they will speak no lies, nor will deceit be found in their mouths. They will eat and lie down and no one will make them afraid." (Zep 3:13)

The LORD has taken away your punishment, he has turned back your enemy. The LORD, the King of Israel, is with you; never again will you fear any harm. (Zep 3:15)

⇒ God's commandments will be obeyed by the nations. There will be national obedience.

**"I myself said, "'How gladly would I treat you like sons and give you a desirable land, the most beautiful inheritance of any nation.' I thought you would call me 'Father' and not turn away from following me. (Jer 3:19)**

⇒ The citizens of Jerusalem will be called holy.

**Those who are left in Zion, who remain in Jerusalem, will be called holy, all who are recorded among the living in Jerusalem. The Lord will wash away the filth of the women of Zion; he will cleanse the bloodstains from Jerusalem by a spirit of judgment and a spirit of fire. (Isa 4:3-4)**

⇒ Believers will call God "my Father."

**"I myself said, "'How gladly would I treat you like sons and give you a desirable land, the most beautiful inheritance of any nation.' I thought you would call me 'Father' and not turn away from following me. (Jer 3:19)**

c. Life in the Millennium will be a life of true worship.
⇒ All nations and kings and people of the earth will worship Christ.

**All the ends of the earth will remember and turn to the LORD, and all the families of the nations will bow down before him, (Psa 22:27)**
**All the earth bows down to you; they sing praise to you, they sing praise to your name." Selah (Psa 66:4)**
**Long may he live! May gold from Sheba be given him. May people ever pray for him and bless him all day long. (Psa 72:15)**
**All the nations you have made will come and worship before you, O Lord; they will bring glory to your name. (Psa 86:9)**
**The nations will fear the name of the LORD, all the kings of the earth will revere your glory. So the name of the LORD will be declared in Zion and his praise in Jerusalem When the peoples and the kingdoms assemble to worship the LORD. (Psa 102:15, 21-22)**
**May all the kings of the earth praise you, O LORD, when they hear the words of your mouth. May they sing of the ways of the LORD, for the glory of the LORD is great. (Psa 138:4-5)**
**And if in a truthful, just and righteous way you swear, 'As surely as the LORD lives,' then the nations will be blessed by him and in him they will glory." (Jer 4:2)**
**This is what the LORD Almighty says: "In those days ten men from all**

**languages and nations will take firm hold of one Jew by the hem of his robe and say, 'Let us go with you, because we have heard that God is with you.'" An Oracle (Zec 8:23)**

⇒ All nations will seek instruction from Christ. Gentiles will become the multiplied seed of David and members of the priesthood of God's true people, the true Israel.

**In the last days the mountain of the Lord's temple will be established as chief among the mountains; it will be raised above the hills, and peoples will stream to it. Many nations will come and say, "Come, let us go up to the mountain of the LORD, to the house of the God of Jacob. He will teach us his ways, so that we may walk in his paths." The law will go out from Zion, the word of the LORD from Jerusalem. (Micah 4:1-2)**
**In the last days the mountain of the Lord's temple will be established as chief among the mountains; it will be raised above the hills, and all nations will stream to it. Many peoples will come and say, "Come, let us go up to the mountain of the LORD, to the house of the God of Jacob. He will teach us his ways, so that we may walk in his paths." The law will go out from Zion, the word of the LORD from Jerusalem. (Isa 2:2-3)**
**Nor will the priests, who are Levites, ever fail to have a man to stand before me continually to offer burnt offerings, to burn grain offerings and to present sacrifices.'" I will make the descendants of David my servant and the Levites [the priests] who minister before me as countless as the stars of the sky and as measureless as the sand on the seashore.'" (Jer 33:18, 22)**
**And I will select some of them [Gentiles] also to be priests and Levites [the priesthood]," says the LORD. (Isa 66:21)**

⇒ There will be a covenant of peace between God and Israel, even the forgiveness of sin.

**And so all Israel will be saved, as it is written: "The deliverer will come from Zion; he will turn godlessness away from Jacob. And this is my covenant with them when I take away their sins." (Rom 11:26-27)**
**I will search for the lost and bring back the strays. I will bind up the injured and strengthen the weak, but the sleek and the strong I will destroy. I will shepherd the flock with justice. (Ezek 34:16)**
**Though the mountains be shaken and the hills be removed, yet my unfailing love for you will not be shaken nor my covenant of peace be removed," says the LORD, who has compassion on you. (Isa 54:10)**

⇒ All of God's people will be purified.

> He will sit as a refiner and purifier of silver; he will purify the Levites [the priests] and refine them like gold and silver. Then the LORD will have men who will bring offerings in righteousness, And the offerings of Judah and Jerusalem will be acceptable to the LORD, as in days gone by, as in former years. (Mal 3:3-4)

⇒ The nations will bless Christ and glory in Him.

> And if in a truthful, just and righteous way you swear, 'As surely as the LORD lives,' then the nations will be blessed by him and in him they will glory." (Jer 4:2)
> All the ends of the earth will remember and turn to the LORD, and all the families of the nations will bow down before him, (Psa 22:27)

4. What are some verses that show that resurrected believers will rule and reign during the Millennium?
⇒ The sovereignty, power, and greatness of the world will be given to believers.

> Then the sovereignty, power and greatness of the kingdoms under the whole heaven will be handed over to the saints, the people of the Most High. His kingdom will be an everlasting kingdom, and all rulers will worship and obey him.' (Dan 7:27)

⇒ The apostles will rule and reign over the twelve tribes of Israel.

> Jesus said to them, "I tell you the truth, at the renewal of all things, when the Son of Man sits on his glorious throne, you who have followed me will also sit on twelve thrones, judging the twelve tribes of Israel. (Mat 19:28)
> Jesus said to them, "You will indeed drink from my cup, but to sit at my right or left is not for me to grant. These places belong to those for whom they have been prepared by my Father." (Mat 20:23)
> "As I looked, "thrones were set in place, and the Ancient of Days took his seat. His clothing was as white as snow; the hair of his head was white like wool. His throne was flaming with fire, and its wheels were all ablaze. Then the sovereignty, power and greatness of the kingdoms under the whole heaven will be handed over to the saints, the people of the Most High. His kingdom will be an everlasting kingdom, and all rulers will worship and obey him.' (Dan 7:9, 27)

⇒ God's people will be heirs of the world, of the whole world or universe.

> He has declared that he will set you in praise, fame and honor high above all the nations he has made and that you will be a people holy to the LORD your God, as he promised. (Deu 26:19)
> It was not through law that Abraham and his offspring received the promise that he would be heir of the world, but through the righteousness that comes by faith. (Rom 4:13)

⇒ God's people will rule with justice.

> See, a king will reign in righteousness and rulers will rule with justice. (Isa 32:1)

⇒ All believers will rule and reign with Christ.

> To him who overcomes and does my will to the end, I will give authority over the nations— 'He will rule them with an iron scepter; he will dash them to pieces like pottery' — just as I have received authority from my Father. (Rev 2:26-27)
> To him who overcomes, I will give the right to sit with me on my throne, just as I overcame and sat down with my Father on his throne. (Rev 3:21)
> You have made them to be a kingdom and priests to serve our God, and they will reign on the earth." (Rev 5:10)
> I saw thrones on which were seated those who had been given authority to judge. And I saw the souls of those who had been beheaded because of their testimony for Jesus and because of the word of God. They had not worshiped the beast or his image and had not received his mark on their foreheads or their hands. They came to life and reigned with Christ a thousand years. Blessed and holy are those who have part in the first resurrection. The second death has no power over them, but they will be priests of God and of Christ and will reign with him for a thousand years. (Rev 20:4, 6)
> If we endure, we will also reign with him. If we disown him, he will also disown us; (2 Tim 2:12)

⇒ The Lord will set up shepherds (leaders) over His people.

> I will place shepherds over them who will tend them, and they will no longer be afraid or terrified, nor will any be missing," declares the LORD. (Jer 23:4)

⇒ God's people will judge or rule over angels. (This may not take place until the new heavens and earth are created.)

Do you not know that we will judge angels? How much more the things of this life! (1 Cor 6:3)

⇒ God's people will be put in charge of all of Christ's possessions.

It will be good for that servant whom the master finds doing so when he returns. I tell you the truth, he will put him in charge of all his possessions. (Luke 12:43-44)

⇒ Believers will rule over unbelieving Jews.

I will make those who are of the synagogue of Satan, who claim to be Jews though they are not, but are liars—I will make them come and fall down at your feet and acknowledge that I have loved you. (Rev 3:9)

Remember: the believers will be in their resurrected bodies and people on earth in their earthly bodies. There will apparently be mingling among the two. What we must keep in mind is this: heaven and eternity are not like what most people think—a spirit floating around on a cloud playing a harp or else a spirit that appears as a ghost or gas-like substance. We will have bodies in heaven and eternity. In fact, we will have our present bodies with one difference: they will be perfected. This is the very purpose for the resurrection: to raise up the very elements of our bodies and perfect them to live eternally in the perfect environment of heaven and earth. Therefore, during the Millennium it will be just like it was when Christ fellowshipped with the disciples after His resurrection. He was in His resurrected body and the disciples were in their earthly bodies. During the Millennium, it will be a common thing for the resurrected Lord and resurrected believers to fellowship with people in their earthly bodies. All will have bodies, some earthly bodies and others heavenly, that is, perfected bodies. Remember: the Millennium will be a new age for the earth. Life upon earth will be entirely different from what it is now. As has been seen in the study above, when Jesus Christ returns to earth, His presence and power will change everything.

| | E. The Return of Satan & His Eternal Fate, 20:7-10 | 9 They marched across the breadth of the earth and surrounded the camp of God's people, the city he loves. But fire came down from heaven and devoured them. | 3 The final armies of the world will be destroyed & Satan condemned forever |
|---|---|---|---|
| 1 Satan is loosed | 7 When the thousand years are over, Satan will be released from his prison | 10 And the devil, who deceived them, was thrown into the lake of burning sulfur, where the beast and the false prophet had been thrown. They will be tormented day and night for ever and ever. | a. The nations will march against the throne of Christ in Jerusalem b. God will destroy the armies before they attack, v.9 c. Satan is condemned forever 1) In the lake of fire 2) With the beast (antichrist) & false prophet |
| 2 Satan immediately deceives the nations: Gog & Magog a. He will gather them to war against Christ b. Their number will be as the sand of the sea | 8 And will go out to deceive the nations in the four corners of the earth—Gog and Magog—to gather them for battle. In number they are like the sand on the seashore. | | |

# DIVISION XII

## THE FINAL TRIUMPH: THE MILLENNIUM USHERED IN, 19:11-20:15

### E. The Return of Satan and His Eternal Fate, 20:7-10

(20:7-10) **Introduction**: this is a shocking Scripture. It tells us this: at the end of the Millennium Satan is going to be set loose from hell and allowed to deceive people again. Why? There are at least two reasons.

1. Satan will be loosed for the same reason that he is allowed to tempt us now: to show man what is in his heart, to show man that he must turn to Christ or else face destruction. People during the Millennium will be no different from any other generation of people: they will have a free will and they will still need to turn to Christ for salvation. Therefore, they have to be shown their need. The fact that they turn to Satan so readily will show people their need for Christ in the most stirring way possible. But note: as with all other generations, most people will reject Christ and choose to go their own way in life. Most people will choose to follow Satan.

2. God will release Satan in order to vindicate the justice of God, that is, in order to show that people deserve to be judged and condemned. When people turn to Satan so readily and oppose Christ so easily, they will be without excuse, unable to say one word against the righteous judgment of God. God's final and eternal judgment will be totally vindicated. Therefore, Satan will be released so that people will see the utter corruption of their hearts and stand speechless before the righteous judgment of God.

This passage is the discussion of *the return of Satan and his eternal fate.*
1. Satan is loosed (v.7).
2. Satan immediately deceives the nations: Gog and Magog (v.8).
3. The final armies of the world will be destroyed and Satan condemned forever (v.9-10).

**1** (20:7) **Satan**: Satan is loosed at the end of the Millennium and he immediately deceives the nations. Who are these nations? Were not all the nations destroyed at Armageddon? Scripture says no, there will still be people upon earth after Armageddon, people who will go through the Millennium.

1. There will be survivors of Armageddon who will become witnesses to the glory of Christ when they return home to their own nations.

**See, the LORD is coming with fire, and his chariots are like a whirlwind; he will bring down his anger with fury, and his re-** buke with flames of fire. For with fire and with his sword the LORD will execute judgment upon all men, and many will be those slain by the LORD. "I will set a sign among them, and I will send some of those who survive to the nations—to Tarshish, to the Libyans and Lydians (famous as archers), to Tubal and Greece, and to the distant islands that have not heard of my fame or seen my glory. They will proclaim my glory among the nations. (Isa 66:15-16, 19)

**Then the survivors from all the nations that have attacked Jerusalem will go up year after year to worship the King, the LORD Almighty, and to celebrate the Feast of Tabernacles. If any of the peoples of the earth do not go up to Jerusalem to worship the King, the LORD Almighty, they will have no rain. If the Egyptian people do not go up and take part, they will have no rain. The LORD will bring on them the plague he inflicts on the nations that do not go up to celebrate the Feast of Tabernacles. This will be the punishment of Egypt and the punishment of all the nations that do not go up to celebrate the Feast of Tabernacles. (Zec 14:16-19)**

2. There will even be some survivors of the bowl judgments which fall upon the earth—some survivors of the catastrophic earthquake that hits all over the world and destroys the ungodly cities of the world (cp. Rev.16:1-21, esp, v.17-21). Remember this earthquake takes place at the same time as Armageddon, when Christ returns to earth. But note: there will be some survivors (v.21).

**Then there came flashes of lightning, rumblings, peals of thunder and a severe earthquake. No earthquake like it has ever occurred since man has been on earth, so tremendous was the quake. The great city split into three parts, and the cities of the nations collapsed. God remembered Babylon the Great and gave her the cup filled with the wine of the fury of his wrath. Every island fled away and the mountains could not be found. From the sky huge hailstones**

of about a hundred pounds each fell upon men. And they cursed God on account of the plague of hail, because the plague was so terrible. (Rev 16:18-21)

3. There will be people who turn to the Lord during the Millennium; that is, people will be saved.

Glorious things are said of you, O city of God: *Selah* "I will record Rahab and Babylon among those who acknowledge me— Philistia too, and Tyre, along with Cush — and will say, 'This one was born in Zion.'" Indeed, of Zion it will be said, "This one and that one were born in her, and the Most High himself will establish her." The LORD will write in the register of the peoples: "This one was born in Zion." Selah (Psa 87:3-6)

Yet it was the Lord's will to crush him and cause him to suffer, and though the LORD makes his life a guilt offering, he will see his offspring and prolong his days, and the will of the LORD will prosper in his hand. (Isa 53:10)

I will make the descendants of David my servant and the Levites who minister before me as countless as the stars of the sky and as measureless as the sand on the seashore.'" (Jer 33:22; cp. Is.53:10)

You are to allot it as an inheritance for yourselves and for the aliens who have settled among you and who have children. You are to consider them as native-born Israelites; along with you they are to be allotted an inheritance among the tribes of Israel. In whatever tribe the alien settles, there you are to give him his inheritance," declares the Sovereign LORD. (Ezek 47:22-23)

4. There will be the nations that are in existence when Christ returns to earth. This shows there will be some survivors within most, if not all, of the nations. There will be few in comparison to the population before the trumpet and bowl judgments and before Armageddon, nevertheless some will survive. It will be the people of these nations and the future generations born during the Millennium that Christ will rule with an iron scepter. It will be these over whom He will execute justice.

"I have installed my King on Zion, my holy hill." I will proclaim the decree of the LORD: He said to me, "You are my Son ; today I have become your Father. Ask of me, and I will make the nations your inheritance, the ends of the earth your possession. You will rule them with an iron scepter ; you will dash them to pieces like pottery." (Psa 2:6-9)

This is what Isaiah son of Amoz saw concerning Judah and Jerusalem: In the last days the mountain of the Lord's temple will be established as chief among the mountains; it will be raised above the hills, and all nations will stream to it. Many peoples will come and say, "Come, let us go up to the mountain of the LORD, to the house of the God of Jacob. He will teach us his ways, so

that we may walk in his paths." The law will go out from Zion, the word of the LORD from Jerusalem. He will judge between the nations and will settle disputes for many peoples. They will beat their swords into plowshares and their spears into pruning hooks. Nation will not take up sword against nation, nor will they train for war anymore. (Isa 2:1-4)

And he will delight in the fear of the LORD. He will not judge by what he sees with his eyes, or decide by what he hears with his ears; But with righteousness he will judge the needy, with justice he will give decisions for the poor of the earth. He will strike the earth with the rod of his mouth; with the breath of his lips he will slay the wicked. Righteousness will be his belt and faithfulness the sash around his waist. (Isa 11:3-5)

"Never again will there be in it an infant who lives but a few days, or an old man who does not live out his years; he who dies at a hundred will be thought a mere youth; he who fails to reach a hundred will be considered accursed. (Isa 65:20)

"Those who consecrate and purify themselves to go into the gardens, following the one in the midst of those who eat the flesh of pigs and rats and other abominable things—they will meet their end together," declares the LORD. "And I, because of their actions and their imaginations, am about to come and gather all nations and tongues, and they will come and see my glory. (Isa 66:17-18)

He will judge between many peoples and will settle disputes for strong nations far and wide. They will beat their swords into plowshares and their spears into pruning hooks. Nation will not take up sword against nation, nor will they train for war anymore. (Micah 4:3)

Then the survivors from all the nations that have attacked Jerusalem will go up year after year to worship the King, the LORD Almighty, and to celebrate the Feast of Tabernacles. If any of the peoples of the earth do not go up to Jerusalem to worship the King, the LORD Almighty, they will have no rain. If the Egyptian people do not go up and take part, they will have no rain. The LORD will bring on them the plague he inflicts on the nations that do not go up to celebrate the Feast of Tabernacles. This will be the punishment of Egypt and the punishment of all the nations that do not go up to celebrate the Feast of Tabernacles. (Zec 14:16-19)

The seventh angel sounded his trumpet, and there were loud voices in heaven, which said: "The kingdom of the world has become the kingdom of our Lord and of his Christ, and he will reign for ever and ever." (Rev 11:15)

Then I heard the angel in charge of the waters say: "You are just in these judgments, you who are and who were, the Holy

One, because you have so judged; (Rev 16:5)

When the thousand years are over, Satan will be released from his prison And will go out to deceive the nations in the four corners of the earth—Gog and Magog—to gather them for battle. In number they are like the sand on the seashore. They marched across the breadth of the earth and surrounded the camp of God's people, the city he loves. But fire came down from heaven and devoured them. And the devil, who deceived them, was thrown into the lake of burning sulfur, where the beast and the false prophet had been thrown. They will be tormented day and night for ever and ever. (Rev 20:7-10)

Then the end will come, when he hands over the kingdom to God the Father after he has destroyed all dominion, authority and power. For he must reign until he has put all his enemies under his feet. The last enemy to be destroyed is death. For he "has put everything under his feet." Now when it says that "everything" has been put under him, it is clear that this does not include God himself, who put everything under Christ. When he has done this, then the Son himself will be made subject to him who put everything under him, so that God may be all in all. (1 Cor 15:24-28)

**2** (20:8) **Satan**: when Satan is set loose at the end of the Millennium, he will immediately deceive the nations. Scripture tells us that everyone on earth during the Millennium *will not be saved*. There will be many whose hearts will not belong to Christ. And remember, Christ will actually be living in Jerusalem where His palace and rule will be centered. Yet the hearts of many will be hard toward Him. How could this possibly happen when Christ will rule for one thousand years, when He will personally guide the rebuilding of the world's cities and bring peace and prosperity to earth? The answer is the same as what is experienced today and has been experienced from the beginning of time. Never forget that God's own Son, the Lord Jesus Christ, came to earth thousands of years ago, yet people not only rejected Him, many denied that He was even God's Son. And today, despite all the clear and unmistakable evidence, most reject and deny Him. Remember this also: the Millennium will be one thousand years long. Think about it: one thousand years. That is a long, long time. People around the earth, as we all tend to do, will begin to fall into a routine. Year after year will pass; then decade after decade and century after century

will pass. Some people will not even meet Christ face to face. They will not go up to Jerusalem for the great Feast of Tabernacles (Zech.14:16-19). As a result, what will happen will be just what has happened since Christ came the first time: people will begin to think of Christ in terms of a mere man. To many people He will be a mere ruler. And note how many will follow the deception of Satan: they will be numbered as the sand of the sea. Note also that they are called by the name of Gog and Magog. These are the names that symbolize the nations that come from the north to fight against God's people. Gog was the king of Magog (cp. Ezk. chapters 38 and 39).

**3** (20:9-10) **Satan**: the final armies of the world will be destroyed and Satan condemned forever. The nations will march against Jerusalem and the throne of Christ to take over the world for themselves (v.9). But there will be no battle. The nations will misinterpret who Christ is, the Sovereign Majesty of the universe. They will let the fact that He has come to earth throw them into thinking He is only a mere man as they are. God will intervene and cause fire to fall out of heaven and consume the armies. The devil will then be taken and cast into the lake of burning sulfur with the antichrist and the false prophet (v.10). And note: they will be tormented day and night forever and ever.

"Then he will say to those on his left, 'Depart from me, you who are cursed, into the eternal fire prepared for the devil and his angels. (Mat 25:41)

For if God did not spare angels when they sinned, but sent them to hell, putting them into gloomy dungeons to be held for judgment; (2 Pet 2:4)

And the angels who did not keep their positions of authority but abandoned their own home—these he has kept in darkness, bound with everlasting chains for judgment on the great Day. (Jude 1:6)

But the beast was captured, and with him the false prophet who had performed the miraculous signs on his behalf. With these signs he had deluded those who had received the mark of the beast and worshiped his image. The two of them were thrown alive into the fiery lake of burning sulfur. (Rev 19:20)

And the devil, who deceived them, was thrown into the lake of burning sulfur, where the beast and the false prophet had been thrown. They will be tormented day and night for ever and ever. (Rev 20:10)

| | F. The Final Resurrection & Judgment of Unbelievers: The Great White Throne Judgment, 20:11-15 | according to what they had done as recorded in the books. | b. The Book of Records |
|---|---|---|---|
| 1 The place of judgment: The great white throne<br>2 The time of judgment: When heaven & earth flee away<br>3 The persons to be judged | 11 Then I saw a great white throne and him who was seated on it. Earth and sky fled from his presence, and there was no place for them. | 13 The sea gave up the dead that were in it, and death and Hades gave up the dead that were in them, and each person was judged according to what he had done. | 5 The resurrection to judgment |
| 4 The basis of judgment a. The Book of Life | 12 And I saw the dead, great and small, standing before the throne, and books were opened. Another book was opened, which is the book of life. The dead were judged | 14 Then death and Hades were thrown into the lake of fire. The lake of fire is the second death.<br>15 If anyone's name was not found written in the book of life, he was thrown into the lake of fire. | 6 The terrorizing punishment of the judgment: The lake of fire which is the second death |

# DIVISION XII

## THE FINAL TRIUMPH: THE MILLENNIUM USHERED IN, 19:11-20:15

### F. The Final Resurrection and Judgment of Unbelievers: The Great White Throne Judgment, 20:11-15

(20:11-15) **Introduction**: the final judgment is coming, that great day when all unbelievers shall stand before God and give an account to God. The final judgment is called the "Great White Throne Judgment." Many deny a final judgment. They smile and scoff at the idea that there is to be future punishment for sins. They laugh at the preaching and teaching of hell. This Scripture stands diametrically opposed to these people. This Scripture declares emphatically: there is to be a final judgment for unbelievers; every unbeliever, small and great, shall stand before God and give an account to God. The declaration is emphatic: all unbelievers shall be judged and punished for their rejection of Jesus Christ and for their works upon earth. Unbelievers shall be judged at the "Great White Throne Judgment of God."

1. The place of judgment: the great white throne (v.11).
2. The time of judgment: when heaven and earth flee away (v.11).
3. The persons to be judged (v.12).
4. The basis of judgment (v.12).
5. The resurrection to judgment (v.13).
6. The terrorizing punishment of the judgment: the lake of fire which is the second death (v.14-15).

**1** (20:11) **Judgment**: there is the place of judgment, the *great white throne* of God. Unbelievers shall stand before the very throne of God, face to face with God and Christ. Standing there they will see exactly what John saw. They will then know that their unbelief and rejection of Jesus Christ was mad and insane behavior. They will know they should have never rejected and cursed God and Christ. They should not have lived for the pleasures and possessions of this world. But it will be too late. Standing there, they will not be standing before the cross of Christ. They will be standing before *the great white throne*, before the throne of God's judgment. Note how the throne is described.

1. The throne of God is a *great* throne. It is far, far greater than any judicial bench of any supreme court. It is greater because God Himself, the Sovereign Majesty of the universe, sits upon it. When He speaks and issues a decision...
   - the decision is final.
   - the decision is for eternity, not just for a life term.
   - the decision can never be appealed, not even once.

But the throne is also great for another reason: its decisions concern a *great salvation*. Everyone who stands before the great white throne of God has rejected the *great salvation of God's Son*. He has rejected the great salvation offered by the *Son of God Himself*. The salvation offered by the Lord Jesus Christ is not just another salvation, not just another way to God, not just one of many ways to God. The salvation offered by Jesus Christ is the only salvation of *God's Son Himself*. This is what makes the rejection of Jesus Christ so serious. Jesus Christ is God's Son, God's very own Son. As good as the morality and teachings of some religions may be, there is only one Son of God. God has only one Son, the Lord Jesus Christ. Therefore, the only person who is ever acceptable God is the person who approaches Him through His Son, the Lord Jesus Christ. As stated, the salvation offered by Jesus Christ is the only salvation there is; it is the only way to God. Why? Because it is the salvation of the *Son of God Himself*. Therefore, it is *the great salvation*, the only salvation that has existed or ever will exist. Consequently, when it comes time to judge those who reject the *great salvation* of God's Son, they will be judged from a *great throne*.

> **How shall we escape if we ignore such a great salvation? This salvation, which was first announced by the Lord, was confirmed to us by those who heard him. (Heb 2:3)**
>
> **See to it that you do not refuse him who speaks. If they did not escape when they refused him who warned them on earth, how much less will we, if we turn away from him who warns us from heaven? (Heb 12:25)**

2. The throne of God is a *white* throne. White stands for purity, holiness, and righteousness. We must never forget: no person is perfect. No person is perfectly pure or righteous. We all have some impurity and some unrighteousness. But not God; God is perfect. He is perfect in purity and righteousness. Therefore, no imperfect person can ever live

with God. If any of us are to live with God, our imperfection must be removed so that we can stand perfect before God.

How can this be done? Only by Jesus Christ. Jesus Christ alone is perfect and sinless. Therefore, the person must believe that Jesus Christ died for his sins, that Jesus Christ actually took his sins off him and died for them. If a person believes this, God counts it so. God actually counts the death of Jesus Christ *for the believer*. Therefore, the believer stands before God perfect and sinless—not because he really is sinless, but because Jesus Christ bore his sins for him and paid the judgment for them. The only person who can ever live with God is a person who has let Jesus Christ bear his sin. If a person wishes to live with God, he must trust the death of Jesus Christ, trust that Jesus Christ died for him.

The point is this: no unbeliever has done this. Everyone who stands before the *great white throne* of God will be bearing his own sins. Not a single *unbeliever* will have trusted the purity and righteousness of Jesus Christ. Therefore, the purity of God's throne will blaze forth in righteousness and condemn the unbeliever, condemn him because he is neither pure nor righteous. The purity and righteousness of Jesus Christ to cover his sins were available, but he rejected Jesus Christ. Therefore, the unbeliever stands in his unrighteousness before God's holy righteousness. Consequently his unrighteousness must be condemned by God's righteousness, and it will be. This is what the great white throne judgment is: the judgment of all unbelievers.

> Let the fields be jubilant, and everything in them. Then all the trees of the forest will sing for joy; They will sing before the LORD, for he comes, he comes to judge the earth. He will judge the world in righteousness and the peoples in his truth. (Psa 96:12-13)

> "At that time the sign of the Son of Man will appear in the sky, and all the nations of the earth will mourn. They will see the Son of Man coming on the clouds of the sky, with power and great glory. (Mat 24:30)

> If anyone is ashamed of me and my words in this adulterous and sinful generation, the Son of Man will be ashamed of him when he comes in his Father's glory with the holy angels." (Mark 8:38)

> And give relief to you who are troubled, and to us as well. This will happen when the Lord Jesus is revealed from heaven in blazing fire with his powerful angels. He will punish those who do not know God and do not obey the gospel of our Lord Jesus. (2 Th 1:7-8)

> Look, he is coming with the clouds, and every eye will see him, even those who pierced him; and all the peoples of the earth will mourn because of him. So shall it be! Amen. (Rev 1:7)

**2** (20:11) **Judgment**: there is the time of the judgment. When will the great white throne judgment take place? When the earth and the heaven flee away. This is a poetic way to describe the destruction of the present heavens and earth that is coming. Remember: God has promised to make a new heavens and earth. To do so, He must first destroy the present heavens and earth. When is this universal destruction going to take place? When the great white throne judgment is going on. Picture the scene! There stand all the unbelievers who have ever lived. Billions and billions of unbelievers stand upon the great sea of glass before the throne of God. Then all of a sudden there is a massive explosion of atoms never dreamed possible. A chain reaction sets off all the atoms throughout the whole universe. A universal atomic explosion destroys the whole universe. Both the heavens and the earth are destroyed by God, destroyed by fire.

Imagine the shock to the unbelievers standing before God in the spiritual world. The idea is that they will witness the fiery destruction of their world, the world upon which they had lived their lives. Note the words "there was no place for them [the unbelievers]." They had lived for the world and their world will be gone. They do not belong in heaven; therefore, there is no place for them. All they had lived for will be gone: money, houses, lands, position, power, fame, popularity, drugs, sex, alcohol, pleasure, possessions, and comfort—it will all be gone. There will no longer be a world for the unbeliever, and they do not belong in heaven. There will be *no place for them*.

> Heaven and earth will pass away, but my words will never pass away. (Mat 24:35)

> By the same word the present heavens and earth are reserved for fire, being kept for the day of judgment and destruction of ungodly men. (2 Pet 3:7)

> But the day of the Lord will come like a thief. The heavens will disappear with a roar; the elements will be destroyed by fire, and the earth and everything in it will be laid bare. Since everything will be destroyed in this way, what kind of people ought you to be? You ought to live holy and godly lives As you look forward to the day of God and speed its coming. That day will bring about the destruction of the heavens by fire, and the elements will melt in the heat. But in keeping with his promise we are looking forward to a new heaven and a new earth, the home of righteousness. (2 Pet 3:10-13)

> Then I saw a great white throne and him who was seated on it. Earth and sky fled from his presence, and there was no place for them. (Rev 20:11)

> Then I saw a new heaven and a new earth, for the first heaven and the first earth had passed away, and there was no longer any sea. (Rev 21:1)

> In the beginning you laid the foundations of the earth, and the heavens are the work of your hands. They will perish, but you remain; they will all wear out like a garment. Like clothing you will change them and they will be discarded. But you remain the same, and your years will never end. (Psa 102:25-27)

> All the stars of the heavens will be dissolved and the sky rolled up like a scroll; all the starry host will fall like withered leaves from the vine, like shriveled figs from the fig tree. (Isa 34:4)

> Lift up your eyes to the heavens, look at the earth beneath; the heavens will vanish like smoke, the earth will wear out like a garment and its inhabitants die like flies. But my salvation will last forever, my righteousness will never fail. (Isa 51:6)

"Behold, I will create new heavens and a new earth. The former things will not be remembered, nor will they come to mind. (Isa 65:17)

**3** (20:12) **Judgment**: there are the persons to be judged. Both the small and the great will be judged.

1. Ordinary men and women will be judged:
   ⇒ Those who are the average and common people of the earth; the blue collar worker, the employees and workers of the earth. They shall be judged.
   ⇒ Those who are the slaves and servants of the world. They too shall be judged.
   ⇒ Those who commit the sins that society considers somewhat small and sometimes understandable: sins of selfishness, hoarding, banking, complaining, laziness, slothfulness, indifference, arguing, gossiping, backbiting, criticizing, immorality, stealing, and lying. They shall be judged.
2. Great men and women will be judged:
   ⇒ Those who are in positions of authority: managers, foremen, supervisors, officers of corporations, owners of businesses, rulers, and kings. They shall all be judged.
   ⇒ Those who misuse their authority, abuse, and take advantage of others, who ignore and neglect others, and in some cases destroy and kill others. They shall be judged.
   ⇒ Those who sin with a daring and a flair, who love their sin and revel in it. They shall be judged.

Every unbeliever on the face of the earth will stand before God and be judged. No matter how small or how great, the unbeliever shall stand before the great white throne judgment of God and be sentenced.
   ⇒ The small and the great shall stand there.
   ⇒ The low and the high shall stand there.
   ⇒ The poor and the rich shall stand there.
   ⇒ The unrighteous and the self-righteous shall stand there.
   ⇒ The nonreligious and the religious shall stand there.
   ⇒ The unknown and the known shall stand there.

No unbeliever will be exempt; no unbeliever will be overlooked or missed. All unbelievers, each in his own time, will be called forward by name and face Him who sits upon the throne. Every unbeliever will have his day in the great tribunal of God.

This will take place on the day when God will judge men's secrets through Jesus Christ, as my gospel declares. (Rom 2:16)
You, then, why do you judge your brother? Or why do you look down on your brother? For we will all stand before God's judgment seat. (Rom 14:10)
But I tell you that men will have to give account on the day of judgment for every careless word they have spoken. (Mat 12:36)
"Therefore, the kingdom of heaven is like a king who wanted to settle accounts with his servants. (Mat 18:23)
So then, each of us will give an account of himself to God. (Rom 14:12)
For you have spent enough time in the past doing what pagans choose to do—living

in debauchery, lust, drunkenness, orgies, carousing and detestable idolatry. They think it strange that you do not plunge with them into the same flood of dissipation, and they heap abuse on you. But they will have to give account to him who is ready to judge the living and the dead. (1 Pet 4:3-5)

**4** (20:12) **Judgment—Book of Life**: there is the basis of judgment. Note exactly what is said.

And I saw the dead, great and small, standing before the throne, and books were opened. Another book was opened, which is the book of life. The dead were judged according to what they had done as recorded in the books. (Rev 20:12b)

There are two kinds of books kept in heaven. Both will be present at the great white throne judgment.

1. There is *the book of life*. This is the book where every human being who has ever lived has his name written. It is the book that includes the names of everyone who has ever lived or ever will live upon earth. God longs for everyone to live with Him forever; therefore, every person's name is recorded in the *book of life*. However, when a person fails to receive Jesus Christ as his Savior, his name is erased from the book, and he loses the right to live as a citizen of heaven with God. Scripture after Scripture tells us this.

But now, please forgive their sin—but if not, then blot me out of the book you have written." The LORD replied to Moses, "Whoever has sinned against me I will blot out of my book. (Exo 32:32-33)
May they be blotted out of the book of life and not be listed with the righteous. (Psa 69:28)
"At that time Michael, the great prince who protects your people, will arise. There will be a time of distress such as has not happened from the beginning of nations until then. But at that time your people—everyone whose name is found written in the book—will be delivered. (Dan 12:1)
However, do not rejoice that the spirits submit to you, but rejoice that your names are written in heaven." (Luke 10:20)
Yes, and I ask you, loyal yokefellow, help these women who have contended at my side in the cause of the gospel, along with Clement and the rest of my fellow workers, whose names are in the book of life. (Phil 4:3)
He who overcomes will, like them, be dressed in white. I will never blot out his name from the book of life, but will acknowledge his name before my Father and his angels. (Rev 3:5)
All inhabitants of the earth will worship the beast—all whose names have not been written in the book of life belonging to the Lamb that was slain from the creation of the world. (Rev 13:8)
The beast, which you saw, once was, now is not, and will come up out of the Abyss and go to his destruction. The inhabitants of the

earth whose names have not been written in the book of life from the creation of the world will be astonished when they see the beast, because he once was, now is not, and yet will come. (Rev 17:8)

And I saw the dead, great and small, standing before the throne, and books were opened. Another book was opened, which is the book of life. The dead were judged according to what they had done as recorded in the books. (Rev 20:12)

If anyone's name was not found written in the book of life, he was thrown into the lake of fire. (Rev 20:15)

Nothing impure will ever enter it, nor will anyone who does what is shameful or deceitful, but only those whose names are written in the Lamb's book of life. (Rev 21:27)

And if anyone takes words away from this book of prophecy, God will take away from him his share in the tree of life and in the holy city, which are described in this book. (Rev 22:19)

2. There are the *books of records*. These books are the records of all the works of unbelievers. When a person's name is found erased from the book of life, then the *books of records* are opened, and he is judged out of them. Note two things.

a. These books are not opened to see whether or not a person is doomed to hell. The book of life tells that. The book of records shows the degree of punishment a person is to receive. A man such as Hitler will be punished and judged much more severely than a petty thief. Both are doomed for hell, but both will not suffer the same amount of punishment.

But I tell you, it will be more bearable for Tyre and Sidon on the day of judgment than for you. And you, Capernaum, will you be lifted up to the skies? No, you will go down to the depths. If the miracles that were performed in you had been performed in Sodom, it would have remained to this day. (Mat 11:22-23)

"That servant who knows his master's will and does not get ready or does not do what his master wants will be beaten with many blows. But the one who does not know and does things deserving punishment will be beaten with few blows. From everyone who has been given much, much will be demanded; and from the one who has been entrusted with much, much more will be asked. (Luke 12:47-48)

b. The *books of records* means that the judgment will be exact and fair. An unbeliever will be treated justly. There is a record of his works, of exactly what he has done and not done. There is a record of secret sins, of the sins committed in the dark and behind closed doors, of ill feelings within the heart, of evil thoughts of the mind. There is a record of all the works of the unbeliever. Therefore, he can be treated with fairness and perfect justice. He will be judged and punished for exactly what he has done, no more and no less.

And that you, O Lord, are loving. Surely you will reward each person according to what he has done. (Psa 62:12)

"I the LORD search the heart and examine the mind, to reward a man according to his conduct, according to what his deeds deserve." (Jer 17:10)

For the Son of Man is going to come in his Father's glory with his angels, and then he will reward each person according to what he has done. (Mat 16:27)

But the one who does not know and does things deserving punishment will be beaten with few blows. From everyone who has been given much, much will be demanded; and from the one who has been entrusted with much, much more will be asked. (Luke 12:48)

Since you call on a Father who judges each man's work impartially, live your lives as strangers here in reverent fear. (1 Pet 1:17)

And I saw the dead, great and small, standing before the throne, and books were opened. Another book was opened, which is the book of life. The dead were judged according to what they had done as recorded in the books. (Rev 20:12)

"Behold, I am coming soon! My reward is with me, and I will give to everyone according to what he has done. (Rev 22:12)

**Thought 1.** Many a person says, "I'm doing the best that I can." He will be judged on that basis. He will be judged for all the good things that he did as well as for all the bad things that he did. But note: he is still doomed for hell. Why? If he did mostly good in his life, why is he still doomed for hell? Because he is not perfect—never has been perfect and never will be perfect—not within himself. His only hope for perfection is to trust Jesus Christ, to trust that Jesus Christ has taken his sins and borne them for him. But the unbeliever does not accept Jesus Christ. Therefore, no matter how mild a sinner he may be, he is still a sinner and imperfect. Consequently, he has to bear his own sins and have them read out loud by God. Standing before God, if the unbeliever had only trusted Jesus Christ to bear his sins for him, he would have been free of sin. There would have been no sin recorded against him. For Jesus Christ would have borne them all; Jesus Christ would have freed the unbeliever of sin and presented him perfect before God. This is the reason *good works and doing the best we can* is not enough. No matter how much good we do, we can never achieve perfection. And to live in heaven with God we must be perfect, for heaven and God are perfect. And God is not about to allow heaven and His presence to become contaminated with sin. Heaven would no longer be heaven if sin were allowed within it.

**5** (20:13) **Judgment**: there is the resurrection to judgment. The *first resurrection* will have already taken place one thousand years before. It was the resurrection for believers (cp. Rev.20:5-6). This resurrection, the calling forth of the dead, is the second and final resurrection, the *resurrection of all unbelievers*. God knows where all the atoms and particles of a person are. The atoms and particles of a person's body may be scattered all over the world, but God knows where every minute element is. And He is going to call forth every human body—every element and particle—of every unbeliever who has ever lived.

Note where the dead unbelievers will come from:

1. They will come from the sea: from the depths of the Atlantic and Pacific oceans, the Mediterranean and Persian seas, the Black and Dead seas. From all the seas of the world the bodies of the dead unbelievers will come—the bodies of those sunken in the wars of human history, in the merchant ships, and in the ships of pirates. Even the bodies of those murdered and dumped in the seas will come forth. There will not be a body ever lost at sea or in any other body of water that will not come forth. All the bodies of unbelievers that have been scattered over the seas of the earth will be brought back together and raised up—all in the flash of an eye—and every body from the seas of the world will stand before the great white throne judgment of God.

2. They will come from death itself and from the graves of the earth (the word translated "Hades" in the New International Version is "grave" in the Greek). All the bodies of dead unbelievers who are in the earth or scattered over the earth shall be resurrected. God knows where every atom and particle of dust is, every element that makes up every unbeliever's body. Therefore, when He calls forth for all unbelievers to stand before Him in judgment, all the bodies of dead unbelievers that lie over the dry land of the earth—they shall all come forth. They shall come out of the great pyramids of Egypt, the jungles of Africa, the rain forests of Brazil, the desert sands of Arabia, the burial grounds of Indians, the battlefields of wars, the alleys and secret places of murder, and the graves of America. Every place upon earth where a human body has fallen or been placed, that body is going to arise. God is going to call forth the atoms or whatever the basic element of human life is; He is going to call those elements together, and the body of the unsaved person is going to stand before the *great white throne* judgment of God. Note that this is exactly what Scripture says:

> The sea gave up the dead that were in it, and death and Hades [the grave] gave up the dead that were in them, and each person was judged according to what he had done. (Rev 20:13)

Note the reemphasis: all unbelievers will be judged *according to what he or she has done*. Every unbeliever can expect to be treated fairly and justly. He shall be judged in perfect justice. He will receive punishment for exactly what he did and failed to do—no more and no less.

**Thought 1.** God has done all He can. He has provided the way of salvation for every person. All a person has to do is to follow that way, to believe in the Lord Jesus Christ and follow Him. And remember: Jesus Christ is God's own Son. The way of salvation cost God the life of His Son. God had to pay the supreme price for salvation; He had to put all the sins of the world upon His own Son and let Him bear all the judgment and punishment for those sins. But He did it; He did it because He loves man. He can do no more. The decision is man's. Man either chooses to believe and follow Jesus Christ or else to face God alone. Following Christ means that Christ bore our sins and punishment. This frees us from sin, frees us because He took them off us and bore them Himself. Therefore, we stand before God free of sin, perfect and acceptable to God. But if

we refuse to believe and follow Christ, then it means that we bear our own sin. We choose to stand before God with our own sin. This is what the *great white throne judgment* is all about. It is the judgment of all those who choose to stand before God as sinners, as bearing their own sins. Therefore, they shall bear them. They shall be judged for their works, for exactly what they chose to do. They shall be treated with perfect justice and equity. They shall...

- bear a punishment that *is equal* to their works.
- bear a punishment that *perfectly matches* their behavior.
- bear a punishment that *measures out exactly* to what they did.

There will be no unfair treatment, discrimination, partiality, or favoritism shown at the great white throne judgment. Everyone will be treated exactly as he himself chose to be treated.

> **"When the Son of Man comes in his glory, and all the angels with him, he will sit on his throne in heavenly glory. All the nations will be gathered before him, and he will separate the people one from another as a shepherd separates the sheep from the goats. (Mat 25:31-32)**
>
> **For he has set a day when he will judge the world with justice by the man he has appointed. He has given proof of this to all men by raising him from the dead." (Acts 17:31)**
>
> **In the presence of God and of Christ Jesus, who will judge the living and the dead, and in view of his appearing and his kingdom, I give you this charge: (2 Tim 4:1)**
>
> **Just as man is destined to die once, and after that to face judgment, (Heb 9:27)**
>
> **If this is so, then the Lord knows how to rescue godly men from trials and to hold the unrighteous for the day of judgment, while continuing their punishment. (2 Pet 2:9)**
>
> **By the same word the present heavens and earth are reserved for fire, being kept for the day of judgment and destruction of ungodly men. (2 Pet 3:7)**
>
> **Enoch, the seventh from Adam, prophesied about these men: "See, the Lord is coming with thousands upon thousands of his holy ones To judge everyone, and to convict all the ungodly of all the ungodly acts they have done in the ungodly way, and of all the harsh words ungodly sinners have spoken against him." (Jude 1:14-15)**
>
> **Let the fields be jubilant, and everything in them. Then all the trees of the forest will sing for joy; They will sing before the LORD, for he comes, he comes to judge the earth. He will judge the world in righteousness and the peoples in his truth. (Psa 96:12-13)**

**6** (20:14-15) **Judgment:** there is the terrorizing punishment of the judgment. If there is any one thing that believers should do, it is to note these two verses. As the great preacher E.V. Hill has said in a sermon: the first reason he accepted Jesus Christ was because he did not want to go to hell. He did not want to be tormented and punished by being separated from God, not forever and ever. Note the verses:

> **Then death and Hades were thrown into the lake of fire. The lake of fire is the second death. If anyone's name was not found written in the book of life, he was thrown into the lake of fire. (Rev 20:14-15)**

1. Death and Hades (the grave) will be cast into the lake of fire. Hades is the place where all unbelievers go after their death. Hades is a temporary place where unbelievers go to await the final judgment. After the great white throne judgment is completed, then all those who are dead and in Hades will be cast into the *lake of fire*. The lake of fire is the final and eternal place of torment where all unbelievers shall be cast.

Note: there are many who say the idea of fire is symbolic, that the *lake of fire* is not real fire. But we must never forget this: if it is not real fire, then it is something far, far worse. For physical and material substances are nothing compared to spiritual and eternal substances. The substance of physical and material fire is nothing compared to spiritual and eternal fire. The human mind cannot conceive how glorious heaven will be nor how terrible the lake of fire will be. Therefore, to say that the *lake of fire* is a symbol does not ease the punishment of hell. Scripture paints the punishment of suffering apart from God as being so horrifying and terrorizing that a person who goes to hell would probably choose fire over the reality of the lake of fire. Remember the rich man and Lazarus: the concern of the rich man in hell was not that he was in a flame of fire, but the torment and suffering he was bearing. He was so concerned over the suffering that he longed for his brothers to escape the suffering when they died (cp. Lk.16:24, 27-31).

> **But the subjects of the kingdom will be thrown outside, into the darkness, where there will be weeping and gnashing of teeth." (Mat 8:12)**
>
> **The Son of Man will send out his angels, and they will weed out of his kingdom everything that causes sin and all who do evil. They will throw them into the fiery furnace, where there will be weeping and gnashing of teeth. (Mat 13:41-42)**
>
> **This is how it will be at the end of the age. The angels will come and separate the wicked from the righteous And throw them into the fiery furnace, where there will be weeping and gnashing of teeth. (Mat 13:49-50)**
>
> **"Then the king told the attendants, 'Tie him hand and foot, and throw him outside, into the darkness, where there will be weeping and gnashing of teeth.' (Mat 22:13)**
>
> **The master of that servant will come on a day when he does not expect him and at an hour he is not aware of. He will cut him to pieces and assign him a place with the hypocrites, where there will be weeping and gnashing of teeth. (Mat 24:50-51)**
>
> **And throw that worthless servant outside, into the darkness, where there will be weeping and gnashing of teeth.' (Mat 25:30)**

2. The lake of fire is the second death. That is, it is eternal death. In the Scripture death means separation from God. Death does not mean annihilation, ceasing to exist, nor ex-

tinction. This life is not all there is. When a person dies upon this earth, he still exists. How? He exists in the next world, in the spiritual world and dimension—the permanent and eternal world, the world that does not age, deteriorate, die, or pass away. The physical world does pass away, but not the spiritual world or dimension. The spiritual world, the next world, is eternal and lasts forever and ever. Therefore, when a person dies upon this earth, that is just the first death. The person is merely separated from this life and world. He merely passes over into the next world, and he exists there forever and ever. But note what happens to the person who dies separated from God. If he does not follow God, if he chooses to be separated from God in this life, then when he passes on into the next world, he is still separated from God. His condition and state never change. He chose to be separated from God; therefore, he shall be separated from God forever and ever.

The point is this: when the unbeliever stands before the great white throne judgment of God, he shall die the second death. He shall be judged to be separated from God. God will know that the man never lived nor followed Him, that the man chose to be separated from Him. Therefore, the man shall die the second death. He shall be separated from God eternally.

The second death simply means to be separated from God eternally. But note how terrible the second death is: the place of the second death is the *lake of fire*.

3. The basis of judgment is the *book of life*. If a person's name is not found written in the *book of life*, then he will be cast into the *lake of fire*. A person must possess the perfect life of Jesus Christ if he is to live forever in heaven with God. If a person does not posses life, the perfect life and righteousness of Jesus Christ, if his name is not written in the book of life, then he is doomed to death. He is doomed to the second death, to the lake of fire.

> **But I tell you that anyone who is angry with his brother will be subject to judgment. Again, anyone who says to his brother, 'Raca, ' is answerable to the Sanhedrin. But anyone who says, 'You fool!' will be in danger of the fire of hell. If your right eye causes you to sin, gouge it out and throw it away. It is better for you to lose one part of your body than for your whole body to be thrown into hell. (Mat 5:22, 29)**
>
> **Do not be afraid of those who kill the body but cannot kill the soul. Rather, be afraid of the One who can destroy both soul and body in hell. (Mat 10:28)**
>
> **The Son of Man will send out his angels, and they will weed out of his kingdom everything that causes sin and all who do evil. They will throw them into the fiery furnace, where there will be weeping and gnashing of teeth. (Mat 13:41-42)**
>
> **If your hand or your foot causes you to sin cut it off and throw it away. It is better for you to enter life maimed or crippled than to have two hands or two feet and be thrown into eternal fire. And if your eye causes you to sin, gouge it out and throw it away. It is better for you to enter life with one eye than to have two eyes and be thrown into the fire of hell. (Mat 18:8-9)**
>
> **"Woe to you, teachers of the law and Pharisees, you hypocrites! You travel over land and sea to win a single convert, and**

when he becomes one, you make him twice as much a son of hell as you are. (Mat 23:15)

They will throw them into the fiery furnace, where there will be weeping and gnashing of teeth. (Mat 13:42)

"Then he will say to those on his left, 'Depart from me, you who are cursed, into the eternal fire prepared for the devil and his angels. (Mat 25:41)

"Then they will go away to eternal punishment, but the righteous to eternal life." (Mat 25:46)

But whoever blasphemes against the Holy Spirit will never be forgiven; he is guilty of an eternal sin." (Mark 3:29)

If your hand causes you to sin, cut it off. It is better for you to enter life maimed than with two hands to go into hell, where the fire never goes out. And if your foot causes you to sin, cut it off. It is better for you to enter life crippled than to have two feet and be thrown into hell. And if your eye causes you to sin, pluck it out. It is better for you to enter the kingdom of God with one eye than to have two eyes and be thrown into hell, Where "'their worm does not die, and the fire is not quenched.' (Mark 9:43-48)

His winnowing fork is in his hand to clear his threshing floor and to gather the wheat into his barn, but he will burn up the chaff with unquenchable fire." (Luke 3:17)

But I will show you whom you should fear: Fear him who, after the killing of the body, has power to throw you into hell. Yes, I tell you, fear him. (Luke 12:5)

"The time came when the beggar died and the angels carried him to Abraham's side. The rich man also died and was buried. In hell, where he was in torment, he looked up and saw Abraham far away, with Lazarus by his side. So he called to him, 'Father Abraham, have pity on me and send Lazarus to dip the tip of his finger in water and cool my tongue, because I am in agony in this fire.' (Luke 16:22-24)

**Thought 1.** Note what a few other Scriptures have to say about hell.

They will be punished with everlasting destruction and shut out from the presence of the Lord and from the majesty of his power (2 Th 1:9)

The tongue also is a fire, a world of evil among the parts of the body. It corrupts the whole person, sets the whole course of his life on fire, and is itself set on fire by hell. (James 3:6)

If this is so, then the Lord knows how to rescue godly men from trials and to hold the unrighteous for the day of judgment, while continuing their punishment. (2 Pet 2:9)

He, too, will drink of the wine of God's fury, which has been poured full strength into the cup of his wrath. He will be tormented with burning sulfur in the presence of the holy angels and of the Lamb. And the smoke of their torment rises for ever and ever. There is no rest day or night for those who worship the beast and his image, or for anyone who receives the mark of his name." (Rev 14:10-11)

And the devil, who deceived them, was thrown into the lake of burning sulfur, where the beast and the false prophet had been thrown. They will be tormented day and night for ever and ever. If anyone's name was not found written in the book of life, he was thrown into the lake of fire. (Rev 20:10, 15)

But the cowardly, the unbelieving, the vile, the murderers, the sexually immoral, those who practice magic arts, the idolaters and all liars—their place will be in the fiery lake of burning sulfur. This is the second death." (Rev 21:8)

On the wicked he will rain fiery coals and burning sulfur; a scorching wind will be their lot. (Psa 11:6)

The sinners in Zion are terrified; trembling grips the godless: "Who of us can dwell with the consuming fire? Who of us can dwell with everlasting burning?" (Isa 33:14)

"And they will go out and look upon the dead bodies of those who rebelled against me; their worm will not die, nor will their fire be quenched, and they will be loathsome to all mankind." (Isa 66:24)

"Surely the day is coming; it will burn like a furnace. All the arrogant and every evildoer will be stubble, and that day that is coming will set them on fire," says the LORD Almighty. "Not a root or a branch will be left to them. (Mal 4:1)

| | | | |
|---|---|---|---|
| **1 The new creation, the new heaven & the new earth**<br><br>**2 The new city of God**<br><br><br><br>**3 The immediate fellowship with God**<br>a. Declared by a loud voice<br>b. The immediate presence & fellowship of God | **CHAPTER 21**<br><br>**VISION FOUR**<br><br>**XIII. THE ETERNITY OF GOD: THE NEW HEAVENS & EARTH & THE NEW JERUSALEM, 21:1-22:5**<br><br>**A. The New Heavens & The New Earth, 21:1-8**<br><br>Then I saw a new heaven and a new earth, for the first heaven and the first earth had passed away, and there was no longer any sea.<br>2 I saw the Holy City, the new Jerusalem, coming down out of heaven from God, prepared as a bride beautifully dressed for her husband.<br>3 And I heard a loud voice from the throne saying, "Now the dwelling of God is with men, and he will live with them. They will be his people, and God himself will be with them and be their God. | 4 He will wipe every tear from their eyes. There will be no more death or mourning or crying or pain, for the old order of things has passed away."<br>5 He who was seated on the throne said, "I am making everything new!" Then he said, "Write this down, for these words are trustworthy and true."<br>6 He said to me: "It is done. I am the Alpha and the Omega, the Beginning and the End. To him who is thirsty I will give to drink without cost from the spring of the water of life.<br>7 He who overcomes will inherit all this, and I will be his God and he will be my son.<br>8 But the cowardly, the unbelieving, the vile, the murderers, the sexually immoral, those who practice magic arts, the idolaters and all liars—their place will be in the fiery lake of burning sulfur. This is the second death." | **4 The perfection of all things**<br>a. Life will be perfected<br><br><br>b. The assurance that God is going to perfect all things<br>1) God assures it<br>2) God's Word assures it<br>3) God's sovereignty assures it<br><br>**5 The citizens**<br>a. Those who thirst for life<br>b. Those who overcome<br>1) Will inherit all things<br>2) Will be sons of God<br><br>c. Those who continue in their sin & reject Christ<br>1) Their identity<br><br>2) Their fate: The lake of fire—the second death |

## VISION FOUR, 21:1-22:21

# DIVISION XIII

## THE ETERNITY OF GOD: THE NEW HEAVENS AND EARTH AND THE NEW JERUSALEM, 21:1-22:5

### A. The New Heavens and The New Earth, 21:1-8

(21:1-8) **Introduction**: What will eternity be like? What will it be like to live with God forever and ever? This chapter of Revelation tells us. All the bad and negative things of this world are going to be conquered and destroyed. All the pollution and impurities, all the ungodliness and evil, all the suffering and pain, all the corruption and death—it is all going to be erased, eliminated, and done away with. The day is coming when there will be no more...

- impure government
- corrupt religion
- bad leaders
- painful suffering
- sin and temptation

This is the glorious message of Revelation. God is going to take Satan and all the ungodly and evil of this world and destroy them. God is going to make a new heavens and a new earth. God is going to make all things new. And when He does, there will be...

- no more tears
- no more mourning
- no more crying
- no more pain
- no more death

This is the great subject of this passage of Scripture: *the new heavens and the new earth.*

1. The new creation, the new heaven and the new earth (v.1.).
2. The new city of God (v.2).
3. The immediate fellowship with God (v.3).
4. The perfection of all things (v.4-6).
5. The citizens (v.6-8).

**1** (21:1) **Heaven and Earth, New**: there will be the new creation, the new heaven and the new earth. The heaven (heavenly bodies in outer space) and earth that we know are going to pass away.

1. All the heavens above—the sun, moon, stars, and planets—are going to be destroyed and remade. God is going to make a new heaven. Think what this will mean. There will be...

- no more violent thunder storms, typhoons, hurricanes, or destructive rains and weather.
- no more stars or solar systems that are burned out.

All of the heavens above will be remade, created anew and made alive. Think how glorious and beautiful the heavens look now when we look up on a starry night. But imagine what they will be like when God recreates them in all the glory and magnificence of a perfect universe. All things within the universe will be alive and reflect the glory and splendor of God Himself. The universe will be perfect, a place where nothing burns out or wears down or wastes away or dies. Think about the light and brilliance and splendor and glory of all the heavenly bodies when God recreates the heavens. Think about what it will mean to have a universe full of *living planets and stars and solar systems*. We cannot imagine the glory and beauty. It is beyond our finite minds. But note the significant point: the Scripture declares emphatically that the heaven is to be remade and recreated into a new heaven (see note, pt.2—2 Pt.3:10).

2. The earth is going to pass away. There is going to be a new earth. The present earth is defective; it is cursed. The earth suffers under all kinds of natural disasters such as earthquakes, volcanic eruptions, destructive storms, floods, scorching heat, deserts, famines, diseases, and death. But the day is coming when God is going to remake the earth. God is going to create a new earth. Think what this will mean.

⇒ No more disasters or destruction.
⇒ No more thorns or thistles or unfertile and unproductive soil.
⇒ No more hunger or thirst.
⇒ No more disease, decay, erosion, or death.

The new earth will flourish and be fruitful, bearing all the good that can be imagined. Think how beautiful, green, lush, productive, and fruitful it will be. Think how peaceful, serene, and comfortable it will be. Think of the security and provision, the abundance and overflowing of every good and perfect gift—the fullness of life that will be possible upon the earth. The earth will be new, perfected by God in every conceivable way.

Note the statement, "there was no longer any sea." This can mean one of two things. The sea will be eliminated, done away with, and the new earth will have no sea. Or it can mean the same thing that is meant with the heavens and the earth. The heavens and the earth and the sea are to pass away and be made anew and recreated. The sea that causes devastation and destruction will be destroyed right along with the earth and the heavens; but when they are recreated, the sea, being part of the earth, will be part of the new earth, part of the new creation.

A perfected earth is beyond our comprehension. But it is exactly what Scripture declares is going to happen. God is going to create a new earth as well as a new heaven.

> I tell you the truth, until heaven and earth disappear, not the smallest letter, not the least stroke of a pen, will by any means disappear from the Law until everything is accomplished. (Mat 5:18)
>
> Heaven and earth will pass away, but my words will never pass away. (Mat 24:35)
>
> But the day of the Lord will come like a thief. The heavens will disappear with a roar; the elements will be destroyed by fire, and the earth and everything in it will be laid bare. Since everything will be destroyed in this way, what kind of people ought you to be? You ought to live holy and godly lives As you look forward to the day of God and speed its coming. That day will bring about the destruction of the heavens by fire, and the elements will melt in the heat. But in keeping with his promise we are looking forward to a new heaven and a new earth, the home of righteousness. (2 Pet 3:10-13)
>
> Then I saw a new heaven and a new earth, for the first heaven and the first earth had passed away, and there was no longer any sea. (Rev 21:1)

> In the beginning you laid the foundations of the earth, and the heavens are the work of your hands. They will perish, but you remain; they will all wear out like a garment. Like clothing you will change them and they will be discarded. But you remain the same, and your years will never end. (Psa 102:25-27)
>
> All the stars of the heavens will be dissolved and the sky rolled up like a scroll; all the starry host will fall like withered leaves from the vine, like shriveled figs from the fig tree. (Isa 34:4)
>
> Lift up your eyes to the heavens, look at the earth beneath; the heavens will vanish like smoke, the earth will wear out like a garment and its inhabitants die like flies. But my salvation will last forever, my righteousness will never fail. (Isa 51:6)
>
> "Behold, I will create new heavens and a new earth. The former things will not be remembered, nor will they come to mind. (Isa 65:17)
>
> "As the new heavens and the new earth that I make will endure before me," declares the LORD, "so will your name and descendants endure. (Isa 66:22)

**2** (21:2) **Jerusalem, New**: there will be the new city of God, the holy city, the New Jerusalem. The idea is that the New Jerusalem will be the capital city in the new heaven and earth. It will be the place where the very presence of God is symbolized. God's presence, of course, will be manifested everywhere in the new heavens and earth, manifested in all of God's glory and majesty. But the holy city will give believers a place with which to identify as they serve God throughout the universe. The next verse shows this. The heavenly city is the tabernacle, the very presence of God that comes down to dwell with man. The New Jerusalem is discussed in detail in the next passage (Rev.21:9f). The point in this verse is to show that God has prepared His own capital city to sit upon the earth. It will apparently be from the New Jerusalem that Jesus Christ will rule the universe and require His servants (believers) to occasionally visit and report on their work (see note—Rev.21:24-27). The Lord's throne will sit in the New Jerusalem and from there He shall rule and reign throughout all eternity. Note that the city comes down out of heaven. It is not constructed here on earth; God has it built in heaven and then moves it to earth. Note also that it is said to be as beautifully prepared as a bride is for her husband. This points both to the beauty of the city and to our longing desire to have God's presence right here on earth with us.

Remember that Jesus Christ told His apostles that He was going away to prepare a place for them. There is the possibility that He was referring to His preparing the New Jerusalem (Jn.14:2-3).

**3** (21:3) **Heaven and Earth, New—Fellowship With God**: there will be immediate fellowship with God. The very tabernacle of God will be set up right here on earth. The tabernacle is a picture of the tabernacle of the Old Testament, the worship center of Israel, the place where the very presence and glory of God dwelt in a special way. The picture is this: when the New Jerusalem, the capital city of eternity, is moved to earth, then the very presence and glory of God will dwell and live right here upon earth. When the New Jerusalem is established upon earth, God's glory and presence will be forever upon earth. God's presence will never again be dulled or removed from the presence of people.

The one thing for which man longs is the presence of God, the glory and fullness of God in all the abundance of life. Man may not know it, but the longing of his heart is for God. Man tries to fill his longing with all sorts of worldly pleasures and possessions, but nothing satisfies—nothing but God, His presence and glory. Until man allows God to fill his heart, he goes through all kinds of negative experiences:

⇒ lack of purpose, meaning, and significance
⇒ emptiness, questioning, and wondering about life
⇒ routineness, dullness, and feeling drained
⇒ insecurity and fear and failure

But when man gives his life to God, he begins to fellowship with God and to experience all the fullness of life. The point is this: in the new heaven and earth the presence and glory of God will dwell with man all the time. Man will never be without the presence and glory of God. He will always experience the fellowship of God's presence and glory. Note how strong the fellowship will be:

**And I heard a loud voice from the throne saying, "Now the dwelling of God is with men, and he will live with them. They will be his people, and God himself will be with them and be their God. (Rev 21:3)**

Four things are said:
⇒ The dwelling, the tabernacle of God, the very presence and glory of God, will be with men.
⇒ God will dwell with them.
⇒ They will be His people.
⇒ God Himself will be with them and be their God.

**Thought 1.** Think how wonderful it will be: we will never be without the presence and glory of God! We will be in His presence immediately and be able to talk and share with God face-to-face. We will be able to fellowship and commune with Him, laugh and rejoice with Him, praise and worship Him, serve and work for Him—all face-to-face. God says He is going to live and dwell with us; He is going to take over the management of our lives, guiding and directing us day by day throughout all eternity. This is what eternity will be like, what the new heaven and earth will be like. The presence and glory of God will be living and dwelling with us right here on earth.

**4** (21:4-6) **Heaven and Earth, New:** there will be the perfection of all things. Note two things.

1. Life will be perfected. This means that the body of man will be perfected; so will the environment and earth. Life will be totally different from what it is now. The very life and utopia for which man has longed will be a living reality. All the sufferings and evil of life and all the bad and negative experiences of life will be gone. Scripture explains the change in the most beautiful and striking way: it declares that "[God] will wipe away every tear from their [believer's] eyes." Imagine a world so perfected that there would never again be a tear shed. Look at what Scripture says:

**He will wipe every tear from their eyes. There will be no more death or mourning or crying or pain, for the old order of things has passed away." (Rev 21:4)**

⇒ There will be no more death: no more aging, murder, killing or war. No more miscarriages or dying children, no more dying mothers or dying fathers, and no more parents who have passed on. No more funerals or cemeteries or burial grounds. Every one will have a spiritual body, a body that will be perfected, made incorruptible and immortal, perfect in strength and honor. There will be no death in the new heaven and earth. God will wipe away the tears of death.

⇒ There will be no more mourning: no more brokenness, disappointment, regret, guilt, failure, weakness, inferiority, inadequacy, or incapability. No more homelessness, starvation, hunger, or thirst. There will be nothing to make us sorrowful. We will be capable and able, successful and fruitful, confident and secure. There will never be a regret or failure to make us sorrowful. We will be perfected. We will be able to live and serve to the fullest degree without any shortcoming whatsoever. God will wipe away all the tears of sorrow in the new heaven and earth.

⇒ There will be no more crying: no more disappointment, arguing, fussing, cursing, divisiveness, drugs, evil, immorality, separation, bitterness, burdens, or heartache—no more bad things that cut the heart and cause the heart and eyes to cry. Every life will be perfected. Everyone will be perfected and live together in love, joy, and peace—never causing hurt to another person. God will wipe away the tears of crying.

⇒ There will be no more pain: no more diseases, accidents, distress, pressure, abuse, beatings, fights, afflictions, or agony. No more emotional or physical pain. No more of anything that causes pain of any kind. God will wipe away the tears of pain.

But note why. It is because God recreates the universe. It is because "the old order of things has passed away." God cannot state it any clearer: the earth as it is now is going to pass away. Note again how clear and exact Scripture describes what God is going to do:

**He will wipe every tear from their eyes. There will be no more death or mourning or crying or pain, for the old order of things has passed away." (Rev 21:4)**

How do we know for sure that God is going to recreate the universe? How do we know that God is going to perfect life for us? *The next point tells us.*

**Thought 1.** Just think! Life will be perfected. The day is coming when God is going to perfect human life. He is going to make a new heaven and earth, a perfect heaven and earth; and He is going to perfect all believers. Everything—all of heaven and earth and all that is therein—shall be perfected. There is no greater hope than this glorious promise of God, the promise that He is going to perfect the universe.

**For the Lamb at the center of the throne will be their shepherd; he will lead them to springs of living water. And God will wipe away every tear from their eyes." (Rev 7:17)**

He will wipe every tear from their eyes. There will be no more death or mourning or crying or pain, for the old order of things has passed away." (Rev 21:4)

For our light and momentary troubles are achieving for us an eternal glory that far outweighs them all. (2 Cor 4:17)

The last enemy to be destroyed is death. (1 Cor 15:26)

When the perishable has been clothed with the imperishable, and the mortal with immortality, then the saying that is written will come true: "Death has been swallowed up in victory." (1 Cor 15:54)

Dear friends, do not be surprised at the painful trial you are suffering, as though something strange were happening to you. But rejoice that you participate in the sufferings of Christ, so that you may be overjoyed when his glory is revealed. (1 Pet 4:12-13)

He will swallow up death forever. The Sovereign LORD will wipe away the tears from all faces; he will remove the disgrace of his people from all the earth. The LORD has spoken. (Isa 25:8)

And the ransomed of the LORD will return. They will enter Zion with singing; everlasting joy will crown their heads. Gladness and joy will overtake them, and sorrow and sighing will flee away. (Isa 35:10)

The ransomed of the LORD will return. They will enter Zion with singing; everlasting joy will crown their heads. Gladness and joy will overtake them, and sorrow and sighing will flee away. (Isa 51:11)

Your sun will never set again, and your moon will wane no more; the LORD will be your everlasting light, and your days of sorrow will end. (Isa 60:20)

I will rejoice over Jerusalem and take delight in my people; the sound of weeping and of crying will be heard in it no more. (Isa 65:19)

2. God assures us that He is going to perfect all things. He gives us three assurances.
   a. God Himself assures us. Note that God Himself spoke from the throne of heaven and declared emphatically that He was going to make everything new:

He who was seated on the throne said, "I am making everything new." (Rev 21:5)

   b. God's Word assures it. God gave a double declaration. He declared that His Words are true and faithful. By true, He means true as opposed to false. He is not lying. He is God; therefore, what He says will happen. By faithful, He means that He will do exactly what He says. We can all count on it. And note: God instructed John to write down all that He said. God wanted us to know about His promise of a new heaven and earth, of a perfected body and life, and He wanted us to be assured of His promise.
   c. God's sovereignty assures it. How? By the power and sovereignty of God. God declares, "I am the Alpha and Omega, the Beginning and the End."

Alpha is the first letter of the Greek alphabet and means *the beginning*, and Omega is the last letter and means *the end*. God is declaring that He is the beginning and the ending, the Creator of all things. All things have their beginning in Him. And He is the end of all things, the consummation and goal and the end and objective of all things. All things find their meaning and being in Him. And He spans all things just as the beginning and end span all things. Therefore, He can do as He wills.

The point is this: God has willed a new heavens and earth. Therefore, He has already spoken it into being. He has already declared, "It is done." The clock is set and the event fixed. The minutes of time are ticking away, and the hour will come when the set time arrives.

The one who calls you is faithful and he will do it. (1 Th 5:24)

If we are faithless, he will remain faithful, for he cannot disown himself. (2 Tim 2:13)

I tell you the truth, until heaven and earth disappear, not the smallest letter, not the least stroke of a pen, will by any means disappear from the Law until everything is accomplished. (Mat 5:18)

Heaven and earth will pass away, but my words will never pass away. (Luke 21:33)

God, who has called you into fellowship with his Son Jesus Christ our Lord, is faithful. (1 Cor 1:9)

"Praise be to the LORD, who has given rest to his people Israel just as he promised. Not one word has failed of all the good promises he gave through his servant Moses. (1 Ki 8:56)

The works of his hands are faithful and just; all his precepts are trustworthy. (Psa 111:7)

The Maker of heaven and earth, the sea, and everything in them— the LORD, who remains faithful forever. (Psa 146:6)

**5** (21:6-8) **Heaven and Earth, New—Believers**: there will be the citizens of the new heavens and earth. Note that God Himself is still speaking. What He is saying is important, so important that He must make the declaration Himself. It is too important to have an angelic messenger declare the message. (God tells us who the citizens of His new heavens and earth will be. But note something else as well: He tells us who will not be.) He warns us that not everyone will live in the new heavens and earth, not everyone will be acceptable to Him. But He shows us how to make sure that we are acceptable, that we do receive the right to become citizens of the new heavens and earth. How?

1. The citizens of the new heavens and earth will be those who thirst for life. God says that He will give the water of life to all those who thirst after it. That is, the person who thirsts after life will be the person who will receive the *water of life*. God is going to give life to the person who thirsts after it; He is going to give the spring of the water of life and give it freely.

To thirst after life means that one thirsts...
   • to know the life that God wants man to live.
   • to know the life that God gives.

- to know the fullness of life that is in God Himself.
- to know the hope of life that God has planned for man.
- to know the perfection of life that God longs for man to live.

Simply stated, to thirst after life means to thirst after the life that God gives, to thirst after God Himself. It means...
- to know God; to fellowship, commune, and share with God.
- to know the salvation, forgiveness, and cleansing of God.
- to know the hope, assurance, and security of God.
- to live for God, to obey and follow God.

The person who thirsts after God will be a citizen of the new heavens and earth.

2. The citizen of the new heavens and earth will be the overcomer. The overcomer is the person who overcomes this world and remains faithful and loyal to Christ. It means the person who remains pure and follows the Lord Jesus Christ. The overcomer is the person who conquers all the temptations and trials of life. Two great promises are made to the overcomer:
⇒ He will inherit all this, all that the new heavens and earth offer.
⇒ He will be a son of God.

**Yet to all who received him, to those who believed in his name, he gave the right to become children of God— (John 1:12)**

**Because those who are led by the Spirit of God are sons of God. For you did not receive a spirit that makes you a slave again to fear, but you received the Spirit of sonship. And by him we cry, "Abba, Father." The Spirit himself testifies with our spirit that we are God's children. Now if we are children, then we are heirs—heirs of God and co-heirs with Christ, if indeed we share in his sufferings in order that we may also share in his glory. (Rom 8:14-17)**

**So you are no longer a slave, but a son; and since you are a son, God has made you also an heir. (Gal 4:7)**

**So that you may become blameless and pure, children of God without fault in a crooked and depraved generation, in which you shine like stars in the universe (Phil 2:15)**

**We proclaim to you what we have seen and heard, so that you also may have fellowship with us. And our fellowship is with the Father and with his Son, Jesus Christ. (1 John 1:3)**

3. The identity and fate of those who continue in their sin and reject Christ is clearly spelled out. What a tragic list it is.
⇒ The *cowardly*: those who do not confess Christ because they fear what others might say; those who are afraid to give up the world and deny self; those who fear taking a stand for Christ; those who fear to fellowship or become identified with Christian people.

**"Whoever acknowledges me before men, I will also acknowledge him before my Father in heaven. But whoever dis-owns me before men, I will disown him before my Father in heaven. (Mat 10:32-33)**

**That if you confess with your mouth, "Jesus is Lord," and believe in your heart that God raised him from the dead, you will be saved. (Rom 10:9)**

**If we endure, we will also reign with him. If we disown him, he will also disown us; (2 Tim 2:12)**

**Fear of man will prove to be a snare, but whoever trusts in the LORD is kept safe. (Prov 29:25)**

⇒ The *unbelieving*: those who do not believe that Jesus Christ is the Son of God, the Savior of the world; those who reject Jesus Christ and His death upon the cross for their sins; those who profess Christ, but live hypocritical lives, who show by their sinful behavior that they do not really believe Him.

**Whoever believes in him is not condemned, but whoever does not believe stands condemned already because he has not believed in the name of God's one and only Son. (John 3:18)**

**I told you that you would die in your sins; if you do not believe that I am the one I claim to be, you will indeed die in your sins." (John 8:24)**

**There is a judge for the one who rejects me and does not accept my words; that very word which I spoke will condemn him at the last day. (John 12:48)**

**The god of this age has blinded the minds of unbelievers, so that they cannot see the light of the gospel of the glory of Christ, who is the image of God. (2 Cor 4:4)**

**Who is the liar? It is the man who denies that Jesus is the Christ. Such a man is the antichrist—he denies the Father and the Son. No one who denies the Son has the Father; [but] whoever acknowledges the Son has the Father also. (1 John 2:22-23)**

⇒ The *vile*: those who are worldly and who live worldly lives; those who reach out to touch and taste the impurities and lusts of the world; those who are stained and contaminated and polluted with worldliness; those who refuse to separate from the pleasures and possessions of this world and refuse to turn to God.

**"Be careful, or your hearts will be weighed down with dissipation, drunkenness and the anxieties of life, and that day will close on you unexpectedly like a trap. (Luke 21:34)**

**Do not conform any longer to the pattern of this world, but be transformed by the renewing of your mind. Then you will be able to test and approve what God's will is—his good, pleasing and perfect will. (Rom 12:2)**

**"Therefore come out from them and be separate, says the Lord. Touch**

no unclean thing, and I will receive you." "I will be a Father to you, and you will be my sons and daughters, says the Lord Almighty." (2 Cor 6:17-18)

It teaches us to say "No" to ungodliness and worldly passions, and to live self-controlled, upright and godly lives in this present age, While we wait for the blessed hope—the glorious appearing of our great God and Savior, Jesus Christ, (Titus 2:12-13)

You adulterous people, don't you know that friendship with the world is hatred toward God? Anyone who chooses to be a friend of the world becomes an enemy of God. (James 4:4)

Do not love the world or anything in the world. If anyone loves the world, the love of the Father is not in him. For everything in the world—the cravings of sinful man, the lust of his eyes and the boasting of what he has and does—comes not from the Father but from the world. (1 John 2:15-16)

⇒ The *murderers*: those who kill and take away the lives of others.

"You shall not murder. (Exo 20:13)

Jesus replied, "'Do not murder, do not commit adultery, do not steal, do not give false testimony, (Mat 19:18)

The commandments, "Do not commit adultery," "Do not murder," "Do not steal," "Do not covet," and whatever other commandment there may be, are summed up in this one rule: "Love your neighbor as yourself." Love does no harm to its neighbor. Therefore love is the fulfillment of the law. (Rom 13:9-10)

If you suffer, it should not be as a murderer or thief or any other kind of criminal, or even as a meddler. (1 Pet 4:15)

Anyone who hates his brother is a murderer, and you know that no murderer has eternal life in him. (1 John 3:15)

⇒ The *sexually immoral*: those who are sexually impure; those who commit sexual immorality or have sex before marriage; those who commit adultery and homosexuality and all other sexual acts that God forbids; those who look and lust, read and lust, think and lust.

"You have heard that it was said, 'Do not commit adultery.' But I tell you that anyone who looks at a woman lustfully has already committed adultery with her in his heart. (Mat 5:27-28)

In the same way the men also abandoned natural relations with women and were inflamed with lust for one another. Men committed indecent acts with other men, and received in them-

selves the due penalty for their perversion. (Rom 1:27)

Rather, clothe yourselves with the Lord Jesus Christ, and do not think about how to gratify the desires of the sinful nature. (Rom 13:14)

Having lost all sensitivity, they have given themselves over to sensuality so as to indulge in every kind of impurity, with a continual lust for more. (Eph 4:19)

Dear friends, I urge you, as aliens and strangers in the world, to abstain from sinful desires, which war against your soul. (1 Pet 2:11)

As a result, he does not live the rest of his earthly life for evil human desires, but rather for the will of God. For you have spent enough time in the past doing what pagans choose to do—living in debauchery, lust, drunkenness, orgies, carousing and detestable idolatry. (1 Pet 4:2-3)

⇒ The *ones who practice magic arts or sorcerers*: those who engage in astrology, witchcraft, devil worship, spiritism, séances, palm reading, fortune telling, and all other forms of false beliefs that claim to reveal and control one's fate, life, and destiny.

Saul died because he was unfaithful to the LORD; he did not keep the word of the LORD and even consulted a medium for guidance, (1 Chr 10:13)

When men tell you to consult mediums and spiritists, who whisper and mutter, should not a people inquire of their God? Why consult the dead on behalf of the living? To the law and to the testimony! If they do not speak according to this word, they have no light of dawn. (Isa 8:19-20)

I will destroy your witchcraft and you will no longer cast spells. (Micah 5:12)

The acts of the sinful nature are obvious: sexual immorality, impurity and debauchery; Idolatry and witchcraft; hatred, discord, jealousy, fits of rage, selfish ambition, dissensions, factions (Gal 5:19-20)

⇒ The *idolaters*: those who worship idols, whether idols made with one's hands or just conceived in one's mind; those who have an image of what God is like and worship and follow that image instead of following the God revealed by the Scriptures; those who put the things of this earth before God; those who give their primary attention and devotion to someone or something other than God.

Therefore, my dear friends, flee from idolatry. (1 Cor 10:14)

The acts of the sinful nature are obvious: sexual immorality, impurity and debauchery; Idolatry and witchcraft;

hatred, discord, jealousy, fits of rage, selfish ambition, dissensions, factions And envy; drunkenness, orgies, and the like. I warn you, as I did before, that those who live like this will not inherit the kingdom of God. (Gal 5:19-21)

For of this you can be sure: No immoral, impure or greedy person—such a man is an idolater—has any inheritance in the kingdom of Christ and of God. (Eph 5:5)

Put to death, therefore, whatever belongs to your earthly nature: sexual immorality, impurity, lust, evil desires and greed, which is idolatry. Because of these, the wrath of God is coming. (Col 3:5-6)

But the cowardly, the unbelieving, the vile, the murderers, the sexually immoral, those who practice magic arts, the idolaters and all liars—their place will be in the fiery lake of burning sulfur. This is the second death." (Rev 21:8)

Outside are the dogs, those who practice magic arts, the sexually immoral, the murderers, the idolaters and everyone who loves and practices falsehood. (Rev 22:15)

⇒ The *liars*: those who tell falsehoods and do not tell the truth; those who deceive and mislead others; those who are gossipers and talebearers and who pass rumors along.

But the king will rejoice in God; all who swear by God's name will praise him, while the mouths of liars will be silenced. (Psa 63:11)

A false witness will not go unpunished, and he who pours out lies will not go free. (Prov 19:5)

[The Lord] who foils the signs of false prophets and makes fools of diviners, who overthrows the learning of the wise and turns it into nonsense, (Isa 44:25)

But the cowardly, the unbelieving, the vile, the murderers, the sexually immoral, those who practice magic arts, the idolaters and all liars—their place will be in the fiery lake of burning sulfur. This is the second death." (Rev 21:8)

Any person who does not repent and turn away from these things—any person who does not turn to God for forgiveness of these things—any person who does not forsake these things—that person will not enter into the new heavens and earth. He will not be a citizen of the new heavens and earth. Where does he go? Scripture is clear:

Their place will be in the fiery lake of burning sulfur. This is the second death. (v.8).

| Outline | Scripture | Outline |
|---|---|---|
| **B. The New Jerusalem, the City of God (Part I): Its Description, 21:9-23** | 9 One of the seven angels who had the seven bowls full of the seven last plagues came and said to me, "Come, I will show you the bride, the wife of the Lamb." | b. The size of the city itself<br><br>c. The size of the wall & gates |
| **1 The last vision given to John**<br>a. The angel with the bowls appears<br>b. He shows John the bride, the lamb's wife<br>c. He carries John to a mountain<br>d. He shows John the great city coming out of heaven | 10 And he carried me away in the Spirit to a mountain great and high, and showed me the Holy City, Jerusalem, coming down out of heaven from God. | **7 The city's materials: Are precious & priceless**<br>a. The materials of the wall<br>b. The materials of the foundation |
| **2 The glory of the city** | 11 It shone with the glory of God, and its brilliance was like that of a very precious jewel, like a jasper, clear as crystal. | |
| **3 The city's walls: Perfect security**<br>**4 The city's twelve gates**<br>a. Guarded by twelve angels<br>b. Have inscribed on them the names of Israel's twelve tribes<br>c. Three gates on each side | 12 It had a great, high wall with twelve gates, and with twelve angels at the gates. On the gates were written the names of the twelve tribes of Israel.<br>13 There were three gates on the east, three on the north, three on the south and three on the west. | |
| **5 The city's twelve foundations: The names of the apostles are inscribed in them** | 14 The wall of the city had twelve foundations, and on them were the names of the twelve apostles of the Lamb. | c. The materials of the gates: Pearls<br>d. The material of the streets: Pure, transparent gold |
| **6 The city's shape & size**<br><br><br>a. The shape is square | 15 The angel who talked with me had a measuring rod of gold to measure the city, its gates and its walls.<br>16 The city was laid out like a square, as long as it was wide. He measured the city with the rod and found it to be 12,000 stadia in length, and as wide and high as it is long.<br>17 He measured its wall and it was 144 cubits thick, by man's measurement, which the angel was using.<br>18 The wall was made of jasper, and the city of pure gold, as pure as glass.<br>19 The foundations of the city walls were decorated with every kind of precious stone. The first foundation was jasper, the second sapphire, the third chalcedony, the fourth emerald,<br>20 The fifth sardonyx, the sixth carnelian, the seventh chrysolite, the eighth beryl, the ninth topaz, the tenth chrysoprase, the eleventh jacinth, and the twelfth amethyst.<br>21 The twelve gates were twelve pearls, each gate made of a single pearl. The great street of the city was of pure gold, like transparent glass.<br>22 I did not see a temple in the city, because the Lord God Almighty and the Lamb are its temple.<br>23 The city does not need the sun or the moon to shine on it, for the glory of God gives it light, and the Lamb is its lamp. | **8 The city's worship: Is focused upon God Himself & the Lamb**<br><br>**9 The city's light: Is provided by God's glory & the Lamb** |

# DIVISION XIII

## THE ETERNITY OF GOD: THE NEW HEAVENS AND EARTH AND THE NEW JERUSALEM, 21:1-22:5

### B. The New Jerusalem, The City of God (Part I): Its Description, 21:9-23

(21:9-23) **Introduction**: the new heavens and earth will have a capital city, a specific place where the presence of God will be centered and where the Lord Jesus Christ will live and rule the universe. Scripture gives us the city's name: it is the *New Jerusalem*. Actually Scripture gives several names by which the capital city will be known:

⇒ The New Jerusalem (Rev.21:2; 3:12).
⇒ The Heavenly Jerusalem (Heb.12:22).
⇒ The Holy City (Rev.21:2; 21:19).
⇒ Holy Jerusalem (Rev.21:10).
⇒ The City of My God (Rev.3:12).
⇒ The Great City (Rev.21:10).

What will the city be like? It is indescribable. How could anyone possibly describe the city of God and of Christ? Think of the stars in the sky, the billions and billions of galaxies scattered throughout the universe. Picture them for just a moment: the vastness, the enormity, the endlessness of the universe. Remember that God is the Creator and Force of the universe, the Sustainer of all things. He is the Intelli-

gence and Power that made all things and keeps all things operating. How could human language describe God? How could human language describe the city where God's presence is centered and where Jesus Christ dwells? This is the problem that John had in trying to describe the New Jerusalem. The city and the presence of God within the city are so glorious that they are just indescribable. There are no earthly things beautiful enough nor valuable enough to be a part of God's city. Therefore, John did all he could: he used the most beautiful and precious things upon earth to describe the city. This passage tells us about the city of God. It tells us what God showed John, what God wants us to know about the New Jerusalem, the city of God, the city where Christ will live and where the presence of God will be centered in the new heavens and earth. Note how it stirs our hearts when we study this passage knowing that we shall be a part of so glorious a future. God has given us the wonderful privilege of being a citizen of God's great city, the wonderful city of Jesus Christ. This is *the description of the New Jerusalem, the city of God.* (See note *New Jerusalem*—Rev.21:2 for more discussion.)

1. The last vision given to John (v.9-10).
2. The glory of the city (v.11).
3. The city's walls: perfect security (v.12).
4. The city's twelve gates (v.12-13).
5. The city's twelve foundations: the names of the apostles are inscribed in them (v.14).
6. The city's shape and size (v.15-17).
7. The city's materials: are precious and priceless (v.18-21).
8. The city's worship: is focused upon God Himself and the Lamb (v.22).
9. The city's light: is provided by God's glory and the Lamb (v.23).

**1** (21:9-10) **Visions of Revelation**: this is the last vision that God gives John, and it is the most glorious of visions. God shows John the New Jerusalem, the great city of God that will be the capital city of the new heavens and earth in the recreated universe. Note who it is that God sends to take John to the city: one of the seven angels who had cast one of the bowl judgments upon the earth. There is symbolism in this: God has a message of warning for the earth—judgment is coming. But God also has a message of hope and glory for the earth: the New Jerusalem, the city of God's very own presence, is also coming to earth; and every person can live with God in the glory of that city. Citizenship is available to all if they will believe in the Son of God, the Lord Jesus Christ, and seek to live in the city with God and His Son.

The angel carries John away in the spirit to a high mountain and shows him the glorious city of God. Eight descriptions are given.

**2** (21:11) **New Jerusalem**: there is the glory of the city (v.11). The glory is the very glory of God Himself.

"[The city] was clothed in God's glory—in all its splendor and radiance. The lustre of it resembled a rare and most precious jewel, like jasper, shining clear as crystal" (*The Amplified New Testament*).

The glory of God gives light to the whole city. God's glory is full of so much light and shines so brightly there is no need for the sun nor for any other heavenly body to give the city light. Just imagine the power and radiance of God's glory—so bright that it is more forceful than the laser beams of light flowing from the sun! It is the glory of God that gives light to the city.

⇒ The glory of God shines all throughout the city, the city actually shines and has a sparkling sheen to it.
⇒ The city shines like the green of a jasper, but it is as clear as crystal.
⇒ The glory of God glitters off the city as though the buildings are crystal clear—everything glitters in the most beautiful green of the jasper.

**Thought 1.** If you have ever walked in a mountain forest when everything is covered with ice from an ice storm, you have walked in the midst of a crystal ice palace. Everything sparkles and glitters—the green needles of the pines, the bare branches of the trees, the small branches and trunks of the saplings, the bushes close to the ground, the leaves lying on the ground. As the glory of the sun strikes the mountain forest, the ice crystals that cover everything in the forest sparkle and glitter just like a crystal ice palace. This is one of the most beautiful sights on earth, a crystal ice forest. Imagine how beautiful the green jasper glistening off the ice crystals would be. This is a very faint idea of the sparkle and glitter of the glory of God throughout the crystal clear city of God.

An angel of the Lord appeared to them, and the glory of the Lord shone around them, and they were terrified. (Luke 2:9)

But Stephen, full of the Holy Spirit, looked up to heaven and saw the glory of God, and Jesus standing at the right hand of God. (Acts 7:55)

And we, who with unveiled faces all reflect the Lord's glory, are being transformed into his likeness with ever-increasing glory, which comes from the Lord, who is the Spirit. (2 Cor 3:18)

The heavens declare the glory of God; the skies proclaim the work of his hands. (Psa 19:1)

**3** (21:12) **New Jerusalem**: there are the city's walls (v.12). The walls are great and very high. The idea is that of protection, of perfect security. When believers reach the Heavenly Jerusalem, they will be behind the walls of perfection. They will be secure from all the evil and enemies of the physical world.

I will remain in the world no longer, but they are still in the world, and I am coming to you. Holy Father, protect them by the power of your name—the name you gave me—so that they may be one as we are one. (John 17:11)

That is why I am suffering as I am. Yet I am not ashamed, because I know whom I have believed, and am convinced that he is able to guard what I have entrusted to him for that day. (2 Tim 1:12)

The Lord will rescue me from every evil attack and will bring me safely to his heavenly kingdom. To him be glory for ever and ever. Amen. (2 Tim 4:18)

Who through faith are shielded by God's power until the coming of the salvation that is ready to be revealed in the last time. (1 Pet 1:5)

To him who is able to keep you from falling and to present you before his glorious presence without fault and with great joy— To the only God our Savior be glory, majesty, power and authority, through Jesus Christ our Lord, before all ages, now and forevermore! Amen. (Jude 1:24-25)

**4** (21:12-13) **New Jerusalem**: there are the city's twelve gates (v. 12b-13). Three things are said about the gates.

1. The gates have the names of the twelve tribes of Israel upon them. This symbolizes that the only way to come to God is through the Messiah of the twelve tribes, the Messiah of the Jews, the Lord Jesus Christ. Scripture says, "Salvation is from the Jews" (Jn.4:22). God sent His salvation, His own Son, into the world through the Jews. Therefore,

the entrance into the Heavenly Jerusalem is only through the Messiah of the Jewish nation. No person can enter the heavenly city unless he comes through the gates of salvation provided by God.

> You Samaritans worship what you do not know; we worship what we do know, for salvation is from the Jews. (John 4:22)
>
> "For God so loved the world that he gave his one and only Son, that whoever believes in him shall not perish but have eternal life. (John 3:16)
>
> Then Jesus declared, "I am the bread of life. He who comes to me will never go hungry, and he who believes in me will never be thirsty. (John 6:35)
>
> "You do not want to leave too, do you?" Jesus asked the Twelve. Simon Peter answered him, "Lord, to whom shall we go? You have the words of eternal life. (John 6:67-68)
>
> Jesus answered, "I am the way and the truth and the life. No one comes to the Father except through me. (John 14:6)
>
> Salvation is found in no one else, for there is no other name under heaven given to men by which we must be saved." (Acts 4:12)
>
> For there is one God and one mediator between God and men, the man Christ Jesus, (1 Tim 2:5)
>
> But the ministry Jesus has received is as superior to theirs as the covenant of which he is mediator is superior to the old one, and it is founded on better promises. (Heb 8:6)
>
> For this reason Christ is the mediator of a new covenant, that those who are called may receive the promised eternal inheritance—now that he has died as a ransom to set them free from the sins committed under the first covenant. (Heb 9:15)
>
> For Christ did not enter a man-made sanctuary that was only a copy of the true one; he entered heaven itself, now to appear for us in God's presence. (Heb 9:24)
>
> To Jesus the mediator of a new covenant, and to the sprinkled blood that speaks a better word than the blood of Abel. (Heb 12:24)
>
> My dear children, I write this to you so that you will not sin. But if anybody does sin, we have one who speaks to the Father in our defense—Jesus Christ, the Righteous One. (1 John 2:1)

2. The gates are guarded by twelve angels: this symbolizes that the entrance to the city is protected. No person is allowed to enter the city unless they are approved by God. A person can enter only if he comes through the salvation that God gave through Israel, through His own Son, the Lord Jesus Christ.

3. There are three gates on each of the four walls of the city, twelve gates altogether. Every direction on earth has three gates:

⇒ The east has three gates.
⇒ The north has three gates.
⇒ The south has three gates.
⇒ The west has three gates.

This symbolizes that everyone on earth is invited to enter the city. There is a wall that faces everyone in the east, and everyone in the north, and everyone in the south, and everyone in the west. And there are three gates facing everyone. Everyone on earth can enter the city. There is no discrimination or prejudice, no partiality or favoritism shown by God. All can come and live as citizens of the city. The only requirement is that they come through the Messiah, the Savior of the world, the Lord Jesus Christ.

> But accepts men from every nation who fear him and do what is right. (Acts 10:35)
>
> I am not ashamed of the gospel, because it is the power of God for the salvation of everyone who believes: first for the Jew, then for the Gentile. (Rom 1:16)
>
> For there is no difference between Jew and Gentile—the same Lord is Lord of all and richly blesses all who call on him, (Rom 10:12)
>
> There is neither Jew nor Greek, slave nor free, male nor female, for you are all one in Christ Jesus. (Gal 3:28)

**5** (21:14) **New Jerusalem**: there are the city's twelve foundations (v.14). They have the names of the twelve apostles inscribed upon them. Note: the twelve apostles are clearly identified as the apostles "of *the Lamb*." This means that the foundation of the city is the testimony of the twelve apostles, the testimony that declares Jesus Christ to be the Lamb of God. It is the *sacrificial death* of Jesus Christ as the lamb of God that makes the city available to people.

⇒ Unless Jesus Christ had died for man—unless He had taken the sins of man upon Himself and sacrificed His life for those sins—no person would ever be free of sin and made acceptable to God. No person could ever enter the city, for every person would still be bearing his own sins.

⇒ Unless a person believes in the Lamb of God, believes that Jesus Christ did sacrifice His life for his sins, that person is not acceptable to God. He will never be allowed to enter the city.

The very foundation of the city is the *testimony of the Lamb* declared by the apostles. Therefore, a person must build his life upon that testimony.

> Consequently, you are no longer foreigners and aliens, but fellow citizens with God's people and members of God's household, Built on the foundation of the apostles and prophets, with Christ Jesus himself as the chief cornerstone. (Eph 2:19-20)
>
> In this way they will lay up treasure for themselves as a firm foundation for the coming age, so that they may take hold of the life that is truly life. (1 Tim 6:19)
>
> Nevertheless, God's solid foundation stands firm, sealed with this inscription: "The Lord knows those who are his," and, "Everyone who confesses the name of the Lord must turn away from wickedness." (2 Tim 2:19)

**6** (21:15-17) **New Jerusalem**: there is the city's shape and size (v.15-17). Three facts are given.

1. The city is square (v.16). There is one side each facing to the east, north, south, and west. Again, the city faces in every direction. Citizenship within the city is available to every nation, city, tribe, language, and person upon earth—available if a person will approach the city through the salvation God Himself has provided for the earth.

2. The city is enormous and, as we would expect of the heavenly city, its size is beyond anything we would ever dream (v.16). It is 1500 miles long and wide and *high*. It towers 1500 miles high! This is a total of 2,250,000 square miles or 3,375,000,000 cubic miles (almost four billion cubic miles)! Picture a huge space station that man might build in a century or two and orbit around the earth. If Jesus Christ delays His coming long enough, the idea that man might be forced to build a large city in outer space to handle the population has already crossed the mind of man. The God who created a moon to orbit around the earth and planets to orbit around the sun has created a city that is far more beautiful than any city man will ever build. It will someday descend from heaven to earth and be the capital city of the universe. God is going to reclaim the earth from all the evil that has engulfed it, and He is going to do the most marvelous thing: make the earth the center of the universe, the place where His very presence will be centered. The earth will be the throne of the Lord Jesus Christ. And the capital city of His rule and reign will be the New Jerusalem. What a glorious picture of the great salvation and sovereign majesty of God!

3. The thickness of the wall and gates is 144 cubits or 216 feet thick (v.17).

**Thought 1.** The size of the city is large enough to take care of all who will enter it. There is room for all who will come to God through His Son, the Lord Jesus Christ.

> **"Turn to me and be saved, all you ends of the earth; for I am God, and there is no other. (Isa 45:22)**
>
> **"Come, all you who are thirsty, come to the waters; and you who have no money, come, buy and eat! Come, buy wine and milk without money and without cost. (Isa 55:1)**
>
> **Go to the street corners and invite to the banquet anyone you find.' (Mat 22:9)**
>
> **On the last and greatest day of the Feast, Jesus stood and said in a loud voice, "If anyone is thirsty, let him come to me and drink. (John 7:37)**
>
> **For there is no difference between Jew and Gentile—the same Lord is Lord of all and richly blesses all who call on him, (Rom 10:12)**
>
> **Who wants all men to be saved and to come to a knowledge of the truth. (1 Tim 2:4)**
>
> **The Spirit and the bride say, "Come!" And let him who hears say, "Come!" Whoever is thirsty, let him come; and whoever wishes, let him take the free gift of the water of life. (Rev 22:17)**

**7** (21:18-21) **New Jerusalem:** there are the city's materials (v.18-21). We must keep in mind that in some cases the gems or precious stones that are mentioned in this passage differed from the valuable stones that we know today. The stones seem to be as follows. (Note the spectacular beauty and variety of color in the city.)

1. The *walls are made of jasper*: a crystal-like rock that is green in color. The crystal green walls sparkle with the most beautiful color as the reflection of God's glory strikes them.

The city is made of pure gold, a gold that is as clear as glass. There is no gold on earth as clear as glass. Imagine a city many times larger than New York or Tokyo or any other major city being made out of pure gold, a gold so pure that it would be crystal clear. Imagine the dazzling gold color of the New Jerusalem as the glory of God strikes it.

2. The twelve foundations are decorated with every kind of precious stone (v.19-20. This information is gathered from William Barclay. *The Revelation of John*, Vol.2, p.273f.)

⇒ The first foundation is jasper: a green rock-like crystal.
⇒ The second foundation is sapphire: a sky blue spotted with gold (cp. Ex.24:10).
⇒ The third foundation is chalcedony: a green stone like the green on a peacock's tail.
⇒ The fourth foundation is emerald: a green, the greenest of all greens.
⇒ The fifth foundation is sardonyx: a stone that has different shades of color, basically white with layers of red and brown breaking the white background.
⇒ The sixth foundation is carnelian: a blood-red stone.
⇒ The seventh foundation is chrysolite: a shining stone with a gold radiance.
⇒ The eighth foundation is beryl: a sea blue or sea green stone.
⇒ The ninth foundation is topaz: a greenish-gold stone that was transparent (cp. Job 28:19).
⇒ The tenth foundation is chrysoprase: an apple green stone.
⇒ The eleventh foundation is jacinth: a violet, bluish-purple stone.
⇒ The twelfth foundation is amethyst: also a violet, bluish-purple stone, but more brilliant than the jacinth.

3. The twelve gates are twelve huge pearls. What magnificent beauty!

4. The streets are made of pure gold, but again the gold is transparent, as transparent as glass.

**Thought 1.** This is a staggering picture of beauty and variety. Imagine the fiery brilliance and splendor as the glory of God reflects off the glistening stones. The beauty is bound to be the most dazzling and staggering sight in all the universe. Do the stones and color symbolize anything? There is bound to be at least this meaning behind such magnificent beauty: the heavenly city is worth any price to enter. It is priceless. No matter what a man has to sacrifice, he is a fool if he does not give up everything he has to enter the heavenly city of God.

> **"The kingdom of heaven is like treasure hidden in a field. When a man found it, he hid it again, and then in his joy went and sold all he had and bought that field. (Mat 13:44)**
>
> **"Again, the kingdom of heaven is like a merchant looking for fine pearls. When he**

found one of great value, he went away and sold everything he had and bought it. (Mat 13:45-46)

But store up for yourselves treasures in heaven, where moth and rust do not destroy, and where thieves do not break in and steal. (Mat 6:20)

Jesus answered, "If you want to be perfect, go, sell your possessions and give to the poor, and you will have treasure in heaven. Then come, follow me." (Mat 19:21)

Sell your possessions and give to the poor. Provide purses for yourselves that will not wear out, a treasure in heaven that will not be exhausted, where no thief comes near and no moth destroys. (Luke 12:33)

What is more, I consider everything a loss compared to the surpassing greatness of knowing Christ Jesus my Lord, for whose sake I have lost all things. I consider them rubbish, that I may gain Christ (Phil 3:8)

In this way they will lay up treasure for themselves as a firm foundation for the coming age, so that they may take hold of the life that is truly life. (1 Tim 6:19)

I counsel you to buy from me gold refined in the fire, so you can become rich; and white clothes to wear, so you can cover your shameful nakedness; and salve to put on your eyes, so you can see. (Rev 3:18)

**8** (21:22) **New Jerusalem**: there is the city's worship (v.22). There is no temple in the heavenly city, for both God and Christ are there. Their presence will be so manifested...

- that the very atmosphere will be heavy with their spirit.
- that every person will be filled with God's Spirit, perfectly filled.
- that every person will be perfectly conscious of God's continued presence.

No believer will be without the full and perfect knowledge of God's Spirit and presence. Therefore, there will be an unbroken worship, communication, and sharing with God and Christ. No matter what service or work the believer will be performing, and no matter where the believer is serving throughout the universe, he will be in unbroken fellowship and communion with God. Therefore, there is no need for a temple and its ceremonies and rituals to pull the human mind into the worship of God.

God is spirit, and his worshipers must worship in spirit and in truth." (John 4:24)

We demolish arguments and every pretension that sets itself up against the knowledge of God, and we take captive every thought to make it obedient to Christ. (2 Cor 10:5)

Finally, brothers, whatever is true, whatever is noble, whatever is right, whatever is pure, whatever is lovely, whatever is admirable—if anything is excellent or praiseworthy—think about such things. (Phil 4:8)

After this I heard what sounded like the roar of a great multitude in heaven shouting: "Hallelujah! Salvation and glory and power belong to our God, (Rev 19:1; cp. Rev.19:1-7)

But his delight is in the law of the LORD, and on his law he meditates day and night. (Psa 1:2)

You will keep in perfect peace him whose mind is steadfast, because he trusts in you. (Isa 26:3)

**9** (21:23) **New Jerusalem**: there is the city's light, the glory of God and of the Lamb, the Lord Jesus Christ (v.23; see note—Rev.21:11).

| | C. The New Jerusalem, The City of God (Part II): Its Citizens & Provisions, 21:24-22:5 | of life, as clear as crystal, flowing from the throne of God and of the Lamb | of continuous life<br>1) Perfectly pure<br>2) Flows out from God & the Lamb |
|---|---|---|---|
| 1 The citizens of the city<br>a. They are from earthly nations<br>b. They walk in the light of God's city<br>c. They are kings<br>d. They have constant, unbroken access to God<br>e. They bring the glory of their nations into the city<br>f. They are guaranteed a perfect life & service | 24 The nations will walk by its light, and the kings of the earth will bring their splendor into it.<br>25 On no day will its gates ever be shut, for there will be no night there.<br>26 The glory and honor of the nations will be brought into it.<br>27 Nothing impure will ever enter it, nor will anyone who does what is shameful or deceitful, but only those whose names are written in the Lamb's book of life. | 2 Down the middle of the great street of the city. On each side of the river stood the tree of life, bearing twelve crops of fruit, yielding its fruit every month. And the leaves of the tree are for the healing of the nations.<br>3 No longer will there be any curse. The throne of God and of the Lamb will be in the city, and his servants will serve him.<br>4 They will see his face, and his name will be on their foreheads. | b. There is a tree of life<br><br>1) Bears all year<br><br>2) For the healing of the nations<br><br>c. There is no more curse<br>d. There is the throne of God & of the Lamb<br>1) Believers serve perfectly<br><br>2) Believers are face-to-face with God |
| | CHAPTER 22 | 5 There will be no more night. They will not need the light of a lamp or the light of the sun, for the Lord God will give them light. And | e. There is the name of God written on their foreheads<br>f. There is eternal light in the city<br>g. There is eternal rule—work & service—for God & Christ |
| 2 The provision of the city<br>a. There is a river of life, | Then the angel showed me the river of the water | they will reign for ever and ever. | |

# DIVISION XIII

## THE ETERNITY OF GOD: THE NEW HEAVENS AND EARTH AND THE NEW JERUSALEM, 21:1-22:5

## C. The New Jerusalem, The City of God (Part II): Its Ciwtizens and Provisions, 21:24-22:5

(21:24-22:5) **Introduction**: the new heavens and earth will have a capital city, a city where the throne of God and of Christ sit. The city is being prepared in heaven and it is beyond description. Its name is the *New Jerusalem* or the *Heavenly Jerusalem*. This was shown us in the previous passage. Now, Scripture shows us the *citizens and the provisions of the great city of God*.

1. The citizens of the city (v.24-27).
2. The provisions of the city (Ch.22, v.1-5).

**1** (21:24-27) **New Jerusalem—Believers—Heaven**: there are the citizens of the Heavenly Jerusalem. Six things are said about the citizens.

1. The citizens are from earthly nations (v.24). They are *the saved* from all the nations of the earth. This again shows us that the gospel is universal; anyone from any nation can be saved. God does not discriminate between people nor show partiality to any person.

2. The citizens walk in the light of the city. This would mean...
* that they walk in the light of the *glory of God*.
* that they walk in the light of *the knowledge of God*, the full and perfect knowledge of God.
* that they walk in the light of *perfection*, perfection of *purity and righteousness* and perfection of *wisdom*, knowing exactly what to do and how to do it.

3. The citizens are kings who bring their glory and honor into the city (v.24). This says two things.
  a. Believers will rule and reign with Christ. They will reign as kings for Him, probably serving Him and overseeing the universe for Him. Remember: the

heavens will be created anew as well as the earth. The billions of heavenly bodies will apparently be made alive and fruitful. Whatever the case, Scripture clearly teaches that believers will rule and reign with Christ and serve Him in responsible positions as kings. (See notes—Rev.14:13; 20:4-6 for more discussion.)

**Jesus said to them, "I tell you the truth, at the renewal of all things, when the Son of Man sits on his glorious throne, you who have followed me will also sit on twelve thrones, judging the twelve tribes of Israel. (Mat 19:28)**

**"His master replied, 'Well done, good and faithful servant! You have been faithful with a few things; I will put you in charge of many things. Come and share your master's happiness!' (Mat 25:23)**

**The Lord answered, "Who then is the faithful and wise manager, whom the master puts in charge of his servants to give them their food allowance at the proper time? It will be good for that servant whom the master finds doing so when he returns. I tell you the truth, he will put him in charge of all his possessions. (Luke 12:42-44)**

**"'Well done, my good servant!' his master replied. 'Because you have been trustworthy in a very small matter, take charge of ten cities.' "His master answered, 'You take charge of five cities.' (Luke 19:17, 19)**

**Now if we are children, then we are heirs—heirs of God and co-heirs with Christ, if indeed we share in his sufferings**

in order that we may also share in his glory. (Rom 8:17)

If we endure, we will also reign with him. If we disown him, he will also disown us; (2 Tim 2:12)

Do you not know that the saints will judge the world? And if you are to judge the world, are you not competent to judge trivial cases? Do you not know that we will judge angels? How much more the things of this life! (1 Cor 6:2-3)

And from Jesus Christ, who is the faithful witness, the firstborn from the dead, and the ruler of the kings of the earth. To him who loves us and has freed us from our sins by his blood, (Rev 1:5)

You have made them to be a kingdom and priests to serve our God, and they will reign on the earth." (Rev 5:10)

b. Believers will bring their glory and honor *into the heavenly city* and give all their glory and honor to the Lord who bestowed it upon them. Believers owe everything they are to God and Christ; therefore they are going to acknowledge and praise God and Christ for giving them so great a salvation. Note that believers will bring their glory and honor *into the city*.

⇒ This speaks as though believers will be serving as kings of nations *outside the city*.

⇒ This speaks as though there will be special occasions when believers will gather *in the heavenly city*, gather to bring the glory and honor of their nations to God and Christ. Read it carefully (the Greek says *eis auten*), for this seems to be the picture being painted. One thing is sure: no matter what we may describe or picture, it is going to be far beyond anything we could ever describe or ask or even think. God's Word emphatically declares this:

However, as it is written: "No eye has seen, no ear has heard, no mind has conceived what God has prepared for those who love him"— (1 Cor 2:9)

Now to him who is able to do immeasurably more than all we ask or imagine, according to his power that is at work within us, (Eph 3:20)

Oh, the depth of the riches of the wisdom and knowledge of God! How unsearchable his judgments, and his paths beyond tracing out! "Who has known the mind of the Lord? Or who has been his counselor?" "Who has ever given to God, that God should repay him?" For from him and through him and to him are all things. To him be the glory forever! Amen. (Rom 11:33-36)

4. The citizens will have constant, unbroken access to God (v.25). The gates are never closed and there is no night in the spiritual world. There is always perfect access into the presence of God, and there is no need for sleep or rest. We will have perfect bodies with perfect strength. In addition, the Holy Spirit of God will fill us to the fullest. The Holy Spirit will give us a perfect knowledge and consciousness of God's presence. He will focus our hearts and minds upon God in a constant, unbroken worship. He will give us an unbroken fellowship and communion and worship of God.

Thought 1. In the new heavens and earth, no matter what work and service we may be doing for Christ, our minds and hearts will be conscious of God's presence. Every thought of our mind will be a righteous and pure thought, a thought that is either upon God Himself or upon something that has to do with our daily lives (like our service and work or fellowship with other believers), a thought that will please God.

For though we live in the world, we do not wage war as the world does. The weapons we fight with are not the weapons of the world. On the contrary, they have divine power to demolish strongholds. We demolish arguments and every pretension that sets itself up against the knowledge of God, and we take captive every thought to make it obedient to Christ. (2 Cor 10:3-5)

Finally, brothers, whatever is true, whatever is noble, whatever is right, whatever is pure, whatever is lovely, whatever is admirable—if anything is excellent or praiseworthy—think about such things. (Phil 4:8)

You will keep in perfect peace him whose mind is steadfast, because he trusts in you. (Isa 26:3)

5. Believers will bring the glory and honor of their nations into (eis auten) the city. This is a continuation of what was said earlier (pt.3). This shows that believers are the kings being spoken about, that believers will be coming from various rules or nations to bring the glory of their nations to God. Again the picture seems to be periodic celebrations of great worship. There will certainly be times when all believers come together from all corners of heaven (the spiritual world or universe) in a great celebration of worship. We would think that the Wedding Supper of the Lamb will not be the only time we will all be brought together to worship our dear Lord.

Note again: Scripture says that as kings we enter "*into*" the city. It is as though we are coming from the far reaches of the spiritual world to bring the honor of our nations to God and Christ. But we must also repeat: whatever the case—wherever we are coming from—our minds could never imagine the glory and majesty of what will really happen. (See pt.3 above for verses and more discussion.)

6. Believers will be guaranteed a perfect life and service. Believers never have to worry about heaven being imperfect or defiled. God is not going to let an imperfect person into heaven, no matter who he is. He is not going to let heaven become contaminated with a single sin. Heaven will always be heaven—perfect, absolutely perfect. No person who has ever sinned will ever enter the city, not until the person accepts the cleansing of Jesus Christ. Unless he accepts the cleansing of Jesus Christ, he is guilty of sin. He still bears his own sin and the pollution of it. Therefore, if God let the polluted person into the heavenly city, the person would contaminate heaven. Heaven could no longer be perfect, clean, or pure. Therefore, God will always keep out any person...

• who defiles (is unwashed from his sin).

• who does what is shameful (detestable, immoral things).

• who lies or deceives.

The only person accepted into the heavenly city are those whose names are written in the *Lamb's book of life*. The person who accepts the sacrifice of the Lamb, the Lord Jesus Christ, for his sins—that person will have his name written in the Lamb's book of life. He will be a citizen of the great Heavenly Jerusalem.

> The acts of the sinful nature are obvious: sexual immorality, impurity and debauchery; Idolatry and witchcraft; hatred, discord, jealousy, fits of rage, selfish ambition, dissensions, factions And envy; drunkenness, orgies, and the like. I warn you, as I did before, that those who live like this will not inherit the kingdom of God. (Gal 5:19-21)
>
> For I tell you that unless your righteousness surpasses that of the Pharisees and the teachers of the law, you will certainly not enter the kingdom of heaven. (Mat 5:20)
>
> I tell you the truth, anyone who will not receive the kingdom of God like a little child will never enter it." (Mark 10:15)
>
> Do you not know that the wicked will not inherit the kingdom of God? Do not be deceived: Neither the sexually immoral nor idolaters nor adulterers nor male prostitutes nor homosexual offenders (1 Cor 6:9)
>
> I declare to you, brothers, that flesh and blood cannot inherit the kingdom of God, nor does the perishable inherit the imperishable. (1 Cor 15:50)
>
> Nothing impure will ever enter it, nor will anyone who does what is shameful or deceitful, but only those whose names are written in the Lamb's book of life. (Rev 21:27)

**2** (22:1-5) **New Jerusalem—Heaven**: there are the provisions of the Heavenly Jerusalem. The provisions are seven.

1. There is a pure river in the city, a river that has the very water of life (v.1). Is there a *real river* in the heavenly Jerusalem or is this to be taken symbolically? Probably both. Certainly the New Jerusalem, being 1500 miles cubic, will have the beauty and refreshment of a running river and of many other bodies of water. We too often spiritualize when we think of heaven, imagining that we will be in some kind of dreamy, unreal world instead of a real world. We must always remember the teaching of Scripture: God is going to *recreate this earth and the heavens of this universe*. This is what He explicitly teaches in the Scripture (cp. 2 Pt.3:10-12; Rev.21:1; etc.).

A recreated world would certainly have the same features that this world has with one exception: it will be perfected. The Heavenly Jerusalem is said to have a particular river flowing through it, and the river has the water of life in it. What does this mean? The verse tells us. Note where the source of the river is: "the throne of God and of the Lamb."

The water of life flows from God and Christ: they are the source of all life that lives in the city. There will be no life there, no person there, other than those who have drunk of the life that God and Christ give. Therefore, the river symbolizes the life that flows out from God and Christ. It will be a constant reminder to us that Jesus Christ is the *living water* who gives us life...

- who *quenches* our thirst for life.
- who *satisfies* our thirst for life.
- who *fulfills* our thirst for life.
- who *completes* our thirst for life.

> Jesus answered her, "If you knew the gift of God and who it is that asks you for a drink, you would have asked him and he would have given you living water." (John 4:10)
>
> But whoever drinks the water I give him will never thirst. Indeed, the water I give him will become in him a spring of water welling up to eternal life." (John 4:14)
>
> On the last and greatest day of the Feast, Jesus stood and said in a loud voice, "If anyone is thirsty, let him come to me and drink. Whoever believes in me, as the Scripture has said, streams of living water will flow from within him." (John 7:37-38)
>
> Then the angel showed me the river of the water of life, as clear as crystal, flowing from the throne of God and of the Lamb Down the middle of the great street of the city. On each side of the river stood the tree of life, bearing twelve crops of fruit, yielding its fruit every month. And the leaves of the tree are for the healing of the nations. (Rev 22:1-2)
>
> The Spirit and the bride say, "Come!" And let him who hears say, "Come!" Whoever is thirsty, let him come; and whoever wishes, let him take the free gift of the water of life. (Rev 22:17)

2. There is a tree of life in the city (v.2). Remember: the tree of life was also planted in the *Garden of Eden* (Gen.2:9). As long as man remained sinless, he was allowed to eat of the tree; but as soon as he sinned, he was not allowed to eat its fruit. The fruit was the nourishment of life; it infused eternal life into Adam's body. Or else, it symbolized the perfect and life-giving environment God had given Adam. Whatever the case, the tree of life is now in the heavenly Jerusalem. Note that two things are said about it.

a. The tree of life bears twelve crops of fruit—one crop each month. The tree bears fruit year round. This symbolizes continuous fruit or continuous life. There is no time that the tree does not bear fruit. It always bears fruit; it provides eternal fruit. Therefore, the person who eats of the tree of life is nourished by its fruit eternally. He lives forever.

There is also another symbol here: bearing the fruit of God's Spirit. The person who eats of the tree of life will bear the fruit of the Spirit eternally.

b. The leaves of the tree of life are for the healing of the nations. That is, they provide a perfect life. The leaves prevent sickness and disease. They give the person who eats them a perfect body. This symbolizes the perfection that Jesus Christ gives, the perfect healing and deliverance from all suffering that He gives, the perfect body He will provide in that glorious day.

> Down the middle of the great street of the city. On each side of the river stood the tree of life, bearing twelve crops of fruit, yielding its fruit every month. And the leaves of the tree are for the healing of the nations. (Rev 22:2)
>
> He who has an ear, let him hear what the Spirit says to the churches. To him who

**overcomes, I will give the right to eat from the tree of life, which is in the paradise of God. (Rev 2:7)**

**And the LORD God made all kinds of trees grow out of the ground—trees that were pleasing to the eye and good for food. In the middle of the garden were the tree of life and the tree of the knowledge of good and evil. (Gen 2:9)**

**And the LORD God said, "The man has now become like one of us, knowing good and evil. He must not be allowed to reach out his hand and take also from the tree of life and eat, and live forever." (Gen 3:22)**

**Fruit trees of all kinds will grow on both banks of the river. Their leaves will not wither, nor will their fruit fail. Every month they will bear, because the water from the sanctuary flows to them. Their fruit will serve for food and their leaves for healing." (Ezek 47:12)**

3. There is no more curse in the city (v.3). The earth is cursed. How? Cursed to aging, corruption, deterioration, decay, death, suffering, evil, disturbance, division, disasters, and on and on. It is cursed because man has chosen to make his own life in this world and to reject God's life. God's life is, as stated above, eternal; His life alone is eternal. Therefore, when man chose to make his own life, he chose to die. Consequently, man brought death and all its evil into the world. Man cursed the earth by his rejection of God and God's life.

But note: the Heavenly Jerusalem has no curse. This means that it is free of evil and death. It is perfect and will last eternally. There is no curse of evil or death in the city. Its citizens are free of the curse; they are perfected forever and ever.

**To Adam he said, "Because you listened to your wife and ate from the tree about which I commanded you, 'You must not eat of it,' "Cursed is the ground because of you; through painful toil you will eat of it all the days of your life. (Gen 3:17)**

**All who rely on observing the law are under a curse, for it is written: "Cursed is everyone who does not continue to do everything written in the Book of the Law." (Gal 3:10)**

**It [the city of God] will be inhabited; never again will it be destroyed. Jerusalem will be secure. (Zec 14:11)**

4. There is the throne of God and of the Lamb in the city (v.3b-4). This means two things.
   a. The Lord's servants will serve God and Christ, operating out of the city. That is, the Heavenly Jerusalem will be the capital city of the universe, the headquarters of the Lord's government and rule and reign. The idea is that we will receive our instructions and do our reporting from the very

throne of God and Christ. We will have access to the very throne of heaven itself. (See note, pt.3—Rev.21:24-27 for verses.)
   b. The Lord's servants will see His face (v.4). We will see Him face to face, actually stand face to face with our wonderful Lord and God: talk with, share with, serve, discuss, worship, praise, and offer thanks; and we will have the right to see Him face to face throughout all of eternity. O the preciousness of the hope! The glory and majesty of the hope! The stirrings and excitement of the hope! Our wonderful Lord has given us a hope that explodes all imagination! We will have the glorious privilege of living face to face with our wonderful Lord!

**Blessed are the pure in heart, for they will see God. (Mat 5:8)**

**Now this is eternal life: that they may know you, the only true God, and Jesus Christ, whom you have sent. (John 17:3)**

**Dear friends, now we are children of God, and what we will be has not yet been made known. But we know that when he appears, we shall be like him, for we shall see him as he is. (1 John 3:2)**

**And I—in righteousness I will see your face; when I awake, I will be satisfied with seeing your likeness. (Psa 17:15)**

5. There is the name of God written in the forehead of believers (v.4). This means possession and security. We shall be wholly possessed by God. We will be His servants and be enabled to serve Him totally and wholly. We shall belong to Him and be under His care and love, direction and guidance, security and safety—eternally.

**Set his seal of ownership on us, and put his Spirit in our hearts as a deposit, guaranteeing what is to come. (2 Cor 1:22)**

**And you also were included in Christ when you heard the word of truth, the gospel of your salvation. Having believed, you were marked in him with a seal, the promised Holy Spirit, Who is a deposit guaranteeing our inheritance until the redemption of those who are God's possession—to the praise of his glory. (Eph 1:13-14)**

**Then I looked, and there before me was the Lamb, standing on Mount Zion, and with him 144,000 who had his name and his Father's name written on their foreheads. (Rev 14:1)**

**They will see his face, and his name will be on their foreheads. (Rev 22:4)**

6. There is eternal light in the city (v.5) (see note, pt.2—Rev.21:24-27; also see notes—Rev.21:11; 21:23 for discussion).

7. There is eternal rule—work and service—for God and Christ (v.5b) (see notes, pts.3, 5—Rev.21:24-47 for discussion).

| | XIV. THE GREAT MESSAGE OF REVELATION: ELEVEN STIRRING FACTS, 22:6-21 | | |
|---|---|---|---|
| **1 The message is trustworthy & true**<br>a. Is of God<br>b. Is prophetic | 6 The angel said to me, "These words are trustworthy and true. The Lord, the God of the spirits of the prophets, sent his angel to show his servants the things that must soon take place." | Omega, the First and the Last, the Beginning and the End.<br>14 "Blessed are those who wash their robes, that they may have the right to the tree of life and may go through the gates into the city. | based on the Lord's Person |
| **2 The message will bring a blessing to the person who studies & obeys the prophecy of this book**<br>**3 The message stirs worship**<br>a. John heard & saw the events<br>b. John was stricken with awe—a sense of worship<br>c. John was told not to worship any being but God & God alone | 7 "Behold, I am coming soon! Blessed is he who keeps the words of the prophecy in this book."<br>8 I, John, am the one who heard and saw these things. And when I had heard and seen them, I fell down to worship at the feet of the angel who had been showing them to me.<br>9 But he said to me, "Do not do it! I am a fellow servant with you and with your brothers the prophets and of all who keep the words of this book. Worship God!" | 15 Outside are the dogs, those who practice magic arts, the sexually immoral, the murderers, the idolaters and everyone who loves and practices falsehood.<br>16 I, Jesus, have sent my angel to give you this testimony for the churches. I am the Root and the Offspring of David, and the bright Morning Star."<br>17 The Spirit and the bride say, "Come!" And let him who hears say, "Come!" Whoever is thirsty, let him come; and whoever wishes, let him take the free gift of the water of life. | **6 The message tells us who will be accepted by the Lord**<br><br>**7 The message tells us who will be rejected by the Lord**<br><br>**8 The message is proclaimed by the Lord Jesus Christ Himself**<br>a. Proclaimed to the churches<br>b. Proclaimed because of who He is<br>**9 The message offers the greatest invitation ever extended to man** |
| **4 The message is to be read & studied by all**<br>a. It is not to be sealed<br>b. Bc. the time is at hand<br>c. Bc. the time is coming when it will be too late to hear it: Repentance will then be impossible | 10 Then he told me, "Do not seal up the words of the prophecy of this book, because the time is near.<br>11 Let him who does wrong continue to do wrong; let him who is vile continue to be vile; let him who does right continue to do right; and let him who is holy continue to be holy." | 18 I warn everyone who hears the words of the prophecy of this book: If anyone adds anything to them, God will add to him the plagues described in this book.<br>19 And if anyone takes words away from this book of prophecy, God will take away from him his share in the tree of life and in the holy city, which are described in this book. | **10 The message must not be tampered with**<br><br>a. A person must not add to the Word<br><br>b. A person must not take away from the Word |
| **5 The message focuses upon the Lord's return & judgment to come**<br>a. Judgment is to be based on a man's work<br>b. Judgment is to be | 12 "Behold, I am coming soon! My reward is with me, and I will give to everyone according to what he has done.<br>13 I am the Alpha and the | 20 He who testifies to these things says, "Yes, I am coming soon." Amen. Come, Lord Jesus.<br>21 The grace of the Lord Jesus be with God's people. Amen. | **11 The message closes with the greatest of all assurances** |

# DIVISION XIV

## THE GREAT MESSAGE OF REVELATION:
## ELEVEN STIRRING FACTS, 22:6-21

(22:6-21) **Introduction**: this passage closes the great book of *Revelation*. It is also the final words of the Word of God, for the great book of *Revelation* is the last book of the Bible. Jesus Christ has sounded forth the great message of *Revelation*. He has revealed the end of time, what is going to happen during the last years of human history. The things He has shown have been astounding. They have caused us to stand in stark amazement at the glory and majesty of God, at His supreme intelligence and power. We have seen God's ability and power to take all the ungodliness and evil of this world and work them all out for good. Think back over what we have seen:

⇒ We saw God holding the great B*ook of Destiny* in His hand and Jesus Christ walking over and taking it and opening it up to reveal the future of the world.

⇒ We saw that the world is going to experience an increase in natural catastrophes—all so destructive that whole areas of the world will be devastated.

⇒ We saw that a great charismatic leader is to arise upon the world scene who will become so evil that he can only be described as a beast. He will be the antichrist, a man who will have the answers to peace and to some of the world's terrible problems. We saw that the world will turn to him because of his answers and that he will actually bring peace and solve some of the massive problems of society.

⇒ We saw that once the antichrist has consolidated his power over a number of nations, he will institute a worldwide loyalty to the state—what might be called a state religion. Every citizen will be required to give his loyalty to the state as the great *provider and protector* of its citizens. We have seen that the antichrist will turn from the good that he will do and launch the worst evil the world has ever known. He will instigate the worst holocaust ever feared by man, a holocaust that will slaughter literally millions and millions of people—people of all religions who refuse to give their *first loyalty and allegiance* to the state.

⇒ We saw that the government, society, and religion of the world will become so evil under the antichrist that God will make the decision to go ahead and judge the ungodly and evil of the world and end world history.

⇒ We saw the judgment of God that will fall upon the earth, the great *seal judgments* that will bring famine and disease and that will kill one fourth of the earth's population.

⇒ We saw the great *trumpet judgments* that will bring violent storms, volcanic eruptions, a meteoric mass, astronomical happenings in space—all so devastating that one third of the earth's vegetation, seas, and water supply will be destroyed. We also saw that there will be plague of locust-like creatures that will torment all the ungodly and evil of the earth. We also saw that there will be a plague of demonic military horsemen which will kill one third of the population of the earth.

⇒ We saw the end come in the seven *bowl judgments* that will fall upon the earth. The bowl judgments are the final judgments that end world history. We saw an ulcerous sore that will hit the human race. We also saw the total pollution of the sea and fresh water supply of the earth and the death of all sea life. We saw that the rays of the sun will hit the earth with a scorching heat, then a pitch black darkness will strike the earth. And then we saw that the most massive military buildup and the largest army ever witnessed by the earth will be launched by the antichrist.

⇒ We saw that the antichrist and his massive army will be destroyed in one moment's time at the last battle of human history, Armageddon.

⇒ We saw that the Lord Jesus Christ will usher in the Millennium, a period of one thousand years when He will rule and reign upon the earth.

⇒ We saw that the Lord Jesus Christ will destroy Satan and the present heaven and earth and judge the dead at the great white throne judgment of God.

⇒ And finally we saw that the Lord Jesus Christ will create a new heaven and earth. And we saw the New Jerusalem, the capital of the new heavens and earth and the eternal rule and reign of believers with Jesus Christ.

This is what we have seen. These are the highlights of what God has revealed to us in the great *Book of Revelation.* Now the point is this: what God has revealed is important to Him. God wants man to know what lies ahead so that he can prepare himself. He has warned man of the terrible things that are coming upon the earth. But He has also given hope to man. There is a better world coming, the most glorious of worlds, a perfect heaven and earth: a world in which there will be no sorrow or tears, suffering or death; a world or righteousness and joy and life. God wants man to know the *message of Revelation.* Therefore, as the Lord closes this great book, everything He says has to do with the overall

message of the book. The message of *Revelation* is so important that the Lord takes the time and space to talk about the message of *Revelation* itself. This is what the Lord has to say about the great *Book of Revelation,* about the message of *Revelation.* Note that eleven stirring facts are given by the Lord Himself and by John.

1. The message is trustworthy and true (v.6).
2. The message will bring a blessing to the person who keeps the prophecy of this book (v.7).
3. The message stirs worship (v.8-9).
4. The message is to be read and studied by all (v.10-11).
5. The message focuses upon the Lord's return and judgment to come (v.12-13).
6. The message tells us who will be accepted by the Lord (v.14).
7. The message tells us who will be rejected by the Lord (v.15).
8. The message is proclaimed by the Lord Jesus Christ Himself (v.16).
9. The message offers the greatest invitation ever extended to man (v.17).
10. The message must not be tampered with (v.18-19).
11. The message closes with the greatest of all assurances (v.20-21).

**1** (22:6) **Revelation, The—Word of God**: the message of *Revelation* is trustworthy and true.

⇒ The message is trustworthy: it can be trusted. It is trustworthy and reliable.

⇒ The message is true: it is not a lie, not false, not a message created by the imagination of men. How do we know this? How do we know that the message of *Revelation* is trustworthy and true?

Note what the verse says:

> **The angel said to me, "These words are trustworthy and true. The Lord, the God of the spirits of the prophets, sent his angel to show his servants the things that must soon take place." (Rev 22:6)**

The message of *Revelation* is from the same Lord God that inspired the prophets of old. The Lord God gave the prophets their message, and He is the One who has given the great message of *Revelation.* It is a matter of belief. We either believe or do not believe that the Scripture is the Word of God. We either believe or do not believe the prophets and writers of Scripture. The Lord Jesus Christ has done just what this verse declares: shown us "the things that must soon take place." We either believe or do not believe that He has done it. But whatever our decision is, we had better listen to what He has to say in the remaining points of this passage. Failure to do so could doom us for eternity.

> **Heaven and earth will pass away, but my words will never pass away. (Mark 13:31)**
> **The Spirit gives life; the flesh counts for nothing. The words I have spoken to you are spirit and they are life. (John 6:63)**
> **Simon Peter answered him, "Lord, to whom shall we go? You have the words of eternal life. (John 6:68)**
> **"No one ever spoke the way this man does," the guards declared. (John 7:46)**

**There is a judge for the one who rejects me and does not accept my words; that very word which I spoke will condemn him at the last day. (John 12:48)**

**He who does not love me will not obey my teaching. These words you hear are not my own; they belong to the Father who sent me. (John 14:24)**

**2** (22:7) **Revelation, The—Word of God**: the message of *Revelation* will bring a blessing to the person who studies and obeys the prophecies of the book. The person who really studies *Revelation* will be blessed in a very special way.

⇒ He will be drawn closer to the Lord, be given a deeper awareness and sense of the Lord's presence.

⇒ He will know what is coming upon the earth in the end time and be better prepared to cope until the Lord comes.

⇒ He will understand more about the ungodly and evil of this world and more about how God is going to conquer all the evil and bring righteousness to the earth.

⇒ He will understand heaven more and be more strongly stirred to long for heaven.

⇒ He will be drawn by the Spirit of God into more and more fellowship with the Lord in preparation for that glorious day of redemption.

On and on the list could go, for the Lord's blessings are endless to the person who truly studies His Word. But note: there is a strong reason for studying and obeying the prophecies of *Revelation*. The Lord says, "Behold, I am coming soon!" The events are about to roll in upon the earth. The idea is that the events are going to happen ever so quickly, one rolling in upon the other. Therefore, we must be prepared, and we must quickly witness to a world lost in crime, drugs, suffering, and death. We must study and study *Revelation*. We must prepare ourselves and do what we can to prepare others, for the Lord and the final days of human history are upon us.

**I tell you the truth, if anyone keeps my word, he will never see death." (John 8:51)**

**"If you love me, you will obey what I command. And I will ask the Father, and he will give you another Counselor to be with you forever— (John 14:15-16)**

**Jesus replied, "If anyone loves me, he will obey my teaching. My Father will love him, and we will come to him and make our home with him. (John 14:23)**

**"I have revealed you to those whom you gave me out of the world. They were yours; you gave them to me and they have obeyed your word. (John 17:6)**

**We know that we have come to know him if we obey his commands. (1 John 2:3)**

**I know your deeds. See, I have placed before you an open door that no one can shut. I know that you have little strength, yet you have kept my word and have not denied my name. (Rev 3:8)**

**3** (22:8-9) **Revelation, The—Worship**: the message of *Revelation* stirs worship. When John heard the prophecies of

the *Revelation*, he was so astounded that he was gripped with a spirit of fear and worship. He actually fell down at the feet of the angel who was delivering the message for the Lord. This was the second time that John had done this (Rev.19:10). Again, the angel rebuked John. He told John to get up, for angels are only servants of God just as men are. He told John to worship God and God alone.

The point is this: the message of *Revelation* should astound us and stir us to worship. But we must make sure that we worship the true and living God and Him alone.

**Thought 1.** The great tragedy is this: so many are worshipping false gods, their own idea of what God is like. They are religious and have been baptized; they attend church and sometimes serve in the church. But they...

• reject Jesus Christ as the Son of God who died for their sins.

• refuse to live a godly and righteous life for Jesus Christ.

• reject the Scriptures as the Word of God.

• reject the *Revelation* as the prophecy of the Lord, the prophecy that reveals what is to happen in the end time.

**Jesus said to him, "Away from me, Satan! For it is written: 'Worship the Lord your God, and serve him only.'" (Mat 4:10)**

**God is spirit, and his worshipers must worship in spirit and in truth." (John 4:24)**

**He said in a loud voice, "Fear God and give him glory, because the hour of his judgment has come. Worship him who made the heavens, the earth, the sea and the springs of water." (Rev 14:7)**

**Ascribe to the LORD the glory due his name. Bring an offering and come before him; worship the LORD in the splendor of his holiness. (1 Chr 16:29)**

**Come, let us bow down in worship, let us kneel before the LORD our Maker; (Psa 95:6)**

**Worship the LORD in the splendor of his holiness; tremble before him, all the earth. (Psa 96:9)**

**4** (22:10-11) **Revelation, The—Bible Study**: the message of *Revelation* is to be read and studied. The instructions of the Lord are clear: the book of *Revelation* is never to be sealed, that is, closed. It is to be read, studied, preached, and taught—always. Two reasons are given.

1. Because the time for the events to fall upon the earth is near. We can never be prepared nor can we prepare others unless we understand what is coming and get ready for the coming events.

2. Because the time is coming when it will be too late to prepare (v.11). The more a person hardens his heart, the less open he becomes and the less likely he will be to change. If we do not repent, turning away from sin and toward God, then our hearts will become harder and harder. If we do not get into the Word of God and the prophecies of *Revelation*, we will be unprepared when the events of the end time hit the earth. Our hearts will be so hardened and our minds so closed that we will be lost eternally.

• We will remain unjust forever.

• We will remain filthy forever.

But, if we turn to God and repent, we will be saved. If we begin to study *Revelation* and do what *Revelation* says, we will be righteous and holy and remain so forever.

But whoever blasphemes against the Holy Spirit will never be forgiven; he is guilty of an eternal sin." (Mark 3:29)

What good is it for a man to gain the whole world, yet forfeit his soul? (Mark 8:36)

Afterward, as you know, when he wanted to inherit this blessing, he was rejected. He could bring about no change of mind, though he sought the blessing with tears. (Heb 12:17)

For in his own eyes he flatters himself too much to detect or hate his sin. (Psa 36:2)

For the evil man has no future hope, and the lamp of the wicked will be snuffed out. (Prov 24:20)

**5** (22:12-13) **Revelation, The—Jesus Christ, Return—Judgment**: the message of *Revelation* focuses upon the Lord's return and judgment to come. Again, the Lord declares: "Behold, I am coming soon!" His return is speedily coming. It is imminent, right at hand. The thrust is for us to prepare. And note why: when He comes back, it means judgment. He is coming back to judge man. The judgment will be based upon two things.

1. It will be based upon the works of man, based upon what we have done. (See notes—Rev.20:12; 14:14-16; 14:17-20 for discussion.)

2. It will be based upon the person of Jesus Christ. Jesus Christ is the Alpha and Omega, the beginning and the end of all things. This means that He is both the Creator and Finisher of the universe. He spans all of time and all of the universe. He began all things and He finishes all things. Therefore, He will finish earth and the heavens above, judge them all. He will judge all who have acted against Him—judge all who have lived ungodly lives, lived contrary to His godliness.

And that you, O Lord, are loving. Surely you will reward each person according to what he has done. (Psa 62:12)

"I the LORD search the heart and examine the mind, to reward a man according to his conduct, according to what his deeds deserve." (Jer 17:10)

For the Son of Man is going to come in his Father's glory with his angels, and then he will reward each person according to what he has done. (Mat 16:27)

For we must all appear before the judgment seat of Christ, that each one may receive what is due him for the things done while in the body, whether good or bad. (2 Cor 5:10)

Since you call on a Father who judges each man's work impartially, live your lives as strangers here in reverent fear. (1 Pet 1:17)

And I saw the dead, great and small, standing before the throne, and books were opened. Another book was opened, which is the book of life. The dead were judged according to what they had done as recorded in the books. (Rev 20:12)

"Behold, I am coming soon! My reward is with me, and I will give to everyone according to what he has done. (Rev 22:12)

**6** (22:14) **Revelation, The—Saved, The**: the message of *Revelation* tells us who will be accepted by the Lord. The best Greek manuscripts say this: "Blessed are those who wash their robes." The only way a person can ever eat of the tree of life is to *wash his robes in the blood of Christ*. No person is ever saved by keeping commandments. Believers, of course, do keep the commandments of God; they keep His commandments because they love Christ and want to follow Him. They do not keep the commandments *in order to be saved*. They believe that Jesus Christ forgives their sins through His death on the cross *in order to be saved*. Then it is that they begin to serve Him and to keep His commandments.

The point is this: the person who is accepted by God is the person who has *washed his robes in the blood of the Lamb*. That is the person...

- who has the right to the tree of life (see note, pt.2—Rev.22:1-5 for discussion).
- who enters into the New Jerusalem, the heavenly city of God (see outline and notes—Rev.21:9-23; 21:24-22:5 for discussion).

We all, like sheep, have gone astray, each of us has turned to his own way; and the LORD has laid on him the iniquity of us all. He was oppressed and afflicted, yet he did not open his mouth; he was led like a lamb to the slaughter, and as a sheep before her shearers is silent, so he did not open his mouth. (Isa 53:6-7)

The next day John saw Jesus coming toward him and said, "Look, the Lamb of God, who takes away the sin of the world! (John 1:29)

He did not enter by means of the blood of goats and calves; but he entered the Most Holy Place once for all by his own blood, having obtained eternal redemption. The blood of goats and bulls and the ashes of a heifer sprinkled on those who are ceremonially unclean sanctify them so that they are outwardly clean. How much more, then, will the blood of Christ, who through the eternal Spirit offered himself unblemished to God, cleanse our consciences from acts that lead to death, so that we may serve the living God! (Heb 9:12-14)

Day after day every priest stands and performs his religious duties; again and again he offers the same sacrifices, which can never take away sins. But when this priest had offered for all time one sacrifice for sins, he sat down at the right hand of God. Since that time he waits for his enemies to be made his footstool, (Heb 10:11-13)

For you know that it was not with perishable things such as silver or gold that you were redeemed from the empty way of life handed down to you from your forefathers, But with the precious blood of Christ, a lamb without blemish or defect. (1 Pet 1:18-19)

He himself bore our sins in his body on the tree, so that we might die to sins and live for righteousness; by his wounds you have been healed. (1 Pet 2:24)

For Christ died for sins once for all, the righteous for the unrighteous, to bring you to God. He was put to death in the body but made alive by the Spirit, (1 Pet 3:18)

**7** (22:15) **Revelation, The—Lost, The**: the message of *Revelation* tells us who will be rejected by the Lord. There are some people who will not be allowed to enter the heavenly city of God. Who are they?

⇒ The *dogs* of society. In ancient days the wild dog was a symbol of roaming about, of being mean and savage, dirty and immoral. Therefore, those who roam about living mean and savage lives, or dirty and immoral lives will never be allowed to enter God's heavenly city.

⇒ The magicians, the sorcerers, the immoral, the murderers, the idolaters, and the liars have already been discussed (see note, pt.3—Rev.21:6-8 for discussion).

For I tell you that unless your righteousness surpasses that of the Pharisees and the teachers of the law, you will certainly not enter the kingdom of heaven. (Mat 5:20)

I tell you the truth, anyone who will not receive the kingdom of God like a little child will never enter it." (Mark 10:15)

Do you not know that the wicked will not inherit the kingdom of God? Do not be deceived: Neither the sexually immoral nor idolaters nor adulterers nor male prostitutes nor homosexual offenders (1 Cor 6:9)

I declare to you, brothers, that flesh and blood cannot inherit the kingdom of God, nor does the perishable inherit the imperishable. (1 Cor 15:50)

Nothing impure will ever enter it, nor will anyone who does what is shameful or deceitful, but only those whose names are written in the Lamb's book of life. (Rev 21:27)

**8** (22:16) **Revelation, The**: the message of *Revelation* is *proclaimed by Jesus Christ Himself*. This is a forceful statement, and it is emphatically stated so that there can be no mistake about the fact: "I Jesus...give you this testimony for the churches." He is the Author of the message of *Revelation*. But note: He sent His own personal angel to bring the message to earth. How do we know that Jesus Christ actually did this? How do we know that Jesus Christ actually sent the message of *Revelation* to earth? Because of who He is.

⇒ He is the "*Root and Offspring of David*." This means that He is the root of David, the root of life, the One who gives life to man. Therefore, He is the One who gave life to David. But He is also the offspring of David. He is the promised Messiah who was to come from the seed and line of David. He is the promised Savior and King who

was to come and save man and rule over the world—all from the throne of David.

⇒ He is the "*Bright Morning Star*." This means two things. The first star to arise is the brightest star, the brightest of all. Jesus Christ is, therefore, the brightest of all beings in all the universe. He is the very Son of God Himself. Second, this is a prophecy of the Messiah: "A star will come out of Jacob" (Num.24:17). Jesus Christ is declaring that He is the promised Messiah, the Star among all the stars of man.

This is the reason we know that Jesus Christ is the Author of the *Revelation*. He is the Son of God, the promised Messiah who gives life and who has the right to judge life. He is the One who knows the future and can warn man and tell man how to prepare for the devastating events of the end time. Being the true Messiah, He is bound to declare the truth to us; He is bound to declare the message of *Revelation* to us.

I no longer call you servants, because a servant does not know his master's business. Instead, I have called you friends, for everything that I learned from my Father I have made known to you. (John 15:15)

However, as it is written: "No eye has seen, no ear has heard, no mind has conceived what God has prepared for those who love him"— But God has revealed it to us by his Spirit. The Spirit searches all things, even the deep things of God. (1 Cor 2:9-10)

And he made known to us the mystery of his will according to his good pleasure, which he purposed in Christ, To be put into effect when the times will have reached their fulfillment—to bring all things in heaven and on earth together under one head, even Christ. (Eph 1:9-10)

He reveals deep and hidden things; he knows what lies in darkness, and light dwells with him. (Dan 2:22)

Surely the Sovereign LORD does nothing without revealing his plan to his servants the prophets. (Amos 3:7)

**9** (22:17) **Revelation, The—Invitation—Come—Water of Life**: the message of *Revelation* offers the greatest invitation ever extended to man:

The Spirit and the bride say, "Come!" And let him who hears say, "Come!" Whoever is thirsty, let him come; and whoever wishes, let him take the free gift of the water of life. (Rev 22:17)

The *bride* is the church, the host of true believers scattered all over the earth. Both the church and the Spirit of God cry out, "Come." And note: once we hear the invitation and come, we must begin to cry out for others to come.

⇒ The thirsty need to come: those who are parched, scorched, empty, craving, burning, laboring, and sweating—all those who need the refreshment, satisfaction, and renewal of the water of life: "Come, come to Jesus Christ, who is the water of life."

The Spirit and the bride say, "Come!" And let him who hears say, "Come!" Whoever is thirsty, let him come; and whoever wishes, let him take the free gift of the water of life. (Rev 22:17c. See note, pt.1—Rev.22:1-5 for more discussion.)

"Come now, let us reason together," says the LORD. "Though your sins are like scarlet, they shall be as white as snow; though they are red as crimson, they shall be like wool. (Isa 1:18)

"Come, all you who are thirsty, come to the waters; and you who have no money, come, buy and eat! Come, buy wine and milk without money and without cost. (Isa 55:1)

"Come to me, all you who are weary and burdened, and I will give you rest. (Mat 11:28)

"Then he sent some more servants and said, 'Tell those who have been invited that I have prepared my dinner: My oxen and fattened cattle have been butchered, and everything is ready. Come to the wedding banquet.' (Mat 22:4)

At the time of the banquet he sent his servant to tell those who had been invited, 'Come, for everything is now ready.' (Luke 14:17)

The Spirit and the bride say, "Come!" And let him who hears say, "Come!" Whoever is thirsty, let him come; and whoever wishes, let him take the free gift of the water of life. (Rev 22:17)

**10** (22:18-19) **Revelation, The**: the message of *Revelation* must not be tampered with. The warning is solemn and emphatic.

⇒ A person must not add to the words of this book.
⇒ A person must not take away from the words of this book.

What happens if a person tampers with the Word of God? If he adds to the words, he is going to suffer the plagues covered in the book. If he takes away from the words, God is going...

• to take away his share in the tree of life.
• to take his share out of the holy city, the Heavenly Jerusalem.
• to take his share out of all the glorious promises of this book of *Revelation*.

When I came to you, brothers, I did not come with eloquence or superior wisdom as I proclaimed to you the testimony about God. For I resolved to know nothing while I was with you except Jesus Christ and him crucified. I came to you in weakness and fear, and with much trembling. My message and my preaching were not with wise and persuasive words, but with a demonstration of the Spirit's power, so that your faith might not rest on men's wisdom, but on God's power. (1 Cor 2:1-5)

We had previously suffered and been insulted in Philippi, as you know, but with the help of our God we dared to tell you his gospel in spite of strong opposition. For the appeal we make does not spring from error or impure motives, nor are we trying to trick you. On the contrary, we speak as men approved by God to be entrusted with the gospel. We are not trying to please men but God, who tests our hearts. You know we never used flattery, nor did we put on a mask to cover up greed—God is our witness. (1 Th 2:2-5)

And we also thank God continually because, when you received the word of God, which you heard from us, you accepted it not as the word of men, but as it actually is, the word of God, which is at work in you who believe. (1 Th 2:13)

And if anyone takes words away from this book of prophecy, God will take away from him his share in the tree of life and in the holy city, which are described in this book. (Rev 22:19)

Do not add to what I command you and do not subtract from it, but keep the commands of the LORD your God that I give you. (Deu 4:2)

See that you do all I command you; do not add to it or take away from it. (Deu 12:32)

Do not add to his words, or he will rebuke you and prove you a liar. (Prov 30:6)

**11** (22:20-21) **Revelation, The—Assurance**: the message of *Revelation* closes with the greatest of all assurances. The assurance is twofold.

⇒ Jesus Christ is the One who reveals and testifies to the things written in *Revelation*. They are not the imaginations and words of men. They are the Word of the living Lord, the Son of God Himself.
⇒ Jesus Christ declares: "Yes—it is true. I am coming soon."

This is the unequivocal assurance of the Lord Jesus Himself. The human heart should shout out: "Amen! So be it! Even so, come, Lord Jesus."

The grace of the Lord Jesus be with God's people. Amen. (Rev 22:21)

Let your gentleness be evident to all. The Lord is near. (Phil 4:5)

You too, be patient and stand firm, because the Lord's coming is near. (James 5:8)

I am coming soon. Hold on to what you have, so that no one will take your crown. (Rev 3:11)

He who testifies to these things says, "Yes, I am coming soon." Amen. Come, Lord Jesus. (Rev 22:20)

# REVELATION
## OUTLINE & SUBJECT INDEX

REMEMBER: When you look up a subject and turn to the Scripture reference, you have not just the Scripture but also an outline and a discussion (commentary) of the Scripture and subject.

This is one of the GREAT FEATURES of *The Preacher's Outline & Sermon Bible*®. Once you have all the volumes, you will have not only what all other Bible indexes give you, that is, a list of all the subjects and their Scripture references, but in addition you will have...

- an outline of every Scripture and subject in the Bible
- a discussion (commentary) on every Scripture and subject
- every subject supported by other Scripture, already written out or cross referenced

DISCOVER THE UNIQUE VALUE for yourself. Quickly glance below to the first subject of the Index:

**ABADDON**
Meaning. Hebrew name of the king of evil spirits. 9:11

Turn to the first reference. Glance at the Scripture and the outline, then read the commentary. You will immediately see the TREMENDOUS BENEFIT of the INDEX of *The Preacher's Outline & Sermon Bible*®.

---

## OUTLINE AND SUBJECT INDEX

**ABADDON**
Meaning. Hebrew name of the king of evil spirits. 9:11

**ABYSS**
Meaning. 9:2

**ADULTERY - ADULTERESS**
Caused by. Partying & failing to separate from the world. 2:20-21
Results. Being sent to hell. 21:8

**ALMIGHTY**
Christ is the A. 1:8

**ALPHA - OMEGA**
Name given to Christ. 1:8; 21:6; 22:12-13

**ALTAR, BRAZEN**
In heaven. Place of the martyrs in heaven. 6:9

**AMEN**
Title. Of Christ. 3:14

**ANGELS**
Function toward believers. Carry out the answers of prayers for God. 8:1-5
Function toward God.
Avenging agents of. 15:1; 15:5-8
To be worshippers of God. 4:1-11; 10:1-7
To bind Satan. 12:7-9; 20:1-3
To serve as messengers. 10:1-7
To surround the throne of God. 7:11-12
Function toward unbelievers.
To avenge God's glory. 15:1; 15:5-8
To execute God's judgment. 8:1-5; 8:6-7
To harvest believers & unbelievers in the end time. 14:15; 14:17-20
In the end time.
To assure Satan's defeat. 20:1-3
To seal, protect from judgment. 7:2-4
Names - Titles. Mighty angel. 10:1
Position in creation.
Ministers of God. 10:1-7

Organized in ranks or orders. 7:1-3
Organized under Michael. 12:7-9
Some are bound. 9:13-15
Some are fallen. 20:10
Worshippers of God & Christ. 5:11-14
Work of. To praise Christ. For seven things. 5:11-12

**ANGELS, FALLEN**
In the end time. War against Michael. 12:7-9
King of. Named. 9:11
Leaders of.
Four fallen **a**. are set loose from the Euphrates river. 9:14-15
Four military **a**. will be set loose to kill men. 9:12-21
Given the key to the bottomless pit. 9:1; 9:2

**ANTICHRIST** (See **END TIME**; **GOVERNMENT**, In the end time; **STATE**, In the end time; **SOCIETY**, In the end time)
Appearance of. Discussed. 6:1-8
Causes. War, famine, pestilence, hunger, starvation, savagery. 6:1-8
Characteristics - Traits.
Attacks believers. Kills multitudes. 7:13-14
Deceiver. 6:1-2
Man of war. 6:1-2
Murderer.
Kills & is responsible for the death of one fourth of the earth. 6:7-8
Kills believers. Two reasons. 6:9
Strife, violence, wrath. 6:1-8
Discussed. 6:1-8; 11:7; 13:1-10; 13:18; 14:9-12; 16:13-14; 17:17-18; 19:20; 20:10
A false prophet. 13:11-18
A political ruler. 13:1-10
Appearance of & description of. 6:1-8; 17:7-14
Arises out of the pit. 11:7; 17:7-8
Cast into the lake of fire. 19:20, 20:10
Makes war against & slays the two witnesses of Revelation. 11:7-10
Mark of. 13:17-18; 14:9; 15:2; 19:20

Power is a given power. 6:1-2; 9:3-6; 13:7
Power of. 13:1-10; 13:2; 17:7-14; 17:9-10
Suffers the wrath of God. 16:1-21
Fate of.
Capital - Babylon destroyed. 14:8; 18:1-24
Cast into the lake of fire. 19:20; 20:10
Judgment to fall upon. 16:1-21
Overcome by the lamb. 17:14
Followers of **a**.
Fate of **a**. followers.
Cast into a lake of fire. 19:20; 20:10
Drink of God's wrath. 14:9-12; 16:21
Overcome by the Lamb. 17:14
Persons not in the book of life. 13:8
Persons with the mark of the beast. 13:16-18; 14:9; 15:2
How **a**. rises to power.
How he gains control of the world. 6:1-2; 6:1-8; 13:1-10; 13:13-17
The political ruler. 13:1-10; see 6:1-8
The religious ruler or prophet. 13:11-18
Methods used by.
Blasphemy. 13:1; 13:5-6
Forming a confederation of power. 13:1-8; 17:7-14
Persecuting believers. 13:7; 13:21-23
Slaying leadership. 11:3-10
War & conquest. 6:1-2, 3-4; 13:1-8; 16:13-14; 17:7-14; 17:15-18; 18:1-24
Working Satanic miracles. 13:2-3; 16:13-14
Names - Titles - Identity.
A political ruler. 13:1-10
A religious ruler. 13:11-18; 16:13; 19:20; 20:10
Beast, The. 11:7; 13:1-10
Death & Hell. 6:7-8
Who he is. 13:1
Nature.

# INDEX

Incarnation of evil. 17:8
"Was...is not...ascends out" of the bottomless pit. 17:8
Number of - mark of: 666. 13:17-18; 14:9; 15:2; 19:20
Origin.
Of Satan. 13:1-5
Out of the bottomless pit. 17:7-13
Power of.
Discussed. 13:2; 17:7-14; 17:9-10
Kings & empires or nations that support. 13:2; 17:7-14; 17:9-10
Chart of. 13:2
Political p. Nations he rules over. 13:1
Rise to p. 13:2-3
Way he secures p. 13:4-8
Prophesies of. Chart on prophecies of Revelation & Daniel. 13:1; 13:2
Warning against.
Should hear. 13:9
Should understand. 13:18
Who escapes from the antichrist.
Believers. 3:10
Those in the book of life. 13:8-10
Those sealed by God in their foreheads. 7:1-8; 9:3-6
Those who keep God's commandments & the faith of Jesus. 13:10; 14:12
Those who reject the beast's mark. 14:9-12; 15:2-4
Those who remain loyal, steadfast. 13:8-10; 14:12

**APOLLYON**
Meaning. Greek name of the king of the evil spirits. 9:11

**ARK IN HEAVEN**
Symbolizes. God's new covenant. 11:19

**ARMAGEDDON**
Discussed. 11:18; 14:17-20; 16:12-16; 19:17-21

**ASIA**
Location of the seven churches of the Revelation. 1:4; 1:11

**ASSURANCE**
In the end.
Believers are assured of being with Jesus. 14:1-4
Day of earth's harvest will come for believers. 14:14-16
Day of earth's harvest will come for the ungodly. 14:17-20
Dead are seen at rest & rewarded. 14:13
Godless government & religion & society will be destroyed. 14:8
Gospel will be preached to the whole world. 14:6-7
Justice will be executed. 14:9-12
Of believers. Will be with Jesus. 14:1-5

**BABYLON**
Destroyed. Under seventh bowl judgment. 16:17-21
In the end time. Will be destroyed by God. 14:8
Judgment. Of both the political & religious B. 17:1-6; 17:7-18; 18:1-24

Political.
Capital of antichrist. 18:1-24
Destruction of. 18:1-24
Religious B. Destroyed. 17:1-6
Traits of. Will be embodied in the antichrist. 13:2

**BACKSLIDING**
Discussed. 2:4; 2:5-6
Of a church. Compromising & permissiveness. 2:18-29

**BALAAM**
Discussed. 2:14-15

**BALAAMISM**
Discussed. 2:14-15

**BEAST OF REVELATION, FIRST** (See **ANTICHRIST**)

**BEAST OF REVELATION, SECOND** (See **PROPHET OF REVELATION, FALSE**)

**BEAST, POLITICAL** (See **ANTICHRIST**)

**BEATITUDES**
Seven b. of Revelation. 1:3

**BELIEVERS**
Fate of.
In the end time during the great tribulation. 7:1-8
Numberless multitude saved. 7:9-17
Sealed & protected from God's judgments during the great tribulation. 7:1-8; 9:4-5
In the end time. Will be martyred by the antichrist. Reasons. 6:9
Marks - Characteristics. Come from all races & nations. 5:9-10
Names - Titles. Kings & priests. 1:6
Nature. New creature. 3:18-20
Warning.
Against being lukewarm. 3:14-22
Against compromise. 2:18-29
Against false profession. 3:14-22
Against idolatry. 2:18-29
Against losing one's first love. 2:1-7
Against permissiveness. 2:18-29
Against Satan's influence. 2:9; 3:9-10
Against spiritual *deadness*. 3:1-6
Against worldliness. 2:12-17

**BIBLE**
Described. Sword of the Spirit. 2:12

**BLASPHEMY**
Sin of.
Religion can be guilty of b. 2:8-11
Will be committed by the antichrist. 13:4-8

**BLESSED**
Meaning. 20:6

**BLINDNESS, SPIRITUAL**
Meaning. 3:16-17

**BOOK OF DESTINY**
Discussed. 5:1-4; 5:5-14

**BOOK OF LIFE**
Described. 13:8
Determines one's destiny. 13:8-10; 20:11-15
Discussed. 20:12
Meaning. 3:4-6

**BOOK OF RECORDS**
Books used to judge unbelievers. 20:12

**BOTTOMLESS PIT**
Meaning. 9:2

**BOWL JUDGMENTS**
Discussed. 16:1-21
Preparation for. 15:1-8

**BRAZEN ALTAR** (See **ALTAR, BRAZEN**)

**BRIGHT AND MORNING STAR**
Name given to Christ. 2:28

**CANDLESTICKS**
Of Revelation. Symbol of the church. 1:13; 1:20

**CARNAL**
Described as.
Complacent. 3:1-6
Looking progressive, but dead. 3:1
Losing one's first love. 2:4
Discussed.
Being corrupted under a man's ministry. 3:14-22
Better cold than lukewarm. 3:15

**CHERUBIM**
Discussed. 4:6-9

**CHRISTIANITY**
Apostate c. to be destroyed. 17:15-18; 18:1-24

**CHURCH**
Described.
Affluent & wealthy, but lukewarm & half-committed. 3:14-22
As candlesticks. 1:13; 1:20
As faithful & alive. 3:7-13
Compromising & persuasive. 2:18-29
Orthodox, but without love. 2:1-7
Persecuted. 2:8-11
Reputable, but dying. 3:1-6
Worldly & corrupted. 2:12-17
Duty.
First d. To be an evangelistic & mission minded c. 3:8
Not to deny Christ. 3:8
Picture of a faithful c. 2:2-3
To keep God's Word. 3:8
What a c. should be. 3:8
Judgment of. Removed by Christ. 2:5-6; 2:16
Local church. (See EPISTLE TO ACTS, Outline; **MISSIONS**; and other Epistles of N.T.)
Ephesus - the orthodox c., but without love. 2:1-7
Laodicea - the lukewarm c. 3:14-22
Pergamos - the worldly, corrupted c. 2:12-17
Philadelphia - the c. that is faithful & alive. 3:7-13
Sardis - the c. with reputation, but dying. 3:1-6

# INDEX

# INDEX

# INDEX

# OUTLINE BIBLE RESOURCES

This material, like similar works, has come from imperfect man and is thus susceptible to human error. We are nevertheless grateful to God for both calling us and empowering us through His Holy Spirit to undertake this task. Because of His goodness and grace, *The Preacher's Outline & Sermon Bible*® New Testament is complete and the Old Testament volumes are releasing periodically.

The *Minister's Personal Handbook* and other helpful **Outline Bible Resources** are available in printed form as well as releasing electronically on WORDsearch software.

God has given the strength and stamina to bring us this far. Our confidence is that as we keep our eyes on Him and grounded in the undeniable truths of the Word, we will continue working through the Old Testament volumes. The future includes other helpful Outline Bible Resources for God's dear servants to use in their Bible Study and discipleship.

We offer this material first to Him in whose Name we labor and serve and for whose glory it has been produced and, second, to everyone everywhere who preaches and teaches the Word.

Our daily prayer is that each volume will lead thousands, millions, yes even billions, into a better understanding of the Holy Scriptures and a fuller knowledge of Jesus Christ the Incarnate Word, of whom the Scriptures so faithfully testify.

You will be pleased to know that Leadership Ministries Worldwide partners with Christian organizations, printers, and mission groups around the world to make Outline Bible Resources available and affordable in many countries and foreign languages. It is our goal that *every* leader around the world, both clergy and lay, will be able to understand God's Holy Word and present God's message with more clarity, authority, and understanding—all beyond his or her own power.

LEADERSHIP MINISTRIES WORLDWIDE
PO Box 21310 • Chattanooga, TN 37424-0310
(423) 855-2181 • FAX (423) 855-8616
info@outlinebible.org
www.outlinebible.org  - FREE Download materials

# LEADERSHIP MINISTRIES WORLDWIDE

## *Publishers of Outline Bible Resources*

### Currently Available Materials, with New Volumes Releasing Regularly

- **THE PREACHER'S OUTLINE & SERMON BIBLE® (POSB)**

**NEW TESTAMENT**

| | |
|---|---|
| Matthew I (chapters 1–15) | 1 & 2 Corinthians |
| Matthew II (chapters 16–28) | Galatians, Ephesians, Philippians, Colossians |
| Mark | 1 & 2 Thessalonians, 1 & 2 Timothy, Titus, Philemon |
| Luke | Hebrews, James |
| John | 1 & 2 Peter, 1, 2, & 3 John, Jude |
| Acts | Revelation |
| Romans | Master Outline & Subject Index |

**OLD TESTAMENT**

| | | |
|---|---|---|
| Genesis I (chapters 1–11) | 1 Kings | Isaiah 2 (chapters 36-66) |
| Genesis II (chapters 12–50) | 2 Kings | Jeremiah 1 (chapters 1-29) |
| Exodus I (chapters 1–18) | 1 Chronicles | Jeremiah 2 (chapters 30-52), |
| Exodus II (chapters 19–40) | 2 Chronicles | Lamentations |
| Leviticus | Ezra, Nehemiah, Esther | Ezekiel |
| Numbers | Job | Daniel, Hosea |
| Deuteronomy | Psalms 1 (chapters 1-41) | Joel, Amos, Obadiah, Jonah, |
| Joshua | Psalms 2 (chapters 42-106) | Micah, Nahum |
| Judges, Ruth | Proverbs | Habakkuk, Zephaniah, Haggai, |
| 1 Samuel | Ecclesiastes, Song of Solomon | Zechariah, Malachi |
| 2 Samuel | Isaiah 1 (chapters 1-35) | *New volumes release periodically* |

**KJV Available in Deluxe 3-Ring Binders or Softbound Edition • NIV Available in Softbound Only**

- **The Preacher's Outline & Sermon Bible New Testament — 3 Vol. Hardcover • KJV – NIV**

- *What the Bible Says to the Believer* **— The Believer's Personal Handbook**
  11 Chs. – Over 500 Subjects, 300 Promises, & 400 Verses Expounded - Italian Imitation Leather or Paperback

- *What the Bible Says to the Minister* **— The Minister's Personal Handbook**
  12 Chs. - 127 Subjects - 400 Verses Expounded - Italian Imitation Leather or Paperback

- **Practical Word Studies In the New Testament** — 2 Vol. Hardcover Set

- **The Teacher's Outline & Study Bible™ - Various New Testament Books**
  Complete 30 - 45 minute lessons – with illustrations and discussion questions

- **Practical Illustrations — Companion to the POSB**
  Arranged by topic and Scripture reference

- **What the Bible Says Series – Various Subjects**
  Prayer • The Passion • The Ten Commandments • The Tabernacle

- **Software – Various products powered by WORDsearch**
  New Testament • Pentateuch • History • Prophets • Practical Word Studies • Various Poetry/Wisdom

- **Topical Sermons Series – Available online only**
  7 sermons per series • Sermons are from The Preacher's Outline & Sermon Bible

- **Non-English Translations of various books**
  Included languages are: Russian – Spanish – Korean – Hindi – Chinese – Bulgarian – Romanian –
  Malayalam – Nepali – Italian – Arabic
  - Future: French, Portuguese

## *— Contact LMW for Specific Language Availability and Prices —*

For quantity orders and information, please contact:
LEADERSHIP MINISTRIES WORLDWIDE or Your Local Christian Bookstore
PO Box 21310 • Chattanooga, TN 37424-0310
(423) 855-2181 (9am – 5pm Eastern) • FAX (423) 855-8616
E-mail - info@outlinebible.org Order online at www.outlinebible.org

# PURPOSE STATEMENT

### LEADERSHIP MINISTRIES WORLDWIDE

exists to equip ministers, teachers, and laymen in their understanding, preaching, and teaching of God's Word by publishing and distributing worldwide *The Preacher's Outline & Sermon Bible®* and related **Outline Bible Resources**; to reach & disciple men, women, boys and girls for Jesus Christ.

# MISSION STATEMENT

1. To make the Bible so understandable – its truth so clear and plain – that men and women everywhere, whether teacher or student, preacher or hearer, can grasp its message and receive Jesus Christ as Savior, and...

2. To place the Bible in the hands of all who will preach and teach God's Holy Word, verse by verse, precept by precept, regardless of the individual's ability to purchase it.

The **Outline Bible Resources** have been given to LMW for printing and especially distribution worldwide at/below cost, by those who remain anonymous. One fact, however, is as true today as it was in the time of Christ:

### THE GOSPEL IS FREE, BUT THE COST OF TAKING IT IS NOT

LMW depends on the generous gifts of believers with a heart for Him and a love for the lost. They help pay for the printing, translating, and distributing of **Outline Bible Resources** into the hands of God's servants worldwide, who will present the Gospel message with clarity, authority, and understanding beyond their own.

LMW was incorporated in the state of Tennessee in July 1992 and received IRS 501 (c)(3) nonprofit status in March 1994. LMW is an international, nondenominational mission organization. All proceeds from USA sales, along with donations from donor partners, go directly to underwrite our translation and distribution projects of **Outline Bible Resources** to preachers, church and lay leaders, and Bible students around the world.

Made in the USA
Monee, IL
26 January 2024

52454357R00175